RAISING THE WORKERS' FLAG

The Workers' Unity League of Canada, 1930–1936

During the Great Depression, the conflicting interests of capital and labour became sharper than ever before. Radical Canadian workers, encouraged by the Red International of Labour Unions, responded by building the Workers' Unity League – an organization that greatly advanced the cause of unions in Canada, and boasted 40,000 members at its height. In *Raising the Workers' Flag*, the first full-length study of this robust group, Stephen Endicott brings its passionate efforts to light in memorable detail.

Raising the Workers' Flag is based on newly available or previously untapped sources, including documents from the Royal Canadian Mounted Police's Security Service and the Communist Party's archives. Using these impressive finds, Endicott gives an intimate sense of the raging debates of the labour movement of the 1930s. A gripping account of the League's dreams and daring, *Raising the Workers' Flag* enlivens some of the most dramatic struggles of Canadian labour history.

STEPHEN LYON ENDICOTT is a professor emeritus in the Faculty of Liberal Arts and Professional Studies at York University. His passion for history is informed by his own life of engagement in the struggles he researches and writes about, including this book about the Workers' Unity League. After joining the Communist Party of Canada (then called the Labour Progressive Party) in 1945 while studying history at the University of Toronto, he soon became a youth organizer, moving to British Columbia.

He knew many of the characters he writes about. Yet, while his admiration for their cause is clear, Endicott maintains a professional integrity in his research and presentation of what can only be considered, whether you agree with them or not, an extraordinary group of militant men and women who have earned their place in Canada's history.

STEPHEN LYON ENDICOTT

Raising the Workers' Flag

The Workers' Unity League of Canada, 1930–1936

UNIVERSITY OF TORONTO PRESS
Toronto Buffalo London

ISBN 978-1-4426-4373-4 (cloth)
ISBN 978-1-4426-1226-6 (paper)

Printed on acid-free, 100% post-consumer recycled paper
with vegetable-based inks

Library and Archives Canada Cataloguing in Publication

Endicott, Stephen Lyon, 1928–
Raising the workers' flag : the Workers' Unity League of Canada,
1930–1936 / Stephen Lyon Endicott.

Includes bibliographical references and index.
ISBN 978-1-4426-4373-4 (bound)   ISBN 978-1-4426-1226-6 (pbk.)

1. Workers' Unity League of Canada – History.   2. Working class – Canada –
History – 20th century.   3. Labor unions – Canada – History – 20th century.
4. Canada – Economic conditions – 1918–1945.   5. Canada – Social conditions
– 1930–1939.   6. Canada – Politics and government – 1930–1935.   I. Title.

HD8106.E54 2012   331.8097109′043   C2012-902653-0

University of Toronto Press acknowledges the financial assistance to its
publishing program of the Canada Council for the Arts and the Ontario
Arts Council.

 Canada Council   Conseil des Arts   ONTARIO ARTS COUNCIL
for the Arts   du Canada   CONSEIL DES ARTS DE L'ONTARIO

University of Toronto Press acknowledges the financial support of
the Government of Canada through the Canada Book Fund for its
publishing activities.

This book has been published with the financial assistance of the
Dogwood Foundation of British Columbia.

To those who, like the heroes of this book, believe that 'history is something to be made while being understood, and something ultimately understandable only when being made'

Vernon Venable

Contents

Contents

Illustrations follow pages 176 and 320

Preface

The history of all hitherto existing society is the history of class struggles.
– Karl Marx and Friedrich Engels, 1848[1]

The Workers' Unity League took shape in Canada in 1930 as a small but feisty organization that aimed to mobilize workers' resistance to the massive unemployment and the general misery of the Great Depression which began in 1929.

Criticizing the mainstream labour movement as being passive in the face of employer attacks on the livelihood of workers, the WUL championed militant class struggle. 'The workers never got anything and never will get anything from the capitalist class,' declared the league, 'unless they fight for it.'[2]

They were Reds at a time when it was particularly dangerous to be a Red in Canada. To a later generation this statement may sound like the start of a fairy tale. But it is not. What unfolds in this account is based on historical records – fact, evidence, proof – and exists within living memory.

Business elites and the wealthy in general were alarmed by the WUL, which clearly didn't just want to get workers a better deal within the existing system, but, over the long haul, wanted to change the system itself. The elites' accustomed control over economic life seemed threatened, and by subversive forces which, they feared, would upset the existing order. They demanded that the Red 'agents of labour unrest' be identified, reined in, and, if possible, stopped in their tracks.

The government of Canada was not slow in responding to the owners' fears. Since the earlier labour unrest in Canada in 1919, at the time

of the Winnipeg general strike, the government in Ottawa had established a secret branch within the national police force to track down
'misguided persons' who sought to upset the established order. In 1931
the government employed a draconian and until then unused section of
the Criminal Code, hurriedly enacted in 1919, to outlaw the Communist
Party of Canada and send its leaders to jail. Following the instructions
of Commissioner A.B. Perry and his successors in the Royal Canadian
Mounted Police, the secret police stepped up its practice of creating personal history files on unsuspecting people, recording 'their ways, habits and antecedents' for possible use in court actions.[3] This pattern of
activity by the police, although a tightly guarded secret, became obvious as events unfolded in the following decades. As a result of informers' reports, many labour organizers served prison terms; many more
were deported. It was indeed a dangerous time to be a Red. Still, these
extraordinary, committed Canadians pushed on.

Since the Workers' Unity League was affiliated or at least associated
with the Red International of Labour Unions, a branch of the Communist (Third) International whose headquarters was located in the USSR,
it was one of those organizations despised and feared by Canada's elite
– there can be no doubt about that. But what did this affiliation mean?
How did 'being Red' affect the work of the organization? What did it
mean to the tens of thousands of Canadian workers – miners, lumberjacks, needle trades operators, the unemployed – who joined with the
WUL in the struggles for justice in the midst of the Depression? Through
the recently available archives of the Third International, this book
brings new perspectives to these questions.

Its organizers trailed everywhere by agents of the Royal Canadian
Mounted Police, the Workers' Unity League was supported everywhere by organizations of immigrant workers (especially the Ukrainian
Labour Farmer Temple Association and the Finnish Organization of
Canada). Encouraged by progressive lawyers, artists, and writers, it was
condemned by editorial writers in the daily press. Trained in Marxism
at schools organized by the underground Communist Party of Canada
(after 1931), members of the Workers' Unity League proceeded by trial
and error, and often with heroic daring, to organize the unemployed, to
build unions where there were none before, to win and to lose countless
battles with the Canadian state and with capitalist entrepreneurs. At its
height, the WUL had won the allegiance of 40,000 workers.

Then, in 1935, the WUL discontinued its separate existence in favour
of its affiliated unions rejoining the older trade union centres. This was

done in the hope of promoting working-class unity and with the prospect of doing something that had eluded it – forming industrial unions
in the auto, steel, rubber, metal mining, pulp and paper, meat packing, shipping, and other large-scale or emerging industries. Was this
act of self-demolition, then, a tacit admission of strategic error by the
militants, the result of outside pressure, or did it reflect a willingness
to consider a new approach under new circumstances? The alternatives
– bread-and-butter unionism (focusing exclusively on getting your own
members a bigger piece of the pie) versus some form of revolutionary
unionism – continue to stir controversy about the example set by the
Workers' Unity League.

A lifetime later, the role of the hardy men and women of the Workers' Unity League, their fleeting and not so fleeting victories in helping,
among other things, to topple a Tory prime minister, as well as their disappointments, have a continuing salience because the same erratic system of private market capitalism that they faced in the 1930s remains in
charge of the Canadian and world economy in a new century. Through
ups and downs, trade wars, fraudulent speculation, dislocations of the
workforce, mass unemployment, growing extremes of wealth and poverty, of privilege and want, ecological disasters, armed conflicts and wars
to gain control of valuable natural resources, the capitalist system continues on, creating 'a world after its own image.'[4]

Confronted with these unpleasant realities, resistance inevitably grows,
and many of the traditions fostered by the Workers' Unity League will be
seen to have their relevance. Those traditions emphasized education in
class analysis followed by class struggle; promoted democratic organization in the workplace and in the conduct of strike struggles; strove to
develop networks of solidarity; fostered public demonstrations; upheld
the practice of analysing mistakes publicly; and, most significantly, put
forward the vision of a socialist alternative to capitalism where public
ownership would replace private control of the means of production,
distribution, and exchange in the economy.

The analysis presented in this book will not satisfy those who see the
Third International as a one-man band conducted from Moscow; for
them Workers' Unity League equals orders from Moscow.[5] But it may
cause some who have considered the Workers' Unity League to be 'a
Canadian success story' and yet at the same time a form of insanity and
sectarian excess[6] to reconsider their harsher judgments.

My approach has been to place the Workers' Unity League in the
larger economic and political currents of society in Canada and abroad,

elements which are important determinants of historical development, and this is the subject matter of the early chapters. There follows an examination of practical activities and experience gained in organizing among coal miners, hard rock miners, garment industry workers, woodsmen, and fishermen, and in light industry and among the unemployed, as the members of the Workers' Unity League sought for ways to build up what they defined as a revolutionary union movement – a designation that is sometimes questioned.[7]

Interspersed and in chapters of a more political nature are the work of conventions of the organization, confrontations with the prime minister, and other matters of special interest. These topics include ways of coping with the government's criminal code, charges of vagrancy, unlawful assembly, rioting, sedition, being called 'foreign agents' etc., and claims that in being willing to defy the law, the league advocated the use of 'force and violence'; the league's affirmation of socialist construction in the Soviet Union as a model of hope for workers everywhere; the existence of, and reasons for, acrid relations between social democrats and communists; the work of revolutionary-minded women in theory and practice; and attempts to introduce democracy in the workplace by shifting the boundaries between management prerogatives and workers' rights.

Within that framework I have aimed to capture, as much as possible, the subjective experience of those who lived the history. This is an effort, in the words of historian Raphael Samuel, 'to personalize the working of large historical forces'[8] with the objective of helping the reader gain the critical perspective of the long view without having to sit in judgment from afar.

When I retired from teaching at York University in the 1990s my intention was to research and write this book immediately. However, several other projects intervened along the way and now it is twenty years later. In spite of the long delay I am grateful for the extra time it has given me to research and reflect more deeply upon a subject that a colleague once warned me 'is fraught.' It is indeed fraught with minefields of many kinds, both real and figurative, making it best for the historian to wear a hard hat when hiking through this exciting terrain.

The records are voluminous. Apart from those of the Communist Party of Canada, by far the most numerous and useful for this study were those gathered by the Department of Labour on strikes and lockouts and those collected by the secret service of the Royal Canadian Mounted Police on communists and others of the left. The police records, some of which have been destroyed but which, nevertheless, still run to tens of thousands of pages, remain partially shrouded in fog under the control of the Canadian Security Intelligence Service. The descriptions and locations of all these collections are listed in the bibliography.

I have many people to thank, including George Brandak, and later Ralph Stanton, of the University of British Columbia Special Collections, who introduced me to its abundant resources on the labour movement of that province. My thanks as well to James Bowman at the Glenbow Archives in Calgary, who provided the same service for Alberta. The staff of the Saskatchewan Archives Board, including Trina Gillis of the government records branch and Tim Novak of special media, were most helpful and attentive to my requests for records of royal commissions and court trials. I am indebted to many archivists and access officers at Library and Archives Canada (LAC), especially those in the Historical Resources Branch of the Government Archives Division, of whom I should mention Ellen Scheinberg and Terry Badgley, who looked for deportation files, and Sarah Gawman, Jay Khosla, Antonio Lechasseur, Doug Luchak, and several others for helping me with the prickly task of arranging access to the relevant Canadian Security Intelligence Service files.[9] My thanks also go to the then solicitor general, Hon. Doug Lewis, for overriding CSIS objections to my seeing the personal history file of Thomas A. Ewen for the years 1930–6.

I want to thank many for sharing their resources and memories with me, including the late Stewart Smith and Oscar Brooks. Also, and with equal thanks, Allen Seager of Vancouver, Garnet Dishaw of Regina, Bill and Arthur Ross and Len Kaminsky of Winnipeg, and Jack Cohen of Montreal. Special thanks to Andrew Cragg, a resourceful and inspired research assistant who is also a talented writer and deserves much credit for chapter 9. Thanks also to the board of directors of the Dogwood Foundation for Socialist Education in British Columbia for their decision to provide seed money to help make the publication of this book possible. I am especially grateful to friends, colleagues, and family members for their comments and suggestions on parts or on the whole of earlier drafts of the manuscript: Meg Luxton, Ester Reiter, David Frank, Ben Shek, Ned Hagerman, Lorraine Endicott, Garnet Dishaw, Nick Aplin, Carl Dow, Bill Devine, and two anonymous readers for the University of Toronto Press. Their advice was of great benefit to the text and to the author who, nevertheless, bears full responsibility for the shortcomings that remain. My appreciation goes to Vivien Endicott-Douglas for helping to collect the photographs, to Marion Endicott and Laura Keresztesi for their assistance with making the index, and to Anne Fullerton for proofreading the text so expertly. My thanks, finally, to the editors Len Husband, Frances Mundy, and Judy Williams of the University of Toronto Press for their continuous support and careful attention in helping to bring this project into the light of day.

Stephen Endicott,
Senior Scholar (retired)
Faculty of Liberal Arts and Professional Studies,
York University, Toronto,
November 2010

Abbreviations

ACCL	All-Canadian Congress of Labour
AFL	American Federation of Labour
CCF	Co-operative Commonwealth Federation
CI Fonds	Communist International (Comintern) Fonds
CLDL	Canadian Labour Defense League
CPC	Communist Party of Canada
CSIS	Canadian Security Intelligence Service
FCWIU	Fishermen and Cannery Workers' Industrial Union
FIU	Fishermen's Industrial Union
FOC	Finnish Organization of Canada
FSU	Friends of the Soviet Union
IUNTW	Industrial Union of Needle Trades Workers
IWW	Industrial Workers of the World
LAC	Library and Archives Canada
LWIU	Lumber Workers' Industrial Union
MWUC	Mine Workers' Union of Canada
NUWA	National Unemployed Workers' Association
OA	Ontario Archives
OBU	One Big Union
RCMP	Royal Canadian Mounted Police
RCWU	Relief Camp Workers' Union
RILU	Red International of Labour Unions
SAB	Saskatchewan Archives Board
TLC	Trades and Labour Congress
ULFTA	Ukrainian Labour Farmer Temple Association
UMWA	United Mine Workers of America

WIR	Workers' International Relief
WLL	Women's Labour League
WUL	Workers' Unity League

RAISING THE WORKERS' FLAG

The Workers' Unity League of Canada, 1930–1936

1

Workers in Canada's Second Industrial Revolution

Swift rivers tumble through the Canadian forests on their way to the mighty
St. Lawrence. Between them, covering vast stretches of the provinces of
Ontario and Quebec, lies a great area of choice timber land, its potential
wealth defies estimate. Year after year, an army of men with axes and saws
invades it, levies tribute for the busy mills dotting the rivers ... seemingly an
endless source of profit to their owners.

−Time Magazine, 27 August 1928

It was a time of considerable optimism in the country. There were profits to be made and jobs to be had. The boreal forests of Canada had
become an immense construction site of capitalism, with pulp and paper
industries joining the new automobile and farm machinery factories in
Southern Ontario and the textile mills of Quebec in prosperous times.
Along with those industries, new chemical, rubber, electrical appliance
factories, and other industries, as well as hard rock mines for gold, silver,
copper, nickel, lead, and zinc in Northern Ontario, in Rouyn-Noranda,
Quebec, in Flin Flon, Manitoba, and in Trail and Anyox, British Columbia, comprise what is sometimes called Canada's 'Second Industrial Revolution.' Gathering momentum since the beginning of the century, the
Second Industrial Revolution, based upon newly available supplies of
electric power, mass production techniques, a growing supply of immigrant labour, and the greater availability of consumer credit, reached its
peak in the years 1924–9 before the great crash and depression of the
1930s.

Pulp and paper manufacture was the largest of the new industries.
It had more invested capital than the others, greater value of output,

as well as higher aggregate salaries and wages paid. At its high point in 1929, the industry had 33,000 workers and indirectly gave work to another 180,000 on the railways, in forestry, in construction and building roads, not to mention other spin-off employment in services and government work. All across Quebec and Northern Ontario, Canadian and American investment bankers, eagerly supported by provincial governments, poured millions of dollars into mills and forestry operations, hydro-electric projects, and railways and roads to anchor this industry's development. The owners of capital engaged in hectic competition to capture the large and growing market for newsprint in cities like Chicago, Detroit, Philadelphia, and New York. By the late 1920s, Canada produced 70 per cent of all newsprint on the world market. Yet, ironically, at the same time the capitalist corporations that achieved this success were on the verge of bankruptcy owing to questionable financial manipulations, unplanned excess capacity, and a glut on the markets.[1]

Companies such as the Abitibi Power and Paper, for example, one of the three largest pulp and paper conglomorates, had mills scattered across Ontario at Iroquois Falls, Espanola, Sturgeon Falls, Sault Ste Marie, and Thunder Bay. Hoping to lure employees and their families to the new frontier of industry, the company, led by Frank Harris Anson, an American, built model towns with stores, restaurants, bowling alleys, schools, and churches. The giant mill at Iroquois Falls, the largest in North America, even had a dairy farm.[2] But so afraid was Abitibi of labour troubles and union organizers that its job-sites sometimes resembled prison camps.

The atmosphere of police surveillance, dangerous work, vicious speed-up, and wretched wages was captured by an employee at the Abitibi Canyon power project near Fraserdale, Ontario, in an article that appeared in the *Worker* in 1930.

The employee wrote that a worker must be shipped into this job by an employment agency. Fraserdale, the closest railway station, was about three miles from the job. This place, he noted, 'bears all the earmarks of the entrance to a prison camp.' When a worker stepped off the train a number of big policemen stepped up and demanded that the worker identify himself by showing a shipping bill from the employment agency or office of the company. If the worker could not produce either of these he was told to get the next train back and the police saw to it that he did. If the worker had the necessary credentials, 'the bulls tell him to open up his baggage' to see what it contained on the pretence of a search for liquor. Then, if the worker had no papers pertaining to organized labour, he was told to put his belongings back together and get on the train that went to the job. The police rode on the train, keeping an eye on him until he was assigned sleeping quarters. For most workers the work day was eleven hours, seven days a week, regardless of the weather. The police were on the job all the time to 'see that you don't come in a minute early at meal times or … stay too long in the toilet.' The rock men or miners were about the worst off. They worked under loose rock and dirt extending from twenty to one hundred feet above them. A landslide buried two workmen who were lucky in getting off with some cuts and broken bones. When the company tried to make the miners in the tunnel work ten hours instead of eight, for eight hours' pay, most of them refused and they were fired. 'They were replaced by another gang and one of these men was killed and another hurt soon after they arrived.' There were about twelve hundred men on this job. Carpenters with tools got 50 cents an hour; trestle men, 45 cents; carpenters' helpers, 25 cents; labourers, 20 cents. All workers paid $1.05 a day for board, one dollar a month for the doctor, 'and four times the price for anything you buy in the line of clothes.' 'Abitibi Canyon,' concluded the correspondent, whose identity was of necessity protected by the newspaper, 'is a good place to stay away from.'[3]

These conditions were a challenge that militant or even just self-respecting workers could hardly ignore, and scattered attempts were made to find redress. One of these, a celebrated case, took place in the woods in 1929 near Thunder Bay where a contractor – the Pigeon River Timber Company – was cutting pulpwood to supply Abitibi Power and Paper and other mills. In an effort to spread an existing strike against low pay, poor working conditions, and mediocre food in the camps, the Lumber Workers' Industrial Union sent two delegates, Viljo Rosvall and John Voutilainen, to contact the pulp cutters in a camp at Onion Lake, about twenty miles west of Port Arthur, near the Shabaqua railway station. The two men, both experienced woodsmen of Finnish origin, set out on foot through the timber land on 13 November 1929 and were never seen alive again by their comrades. The union claimed foul play and that the men had been murdered; the other side spread rumours such as that the woodsmen had absconded to the USA with union money. The provincial police made perfunctory investigations. Five months later, when the snow melted, the bodies of the two men, with bones broken and clothes torn, were found half a mile apart in the bed of a shallow creek running into Onion Lake. The coroner's verdict was 'accidental case of drowning' and nobody was ever charged. In spite of a huge funeral during which 5,000 mourners marched through the streets of Port Arthur, and other protests, it took over sixty years before 'the two union men who never died' gained general recognition by their induction into the city's Labour Hall of Fame and the naming of two small lakes in their honour near Onion Lake by the Ontario Historical Board.[4]

'The Canadian bourgeosie is young and arrogant,' wrote K. Finn, a Finnish immigrant journalist, saying that it would be hard to find a ruling class anywhere that had created its riches 'by such dirty robbing, murdering and exploitation of the workers and the natives.' For workers who did not want to believe that 'the bourgeoisie was as mean and arrogant as it showed itself to be,' he said, it was time to cast away illusions.[5]

Simultaneous with the spread of the pulp and paper industry on the rock-bound lands of the Canadian shield, there came a rapid development of mining and smelting for non-ferrous minerals. Stock promoters were quite ecstatic about the possibilities of the mines, the 'treasure box' of the north. In the decade of the 1920s the output value of the six metals – gold, silver, nickel, lead, zinc, and copper – tripled across Canada to $150 million and the number of workers involved rose from 10,000 to 23,000. Several new millionaires emerged in Toronto, Montreal, and Vancouver, but the low wages and dangerous working conditions in the mines were little different from those of the Abitibi Canyon, and although spontaneous protests and revolts by workers were not uncommon, the presence of union organizers capable of overcoming security fences was just as rare. The structured mal-distribution of wealth and purchasing power that was to lead to the catastrophes of the 1930s, write historians John Thompson and Allen Seager, 'was a constant factor in Canadian economic life.'[6]

Among the other fast-rising manufacturing industries in this new economic era, none was more important or of greater significance for Canada's development than the automobile factories. In the 1920s, total capital invested in the business rose from $40 million to $98 million and the number of workers involved in building motor vehicles by 1928 was 13,000, mostly in southern Ontario. Through mergers and buy-outs, a score of small Canadian companies, such as the McLaughlin Motor Car Company of Oshawa and the Gray-Dort Motor Company of Chatham, Ontario, were absorbed into the Canadian branch plants of the 'big three' of the United States – Ford, General Motors, and Chrysler – which soon dominated the Canadian scene. Underpinning the production and spread of the automobile was its need for steel, glass, rubber, fabric, batteries, electric fixtures, precision machinery, oil and gasoline, service stations, mechanics, licensing bureaux, insurance agents, and road builders, all of which had a ripple effect throughout the economy, stimulating growth in many directions.[7] And lured by Ford's policy of 'high output, low prices, high wages,' workers flocked to Detroit and Windsor to get jobs in the industry.

Inside the automobile factories, however, there was a harsh reality of assembly-line speed-ups, industrial accidents, tyrannical overseers, and unexpected layoffs. 'Nowhere in the world were the workers exploited more systematically and heartlessly,' wrote William Z. Foster, chairman of the American Communist Party, in commenting on the autocratic rule of the automobile kings and their highly developed union-smashing techniques, including hired provocateurs who posed as union members and a network of labour spies. 'Never before has competition between the automobile trusts been so fierce,' observed Harvey Murphy, the youthful secretary of an early Canadian attempt to build a union in the industry in 1928. The workers' share of an industry that was headed for a crash, said Murphy, was the prospect of being burnt out in a few years unless the ruthless speed-ups, wage-cuts, and longer and longer layoffs could be checked.[8]

Another major sector of the Second Industrial Revolution was the textile industry, which in its cotton, woollen, hosiery and knit goods, and silk and rayon factories employed over 56,000 workers by 1929, of which 43 per cent were women and girls.[9] The largest of four conglomerates controlling the industry in Canada was Dominion Textiles of Montreal, with sales of $21 million in 1929 and headed by such pillars of society as Sir Herbert Holt (president of the Royal Bank of Canada), Sir Charles Gordon (president of the Bank of Montreal), and his son G. Blair Gordon.

The handful of millionaires who ran the textile industry had a particularly hard resolve, easily comparable to that of the 'automobile kings.' In every factory they had efficiency experts at work devising new speed-up schemes which, together with new machinery, increased production enormously. This process also intensified the labour of the workers involved. It was not unheard of in some factories for one girl to operate as many as ten looms for a mere $10.00 a week. In the years since 1921 the companies had pushed down wages of their workers by as much as 40 per cent and extended the work week to fifty or fifty-five hours. Within the operations of a mill, a carder getting 44 cents per hour in 1921 received 30 cents in 1928, as did a loom fixer who formerly earned 53 cents. A ring spinner dropped from 26 ½ cents to 17 cents an hour.[10] The workers had a saying: 'If you cut Sir H. Holt he would bleed ice-water.'[11]

Apart from merciless exploitation of their workers, the textile barons also engaged in scandalous stock market frauds and tax evasions, becoming multi-millionaires in the process. Their behaviour was such that a public outcry forced their peers to establish a royal commission of investigation. The lead counsel of that commission, J.C. McRuer, later chief justice of Ontario, described their activity using these words:

> A shameful, sickening, story of heartless exploitation and wholesale robbery by men prominent in the public life of Canada. Inordinate greed, barefaced lying and criminal fraud, characterize the careers of this gang of high-class crooks.[12]

These were the leaders in the cotton manufacturing industry and simultaneously presidents of Canada's largest banks. A 'spirit of unrest permeates every textile factory,' wrote Rebecca Buhay, director of the Women's Department of the Communist Party, in 1931. Wildcat strikes had broken out here and there, but the textile industry was virgin soil waiting for a method 'of drawing these masses of women and girls into the struggle' against the intense exploitation.[13] In this connection McRuer warned the textile owners of 'devastation of drastic industrial revolution' unless the workers received the measure of justice to which they were entitled in a democratic country.[14]

When the Great Depression struck at the end of 1929 and brought a halt to the surging economy of the Second Industrial Revolution, the Canadian labour movement was ill prepared to defend workers against drastic attacks on their living standards. Wage cuts and lay-offs, factory closings and line-ups for relief, defaulted mortgage payments and evictions were the order of the day, crying out for protest and acts of resistance. But the days of the Winnipeg General Strike and such militant unions as the One Big Union in 1919, a time when workers 'created their own organizations, marched off the job in record numbers, engaged in defiant acts of solidarity, and made bold new demands,'[15] were long gone, replaced by a shrinking and increasingly conservative and complacent labour movement led by the international craft unions of the American Federation of Labour/Trades and Labour Congress of Canada (AFL-TLC). A Conservative government in Ottawa felt comfortable in selecting one of their number, Gideon Robertson, to be in the Senate, and he became minister of labour.

A brief exception to the general downward trend of the labour movement was the formation of the All-Canadian Congress of Labour in 1927 as a centre for unions built on an industrial rather than craft basis. Led by A.R. Mosher, a social democrat and president of the Canadian Brotherhood of Railway Employees, the ACCL represented a rare moment of co-operation between communists and social democrats in the labour movement. In this organization 50,000 unionized miners and lumber and building trades workers, as well as railroaders, agitated against foreign control of Canada and its unions and for industrial unions to replace the obsolete form of craft unions. For a time its leaders expressed a common admiration for the progress of building socialism in the Soviet Union as an alternative to the capitalist system.[16]

Reflecting some deep divisions of opinion in the Canadian labour movement of the time, Tom Moore, president of the TLC (which had 203,000 members in 1929),[17] greeted the formation of the ACCL with derision and disdain. He said it should be called the 'All-Red Congress of Labour.'[18] The ACCL, through its new journal, the *Canadian Unionist*, made spirited replies. The AFL-TLC name-calling, it said, was 'only another scarecrow,' and it considered any attack from that quarter to be a compliment. The war of words grew heated as the *Canadian Unionist* ran articles about 'the labour-faker ridden' American unions – 'capitalist agents at work within the unions.' The 'Honourable' Gideon Robertson, vice-president of the Order of Railway Telegraphers and soon to be labour minister again, was singled out by the ACCL for special mention as having all of the attributes of the successful capitalist agent: 'a rhinoceros hide, an automatic handshake, and a not altogether exaggerated regard for the truth.' Off the backs of the working class, this man had scaled 'the entire gamut from the garden variety labour-faker to the dignified position of capitalist Labour Lieutenant extravaganza,' all the while 'browsing on the field of organized labour.'[19]

This kind of rhetoric, colourful and satisfying at the moment, was not uncommon in the labour movement at the time and it soon escalated as the communists and social democrats rediscovered their mutual incompatibilities within the newly founded ACCL.

The immediate issues underlying their historic rift, to judge by columns in the *Canadian Unionist*, were, for the social democrats, 'the communists' conceit' in thinking that anyone who did not agree with them was 'either a knave or a fool,' their bad manners, and their aggressive, crusading tactics in Salvation Army fashion.[20] For the communists it was the ACCL's tendency to rely on poaching members from other unions rather than initiating organizing drives[21] and, perhaps even more important, their ideological sympathy for something called Mondism.

Mondism took its name from Alfred Mond, the first Lord Melchett, a British politician – minister of health for a short time – and a man of considerable means, a multi-millionaire in fact. He was the founder and chairman of Imperial Chemical Industries, one of Britain's largest corporations, manufacturing explosives, fertilizers, insecticides, dyestuffs, industrial chemicals, paints, and printing materials. He owned one of the big nickel mines in Sudbury, Ontario. After the bitter general strike in Britain, in 1926, he had come up with a plan for team play and harmony in industry to replace strikes and he persuaded the social democratic head of the British Trade Union Congress to join him on a tour of that country to popularize his ideas. The editor of the *Canadian Unionist* gave much publicity to Mondism and editorialized that 'buyers and sellers of labour power ... may have little respect for each other, but they can seldom gain anything by standing aloof or by brawling in the marketplace.' In his report to the second national convention of the ACCL at the end of 1928, Mosher said his executive was watching 'with interest' the progress in England of the Mond plan for an industrial peace between Capital and Labour and thought it would be 'unwise' for labour 'to refuse their co-operation, keeping in mind the general welfare of the workers and the people of Canada as a whole.'

Before long and increasingly, the *Canadian Unionist* began soliciting and gaining display advertisements from some of the largest corporations in Canada – the banks and oil companies, distilleries, the T. Eaton and Robert Simpson companies, Canadian Industries Ltd (Alfred Mond's branch company in Canada), Dominion Textiles (Montreal) Ltd, National Steel Car Company (Hamilton), Canadian Western Lumber (Fraser Mills, BC), Canadian Collieries (Dunsmuir) Ltd – many of them the very worst examples of non-union, open shops that the communists were determined to organize.

With the communists shouting epithets such as 'labour fakers' and 'social fascists' (socialists in words, fascists in deeds), and the social democrats decrying 'anarcho-communists' and 'puppets of Moscow' in mutual vituperations, their co-operation began to unravel rather quickly.

The basic differences that emerged within the ACCL between the social democratic tactic of Mondist *class co-operation* (sometimes termed *class collaboration* by its critics) and the communist preference for *class struggle* tactics would present themselves as a fundamental feature of the labour movement for decades to come. As the Great Depression began, these differences played themselves out most dramatically in the coalfields of Alberta. When faced with the expiry of union contracts in

1930 and the demand of the coal bosses for more wage cuts and other concessions, Frank Wheatley, vice-president of the ACCL, president and secretary of the Mine Workers' Union of Canada, and a close colleague of Mosher, took a soft line, proposing a royal commission to investigate the mining industry and a conciliation board to settle the issues. In contrast, the youthful and abrasive communist organizer, Harvey Murphy, demanded preparations for a strike. Workers never get anything unless they are prepared to fight, said Murphy; it was a matter of 'Strike or Starve!' In a surprising result, for Wheatley, the miners, in response to Murphy's efforts, voted in a recall ballot to remove Wheatley from office, ending his career as a union official.[22] (See chapter 3.) More and more, communist and social democratic leaders in Canada became bitter enemies. While their socialist visions of the future may, in some cases, have been quite similar, their strategies and tactics for getting there were often many miles apart and as a result they often carried their sectarian in-fighting to exaggerated lengths.

As the project for building the All-Canadian Congress of Labour faded, an old but urgent question posed itself to the communists: How could they help militant workers gather up their forces to influence the direction of the labour movement? How could union organizers reach the workers in the camps of the Abitibi pulp and paper operations, in the hard rock mines of Alfred Mond, in the spy-infested automobile factories run by Henry Ford, the exploited women and girls in the mills of Sir Herbert Holt and the other textile barons? How could they build effective trade unions to confront the 'gang of high-class crooks' who currently dominated the public life of Canada?

Hitherto the communists had relied on building up the Trade Union Education League, a body founded by the American communists in the early 1920s as a vehicle for carrying out their program in industry by working within the mainstream unions. Sensitive to the criticism that the TUEL would be just another 'dual union' like the One Big Union and a cause of unforgivable disunity in the labour movement, the communists took great pains to say that it was *not* a union at all, but a 'purely educational body.'[23] But by the end of the decade in both the United States and Canada the effectiveness of the TUEL had declined. Battered as it was by the policy of many unions to expel radical members, and weakened by visions of prosperity in the working class as capitalism made economic advances in the Second Industrial Revolution, the TUEL, according to its leaders, was more or less moribund by 1928.[24]

It was at this juncture that a new answer to the problem began to take shape, an answer that, like Alfred Mond's program, came from the other side of the Atlantic Ocean. Coinciding with the start of the great crisis in the industrial system of capitalism and building upon the theoretical weight and practical experience of the Red International of Labour Unions of the Third (Communist) International,[25] centred in Moscow, the new direction had a certain undeniable logic and attraction for radicals. Cautiously at first and then with increasing vigour, the Canadian communists adopted a new path in their odyssey to find a way to participate in the class struggles in Canada and to influence the course of politics in a manner favourable to the working class. In spite of the pitfalls of *dual unionism*, they would aim to build a new, more militant, trade union centre.

2
The Red International

The Workers' Unity League was organized on the instructions of communist officials in Moscow ... its plan of action ... is dictated from Moscow,
and ... it subsists principally to carry out the instructions of its masters, and
is much more concerned with Russian praise than with Canadian welfare.

Hon. W.H. Price, attorney general for Ontario[1]

It would be misleading to depict Comintern and its component parties in
the early nineteen-thirties as a monolithic structure responding blindly to
the dictates of a single supreme authority.

E.H. Carr, British historian[2]

The communists of Canada were a section of the Third (Communist)
International, whose headquarters were in Moscow. As their recruiting
propaganda showed, they were proud of this fact.[3] They considered the
Third International ('Comintern' for short) to be 'the general staff of
all Communist Parties,'[4] leading an offensive against capitalism. But at
times they had to disguise their links to what many Canadian politicians
and other Western leaders considered an irritating and possibly a dangerous centre of socialist revolution. Canadian delegates to the headquarters of the Comintern, therefore, often used pseudonyms to avoid
arrest when returning home, and, to elude spies in the Royal Mail, they
sometimes established more secure channels for sending communications back and forth between Toronto and Moscow. These elements, plus
the emergence of police agents secretly planted among their organizations by the government, have contributed to an aura of mystery surrounding some activities of the Canadian section of the Comintern and
its associated Red International of Labour Unions.

On the one hand, political leaders in Canada did their best to portray the communists as an international conspiracy organized and financed by Moscow to subvert the constitution and the British way of life. They claimed the communists aimed to do this by 'force and violence' and 'armed uprising.' At first glance the formulation of early theses of Lenin's Third International, with phrases like 'only the forcible overthrow of the bourgeoisie' could lead to the submission of the exploiters to the will of the majority, lent some credence to that idea.[5] The Third International, so the argument ran, found willing and subservient men and women who took 'orders from Moscow' to accomplish their insurrectionary work, all to the detriment of the working people they claimed to serve. This was sedition, if not treason. Lawyers and judges hammered away at this theme in the numerous trials of arrested activists, at deportation hearings of strikers, in the media, and through special publications.[6] Not surprisingly, the communists had a much different understanding of the place of the Third International in Canada. Either way, its dimensions and influence were of such importance that the general outlines and controversies surrounding the subject need to be explored and grasped – an inescapable and intriguing necessity for understanding the Workers' Unity League, its work and purposes. A brief introduction to the complexities of this matter is the purpose of the present chapter.

In the late 1920s and early 1930s, when young Canadian workers set forth to work or study in the headquarters of the Third International, it was an intensely dramatic moment in their lives. There was the excitement of an ocean liner crossing the Atlantic, arrival in England, France, or Hamburg, Germany, and after a few days to make contacts and arrangements for further travel, an exciting and slightly nervous train ride crossing frontiers of countries barely on speaking terms with the Soviet Union. At last to arrive in Moscow, and Red Square, Lenin's tomb, symbols of the Great October Revolution that was barely ten years old.

The first to participate in this high adventure was Stewart Osborne Smith, son of Rev. A.E. Smith, a Methodist minister of Brandon, Manitoba, and not yet nineteen in the spring of 1926. Other Canadian communists, including Jack MacDonald, Maurice Spector, and Tim Buck, had come earlier for short periods of time to attend congresses and meetings, but young Smith was the first to set down his feet on a two-year extended stay for study and work. He was followed in the next dozen years by a host of other Canadians, some of the most prominent of whom were Charles Marriott, Leslie Morris, Oscar Ryan, Sam Carr, John Weir, Harvey Murphy, James Litterick, Charles Sims, Norman Freed, Annie Buller, Bill Rigby, and Tom Ewen.

Smith lived in a small hotel, on Tverskoi Street, down the road and around the corner from the Lux Hotel where most of the delegates to the Third International stayed. He divided his time between studies at the newly opened International Lenin School and, as the responsible person (called a referent – someone to whom matters are referred) for Canada, working at the secretariats of the Comintern and the Red International of Trade Unions – setting the pattern for those that followed.

The curriculum and culture of the International Lenin School had a strong influence in shaping the cadre of young men and women who would lead the Workers' Unity League. The school, which was located at 25a Vorovsky Street, was in the central core area of old Moscow not far from the famous Arbat market. The building was said to be a former palace of Catherine the Great.[7] One of the largest rooms, perhaps Catherine's bedroom with its great painted ceilings, was the dining room. Smith roomed with a German student whose pseudonym was Karl Adolphus, and he never learned his real name. 'We studied hard,' Smith told me when I interviewed him many years later, 'and I had difficulty with the chief instructor of the English sector. I've forgotten his name. He was a Hungarian of the Bela Kun revolution ... The head of the school was Klavdiya Kirsanova, wife of the minister of culture in the government.' Altogether there were about 200 students and they each received a small stipend while enrolled in the school. 'I had tens of thousands of roubles in the bank, from articles that I wrote,' recalled Smith. 'Anytime an event happened in Canada I would be asked to write articles for this or that paper and they paid me.'[8] Smith was an apt learner, became fluent in German, the official language of the Third International, and did well.

Sensational claims to the contrary,[9] bomb-making and espionage techniques were absent from the curriculum of the school. Students studied the philosophical world outlook and method of Marxism-Leninism, the history of the Russian Revolution, how to apply Marxist philosophy to the understanding of historical problems, knowing the difference between strategy and tactics, the value of criticism and self-criticism, and related matters. They also took part in work experience projects in the factories and farms of the Soviet Union to learn about the building of socialism in real life.

Another thing students absorbed from their instructors was the importance of *parti´ness* – having a sense of commitment or loyalty to the movement. As they studied the history of the First International (the International Workingmen's Association, 1864–76), the Second (Socialist) International (1889–1916, and after a brief hiatus down to the present), and the Third (Communist) International (1919–43), they knew that parties trying to guide themselves by the social science of Marxism had made errors and would get into blind alleys, but these detours were ephemeral. Like sailing ships in a squall, the party would right itself and surge ahead. That is what members hoped for and believed. What the students experienced from their life in the Soviet Union and in their stints of practical work experience only served to strengthen such convictions in most of them. To unsympathetic observers, to those who had no interest in the method of Marxism or in the discoveries that Karl Marx had made about class struggle and the economic patterns of capitalism, such *parti´ness* was something to be abhorred or perhaps pitied and despised as a willingness to be supervised from afar. But for someone who had decided to become a revolutionary it was not a matter of supervision, but of discipline. And mainly voluntary self-discipline – along with the possibilities of participation that were felt to be genuine and meaningful, though sometimes uncomfortable.

For the other parts of his assignment, to act as referent for Canada, Smith went over to the Comintern headquarters and to the head office of the Red International of Trade Unions.

The CI offices were located on Mokhovaya Street near Okhotny Riad (Hunter's Square) opposite one of the entrances to the Kremlin, the historic fortified complex at the centre of Moscow which housed the executive branch of the Soviet government. Smith remembered the place as a shabby white building, three or four stories high. Inside delegates and workers from all the main countries of the world, from Europe, Asia, Oceania, Africa, and the Americas, people of varied experiences and temperaments, came together, the one place on the globe where they could escape the harassment of the propertied classes and the colonial rulers. 'Day in and day out,' according to a young American participant, Joseph Freeman, 'they gathered and collated the experiences of the working class in all lands … they exchanged opinions with all the parties; they outlined policies, democratically arrived at, for the direction of the struggle for a new world.'[10] It was a stimulating environment beyond all Smith's expectations.

In the Comintern building, with its meeting rooms and library, well stocked with government publications and statistics from around the world, annual reports of business corporations, publications of the labour movements, newspapers of the communist and social democratic parties, and *The Times* of London or the *New York Times*, Smith kept up to date with the world and did his homework. Here, too, he met and was on speaking terms with Nikolai Bukharin, and then Dimitri Manuilsky and

Otto Kuusinen, top leaders of the Third International from the Russian delegation.[11] Fellow student Joseph Freeman provides an intimate portrait of some of the these leaders and their working style:

> Here was Kusinin [*sic*], of the presidium, a Finn of forty-six, with years of struggle and suffering behind him, pure in his devotion to the cause; a quiet deliberate, slow-speaking man, cautiously sifting facts. Mistakes were dangerous; too much was at stake. He turned your mind inside out, asking a thousand questions about your country, your Party, your labour movement. He carefully probed everything you knew, and everything everybody else knew, before coming to any conclusion of his own. He reminded you of [a professor] on campus, with his lined sallow face, his scientific meticulousness ... Manuilsky, also of the presidium, had the same thoroughness; he, too, examined and cross-examined men and documents before arriving at decisions, but his method was different. He drew you out by humour; he rocked your memory loose by anecdote and laughter ... He kidded you into remembering what you had forgotten ... The methods were different but the results were the same.[12]

Mostly Smith's finished reports ended up with Kuusinen, the member of the executive committee of the CI with overall responsibility for its Anglo-American Secretariat. This was a logical step since 60 per cent of the membership of the Canadian party were Finns – Red Finns who had arrived in Canada after the Whites won the Finnish civil war in 1918.

The Anglo-American Secretariat encompassed all the English-speaking countries and it was headed by Kurt Eckert, a German, who, according to Smith, 'was very familiar with U.S. and British Communist Party affairs.'[13] A staff of translators, stenographers, and typists led by a senior political secretary from each of Britain and the United States, as well as national representatives or referents (such as Smith) from Canada, Australia, South Africa, Ireland, India (which was a British colony at the time), and later New Zealand, carried on the day-to-day work of the 'A-A Secretariat.' The method of work for communicating with the sections in the various countries reflected a noticeable national ethos: referents from each country drafted the documents or letters and then, with a German translation, they circulated around for notations or minutes by the members of the Anglo-American secretariat. Taking these comments into account, the national representative would then redraft them and the documents would be dispatched under the name or seal of the secretariat. The form, tone, and content of letters and directives of the

Comintern most often were the product of discussion and agreement by national and international participants.[14] 'I never wrote a document that I didn't agree with,' Smith insisted.[15]

Sometimes the Canadians delayed implementing policy adopted by the Comintern or the Red International of Trade Unions, even acting contrary to the directives and advice, either because of disagreement with them or because they seemed impractical, as in the case of mining policy or organization of the unemployed movement. Canadian representatives, at least, could find room for expression of their ideas in the working out of policy about the Workers' Unity League. Moreover, it was expected of them. The easy characterization of participants in the international organizations as subservient pawns and foreign agents is superficial, an interpretation stemming from misinformation or political bias. At the same time, it cannot be denied that the common recognition of the leading position of the Soviet Communist Party in the Comintern (it was the largest party and had achieved state power) made it difficult to suspend belief when aspects of the Soviet Union's foreign and domestic policies deserved closer scrutiny and questioning by fellow members of the organization.

Smith, who was to play a prominent part in the Canadian communist movement,[16] was not an easy character to work with and he was certainly no pushover. He was flamboyant in speech and verbose in composing official documents. He was always coming up with jaunty, dogmatic, self-evident 'truths' which he liked to drive home with theoretical-sounding flourishes. Reading the Comintern archives, even seventy-five years later, it is not hard to detect the documents produced by his handiwork.

The robust character of the young Canadian students at the Lenin School and the candour of their relationships are illustrated in a lengthy handwritten letter sent by Leslie Morris to Smith complaining of his treatment of some articles Morris had mailed from Moscow for publication in the *Worker*. Smith, by now back in Toronto, had said Morris played 'the role of confusionist by obscuring the issues of the struggle' and accused him of 'somersaults.' Morris was furious. 'Jump off your high horse, Stewart, before you fall! Bugger you and your pharsical [*sic*] humbug … You should not be so high-falutin in your approach to comrades. I tell you straight – well-meaning as you may be – that this attitude doesn't fizz on me after 18 months in the Lenin School with as good a record as you, I am sure. So that is that.'[17] Personal rivalry and animosities aside, these were people, mostly men, of unusual ability and strength of character, eager to make their contribution to a cause.

Apart from providing scholarships for a limited number of young revolutionaries from other countries to get what amounted to a university-level education in Moscow, what other material aid did the Russian Revolution give to its friends around the world? And did the executive of the Comintern use financial aid as a means of expressing approval or disapproval of its sections? These are questions of frequent speculation.

Perhaps the most famous cases of material support from the Comintern were with Britain and China. At the time of the coal miners' general strike in 1926, British and Soviet trade unions were linked by the Anglo-Russian Trade Union Committee. As a gesture of solidarity with the British miners, Russian miners raised 10 million roubles for strike support, but the British Trade Union Congress was too embarrassed and refused to accept the funds.[18] In the case of China, the Soviet government successfully sent a boatload of arms and Michael Borodin as political adviser to help Sun Yat-sen's Kuomintang (Nationalist) Party in the 1920s in its effort to unify China against the regional warlords who were being bolstered by various Western powers and Japan.

Another less ostentatious way of giving aid to its friends was through the regular trading networks and banking facilities that the Soviet Union was establishing in Western capitalist countries. Arcos in London and Amtorg in New York City, for example, were Soviet companies that arranged commercial transactions – the selling of Russian raw materials and the buying of industrial equipment and machinery. The sums of money involved here were in the tens of millions and it was well within the capitalist 'rules of the game' to pay commissions or fees of various kinds; at least that is what Amtorg said when questioned. There was nothing to stop some of the commissions from going to supporters of the left. The famous American entrepreneur and millionaire Armand Hammer played such a role. After talking with Lenin, he established a pencil factory, a branch of an automobile company, and other enterprises in Russia, and for the privilege he agreed to pay some of the necessary fees and commissions to the New York account of what was in fact the American section of the Comintern.[19] There was undoubtedly something fictitious, but according to prevailing practices of the markets there was nothing illegal about such transactions. Funds could also be paid as commissions for services rendered in distributing Soviet films and publications in foreign countries or Soviet purchases of subscriptions to the communist press to stock its libraries. All these things undoubtedly happened and, based upon their suspicions, the bourgeoisie raged about it from time to time.

But was there any form of direct subsidy from the Third International to its section in Canada? I asked Stewart Smith about this. 'I made representations to get some money for the Canadian party, but I never succeeded,' was his reply. 'I think they did send some in the 1940s maybe. I don't know.'[20] Courtland Starnes, commissioner of the RCMP, stated in 1930 that 'no evidence has been procured of direct subventions to any of [the Canadian communist] journals by Moscow; they are nearly, if not altogether supported by money raised in Canada.'[21]

Available records of the Third International on financial dealings with Canada in the 1930s remain sketchy. Perhaps more details will emerge.

But there is enough evidence to suggest that although the material aid was intermittent, requiring constant requests, negotiation, and persuasion and subject to some kind of performance criteria, it was nevertheless helpful and possibly amounted to between 10 and 15 per cent of the party's budget – on occasions when it was available. As suggested earlier, for some observers the existence of a financial connection turned local sections into 'yes men' of the Third International. That is what the severest critics said. It might have been true in some cases. But to keep such matters in perspective it is worth recalling that most organizations with international operations – whether central intelligence agencies and their covers, multi-national businesses and their clients, churches and their missionaries, the American Federation of Labour and its branches, or the Communist International and its sections – had their financial connections. It was something to be expected, praised or criticized depending upon the interests and objectives involved.[22]

The organization in Moscow of most practical importance for the Canadians engaged in the activities of the Workers' Unity League was the Red International of Trade Unions, sometimes thought of as the economic wing of the Third International, also known by its Russian name, *Profintern*. Located in the Palace of Labour, a few blocks east of the Kremlin, at 12 Solianka Street, 'in another of those white four or five storied buildings running along the street typical of European cities,' according to Smith,[23] it was led by the formidable Alexander Solomon Lozovsky. Unlike Kuusinen over in the Comintern secretariat, once described, perhaps unfairly, as 'a competent official of no great intellectual stature or strong personal convictions,'[24] Lozovsky was an able person of wide trade union experience with strong opinions, persistent activism, and historical perspective. He led the RILU as its general secretary throughout its existence from 1921 to 1937. A young Canadian, Joseph Knight, representing the Central Council of the One Big Union in Winnipeg, attended the founding conference of the RILU in July 1921 and provides a vivid impression of the Russian leader:

> Lossovksy [*sic*] of the Russian Metal Workers' Union was chairman of the Praesidium. He has a comprehensive knowledge of the International Trade Union movement, and when living in Paris was for many years secretary of the French Metal Workers Syndicate. He is a forceful and convincing speaker – very quick at repartee, but delivering his counter strokes with utmost good humour … To preside over a congress of 342 delegates from 42 countries is in itself no light task … Young, being only yet 34 years of age, he seems destined to leave his mark on the international movement in the near future.[25]

Lozovsky's ideas, his writings and speeches, circulated widely in the communist movement, including in Canada. On the fiftieth anniversary of Marx's death, in 1933, he published *Marx and the Trade Unions* as 'a starting point' in the complicated task of making a Marxist analysis of 'the theoretical and tactical principles' of the international revolutionary trade union movement.[26] This book became a text at Canadian and American party schools in the 1940s and 1950s and many of its ideas came to inform the attitudes of left-wing trade union organizers across North America.

As the 1920s shaded into the 1930s, Lozovsky argued for three main points of attention in the international trade union movement: the unemployed, the building of independent or 'Red' trade unions where appropriate, and broadening the basis of strike strategy, all three points employing 'the tactic of the united front from below' (which was, in essence, the same tactic used by the 'new social movements' of Europe and America in the 1970s and 1980s). There had been too much empty talk about the united front, Lozovsky said. The united front 'in a Bolshevist sense,' according to him, signified joint action against capital by the communists and members of the revolutionary trade unions with workers belonging to social democratic parties, members of the reformist unions, and unorganized workers. But apart from that general statement about the united front, an 'all-embracing instruction' could not be invented since a different specific approach was necessary in each factory, in each industry, in each country. There had been too much sameness up to the present, not enough flexibility. The main thing was to have a definite line of policy. What was important, said Lozovsky, was that the organs of the united front be 'formed for struggle against the employers, be elected by the workers in the factories, consist of workers of various tendencies, and not replace revolutionary trade unions.' In other words, he advocated maximum organizational flexibility and non-sectarianism. Moreover, communists should give up reliance on spontaneity, waiting for something to happen, shilly-shallying.[27] Lozovsky's militant rallying cry was 'to the factories! to the work-shops! to the masses!' If communists were a vanguard, they should not be content with following at the tail of events, they should take a lead. Lozovsky's plan of action was ambitious, demanding, confrontational, and not a little prone to disappointments. His critics said his program was left-sectarian and extreme; he criticized their opportunistic delays and evasions. In his view his was the way to advance Marx's 'basic idea' of the economic struggle of the working class, namely the necessity of 'turning the working class into a class for itself, drawing the line between the working class and the bourgeoisie, uniting the working class, consolidating its forces, and setting up the working class against the bourgeoisie.' This idea, he said, is 'woven like a red thread into the entire texture of Marx's writings and actions.'[28] The aim was to raise the workers' flag.

Many of his comrades resisted Lozovsky's new program. The leadership of the Soviet trade unions, for example, preferred the tactics of 'the united front from *above*' – emphasizing relations with the *leadership* of reformist unions – as symbolized by the now defunct Anglo-Russian Trade Union Committee. Leaders of the main communist parties in Western countries were divided in their reactions, and many, including those of Italy, Britain, and the United States, were less than enthusiastic. However, the theses proposed by Bukharin (and backed, possibly initiated, by Stalin), adopted by the Sixth Congress of the Comintern in the summer of 1928, which foresaw the capitalist world economy entering into a new phase of turbulence and crisis, a sharpening of the danger of war and of the class struggle – a 'third period' since the end of the First World War and summed up as 'class against class'– had given strong support to the impetus of Lozovsky's militant program, his 'new tactics, new methods of struggle' for trade union development.[29]

Lozovsky put continuous and unrelenting pressure on the American communist party to adopt some of the new methods of struggle, urging them to stop 'dancing around the AFL,'[30] a process that the Canadian communists watched with great attention. Of the 26 million American workers, Lozovsky noted at an international gathering, only 3 million were in unions; but instead of trying to organize the rest, the American comrades indulged in 'their own particular disease – fear of "dual unionism," of parallel unions.[31] By 1929 William Z. Foster relented and withdrew his opposition to the possibility of 'dual-unionism' in favour of the formation of new, communist-led unions for the poorly led or unorganized miners, textile, needle trades, auto, steel, tobacco and agricultural, and other workers. At the end of that summer, 690 delegates from eighteen states and a fraternal delegate from Canada attended a convention of the Trade Union Education League in Cleveland. The purpose of this convention was to transform the TUEL from an organization that worked as a minority movement within conservative unions into the Trade Union Unity League, a trade union centre mandated, among other things, to organize the unorganized into industrial unions independent of the AFL.[32] This was a radical change of direction. Spirits were high at the convention, but in their hearts the delegates may well have sensed the new direction was fraught with dangers, not least from vigilante mobs, the Ku Klux Klan and other terrorist organizations who would be stirred up by employers and local authorities as the communists moved into action.[33] To some, the new direction smacked of adventurism, of 'leftism,' but for the majority, to remain with the status quo suggested the slough of opportunism, passivity in the face of a chance for badly needed advance.

The Canadian communists, also on Lozovsky's urgings, had already begun trying to organize independent, Red-led unions — among lumber workers, miners, needle trades, and auto workers[34] – some of them undoubtedly *dual unions* – but they were not quick to follow the American example in starting a new national trade union centre. Lozovsky had sent a letter to Toronto in February 1929 to that effect, but the wording was cautious. Drafted by the Anglo-American Group (sometimes called by its German name, *landergroup*) at the Red International of Trade Unions (where Leslie Morris, Sam Carr, and John Weir were the most prominent Canadians after Smith's return to Canada in late 1928), the letter proposed the formation of 'a broad left wing opposition movement' in Canada. This 'opposition movement,' according to the letter, was *not* to be 'a Third Trade Union centre' rivalling the TLC and ACCL. At the same time it was to have its own separate headquarters, a platform, its own press, and local union memberships leading to a national conference to found an organization.[35] A careful reader of this document could therefore wonder what difference there was between this 'opposition movement' and a 'trade union centre.' The hesitations and uncertainties which the Canadian party had about the direction of its trade union work were not resolved by Lozovsky's directive.

A follow-up letter from the secretariat of the Third International, in April 1929, made no mention of a separate trade union centre.[36] A little later at the party's sixth national convention in June 1929, however, resolutions spoke of building 'a revolutionary Canadian Centre' affiliated to the RILU as well as 'a broad Left wing movement' for radical workers still in the AFL, ACCL, and the Catholic unions.[37] After the convention the party's enlarged central executive committee named personnel to an elaborate network of program committees for different industries which would stir activity leading to a national conference for the creation of something called the National Trade Union Unity League, a name similar to that of the American revolutionary trade union centre.[38] But then nothing much happened. The Canadian party was either unable or in no hurry to follow the example of the American communists. It was six months before it decided to launch the Workers' Unity League and another two and a half years before the first formal convention of the new national centre actually convened.

There were several palpable reasons for this delay.

To begin with, in the summer of 1929 the Third International's forecast about the general crisis of capitalism and the growing radicalization of the working class raised a certain amount of scepticism. These conditions were not yet readily apparent in Canada,[39] at least not before the panic of the New York stock market crash in October of that year and the growth of bankruptcies, lay-offs, and unemployment. In this case, was it necessary or possible to rush ahead with new, militant tactics of trade union organization? Some communist activists thought it was not urgent.[40] Organizers like John Stokaluk of the Alberta coal miners, and J.B. Salsberg of the needle trades workers in Ontario and Quebec, were quite content to continue working in their newly established relationships with the social democratic leaders of the All-Canadian Congress of Labour. Furthermore the harsh tone of Comintern rhetoric about denouncing the social democrats as 'social fascists,' mainly in response to German experiences,[41] seemed hardly credible in Canada, leading many Canadian communists in the Workers' Unity League to neglect the use of that phrase in their reports, articles, and letters in favour of continuing to criticize reformists and social democrats as 'labour fakers' or perhaps more pungently as 'labour fakirs.'[42]

Another factor was that the leading lights of the party were engaged in an acrimonious debate over higher strategy of revolution in Canada. Was Canada still a colony, they asked, her bourgeoisie oppressed by British and American imperialism? Or was Canada a full-fledged capitalist state in her own right? This was an important distinction, it was claimed, because the status of Canada would determine which was the primary road to revolution, through the *outer* or the *internal* contradictions of capitalism.

The previous leading thinker of the party had developed a thesis that Canada was still a colony and therefore it was the *outer* contradictions that were the key. In this case, according to Maurice Spector, the road to revolution would be through the struggle for Canadian independence, a national liberation struggle.[43] By implication, the Communist Party would become an ally of the bourgeoisie in a fight against the British and American oppressors of Canada.

It was a fairly common belief of many political thinkers in those days that strained relations between England and the United States, the Anglo-American rivalry after the First World War, were so intense that armed conflict between them was a distinct possibility. The British, impoverished and indebted by the Great War, resented the increased power of the United States, its large and growing navy and its dominance of world financial markets. It was Churchill who wrote in July 1927, 'No doubt it is quite right in the interests of peace to go on talking about war with the United States being "unthinkable." Everyone knows that this is not true.'[44] 'War between Britain and America,' predicted Jack MacDonald, general secretary of the Communist Party of Canada, in the summer of 1929, 'means civil war in Canada, with a rapidly developing revolutionary situation': the British-connected Canadian capitalists, grouped around the Bank of Montreal, would find themselves engaged in civil war with the U.S.-related capitalists of the Royal Bank of Canada. The communists, the argument continued, would lead the workers to turn a liberation *cum* civil war into a revolutionary insurrection in favour of a Workers' and Farmers' government in Ottawa.[45]

Stewart Smith was especially enthusiastic. When he first returned from Moscow in 1928, Smith gave an extensive interview to a reporter from the *Toronto Star* in which he elaborated the civil war thesis and was reported as saying that 'in a very short time the streets of Toronto will be running with blood.'[46] This insurrectionary scenario was a great embarrassment to everyone, and luckily the editor of the *Star* pulled the story from the next edition.

Sam Carr and his younger colleagues at the International Lenin School took an opposite view, saying that the *inner* contradictions of capitalism were the more decisive for the prospects of revolution. Citing official statistics, they argued that the Canadians owned 80 per cent of the national wealth of the country and their capitalists had 66 per cent of all investments, thus apparently proving that they were still in majority control. And even the American investments, nominally with about 19 per cent of the total, and the British with 13 per cent, had the support and co-operation of Canadian financial institutions.[47] It was nonsense, they said, to think that the Canadian bourgeoisie would be allies of the working class in a war of liberation. The way forward for the working class, therefore, lay in another direction. It was to confront resident capitalists and financiers and their ideological apologists and political helpers, in struggle. And that struggle should take place in and around the factories, mines, and mills of the 'second industrial revolution.' The Canadian bourgeoisie was 'the main enemy of the Canadian proletariat'; it was 'the chief and most active agent of the imperialists in their attacks upon the Canadian working class.'[48] Since the current emphasis of the Comintern was 'class against class,' Carr's version, if for no other reason, won the support of the Anglo-American Secretariat. Cynics would say Carr's hard-edged position was instigated or at least inspired by contacts in the Russian Communist Party briefing him on a *left vs right* leadership struggle between Stalin and Bukharin then taking place there,[49] but there is no such direct evidence. Later Smith called Carr a 'Stalinist' as a term of reproach.[50] The whole process was perhaps not of immediate interest for many on the left in Canada, but the debate was important, Carr once observed, 'because you don't start arranging the furniture until you first know the shape of the house.'[51] The resolution of the controversy in early 1931 in favour of Sam Carr's position set the new direction in Canada, while at the same time it consumed much intellectual and emotional energy of leading people during a time of many transitions.[52]

Perhaps the most important reason for the slow response to adopting the new strategy for trade union work lay in the size, composition, and structure of what was a very small communist party – so small and so weak that it was not on Lozovsky's list for special attention.[53]

The exact size of the Canadian communist party at any given time was not easily gauged because its method of record-keeping by individual membership books and the sale of monthly dues stamps was not well observed. There were many complaints about this from the national office and the centre often had to guess at the numbers. When Stewart

Smith gave an account of his eighteen months of leadership, in mid-1930, he proudly claimed between 3,700 and 4,000 members 'as a factual estimate.'[54] A short seven months later, when his rival, Sam Carr, became national party organizer, he reported only 1,300 members. This infuriated Smith, but the information led a referent in the Third International's secretariat to comment dryly that 'recently for the first time the C.P. of Canada has began [*sic*] to give information about the organization situation of the Canadian party ... some 1,300 paid up members (previously reported to be 4,000).'[55]

The social composition of the Canadian party was considered to be 'quite good,' made up largely of workers – 'proletarian comrades working at the bench.' But after almost ten years it remained largely an immigrant party 'only poorly connected with the basic sections of the Canadian working class.' Although the overwhelming majority of the population was made up of Anglo-Celtic and French-Canadian workers, 95 per cent of the party membership was confined to three other language groups – Finnish with 60 per cent, Ukrainian with 25 per cent, and Jewish with 10 per cent. Such a national composition was a serious barrier between the party and the majority of workers which still had to be surmounted before it could call itself and act as a Communist Party 'leading and reflecting the interests of the Canadian workers.'[56] Sporadic attempts to change this situation were sometimes called 'bolshevizing' the party – making it more worthy of its proud namesake.

That is not to say that the immigrant composition of the party was without its advantages for communist activity. The very process of chain migration from the old country meant that homogeneous groups gathered together in certain geographic centres for mutual aid and collective activities of a social, economic, and political nature. The Red Finns in Sudbury, Port Arthur, and the lumber camps of Northern Ontario, for example, built their consumer co-operatives and community halls for economic, educational, social, recreational, and sporting activities, raised money to publish the daily paper, *Vapaus*, with a circulation of 3,000, organized a lumber workers' union, and by joining the Finnish Organization of Canada, automatically became members of the Communist Party. Like-minded Ukrainians who settled the west, the prairies, and the coal mining villages in the Rocky Mountains formed their Ukrainian Labour Farmer Temple Association in Winnipeg and built 114 halls[57] across the country as places for their social and educational activities; they published the *Ukrainski Robitnichi Vesti* (Ukrainian Labour News) three times a week in 10,000 copies. The Jewish tailors and dress-makers, cap makers, and fur and leather workers found employment in the factories of Toronto, Montreal, and Winnipeg and built their unions, and like-minded ones raised money for the publication of *Der Kamf* (Struggle); and in Hamilton revolutionary-minded Hungarian immigrants built an organization and published *Munkas* (The Worker). Altogether a dozen or so different language federations such as these provided a priceless support system and strategic reserve for the labour movement and its communist militants as the fierce class struggles of the depression era unfolded.[58]

For better or worse, the Communist Party's 'immigrant composition' greatly influenced its structure, leading it, in practice, to become a federated rather than a centralized organization as required under the statutes of the Third International. This federal structure (it was decried as a 'social democratic' hangover) inevitably affected the political activities of the party. The Finns and the Ukrainians, in particular, had the practice of selecting their own representatives to sit on the leading bodies and they in turn decided which of the party's policies should be brought back for action by their members in the language organizations. And which could be ignored. There were, in effect, three centres of authority in the party. Although the language organizations had come into existence on the platform of class struggle and nominally conducted their work under this slogan, 'actual living and continual participation in the class conflicts of the Canadian working class,' declared a resolution of the Third International, 'has not been as it should be, in the centre of their activities.' Instead the various cultural activities, orchestras, and drama groups 'became an aim in themselves.' The party members busied themselves in the affairs at the halls, which 'led to weakening of the Party as a whole' and 'further segregated the mass organizations' from the general struggle of the Canadian working people. Furthermore, the isolation of these organizations led 'to the development of "immigrant" ideology, striving for respectability in the eye of the ruling class,' and strong legalistic worries about the safety of their benevolent insurance associations or property investments in the halls, sometimes causing them to withdraw their use in service of strike struggles and other vital campaigns.[59]

For half a decade, the leading bodies and conventions of the party had regularly condemned this ideology as 'right opportunism' and had passed resolutions to end the federated functioning of the party, and just as regularly these resolutions were ignored. Stewart Smith, newly appointed national organizer after returning from the headquarters of the Third International, decided to put an end to this state of affairs in 1929 and he proceeded to create havoc. 'The report of Smith is good,' said one of the Ukrainian party leaders at a conference, 'but it's like a razor, you can both shave and kill yourself.'[60]

Smith took special aim at the Finnish Organization – the main membership base of the party and source of its finances. He went to Sudbury armed with a decision of the central executive and was given forty-five minutes to address the membership (at a meeting which took place near midnight on 7 November 1929, following a celebration of the Russian Revolution). In his speech he quoted Otto Kuusinen about the influence of social reformism and opportunists, 'dragging at the tail, their vacillating passivity, their constant adaptation to the passing moment, this is the greatest danger we have to avoid.' When Smith concluded, some young men unceremoniously ushered him out of the hall. He was shocked and declared that a pogrom atmosphere existed.

After his departure from the meeting, the Finnish leaders spoke many bitter words of resentment against 'blindly following instructions' and attacked the 'present gang of leaders' of the political committee of the CPC headed by Smith. Smith retaliated by suspending and expelling several leading Finns from membership in the party. They responded with a request to the Third International for a commission of investigation, saying that an attempt to enforce decisions on a mass organization 'by mere discipline is a mistake,' and 'this is what the present party leaders are doing. By such conduct workers are trained into submissive slaves as they are trained by the Catholic Church.'[61]

Kuusinen acted on the request for a commission, sending his wife, Aino Kuusinen, and another leading Finn, Karl Manners, to Canada early in 1930. The upshot was a face-saving compromise, but all the Finnish leaders were restored to their former positions.[62] Unfazed, when Smith was next in Moscow, in the summer of 1930, he calmly wrote to Tim Buck about Manuilsky telling him that he, Smith, had been singled out in the Third International as 'a very bad example,' giving the impression that 'we had expelled all the good elements from the party and kept all the bad ones.'[63]

In the meantime Buck, refined and mild-mannered compared to Smith and on sick leave because of Bell's palsy, a temporary paralysis of the facial nerves, had also made a trip to Moscow, seeking to clarify outstanding issues and to establish his presence as the new general secretary of the Canadian party. He had cordial private meetings with Lozovsky and with Kuusinen and his wife in early January 1930, but otherwise only desultory conversations for weeks before he could arrange a serious hearing with the Anglo-American Secretariat. As a result of Sam Carr's campaign about the 'status of Canada' and Smith's mishandling of the Finnish question, the American secretary, Joe Fineberg, who 'for all practical purposes,' said Buck, was in charge of the secretariat, expressed doubts as to whether the new leadership was able to carry out the line of the Sixth Congress of the CI. The general impression in the Third International, wrote Buck to his comrades back in Toronto, is of a Canadian section that is 'organizationally impotent, incorrect politically ... full of illusions about the "independence" slogan, ready to issue slogans for the defense of (capitalist) Canada. It is a conciliatory leadership that sets itself not to fight the right danger but to win control of the apparatus, a leadership that ignores the menace of war against the Soviet Union.' To put the matter briefly, 'it was virtually a case of an already discredited leadership knocking at the door.'[64] Buck warned that there was even 'talk of organizational measures,' namely a threat to remove the 'new' leadership of the party.[65] To top it off, as already related, a request for some financial aid was turned down on what Buck thought were flimsy grounds.

All these matters created heavy preoccupations for the communist activists in Canada. Given their small numbers and constant harassments from the 'red squads' of the police, it seemed there was little time or energy for much else.

But as the summer of 1929 turned into autumn, the state of political doldrums in the country, or parts of it, began to change. There were outward signs of renewed restlessness by working people, signs that the class struggle was beginning to stir again. At first a little here and a little there – demonstrations for free speech on the street corners and on the lawns of Queen's Park in Toronto and other parts of the country, strikes in half a dozen coal mines in Cape Breton, hundreds of steel railway car builders spontaneously walking off the job in Hamilton (juxtaposed in the press by the hooded Ku Klux Klan marching a thousand strong through the city with their burning crosses on the mountain), a thousand pulp cutters for Abitibi Power and Paper in northern Ontario stopping work to protest wage-slashing (and the murder of two of their union organizers) – and after the crash of the New York stock exchange at the end of October, increasingly widespread anxiety and unrest especially among the growing ranks of the unemployed. For the Trades and Labour Congress of Canada it was still business as usual.[66] And while the All-Canadian Congress of Labour took a combative stance, observing that great distress prevailed among the people and declaring that 'the struggle within industry must continue,'[67] it had doubts about the strike weapon, preferring arbitration and conciliation with the boss. Perhaps, then, it was time for the communists to take up the long-simmering challenge of building a new, revolutionary trade union centre capable of organizing the unemployed, of offering unhesitating support and direction to workers in their spontaneous actions and strike struggles, and of raising sights about the rightful place of workers in Canadian society as creators rather than servants.

Two new messages came from Moscow in October 1929, one from the secretariat of the Third International and the other from the Red International of Labour Unions. The first one, carried by hand to Toronto by Leslie Morris, dealt mainly with other matters but referred briefly to the formula of 'a broad Left-wing movement' that 'will eventually' develop into a revolutionary trade union centre.[68] The message from the RILU, drafted by its Anglo-American Section, struck a more urgent tone. It reiterated some of the themes of Lozovsky's February 1929 letter and added that the transformation of the ACCL into 'a mere tool of capitalism' and other developments in Canada 'force us to take up the question of establishing a revolutionary trade union centre.' It spoke of new strike tactics, 'following the Strassburg Resolution,' and proposed a workers' delegation from Canada to the USSR as a means of stimulating interest in building the new organization.[69]

Nothing happened for another two months and then one day in mid-December 1929, 'the little band' took a decision to start 'an opposition Centre.'[70] Unlike the Americans with their big founding convention for the Trade Union Unity League, the Workers' Unity League of Canada began its life without fanfare, on a provisional basis with a shoestring budget. Its origin bespoke caution, trying to avoid some purely ceremonial act of creation. Its provisional general secretary was a newcomer to the city. As it turned out, he had but eighteen months on the job before the state arrested and jailed him in Kingston Penitentiary as 'an agent of revolution.' But by then he and his comrades had gained some valuable experience for constructing a remarkable national trade union centre that within four years came, by its own estimate, to encompass 40,000 members. His name, at that time, was Thomas A. Ewen.

3

Getting Started

The working class and the employing class have nothing in common. There can be no peace so long as hunger and want are found among millions of the working people and the few, who make up the employing class, have all the good things of life.

Preamble, IWW Constitution (1905)

Don't wait too long to get wise to yourself ...
Misery or triumph,
You've got to be either the anvil, or the hammer.

J.W. von Goethe[1]

Things are going to be hot this winter and the more we prepare now ...
the better shape we will be in to meet the shock.

– T.A. Ewen, National Secretary,
Workers' Unity League of Canada, 12 June 1931[2]

Tom Ewen was an aimiable man. On the shy side, he was possible, at first, to mistake for an innocuous sort. The Special Branch of the Royal Canadian Mounted Police, for example, described the man who became head of the Workers' Unity League, in a secret report to the prime minister in 1931, as 'well and quietly dressed,' having a 'very earnest and quiet, very pleasant' manner and a 'jaunty gait.'[3]

In fact, Ewen was an outspoken person, determinedly expressing his views on questions of the day, the strategy and tactics needed for advancing the cause of workers. His favourite motto, taken from Goethe, was 'Misery or triumph, you've got to be either the anvil, or the hammer.'

He picked the hammer. His rhetoric, clear and spiced with sardonic wit, enlivened many a newspaper column and encouraged workers in the midst of strikes. For fifty years Ewen provided inspiration to the movement he helped to lead.

Born in Stonehaven, a village along the Kincardine coast, in Scotland, Ewen had parents who were so poverty-stricken that his mother had to go to a poorhouse to have her baby. Both parents died early, leaving him an orphan when he was but a toddler. A childless couple took him in. With Annie Wishart 'lavishing her boundless love on a homeless waif,' and filling his head with fairy tales and stories of Scottish rebels and outlaws, Ewen recalled these as the happiest years of his childhood. At the age of nine he was sent by the Poor Inspector to a fishing family, an uncle and aunt who were strangers to him, but eager to have his labour. They were stern Scots Presbyterians and under the eyes of these hard taskmasters Ewen performed a heavy load of chores and attended school until grade 6. In addition to household tasks and homework, the young boy was required by his Aunt Susan, who could not read, to read aloud the *Weekly People's Journal for Aberdeen and Kincardineshire* from start to finish. She also demanded that he read aloud various classics for which, in his words, she had 'an insatiable hunger' and a 'profound respect.' In an atmosphere of quasi-hostility a bond grew between them. She taught him to read as the author meant it to be read, 'with understanding,' and Ewen became imbued with the classics of Shakespeare, Blake, the Bible, Dickens, Thackeray, Walter Scott, and of course 'the poems of our immortal Burns.' 'To two toil-worn women of my childhood days,' he wrote in his old age, 'I owe a very deep debt of gratitude. From them I learned of men and women of other days whose songs and writings and poems, pulsating with the breath of struggle and revolt, had lightened the dark corners of hardship, poverty and despair; of poets and writers whose works had bestowed incalculable riches upon poor people everywhere.'[4]

At the age of thirteen he left home to work for fishermen and farmers as a general roustabout or horse flunky until settling into a four-year apprenticeship to become a blacksmith, learning, amongst other skills, the science of horse-shoeing. Married and a father by the age of nineteen, he was attracted by the pamphlets of the Canadian Pacific Railway agents. He and his wife, Isobel Taylor, decided in 1912 to emigrate to Canada in the hopes of a better life.

Ewen went first, with a contract as a farm labourer in rural Manitoba. When that proved intolerable, he broke his contract and moved into the nearby town of Morden and a better-paying job. Within a year he had saved enough to bring over his wife and their baby daughter, Jean. The family soon headed to Winnipeg where Ewen had even better luck as there were many horses to shoe. While there, he and a group of friends used to attend Sunday meetings in Market Square, listening to orators, picking up pamphlets of the Socialist Party of Canada, and beginning their study of revolutionary Marxism. It was in Winnipeg that the Ewens' second daughter, Isobel, was born. Then in 1914 the family headed to Swift Current, Saskatchewan, looking for better opportunities

In his fourteen years in Saskatchewan, during which he ended up in Saskatoon, Ewen worked at many jobs – blacksmith, auto mechanic, harvester, threshing machine operator, and general handyman – taking responsibility for supporting his growing family. Along the way, disaster struck when the post–First World War Spanish flu epidemic hit Saskatchewan, leading to the death of thousands, including his wife. In his sorrow Ewen described her as 'a brave, strong and courageous woman who gave of her best to all about her until she, too, passed into the shadows.' Thus by 1920 Ewen was left alone with four children under the age of nine. Even for a person 'steeled in the crucible of hard times,' as he put it in his autobiography, this was a crushing blow. But he determined to keep his family together because his own childhood experiences revolted against condemning his motherless children to a like fate.[5] While relations with his feisty eldest daughter often became argumentative, he found great support in this task from Isobel, who, with 'matchless courage and love,' he wrote, 'took on the role of "Mother" to all of us.' Ewen was heart-broken when Isobel died of tuberculosis at the age of thirty-six in 1950.[6]

During his years in Saskatoon Ewen and several friends made contact with the newly founded branch of the Communist Party and decided to sign up. While still working at his trade, 'as one of the highest paid mechanics in Western Canada,' he rapidly became a leading light in the party branch, and in 1927 the national party office in Toronto appointed him full-time organizer for Saskatchewan and Manitoba out of Winnipeg, where he moved with his family. Less than two years later he received another call from Toronto appointing him national industrial director, to replace Tim Buck, who became general secretary of the party. In this unfamiliar capacity, the rapidly promoted Ewen had the task of relocating his family again and helping to start up the Workers' Unity League.[7]

It was on an unusually mild Christmas morning in Toronto, in 1929, that Ewen and Charles Sims hurried past the Canada Bread Company billboards assuring boys and girls that 'There is a Santa Claus.' The men took little notice as they had something else on their minds. They were anxious to hold a meeting of the Communist Party's industrial department at 650 Bay Street in order to set the wheels rolling, at last, for a revolutionary trade union centre in Canada. They decided to send out announcements to all the district offices of the Communist Party, and to signal the importance of the event they would append the latest letter of the Red International of Labour Unions. In his covering letter, Ewen urged that this act of creation be seen in the context of 'great class struggles,' especially in the new, unorganized industries. He predicted that these struggles would involve the mounting rolls of unemployed workers as 'part of the revolutionary working class movement.' In addition the men despatched letters to trade union activists across the country requesting their support for a manifesto, asking permission to advertise their names as a provisional committee for the Workers' Unity League, and for authority to print their names on the stationery.[8] It was a fruitful morning's work.

Responses were quick and, after a few weeks, Ewen was able to print a respectable-looking letterhead with twenty-two names. The figures were listed as follows:

MINERS' SECTION, COAL: Jas. Sloan, Lethbridge, Alta., J.B. McLaughlan, Nova Scotia, J.B. Milley, Nova Scotia, M. Clark, Nova Scotia, A.J. McNeil, Nova Scotia. MINERS' SECTION, METAL: Jim Barker, Nova Scotia, J. Kostinuik, Sudbury, Ont., M. Parker, Sudbury, Ont. LUMBER WORKERS: A. Hautamaki, Port Arthur, K. Salo, Port Arthur. RAILROAD: J. Lakeman, Edmonton, Alta., T.A. Ewen, Toronto. NEEDLE TRADES: Max Shur, Toronto, A.S. Buller, Toronto, G. Gershman, Montreal, Que., M. Dolgoy, Winnipeg, Man. METAL WORKERS: T. Raycroft, Sudbury, Ont., G. Ironberg, Hamilton, Ont. BUILDING TRADES: M. Bruce, Vancouver, B.C., W.W. Findlay, Vancouver, W. Swift, Toronto, Ont. FISHERIES, B.C.: T. Hayna, Vancouver, B.C. AUTO WORKERS: G. Wandon, Windsor, Ont., A. Seal, Windsor, Ont.

These names decorated an impressive masthead under the logo 'CLASS AGAINST CLASS' – Canadian Section – RED INTERNATIONAL OF LABOR UNIONS.[9] By now Ewen had also rented a separate office, a room on Lombard Street in the heart of Toronto's financial district. It was a ten-minute walk from the headquarters of the Communist Party, on Bay Street, where he served concurrently as acting general secretary (dur-

ing Tim Buck's prolonged sick leave). As a psychological irritant perhaps, and as a security precaution, certainly, the communists preferred
to locate their quarters in up-close proximity to where the captains of
industry and the leaders of finance carried on their operations. Whatever the reasoning behind office location, it was important for the WUL
to establish an independent identity separate from any political party,
with its own address.

Ewen prepared a draft constitution to lay down the rules and set out a
dues structure governing all sections of the league until its first national
convention, whenever that might be. Imbued with the class-struggle
spirit of the Industrial Workers of the World and patterned directly on
the earlier-established Trade Union Unity League of the United States,
this constitution proclaimed the organization's immediate and long-
term aims. These were to organize Canadian workers (skilled, semi-
skilled, and unskilled) into industry-wide unions created on the basis
of widest rank and file control; to defend and improve the conditions
of the working class; to organize unemployed workers as an integral
part of the working-class movement; and to develop left-wing groups in
the 'reformist unions' as a means of winning their members to support
industrial unionism. The long-range aims, expressed in terms more akin
to those of a political party than to those of a trade union, were to mobilize workers for the 'complete overthrow of capitalism and its institutions
of exploitation,' and for the 'setting up of the State Power of workers
and poor farmers through a workers and farmers government.'[10] Anxious to distinguish the league from what he saw as the lethargy of the
old trade union establishment, Ewen employed the word 'revolutionary'
half a dozen times in the brief preamble, which ended with the famous
slogan of Marx and Engels's *Communist Manifesto*, 'Workers of the World
Unite!'[11] For the moment he was not thinking about how all this might
sound when organizers were hauled before a judge in a court of law.

After this assertive beginning, the first year of building the league was
slow, often discouraging work. A conference of trade unionists representing 24 organizations, sponsored by the Workers' Unity League, was
held in Toronto in May 1930, and delegates appointed commissions for
the development of campaigns in the auto industry, in steel, in textiles,
among the unemployed, for youth and women, and within the AFL-TLC
and ACCL unions. Ewen referred to this as the inaugural conference
of the WUL.[12] But Communist Party members and progressive workers
employed in unorganized mines, mills, and factories such as Massey Harris in Toronto, the Ford Motor Company in Windsor, and the Interna-

tional Nickel Company in Sudbury, places often bristling with company informers, were understandably cautious. Leaflets, manifestos, posters, and stickers were printed by the thousands, protesting wage cuts, speed-ups and unfair practices, arbitrary dismissals, and other grievances, in the name of an underground union group or the Workers' Unity League itself. But, as Ewen admonished a frustrated young league organizer in Sudbury, the task could not be done by issuing leaflets; 'otherwise the job would have been completed years ago, and we would now be in the period of the millennium.' There had to be follow-up work. Industrial unions could only be built in struggle, and the business of communists, he said, 'is to prepare, advocate, agitate and develop these struggles.'[13]

The logical place to start building the league was with the left-led industrial groups and unions already in progress – small nuclei among the steelworkers, auto workers, hard-rock miners, lumbermen, and the already functioning unions encompassing coal miners and garment workers where other unions already existed. All of these workplaces had their histories, peculiarities, and special challenges, which were magnified by the onset of the economic depression in 1929 and the intensifying drive by employers to reduce costs.

The difficulties besetting the 2,000-member Industrial Union of Needle Trades Workers, formed in 1928, were compounded by the resignation of its talented chief organizer, J.B. Salsberg, and his temporary expulsion from the Communist Party in late 1929. Ewen, in later years, described Salsberg as 'not all we would wish for in a strictly inner-family sense,' yet still one 'of the most devoted fighters for the people this or any other country ever had.'[14]

But in 1929, Salsberg, who had just succeeded with great flair in building up the needle trades industrial union on a united front basis with Aaron Mosher of the All-Canadian Congress of Labour,[15] was unhappy about the new direction of the Communist Party in the 'third period.' The new course, as described earlier, proposed to cancel such united fronts 'from above' (with the leaders) in favour of confrontation with the bosses, class-struggle, and united fronts 'from below' (with the rank and file). Among the trade unions, it pitted the model of shop-floor unionism, and the threat of work stoppages to enforce the terms of contracts, against the less confrontational social democratic model, which, while it allowed for the possibility of striking, preferred management-labour cooperation and a third-party arbitrator to settle grievances.

Salsberg was especially unhappy with the overbearing tactics of Stewart Smith, and at a party convention, he confronted the party's new national organizer. Since Smith's return from the Lenin School, according to Salsberg, he had 'assumed the air of a pompous professor.' He displayed great impatience and irritation at anyone who failed to heed his every remark. Salsberg offered some advice: 'Comrade Smith will have to learn to become a communist leader, a leader and teacher of workers who are not all accustomed to classroom manners.'[16]

Salsberg, at age twenty-six and five years older than Smith, would sit on the sidelines for a year and a half until he decided the other position was right after all, whereupon he applied for readmission and was taken back into the party. He became the dynamic WUL organizer for Southern Ontario, the leader of many confrontations and strike battles and later an elected communist member of Ontario's provincial parliament at Queen's Park.[17]

Of course, there were other able young men and women militants in the needle trades field – including Joshua Gershman and Myer Klig in Montreal, Annie Buller, Norman Freed, and Max Shur in Toronto, and Pearl Wedro and Max Dolgoy in Winnipeg. They and others soldiered on, hoping to make a dent among an estimated 30,000 workers in the sweatshops of the garment industry – 90 per cent still untouched by union organization.[18] They appealed to the RILU for financial assistance[19] but received no apparent response. In 1930–1, they had modest successes, especially among the Jewish immigrant garment workers.[20] But the field was rife with factional disputes. As well, it was populated by countless unions of tailors, dressmakers, cloakmakers, hatters, raincoat-makers, glove-makers, button-hole-makers, furriers, cutters, pressers, sewing-machine operators, finishers, and so on, each jealously guarding its respective jurisdiction, and largely ignoring the unorganized majority. The barriers to creating an all-inclusive industrial union were thus formidable. At the same time the employers, many of them former workers and now small-time, fiercely competing entrepreneurs, were deaf to pleas for improved working conditions. Instead they encouraged divisions among the workers and drove wages down below subsistence levels.[21]

When Gershman wrote a gloomy letter from Montreal at the end of 1930, saying that the needle trades union had been unable to conduct any struggles, Ewen sympathized with him. They were seriously handicapped by the lack of any French-speaking members, and this would have to be rectified by 'scratching our brains' on how it could be done. Apart from that, Ewen wrote, the new 'shop delegate system' of choosing union representatives right from the shop floor (shop-floor unionism), while fundamentally correct, somehow often led to the same old gang coming to the fore, a gang 'who cannot produce results no matter how much we shuffle them around.'

Ewen used the new *Needle Worker* paper as an example of the problem. Here was a paper that ought to be of great assistance in mobilizing the workers by reflecting their daily struggles. 'But what do we find?' he asked rhetorically. The same old stereotyped over-the-top materials 'that fly clean over the heads of the workers.' 'When we speak of "periods" first, second or third — of rationalization and radicalization and so on to each other,' he continued, 'we know what is meant, but to the workers we might as well address our communications in Greek as write in this manner.' Until this changed into language that the workers used and understood, the union and the Workers' Unity League would remain a propaganda sect – 'nothing more, nothing less.'[22]

The Lumber Workers' Industrial Union was another ready-made part of the Workers' Unity League's beginnings. Largely composed of Finnish immigrant workers in Northern Ontario, it, too, was not in good shape. The economic crisis affecting lumber, pulp-cutting, and agriculture had put as many as 50 per cent of the union's members in Ontario into the ranks of the unemployed. The union was heavily in debt. In British Columbia, where the lumber companies kept a blacklist against militants, the union's branch was barely alive with just fifty members, most of whom were also unemployed.[23]

Ewen rode the CPR to Port Arthur, in April 1930 (and again in April 1931), to bring greetings from the WUL to the lumber union's annual convention, and to consult with the Communist Party's fraction in the union. As the train rolled through the boreal forests north of Superior, he reflected on the union's history and its problems, including the tremendous difficulty of maintaining union conditions in the lumber camps:

In Northern Ontario the lumbering industry must penetrate deeper and deeper into the wilderness. Camps may be from 20 to 40 miles from the nearest town and miles from each other; from 50 to 100 men may be employed in each camp. When a strike is called to enforce union conditions, sufficient pickets must be left in the camp area with food and shelter provided. The balance must trek to the nearest town involving a hike of possibly twenty miles or more through a veritable wilderness held in the grip of winter. There, they must be maintained by the Union on picket duty at the local slave markets and the railway stations, to keep the workers, who have been duped by the agents of the bosses, from scabbing. In spite of this vigilance, numerous scabs are toted out by the companies in motor trucks etc., where a number invariably refuse to scab and become a charge upon the lumber workers for food and transportation back to town.[24]

Ewen was not optimistic about the industrial lumber union's immediate future. For one thing its leader, Alf Hautamaki, was a party member about whom Ewen had received a number of complaints. A fine speaker and self-taught editor of the union's newspaper, *Metsatyolaisten* (Lumberworker), but now in poor health, Hautamaki wished to be relieved of his duties. That couldn't be arranged until the following year, when Emil Whalen (also known as Wilen) took on the job as secretary. Unfortunately, the authorities deported Whalen for his activities in support of Port Arthur's unemployed bushworkers, and it wasn't until the following year that a new, stable leadership emerged with Kalle Salo and Jack Gillbanks.[25]

Another concern for the union stemmed from the seasonal nature of the lumber industry. Most of the pulp cutters were farm labourers when the bush camps were not operating and many headed out West in the summer to participate in the prairie wheat harvest. How could the union keep in touch with them, defend their interests, and at the same time keep up the union's financial base? Ewen's modest proposal, suggested by the RILU, was to change the name of the union to Lumber and Agricultural Workers' Industrial Union of Canada, the better to reflect the work of the membership. This would also allow organization among the migratory farm workers whom the lumber companies otherwise used to break strikes. The convention of 1930 accepted this change, but by now the move was somewhat academic as mechanized combine harvesters were rapidly replacing the itinerant harvester in the prairie wheat economy.[26]

A further challenge for the union came when the government in Soviet Karelia asked it to send a contingent of skilled Canadian lumberjacks to train Karelians and to help them achieve the goals of the first Five Year Plan in the timber industry. Karelia was an area of the Soviet Union adjoining Finland, largely populated by people of Finnish origin and therefore an appealing prospect, especially for unemployed Finnish-Canadian workers. The union responded enthusiastically, perhaps expecting to send a few hundred woodsmen, but the exodus became a veritable stampede as the commissar in charge of the Karelian Timber Trust began an extensive private correspondence with prospects. In spite of attempts by the Anglo-American Secretariat of the Third International and by the Canadian party to limit the flow, between 2,000 and 3,000 left for the Soviet Union, severely depleting the supply of the most committed members of the union in Ontario.[27]

All these matters, as well as continuing factional struggles in the Finnish Organization of Canada, delayed the revival of the LWIU. But at least Ewen had the satisfaction, after his address to the convention, of witnessing the union deciding to affiliate with and pledge itself to work for the objectives of the Workers' Unity League. Their support would be invaluable.

Ewen began the WUL's mining campaign among the coal miners of Nova Scotia. There were 12,000 of them, many unemployed as the result of technological advances that had increased the output of coal per man. In March 1930 Ewen travelled to Cape Breton to attend a convention of miners disgruntled with the leadership of the United Mine Workers of America, who gathered together in the Temperance Hall in Sydney. The purpose of the two-day convention was to consider establishing a new miners' union to replace District 26 of the UMWA. Although the UMWA held contracts and the check-off of dues for most of the mines, it was discredited among a significant portion of the membership. They believed that John L. Lewis, the UMWA leader who sacked the outstanding, militant leader of District 26, J.B. McLachlan, during the coal strike of 1923,[28] had also sabotaged the subsequent general strike in 1925. Bitter feelings abounded. Under Lewis's leadership, the UMWA in North America had fallen from 600,000 to only 100,000 members.

With J.B. McLachlan in the chair, the Sydney convention, which had representation from eight local unions that encompassed about 4,000 miners, listened to Ewen's presentation and took a formal decision to launch the Mine Workers' Industrial Union of Nova Scotia. But there was a noticeable hesitancy about the idea and even some not so subtle inferences that the participation of communists would be detrimental to the success of a new union. By the end of the two days when the nominating committee, as expected, proposed McLachan for president, he abruptly declined and could not be persuaded to change his mind. If he was going to go back into office, he declared, 'it will be with the vote of the rank and file.'[29] And that was that. Such was the prestige of 'Old Jim' that a new union could not be built without his support.

In post-convention reports from Jim Barker, the young Nova Scotia district organizer of the Communist Party (a person McLachlan contemptuously dismissed as an 'office boy' sent down from Toronto), Ewen learned that McLachlan and his friends did indeed want a new

union, but one without international connections – to Moscow or anywhere else. Ewen was appalled. 'This we will never do,' he blustered. He
believed the Nova Scotia radicals had succumbed to the combined pressure of the Dominion Steel and Coal Corporation (formerly the British Empire Steel Corporation), the major employer in industrial Cape
Breton, the UMWA, which he considered the company's handmaiden in
the labour movement, and the political offensive of the Catholic priests
who took their cue from Rome. Ewen told a gathering of party leaders
in Toronto that McLachlan and other local leaders 'were not prepared
to carry out this program,' and in a few weeks all activity for the Workers' Unity League in Nova Scotia 'practically ceased.'[30] Outwardly calm
but inwardly furious, Ewen expressed a fleeting thought to Barker that
McLachlan should be treated the same as 'the rest of the trade union
fakers unless we have reduced ourselves to mere sentimentalists.'[31] Fortunately, he kept these thoughts well bottled up because less than two years
later, at the WUL's first annual convention and with Ewen already behind
bars in Kingston Peniteniary in Ontario, McLachlan would emerge with
his reputation intact in the eyes of militant workers and become national
president of the league.

The situation in the Alberta coal fields was quite different from Nova
Scotia, although not without its own complexities. There, the grasp of
the UMWA in District 18 had already been severely weakened. Five years
earlier a section of the union led by communists had broken away to
form the Mine Workers' Union of Canada and successfully challenged
the UMWA's rule. District 18 of the UMWA continued to exist, but the
rival Canadian union held sway in many of the mining camps.

Although originally founded on the initiative of the communists and
their radical allies in 1925, the leadership of the MWUC had since passed
into the hands of the social democrats and especially Frank Wheatley,
who was concurrently vice-president of the All-Canadian Congress of
Labour. Wheatley, as previously related, favoured bargaining with the
mine owners on the basis of arbitrations and conciliation boards and, if
necessary, by reference to royal commissions to determine whether and
how the coal industry could actually afford to pay the miners more.[32] The
communists, while recognizing that the market was changing, especially
with the coming of diesel locomotives on the railways, argued that workers, far from accepting imposed or negotiated lay-offs and speed-ups,
must share in the gains of technological change, through strike action if
necessary. Given the balance of power in Canadian society, they regarded
the strike, in Ewen's words, 'as labour's key weapon in determining the

social and economic returns for the sale and use of its creative labour power.'[33] It was this message that they now brought to the Alberta coal fields in a powerful organizing campaign led by the fledgling Workers' Unity League.

The messenger was a young green-horn named Harvey Murphy, barely twenty-three years old but already seasoned by participating in organizing and strike battles in Ontario.[34] A stocky, powerfully built person with a balding head, he arrived in Edmonton in late December 1929 as district organizer of the Communist Party – a party that would claim his lifelong allegiance.

Murphy is a hard man to pin down. Several enthusiastic biographers who wanted to write his biography tried, but gave up. When I asked a son, who is an author, why he didn't record his father's colourful life, he replied: 'With Harvey you could never tell what was what. He even had two birth dates!' Admittedly this is a handicap. But anyone wishing to know about the Workers' Unity League of Canada must try to discover his footsteps because, as historian Allen Seager has written, Murphy left 'an indelible imprint on the history of the working class movement of this country.'[35]

The eldest son of poor Jewish immigrants, Murphy arrived in Berlin (Kitchener), Ontario from Poland with his parents shortly before the First World War. The family, which later moved to Toronto, and grew to have nine children, was orthodox in its religious practices, the father, Sam Chernikovski, being a kosher butcher. Murphy left school at age thirteen to work at various odd jobs and apprenticed as a plumber/steamfitter. Finding that people with names ending in '-ovski' faced discrimination in applying for plumbing jobs in Toronto, he changed his to Patrick Harvey Murphy.

Murphy became aware of the radical politics of the labour movement at the end of the Great War, joining the Young Communist League by the time he was sixteen. This action led to a break with his father. By now, young Murphy had new heros: J.B. McLachlan, Tim Buck, Becky Buhay, and Maurice Spector, before Spector left to join the Trotskyists. Murphy was especially fond of Buck, at whose home he spent many informal hours during his early years in the movement. It was Buck who noticed how precocious the young man was and proposed sending him to Alberta at the end of 1929 to revive the fortunes of the party there and to start building the Workers' Unity League.

Murphy's instructions relating to the roughly 8,000 Alberta coal miners were to help them give expression to their fighting spirit. He was to inspire the rank and file with the possibility for strike action in support of a union wage scale. Through the columns of a newspaper which he would found and by mass demonstrations and marches into camps run by strike-breakers, he was to stir up the necessary forces to capture the leadership of the existing Mine Workers' Union of Canada from its passive president, Frank Wheatley, and in the process rout the remains of District 18 of the United Mine Workers of America. He was to try to convince newly invigorated unionized miners in the MWUC to become part of the Miners' Section of the Workers' Unity League and by extension join the world-wide struggle of miners led by the Red International of Labour Unions. And finally, he was to unite the mass of unemployed and the unionized workers to force various levels of government into providing adequate relief and unemployment insurance for the growing ranks of the jobless.[36] It was a grandiose vision, a tall order for the young organizer, who up to now had only the slightest connection with miners. His mentors, especially Buck and Ewen, saw his task as a fairly long-range proposition. But to the astonishment of everyone, perhaps even Murphy himself, he was able to deliver big victories in relatively short order. These victories came in spite of confusion and some formidable obstacles.

Confusion arose from the fact that the Workers' Unity League plan for organizing miners in Alberta was seriously at odds with the policy proposed by the Red International. The Mining Section of that body favoured building entirely *new national unions* for energy workers in countries like Canada and the United States. Such unions would combine oil workers and coal and metal miners from across the country. The Anglo-American Section of the Red International argued, not without logic, that this would reflect the coming shape of the energy industry in these countries, and its increasingly monopolistic markets, and would improve the bargaining power of the workers as they changed employment from one sector (coal) to another (oil and gas). They would have a name something like the Industrial Union of Mine, Oil, and Smelter Workers. In theory it seemed like a reasonable proposition. As for the plan to capture the leadership of the Mine Workers' Union of Canada, the secretariat of the Red International of Labour Unions opposed this idea, thinking it would be a hollow victory even if left-wing members succeeded in taking over that office. It was an unlikely possibility, and such 'success' would not do much to win the hearts and minds of the miners or build a revolutionary union. This latter, central aim, could only be achieved by grass-roots organizing from the bottom up at the pit head.[37]

Murphy's advisers, however, especially Buck and Ewen, thought otherwise. They believed that the Alberta miners would not be sympathetic to any attempt to establish yet another miners' union, especially when barely five years earlier the communists had led them in creating the Mine Workers' Union of Canada. Why not try to set the existing union back on its militant track? The social democrats had not had time to consolidate their control of the local unions, the communists reasoned, and therefore it would be possible to gain more than the central office of the union. As for the other concern of the Red International – to establish a national union connecting all miners and oil and energy workers – the Canadian leaders argued that this link could be accomplished by having the far-flung districts in Nova Scotia, in northern Ontario and Quebec, and in Alberta and British Columbia form a federation through their affiliation to the Miners' Section of the Workers' Unity League.[38]

Sparring between Toronto and Moscow on this question continued for the next few years. Prizing unity at all times, members of the Third International had their own unwritten rules about the proper method of discourse. A letter flowing from a higher to a lower level, whether in Canada or from abroad, could be blunt: *'your actions are wrong.'* A critical or dissenting communication from a subordinate unit, however, proceeded differently. It would raise doubts, ask questions, request clarifications of policy, and emphasize the importance of flexibility and the avoidance of mechanical decisions. It skirted confrontation. Every comrade who had attended a party school in Canada understood these protocols of debate. Such circumspection might seem strange to an outsider, and its real significance might pass unnoticed, or be scoffed at by critics of the early Communist Party. But this method of 'freedom of discussion, unity of action' (known as 'democratic centralism') was the way in which the unity and fighting spirit of the organization could be maintained while allowing for a degree of democratic consultation from top to bottom and vice versa. The argument over mining policy in Canada and the way in which the argument proceeded refute the idea promoted by some historians that the Russians were 'the masters' and that lower units of the Communist International were everywhere necessarily obedient to 'foreign dictation.'[39] Possibly well-intentioned in attempting to warn future activists about pitfalls in some forms of international solidarity, that claim – especially when the presence of national representatives within the CI structures is borne in mind – is superficial, often misleading and tinged with political bias.

In Alberta, Murphy plunged ahead with his assignment. Greeted at

the Edmonton train station by Jan Lakeman, Joe Farbey, William Niki-
foruk, and other members of the Communist Party's district executive
committee, Murphy could hardly wait to be on the move again. There
were people to be energized and, as he expected, opposition within the
party to be overcome. Apart from Edmonton and Calgary, and some
farming communities, the main base of the party in Alberta was among
miners, and he soon headed out to make the rounds of the party units in
the mining camps – Luscar, Nordegg, and Canmore on the western edge
of the province, south to Drumheller and Wayne in the Red Deer Valley,
further south to Lethbridge and Coalhurst, and finally up to the Crowsnest Pass in the Rocky Mountains. There over 2,000 miners[40] in Bellevue,
Blairmore, and Coleman on the Alberta side of the pass, and Corbin,
Michel-Natal, and Fernie, in Eastern British Columbia, constituted the
heart of the left-wing strength.

Everywhere he went, Murphy held meetings or met miners informally
where they gathered after work, sharing his views about the deteriorat-
ing economic situation and his plans for militant action. These included
building units of the Workers' Unity League as a kind of left-wing caucus
among the miners to urge unity among the various competing unions
and unorganized camps; encouraging militants to become delegates to
the wage scale conference that the MWUC was going to hold in mid-February 1930; creating pressure on Wheatley for strike action in support
of the expected demands of the conference, and, failing that, spreading
the idea of replacing Wheatley as president of the union. Wheatley, said
Murphy, is a 'good leader for miners who are standing still as a row of
fence posts.'[41]

In Lethbridge, Murphy convinced the secretary of the MWUC local,
James Sloan, a non-party member, to become head of the Miners' Section of the Workers' Unity League in Alberta, and made plans with him
for starting a semi-monthly miners' newspaper, the *Western Miner*, as the
voice of the WUL in Alberta. To start things off, Sloan said he could
arrange for his Lethbridge local to take 25 cents per capita from each of
its 700 members to get the first issue out. By mid-February 3,000 copies
of the first issue of the *Western Miner* rolled off the press in Lethbridge.
'The situation is splendid for the party in the Mining fields,' Murphy
wrote to the political committee of the Communist Party in Toronto.
The miners, he said, 'want leadership.'[42] In response to police brutality
at demonstrations of the unemployed that he addressed, Murphy was
publicly demanding the abolition of the Alberta provincial police.

At Wheatley's request, Murphy met Wheatley face-to-face in Calgary in

February 1930, during the wage scale conference. Murphy thought the union president was 'pretty nervous.' With most of the mining contracts due to expire at the end of March, Murphy told Wheatley that his position, and that of the party he led, 'was out for to fight' and to strike if necessary to gain the 7 to 15 per cent, or even 27 per cent wage hike in some cases, that the scale conference had decided upon. Wheatley disagreed. It was the duty of the union miners, he said, to avoid a strike pending the rehabilitation of the industry. Wheatley said Murphy's policy was 'strike and starve.' He accused the Workers' Unity League of favouring chaos so that Russia could gain the market for coal in Canada. Ignoring the taunt, Murphy replied that 'the owners' problem is none of your business; if they cannot carry on the business, the state must do so.' He reminded Wheatley of his own public stance in favour of nationalizing the coal mines. Or was that just electioneering demagogy? Now, at a time of crisis, was the moment when such a change in national coal policy could and should take place! Wheatley became uneasy, perhaps sensing that, from the point of view of the miners, the younger man had the higher moral ground. After two and a half hours of arguments, according to Murphy, Wheatley said: 'Well, I guess I am getting too old to be president.'[43]

Then, just as the wage scale conference ended, something extraordinary happened. Murphy received new and different instructions from the political committee of the party in Toronto. He was to tone down his militancy and not push for a strike; the miners were not ready to remove the Wheatley machine. Instead, the party should agitate for the abolition of the check-off of union dues as a means of achieving Wheatley's eventual ouster. Ewen had got cold feet.

Murphy and his comrades were dumbfounded. Your instructions 'shocked us cold,' he wrote Ewen. 'Only by the mass marches of the union miners can these places be organized,' he exclaimed. 'How are you going to organize the unorganized and build the union if not with strikes?' The Alberta leaders asked for clarification of what they considered to be 'a wrong line.'[44]

In reply, Ewen scolded Murphy, saying he would need 'occult powers' to understand the situation as Murphy saw it. He complained that Murphy had never talked before of 'hunger marches,' not to mention the 'damned fool demand at this stage of the game' for the abolition of the Alberta provincial police. Is that the unparalleled level of 'the revolutionary tempo of the miners' in Alberta these days? he asked sarcastically.[45]

Apart from the vacillations of the party's national leadership, Murphy

faced a further difficulty in the continuing opposition of the Ukrainian party members to the 'third period' tactic of 'class against class.'
Attempting to discredit the new district organizer, the secretary of the
party group in Drumheller, Alberta, a Ukrainian miner, sent a scurrilous
letter to the centre demanding his recall.[46] But it was John Stokaluk who
gave Murphy the most grief.

A coal miner, a veteran union organizer, and a respected member
of the district executive committee of the Communist Party in Alberta,
Stokaluk had been attending a national school of the Ukrainian Labour
Farmer Temple Association in Winnipeg when Murphy arrived on the
scene. Upon returning to Alberta, instead of reporting to the young
Murphy, Stokaluk went straight to his base at Coleman in the Crowsnest
Pass, where Wheatley took him on as a paid organizer for the union.
Many of the Ukrainian miners held him in awe.

Stokaluk proceeded to sabotage Murphy's efforts by ignoring party
instructions. He refused to distribute the first issue of the *Western Miner*
in the Crowsnest, saying that its message was confusing, and circulated
his own paper among the miners, opposing strike action. He and Wheatley hoped to win the check-off of dues away from the UMWA by adopting
a co-operative attitude towards the employers and they argued that this
was the best way to strengthen the Canadian union. Murphy and the
majority of his executive committee disagreed. The workers' interests
and those of the Canadian union could only be advanced by its becoming a fighting organization. Murphy wrote Stokaluk, pointing out that he
had disobeyed party directives and saying that the situation was too critical to allow anyone, 'be it you or anyone else,' to flout party committees
and do what he pleased. Warning him that he had been the subject of
a motion of censure for spreading disunity and defeatism, Murphy said
that failure to report to the District Executive Committee would lead to
his suspension. Furthermore, since he was working for the MWUC, he
must, according to party policy, refund to the party all wages he received
in excess of the party scale.[47]

Not leaving anything to chance, Murphy organized a meeting of all
the communist miners of Southern Alberta, including Stokaluk, in Lethbridge mid-March. This meeting, which was well attended and authoritative, decided to endorse a call from the Coalhurst local of the miners'
union for a 1 April strike deadline and for a unity convention later in
the same month to consolidate the militant program. When Stokaluk
continued to circulate a no-strike statement for signatures, the meeting
voted for his expulsion. Stokaluk 'came into the meeting as the big man,'

reported Murphy, 'and went out in the end … a pretty small gink.' He urged the political committee in Toronto not to waver.[48]

But waver it did. The party centre believed that unifying left forces 'for the coming decisive events' was a key consideration, and appealed to the Alberta district membership to unify their ranks. While affirming that 'those who persist in open right-wing opposition' had to be opposed,[49] the centre, nevertheless, dispatched a telegram setting aside Stokaluk's expulsion. As a consequence, the 1 April strike call fizzled out. Then, on 4 April, the centre changed its mind again, lifting its annulment of the district's action against Stokaluk and issuing a statement on his expulsion from the party.[50] Stokaluk was advised of his right of appeal, right up to the Comintern if he desired. He took that path but with little effect. However, such was the enduring importance of the Communist Party to Stokaluk that a year later, after suitable public apologies about breaking discipline and, perhaps more importantly, after the Ukrainian section of the party had at last decided to participate in the new policy of 'class against class,' he appealed for reinstatement. The party overcame the costly schism by accepting the talented organizer back into its ranks again, and into a leading role.[51]

Wheatley, meanwhile, was fighting hard for his position as president of the union, but an incident in the Lethbridge local, where Sloan was the secretary, did not help his cause. One day a gang of right-wingers, accompanied by policemen (organized by some priests, according to Murphy), arrived at a meeting and Wheatley looked on as the local president, a CP member, was beaten up, 'chairs were smashed,' the executive ousted, and a new one elected on the spot. News of the incident spread like wildfire through the district and did no credit to Wheatley. There were other violent incidents. An amateur boxer in the miners' union, 'Kid Burns' (Lewis McDonald's nickname), who was a disaffected former party member, knocked out one of Murphy's teeth at another meeting and threatened to knock out some more. Momentarily, Murphy wondered if the reactionaries were gaining the upper hand.[52]

The flow of the struggle soon changed again, however, with the unexpected resignation of Wheatley's vice-president. This opened the way to a district-wide by-election. When the Workers' Unity League forces nominated Sloan for the post and he won handily over Wheatley's nominee, the momentum was unstoppable. Before long, Wheatley himself was the subject of a recall vote and removed from office, and, in a district-wide ballot, James Sloan became the new president.[53]

The Workers' Unity League now appeared to have the lead – a full-fledged union, up and running. But any celebrating was premature as the new leadership had two serious hurdles to overcome. The first test of its mettle was at a small coal mine in northern Alberta; the second a surprise during the union's upcoming annual convention.

At the McLeod River Collieries in Mercoal, Alberta, a majority of the eighty miners who worked there had signed up with the Mine Workers' Union of Canada.[54] But when the existing union contract was open for renewal in June 1930, the operator arbitrarily ignored the claim of the Canadian union and re-signed a two-year contract with the United Mine Workers of America. Angry that they would have to pay a $2-per-month check-off of dues to the American union to keep their jobs, the miners went out on strike. The local detachment of provincial police escorted non-union members through boisterous picket lines, and the company began hiring unemployed miners to keep the mine open. This was a challenge that could not be ignored. Sloan and Murphy hurried over to give a hand. Murphy persuaded the men at nearby Cadomin, the most important mine in the northern sub-district, to support their brothers by a vote of three to one, and soon he was leading a ten-mile march of 150 men to bolster the picket line at Mercoal. Sloan, too, was busy, addressing mass rallies of strikers and collecting strike relief from their supporters. The mine was forced to close for ten days.[55]

The Alberta United Farmers' government, headed by Premier J.E. Brownlee, generally considered to be of social democratic persuasion, responded to the operators' appeal for help by sending in reinforcements – over a hundred police and 'specials' armed with machine guns, rifles, revolvers, and tear-gas bombs. According to the *Edmonton Journal*, this was 'the largest gathering of the provincial force in its history,' and this action was taken 'in spite of the fact that the new Canadian organization has secured a strong hold in this area and is now in control in the majority of the neighboring mines.'[56]

Tempers flared, and there was some booing and shouts and some shoving, termed 'colliery riots' by another Edmonton paper,[57] and police charged several members of the MWUC, including its president, Sloan, with unlawful assembly, assault, or incitement to riot. Burdened with court costs and the need to support the families of the Mercoal strikers, the union could not continue the struggle beyond five months. But under its new leadership, it had shown its grit. The workers had put 'a real fear into the hearts of the coal operators and the social fascists AFL leadership,' said Murphy.[58] The strike was a forerunner of greater struggles to come as the miners prepared for combat against unbearable, starvation conditions and the system that was responsible for them. At least, that was Murphy's prediction and he hoped to be leading them when the time came.[59]

It is ironic that as Murphy and the Workers' Unity League led the immigrant coal miners of Alberta in exercising their rights to picket, to free speech, and to free assembly and association, all celebrated institutions of British liberty, their critics condemned them as prescribing 'a policy of mob violence, of open terror,' and of urging 'productive workers to abandon their jobs and to prepare for armed insurrection.' A close reading of the evidence suggests that nothing could be further from the truth, as even the *Edmonton Journal* recognized.[60]

The other hurdle for the WUL's mining campaign occurred at the 5th Annual Convention of the MWUC in September 1930. After Sloan and the new executive were voted into office, the anti-WUL forces raised an awkward objection. The convention, they argued, had no right to decide to affiliate to the WUL because the membership had not been consulted on this important matter. Since both the miners' union and the WUL were rank and file organizations, they argued, there should be a referendum. Although the communists were fearful of the result, there was no way to deny the challenge. They would have to welcome the idea, but they would not be in a hurry. They would stall to give the new union executive time to show their fighting capacities. Not until eight months later, in the spring of 1931, did the union put two questions on a referendum ballot: 'Are you in favour of affiliation with the Workers' Unity League?' and 'Are you in favour of an extra 5 cents per capita per month for *The Western Miner*?' A short, furious campaign in all the mining camps where the MWUC had locals led to a tensely awaited but a highly satisfactory result for the communists: 1,779 in favour of the WUL to 638 opposed, and similar support for the paper.[61]

It was a historic victory, a time for celebrations all right, but by now its chief architect, Murphy, was long gone from his assignment in Alberta and found himself in Moscow, a student at the International Lenin School. During his stint in Alberta as district organizer for the Communist Party, he had made a lot of enemies – one party comrade predicted that he would be lynched if he ever came back[62] – and he had also won high praise. Malcolm Bruce, a senior member of the political committee of the Communist Party and editor of the *Worker*, who was not a personal admirer of Murphy but who made two visits to Alberta during the WUL miners' campaigns of 1930–1, said it was a mystery to him how the miners had retained their faith in the communists, but they had. The party in Alberta, he wrote to Ewen, has made a 'wonderful recovery' and its prestige and influence 'is greater than anywhere in Canada.' In his judgment, it was now the leading district.[63]

But, at heart, Murphy was unhappy with his time in Alberta. For one thing he was homesick. 'Believe me,' he wrote Ewen, 'I miss the Toronto Island, the Jewish restaurants, hot corn beef, and herring ... the political life in Toronto and all the gossip, Stewart Smith's five points, Sims crying and tearing his hair ... Becky Buhay's tears ... I also need a drink.'[64] Also, in the heat of the battle, he had felt in over his head and lacking in necessary theoretical understanding. 'We have a division in the Party,' he complained, 'between promising young favourites that should be educated and those that only are fit for mass work and I curse all the time at this when I am called upon to do work that a well-trained comrade should do ... for the first time in my Party life I feel the great needs of them things I ain't got. I wish you would propose that I be taken out as D.O. and left as an organizer of the WUL and left-wing work generally.'[65]

What Murphy wanted most of all was a chance to go overseas as part of the Canadian delegation to the Fifth Congress of the Red International of Labour Unions in the late summer of 1930. He wanted to visit 'Mecca.' His wish came true, although not exactly as expected, when the next phase of activities important to the establishment of the Workers' Unity League shifted overseas.

4
Going to 'Mecca'

The impact of the Soviet Union on the western world has been a decisive historical event, though it may be difficult to assess its consequences with precision.

– E.H. Carr, *The Soviet Impact on the Western World*, vii

In the English-speaking world, seasoned members of communist parties often referred to Moscow as 'Mecca.' It was a curious and distinctly self-mocking metaphor. How could the world's most famous headquarters of scientific socialism be compared with a centre for religious pilgrimage? This was not an expression that would appear in any official or formal Communist Party document, but it surfaced frequently in private correspondence and conversations. On the one hand, it functioned as an insider joke to throw an eavesdropper or prying eye off the track. On the other it hinted at Moscow as a place for people needing spiritual renewal. And in a contrary way, it implied a sense that Moscow was the seat of the movement's inspiration, and the inherent pitfalls in any blind faith.

There were many pilgrimages to Moscow in the early 1930s and not just by revolutionaries or would-be revolutionaries.

In the first place there were the contractors and business entrepreneurs of all sorts and descriptions, friendly and unfriendly to the planned economy of Soviet Russia, who came hoping to land contracts. In its first Five Year Plan (1929–33), the Soviet Union built hundreds of new electric power stations and factories, including industries previously unknown in Russia, such as chemical, machine building, tractor making, and automobiles. Substantial foreign investments poured into coal mining, the oil industry, and the manufacture of iron and steel. Arthur

McKee and Company from Cleveland, Ohio, for example, won a concession, in 1930, to build an integrated iron and steel complex beyond the Ural mountains at Magnitogorsk which would replicate the largest and most advanced plant of U.S. Steel at Gary, Indiana. There was an explosion of industrial expansion and many of these developments required foreign engineers, technical advisers, specialist consultants, supervisors, and skilled workers.[1] To fill these needs, there was no shortage of applicants from the capitalist countries of the world, including Great Britain, Germany, the United States, and Japan, as thousands of people sought to escape the grip of economic depression in the market-driven economies. The case of lumberjacks from Canada has already been mentioned.

And it wasn't just businessmen who made the journey. Journalists, writers, artists, religious thinkers, scholars, and other professional people lined up to gain entry to the Union of Soviet Socialist Republics, which appeared, for many, as a beacon of hope for a fairer, more just world. They were an eclectic mix: Maurice Hindus, prolific writer; Lement Harris, wealthy American stockbroker's son; George Bernard Shaw, acerbic playwright; James S. Woodsworth, independent labour member of Canada's parliament; Sidney and Beatrice Webb, Fabian socialists; George Williams, Saskatchewan farm leader, and hundreds more. They had myriad questions to ask of the Soviet Union. What was the secret of Russia's success? they wanted to know. Did the Russians use forced or prison labour to dump goods on the world market? Was there freedom of religion? Had marriage been abolished? Were there trade unions? How did collective farms work? What were Soviets? What were the realities of Communist Party rule? Were the workers in Russia building a new world, as some claimed, and did it have any planetary significance? Most of them went home favourably impressed to one degree or another.

Much has been written about these 'political pilgrims,' as they were labelled during the Cold War against communism,[2] and most of the writing has been in a derisive vein about people estranged from the social systems in which they lived wanting to discover the well-springs of a new, dynamic society, wishing to evaluate the progress of such a vast experiment in social change as was found in the USSR, or hoping to find reassurance in the possibilities for human progress. The path described by these writers usually starts with an initial condition of naive belief, moves on to uneasy doubts, and, finally, some years later, to ashamed unbelief and regret.

It was in this milieu that the Workers' Unity League of Canada sent its own representatives to the Soviet Union in the late summer of 1930.

They also wanted to learn how the idea of socialism, which the leaders, at least, subscribed to, was getting along in the Soviet Union and, in addition, they wished to gain ideas about the international movement, and how they might improve their own work in Canada. For these purposes, a delegation of five women (including two trade unionists), led by Rebecca Buhay, and a group of six male trade unionists, led by Tom Ewen, arrived to attend the much-anticipated Fifth Congress of the Red International of Labour Unions and two subsidary conferences composed of miners and working women.[3]

As might be expected, the delegates felt a keen sense of anticipation when they reached the Soviet Union for the first time in their lives. On hand to greet them and to help them get oriented were Stewart Smith and Sam Carr, two seasoned Canadian participants in the world of 'Mecca.' They would go on tours of cities and towns, of factories, mines, oil refineries, collective farms, hospitals, schools, museums, and workers' living quarters in different parts of the country. But first there was the main event.

At one level it was not difficult to settle in to enjoy the drama of the moment. The Sixteenth Congress of the Communist Party of the Soviet Union had just concluded its sessions in Moscow and now the Red International of Labour Unions would occupy the stage for the last two weeks of August. Its sessions took place in one of the city's most famous buildings, the former Noblemen's Club, built in 1780, at the corner of Okhotny Riad and Pushkin Street, just west and in full sight of the Kremlin. After the Bolshevik revolution of 1917, this magnificent clubhouse became the Trade Union Hall of Columns. The Moscow trade unions organized grand receptions for the delegates. Groups of workers from different factories brought greetings and flowers for each of the more than 500 representatives from fifty-five countries. After the concluding speeches, the delegates proceeded into the street singing the 'Internationale' to meet a great mass demonstration of Moscow workers in honour of the Fifth Congress. 'The whole square was decorated with red placards,' according to a newspaper report, and 'the march past of working men and women, employees, students, scholars, and pioneers, across the whole breadth of the square, lasted more than two hours.'[4]

All this inspired the Canadian delegation, as did speeches of delegates from revolutionary China, from colonial India and the Philippines, from Cuba and Latin America, South Africa, Syria, Australia, and from most European countries. James Ford of the United States, representing the International Trade Union Committee of Negroes, spoke of the heroic efforts to organize the black workers of Alabama in the midst of trumped-up charges and lynchings by the Ku Klux Klan. The Canadian participants chose Pearl Wedro, needle trades worker and union organizer from Winnipeg, to speak for Canada in the plenary session of the Congress of the RILU.

Most of all they listened to, and pondered, the five-hour report of the stocky, bearded general secretary and leader of the Red International, Alexander Lozovsky, who, according to press reports, was greeted with 'tumultuous applause and the singing of the "Internationale"' when he arrived at the podium. Here was a formidable man with a legendary reputation. Reputed to be close to Stalin in his thinking, a long-time supporter of 'bolshevization' in communist ranks, protagonist of Red (communist-led) trade unionism, and persistent critic of social reformism, he has been pegged by subsequent historians as a hard-line leftist – sectarian,[5] inflexible, and prone to 'adventurism' – a strident ultra-revolutionary thought to be typical of the 'third period' in the history of the Third International.[6] How apt was this description of Lozovsky's leadership from the perspective of the Fifth Congress of the RILU? How did the Canadians understand his urgings?

Lozovsky's report, spread over two days, cannot be easily summarized.

As expected, he began by analysing the crisis convulsing the capitalist and colonial world. From there, he contrasted the decay of capitalism with the rise of the USSR, which, he said, had proved to the whole world what the proletariat was capable of accomplishing when it developed its latent energy and creative power. And now, in view of the growing danger of war, and war preparations against the Soviet Union, defence of the socialist revolution and its Russian birthplace constituted a principled criterion of proletarian solidarity for the trade union movement led by the RILU.[7] Such introductory comments were standard in Comintern thinking at that time.

Then, abruptly, in the middle of his speech, as if suddenly remembering why this particular audience had assembled, he announced: 'we have come to the central task of the present Congress – to the organization of economic struggles.'[8]

He wanted to talk about strikes, 'one of the sharpest weapons of struggle,' and he did so at length and in great detail. Too often, he said, sections of the RILU had 'prepared them badly and conducted them still worse.' He insisted that at the present moment 'the essence of revolutionary trade union tactics' meant fewer abstract slogans and more attention to the direct demands of the workers, their day-to-day needs for better wages and working conditions, safety regulations, social insurance, housing conditions, and women's and young workers' concerns.

Lozovsky reminded everyone that workers think a great deal before they decide to go on strike and do so because they are quite serious about defending their own interests. 'We often jump from one demand to another and in the end we forget where the strike began,' he said, whereas the workers who go on strike want, first of all, to achieve what was demanded at the beginning of the strike. Thus, when strikes are badly prepared and demands not clearly formulated, the workers are split, he explained, and they lose faith in their power and in the possibility of victory. Militant unionists then forfeit the opportunity that strikes provide as 'schools of solidarity, where militant class contact among the workers is hammered into shape,' and where workers learn to fight the triple alliance of the bourgeois state, the employers, and the reformist trade union bureaucracies. Properly led, he said, the strike movement trained the workers for the struggle, helped to reveal the close relation between economic and political issues, and 'markedly [brought] out the fundamental aims of the strike movement' – the forging of the dictatorship of the proletariat and the overthrow of bourgeois class rule.[9]

In many ways, Lozovsky's report was a sombre reminder of difficulties facing a militant trade union movement. It did not sound as if he expected revolution to arrive any time soon. Although some gains had been made since the previous congress, especially in the colonial and semi-colonial parts of the world, Lozovsky reported a stalemate or serious losses for the Red International of Labour Unions in the main citadels of capitalism. Neither Germany nor Great Britain had any independent revolutionary trade unions – only poorly functioning minority movements within the reformist unions. In the USA, France, Czechoslovakia, and Japan, the memberships of revolutionary unions had fallen. The Italian unions, under the hammering of Mussolini's fascism, had quit their membership in the RILU; Canada received but scant mention in passing. 'If we cast a cursory glance at the political map of the world,' said Lozovsky, 'we see that the revolutionary trade union movement is illegal and semi-legal, in at least 30 countries,' and 'we know of tens of thousands of supporters of the RILU suffering in jails and cut off from active life altogether.'[10]

The origin of these losses, according to Lozovsky, was mainly to be found in the 'unheard-of persecutions of the revolutionary workers' movement in all countries.' Arrests, breaking up of organizations, the illegal seizure of their premises, the suppression of the workers' press

– all these were 'links of the long chain of capitalist attacks' on the agencies of the working class. Strikes had been stubbornly opposed not only by the bourgeois governments and employers' organizations, but also by the reformist trade unions, and their combined actions had acquired 'an extremely violent character' in recent years. Hardly any of the strikes proceeded peacefully, and, in all countries, 'even in the so-called democratic countries,' the 'whole power of the ruling classes' was brought into play to crush the resistance of the workers. The bourgeoisie sent out police and soldiers, made mass arrests, murdered leaders, 'openly or in the dark,' shot at pickets, brought truck-loads of strike-breakers under police protection to the factories and mines, organized special gangs, and used anti-strike legislation or compulsory arbitration to crush the movement. 'We are not blind to the difficulties,' said Lozovsky, 'but we are not willing to surrender.'[11]

That difficult objective situation, however, did not explain everything. There were still many elementary shortcomings in the work of the revolutionary unionists that contributed to the defeats. Often, strikes broke out catching RILU members unawares, revealing the leadership's tendency to lag behind the fighting spirit of the masses. Sometimes there was inadequate preparation for a strike, including lack of prior discussion of definite demands by all interested men and women workers, not just by a few leaders. And there was the habit of choosing strike committees by a small circle of people instead of having them elected by all workers in the shop, both union and non-union members having a vote. Lozovsky elaborated on this question in a way that highlighted his belief in the power of union democracy.

There are comrades, he said, who object, thinking, 'If we begin to elect any leading organs, then we risk the danger of reformists being elected, and the reformists will betray the strike.'

'True enough,' he responded, 'the reformists will undermine every strike. But do you think if we create a strike committee artificially, that we shall thereby improve the position of the strike? Not at all. Let the workers elect the strike committees they want. If we are in the minority, it is up to us to warn … that the policy of the reformist majority means retreat and defeat, but let this organ be really elected by all the workers, and, in the process of the struggle, in the process of the class collisions, as the contradictions become more and more intensified, the workers will support that section of the strike committee which really express[es] their militancy, which really embod[ies] all their demands and give[s] a revolutionary lead to the struggle.'[12]

There were other fundamentals of strike strategy that he tried to hammer home. A real strike committee, he said, did not issue 'orders' and was valuable only when it made daily reports to the workers and did not lose touch with them for a single moment. Such a committee had the ability to counteract demagogic slogans and 'leftist manoeuvring,' which frequently caused confusion in the midst of a strike. It avoided becoming enmeshed in behind-the-scenes negotiating by reporting immediately to the strikers on everything that took place in meetings with the employer. And it knew when to beat a retreat and return to the enterprise in orderly fashion. 'We must not think that every struggle is a final and decisive battle,' said Lozovsky, 'they are only skirmishes ... Defeat is not a disgrace.' The worst thing was to drag out a strike to the point of complete exhaustion and disorganization of the strikers. In his speech, Lozovsky drew heavily on the deliberations of a conference of West European trade unionists, apparently held in Strassburg in early 1929, and whose conclusions were summed up in 'The Strassburg Resolution on Strike Strategy and Tactics.' This resolution, he said, should be endorsed and carried forward. It became an essential guide to the revolutionary trade unionists of Canada.[13]

Unless one considered the very notion of organizing strikes and demonstrations in the midst of an economic depression to be foolhardy madness and a form of ultra-leftism, as some did, there was, in fact, little hint of 'adventurism' in Lozovsky's wide-ranging urgings of what he called the central task of the Red International: to fight for the economic demands of the working class. As the Canadians listened to him, they felt there was a great deal to learn, considerable room for self-criticism, and much practical work to be done.

Lozovsky, of course, spoke of many other related issues, such as the organization of the unemployed; the struggle against fascism (especially in Austria and Germany); the organization of workers' self-defence corps; work in the reactionary and reformist unions; organizing the unorganized workers; building the united front around struggles; and the consolidation of the independent Red unions. These were all considered to be important tasks. Knowledgeable observers have noted that he held back on advocating a favourite theme – the establishment of *new* independent Red unions where reformist unions already existed – because other leaders of the Comintern expressed ambivalence, fearing the growth of sectarianism and isolation from the mass of workers.[14]

Finally, scattered through different parts of Lozovsky's speech were references to the nagging but all-important question of conflict and unity between communists and social democrats in the trade union movement. He dwelt on the notion that the social democratic *leaders* were the main organizers of the capitalist attack on the workers and that this was 'the most outstanding feature of the present period of class struggles.' They operated by pacts of non-aggression between workers and capitalists (see the discussion of 'Mondism' in chapter 1 of this book). They promised 'socialism without revolution, liberty without struggle, and utmost happiness without misery and sufferings.' Giving numerous examples, he said that this behaviour, including ruthless, repressive actions in the places where social democrats held state power, weakened support for the daily struggles of working people for decent wages and better conditions. The difference between revolutionaries and the reformists, he emphasized, 'is not that the reformists are for reforms and we are against them, but that we are striving for reform by way of the class struggle; they, on the contrary, want to achieve them by means of class collaboration.'[15]

At the same time, Lozovsky criticized as 'left sectarianism' a tendency to lump together the social democratic leaders and the workers who followed them, and in 'not knowing how to work – often not wishing to work – in the reformist trade unions for the realization of the united front from below.' That is, in fighting against the compromises of reformism and in favour of more militant class struggle, there arose a danger of estrangement from the mass of workers.[16]

Nowhere was the struggle between the social democrats and the communists in the trade union movement more acute than in Germany. Both groups had a popular following and each hoped to become the dominant force, although the social democrats were far ahead. Each side hurled insults at the other. Lozovsky praised the efforts of the German section of the RILU and recommended it as a fine example to the delegates at the Fifth Congress. What he did not say, perhaps did not realize at the time, or avoided mentioning because of the outcast Trotsky's advocacy of rapprochement with the social democrats,[17] was that given the alarming growth of chauvinistic nationalism in Germany by 1930, as represented by the rapid rise of the fascist Nazi Party, which presented itself as 'national socialism,' neither the communists nor the social democrats could win big victories for the labour movement on their own. They needed a united labour movement.

As table 4.1 shows, the Nazis increased their popular vote by eight times in the September 1930 election to become the second largest party in the Reichstag. It was a sensational result. In spite of this alarming situation, however, each side of the German trade union movement con-

Table 4.1 Number of votes in German Reichstag elections

Year	Social Democrats	Communists	Nazis
May 1928	9,146,000	3,262,000	809,000
Sept 1930	8,572,000	4,590,000	6,401,000
July 1932	7,951,000	5,278,000	13,372,000
Nov 1932	7,231,000	5,971,000	11,750,000

Source: Gerhart Eisler, Albert Norden, and Albert Schriener, *The Lesson of Germany: A Guide to Her History* (New York: International Publishers, 1945), 101, 105, 108.

tinued to speculate on the mistakes of the other, trading vituperations and accusations such as 'anarcho-communist' or 'social fascist' in what was an incalculable political blunder. For the next two and a half years, as the Nazis gained popular support, the two working-class parties were unable to keep their differences within bounds. It wasn't until after Hitler seized power, in January 1933, that the German communists, with the support of the Third International, offered an olive branch without conditions attached to the social democratic leaders, and began to talk once more of a 'united front from above' as well as 'from below' to halt the Nazi drive to power.[18] But by then it was too late. In short order, as everyone knows, the most militant working-class leaders of both groups found themselves in exile or in concentration camps and their parties outlawed. Along the way, Lozovsky undoubtedly contributed to the sectarian debacle of the German communists.

This discussion of Germany was of great interest to the Canadian delegates in the Moscow congress, although much of it had an academic flavour. As yet, Canada did not have its own social democratic party with national reach – not until the Co-operative Commonwealth Federation (CCF) was formed in the summers of 1932 and 1933. The greatest challenge at the moment was how to go about opposing the employers' wage-cutting drive, how to develop organization among the growing ranks of the unemployed, and how to reach the great mass of still unorganized workers. It was on these topics, and on internal organizational difficulties, that the Canadian participants concentrated their interest and sought to clarify their thinking.

While the members of the Canadian trade union and women's delegations left for tours of the Soviet Union after the conclusion of the RILU Congress, their leaders, including Ewen and Buhay, Stewart Smith, Sam Carr, and John Navis (of the Ukrainian section of the Canadian party), stayed behind in Moscow for six weeks of discussions in a Comintern commission that dealt with such topics as 'the Canadian question' (was Canada a colony or sovereign nation?), the 'Ukrainian question' (should cultural activity among new immigrants reflect more of the class struggle?), trade union work (how to build the Workers' Unity League), work among miners, 'participation in the proletarian women's movement,' and 'the agrarian question' (working out farm policy).[19]

The Canadians drafted resolutions and position papers on these topics which ultimately went up to the political secretariat of the Third International where Dimitri Manuilsky and Otto Kuusinen presided.[20] As expected, Kuusinen took charge and, at a meeting of the Canada commission, he astonished everyone by delivering a two-and-a-half-hour speech. The record of this talk does not seem to have survived but, from scattered references, it appears that Kuusinen, in effect, seconded the emphasis that Lozovsky had placed on the primary importance of *economic* struggles of the workers; the plight of the unemployed, who now reached 300,000 in Canada; organizing in the factories, mills, and mines; and the need to learn more about strike strategies. Carr summed up the feeling with the comment: 'Old Kuus made a great speech ... and I am certain that it provides an excellent base for the future activities.'[21]

Apart from some particular ideas about strike strategy and methods of organization among the unemployed and in workplaces, perhaps the most important result of the meeting was something more general: it was the added prestige such a high-level encounter gave to the Canadian communist leaders. This would help them in their major home constituencies of radical Finnish and Ukrainian immigrant workers who followed developments in the international communist movement with great interest.

The only exception to the political secretariat's vote of confidence for the Canadian leaders was Smith, who, they recommended, should stay in the Soviet Union for an undetermined period. He was to 'learn from the school of practice' to 'gain international experience,' and, incidentally, to help strengthen Comintern capabilities for drafting documents. It was an unspoken punishment for his offensive against the Finns in Sudbury, Ontario, in the autumn of 1929 (chapter 2). For the other leaders of the Canadian party, an unpleasant result of this unexpected lay-over of Smith was that, during the next year or so, they were destined to receive a stream of letters and official resolutions from the Comintern couched in Smith's abrasive, verbose, peremptory language, and they felt obliged to spend precious hours preparing defensive replies.[22]

As to the group of Canadian trade unionists who came to Moscow that summer, they were, from Ewen's point of view, a 50-50 proposition. Only half of them had been chosen by representative assemblies of workers and therefore felt a personal sense of responsibility to report back on their impressions of the Soviet Union. As for the others, including a coal miner from Alberta, a railway shop worker from London, Ontario, and a boot and shoe worker from Toronto, Ewen couldn't even persuade them to take notes on what they were experiencing. He doubted they would become revolutionary assets. When Lethbridge miner Jerry McLeod, for instance, discovered that the Red International would not be paying a $5 per diem, he became a different person, grumbling about how much money he had lost by not staying home and working that summer. 'He was there,' said Ewen, 'but did not see the biggest thing ... like the small boy who went to the circus but did not see the elephant.'[23]

It was not much better with the women's delegation. Buhay, like Ewen, had not been able to accompany her group on the tour outside Moscow since she was engaged in top-level committee meetings; as a result, there was no one to provide historical and political perspectives during the tour about the larger context of the Five Year Plan for the construction of socialism. What made an impression on some of the Canadian women was not the new factories and marvellously equipped workshops, but the shortage of consumer goods and the long queues for daily necessities, which they saw almost everywhere. One of them, Anne Whitfield, from a mining family in Glace Bay, talked about 'telling the truth when I get home.' Alarmed by this, Buhay persuaded the Russian hosts to arrange another tour around the country, which she personally led. Accounts of people seeing the same things and coming to opposite conclusions about life in the Soviet Union were not uncommon.[24]

The most detailed, scholarly work about the USSR between the two world wars was written by Sidney and Beatrice Webb, who were British socialists, and members of the Fabian Society. They had many profound differences with the Communist Party, but prided themselves on having a rational approach to understanding changing societies. They were patient with the Soviet Union and were generally favourably impressed by what they discovered. They preferred a political system of liberal democracy but they accepted the necessity of dictatorship by a party like the Communist Party in a country with the historical traditions of tsarist Russia. Their book, *Soviet Communism: A New Civilization?* was first published in 1935 and ran to almost 1,200 pages in two large volumes. After reviewing the criticisms put forward by the anarchists, Trotsky, and others about the Five Year Plan being a betrayal of socialism, nothing but state capitalism, etc., the Webbs said: 'everyone is free to call anything by any name that he pleases,' but what the workers of every country mean by socialism 'is the supersession of the landlord and the capitalist, together with the profit-making motive, by collective ownership, in a condition of social equality, with the universalization of security by the appropriate organization of social services.'[25] They removed the question mark from their book's title in the second printing in 1937.

Favourable impressions of the socialist experiment in the USSR continued to be held through 1945. They were bolstered by the heroic feats of the Red Army in stopping and then defeating the German Nazi onslaughts that had subdued most of Western Europe. This positive image was portrayed, for example, by David Lewis and F.R. Scott of the CCF in their book, *Make This Your Canada*. In another book, published in 1946 by the widely respected British professor E.H. Carr, the author judged the Soviet impact on the Western world to have been 'a decisive historical event,' helping to mould the Western world in the previous quarter-century, sometimes with the West's own ideas that had lain forgotten or neglected, and which seemed suggestive of what was likely to happen in the future.[26]

Such a prospect, of course, alarmed other Western leaders, and, as a counter-measure, their great champion, Winston Churchill, hosted by President Truman, travelled to Fulton, Missouri, in March 1946, to deliver his famous apocalyptic speech about an Iron Curtain in the middle of Europe, allegedly created by Stalin. The American president followed Churchill's lead in 1947 by announcing the 'Truman Doctrine,' which proposed to place American economic power, diplomacy, and armed forces at the service of a world-wide crusade to stop the spread of communism, beginning with the underwriting of the shaky right-wing governments of Greece and Turkey. By now the Cold War was in full swing and the paradigm of many Western intellectuals for thinking about the Soviet Union swiftly changed from that of a gallant ally in the fight against fascism to a despotic, totalitarian system devoid of redeeming features. And, in 1956, when Stalin's heir, Nikita Khrushchev, revealed hitherto unknown details of the internal affairs of the Soviet Union and especially of the 'Great Terror' of the 1930s, and marked Stalin as an evil tyrant, the prestige of communism in Europe and North America evaporated.

What of the campaigns of the Workers' Unity League in the 1930s, then, 'to defend the USSR,' and to 'support socialism as the hope of the future'? Had they been a mirage, a colossal mistake? Had the Webbs been misguided and naive? These questions are important for any judgment of the path taken by the Workers' Unity League, since much of its organizers' dynamism rested on a belief in the possibility of an alternative to capitalism, of a socialist commonwealth such as was arising in the East under the 'dictatorship of the proletariat.'

Just when the Cold War generation of scholars and journalists thought they were writing the final obituaries for socialism at the end of the twentieth century ('the end of history,' some thought), a new generation of Western scholars began emerging: young people fluent in the Russian language, able to live and work in the former USSR, and having permission to comb through its newly opened historical archives. With the 'threat' of communism gone, they began to depict, here and there, a new, more promising account of 'the building of socialism.' One of the most compelling, nuanced narratives by this new breed of scholar came from the pen of Stephen Kotkin of Princeton University, later head of that institution's Russian studies program. Basing himself on a micro-analysis of the revolution in Magnitogorsk, in 1995 Kotkin published his thesis in a large book called *Magnetic Mountain: Stalinism as a Civilization*. In this book, he carried forward E.H. Carr's notion that the Soviet experiment, while rooted in the rejection of capitalism, was built upon notions of the Western Enlightenment and should be recognized as part of the mainstream of European culture. The defining characteristic of socialism, he discovered, was no private ownership of land or the means of production or the hiring of wage labour; no exploitation of labour as a commodity. Whatever vacillations existed, that was what, in Kotkin's view, made the USSR a distinct civilization. In the 1930s, when the iron and steel complex at Magnitogorsk was under construction, 'the Soviet people were engaged in a grand historical endeavour called building socialism.' They searched for socialism in housing, city building, popular culture, the economy, methods of management, population migration, social structure, politics, values – everything from styles of dress to modes of reasoning. The search was based on a non-capitalist orientation and there was much to discover. He found that despite the violence and hatred that was unleashed during Stalin's rule of terror, the USSR 'meant something hopeful.' It stood for 'a new world power, founded on laudatory ideals and backed up by tangible programs and institutions: full employment, subsidized prices, paid vacations for workers, child care, health care, retirement pensions, education and the promise of advancement for oneself and one's children.' Much was being pioneered. At the same time, belief in Soviet socialism, 'as in all matters of faith, was never without ambivalence, confusions and misgivings.'[27]

In many ways, Kotkin's portrait of socialism in the USSR was the one that Canadian militants of the Workers' Unity League recognized and believed in the 1930s. When they visited 'Mecca,' even if some had reservations, they could picture a grand design and saw for themselves, albeit only in glimpses, the fulfilment of the living stream of history. Such hopefulness gave strength and courage for mundane struggles. It made the existence of the USSR something urgent and worth defending, and it became the meaning, the central core, of proletarian internationalism. Recent scholarship is re-establishing that all was not mirage and myth. There was more to the Soviet Union than Stalin shooting his enemies, which he considered to be many. In view of revelations after Stalin died about the dark side of the Soviet experiment, some people still feel uncomfortable about accepting such truth. But it is safe to say that there were many admirable achievements in the five year plans. And if, in the future, people still wish to create a social alternative to the devastations of capitalist individualism, it is likely that there is much to learn from the path of socialist collectivism in the USSR. It is certain that if the strongly held beliefs and motivations – the actions, the achievements and mistakes – of the Canadian and other communists of the era are to be understood, the experience of the USSR in building socialism needs to be further explored and not lost to history.

5

1931: Trial by Fire

We are entering the period when the iron heel of capitalism will openly seek to crush us at every turn.

– T.A. Ewen, 17 December 1930[1]

This is a land of freedom where men may think what they will and say what they will, so long as they do not attack the foundations upon which our civilization has been built ... it is not just nor right that ... we should permit such action by words or deeds as may tend to unsettle confidence in the institutions and customs under which we live ... we will ... free this country from those who have proved themselves unworthy of our Canadian citizenship.

– Prime Minister R.B. Bennett, 29 July 1931, Hansard, 4278

When Ewen returned from the meeting of the Red International of Trade Unions, he was imbued with determination to build the Workers' Unity League into a revolutionary organization worthy of the name. The message he brought back was a stark one: that the WUL would have to stand on its own feet or die still-born. In financial affairs, especially, it would have to be self-reliant, getting rid of any notions about subsidies from abroad. The budget commission of the Red International had made this abundantly clear.[2] And he was irritated by those who offered members a trip to Moscow or a stint at the International Lenin School as some kind of reward. 'We have got to hold this institution in a higher regard than merely giving members a trip in recognition of their services, or "saving" by sending them on a trip,' he wrote to one organizer. 'It looks too much like revivifying a dead horse.'[3]

   In order to transform the Workers' Unity League 'from an idealistic
imaginary centre of "hope,"' as many regarded it, 'into a living centre
of revolutionary struggle,' he wrote in Bulletin No. 1 of the WUL in
December 1930, certain elementary organizational obligations had to
be fulfilled, such as an affiliation fee from every national union, industrial league, or opposition group within the reformist unions, ordering
of membership cards and constitutions from the national office, and
sending in 5 cents per capita out of the 50 cents collected in dues each
month from every member.[4] When organizers complained that workers could not afford the dues, Ewen was adamant about keeping to the
WUL schedule. 'After all,' he wrote to his organizer in Sudbury, 'if we
cannot convince these workers that a union is worth 50 cents a month,
then there is something the matter with us or they do not want a union,
and consequently it does not matter what the price is.'[5] Dues for unemployed workers were 5 cents per month, with 2 cents the share going to
the national office.
   Aside from having a Workers' Unity League with empty coffers, Ewen
was frustrated by reports coming in from the main centres on their failed
attempts to build up the league. Local conferences for that purpose
had been held in places like Vancouver, Calgary, Edmonton, Winnipeg,
Southern Ontario, and Montreal, but so far little had been accomplished.
There was much confusion and discouragement.[6] Instead of finding ways
of drawing in workers, 'whether "left," "right," or "centre,"' who would
accept the program of the WUL, these conferences most often decided
to turn the existing industrial departments of the Communist Party into
local or district councils of the WUL. The 'mere reshuffling of the Party
and the [Youth] League and giving ourselves new titles,' Ewen observed,
only aided stagnation and increased confusion without developing a
trade union movement that would be 'far broader than the Party.' 'Our
comrades,' he wrote, 'are attempting to put the roof on a structure
before the simple job of laying a foundation has barely been started,'
and then they 'feel pained and surprised because the structure comes
down about their ears.' The characterization by the executive committee
of the Third International that 'we are only a propaganda sect' remained
to all intents and purposes correct, according to Ewen. The Canadian
communists, he said, had not yet learned 'that the masses can only be
reached thru the trade unions.' He urged that instead of 'embracing the
whole universe at one and the same time,' the local comrades select a
few industries according to local conditions and concentrate there on
the 'three main tasks' (aside from work among the unemployed on a

national scale) which were (1) consolidation of national revolutionary unions already in existence (needle trades, lumber workers, and miners) by having every party and youth league member eligible for membership get into these unions and become active; (2) building industrial leagues in unorganized industries by conscripting all comrades and members of mass organizations (Ukrainians, Finns, and others) into the leagues of a particular industry where they are employed, thus forming a nucleus where directives could be carried out, and (3) organization of opposition groups in the reformist unions of the AFL which could draw broader sections of workers into discussion of questions of importance to the shop in question.[7]

In moving from the floor of the union local to the *shop floor* as the locale of work, Ewen urged that his comrades discard 'hysterical agitation and propaganda,' which turned workers away in disgust. They should create popular programs of the demands of the workers instead of 'unintelligible demands' that were class-conscious but had 'nothing in common with the daily struggle as the worker sees it.'[8]

Apart from its own confusions and hesitation, there was the growing resentment and wrath of the property-owning class, the bourgeoisie, against the audacity of the Workers' Unity League in helping workers exercise their democratic rights – especially the right to assemble and to picket. Things were especially difficult in Quebec. After Ewen joined a small picket line of needle trades workers there, in December 1930, he reported 'scenes of struggle that for brutality surpasses anything as yet existing in Canada.'[9]

Many troubling questions arose as the Workers' Unity League urged its members to raise their antennae in the workshops and other places of class confrontation. From Vancouver, organizer George Drayton wrote asking for advice – 'some simple directions and guide for the members'– as to how to form a shop group, taking cognizance of the shop spies, the blacklist system, the backwardness of the workers, the national prejudices of the native-born workers and the British-born, 'and all the other obstacles we stack up against.' Another member, in Cranbrook, British Columbia, had organized forty-five men and women into a unit of the National Unemployed Workers' Association. What should we do next, he wanted to know. Steve Forkin, of Saskatoon, wrote about the difficulty of obtaining police permits to hold demonstrations. From Winnipeg, Ben Winter, pseudonym for Victor Friedman, reported that the organizer of a clandestine local of the Packing House Workers' Industrial Union at the Swift meat packing plant had been discovered, probably by a stool-pigeon, and fired for union activity. The Winnipeg committee of the WUL pondered its options: should it secure legal advice, organize a boycott of the products of Swift, or perhaps call a strike? If the latter, was there anyone who could step forward to lead it?[10]

On all these and other critical matters, Ewen worked with passion and wit to give a lead. The steady flow of correspondence between the national office and its subordinate units in the provinces, captured in police raids in August 1931, continues to reveal more about the political culture of the Workers' Unity League in this formative period, its inner workings and revolutionary nature, than any number of printed resolutions or draft constitutions.

In speaking of what to do in the face of blacklists, company spies, and ethnic prejudice among fellow workers, Ewen pointed to shortcomings in the practice of liberal democracy. 'Since legality and democracy are denied the workers in their right to organize,' he wrote, 'the question presents itself that other means have to be found.' He referred to underground shop papers and secret meetings with workers. 'It is quite permissible for our comrades to lie like hell on the question of membership in the Communist Party,' he said, 'and to govern their actions accordingly ... scruples have to be scrapped.' 'In this period,' he ventured, 'the end justifies the means in all activity.'[11]

To the organizer of the unemployed in Cranbrook, BC, Ewen urged patient efforts. There was no magic formula. It was through paying attention to the little things happening to workers and their families, as well as by large demonstrations, that the Workers' Unity League would grow stronger. 'Get a good working committee,' he urged, 'one that will place every case of working class victimization resulting from unemployment before the local civic administration.' They should take up the everyday needs of the workers, immediate relief, free food, milk for children, clothes for the unemployed workers and their dependants. These were the immediate things on which a council of the National Unemployed Workers' Association could be built. The one determining factor of success on the part of the workers, Ewen wrote elsewhere in congratulating an organizer in Burnaby, BC, for a successful meeting with the municipal council, 'is the existence of a well-organized, determined body that refuses to starve submissively,' and which makes this perfectly clear to the powers that be. 'Certainly the bosses do not like demonstrations but conditions throughout the country are such that the workers are demonstrating anyhow since there isn't anything else to do.' As for the larger political aims of adherents of the Red International, Ewen reminded

his co-workers that these would be advanced by broadening out the economic struggles in appropriate fashion and turning purely economic
demands into a struggle for class demands, such as unemployment insurance paid for by the state.[12]

On the question of seeking police permission to carry on the work of
organizing the unemployed, Ewen was adamant. He advocated disobedience. On principle he did not think that at any time from now on the
unemployed should govern their activities within the prescribed limits of
police permission. 'I think it is a recognized fact of revolutionary principle,' he wrote to his organizer in Saskatoon, 'that since we do not require
a legal permit to starve, neither do we need one to resist it, as otherwise our resistance will be materially narrowed down and consequently
futile.' As the research of legal historians Judy Fudge and Eric Tucker
demonstrates, the WUL organizations 'manifested a willingness to break
the law if necessary' to make their demonstrations and strikes effective,
and 'working class Canadians became more willing to engage in civil
disobedience' to protect their interests as the regime lost its legitimacy.[13]

Ewen gave much thought to the questions raised by the Winnipeg
Swift workers as a result of the management firing their organizer. He
rejected the idea of trying to persuade people to boycott Swift' products.
He said the suggestion reminded him of the Trades and Labour Congress, and since working-class revolutionary consciousness had not as yet
developed to a very high degree, 'to speak of boycotting is like trying to
empty Lake Winnipeg with a tin can.' A boycott presupposed a highly
developed labour movement, something which did not exist as yet, and
was an expression, in Ewen's opinion, of the worst kind of trade union
legalism, only equalled 'by seeking "legal" advice from a shyster lawyer'
and hoping that through the machinery of the capitalist state, a worker
would be 'reinstated as a respectable and "law-abiding" member of that
state.'[14] That left the option of a strike. And who would lead the fight?

Even though less than one-third of the workers at Swift were organized, Ewen proposed that '*every effort and attempt must be made to organize
a strike struggle*' (his emphasis). There were two plain issues: the right to
organize and the right of collective bargaining. 'The fight is inevitable,'
said Ewen, and because the boss does not like union organization, he
precipitates a fight 'which very often finds our Sections in a compara-
tively weak state,' and generally speaking, not in a position to engage in
a struggle. It was just at this point, he warned, 'that many good comrades
waver and follow a "right" line by saying, "wait until we get stronger",
"our Union is too weak."' This, in Ewen's opinion, was where the parting

of the ways took place between the old and the new. Those arguments belonged to the old school. The new school of revolutionary struggle, when faced with such a situation, he argued, 'has no other alternative left than to fight.' 'We are right in not precipitating a fight when we know we are in a weak position,' he said, 'but when a fight is precipitated upon us thru any action of victimization on the part of the boss – then we have one policy – strike.'[15]

Finding effective leadership to conduct a strike was admittedly a problem. What should be the characteristics of such leaders? Ewen noticed in the minutes of the Winnipeg WUL Council that there was reported a lack of good speakers. While the development of these was important, Ewen cautioned against turning union meetings into purely propaganda and agitational affairs. For the elementary training of union leaders, he thought it advisable to have weekly classes of the best elements in the district but 'on no account' should the aim be to produce 'good spouters' who could make an excellent spiel on revolution but who were 'as helpless as a baby' when it came to worrying out the hard facts of necessity in the everyday life of the workers in the shops. To draw workers into the union, he said, we 'must more and more initiate the personal appeal'; visit them in their houses, talk with them, convince them, 'see that they get a firm grasp of what we are attempting to do, make them feel as they are a part of this Union,' and 'on no account try and cram the three volumes of Marx down their throats in one night.' 'By all means send speakers to the local meetings,' he said, 'but insist that they talk shop.'[16] In building the new industrial unions, great patience and tact were required to convince the workers on a program of direct action. After a list of demands was drawn up and thoroughly discussed by the workers involved, it should be presented to the boss with an ultimatum of a strike. If the boss rejected these demands then the entire district council of the WUL should stand behind the union in organizing relief and strike support.[17]

Still, the insistent question remained, who will lead a strike? Ewen recalled being in the sessions of the Red International in Moscow and feeling that tasks set were entirely beyond realization, and he used to be continually harping on the lack of forces. Apparently Kuusinen got fed up with this and spoke up, saying, among other things, that 'in every struggle the workers will supply the forces.' Kuusinen's intervention made a deep impression which Ewen tried to pass on to his old friends in the Winnipeg organization. 'In the everyday humdrum life of trying to develop a new leader,' he wrote, 'this seems to be a slow uphill job, but when the workers are on the picket line and the breadline, we have to admit that Kuusinen is right.' Following Kuusinen's advice, Ewen said that in developing working-class cadres, the WUL should not fall a victim to 'right wing sectarianism' by being afraid that rank and file workers could not be entrusted with this or that job because they might make a mistake or that they were not sufficiently politicized. In times of comparative calm, such workers should be put into leading positions, given help and advice, but the WUL should never permit the monopolizing of the leading positions by Communist Party members because, 'when this happens, at the end of the trail, we come back to where we started from.' Every struggle developed new forces, and 'conditions themselves' would determine the extent of the ability of these forces. Ewen said that he had found, in the many scraps he had been around since moving to Eastern Canada, that 'there are a hell of a lot more good proletarian fighters outside the Party than in it,' and it was the WUL's business in organizing the daily economic struggles of the workers 'to search these elements out and develop them previous and during the fight.' The old idea of communists leading the economic struggles *from the outside* was obsolete. The new idea of 'facing to the factories'[18] was to agitate and prepare for struggles at the point of production. 'We shall have many defeats,' Ewen agreed, 'but no single strike was fought under revolutionary leadership without some gains.' And he thought an episode like Swift (where no strike took place) 'must never again be permitted to develop without resistance and by resorting only to "legal" methods,' because by doing so 'the Revolutionary movement is compromised before the workers and shatters their confidence.'[19]

Underneath a brave exterior, Ewen sometimes felt discouraged, and for a number of reasons. He poured out his heart to an old friend in Saskatoon. Lamenting an organization which was financially 'as barren as the Sahara,' he reported that the Toronto police had just tried to put him 'out of business.' When the police arrested him and took him to a police station after a municipal election rally, in December 1930, he received a vicious blow to the face that knocked out most of his teeth – necessitating a complete set of dentures. It was a foretaste of things to come. He was back in the office, he wrote ten days later, 'feeling "tender" but still on top.' He confessed that were it not for a 'perspective,' he would feel like taking up a homestead in Saskatchewan. He was coming West in the spring and said he was going to try to stay there if possible. 'This idea does not originate from the close attention of the police,' he wrote, 'as this will soon be general, if not already so, but from the point of view that a trade union movement will never be built in Canada with the centre in Toronto.' If ever provincialism was manufactured in the ideology of revolutionaries, he maintained, 'it is here that this is most pronounced, and the Toronto complex is that nothing outside of it matters,' with the result that all members of a central body become local leaders and never get past this.[20] At the beginning of March, 1931, he found himself sitting in the Don Jail once again, for two weeks, after the 'Red Squad' of the Toronto police had taken another run at him at a local demonstration.

There were seven strikes in greater Winnipeg in 1931, as recorded by the Department of Labour, four of them led by the Workers' Unity League, of which two – at a metal working foundry and a small furniture factory – were successful, with the workers resisting a wage cut and making some modest gains. These strikes, especially the week-long one involving eighty-five workers at the Dominion Wheel and Foundries in Saint Boniface and led by the fledgling Metal Workers' Industrial Union, aroused considerable enthusiasm as an example of hard-hitting 'revolutionary strike strategy.' In this case when the boss, G.J. Baetzhold, rejected the workers' demands, refused to meet a union delegation, and posted a notice advising their committee to disband itself, the well-prepared strike began.

Crucial initial support came from unemployed workers. Already alerted to such possibilities and organized into the National Unemployed Workers' Association by the WUL, the unemployed, 200 strong and banners waving, arrived to bolster the picket line on the very first morning of the work stoppage, while the somewhat astonished city and provincial police looked on from across the road. From the Workers' Centre, an old church building on Bannatyne Street in downtown Winnipeg, and from the Ukrainian Labour Temple in Saint Boniface, the local branch of Workers' International Relief, led by Rose Shelley, prepared food for the picket line and collected donations of all kinds to support the strikers. The WIR was a loosely knit but permanent organization being established by the Red International of Labour Unions to publicize need and to collect and distribute relief during strike struggles in all parts of the world. Among its honorary patrons were such outstanding persons as Professor Albert Einstein, Henri Barbusse, Theodore Dreiser, Maxim Gorki, and Upton Sinclair.[21]

Claiming that the trouble-makers were just a small handful of communists, Baetzhold demanded more police protection to escort strikebreakers into the factory, but the mayor of Saint Boniface was wary. In response to the employer's refusal to negotiate, the union maintained round-the-clock-picketing of the plant and organized a mass rally of strikers and their families at city hall. 'The parade and subsequent meeting on the grounds outside the building,' wrote the *Manitoba Free Press*, 'were orderly.'[22] Inside, after two representatives of the union received a sympathetic hearing by the city council, the mayor accepted the strikers' invitation to help effect a settlement by requesting the Department of Labour to send its mediation officer to the scene. That officer persuaded Baetzhold to meet a committee of the strikers face-to-face, and shortly afterwards a settlement, conceding most of the strikers' original demands, emerged. The jubilant strike committee placed their proposed settlement before a meeting of the strikers and it was accepted in the same spirit. Within a week the Metal Workers' Industrial Union and its supporters had gained de facto recognition of a continuing union committee in the shop, an achievement that sent ripples of excitement and appreciation through the Winnipeg workers' movement.[23]

A decisive factor in the strikers' success lay in sympathetic support from the wider community, particularly the unemployed workers' association and the Ukrainian Labour Farmer Temple Association. Such a strategy of mass solidarity was especially possible in Winnipeg with its large population of workers and their militant labour traditions.

In smaller centres, it was much more difficult for the Workers' Unity League to make gains, especially so in the Quebec of that day, as illustrated by the failed strike of 300 workers at the Bruck Silk Mills in Cowansville, a village of 1,800 people in the Eastern Townships.

In a community largely dependent on this one employer, the manager of the Bruck mill decided to introduce a 25 per cent wage cut to bring his costs more in line with those of mill owners in other nearby villages, and he made calculated preparations. This was after an earlier 10 per cent reduction. For several weeks he sped up production to gain a stockpile of finished products, and then at a mid-week point in the beginning of March, 1931, he abruptly closed down production and sent the workers home. When they returned a few days later to pick up their pay, they found a notice in their envelopes announcing the 25 per cent cut in wages.

Except for several workers who had been members of the National Textile Union in the United States, none of the workforce, many of them young girls from surrounding farms, had any previous knowledge of union organization. Nevertheless, some of the workers decided to try to organize resistance, and they chose a committee of seven to take the lead. On Monday morning they put up a picket line, which prompted the boss to declare a lockout for a week. While the priest at Sunday mass had denounced the strike and warned the strike committee against any disorders, talk of 'union' and 'strike' continued to percolate among the workers. Through personal contact, a message was sent to the Workers' Unity League in Montreal requesting assistance. Fred Rose and several companions, members of the Young Communist League, arrived a few days later to see what could be done. As they circulated among the workers, they sensed a strong anti-communist sentiment. A weaver commented that the company was trying to treat the workers like slaves as in Russia. When Rose proposed a leaflet to let surrounding communities know of the situation, the idea was opposed on the grounds that the priest had said issuing a leaflet would be a communistic thing to do. Nevertheless, following the guidelines of revolutionary strike tactics, a leaflet was issued and a list of demands formulated, and a mass meeting took place in the village theatre. There Rose spoke about the Workers' Unity League, criticized the AFL and Catholic unions for their passivity, and proposed that an enlarged strike committee of twenty be elected on the spot and that a mass picket take place on Monday morning when the plant reopened. These steps were agreed to, but then someone challenged Rose and his companions as to what union they belonged to; others shouted out that they wanted to join a union right away.

The Montrealers were ill prepared for this turn of events. The WUL did not have a textile workers' union, not even in embryo, no membership cards, no outline of a constitution. They decided to enrol applicants directly into the Workers' Unity League, but when they looked carefully at the WUL card, they saw that it had the phrase 'Section of the RILU' printed on the cover, and inside they thought they saw the words 'open to anyone who accepts a program of class struggle.' *Sacrement!* While the workers might not know what the initials RILU stood for or the Marxist flavour of the term 'class struggle,' the priest and the media would surely soon make that clear, and 'we would be kicked out,' said Rose. What should they do? Making a quick decision, he and a companion made a hurried trip back to Montreal to have a new batch of WUL cards printed – minus the unsuitable wordings – and then returned to sign up the Cowansville workers. On the following Monday, when the plant reopened, there was a large and boisterous picket line. The police arrested four girls charged with assaulting a scab, and the priest and some helpers went to work, visiting strikers' families. The next day, there was a poor turnout, and very quickly the strike fizzled.

What didn't fizzle out was an intense debate within the Workers' Unity

League about the lessons of this experience and how communists should conduct themselves in such a hostile environment. When the WUL committee in Montreal wrote to the Toronto headquarters during the strike asking for advice and help, Ewen was serving a sentence in the Don Jail, leaving Tim Buck to reply. Buck thought it was a mistake for the WUL organizers to conceal their political identity for more than two or three days – enough time to make some initial contacts – otherwise there was the danger of being exposed as communists sooner rather than later, before they had a chance to explain and develop the revolutionary strike methods. It would be regrettable if the communists lost the possibility of participating in the leadership of the strike through coming out openly as revolutionaries, but 'if it should happen as is likely that the strike will be betrayed,' Buck wrote, 'then I think you will all agree that it is far better that the workers should say "the Communists were right after all", than that they should think that our Party agreed with the policy of betrayal.'[24]

When Ewen emerged from jail he sharpened the criticism. Although as a matter of expediency he also thought it all right to 'hide the face of the Party' in some situations, especially in the province of Quebec 'with its religious mania against communism,' nevertheless he believed it 'absolutely impermissible' to hide the face of the revolutionary trade union movement, of the RILU, 'to the extent of obliterating this from the membership cards.' Ewen included a surprising observation. Better, he said, to have left the question of organizing a union entirely out and to have concentrated on the tactics of successfully pursuing this strike 'rather than to make such a compromise.'[25]

Rose disagreed. He drew up a lengthy report describing the strike and its lessons and defending his actions. 'I for my part cannot see how we could have acted different than we did,' he wrote. 'It is not necessary to use the phrase "hiding the face of the Party" in every instance.'[26]

His report caused the national textile fraction of the WUL to soften Ewen's earlier criticism 'to some extent.' The 'extreme ideological backwardness' of the French-Canadian workers and the 'pernicious influence of the Roman Catholic Church' in every economic struggle, they agreed, made it necessary for the communists to work very carefully, and even in certain conditions 'to conceal our identity from the main body of the workers.' But, the fraction insisted, an effort to build a 'firm nucleus of the best elements' should always be attempted. And backing Ewen up, they declared that by no means should 'complete obliteration of our identity' be permitted to the extent of submerging mention of the RILU when promoting the WUL. They also criticized Rose's distortion of the wording on the WUL membership card. Contrary to his assertion, the term 'class struggle' did not appear there. The statement on the membership card was less strident: '*The WUL shall include all wage workers and their labour organizations in industry and agriculture, regardless of age, race, colour or sex who subscribe to its programme of struggle.*' They summed up Rose's leadership in the Cowansville strike as 'rank opportunism.'[27]

There were other important strikes in 1931 that helped to test the meaning of Alexander Lozovsky's 'revolutionary strike strategy' in Canada: the first at the coal mines of Bienfait, Saskatchewan, and others at the sawmills of British Columbia.

The strike at Bienfait, involving 600 miners, lasted for thirty days from 8 September to 8 October and ended shortly after the RCMP shot and killed three miners and wounded a score of others during a miners' demonstration in the nearby town of Estevan. This tragic result is sometimes blamed on the miners and especially on the organizers of the Workers' Unity League as an example of the 'reckless adventurism' dictated by the 'third period' leftism of the Third International. Another interpretation, placing responsibility where it more properly belongs, is possible, and, based upon the voluminous historical records on the Bienfait strike, I wrote a book to that effect as a result of conducting research for this present text.[28] The conclusion of that book is that

> In the fullness of time the rumours and gossip, the usual account of the communist organizers as a group of violence-prone criminal conspirators has been redressed. Historians and the labour movement in Saskatchewan are coming to view the lead given by the Workers' Unity League and the activities of the group of Bienfait miners inspired by the ideas of Marxism in a more objective fashion: it was the president of the coal operators, not the union leaders, who advocated violence; it was the government's police who practised conspiracy and used firearms. And it was the workers, and Sam Scarlett, Annie Buller and their comrades who went to jail or exile or on a blacklist for exercising their democratic rights.[29]

The high drama of the miners' struggle, their systematic abuse and exploitation by 'red-baiting politicians and hysterically anti-labour bosses,'[30] will not be re-created here. It is rather, the theory and practice of the Workers' Unity League organizers as they led this battle, trying to implement the 'united front from below,' that merit closer attention.

The salient points of the 'united front from below' may be recalled from Lozovsky's exposition of revolutionary strategy at the Fifth Congress of the RILU (and the Strassburg Resolution). Lozovsky had warned against any conspiratorial approach by militants: important decisions should be made by all the workers in a potential strike situation. He stressed the importance of clear and understandable economic demands arising from the actual situation in the mining pits that 'must be discussed by all workers.' In the case of favourable conditions for a strike, a strike committee should be elected by all the workers. 'Workers of all beliefs and affiliations must be able to participate in these elections, the organized as well as the unorganized,' otherwise the strike would fail. These were strong urgings for democratic participation by all involved. There were several other important questions. Consideration had to be given to the offensive of the bosses and to the diversionary tactics of the reformist, business-as-usual unions, and to how to paralyse these efforts in the course of the struggle. How were the unorganized, the unemployed, the youth, and women workers going to be drawn into the struggle? How was the whole working class and its sympathizers in the wider community to be mobilized to aid the striking workers in achieving their demands? Without solving these problems, there would be little of a united front.[31]

When news of the miners' rising discontent about a new round of wage cuts being proposed by the mine owners in the Bienfait coalfields reached the Western Canada centre of the Workers' Unity League in Winnipeg, in August 1931, the organization decided to send Martin Joseph Forkin, one of its most experienced leaders, to see what could be done.

Fortunately for Forkin, there was already a firm nucleus in place. A month earlier, Sam Carr, national organizer of the Communist Party, had stopped over in Bienfait while on a tour and helped to establish a unit of that party. This unit brought together people from the two most numerous and influential ethnic groups in the village – the Anglo-Celts and the East Europeans. The latter group, of peasant background and mainly from Western Ukraine (then under Polish rule) and Lithuania, including the families of Alex and Tekla Boruk, John and Mary Bachinsky, Peter and Stella Gemby, and John and Ursula Billis, had established a branch of the Ukrainian Labour Farmer Temple Association and their hall became a valuable base of activity during the coming strike. The Anglo-Celts consisted of John and Mary Harris, Martin Day, Fred Booth, and perhaps others – militant British coal miners who had emigrated to Canada following the defeat of the General Strike in support of the coal miners of Britain in 1926 – people well experienced in building workers' unions in the context of British institutions of free speech and assembly and the right to picket when on strike.

With the help of the local militants, Forkin was able to establish a committee with representatives from all six of the deep-seam mines in the district (but not from Truax-Traer, the newly started, American-owned, open-pit mine), and in short order, half the employed miners had signed lists stating their desire to join a union. On Forkin's request, the Mine Workers' Union of Canada in Calgary sent an organizer with union books and cards and began signing up members. Two days later, on 20 August, Crescent Collieries fired John Adams, who, according to the local paper, was 'organizing the foreign workers' in the mines. Martin Day, head of the pit committee at Crescent Collieries, promptly led a small delegation to call on the manager to see if he would reinstate Adams. The manager refused to give any reason for his dismissal or to reinstate him. The next morning, in the style of Fifeshire miners of Scotland where he was from, Day led all fifty workers at the colliery in dropping their tools and walking off the job; the miners in several other collieries expressed their willingness to have a sympathy strike if necessary. This was a strong display of unity and a promising beginning.

On the following Sunday, Forkin and his committee organized a family picnic down by the Souris River, near the two largest mining camps, attended by 1,200 men, women, and children. They heard speeches, some of them fairly cautious. The most important speech for stirring up enthusiasm and which helped set the tone for things to come was by Sam Scarlett, 'a ruddy-faced square-built worker with a husky voice,' who had come from Saskatoon to give Forkin a hand. For years, Scarlett had been an anarcho-syndicalist of the Industrial Workers of the World (IWW) but he had recently joined the Communist Party, and this was his first party assignment. He was a legendary working-class leader; so much so that when the RCMP headquarters learned of his arrival, they headed their whole file on investigations into the Bienfait strike as 'Sam Scarlett – Communist Agitator.' The central theme of his speeches for the next six weeks was that our society was divided into two classes, 'the exploiter and the exploited [and] between them there is nothing in common,' and he would go on to trace out the pattern of another and better tomorrow. His convictions were contagious, and he could move people to laughter and to tears. The manager at Crescent Collieries caved in the next day and rehired Adams. The confidence of the miners began to soar.

Next came James Sloan, from Calgary, the new president of the Canadian Mine Workers' Union. Sloan, like Forkin a quiet but effective speaker, addressed an open-air meeting of 1,000 people in Bienfait and another one in Estevan Town Hall, where he declared that the conditions in the Bienfait coalfield were the worst he'd ever seen. With Sloan presiding, all the pit committees met together for the first time, and Local 27 of the Mine Workers' Union of Canada was born. The meeting proceeded to elect Dan Moar, an ex-serviceman working at Crescent Collieries, as president, John Harris as vice-president, and Harry Hesketh, a miner of the British Independent Labour Party tradition who had worked in the area since 1903, as secretary-treasurer. They were all able leaders, no doubt, but by deliberate choice, the union had pushed Anglo-Celts into the leadership to the exclusion of all others, an opportunistic manoeuvre at odds with WUL principles, taken with the best of intentions to deflect attacks by the employers and conservative politicians claiming that the union was 'just a bunch of foreigners' who ought to be sent home. Here, though, was potential for stirring up resentment among sections of foreign-born miners.

The following week, union activists met to investigate complaints and gather material for a meeting with the operators. Mass meetings were held among the miners and their families in preparation for the possibility of a strike. WUL organizers explained how unions worked in other coalfields and promised, in an unspecified way, the support of the Red International of Labour Unions, which, they said, had 28 million members. This was a rash and unlikely promise that opened the door wider for anti-communist attacks by the owners.

Sloan answered questions asked by the miners and their wives. He explained the arm's-length relation of the Communist Party to any trade union; he assured them they did not become communists by joining the miners' union. He told them that they had the sympathy of the people, including the local detachment of the RCMP, and 'not to spoil this sympathy by violence.' Forkin and Scarlett went to local meetings of farmers, churches, and other community groups answering similar questions and to describe the situation, seeking food and relief contributions, and to ask the farmers not to engage in strike-breaking. By then the union had signed up almost all the miners.

Twice the union invited the operators to a conference to reach an agreement on wages and working conditions, and twice the operators refused to attend. 'We will not meet with the representatives of the Mine Workers' Union of Canada,' said C.C. Morfit, president of the operators' association, 'because they are communistic,' and the union 'is an emissary of the Third Internationale.'

On Monday evening, 7 September, after the operators failed a second time to show up for negotiations, union activists met late into the night to make final preparations for a strike. The men hurriedly formed a strike committee composed of the executive of Local 27 and four committeemen from each of the mines – twenty-eight in all – and they would be the picket captains. At the same time, fifty women met in the Ukrainian Labour Temple to form a women's auxiliary of the union.

The strike began the next morning, with all deep-seam mines ceasing production.

The hurried deadlines, and the failure to organize open elections for the strike committee or to circulate the precise strike demands among the membership or *even among the executive* in advance of the strike, were major departures from revolutionary strike strategy, leading eventually to an atmosphere of discontent and internal dissension that would have serious consequences for the success of the struggle.

Since there is no record of the conversations among the WUL leaders during these days, the reasons for their hasty, secretive actions are a matter of conjecture. Partly it was accidental. Sloan's impatience to meet or confront the employers was understandable because later in the week he had to be back in Calgary for the opening of the sixth annual convention of the Mine Workers' Union of Canada, of which he was president. Apart from that, Sloan was an experienced and able negotiator who was not a Communist Party member but had acquired a solid reputation among the miners of Alberta (where wages were higher than in Saskatchewan), and he had his own ideas about what was most important. On the second day of the strike, when he had to leave Bienfait for Calgary, and would be gone for ten days, he unaccountably took the only copy of the detailed demands of the union. His only instruction to the strike committee was that if the employers decided to negotiate in his absence, the committee should insist on the first point, namely recognition of the Mine Workers' Union of Canada as the bargaining agent of the men. Without union recognition, Sloan reasoned, any other concessions gained would be unenforceable, leaving the employers free to continue on as always. Forkin and Scarlett argued that there should be no preconditions to opening negotiations for a settlement, but the strike committee was with Sloan.

In the absence of President Sloan, the operators quickly reversed their position, announcing their willingness to negotiate with the strike committee. After a brief meeting the operators publicized the sole demand put forward by the miners: their demand for union recognition. The strikers, they said, had presented nothing requiring redress and they immediately launched a campaign to discredit the union. According to the employers' propaganda, spread by the press, especially by the *Mercury* of Estevan, the union was nothing but a conspiratorial organization affiliated to the Third International, power-hungry and interested only in revolution. Sloan's strategy had opened the door for the operators, and in his absence they clearly put the miners on the defensive.

Later, when analysing the lessons of the strike, Ewen criticized what he considered to be the 'stupendous errors' of the WUL organizers. Sloan's strategy of putting 'union recognition' ahead of all other demands, he said, was 'the rock upon which certain victory was battered into partial defeat.' The 'twin brother to this class stupidity,' he continued, was the atmosphere of 'secret conspiracy that predominated the activities of the Strike Committee and their relationship with the miners throughout the strike.' This included the failure to submit the strike demands to a membership vote, and failure to issue any strike bulletins that could reply to the operators' lies and could publicize the preparations for the fateful parade into Estevan where the murderous confrontation with the police took place. When remembering the neglect of 'the most elementary principles of revolutionary trade unionism,' Ewen marvelled that such tactics did not completely wreck the faith of the miners in their union.

Then there was the open-pit mine, which was shipping record amounts of coal. At a meeting to discuss the situation, people had different views on what should be done. Scarlett joined with those who thought the miners, in their overwhelming numbers, should take over the Truax-Traer mine, but this risked violent confrontation with the police. Forkin convinced the majority of the strike committee to take a different course, of trying to persuade the wider community of the justice of their cause and seek their support to pressure the operators into negotiations to settle the conflict.

The Bienfait strike ended thirty days after it began without Local 27 of the Mine Workers' Union of Canada winning union recognition. But not all its efforts were in vain. In a few short weeks in the summer of 1931 the miners managed to form a union encompassing the whole deep-seam minefield; they brought the unemployed onto their side and won the sympathy of the farmers; they conducted a month-long strike against the mining companies and forced the appointment of a Royal Commission to consider their situation. In the wake of a sympathetic stand by the commissioner, Judge E.R. Wylie, they wrested a number of concessions from the mine owners, including cancellation of a 10 per cent wage cut, the recognition of the miners' pit committees, the right of miners to elect their own checker at the weigh-scales, and the promise of no black-list. But without a union that the operators had to respect, these gains, as Sloan had warned, could not be maintained for long.

The tragic events of 29 September 1931, which became known as Black Tuesday in Estevan, have already become part of the lore of Canadian labour history. When the striking miners and their families drove into town to publicize their cause – with banners that read 'We will not work for starvation wages; We want houses, not piano boxes,' and 'Down with the company store' – armed police stopped their motorcade, and in the ensuing melee killed three men and wounded a score of others. The miners were driven helter-skelter back to the coalfields, their leaders and the wounded hunted down like criminals. In an atmosphere of police terror, the militant miners stood firm, raised $100,000 in property and cash bail for their arrested comrades, testified in court, and appeared before the Royal Commission to state their woes and offer proposals to change the rules governing the mining industry. The next time around, a decade or so afterwards, the same miners' local union (under a new name) would win some strikes and take permanent root in Local 7606 of District 18 of a reoriented, now militant, United Mine Workers of America.

For the thousands of militant workers swept up by the police and actually brought to trial in court during these years, the Workers' Unity League relied on the help of the Canadian Labour Defense League headed up by Rev. A.E. Smith of Brandon, Manitoba. Smith, like Rev. J.S. Woodsworth, had left the pulpit for the platform in the 1920s. Apart from raising money to pay for unavoidable legal costs and publishing the *Canadian Labour Defender*, Smith specialized in helping workers to defend themselves, coaching them not to quibble over points of law or to beg for mercy but to speak to the jury as a worker defying the capital-ist state and to use the occasion to outline the demands of the workers' movement.[32] In the aftermath of the Bienfait strike, when the police laid charges of vagrancy, unlawful assembly, and riot against more than thirty men and women, Smith hurried to the Estevan court house to help pre-pare sixty-eight witnesses for the defence.[33]

The Workers' Unity League helped to organize several successful or partially successful strikes against wage cuts in British Columbia in 1931, including a ten-day strike of 500 fishermen at Berkley Sound, Vancouver Island, and walkouts from sawmills at Barnet Mills and Port Moody, near

Vancouver. The most consequential saw-mill strike, one lasting almost two and a half months and involving 650 workers, in which the Workers' Unity League organizers successfully tested and practised Lozovsky's strike strategy in spirit if not in every detail, took place in the municipality of Coquitlam, at Fraser Mills, in what was said to be 'the largest saw-mill in the British Empire.'[34]

This strike has been documented and carefully analysed by Jeanne Meyers in 'Class and Community in the Fraser Mills Strike, 1931.'[35] The author states that it was 'the marriage of communist organizational talent and the internal features of the community' which gave the strike a firm foundation. The workforce had an extraordinary cohesion, based on a 'tightly bonded' community of French-Canadian workers in Maillardville (who had been brought by special train from Quebec twenty years earlier by priests, Father O'Boyle and Father Maillard, to work in the mill), and an ethnically mixed population of 150 Chinese, Japanese, and East Indian contract workers, over 100 Scandinavians, and 65 British immigrants, many of whom lived in the adjacent company town of Fraser Mills. Business leaders considered Fraser Mills to be a model industrial village and a worthy focal point for family life; there was no history of labour strife.

But after Canadian Western Lumber Company, faced with shrinking markets and lower profit margins in 1930–1, embarked on a series of wage cuts and other assaults on working conditions, the mill workers, brought together by 'a high degree of residential concentration,' proved themselves to be effective fighters to maintain decent living standards and, as Meyers observes, 'many fought for the Red Flag.'[36]

When J.T. (Tom) Bradley, age twenty-five, organizer for the Lumber and Agricultural Workers' Industrial Union, arrived in Maillardville in the summer of 1931 and found room and board with Mr and Mrs Andy Rocheleau, he had few contacts in the giant mill.[37] But as news of his purpose spread, the workers, who had seen their income drop by one-third during the previous eighteen months, willingly signed up for the union. While it is true that consumer prices fell by about 20 per cent during the same period, still, 'the loss of real income [was] most definite,' and by summer's end, before the strike began, 50 per cent of the employees had a union card.[38]

Taking the debate around the Cowansville strike to heart, the union organizers made no attempt to hide the participation of communists in the union drive. For the guidance of leading millworkers, George Drayton, provincial secretary of the Workers' Unity League, proposed to distribute copies of Lozovsky's 'Strike Strategy.' And in response to the activities of H.J. Mackin, president and general manager of the Canadian Western Lumber Company, and the priest, Father Teck, in warning against communistic activities, Glen Lamont, head of the BC Section of the Lumber Workers' Industrial Union, came to speak, saying, 'we intend to fight the Fraser Mills company and the Federated Timber Mills of B.C. not on the basis of communism but on the basis of bread and butter.'[39] Lamont issued a leaflet in which he outlined the union's affiliation to the Workers' Unity League, Canadian section of the Red International of Labour Unions. 'Does this mean that the union is controlled from Moscow by a little clique of communists?' he asked rhetorically. 'Most decidedly not.' And then a series of questions and answers: Are there communists in the union? Why certainly. There are communists in all organizations of the working class. Do they control the union? They do not. Does the union follow the policy of the communists? Only when that policy is accepted by the majority of its members. The membership alone decides the policy of the union, and all members have absolutely the same right. The union does not discriminate in any way among its members. It is an industrial trade union organization for all workers in the industry, irrespective of race, sex, nationality, colour, or creed. Only policies supported by the majority can be adopted and that includes the decision to start a strike or to terminate one. In all cases where a strike takes place, it is the first duty of the shop committee to see that a strike committee is elected. In short, Lamont's answer to scares about communist conspiracies spread by church, business, and the state was the commitment to practise democracy within the union.[40] The conduct of the Fraser Mills strike, from the union's side, demonstrated this commitment, the essence of revolutionary unionism, and is one of the best documented examples of the Workers' Unity League's efforts to carry out the 'united front from below.'

Since this struggle is so ably served by Jeanne Meyers, only a thumbnail sketch is given here as a reminder of how a well-executed strike proceeded in this period.

On 14 September, a meeting of 266 union members took place in the parish hall to consider strike action and to draw up a list of demands. In a secret vote, 181 were for a strike and 81 against, with four spoiled ballots. The next day a small committee took five demands, which included a 10 per cent increase on all wages and union recognition, to H.J. Mackin, the general manager. Mackin simply said 'No.' Another mass meeting the following day upheld the earlier decision to support demands with strike action by a vote of 251 to 71. By now the list of demands had grown to include matters affecting the 'Oriental workers,' reflecting the union's determination to combat racism. The next morning a picket formed, closing down the operations of the mill. It was a formidable line, several hundred strong (some claimed 1,000 participants), joined by some members of the Asian workforce and reinforced by 150 unemployed loggers from Vancouver. The union quickly formed a strike committee of thirty-one members, mostly from the French Canadians, but encompassing the other ethnic groups including two Asians, and it selected picket captains to control any outbreaks of violence or other misbehaviour. Tensions grew as police placed machine guns at the entrance to the mill and brought in mounted reinforcements from Vancouver. On the third day of the strike, on orders from the provincial authorities, the police drove the pickets away from the mill gates and arrested ten people, charging them with unlawful assembly. The commissioner of BC Police, J.H. McMullin, assured Mackin that should he wish to open the mill, he would be given 'ample police protection.'[41]

Throughout the two and a half months, the strike committee met at 10 o'clock most mornings to listen to reports of the various committees – publicity, transportation, strike support (they called it 'a bumming committee'), relief, sports – and to make plans to mobilize the strikers and their families for the multitude of tasks at hand: keeping the picket line going, preparing strike bulletins, supporting the arrested strikers, organizing mass meetings to sustain morale or to hear any reports of negotiations with the company, staffing a kitchen that prepared five or six hundred meals a day, approaching community organizations, local merchants, farmers, and ACCL and TLC unions for donations and supplies of food,[42] organizing sports events, concerts, dances, rummage sales to help generate funds for the strike, running a barber shop, a shoe repair, and other activities to service the needs of the members.

A branch of the Women's Labour League mobilized ninety women to assist the strike work. The women not only organized the relief work and staffed the strike kitchen, but also took part in picket line support and in demonstrations, sometimes bringing their children. The reporter of the *British Columbian* caught an unforgettable image of this aspect in reporting a demonstration at the Coquitlam municipal hall on Friday 25 September: 'While provincial police mounted guard on the hall,' he wrote, 'a crowd gathered on the lawn, the boulevard and across the road. Fifty children of school age, marching two abreast, were brought from Millside school, led by a determined looking lady with a stout stick.'

The united front negotiating teams, elected afresh by the strikers for various occasions, brought together different strands of experience and outlook: Harold Pritchett, chairman of the strike committee and a supporter of the social democratic Independent Labour Party at that time; H. Boissé or other communion-taking members of the Maillardville parish; Mariyama from the Japanese contract workers; Tom Bradley, organizer of the provincial WUL and the Lumber Workers' Industrial Union.

Eventually, after the Comox Logging and Railway Company, of which Mackin was president, had to lay off 300 loggers for lack of orders from the mill, Mackin, blocked in an attempt to set up a company union, offered to settle the strike. His terms were favourable to the workers: restoration of an earlier wage cut, increase in the rate paid for shingles, no discrimination against union members, and willingness to meet with an employees' committee to consider future grievances (though not formally with the Lumber Workers' Industrial Union).[43] Reeve R.C. Mac-Donald of Coquitlam, who helped mediate on behalf of the strikers in the late stages of the struggle, read out the terms of the proposed settlement to a packed meeting in the union hall. In the context of the Depression, when markets for lumber were weak, it was a substantial victory for the workers even though it fell short of their goals. The pattern of wage cuts had been checked and as an entry in the Strike Log said, 'tonight's meeting brought joy in the ranks of the striker.'[44] The acting national secretary of the Workers' Unity League, Harvey Murphy, sent a telegram of congratulations from Toronto hailing a 'splendid victory.'[45]

But as in the case of the coal miners in Bienfait, the victories gained were bitter-sweet. Without recognition of their militant union, there was little possibility for the mill workers to keep their gains in the face of an artful and relentless operator. Within four months, Pritchett was leading a delegation to the Coquitlam municipal council requesting its support in persuading the mill management to live up to its promises about wage rates, no discrimination, and willingness to meet a workers' grievance committee. Pritchett, himself, was soon laid off, swept up in a surge of blacklisting and forced to spend the next several years on relief. Yet the strike *had* brought material benefit for the workers and a measure of new-found respect; for the communists it provided valuable lessons on how to conduct strike struggles, and, not insignificantly, an influx of new party members, including Harold Pritchett, who, as president of the International Woodworkers of America a few years later, became a major figure in the labour movement of British Columbia, leading its largest union.

The Workers' Unity League made its greatest mark in this turbulent year through taking up the cause of the unemployed. By the June 1931 census count, the number of jobless in Canada exceeded 469,000, which was over 18 per cent of the labour force, and that number rose to an unimaginable 30 per cent (over 1,000,000) in the next two years.[46] Truly, as Sir Edward Beatty, president of the Canadian Pacific Railway, Canada's largest corporation, told a meeting of his shareholders, 'the world has been visited by an economic storm of unparalleled violence.'[47] The legitimacy of the capitalist system itself seemed uncertain, and its leaders, both corporate and in government, felt considerable panic. So alarmed was the minister of railways, in July 1931, that he urged his prime minister to act swiftly. 'We may hesitate too long,' he warned Bennett, 'and have serious riots verging on revolution as hungry men can hardly be blamed for refusing to starve quietly.'[48]

The attitude of the main-line parties and the attempts of the Conservative government to cope with this 'disease of capitalism' are detailed in James Struthers's masterful study, *No Fault of Their Own*. He suggests that the government's response was shaped by three things. The first was the nature of the export-oriented economy, which relied on a large mobile workforce to maintain its railways and to run primary resource industries (wheat farming, fishing, mining, forestry) that operated only eight months of the year. There was no system of unemployment insurance and such vulnerable seasonal workers made up 40 per cent of the country's workforce in the 1930s. These mostly unskilled workers never had and never could expect to have regular year-round employment. Yet somehow they had made do up until now and should be expected to do so, so the argument ran. Any other course of action, it was claimed, would be too expensive and might bankrupt the country. Meanwhile the government's immigration policy constantly augmented their numbers; the creation of an over-supply of labour for the peak periods of summer and autumn was a necessary part of the scheme from the point of view of capital. During the four months of winter or when industry stalled because of fluctuating world prices, the workers had to fend for themselves. All the while, Prime Minister Bennett and his closest advisers acted on the belief that the lack of jobs was part of the usual seasonal unemployment problem that would disappear in the spring and was not the symptom of a deeper, recurring, cyclical crisis of capitalism.[49]

The structure of Canada's federal system of government was the second factor affecting the way the federal government thought about offering unemployment relief. Since the British North America Act of

1867 assigned responsibility for 'property and civil rights,' including social welfare, to the provinces, it was widely assumed that such matters were local concerns. Thus except in time of national emergency, the federal authority could advance legal reasons as to why it should not intervene or why it could not adopt a much-discussed system of unemployment insurance such as already existed in Great Britain and many other countries. But, according to Struthers, the constitution and its division of powers 'provided the excuse but not the reason' for the inaction of the main-line parties.[50]

The third factor and the real barriers to action were more ideological than fiscal or legal. They were related to assumptions about poverty and the meaning of work which Canada's elite inherited from the nineteenth century. Attorney General R.H. Pooley of British Columbia, for example, lectured a leader of Victoria's unemployed: 'The human race was meant for work either mental or physical according to the particular qualifications of the individual. Life is not a place for dreamers ... the person inclined to work rather than dream will find the work to do.'[51] Pooley, in the British 'poor-law' tradition, presumed that a healthy unemployed man was idle deliberately. Idle workers and their families, therefore, had to be made uncomfortable. If relief was necessary to avoid starvation, it should only be available with a severe means test in which public servants and neighbours acted as watchdogs so as to ensure social stigma. Opponents of publicly funded relief, like Mr Pooley, urged taxpayers to ask why they should support idle men to remain in the city when there was work to be done on the rural frontier. The slogan 'Go Back to the Land,' where thousands of farmers were going bankrupt, served, as Struthers observes, to provide 'an excellent rationale for maintaining a constant "reserve army" of the unemployed so that the supply of labour could be kept cheap and available.'[52]

R.B. Bennett campaigned in the election of 1930 promising to do something about unemployment, and after he came to power that summer he acknowledged that unemployment had 'become national in its importance.' Nevertheless, he continued to insist that relief was still 'primarily a provincial and municipal responsibility' to which the federal government would make only an indirect support. His administration proceeded to fund a hodge-podge of relief measures, beginning with the Relief Act of 1930, which provided millions of dollars for relief or to create relief works, but all framed with an eye to enforcing the Puritan work ethic. In the spring of 1931, in response to cries from provincial premiers for help in removing from the cities thousands of jobless, hungry, and increasingly angry young workers who were being disturbed by 'communistic agitation,' Bennett rushed the Relief Act of 1931 through Parliament on Dominion Day. It authorized funds for work camps in remote areas outside urban centres to build roads, bridges, culverts, exhibition grounds, school grounds, mental hospitals, airfields, the Trans-Canada highway, and other infrastructure; the pay would be $2 per day less 85 cents for board and lodging. Soon British Columbia had 237 such camps holding 15,000 of the single unemployed, a great majority of whom, according to a provincial government report, were physically unfit for work because they had been undernourished and 'living on the verge of starvation for some considerable time.'[53] Bennett also provided coercive measures to back up the terms of the Act: fines of up to $1,000 and prison terms up to three years for anyone disobeying orders or regulations. In this way it was believed that 'any communist opposition to the removal of single men from the cities would be effectively crushed.'[54] For good measure and to underline his implacable opposition to communism, Bennett's government placed an embargo on trading relations with Soviet Russia in 1931.[55]

The Workers' Unity League had early on pledged itself to help organize the unemployed workers, one reason being to prevent them from being used as strike-breakers. Also, the league wanted to link their activities with the general struggle of 'the revolutionary workers' movement.' With slogans like 'Work or Maintenance' and 'Non-Contributory Unemployment Insurance,' the league organized local conferences of unemployed workers, beginning in the spring of 1930. The Toronto-area conference elected a full-time organizer whose purpose was to hold a national unemployed conference. Until such a conference was possible, a uniform dues card in the name of the National Unemployed Workers' Association would be issued so that 'the work could be uniform' and the 'forces could be united.' The organization would publish a monthly unemployed organ.[56]

In spite of the efforts of the national organizer, Harvey Jackson, and sporadic local activities (which often drew the unwelcome attention of the police, especially in British Columbia), the WUL's efforts to mobilize the unemployed made slow progress. By year's end, Ewen reported that co-ordination was still lacking, there was as yet no nation-wide unemployed movement, and he was still trying to work out a suitable program of demands, organization, and general activity. Leslie Morris, a leading communist by now, criticized existing efforts as being too isolated from the left-wing movement and from the 'class struggle unions.' The

usual method that was practised at the moment in organizing the unemployed, he said, 'is the formation of a local organization ... that finds its
chief activity in "begging" expeditions to the City Council or the Provincial governments.' And the usual fate of these organizations was 'the
watering-down of the maximum political demands for "Work or Wages"
and "Non-contributory Insurance" to demands for immediate relief,' for
'coffee and doughnuts.'[57]

All this was about to change. At the start of 1931 an enlarged meeting of the central committee of the Communist Party assembled in
Hamilton, Ontario, bringing together leading members from all over
the country. At this meeting the main topic of conversation was how to
build up the Workers' Unity League and especially its campaign among
the unemployed workers; how to increase pressure on the various levels of government as a way to awaken people's political consciousness.
The participants planned a two-pronged offensive made up of, first, a
national petition to the federal government, demanding a system of non-
contributory unemployment insurance and immediate relief measures,
and second, street rallies to back up these demands.[58] In this conversation, a most important new development was the fact that the leadership
of the Ukrainian and the Finnish wings of the party had decided to drop
their opposition to the militant politics of 'class against class' of the world
communist movement. Now, in a 'decisive turn,'[59] they would lead their
members wholeheartedly into the battles of the Great Depression. This
would make a great difference. Between them, these wings of the movement included 85 per cent of the Communist Party members and they
controlled over one hundred assembly halls scattered across the country.
The halls increasingly would align their cultural, sports, and social activities to the campaigns of the labour movement and they became hives of
industry, inspiring their members to acts of public daring and self-sacri-
fice, risking imprisonment and, in some cases, deportation. And, with
their support, the WUL was able to launch its own six-page bi-monthly
newspaper, *Workers' Unity*, as a voice for the unions, the unemployed, and
the women's movement that it aimed to organize.[60]

Another matter prompting close attention from the communists was
the increasing pressure from the police forces across the country. From
the commissioner of the RCMP down, the police were mobilized as
never before to deal with what was called 'the communist menace.' The
police frequently arrested demonstrators, picketers, and street-corner
agitators on various grounds and took the administration of 'justice' into
their own hands. Instead of laying charges to come before a judge, they

physically assaulted their prisoners in the station before turning them out onto the street again to nurse their bruises. This illegal practice was especially prevalent in Toronto where lower-level judges sometimes gave the benefit of the doubt to street orators and demonstrators. For example, after Detective-Sergeant William Nursey's 'Red Squad' arrested Beckie Buhay at a large street-corner rally at Soho and Queen streets and charged her with obstruction and vagrancy, Judge Garrow dismissed their case, saying that the Eaton's Santa Claus parade also obstructs people from going about their business but the participants could not be charged with vagrancy. And when they apprehended Charles Sims, Lillian Himmelfarb, and others for distributing a leaflet which allegedly 'advocated ... the use, without authority of law of force, violence, terrorism ... to persons or property ... as a means of accomplishing governmental, industrial or economic change' contrary to Section 98 of the Criminal Code, Judge Denton quashed the charges, saying that while the circular contained 'very strong and very objectionable language,' in his opinion it did not contravene the law. The words 'revolutionary struggle,' he said, did not necessarily mean the use of force and violence.[61] 'Red Squad' officers, therefore, often preferred to take the administration of justice into their own hands, and Ewen was no stranger to their terror tactics.

Then there was the problem of the adventurers and anarchists within the ranks of the workers' movement. An organizer of the Workers' Unity League in Winnipeg, Joseph Forkin, and others complained that some activists, such as unemployed leaders James Beattie, Jack Hudson, and Charles Sims, sought unnecessary clashes with the police and, in trying to 'put it over the police,' were in danger of forgetting the purpose of the rally or demonstration. Ewen disagreed. The only theory comrade Beattie has, he said, 'is to get a punch at the police, and that is a very good theory, in my opinion.' Beattie, he continued, was 'a good element, he wanted action.' Possibly his type was hard to control, 'but certainly it is a type that should not be condemned by the Communist Party.' It was out of these types, Ewen argued, that the leadership of the unemployment and other movements would develop. He conceded, though, that 'these comrades have to come to realize that there is something more in the duties of a Communist than getting arrested and making yourself known. We have got to try to develop ourselves.'

Forkin, who had, for a short time, been a policeman, was still uncomfortable. 'We have to appeal to the police as workers with sympathies for fellow workers,' he contended. He said he knew some policemen sympathetic to the Communist Party and thought the party should issue bulletins to them. In this debate Ewen agreed that there were some police, especially in Winnipeg, more or less sympathetic to the working class. 'But we must regard the police not as an individual,' he said, 'but as a body, – as the strong arm of Capitalist Democracy – and our approach to the police is not through bulletins appealing to their sentiments, but through black-jacks.' The communists resolved to form a Worker Defence Corps as 'a permanent and well-disciplined proletarian organization,' trained to protect speakers on the street corners and for defence against gangsterism on picket lines and other attacks on workers' activities.[62]

When the national secretary of the Workers' Unity League turned up on the steps of Parliament, in mid-April 1931, leading a delegation of unemployed workers and armed with a notarized affidavit confirming over 94,000 signatures to a petition, Prime Minister Bennett agreed to meet them in the Railway Committee Room. This was the first of half a dozen delegations that organizations associated with the Workers' Unity League would send to meet this prime minister and his cabinet over the next four years.[63]

In requesting the interview, Ewen had written a lengthy letter to the prime minister, stating the case and enclosing a copy of the petition and a draft of a Federal Unemployment Insurance Bill. Unemployment in Canada, as in all highly developed capitalist countries, he wrote, was an integral part of the economic life and structure of the country, not some seasonal phenomenon; the breadlines, flop-houses, and other 'most humiliating forms of capitalist charity' used to deal with the problem only compounded the sufferings of victims; all workers whose services 'are rendered unnecessary by the development of the productive forces,' he said, must be 'provided for definitely and unequivocally, as part of the cost of industry.' This was the case for unemployment insurance. And this insurance must be at the expense of the state and the employers; otherwise *contributory* unemployment insurance would 'only mean a further slash of the miserable wages of the still employed workers and an attempt to make the workers shoulder the burden of the crisis.' Ewen stated that the demand for 'Non-Contributory State Unemployment Insurance' contained in the draft Bill and supported by 94,136 signatures should not be construed as an agitational step, but rather as an urgent need. In a final comment on the six-week signature campaign he maintained that names were gathered under conditions 'of a most vicious ... terror': workers canvassing for signatures had been beaten by police officers, lists

of signatures were destroyed, and workers were intimidated against signing; throughout the country, he said, there was 'already in effect a virtual
reign of terror against the working class movement.'[64]

Bennett, flanked by his despised labour minister, Senator Gideon Robertson, had been well briefed by his security staff, especially about Ewen.[65]
In his reception of this petition, which bore an unprecedented number
of names, and his 'welcome' to the men and women who brought it
to the nation's capital, Bennett was alternately furious and condescend-
ing. 'Demand?' he asked. 'What right have *you* to demand anything!'
He expressed the opinion that the delegates represented the shiftless
section of the population who did not practise thrift, who did not invest
their earnings prudently, and who therefore were bound to suffer during temporary periods of depression. Or perhaps they had gambled too
much on horse-racing? He assured them that he was once as poor as they
were and expressed his sorrow that the secretary of the Workers' Unity
League was a fanatic. He abruptly asked all of the thirty-four delegates to
state their names and countries of birth, hoping to demonstrate before
the press that they were 'foreigners.' In responding to the petition the
prime minister stated that 'neither this government, nor any other government that I am a member of will ever grant unemployment insurance. We will not put a premium on idleness.' He hoped on this there
would be no misunderstanding.[66]

Even as the prime minister talked, tens of thousands of employed
and unemployed Canadian workers demonstrated on the streets of the
country's major cities in support of the delegation to the nation's capital. These demonstrations followed earlier protests on 25 February 1931,
as part of an international day of struggle against unemployment, and
would be succeeded by some of the largest May Day rallies in recent
times on the same theme. The numbers of demonstrators ranged from
76,000 in February to 85,000 in April with the largest actions in Winnipeg (estimated at 15,000), Toronto (13,000), Sudbury (8,000), Montreal,
Hamilton, Windsor, and Regina (5,000 each), Fort William, Edmonton,
Two Hills (Alberta), and Vancouver (3,000 each).[67] In spite of some
muddles and confusion (in Montreal, for example, no speakers showed
up to address the multitude), these were the largest and most militant
demonstrations ever held until that time in Canada under the leadership
of the communists.

Even for the organizers, the surge of anger from the unemployed
citizens was unexpected. At the community of Two Hills, Alberta, it was
reported that thousands of 'aged farmers and their wives' from fifty

miles around gathered to parade behind young farmers carrying the
Red Flag and banners demanding relief.[68] Occasionally, harried organizers appeared to be unnerved, as this report from the Communist Party
in Sudbury illustrates:

> Preparations ... were not bad. Several mass conferences (a bad term that we
> must drop, I suppose) were held, leaflets printed and issued. *Vapaus* also pre-
> pared the campaign as good as it could ... But this is only as to the agitation
> and propaganda. The organization of the affairs were under all critics [i.e. a
> lot of criticism]. And for this we all – myself included — have the responsibil-
> ity ... At the time appointed the masses were mobilized to an extent unfor-
> seen in Sudbury, but we were not able to lead them organizationally. The
> demonstration started with a mass meeting in Liberty Hall at 1 o'clock. But
> already at that time there were very large masses outside the hall. [There was
> no more room in the hall.] Notwithstanding that the boys let the mass meet-
> ing last a whole hour without any connection with the masses on the streets,
> which began to become impatient being slightly disturbed by the police.
> After the mass meeting large crowds at once joined the demonstrators and
> the procession moved a hundred yards or so. But there began the attack of
> the police forces, reinforced with the police of Copper Cliff and other plac-
> es. The main battle took place just before the *Vapaus* building. One police-
> man was knocked down and injured very badly, maybe he loses his sight.
> Notwithstanding the police forces a big deal of demonstrators – disorderly
> of course – continued their march towards the police station and City Hall.
> There went also the deputation under the leadership of Mike [Kostaniuk,
> head of the local mine workers' union] and was met by the mayor. (I'm sorry
> you can't read the *Vapaus*, there I have written all these things in a manner
> which constitutes one of the finest pieces of proletarian reportage ever deliv-
> ered in America.) ... Our main weakness ... lack of any organizational prep-
> aration and leadership of the demonstration caused by a certain uneasiness,
> by a certain confusion as to how to deal with the police. On the other hand
> nobody of us had waited such a big participation on behalf of the masses,
> may be it could be characterized as a certain, slight underestimation of the
> preparedness of the masses to demonstrate and – fight.
>
> The demonstration has had a – I dare to say – tremendous impression
> upon the people here including the bloody Sudbury Finns. The [munici-
> pal] officials have become very polite to the unemployed who ask cards to
> the soup-kitchen etc. ... two weeks ago the only answer given to the unem-
> ployed was: go to Burwash! [the nearby provincial jail] ... There are among
> the masses especially among the Ukrainians a certain amount of rather

strong 'left' tendencies (talking about the preparation to riot, seizure of the whole Sudbury etc.). But I think that it will not be a very difficult task to clean out such sentiments. On the next day the District Bureau meeting took place with a very serious self-criticism [and a decision] to make certain modest but real concrete steps in the question of defence corps, i.e. in the organization of demonstrations.[69]

In this internal report from the largest base of the Communist Party in Canada, it is apparent that its leaders were preparing neither themselves nor their followers for a 'barricade revolution' to overthrow the state. At this stage they were mainly concerned with not starving to death quietly. They evidently believed, as did Marx and Engels in their famous *Manifesto*, that the lessons of revolution would be learned in the course of the daily struggle.

The response to the unemployed demonstrations varied widely. They included improved manners of civic officials and supportive telegrams to the prime minister by civic officials such as Mayor David Croll of Windsor saying that after the city council had received a delegation from a large demonstration it had gone on record in favour of unemployment insurance. Other, less sympathetic, mayors and the Employers' Association of Manitoba demanded that the government act urgently to declare illegal any sections of the Communist International operating in Canada.[70]

Bennett was ready to act. And there began a series of events that have been characterized by historian Lorne Brown as 'the most severe and extensive repression in our country during peace time in the twentieth century.'[71] The repression included increased police surveillance of activists; attacks on demonstrations; arrests, beatings, imprisonment, and deportation of leaders without trial; breaking up picket lines; raids on private homes and on the offices of left-led organizations, 'sometimes on the pretext of a liquor search, seldom with a search warrant';[72] confiscation of materials; and encouragement of the legionnaires, the Ku Klux Klan, and other right-wing vigilante groups. By mid-1931 the Canadian Labour Defense League found itself handling scores of court cases – 119 arrests in the last two weeks of June alone – of people accused of everything from vagrancy and obstruction of police to assault and charges of seditious conspiracy. According to Communist Party records, the state arrested 720 of their members in 1931, sentenced 155, and deported a large number. The ruling power recklessly prosecuted communists for their political activities while violating the common law constitution it claimed to be defending.[73]

These were the 'ordinary' occurrences of harassment. Then there were the extraordinary measures striking at the right of communist or communist-led organizations to exist. Even as the prime minister was receiving the unemployment delegation of the Workers' Unity League in April 1931, his government was in secret negotiations with the province of Ontario to outlaw the Communist Party. In what historian Lita-Rose Betcherman calls a 'council of war,' the federal minister of justice, Hugh Guthrie, had met with senior police officials from across the country, in February, to plan for what they hoped would be the banning of communism and the quelling of radical activities associated with the unemployed movement. 'We are going to strike a death blow at the Communist Party,' said ex-military commander and commissioner of the Ontario Provincial Police, V.A. Williams.[74] Prime Minister Bennett told Parliament that his government would 'free this country from those who have proved themselves unworthy of our Canadian citizenship.'[75] To help him in this task he appointed a zealously anti-communist and wealthy military man, Major General Sir James Howden MacBrien, who had been chief of staff of the Canadian Army from 1923 until 1927, as the new commissioner of the Royal Canadian Mounted Police.

The arrests in August 1931, the trial and conviction of the top eight communist leaders, including Tom Ewen, not for any overt action on their part, but for guilt by association, their sentencing to five years' imprisonment, and the virtual outlawing of the Communist Party in Canada under Section 98 of the Criminal Code has been related many times and need not be reconstructed here at any length. This action was conducted under a statute that Ontario Attorney General William H. Price defended as necessary to save the foundations of Christian civilization, protecting citizens 'against red revolution and civil war, against the fire and sword of armed rebellion.'[76] Of the same statute, McGill University law professor F.R. Scott said it was 'unequaled in the history of Canada and probably of any British country for centuries past' for its 'restriction of the rights of association, freedom of discussion, printing and distribution of literature, and for severity of punishment.'[77] The House of Commons had tried several times to repeal the obnoxious legislation in the later 1920s but had been thwarted by the Conservative majority in the Senate.[78]

Following the jailing of the Eight, the government, for good measure, swooped down on the offices of the Finnish and Ukrainian wings of the movement, picking up ten editors and organizers in Winnipeg and Sudbury and spiriting them away to the immigration sheds in Halifax.

There, after summary hearings, they were deported under terms of the Immigration Act.[79]

In the long run, the imprisonment and deportation of communist leaders did not yield the results Prime Minister Bennett and his friends had hoped for or expected. Instead of being held in disgrace, the popularity of the communist cause steadily increased over the next few years and when the Eight were released from jail they were welcomed by enthusiastic crowds of well-wishers, including a rally of 20,000 Toronto citizens that over-filled the Maple Leaf Gardens hockey rink. Scott speculated that one day there might well be 'a monument in Toronto to the memory of Tim Buck and his fellow-accused.'[80] Here and there, communists started to get elected to municipal councils and even to a provincial legislature, and when the party held its first public convention after the repeal of Section 98 of the Criminal Code, in 1937, some of its plenary sessions took place in Toronto's 5,000-seat Mutual Street Arena. This turnabout was a lesson on repression that the leaders of the Canadian state remembered warily when strident cries rose again to ban the communists during the Cold War of the 1950s.

By some turn of fate, or quirk in the mind of Ontario supreme court justice William Henry Wright, the Workers' Unity League (and the Young Communist League) were not included in the prohibition of communists after the trial of the Eight. Only the Communist Party of Canada was on trial, said Justice Wright, much to the chagrin of the crown prosecutors. While there was no doubt that Tom Ewen, general secretary of the WUL and one of the Eight, would be out of circulation for the next few years, the WUL, in spite of a contrary and much-publicized opinion by Judge Ousley in Moose Jaw, Saskatchewan, was apparently still entitled to claim, and to assure its members, that it was a legal entity.[81]

It was in these anxious and slightly ambiguous circumstances that the Workers' Unity League began to refashion its leadership and to compose its manifestos for the tasks ahead.

6

Red Blairmore

In these hard times the results of 1931 must be considered exceptionally good ... a net profit equal to 5 per cent of the capitalization constitutes a very good result; we made 10 per cent.

– G.A. Vissac, general manager, West Canadian Collieries Ltd.,
Blairmore, Alberta, 12 January 1932[1]

It is virtually impossible for a majority of the men employed, especially married men with families, to make ends meet, a condition which has resulted not only in suffering and privation, but has engendered grave unrest. Men who are physically below par through insufficient food and inadequate clothing, who suffer themselves and see their families suffer, turn readily to any doctrines that seem to offer a way out ... The need is immediate and urgent, the distress is real and serious.

– Bituminous Coal Mine Operators to W.A. Gordon, minister of mines,
urging government subsidies for the coal industry, February 1934[2]

This movement by the workers of Blairmore is a protest against injustice; we saw we were getting nowhere. Private ownership of the mines and railways and their operation for profit was steadily making the plight of the workers more and more intolerable. There was a strike – seven months it continued. It was then that this drive for control started. And it has continued. And is going to continue.

– William Knight, picket captain and coal miner, mayor of Blairmore, May 1935[3]

The first major scene of battle for the Workers' Unity League, after the imprisonment of Ewen and the other communist leaders, was in the

Rocky Mountains, especially among the coal miners of the Crowsnest Pass and centred in the town of Blairmore. And once more the irrepressible Harvey Murphy, agitator *par excellence*, now a semi-graduate of the prestigious International Lenin School, was on the job directing operations for the league in Alberta. In the tumultuous year of struggle that lay ahead, in 1932, when Murphy ended up in Lethbridge jail serving three months hard labour, he showed his mettle, provided one of the finest hours of his long years as a militant labour organizer, and gave considerable substance to his later claim of being 'the reddest rose in the garden of labour.'[4] Modesty was not one of his more prominent characteristics, and along with spectacular feats in confronting the tight-fisted coal operators, mistakes were made, perhaps some of them avoidable had Murphy had the patience to follow Lozovsky's revolutionary strike strategy more carefully. Nevertheless, through the vicissitudes of seven months and a surprising aftermath, the Pass Strike of 1932 became both a storied event in the history of the Canadian labour movement and a hard-edged learning ground for future struggles.

Set in the broad valley of the Crowsnest River with its colourful carpets of lupin, blue clematis, fireweed, and other wildflowers, flanked by serene and majestic mountain peaks, Blairmore had started out as a mere railway siding along the Canadian Pacific Railway. The new 'Crow' line, completed in 1898, was built primarily as a means of hauling the burgeoning prairie wheat crop to international markets through the port of Vancouver. With the discovery of bituminous coal in the Pass, a superior grade of coal for steam locomotives, and the subsequent opening of mines at Blairmore and Coleman and several other places down the river at Frank, Bellevue, and Hillcrest, the population of the Pass (including the mining camps at Michel, Corbin, and Fernie on the British Columbia side) grew rapidly. Very soon scores of entrepreneurs began arriving – butchers, bakers, grocers, and pharmacists; clothing, hardware, and blacksmith shops appeared; auto repair, shoe repair, second-hand furniture, jewellery, photography, billiard halls and bars, cafés, Chinese restaurants, and several full-fledged hotels, to serve the mining population. There were some solid brick and mortar buildings along the main streets, including an opera house. Schools and sports arenas as well as the buildings of mutual aid societies that reflected the diverse ethnic origins of the population sprang up; on the outskirts of Coleman there stood a meeting hall of the radical Ukrainian Labour Farmer Temple Association. Churches appeared early on, their leaders inviting the people of the Pass to join moral crusades to overcome the area's reputation for drinking, gambling, prostitution, and radical ideas.[5] Labour unions had made their presence known through the Western Federation of Miners, followed by the One Big Union and the United Mine Workers of America. A majority of the Crowsnest Pass miners were among those who gave a strong welcome to the formation of the Mine Workers' Union of Canada in 1925 as a replacement for the increasingly complacent American-based United Mine Workers union.

At the heart of the Crowsnest communities on the Alberta side of the Pass, the base of their existence, lay four substantial coal companies and behind them Canada's largest and most powerful corporation, the Canadian Pacific Railway, a company that normally bought 90 per cent of their output.[6]

Hillcrest Collieries Ltd, the smallest of the large operators and a subsidiary of a Montreal company controlled by Sir Herbert Holt and Sir Charles Gordon, operated on privately owned land and was a constant thorn in the side of the unions; the management there formed a home local or company union and for many years thwarted successive unionization drives.

Coleman, with a 1931 census population of 1,704 and another 1,000 people living in 'bushtown,' adjacent to the town limits, was the largest centre and had two operators, the McGillivray Creek Coal and Coke Company and the International Coal and Coke Company, both with 'double A' credit ratings. The International Coal and Coke Company, which also supplied Coleman with its light and water through a subsidiary company, had a capital stock of $3 million and listed assets of almost $5 million on the Toronto Stock Exchange. The general managers of these mines, George Kellock and O.E. Whiteside, were well experienced, having been at their posts for many years; Kellock had himself been a miner. The labour recruitment policies of these men favoured Canadian- and British-born workers over others by a margin of 2:1, resulting in a workforce composed largely of Anglo-Celts, followed by substantial groups of Slavs and Italians. The ethnic mix played a significant role in the coming strike.

The largest operator on the Alberta side of the Pass was West Canadian Collieries Ltd with mines in Blairmore (the 'Greenhill' mine) and in Bellevue. In a normal year, West Canadian produced about 40 per cent of the bituminous output in the district and as the leading operator it became the focus of union organizers. The company, which was owned by French capitalists headed by the already wealthy Alphonse Wicart, managing director, had a headquarters in London, England,

and, as might be expected, added a sizeable group of French and Belgian French-speakers to the mix of Anglo-Celts, Slavs, and Italians in its workforce. The general manager in Blairmore was the ever alert G.A. Vissac, aided by general superintendent L.P. Roberts. Vissac responded to the desire of the principals in France to be kept well informed about progress in Canada by sending frequent, detailed, and candid reports on the political economy of the company; happily a selection of this voluminous correspondence is available for historical researchers at the Glenbow Archives in Calgary.

As the depression deepened, Vissac, who was also head of the Association of Bituminous Mining Operators in Alberta, took stock of the industry's position. It was not a happy picture. Markets for the prairie wheat crop had contracted, reducing rail shipments and therefore shrivelling the demand for coal. Sales of bituminous to the railways plummeted. The general business situation, he wrote, 'is admitted to be the worst in the last twenty-five years' and was going to be a 'real test' for the company. 'We must be more careful, more watchful than ever,' he wrote, and he promised that 'everything will be squeezed down to the limit.'[7]

On the wider scene Vissac welcomed the Conservative election victory of 1930. 'It is unfortunate that all of our Canadian Directors are Liberals,' he mused, but he thought the Conservative Party 'will surely attempt to help us.' He reassured his principals that he had some 'very good friends in the party.'[8] By early 1932 he was thinking that the worst was over in Europe: 'the Hitlerites will take full control of power in Germany next April,' he predicted, and he thought this would be for the benefit of everybody but France, since the Nazi party had 'already concluded alliances with Britain and Italy and ... with the U.S. bankers.' While he did not wish to comment on the right or wrong, he could see better markets for Canada in these developments, which meant 'a switch of power and prosperity from France, a small customer, to Britain our largest customer.'[9]

Always conscious of the importance of political will in business affairs, Vissac described how he would try to enlarge the market for Alberta's bituminous coal. He was organizing his fellow operators into a 'unanimous delegation' to meet the new prime minister, R.B. Bennett, to request a subsidy to the railways of $1 per ton for all railway coals used in Ontario. This would create an annual new market of two million tons for Western Canada's bituminous coal and it was the only way to compete with American coal operators who were currently sending ten million tons into Ontario. The mine workers' unions generally supported this demand, but compared to the Nova Scotia operators, who achieved almost two million tons of assisted shipments to central Canada by the end of the Conservative Party's term in office in 1935, Alberta had to be satisfied with 320,000 tons.[10] Still, it was better than the pittance the Liberals had offered.

In his reports and in his appeals to the government, Vissac often referred to the plight of the miners and their families and the danger that their extreme poverty posed for the peace and tranquillity of the community. He avoided the word 'starvation.' With employment at 'a seriously low ebb,' he wrote the minister of mines, 'it is virtually impossible for a majority of the men employed ... to make ends meet, a condition which has resulted not only in suffering and privation, but has engendered grave unrest.' There was 'a lot of destitution' in the district. Some miners, according to his reports, earned less than $400 a year. Men who were physically below par 'through insufficient food and inadequate clothing,' who suffered themselves and saw their families suffer, he said, turned readily 'to any doctrines that seem to offer a way out.' A sad conclusion from the 1930 provincial election results, for Vissac, showed that 'the Communist party has been making very serious gains in our district.' He did not want to 'see the majority of our men slip to the party of disorder.'[11]

In spite of his expressed concerns about the miners' welfare, Vissac prepared to squeeze the men still further. He had reason to be confident of the efficiency of his organization to such an end. 'In these hard times,' he wrote to the owners, on the eve of the historic seven-month strike against his company, 'the results of 1931 must be considered exceptionally good.' It is generally admitted here, he continued, 'that a net profit equal to 5 per cent of capitalization constitutes a very good result; we made 10 per cent.'[12] With a victory over the union, he told Wicart, he hoped to fortify the company by arranging a three-year contract with successive wage cuts of 10 per cent in the first year and another 10 per cent at the end of the second.[13] If only he could get rid of the miners' union – 'les rouges' as he called them. It was to this burdensome task that he began to dedicate his energies. Quite possibly Vissac did not consider the bitter fact that, by transferring just one or two percentage points of the unusually high profits of his company to the wages account, he could have provided every miner working at the lower half of the scale an annual wage of $800, the level of a semi-skilled worker in Canada at that time.[14]

Combating starvation and striving to achieve a decent wage for the workers, helping them to check the decline of their living conditions and to gain a larger share of the results of their work, was not part of Vissac's mandate. That would be the central task of the Mine Workers' Union of Canada (MWUC).

Since 1929 the average yearly earnings of Alberta miners had been 'steadily decreasing,' wrote John Stokaluk, secretary-treasurer of the union in December 1931, in his call to the mining camps to elect delegates for the coming wage scale convention. In fact the average yearly earnings were lower than at any time since the war, he said, and the value of wages had declined much faster than production or commodity prices with the result that 'want or hunger is present in every miner's home.' Without actually cutting the wage rate but by their system of 'short time and speed-up,' the company had succeeded in raising a ton of coal for a cost of $1.61 in 1931 compared to $1.83 in 1929. The average annual earnings per employed miner during the same period dropped from $1,372 to $919 – a decline of 33 per cent. This was no time for complacency, especially as the company was still able to gain handsome profits for its shareholders.[15]

The 8,000 coal miners of Alberta (2,000 surface and 6,000 underground workers) were badly fragmented in their ever-shifting union affiliations, some still in the American-based union, others in company-sponsored 'home locals,' and less than half in the Mine Workers' Union of Canada, affiliated to the Workers' Unity League.[16] This fragmentation was not the best position from which to take on the coal operators.

Nevertheless, since its convention in September 1931 when the leadership of the Workers' Unity League found favour, the Canadian union had strengthened itself in some respects. The convention showed signs of concern to have only dedicated men in the leadership, by making a reduction in the pay and expense accounts of the union's leading officers with the president's salary pegged at $140 a month – down from $180. This new level was subject to change only in proportion to the prevailing wage scale of the miners.[17] Other amendments included clauses prohibiting national officers from having shares in mines, beer parlours, or liquor stores and, perhaps reflecting previous experience, forbidding them to hold two salaried positions at one time.[18] A strike could take place only after a referendum vote and 'a majority decision shall prevail.' In another new departure, the constitution stipulated that contract agreements signed with the operators should not have provision for the intervention of the provincial or federal departments of labour 'in the capacity of an arbitrator or conciliator';[19] the union preferred direct negotiations between the boss and the workers and *mediation* only in case of dire necessity. The constitution provided for the establishment of a youth section and women's auxiliaries; it exonerated unemployed members from payment of dues while still remaining in good standing and it expected such members to take part in the unemployed workers' movement.

Two sensitive issues not mentioned in the new rules were the common practices of employer 'check-off' of union dues from the pay envelopes of the workers, and a 'stagger system' whereby available work was supposed to be shared equally among all the miners on a rotation basis. The Workers' Unity League, and the Red International as well, strongly opposed both of these practices in present circumstances.

In the case of the 'check-off,' if there was no law requiring the owners to deal with a union democratically chosen by the majority of their employees, then the owners could give the dues money they collected to whatever organization they pleased, including their own company union; far better, according to the WUL, that the workers gather the union dues themselves on a voluntary basis without the compulsory check-off by the operators even though it meant less certainty and more work for union activists.

Proposals by the WUL to abolish the 'equal sharing of work' or 'stagger system' met with strong opposition from the Crowsnest miners. The 'equal sharing of the work' had become a touchstone of solidarity among them. Many a work stoppage occurred when pit bosses showed favouritism or discrimination in the distribution of available work. Murphy and his colleagues argued without much effect that the practical result of the 'equal division of work' was to pull down the general wage level. With everyone rotating in for a few days each month and living at a starvation or semi-subsistence level, the only side to benefit was the boss, who then kept a vast reserve of labour always on tap. This practice masked the true extent of unemployment and put the burden on workers still on the job, 'who must share their little piece of bread with their unemployed brothers.'[20] Better, the WUL organizers asserted, to campaign for a five-day work week with a guaranteed minimum weekly wage for those working in the mines, and for those without work to demand full maintenance by state-run, employer-financed unemployment insurance. But when the question was debated at membership meetings the miners insisted that in fighting against layoffs the demand for work to be divided up equally was crucial to the survival of the union. Otherwise the operators would weed out the militants, who would have to leave the camp. In that case

it would be impossible to form pit committees and the union's affiliation to the Workers' Unity League would soon be reversed. The fight for
the 'equal division of work' to give the militants an even break with the
'suckers,' the miners argued, was one of years' standing and had been a
successful fight. And where the miners had been able to retain a share of
the work for the militants, they had also been able to get one or two days'
unemployment relief from the municipal authorities as a supplement to
everyone's wages.

In the face of these realities, the Workers' Unity League decided not
to press the conversation for the time being, especially as the union's
new constitution provided that local units had 'the power to determine
all questions pertaining to Local questions and conditions.'[21] Instead
the WUL published a program for the Canadian mining industry that
ignored the issue but provided eleven demands on which the miners
could concentrate their energy. These included the demand for a six-
hour working day for underground workers and seven hours for surface
workers, increased wages and a guaranteed minimum wage, social insurance on a *non-contributory* basis to provide full wages during sickness,
accidents, unemployment, and old age, to be administered under the
control of workers' organizations; mine inspections by labour protection
committees elected by the miners; one month's holiday for underground
workers and two weeks for surface workers with full pay; recognition of
Pit and Mine Committees elected by the miners; equal pay for equal
work on all jobs; prevention of hiring young people under eighteen
for work underground and a reduced working day for young surface
workers; abolition of all overtime and stretch-out shifts, and two fifteen-
minute rest periods in each shift. This program was adopted by delegates
to the Mine Workers' Union of Canada at its convention in 1931.[22]

With the two-year collective agreements expiring on 31 March 1932,
the Workers' Unity League and its affiliated miners' union had a five-
step plan for achieving a new, and if possible district-wide, collective
agreement with the coal operators of Alberta and southeastern British
Columbia. First, the Mine Workers' Union of Canada would send out
invitations far and wide to a united front wage scale convention to be
held in Calgary in mid-January to discuss the possible terms for a new
agreement. That convention would elect a broadly representative united
front policy committee charged with convening a similarly representative united action convention in Lethbridge two months later to sum
up the discussion, to finalize proposals, and to make detailed plans for
strike action should the operators balk. Then on 31 March union repre-

sentatives from each mine would request meetings with the operators to arrive at a new agreement. Allowing two weeks for negotiations to take place, the united policy committee would organize a referendum vote on possible strike action on 11 April. If the mandate for strike action was positive (and the negotiations at a standstill), the final step would be for the united policy committee to initiate and lead a district-wide general strike at a time favourable to the miners.[23]

That was the plan. But the actual strike began in a far different and uncomfortable manner six weeks before the projected strike vote was scheduled to take place.

It started over a relatively minor incident at the Greenhill mine: the firing of a young driver, John Zemek, for 'insubordination' and for swearing at a pit boss. Zemek made the required verbal apology, but Vissac, wanting to goad the union, demanded an apology in writing. The local union leaders found this demeaning. But instead of a work slow-down or 'work to rule' protest, the sub-district executive, in the absence of Murphy and the district leaders of the union, called the workers off the job on 23 February and the next morning the Bellevue miners came out in sympathy. Suddenly there were 700 miners on strike, a strike for which no strike vote on an approved program had been taken at the mines, no large strike committee elected as required by the revolutionary strike tactics of affiliates of the Workers' Unity League, and for which there was little strike fund preparation. Feeling confident in their strength, the next day, 25 February, the local union presented Vissac with its demands for a new contract. This was a seventeen-point document containing the Wage Scale Convention call for a 10 per cent wage raise plus local demands such as free coal to the miners and 40 per cent reduction in house rent.[24]

For some time Vissac had been alarmed by the growing militancy of the miners. 'We must have discipline in our mines,' he muttered. And 'if we want to retain the management of our mines, if we want discipline, order and peace,' then 'we must clean up the red element.' He was prepared to face a long strike and, as it turned out, at minimum cost, because the CPR management hurried to assure him that his business would be protected. When the mines resumed work, the railway promised to take additional tonnage 'to make up for the tonnage you are losing during the tie-up.' With this firm assurance Vissac vowed never to reopen the mines until he got a new agreement settled, got just the number of men needed – no more turns of work – and laid off all the agitators. The reds, such as Joe Krkosky Jr and William Peters at Blairmore, William Olensky and John Price at Bellevue, Rick Sudworth and

Andrew Dow at Coleman, were 'active, energetic and determined,' Vissac conceded, but they were a minority, 'not over 20 per cent,' and while the rest were 'absolutely inert at the present time' they would 'shake the reds out' after they had suffered. He was prepared to 'fight it out to a finish' and he ignored the seventeen demands. The next day, 26 February, he ordered the miners to take out their tools, shut down the mines, and put the horses out to pasture.[25]

Within several weeks, on 24 March, the miners at Coleman came out in support of the strikers at West Canadian Collieries. They had had several short work stoppages over 'no discrimination and equal division of work' and they too were fed up with the harassing tactics and favouritism displayed by the bosses. This brought a surge of enthusiasm to the strikers' ranks, but now a total 1,400 miners and their families had to be helped and kept from hunger by the union's relief activities. It was a gigantic challenge.

A strategic weapon for the miners in this situation was Harvey Murphy. It would be difficult to overestimate his role. Whether present or not at the start of the strike, he was the leading figure of the Workers' Unity League in Alberta and he had to take responsibility for it. For the mistakes made, Murphy received heavy criticism from the national centre of the league, who said the strike could have and should have been avoided until later.[26] He even wrote a self-criticism and had it published in the *Canadian Miner* in the midst of the struggle.

'This is not a confession,' he said. 'We have nothing to be ashamed of – anyone can make a mistake – but only a fool makes them twice or more.' The main mistake had been to rely on the leaders of the union in the manner of the reformists without drawing all the members into activity. There had been the old idea, wrote Murphy, that 'when a strike is on, the rank and file are on a holiday, while the Union Executive do[es] all the work, works out the plans, raises the relief, and reports back to the members when the strike is over.' In a revolutionary union 'a large strike committee should be elected at the beginning … a strike committee that will discuss EVERY important question' and will hold frequent meetings and report to the strikers regularly. A union executive of five or seven was not enough. All sections of the strikers should be represented on the strike committee, and it should have the confidence of the whole of the rank and file. If some committee members waver, the strikers should replace them and elect new ones. 'A strike committee does not include those who oppose the strike.' Picket lines were important. Every member of the miners' families 'must be prepared for picket duty.' A picket line is

not a mob, he said, 'it is an organized strike defense against strike break-
ers.' Murphy maintained that the miners in the Pass were correcting the
errors 'to some extent' and he was publishing his article so that other
workers 'can learn from our mistakes.'[27]

A turning point in the strike occurred in early April when the miners'
committees discovered that the coal operators demanded they repudiate
the Mine Workers' Union of Canada before any negotiations could take
place. This the great majority of miners refused to consider. The referendum vote to strike, if there was a wage cut, had already passed 673 to
94 in the Crowsnest mines and on 15 April a huge meeting took place in
Coleman which voted to continue the existing strike until three demands
were won: no wage cuts (which had been proposed by coal operators in
Coleman), no lay-offs without maintenance (proposed by West Canadian
Collieries), and the right of all workers to belong to whatever organization they wish and to have their elected representatives received by management for the purposes of negotiating a collective agreement.[28] With
three cheers for the Mine Workers' Union of Canada, the aims of the
strike were crystallized at last and from now on it would be hand-to-hand
combat in a figurative, and sometimes literal, sense.

As the tumultuous events of the strike developed – attempts by the
operators to reopen the mines, massive picket lines, demonstrations,
marches and rallies, clashes with the mounted police, the arrest of scores
of men and women on the picket lines, secretive efforts by the mine
managers to form company unions, a fiery cross of the Ku Klux Klan
burning on the mountainside, charges of arson, formation of a Citizens'
League to counter the union, picnics where the union women led by
Mary North served a thousand meals – Murphy intensified his whirlwind
tours in the province and in southeastern British Columbia. Speaking
as a national organizer of the Workers' Unity League, he addressed
audiences big and small, from a few dozen miners in isolated mining
camps to thousands of unemployed workers in Edmonton and Calgary.
He spoke to meetings of the newly formed united front policy committees, to the Canadian Labour Defense League, to the Ukrainian Labour
Farmer Temple Association, and to units of the Finnish Organization of
Canada, hoping to mobilize the supporters of the left to aid the strikers. He paid special attention to locals of the Farmers' Unity League,
the Workers' International Relief committees, and other groups such as
the Doukhobors in nearby British Columbia. The Doukhobors, he said,
'knew what oppression meant, and they gave us great amounts of food
from their little farms.'[29] By the end of March almost thirty tons of food

relief had reached the Pass — potatoes, flour, meat, butter, and eggs.[30] But it was not enough.

As the weeks passed Murphy's reputation grew in stature – as a hero to the workers and their families, according to an RCMP detective assigned to his case,[31] or a dangerous plague to be eliminated as soon as possible, in the opinion of the coal operators. The latter bombarded senior levels of government with impassioned pleas to lock this man up or send him away somewhere.[32] The Citizens' League decried law-breakers, those who disturbed the peace, and they trashed 'non-English speaking immigrants bringing ideas from foreign countries.'[33]

The Alberta premier, J.E. Brownlee, hesitated to intervene, since he had been elected with labour support, and the Conservative prime minister, Bennett, whose parliamentary seat was in Calgary, seemed reluctant too.[34] Among the top officials it was Commissioner General J.H. MacBrien of the RCMP who was eager to oblige and kept himself informed by scanning the frequent secret police reports for the possibility of criminal proceedings against Murphy.

Murphy's effect as a speaker is not easy to define. Sometimes it was his gestures, or tone of voice or pauses, as much as what he actually said that made an impact on his audiences during his one- or two-hour performances. He was a stump orator, speaking off the cuff, without notes, yet well informed, and he loved to talk.[35] He was blessed with a confident, good opinion of himself and an ironic tongue, and by his outgoing personality he became one of the most popular speakers for a generation of the radical left in Canada. Sources as different as the editor of the *Worker* and the half-dozen officers of the RCMP assigned to tail him at this time attest to Murphy's aura.

The veteran editor of the *Worker*, Malcolm Bruce, who had often campaigned with the young man and who now sat in Kingston Penitentiary for his efforts, lampooned Murphy's restless personality. 'An Alleged Autobiography of Harvey Murphy,' written in jail in 1932, is a chronicle by Bruce in the style of Lord Byron's *Childe Harold's Pilgrimage*, depicting a conceited, under-achieving candidate for greatness, and it concludes with 'An Alleged Reply by Murph' that evokes underlying tensions and a sense of humour among the communist leaders:

CANTO the SIXTH
(Extract)
Although my fame had spread both far and near
And as a Leader I had not a peer,

I felt I'd exercise a greater rule
If I would browse a while in Lenin School,
Erase the bad impressions of the past
And show the Duke that I was not declassed.
It took three years for Taffy, Sims and Carr,
The Duke and Weir – slaves to the samovar –
But brains like mine in nine short months could learn
All stored-up knowledge of the Comintern ...

AN ALLEGED REPLY BY MURPH
(Extract)

Who is this libelous and leprous swine
Who prostitutes the art of verse and line
To spin irreverent biography
And call the sorry tripe a work of mine?

While I in Labor's cause throughout the West
To Brownlee's janissaries bared my breast
This moron scribbles his buffooneries
In house security as Bennett's guest.

While I inspire great proletarian throngs
He's sloughed up where he properly belongs –
A jailhouse poetaster with vile pen
Salaciously inditing lecherous songs.

'Tis jealousy inspires his owlish screech,
His creaking doggerel and noisome speech –
'Base envy withers at another's joy
And hates that excellence it cannot reach.'

(With apologies to Lord Byron, *Childe Harold's Pilgrimage* and *English Bards and Scotch Traducers*. 'The Duke' refers to Stewart Smith, 'Taffy' to Leslie Morris.)[36]

The police surveillance file on Murphy contains considerable information on his activities, his oratory, and his reception by the public during the period of the Pass Strike.[37] Half a dozen RCMP officers and other special agents tracked him, sometimes two or three at the same time. After attending one of his meetings they would return to their rooms and write reports, occasionally as much as 1,800 words, and sum up their impression. Their special task was to provide evidence that could be made the subject of a prosecution that would allow the government to take control of Murphy under the sedition law of the Criminal Code. Their quarry was quite aware of their presence and at public meetings he would often make taunting remarks about the RCMP as a 'finely developed stool-pigeon agency,' or 'uniformed thugs who shot down our brothers in Estevan.' Sometimes he quoted from the definition of sedition in Lord Halsbury's *Law of England*, volume 9, page 462, to the effect that it is 'an intention to bring into hatred or contempt or to excite disaffection against the King or the Government ... or to incite any person to commit any crime or breach of the peace,' his purpose being to entertain the audience and rebuke the government's sleuths for their attempt to intimidate legitimate criticism.[38]

Invariably Murphy would begin his talks with some arresting statement such as 'the time had arrived when the miners were face to face with the absolute necessity of quietly and peacefully starving to death or else starve fighting.' Then he would decry the role of government and business, of banks, loans, interest and dividends, the wages system, and profit as 'weapons of the Capitalists in oppressing the working class and the cause of the industrial crisis throughout the world.'[39]

Sometimes, to the delight of the crowds, Murphy walked perilously close to the edge of sedition. Sergeant E.O. Taylor, Banff Detachment, after attending a miners' meeting in Canmore, had Murphy responding to a government announcement on relief saying, 'there will be no more relief after April 1st, and if the Governments allow men to go hungry and they die it is murder. Says there is only a pane of glass between a hungry man on the street and something to eat.' Was this not some kind of incitement to commit a crime? Outside the post office in Coleman, Murphy urged a meeting of several hundred people on the evening of 4 May to express solidarity with the miners. He told them that if they stood together they would be bound to win and urged them to join the picket in the morning 100 per cent and that nothing could stop them, 'not even the Mounted Police,' which the operators 'had brought in to break the strike.' To which an excited heckler shouted, 'Try them!'[40]

In reply to another heckler who asked how he made his living and accused him of fleecing the miners, Murphy is reported to have answered, 'I do not need to worry about my tea and sandwiches; I get mine direct from Moscow.' This remark briefly excited some senior police officers into thinking Murphy had admitted to being a paid agent of Moscow, something they had long wanted to prove. Murphy was not inclined to shy away from a Moscow connection. A police informant at a rally in Edmonton's Market Square had him delivering a rousing peroration: 'The capitalists say we are affiliated to Moscow, we are, and we will never renounce our affiliation to Moscow. We are proud of Moscow. The bourgeoisie say the Workers' Unity League is red, sure its [*sic*] red and it will be redder yet. There was a little czar who outlawed the communist party, and what happened? The party went underground, and a few years later bango, the czar was underground six feet and the communist party on top. They can outlaw the communist party, but it will never die. We will fight capitalism, and hound it to destruction and to its grave.'[41]

Murphy's narrowest escape from prosecution for sedition happened at the May Day rallies in Coleman and Blairmore, in 1932, where the RCMP had five officers present to pay close attention to the speeches. The first speaker, Andrew Dow, in reply to a question, had told his hearers that in the event of another world war, they should not enlist but stay in Blairmore. Commenting on that statement, Murphy was reported as follows: 'I say to you go into the army, and get your rifles and learn how to use them but don't use them against your fellow workers, but against Capitalism. In the last war the Russians fought against the Germans for two years before they realized that they were fighting workers such as themselves. Then they turned their rifles on their bosses and cleaned up the czar. He's not there now. We've got lots of czars like him in Canada, but they don't have crowns.'[42] The officers qualified their reports by saying the statement was not verbatim, but was substantially what he had said.

On reading these accounts, Inspector K. Duncan, RCMP commander in the Lethbridge West area, became confident that under all circumstances 'we have ample evidence on which to prosecute this man for Sedition.' After receiving the approval of his superior in Edmonton, Duncan issued a warrant for Murphy's arrest with the information that on 2 May he did 'speak seditious words, with intent to raise dissatisfaction and discontent amongst His Majesty's subjects and did at the same time and place speak seditious words with intent to provoke disorder.' But before the warrant was served it was referred to the law officers of the Crown, who urged caution and warned that the charge would not succeed because of the generality of the terms in which the statements were made, because the statements were not obtained verbatim, and because on previous occasions Murphy had instructed his followers that violence must not be resorted to on any account. The lawyers did, however, recommend going ahead with a lesser charge of Murphy being a member of an unlawful assembly that was 'likely to disturb the peace tumultuously.'[43]

Generally speaking, except for the RCMP sergeant in Fernie, BC, who found Murphy to be 'absolutely uneducated' and not 'at home in the English language,' the rest of the officers who tracked him were considerably impressed. 'As usual Murphy was well received by the crowd,' wrote Constable J.A. Simpson, of Coleman, 'and kept them in good spirits with his witty remarks about different People, the Government and the Police.' Corporal J.J. Weaver, in charge of the Blairmore detachment, reported on Murphy, saying, 'he is a fluent speaker and has the advantage over other agitators who have appeared in this district in that he has no difficulty in finding words to fully express himself.' He 'wield[s] a not inconsiderable influence amongst the rank and file of the coal miners.' Covering a meeting of the Canadian Labour Defense League in Edmonton's Gem Theatre, Constable D. Mighall said Murphy spoke for an hour and twenty minutes and 'held his audience better than any other radical speaker of this City. Murphy is very eloquent and has the personality which enables him to put it over. In my opinion Murphy is a very smooth and dangerous man.' These and other estimations give a strong indication of the powerful influence Murphy had on the miners and on their determined struggle to defend the interests of their class.[44]

May Day in the Crowsnest in 1932, in the middle of the general strike, was unusually enthusiastic. At least that is what many of the local people felt. The schools were closed by 10 a.m. to allow the children to join their parents and miners from all parts of the pass to meet in Coleman. There they lined up in picket formation and, led by the miners' brass band, marched the four miles into Blairmore carrying banners inscribed with the demands of the strike and the unemployed and denouncing imperialist war. After a number of speakers addressed the mass meeting from the bandstand, organized sports and games took place, followed by the Workers' International Relief feeding everyone.[45] There was a high sense of camaraderie.

Misunderstanding the temper of the workers, Vissac decided at this juncture to have a test of strength by reopening the West Canadian Collieries mine at Bellevue. He had been concentrating mine officials there, former officials, fire bosses, and maintenance men, sixty-five in all, and contacted the RCMP about his plan. Apparently with the approval of the Alberta attorney general's office (Premier Brownlee was also the attorney general), the RCMP sent a force of seventy-five men, mounted and armed, to Bellevue. Then at 11 a.m. on 3 May Vissac publicly announced the mine would open the next day and invited men to sign on. He claimed to have forty-five volunteers.

The union got wind of the plan and quickly sent truckloads of miners all night to Bellevue from Blairmore and Coleman. In spite of their efforts, the strike-breakers got into the mine 'without too much damage' on the morning of the 4th.[46] As this news spread, union men gathered in the Crowsnest towns and heard Murphy and Stokaluk urging a 100 per cent turn-out to the picket lines in the morning, and urging the women to come out in full force. 'It has been said that a woman's place is in the kitchen,' Murphy shouted, 'but what was the use of her being there if there was nothing to eat in the kitchen!' Mary North, Julia Johnson, and other active women went door-to-door recruiting women for the picket line.

Vissac noted that strong preparations were being made for the 5th, so he decided to rush the men through the picket lines by trucks. But that morning 1,200 men, women, and children were picketing. It was a daunting sight. The mounted police, Vissac observed dryly, 'had considerable trouble trying to handle the crowd, with women and children particularly hard to go through.' Hand-to-hand fighting occurred, stones were thrown at the trucks, two of Vissac's men were wounded and a dozen picketers arrested. Hoping to render the strike leaderless, the police issued a warrant for Murphy, charging him with 'unlawful assembly.'

Vissac tried to get some relief by asking Kellock and Whiteside to reopen their mines, but the Coleman operators claimed they could not get sufficient men to go to work. He then decided to make a strategic retreat, explaining his decision to the French shareholders: 'The next day a fierce battle was certain with blood-shed and bad feelings left for years. I went to the pickets that night and asked them to cut out the rough stuff; they promised they would; then I promised to have the mine idle the next day.' In the meantime, he said, 'we have had a chance to uncover the red leaders,' several of whom would be prosecuted; the test opened the eyes 'of many good Britishers, and of the police.' He noted the appearance of a branch of the Ku Klux Klan and the fact that 'some fighting has already started.' When the situation was ripe, he wrote, 'we may be able to make another test.' His position was adamant: 'We will never deal with the present union. We will never hire again the red leaders ... We must have the workers under our absolute control.'[47]

The Coleman operators were also working assiduously to undermine the Mine Workers' Union of Canada and they had enticed two of the local union leaders over to their side to help them build a company union. These men, William White and D. Gillespie, succeeded in taunting their former comrades into agreeing to a secret ballot to determine who should be the committee to conduct negotiations with the operators. Murphy was furious when he learned of this. 'Here we have already exposed them as strike-breakers,' he said, 'and then we "legalized" them by forming a joint committee of three from each side to draw up a ballot and conduct a vote.' This was nonsense, he said. There were only two 'sides' – the workers and the bosses – to every struggle, and if the elected strike committee in the opinion of the strikers doesn't represent their 'side' correctly, 'then openly bring this up at a meeting of the strikers and elect a committee that does ... but there are no two "sides" among the workers.' As for taking a secret vote during a strike, Murphy thought there was 'something fishy' about a striker who is afraid to stand up and vote in front of his fellow workers in his own way.[48] In spite of everything, the radical leaders of the Coleman local handily won the secret ballot 319 to 218, allowing them to remain as the committee to negotiate with the operators.[49]

Encouraged, however, by the size of their following, which had been revealed by the vote, the company-led insurgents continued their activities. In this they were supported by the formation of a right-wing Citizens' League led by the Protestant clergy, by the Ku Klux Klan, and by appeals to the 'loyal British element' against the 'foreign bolsheviks.' On the night of 13 May a giant fiery cross, symbol of the Ku Klux Klan, burned on Goat Mountain on a bare spot just above the Blairmore cemetery and in full view of the townspeople. Threatening notices reading 'Reds Beware, Watch Your Step – KKK' were pinned on the union hall and on the homes of prominent union members. A shot was fired from ambush into a car in which John Stokaluk was riding.[50]

Keeping up their offensive, the as yet unannounced company union organizers engineered a ballot the next day which they won 292 against 237; a majority of 55 for a return to work.

Three days later, on 17 May, when the Mine Workers' Union of Canada local called a meeting in the Coleman Opera House to consider the attempt to break away, an unexpected turn of events occurred. On a motion from the floor George Gaseoff, president, and Andrew Dow, secretary, the officers of the MWUC local, were unceremoniously voted out of office. Immediately they were replaced by White and Gillespie, organizers of the strike-breaking company union. At this unpleasant surprise, according to the press, the union supporters became enraged, 'chairs were heaved through the air, blows were exchanged in hand-to-hand fights. Almost every window in the Coleman Opera House was broken in the hectic gathering of 600 miners.'[51] As the meeting dissolved in disorder the RCMP were on hand to arrest three strikers. In the wake of these events the supporters of former union president Frank Wheatley could well savour their revenge.

In a last-minute attempt to stem the collapse of the Coleman local, Murphy and Stokaluk, led by a piper, headed a column of 400 men and 60 women from Blairmore to give support to their beleaguered comrades in Coleman. The marchers, wending their way through the mountains to the weird, whirling music of the bagpipes, resembled a scene from a movie in British India. The strikers succeeded in temporarily blocking the organizing meeting of the new union for a few days, but when it became obvious that the companies would succeed in reopening the mines, the MWUC leaders had to admit defeat. They called an end to the strike in Coleman and urged their members to join those going back to work in order to avoid being shut out. The men, all but 70 who were blacklisted, returned to work on 26 May; the company union held sway in Coleman for the next seven years.[52]

The strike against West Canadian Collieries in Blairmore and Bellevue, however, remained solid and would continue for another three months.

Vissac bemoaned his fate. 'We are in an extremely sad and painful situation,' he said. 'We have still to deal against a solid wall … the workers are powerfully organized and entirely in the hands of their leaders.' He informed the shareholders that he had helped to organize a 'new union of moderates' but unfortunately they controlled only 10 to 15 per cent of the workers. Criticizing the hiring practices of previous managers, he regretted that his British miners were in such a minority. 'They are generally patriots and do not easily accept the red flag,' he said, compared to the Italians and Slavs, who, he added patronizingly, were 'hard working and obedient, but too easy to lead and incapable of opposition.' The moderate union (composed mainly of British miners) was 'following his advice,' he said, without a hint of irony, 'organizing meetings now and collections.'[53]

With the help of the fire bosses and management personnel, Vissac was at least pleased that the Bellevue mine was shipping about 2,000 tons of coal every two weeks. It was a continuing challenge which the miners could not let pass.

Picket lines remained strong. Mass demonstrations and parades of various kinds took place frequently to keep the strike-breakers on alert, while picnics, dances, and other social and sports events were organized

Table 6.1 Employees at Blairmore mine

	British	Foreigners	Total
New Union (Moderates)	111	36	147
Red Union	57	443	500

Source: 'Labour Situation,' Glenbow Archives, WCC Papers, file 101, 28 July 1932.

to encourage the strikers' morale. 'This strike is different from any other strike,' wrote a miner's wife in the *Worker*. 'Before everyone was idle, but now everyone is busy – it is a question of the right to live.' Children's clubs were being created and the organizations of working women registered growth. Different nationalities were being brought closer together. 'This solidarity between nationalities,' the same correspondent said, 'is something new here and is a positive gain from the strike.' On another theme she remarked that there were 'plenty of police stationed at Blairmore.' 'They even played ball with the miners,' she said, and the miners won. 'Otherwise it seems only like an intervening peace in a time of war.' She was certain that the miners were going 'to stick to their ace-card, their militant WUL union' because it was an effective fighting instrument and a barrier in the path of the bosses' wage-cutting plans.[54]

Vissac continuously took stock of his situation, looking for a time that was ripe. But in mid-July his calculations showed that the balance of forces was still not favourable. By their 'ignorance and imbecility,' he raged, the foreigners, the Italians and Slavs, allowed themselves to be held under 'the yoke of agitators.' He illustrated this dramatically by a table of his employees (see table 6.1).

Unable to risk a direct confrontation, Vissac organized pressure on Brownlee for more police activity in Blairmore and Bellevue, especially to put an end to 'public disturbances in the form of parades.' The premier, however, continued to be cautious. He told Vissac that the operators had 'added unnecessary fuel to the fire by adopting a system which practically means blacklisting a number of workers,' and it was not surprising if men 'who see no future hope of work of any kind, resort to extreme measures.' He suggested the company reconsider its stand.[55] The next day, however, Brownlee abruptly changed his mind and ordered the RCMP to stop all parades in the Crowsnest Pass. This led to the arrest of almost 100 strikers who defied the order. Murphy called it the imposition of martial law. The act that stirred Brownlee into action, apparently, was a parade of children through the streets and around Vissac's house singing a parody on 'Mademoiselle from Armentiers' about the police bringing the scabs to the mine, which, according to the *Lethbridge Herald*, 'greatly stirred citizens all through the Pass.'[56]

The strike committee, seeking once more to find a negotiated settlement, elected a delegation to interview Premier Brownlee on various strike occurrences and to demand relief for the discriminated Coleman miners. Brownlee agreed to come to the Pass to investigate and to hold talks with both sides. From his intervention came the 'Brownlee Accord,' which brought an end to the strike on Labour Day 1932. The 'Accord' allowed both sides to claim a partial victory. It included the renewal of the former agreement without any wage cut or check-off, and the company agreed to drop its blacklist: there would be no discrimination against the strikers. The company, on the other hand, gained the right for a committee of the fifty men in its new union to sign the agreement separately, thus establishing a 'Home Local.' In addition the company insisted on 'Clause No. 3' saying it would rehire 'as rapidly as ... business conditions make it possible.'[57] Brownlee promised that the government would provide outdoor relief work for any miners waiting to be rehired. In addition the company agreed to free coal, light, and water for the miners.[58]

The miners suffered some hard blows in the wake of the settlement. The vacillating premier turned out to be no friend of the militant miners. He reneged on his pledge to provide relief,[59] and although he had been adamantly opposed to 'any open threats' to permanently lay off a certain number of the miners' leaders, company records show that he knew Clause No. 3 gave Vissac the same power in disguised form and that the operator intended to use that power to 'prune the union.'[60]

Vissac would have preferred a 'complete break' with the 'destruction of the red union' through 'a series of battles and the spilling of blood,' he told his shareholders, but after Brownlee's intervention he took the indirect method to 'consummate its end.'[61] The principal benefit of the 'Brownlee Accord' to the company, he said, had not been the elimination of 50 reds, but of 150. 'It is a terrible lesson for them,' Vissac wrote, 'which will bear fruit.' In addition, he reported that 'we have profited from these circumstances to eliminate all those who are not useful' by reason of age or sickness. 'In normal times,' he added, 'it is difficult to get rid of them.'

Another affront to the strikers was the imprisonment of Murphy. On the advice of their union and at the direction of the Alberta attorney general's office, virtually all the others arrested during the six-month strike pleaded guilty and were given two-year suspended sentences. Murphy refused to plead guilty and was booked for trial on the more serious charge of 'unlawful assembly' at the picket line in Bellevue on 4 May. He pleaded 'not guilty' and was tried in the Supreme Court of Alberta at McLeod by Justice Frank Ford. He was found guilty by the jury and sentenced on 18 October 1932 to three months' hard labour in Lethbridge jail. The crown prosecutor at the preliminary hearing was J.E. Gillis, the same man who was lawyer for the West Canadian Collieries. The outcome of the trial is somewhat of a mystery since the sworn information of the police, on which Murphy was arrested and charged, stated that although he was at the entrance to the West Canadian Collieries washhouse on that day he 'took no active part in the disturbance or performed any act of violence.' As for the men who were crossing the picket line and proceeding down into the mine, Murphy, according to the police report, 'addressed the crowd nearby complimenting them on their turn out but urging no acts of violence.'[62] Since the RCMP destroyed their large secret file on the Crowsnest Pass Strike (file 175/7717) thirty years later, before it could be transferred to the public archives, it is not possible to determine if or how the evidence against Murphy was rigged by the RCMP as it had been in the trial of Annie Buller in Estevan a year earlier.[63]

What was the legacy of the six-month Crowsnest Pass Strike of 1932? Was it a fool's errand? Or was it a portent of stout-hearted resistance? Leading figures of the communist movement were still heatedly debating this question several years later. On the one side were Murphy and his group of supporters in the Alberta district of the party, including John Stokaluk at this point in time, and on the other Stewart Smith, acting general secretary of the underground Communist Party, and probably the national mining committee of the party in Toronto, which would have included, at this time, James Litterick, acting secretary of the Workers' Unity League and Charles Sims, its national organizer.[64]

The top leaders, while allowing for some small successes, were adamant that the strike had been a colossal blunder, the result of unfounded optimism about the strength of the left and opportunist errors in the conduct of the struggle. Murphy, it was argued, had been guilty of 'leftist leaps' and 'a right opportunist perversion of the party line.' He had placed his hopes in some 'easy, spectacular' action that would quickly and all at once bring all the miners on side. But in practice what had happened?

In a short few months the membership of the Mine Workers' Union of Canada in Alberta had plummeted to less than 1,000; many locals of the MWUC had disappeared altogether (Coleman, Cadomin, Lethbridge, and the North Branch), being replaced by 'Home Locals' sponsored by the companies; the reformists were now in the lead of the majority of the miners; the 'united front conferences' in Alberta had been no united front at all, as shown by the fact that 'the machinery to carry out the decisions' after the conferences was still the officials of the MWUC; it was the same with the supposedly 'mass strike committees' that were belatedly elected but hardly functioned; the demand of the scale convention (wage raise of 10 per cent) had been 'incorrect,' creating confusion among miners who looked on it as unrealistic, impossible for strike action and only later corrected; the party units and fractions did not play a proper role and where they functioned at all, they 'functioned badly, and spasmodically'; a district or sub-district strike could have and should have been avoided until a real united front from below had been organized in the mining pits; finally, the failure 'to retreat at a sufficiently early date' (after the debacle at Coleman) in the face of a prolonged struggle was a serious error. The strike, in sum, had been conducted by a small cabal in the traditional way of the reformists without regard to 'elementary revolutionary strike strategy.' The source of this mistake was the theory that when a revolutionary union embraced the masses of striking workers, 'broad elected strike committees to lead the strike and to conduct the negotiations' were unnecessary. This had been the downfall of the strike.[65]

It was quite an indictment, almost as harsh as that being spread by the leaders of the American-based union,[66] and it offered a glimpse into the active inner life and sometimes sharp debates within the communist movement of the time.

Murphy did not take kindly to being portrayed as a bureaucrat – in effect a dictator – and a factionalist. He argued that the leadership in Toronto underestimated what had been achieved and were heading in the direction of liquidating the revolutionary union by their stress on the united front and the need to work within the Home Locals and the American union. How many members were actually capable of doing this, he wanted to know. He recognized some errors, such as the need for more democracy, and he promoted a constitutional amendment that was passed at the MWUC annual convention, in September 1932, stipulating that in the case of a strike preparation, before the men departed for home a large, representative strike committee should be elected to lead the strike.[67] But his main argument, along with Sloan and Stokaluk and the other Alberta miners' leaders, was that from the Crowsnest Pass Strike the operators and the miners clearly understood that the Mine Workers' Union of Canada, alone, was 'the champion of the miners and the main obstacle in the way of the boss class wage-slashing campaign.' As long as this union lived the coal barons would be faced 'with a militant struggle on all fronts.'[68] This was at a time, they pointed out, when workers in practically every other industry and locality in Canada – the railways, manufacturing, logging – were working at reduced rates. The resistance offered by the striking miners and their families was, therefore, no mean achievement, no mere exercise in futility. The workers had gained 'a sense of self-respect and collective independence.'[69] Was this not the larger long-run aim of the Workers' Unity League?

Emerging from the furore, the Mine Workers' Union, although weakened, continued as a vital force in the Crowsnest Pass and demonstrated this in a number of ways. Partly it shifted its attention to neighbouring mines such as those at Fernie and Michel, British Columbia, where, according to Vissac, the Crows Nest Coal Company abjectly caved in to the union, leading to large celebratory parades on the following May Day. Vissac also noted that the political agitators 'keep very busy in our camps' and accordingly the membership of his new union did not show 'any strong tendency towards increasing.' In spite of his 'cleansing efforts,' militants such as Joe Krkosky Jr, Sam Patterson, and John Price remained on the payroll of his mines and were continuing leaders of Local No. 1 of the MWUC.[70] Sensing the way things might go, the head office of West Canadian Collieries, in France, urged Vissac to be 'diplomatic' in his management decisions.[71]

An indication of the Pass Strike's indelible legacy lay in the next municipal election in Blairmore, in February 1933. Here the miners ran a full slate – mayor, council, school board – against the nominees of the Citizens' League and elected all their candidates save one school trustee. It was a major triumph that made headlines far and wide. Under the leadership of the new mayor, coal miner William Knight, who had been a picket captain in the recent strike, one of the new council's first defiant acts was to appoint Murphy as town solicitor. To the din of tirades from pulpit and press about the dangers of revolution and atheism, the workers' administration was not able to introduce socialism, but it brought about changes big and small to favour the hitherto disadvantaged. They discharged the police chief, fire chief, and other personnel of the former administration and gave their positions to unemployed miners; they discovered that the town treasury had been pilfered of up to $4,000 and that some of the supposed 'best citizens' had neglected to pay their property taxes for years. The council's solicitor found that some company officials

had been living as tenants in the Greenhill Apartments and avoided paying municipal taxes, so it struck them off the voting list, a move which
the company officials appealed in vain to the Supreme Court of Alberta.
The union miners had been paying 5 per cent of their earnings to the
Workers' International Relief to support their unemployed brethren;
now the council decided to levy a 5 per cent surtax on the businesses for
the same purpose. Murphy thought up an unusual way of having the burden of taxation fall on those better able to pay: a dog tax. It was a graded
tax according to the breed and was heaviest on the purebred Alsatian
police dogs that the coal company officials and other businessmen liked
to own. The workers found all this a great topic of conversation, but the
business people tried to put across a tax strike and for a time the verbal
battles became as sharp as they had been during the strike.[72]

Tempers flared even more when the Workers' Town Council declared
May Day and 7 November, the anniversary of the Russian revolution,
civic holidays – holidays with pay for civic employees. After an attempt
was made to shoot Tim Buck in Kingston Penitentiary and after Rev.
A.E. Smith of the Canadian Labour Defense Committee came to town
to denounce that act, the workers' town council changed the name of
the main street, named after Queen Victoria, to Tim Buck Boulevard
and spent some money to create flower beds, rockeries, and illuminated
signs along the roadway. Later, when Buck visited Blairmore after his
release from jail, in 1935, the mayor proclaimed a civic holiday; at a
meeting in Columbus Hall chaired by Murphy, and attended by about
1,000, the mayor presented the Canadian communist leader with 'the
keys to the town.'[73]

Before long the *Toronto Star* sent a reporter out to the Rocky Mountain
town to see what all the fuss was about. He found that Blairmore and
its 'blue-jumpered' mayor, a 'tall, lean, straight-talking Englishman' who
'did his bit overseas during the war,' had done some startling things all
right, but the reporter wrote a rather objective account for his newspaper. In response to a question, the mayor said he didn't think there
were any real communists on the town council or school board, but they
were all in sympathy with the communists. They had a Workers' Council
linked to communism, the mayor affirmed, through their union, part of
the Workers' Unity League which was affiliated with the Third International, which he considered gave 'mighty good leadership.' The drive for
control, Knight said, started in the seven-month strike and it would continue. The movement of the workers of Blairmore was a protest against
injustice; they saw they were getting nowhere. 'Private ownership of the

mines and the railways and their operation for profit was steadily making the plight of the workers more and more intolerable.'

'We are now going to look after our workers,' said Knight; 'you can call it a five-year plan, if you like.' That didn't mean they were going to override the rights of others in town. Everyone would get a fair deal. He was proud of what his administration had accomplished in two years and he thought it had 97 per cent of the citizens behind it. In the second re-election their whole slate went in by acclamation. The mayor outlined some of the accomplishments: six miles of roads and sidewalks built in the section of town occupied by the workers where there had been none before and a gravel-crushing and loading machine purchased for this work; a $5,700 snow plough bought to keep the roads open; a first-class road maintainer; an automatic fire alarm system installed; two parks under construction; waterworks rehabilitated; a drainage system introduced to solve the flood problem; a system of garbage collection instituted; the minimum light rate cut from $1 to 50 cents, helping the poor; and a business tax imposed, based on rental values, but the mill rate cut by two points. Blairmore was out of debt and had no debenture payments to meet; neither the mayor nor the councillors were paid, they all worked in or around the mine.

The school board had a similar proud record for its 464 students. Average attendance was over 90 per cent; teachers were all members of the Alberta Teachers' Alliance; their salaries had not been cut and they received a raise of $50 to $75 each year until they reached a maximum of $1,400 in the public school and $2,300 in the high school. The board had maintained a high standard; it had purchased the more affluent West End school from West Canadian Collieries and had paid for it; it had introduced a dental service at a cost of $1,400 a year and a music program under a qualified supervisor. Communistic teachings, which included atheism, were inculcated, but not in the schools. The Young Pioneers and the Young Communist League and other units were active organizations 'playing a prominent part in the public demonstrations.'

From outward appearances, the *Toronto Star* reporter concluded, life went on in Blairmore much the same as in other Canadian towns. It was quiet and orderly and not so startling – except for the illuminated signs at night on Tim Buck Boulevard. Even those from the business and professional classes whom he spoke to said, 'Knight has not done so badly.'[74] The Workers' Town Council continued in power for the next two decades.[75]

As for Murphy, he felt at home in Blairmore, especially after he fell in love with Isabel Rae, daughter of a coal mining family who had moved West from Joggins, Nova Scotia, in the 1920s. The two of them, in a life-long partnership, raised three children, and after several more eventful decades of organizing hard rock miners and mill and smelter workers across Canada, Murphy, at the age of seventy-one, finally came home to rest in the little cemetery on Goat Mountain, overlooking Blairmore and the broad valley of the Crowsnest River. Friend or foe, he left an indelible memory in the minds of his contemporaries as the 'reddest rose in the garden of labour.'

7

August 1932:
Confronting the Prime Minister

Ottawa, Aug. 2. – The workers' economic conference met in Ottawa to-day and, in a few hours, created a greater furore than the delegates of empire have in ten days.

– Toronto Star, 3 August 1932

As the still, hot summer days of July descended upon Ottawa, the British Empire's pre-eminent leaders began arriving for the Imperial Economic Conference of 1932. They had crossed the Atlantic Ocean and sailed up the Gulf of St Lawrence to the ramparts of Quebec aboard the Canadian Pacific Railway's flagship, the *Empress of Britain*. From Africa, Asia, Australia, New Zealand, Newfoundland, and the Irish Free State they came; the Empire still boasted of having a quarter of the human race and the same proportion of the world's territory.

Heading the list of participants was the sixty-person delegation of the United Kingdom led by its lord president of the Council, Rt. Hon. Stanley Baldwin, and chancellor of the Exchequer, Rt. Hon. Neville Chamberlain. The minister of war came too, as well as those in charge of dominions, colonies, trade, agriculture, and fisheries; the delegation included leaders of the British Chambers of Commerce and the British Federation of Industries, and the general secretary of the General Council of the Trades Union Congress, Walter Citrine. It was a decidedly high-powered group representing social forces that backed both the Conservative and Labour Parties, who were temporarily in a coalition National Government to deal with the chaos that war debts and the great depression were wreaking upon the British economy.

In honour of the occasion, banners, flags, and streamers festooned downtown Ottawa, and gala social events welcoming the famous guests were held in the imposing Chateau Laurier. The business sessions of the conference took place up on Parliament Hill and as the delegates gathered there a battery fired the royal salute while the carillonneur of the Peace Tower rendered a version of Sir Edward Elgar's 'Land of Hope and Glory.' Following the 'pomp and circumstance,' including a special message from King George V and customary expressions of loyalty to the Crown, the conference elected Mr Bennett, prime minister of the host country, as chairman of the gathering. He gave the first speech.

Bennett tried to set a broad, welcoming tone for the conference, calling for closer economic co-operation and reciprocal trade agreements within the Empire. In this speech it soon became apparent that he had another preoccupation: how to isolate and if possible shut down the Soviet Union's surge into world markets, especially its competitive trade into the British market for primary products such as lumber, coal, wheat, and asbestos in which Canada had a special interest. By embargoes, tariffs, and quotas the British Empire, at least, the prime minister thought, should be made safe for its own members. This was his plea and he couched it in robust ideological overtones. 'State-controlled standards of living, state-controlled labour and state-aided dumping dictated by high state policy,' he declared, 'conflict in theory and in practice with the free institutions of the British Empire. The subordination of individual right and liberty to a national economic plan affronts our whole idea of national development.' The British Empire should be active in the defence of its institutions, Bennett urged, by 'providing safeguards against unfair state-controlled competition.'[1] This sort of talk, appealing *for* state intervention to combat the same, seemed to confirm the predictions of the communists about some deeper purposes of the conference.

The British delegation, it turned out, did not agree with Bennett. Diplomatically but firmly, Baldwin said he preferred the method of lowering of barriers among Empire countries rather than raising them against others.[2] The fact was that Britain imported 25 per cent of her lumber requirements from Russia at favourable prices, and was selling to her substantial orders of machinery and other manufactured goods. The British cabinet recognized that if the USSR could not export to the United Kingdom she would be unable to repay the short-term credits of up to £8 million which were financing British exports. Hence they 'looked forward to a new Anglo-Soviet trade agreement – not toward the embargo which Bennett sought.'[3] Canada, as the communists were quick to point out, could have had a similar Russia trade deal to sell $10 million worth of Massey-Harris tractors.

The Imperial Conference continued on for several weeks in closed meetings during which, according to the *Ottawa Citizen*, the Soviet trade issue became 'one of the turning points of the conference.'[4] In the end a general resolution, avoiding any ringing declarations, announced that participants had negotiated many reciprocal preferential tariffs which it claimed would 'ensure that the resources and industries of the Empire are developed on sound economic lines,'[5] while Bennett continued his policy of embargo.

When news of the Imperial Economic Conference first began circulating in Canada, in the spring of 1932, the semi-underground and illegal Canadian Communist Party was mulling over its none too favourable options.

The federal government, not content with locking up the party's eight top leaders, had begun kidnapping officials of Ukrainian and Finnish immigrant societies, spiriting them away in the middle of the night to dockside immigration sheds in Halifax for deportation – even though some of them had lived in Canada ten to twenty years. Provincial and municipal police forces took similar stringent actions against 'the Reds' and the activities of the Workers' Unity League. As the date for the Imperial Conference drew near, the Canadian Labour Defense League observed that 'a veritable reign of terror' had been unleashed against workers and their organizations. One by one, the rights of freedom of speech, freedom of assembly, freedom of the press and organization, and of *habeas corpus* were 'being wrested from the working class.' According to the Canadian Labour Defense League, 456 people had been arrested for working-class activity in the first six months of 1932; 33 workers were deported on political grounds and another 49 held for deportation; there were 103 raids on workers' homes and halls; 125 workers were wounded or beaten by the police; 53 hall and outdoor meetings were violently smashed by police; and 100 workers were serving jail and penitentiary terms. Ten halls of the Ukrainian Labour Farmer Temple Association had been burned to the ground and two partially destroyed. In Toronto alone, 6,000 bailiffs' warrants were issued in 1931 on behalf of mortgage and loan companies. In some centres unemployed workers on the verge of starvation were forced to sign voluntary deportation slips in order to receive relief.[6]

Perhaps it served the purpose of the Bennett government, the *Manitoba Free Press* observed dryly, 'to have people talking about communists, mounted police and deportation, instead of about the shortcomings of the Government and its failure to fulfill its election campaign.'[7]

To top matters off, a report circulated at Comintern headquarters in Moscow to the effect that the Canadian communists did not want to believe the bourgeoisie was 'as mean and arrogant as it showed itself to be,' and that their attacks had 'brought about partial and temporary wavering and timidity in the ranks of the Party.'[8]

In these circumstances of harsh repression, unprecedented in the English-speaking world (except perhaps for British India), the communists desperately wanted to hold a much-postponed national gathering of the Workers' Unity League. After two and a half years of existence it was time to clarify WUL strategies, to establish a recognizable leadership core, and to rally members of the league. How should they proceed?

One decision was to send a new envoy to the Third International for consultations and to press for some help. This envoy was 'Morgan,' a pseudonym for Norman Freed, a promising young activist in the needle trades and brother-in-law of the imprisoned Sam Carr. After various delays Freed arrived in Moscow in the early summer of 1932 to brief Kuusinen and, as was customary for newly arrived delegates, to give a general report to the Anglo-American Secretariat on Canadian developments.[9] He came to seek advice on how to work under conditions of illegality, to request the transfer of some 'developed comrades' into the Canadian field, 'new people not personally known to the espionage agents of the state,'[10] and possibly to make some financial requests. He found the group of Canadian students at the Lenin School engaged in academic exercises, busily preparing defensive reports on various subjects for some plenary sessions of the executive committee of the CI and of the Red International of Labour Unions.[11] He also found a letter to be sent from the Anglo-American Group of the RILU to the Workers' Unity League with suggestions for a national gathering. Freed stopped this letter, he said, because it would have arrived too late to serve any purpose.[12] After hearing Freed's short report on trade union work, the RILU decided to send a cable and to publish an article in *International Press Correspondence*, 'laying down a general line.'[13] It is not clear that Freed achieved any financial aid. Mainly he held discussions with co-workers from other British Empire countries about something else. It was the Communist Party's daring decision to hold a mass Workers' Economic Conference in Ottawa to coincide with and as a foil to the Imperial Economic Conference.

The workers' conference was formally initiated by an *ad hoc* committee, the 'National Committee of Unemployed Councils.'[14] The organizing committee proposed a program of struggle against the wage-cutting offensive of the employers and against 'the appalling increase of unemployment, poverty and destitution.' At the same time it declared the Imperial Economic Conference to be a 'united front of employers and governments to conserve their profit at the expense of the workers,' a conference whose organizers were promoting war preparations, especially directed against the Soviet Union, 'as a way out of the crisis.' Apart from the Bennett government's hostility to the Soviet Union, Japanese aggression in China – seizing the Manchurian provinces, taking over joint Russian-Chinese railway assets, and placing troops along the border with Soviet Russia, according to the conference organizers – had received the tacit support of Britain, Canada, and other members of the League of Nations. To the communists these developments appeared as harbingers of a wider war, and they said so.

The conference call, signed by George Winslade, secretary, invited the shops, mines, and mills, all trade unions and other working-class organizations, 'irrespective of political or trade union affiliation, creed or nationality,' to send two delegates to this Workers' Economic Conference. In the published documents of the conference and in reports of it in the *Worker* and in the daily newspapers, there were no exclusions, no warnings about 'labour fakirs,' 'betrayals,' or 'social fascists.' In a time of much sectarian jostling on the left, a time when an anxious Communist Party saw the social democratic forces in Canada gaining momentum with the birth of the CCF, this was a remarkable initiative, worthy of notice. It appeared to foreshadow, on native soil, the inclusive politics of 'the popular front' promoted by the Third International in the second half of the decade.[15]

In this respect a small but important and puzzling fact is that still lying in the Comintern archives, in Moscow, there are two *unpublished, undated*, draft documents which are clearly related to the Ottawa conference. They are titled 'Resolution on Future Tasks Unemployed Councils' and 'Manifesto.' Although anonymous, they are written in the inimitable sectarian style of Stewart Smith. One of them has a heading 'Beware of Fakirs'; social democratic members of parliament Abe Heaps and J.S. Woodsworth of Winnipeg and Angus McInnis of Vancouver are named and it is claimed that they 'betray the interests of the class they profess to represent,' they use the workers' movement for their personal and political advantage, they try to turn the workers away from struggle and 'in essence and fact' support the Bennett program. This was vintage sectarian rhetoric of the kind of which Smith was a past master; but there is no evidence that these documents were actually presented or voted upon at the Workers' Economic Conference. The archive is silent on why this happened, leaving a speculation that the local organizers felt the divisive rhetoric did not fit the temper of the gathering and performed their own editing.[16] It was a time, evidently, to refrain from sectarian argument.

To get the conference rolling, the National Committee of Unemployed Councils sent out 2,500 conference calls, with draft resolutions attached, and it expected local unemployed militants to follow up by personal visits to organizations to see that delegates were actually elected to Ottawa; in cases where the secretary had thrown the call 'in the basket,' militants were to ask permission to speak on the floor of membership meetings to urge participation. The organizers aimed to get 1,000 delegates elected and to raise $5,000 for accommodations and food, leaving it up to the participants to get themselves there – 300 from west of Winnipeg – by 'riding the rods' or 'side-door Pullman' – methods already perfected by thousands of Canada's unemployed workers. It was an audacious plan.[17]

The immediate impetus for this 'On-to-Ottawa' trek, precursor of a more famous one three years later, came from the idea that when faced with repression the best response was not to retreat into dimly lit cellars but to carry out some public activity, as spectacular as possible, so as to gain attention for the plight of the people and for the solutions offered by a united front led by the communists. If successful it would allow militant workers to emerge from the dark corners and by dint of a broad public campaign in the presence of major world leaders to generate significant support for the demands of the unemployed and for a working-class program that could be tied to the first national convention of the Workers' Unity League. Even if the trek did not visibly and immediately change the course of Canadian politics, as its organizers must have realized would be the case, such a gathering could regenerate the determination and morale of the left and baptize many new workers into the world of organized resistance and collective struggle. It seemed to be a gamble worth taking.

Prime Minister Bennett was decidedly unhappy and perhaps a little apprehensive about the thought of a thousand unemployed workers descending on the capital in the midst of the British Empire's summit meeting. His disposition was not improved by publicity which reached his desk. In one letter published by the *Ottawa Citizen*, the district secretary of the workers' conference cited official figures of 750,000 unemployed in the country. Urging support for the conference, he wrote that this gigantic army, along with their wives and children, were 'existing between the borderline of starvation and death.' Not a hundred miles

from the Parliament Buildings, he said, about 200 unemployed workers, the majority of them ex-servicemen, were living with their wives and
children in tents 'under conditions that defied description.' He challenged anyone to verify this fact by a trip to Mechanicsville, where the
first thing to catch the eye was a French-Canadian family of eight clothed
in the most primitive fashion and the mother in an advanced state of
pregnancy.[18] Another piece of paper to pass through Bennett's hands
was a leaflet by the Working-Class Ex-Servicemen's League of Vancouver
listing demands and calling all vets to join the trek to Ottawa. 'The sun
is shining and here is a chance to shake the dust from your shoes for a
while ... Plenty to eat on the way and every trekker a buddy. Here is a
chance to do something for yourself and the rest of humanity.'[19] Handwritten posters began to appear around the country, at railway under-
passes and in city parks, 'On to Ottawa, August 1st.'

To deal with the prime minister's worries, General MacBrien, RCMP
commissioner, called a meeting of CPR and CNR executives in his
office early in July. Here he requested the co-operation of the railways
to remove riders from the freight trains. The government wished this
operation to be carried out without publicity, he said. When the railway executives hesitated about enforcing the Railway Act after having
allowed thousands to disobey it at will, MacBrien promised to send extra
RCMP officers at points between Calgary in the west and Moncton in the
east, to back up the railway police and to make selective arrests whenever they found men carrying credentials to the Ottawa conference. The
railways accepted the government's proposal and at various points they
located tourist carriages on spur lines hidden from the main line as temporary headquarters for the RCMP, preventing the casual observer from
suspecting their presence.[20] Police also contacted local magistrates along
the route, seeking their 'co-operation.' The RCMP proposed 'an agreement for all Magistrates to deal with offenders in the same manner ...
by imposing a penalty of say $10 ... with a minimum of 30 days,' which
would serve the purpose of 'impeding trespassers' during the Ottawa
meetings.[21] Local police were cautioned about making wholesale arrests
for lack of jail space.

In early July the Canadian Labour Defense League learned that the
government had further plans in preparation for the Workers' Economic
Conference. It reported that 150 RCMP officers from Regina were being
brought to Ottawa; 800 members of the Royal Canadian Dragoons of
Toronto were going to Ottawa for 'camp duty,' and 1,500 Highlanders
from Montreal were on the move to Hull.[22]

Soon hundreds of unemployed men and an increasing number of women[23] were being put off trains at Calgary, Swift Current, Moose Jaw, Regina, Saskatoon, and eastern regions as constables riding on the box cars kept watch over the eastbound freights. The transients began gathering in 'jungle towns.' When the mayor of Calgary complained to Bennett that the RCMP were removing unemployed transients bound for Ottawa and that large numbers were congregating in Calgary due to this action, Bennett sent a deceptive telegram in reply. The action was being taken to remove hobos, he said, 'because it was requested by officials of the Canadian transportation companies.'[24]

Confronted by the police blockade, determined trekkers found ways to circumvent it. Mabel Marlowe, of Port Arthur, and Helmi Anderson, of Vancouver, were among those who walked around the check-points, travelled short distances by boat, hitch-hiked with truckers, or rode in cattle cars. Trains brought to a halt unexpectedly at small stations in the wilderness of Northern Ontario with their passengers ordered to depart found themselves full again a hundred miles down the track and the performance had to be repeated. Sympathetic railway workers assisted the dust-covered travellers. In one case the RCMP discovered sixteen men arriving in Ottawa after being sealed in a car by a trainman at North Bay. A sergeant in Regina reported, on 27 July, that conditions did not look good. 'I anticipate trouble at any time,' he wrote. 'The men are now getting desperate and resort to any means to getting east; it has been found necessary at times to resort to some handling before they could be removed ... It is a mystery to me where they are securing their food.'[25] Another source said that many men 'of foreign birth' had been passing through North Bay and 'flaunted *The Worker* ... from their hip pockets,' instructing men and women to proceed to Ottawa for the assembly on 1 August.[26]

While on an early morning patrol a week before the opening of the conference, J.W. Phillips, RCMP superintendent in Ottawa, found 203 transients in the vicinity of Hurdman's Bridge. They were given one meal a day 'at the temple,'[27] he said, and then told to go out and beg and find places at the several dumps. Phillips felt encouraged. There would be no demonstration 'of size or consequence,' he predicted. He found the local followers generally 'are afraid' and in spite of Dominion-wide requests for money 'they have had no success and they are without any funds whatever.'[28] The *Mail and Empire* of Toronto echoed this sentiment, saying that the demonstration in Ottawa was the work of 'agents of Moscow,' but that their every move was known to Major General J.H.

MacBrien, whose 'spies have walked with small contingents marching towards the capital on foot.' The police superintendent predicted that the demonstration was 'likely to prove a fiasco.'[29]

Conference organizers, meanwhile, had applied to Ottawa municipal authorities for financial aid and for permission to use the coliseum as a conference assembly hall. Refusal of these requests provoked the *Ottawa Citizen* to say that the unemployed could hardly be refused the right to assemble, and it suggested a better way should be found to handle the advent of a large contingent of destitute men than reliance on force alone. Perhaps, the paper wondered, the churches and other relief machinery in the city could help to allow the unemployed 'a reasonable opportunity to express themselves.' After all, the editor said, 'it has long been the privilege of the most humble subject to lay a petition at the foot of the throne.'[30]

Signs of support from the liberal middle class were encouraging, but without waiting upon their charity, the militants of the Workers' Unity League, who were by now quite numerous in the city, prepared the grounds for the conference. They rented an abandoned garage on Gladstone Avenue, a mere mile from Parliament Hill, for $20 for four days, and proceeded to construct a speakers' platform and rows of benches. Along the edges they spread two inches of sawdust covered by canvas to serve as sleeping quarters for several hundred delegates. An empty house and the Ukrainian Labour Temple on nearby Arlington Avenue served as kitchens and dining halls with dishes rented from McIntosh and Watts on Bank Street. A sympathetic farmer billeted many of the trekkers. Letters were delivered to wholesale merchants explaining the purposes of the march on Ottawa and saying that 'properly accredited' Workers' International Relief members would be visiting them on or about 27 July for contributions of funds, food, and clothing.

The proceedings of the workers' conference can best be recreated through the colourful and sometimes conflicting reporting of bourgeois journalists who were given full access by the conference committee, and through the reports of one of MacBrien's clandestine agents. The *Ottawa Journal* said 675 delegates had arrived and were crowded into a former garage at 577 Gladstone Avenue, where participants were 'cheering to the echo' demands for non-contributory unemployment insurance, shorter working days, and discontinuance of the 'police terror.' The correspondent noted the variety of speakers addressing the conference – union delegates, Alderman Tom Raycroft of East Windsor, and several women including Helmi Anderson, a frail, older woman from Vancouver,

Mabel Marlowe, an eighteen-year-old who brought 'revolutionary greetings' from Port Arthur, and Annie Buller, 'a delegate from the coal fields of the far west.' He noted that Anderson and Marlowe had both travelled by freight, evading police blockades, to reach Ottawa.[31]

The *Toronto Star*, in its extensive coverage, gave a fair summary of the proposals of the conference as miners from the Maritimes, lumbermen from British Columbia, and industrial workers from Toronto and Montreal demanded from the government immediate relief in the way of unemployment insurance payments, and then, subsequently, changed working conditions and hours, repeal of tariffs and taxes on the necessities of life, abolition of rent, taxes, and debts of poor farmers, cessation of 'police terrorism,' and abolition of the Russian embargo.[32]

Harvey John Hickey, correspondent of the *Mail and Empire*, put the number of delegates, more accurately, at 500. He concentrated on the 100 war veterans in attendance. 'Blistered and ragged,' he wrote, most of them having travelled by freight car from British Columbia and the prairies, they were awaiting the chance to interview Premier Bennett. Everyone was 'encamped in an empty house, a garage and along railway tracks at the end of Arlington Avenue.' Five of the veterans, led by Captain John McLennan of Hamilton, DFC and Military Medal, visited the press centre at the Chateau Laurier to give a briefing. They supported the demands of the workers for non-contributory unemployment insurance, and in the meantime wanted cash relief at the army scale of $1.10 per day and free medical service for all veterans. If demands were not met they threatened to bring 15,000 ex-servicemen to Ottawa from all over the country, as the U.S. veterans' 'Bonus Army' had done in Washington.[33]

The police undercover agent also described the scene on Gladstone Avenue, where, he said, 'a large number of delegates slept on the floor of the garage, others slept in adjacent fields and in box cars at a nearby railway track.' He gave details of the opening day's proceedings.[34] Veteran trade unionists James McLachlan of Glace Bay, NS, and Alex Gauld of Montreal were chosen alternating chairpersons for the day. Harvey Murphy of the Workers' Unity League in Alberta brought greetings, telling of the militant five-month strike of the Crowsnest Pass coal miners. Proceedings were interrupted briefly when fifty 'hunger marchers' arrived from Verdun, Quebec. Sent off by a rally of 2,500 people in the suburbs of Montreal, the Verdun marchers had travelled the 120 miles to Ottawa on foot to demonstrate their determination. The delegates came to attention as George Winslade, of Trail and Vancouver, BC, secretary of the conference, presented his report on behalf of the National Committee of Unemployed Councils. He outlined the worsening conditions of the unemployed and employed workers, and contrasted the purposes of this conference with those of the Imperial Economic Conference meeting concurrently in Ottawa. He introduced some goals of the conference, emphasizing immediate demands and the enactment of the non-contributory unemployment insurance bill. He also spoke of his experience in unemployed demonstrations in Vancouver. Then, to everyone's surprise, he read a letter from the Rt. Hon. R.B. Bennett, whom he referred to as 'the old man himself.' The letter stated that the prime minister of Canada would receive a delegation of seven accredited delegates in his office at noon on Tuesday, 2 August, provided none of the members were communists. Amidst scenes of wild excitement in the afternoon, with Annie Buller, whom the *Toronto Star* described as 'a Saskatchewan Amazon,' in the chair, they adopted a resolution of 'demands' and chose seven delegates to represent them. These were George Winslade; Thomas Raycroft, ex-serviceman, East Windsor alderman; A. Bailey, hunger marcher, Verdun; P. Ritchie, French-Canadian youth; K. Slusky, miner, Crowsnest Pass; Lillian Wilkinson, woman delegate, North York; and J.B. McLachlan – several of them well-known communists. In spite of police warnings not to assemble on Market Square, the delegates planned to go there the next day to reinforce the delegation elected to meet Bennett in his office.

Meanwhile another highlight of the conference emerged from the caucus of the ex-servicemen. This followed shocking news about a massive assault on ill-fed war veterans and their families in Washington, DC. Ordered by President Hoover to clear out the 15,000 'bonus army' that had gathered in the capital for several weeks to claim payment of promised bonuses, the U.S. Army with fixed bayonets and tear gas, cavalry charges, and tank support emptied the streets of the capital and routed 10,000 inhabitants of the main encampment located on the flats by the Potomac River. Under the command of General Douglas MacArthur, and Majors George C. Patton and Dwight D. Eisenhower, the army sent the ramshackle camp up in flames. In the process two veterans and two babies lost their lives. Ottawa delegates were outraged by this news. The images fuelled their anger and gave even more meaning and sense of urgency to their own commitments and to their attendance at the conference. They were, therefore, more than willing to endorse a telegram to Hoover condemning the 'brutal and bloody treatment of the ex-servicemen in Washington' and holding the U.S. president 'responsible for the death of these brave workers,' and for the maintenance of their widows and orphans.[35]

The highlight of the Ottawa conference was undoubtedly the meeting with the prime minister and the widespread coverage of that encounter by reporters present from the daily newspapers. According to them, Bennett was 'friendly but firm' as he welcomed the workers' delegation into his office. Some remembered that he shook hands all round. For almost an hour he conducted an unusual interview, parrying the delegation's demands, saying they were off the mark, contrary to law, or matters of provincial jurisdiction, all the while carrying on an informal Socratic-type lesson, inviting questions and interruptions, alternating between patronizing remarks and angry outbursts. This was just the latest of several times that Bennett had met delegations led by or inspired by the Workers' Unity League and in some strange way he seemed to enjoy the chance to cross swords in the full glare of publicity. To the *Worker* the prime minister's interview showed that Bennett 'dared not refuse to receive a delegation representing nearly a quarter of a million workers of Canada.'[36]

Sitting at his desk, with Labour Minister W.A. Gordon and Justice Minister Hugh Guthrie on either side, and attended by twenty reporters, the prime minister leaned on his elbows listening attentively as Winslade, leader of the delegation, made what a *Toronto Star* reporter thought was 'a very reasoned and orderly presentation of the case.'[37] With the program of the delegation being put forward as a series of 'demands,' the prime minister interrupted briefly:[38]

BENNETT: Perhaps 'demand' could be replaced by 'request'?
WINSLADE: No. I have been mandated by the conference resolution to 'demand.'
BENNETT: Very well then.

Stripped to the core, this is what Bennett and his ministers heard:

We demand enactment of a workers' non-contributory unemployment insurance bill and pending enactment, cash relief at the rate of $10 per week with $2 per week for each dependent.
We demand the seven-hour day and the five-day week with no reduction in pay. Full union wages for all relief work. Abolition of the forced labour system. Abolition of child labour for all children under sixteen.
We demand repeal of all tariffs and taxes which hold up prices on necessi-

ties of life and constitute a monopoly attack on the standard of living of the workers.

We demand immediate cessation of the police terror and violence regime throughout Canada. The repeal of Section 98, immediate release of Tim Buck, Ewen, Carr, Popovich, Hill, Boychuk, Bruce, Bill Cacic, and all workers imprisoned for their labour activities. Stoppage of the kidnapping and deportation policy, restoration of the rights of free speech, assembly and organization.

We demand immediate release of the thirty-two Indian trade union leaders now lying in Merut prison for three years without trial. Release of the 55,000 Indian political prisoners. Self-determination for India and withdrawal of all British troops from the colonies.

We demand no shipments of food or war materials to Japan. Withdrawal of Premier Bennett's war embargo against the Soviet Union. All military and naval expenditures for the relief of the unemployed workers and poor farmers in Canada. [In making this point Winslade mentioned his own war service and said that all veterans were opposed to further wars; the last war having only made millionaires of the likes of Joseph Flavell.]

We demand exemption of all poor farmers from taxes, debts, and rent payments. Adequate emergency relief for the poor farmers at the expense of the rich. Enactment of the Farmers' Unity League Farm Relief Bill.

Keeping calm, at first, Bennett turned to other members of the delegation, inviting their comments. Lillian Wilkinson, a mother of five, with an unemployed husband, was the first to stand up to educate the chief executive of Canada:

WILKINSON: Mr Bennett, families of seven on relief are getting only $4 a week in North York and young girls, out of work, are being forced on to the streets.
BENNETT: I've heard that claimed before, but it is not so.
WILKINSON: You don't know. (*She thumped on the prime minister's desk, tears welling into her eyes.*) The women of Canada are not going to see their kids starve and go without shoes. You don't know; you have enough to eat.

The prime minister leaned over and took her hand.

BENNETT: There, there, Mrs Wilkinson, you mustn't do that. There is a well-organized system to deal with relief in North York and they will see that no child starves. If your children are in want I will immediately take up this matter personally and see that relief is granted.

WILKINSON: I'm not speaking for myself but for other women all over Canada. (*Growing more agitated.*) This thing can't go on. We can't see our children want.

BENNETT: You mustn't get bitter.

WILKINSON: If we are bitter it is you who have made us bitter. We women can't go on bringing kids in this world just for them to starve. Four dollars a week for a family of seven! No wonder we get bitter.

Fellow delegate J.B. McLachlan, pulling on his straggly mustache, rose to support Wilkinson.

MCLACHLAN: (*Speaking quietly*) Mr Bennett, we put it to you. What would you do if you had no work, your wife and children had no food, the rent was unpaid and you were in debt? What would you advise us to do?

BENNETT: We have told the provinces we will assist them to provide relief for every family in need. We are trying to provide food and clothing for all, and in time of peril that is all we can hope to do. So far as this government is concerned there will never be any [non-contributory unemployment insurance] legislation passed. Where would the money come from?

MCLACHLAN: This country is very rich. There are people of wealth, including you, holding shares in institutions such as the CPR and the Consolidated Mining and Smelting Company.

BENNETT: Thank you for the opportunity of stating definitely and publicly that I hold no shares in the CPR or in Consolidated Mining and Smelting Company. No, there are the savings of a great many people. The country is rich in raw materials. You want me to take from the people's savings to give to others.

When attention turned from the demands of the unemployed to police terrorism and Section 98 of the Criminal Code, Bennett lost his calm. According to the reporter of the *Toronto Star*, 'he pounded his desk in his denunciation of those who would destroy law and order.' Eyes flashing as he leaned toward his visitors, he said, 'This is a democracy and our laws represent the considered judgement of the people ... You break those laws and I say that as inevitably as the sun rises, you will pay the full price for it. Let that be clearly understood.'

Wilkinson, Winslade, and McLachlan made several interjections: five times the elected House of Commons had tried to repeal Section 98 of the Criminal Code and five times the unelected Senate had rebuffed its will. What was democratic about that? Workers jailed under Section 98 were kept there while swindling stockbrokers had been released before completing their prison sentences. Why the hypocritical double standard?

The brokers 'were released on ticket-of-leave,' snapped Bennett, 'just as anybody might; they made restitution and served half their term.'

Bennett made considerable efforts to persuade the delegates of his views on other issues. As president of the Imperial Conference, he promised to communicate the representations with respect to political prisoners in British India, but dwelt at some length on 'the British uplifting of the three hundred millions of India' as 'one of the brightest spots in history' and praised the 'the administration of British justice.'[39]

As for Japan (which was busy invading China at that moment at Shanghai and in Manchuria), Bennett saw no reason for any embargo and he claimed no war materials were being shipped out of Canada anyway since there was a law forbidding it.

He defended his embargo on Russian trade on the grounds of unfair competition by a state monopoly and he rode his hobby horse that Soviet low-price 'dumping' of lumber, wheat, and asbestos into the English market was 'a menace to world civilization.'[40] 'Do you believe in unfair competition?' he asked rhetorically. 'Do you believe the workers of this country should not have a fair chance in honest competition?'[41]

When he went on to disparage unfair labour conditions in the Soviet coal mines, McLachlan jumped up to challenge him. This resulted in a heated exchange that ended the interview. 'Ye can no tell me lies about the Soviet workers, Mr Bennett,' said the fiery Nova Scotian. 'I spent six weeks in the mines with them in the Soviet Union! … Although only one sixth of the world is under the workers' management, this part, which is Russia, has paved the way for the rest of the workers of the world to follow. And follow they must if they want to enjoy the fruits of their labour.'[42]

The prime minister had made himself accessible to the workers' delegation and that was to his credit; the *Mail and Empire*, advocate for the business class, was pleased that he had been 'firm' with the unemployed; but on most counts, as the *Toronto Star* demonstrated in its extensive coverage, it had not been a good day for Mr Bennett.

Out on the streets of Ottawa there was a further demonstration of the liberal democracy and 'rule of law' that the Tory prime minister had attempted to idealize. The municipality had denied the Workers' Economic Conference use of the municipal coliseum to hold its meetings;

it forbade the delegates to gather in Market Square, a traditional space for assemblies in Canadian cities, and the Dominion government ruled its extensive park space out of bounds for a rally. If they could have their way, the powers in Ottawa, in honour of the Imperial Conference, would have the city buttoned down tight except for a decrepit little street in the south end.

But the organizers of the Workers' Economic Conference felt otherwise. They were determined that supporters who had streamed into Ottawa from all parts of the country, in spite of an attempted government blockade, would have a chance to make their stand in the heart of the capital city: they would ignore the 'rule of law' in favour of honouring the 'right of assemblage.'

Volunteers, therefore, handed out thousands of mimeographed, bilingual leaflets on Monday, 1 August, calling upon citizens to 'Demonstrate against Hunger and War' the next day in Market Square at 1:30 p.m.[43] A crowd of six or seven thousand showed up – participants and onlookers.

As related in the *Toronto Star*, the delegates to the Workers' Economic Conference, numbering about 500, wearing red arm bands, and singing the 'Red Flag,' paraded across the city to Market Square. There city police and the RCMP quickly dispersed them without disorder. The delegates then scrambled to the nearby park. To the cheers of the audience, speaker after speaker 'extolled Sovietism and exhorted the unemployed to assert their rights.' As Mabel Marlowe, the eighteen-year-old from Port Arthur, spoke, police rushed through the crowd using 'fists, batons and boots,' arresting many who 'showed signs of fight.' Lillian Wilkinson, fresh from her interview with the prime minister, was one of those arrested. A banner was hoisted up inscribed 'Fools slave, men fight.' To watching journalists it seemed to be a signal, whereupon the 'Reds' sat down on the ground and refused to budge. Police picked them up bodily and if they sat down again used a club. Boos and jeers 'roared out from the crowd,' and the police turned their attention in that direction, moving bystanders along after whacking a few heads with their billies. Over on Parliament Hill, while the crowd of unemployed 'surged against the wrought iron and stone fence' which surrounds the Hill, anxious Mounties marched back and forth 'with eyes alert,' according to a *Toronto Star* reporter, and admitted no one inside the gates without inquiry.[44]

'In a few hours,' observed Canada's largest circulation newspaper, the workers' economic conference meeting in Ottawa 'created a greater furore than the delegates of the empire have in ten days.'[45]

The official organ of the Workers' Unity League summed up the conference by reflecting on the delegates who had come from the point of production, from the bread lines, from the shacks of working-class neighbourhoods. They had little or no expense money and they slept on the sawdust in the old garage with no complaints, not a murmur. Their only conversation was their 'experiences along the line of travel,' the 'building of the unemployed movement,' and their 'demands on Bennett and his Government.' Those delegates were part of 'the cream of the revolutionary working class of Canada,' it said, and if Bennett could have heard them as they rested on the sawdust, 'he would see the writing on the wall.'[46]

With no time to waste, a large group of the participants in the Workers' Economic Conference, 140 to be exact, hurried away in high spirits to attend the first national congress of the Workers' Unity League. The congress had been announced to take place in Toronto, but this was to throw the government and its police agents off the scent for a while. It actually opened in Montreal, at 10:00 a.m., on 5 August.

8

The First Congress of the
Workers' Unity League 1932

The First Congress of the WUL represents a historic landmark in the consolidation of the revolutionary union movement and the organisation and leadership of the struggles of the Canadian workers against the capitalist offensive upon our standards of living.

> –Resolution Adopted at the First Congress of the Workers'
> Unity League, Montreal, August 1932

The Communist Party is firmly convinced that [a new economic and social order] can only be brought about through violence and bloodshed and with, at least, a temporary dictatorship. They can think only in terms of Russia. We in the CCF believe that it may be possible to bring about fundamental changes in Canada by peaceable and orderly means. Only the event will prove whether we are right.

> – J.S. Woodsworth, MP, *Winnipeg Free Press*, 19 January 1933

Today there are hundreds of independent neighborhood unemployed organizations; almost every large city has one or more ... most of them under reformist ideology and leadership, some of whom are putting up militant struggles over the heads of their leaders.

> – J. Burns [pseud. of Stewart Smith] *Workers' Unity*, August–September 1932

There was much talk of sectarianism in speeches at the first congress of the Workers' Unity League. Actually, two kinds of sectarianism.

The first kind was the sectarianism of going it alone. This sectarianism arose from a variety of sources: a sense of superiority; lack of trust; criticism of others' personal habits such as drinking, gambling, and church-going; or perhaps inertia, an absence of resolve, insufficient nerve to go out in search of allies for some campaign or act of resistance. The need to reach out might be as varied as helping a neighbour facing eviction, a demand at city hall for adequate relief, help to a beleaguered picket line. Speaker after speaker exhorted each other that the remedy for this type of 'sectarianism' within the ranks of the Workers' Unity League was to initiate a 'united front from below,' that is to say, to approach neighbours, workmates, acquaintances, strangers, members of other organizations, to build coalitions in favour of taking some part in the struggle. This sectarianism was mainly about questions of practice.

The second type of sectarianism was ideological. It concerned strategy and tactics for advancing the cause of working people. This kind of sectarianism was about questions of principle that needed to be debated and clarified. Anarchists, communists, social democrats, Trotskyists, and others on the left held divergent views on the relative value of parliamentary representation, the strike weapon, 'class struggle' versus 'class collaboration,' 'Mondism,' reform and revolution, the origin and place of 'force and violence' in social change, 'building socialism in one country,' and other related questions. As a result of these differences their debates would descend into vendettas of bitter name-calling, the tone often exaggerated by *agents provocateurs* or the zeal of the newly converted, using terms such as opportunist, traitor, betrayer, disrupter, splitter, 'agents of Moscow,' 'agents of the boss,' 'social-fascists,' 'fakir,' 'carrion, renegades, spawn,' hypocrites, demagogues …

This kind of sectarianism plagued the socialist movement from its very beginnings, as the writings of Karl Marx testify. 'The sect views its *raison d'être* and its *point d'honneur* not in what it has *in common* with the class movement,' Marx wrote, 'but in a special shibboleth that distinguishes it from this movement.' The ideas of sects could be a form of enrichment and were justified historically, Marx thought, when the working class was not yet sufficiently mature for an independent historical movement, but as soon as it reached that degree of maturity, all sects were 'essentially reactionary' because they demanded that 'the class movement subordinate itself to a special sectarian movement.' That was what the history of the International showed: 'the obsolete seeks to renovate and maintain itself within the newly won forms.' Lozovsky knew and wrote about these judgments of sectarianism as he led the Red International in the early twentieth century.[1]

Sectarianism took on new significance in Canada in the summer of 1932 with the founding of the social democratic Co-operative Commonwealth Federation (CCF) in Calgary. This happened in the same week as the Workers' Unity League held its first congress in Montreal. There were now two potentially formidable competitors on the road to socialism in Canada; how would they interact during this time of economic chaos and heightened class struggles? For the communists, the Workers' Unity League congress was a 'first test' and it had a surprising element.

The congress opened on a Friday morning, 5 August 1932, with J.B. McLachlan, fresh from his triumphs at the Workers' Economic Conference, in the chair. There were ninety-eight delegates representing ten affiliated unions, an equal number of 'Left Wing Shop Groups,' and thirty-four fraternal representatives from organizations such as Unemployed Councils, the Canadian Labour Defense League, and the Workers' International Relief.[2] McLachlan was an experienced chairperson of union meetings and the opening formalities proceeded with dispatch: the appointment of a credentials committee of three; brief greetings from various places and organizations – British workers, the striking coal miners of Alberta, the Canadian Labour Defense League, and the Workers' International Relief; the election of a congress committee of eighteen members and the formation of sub-committees on resolutions, finance, program, and constitution.[3]

McLachlan then introduced James Litterick, national secretary of the WUL, to make the opening report, and he was followed with co-reports by Harvey Murphy on organization, George Winslade on the unemployed movement, and Joshua Gershman, garment workers' organizer, on the Red International. Gershman had recently returned from representing Canada at the eighth session of the Central Council of the RILU in Moscow.[4]

Litterick, thirty-one, was a relative newcomer to the movement. After joining the Communist Party in Scotland he had migrated to Canada in 1925 and worked in the forests and mines of British Columbia for a few years. The Canadian party discovered him and appointed him as an organizer, moving him to Montreal when the WUL was founded in 1930. He did well and after Tom Ewen was sentenced to Kingston Penitentiary, Litterick became acting national secretary. A few years later, in the 1936 Manitoba general election, he became the first communist ever elected to a provincial or state-level legislature in North America.

On this day Litterick spoke about 'the new offensive against the workers and the tasks of the WUL.' It was a brief but far-ranging report, delivered in a reasoned tone without hint of narrow sectarian clamour. He cited facts to show that capitalism was in a 'definite state of collapse.'

The point was to check the capitalists' way out of the crisis, their wage cuts, lay-offs, part-time work, government budget cuts, and other measures that placed the burdens of the crisis on workers, small farmers, sections of the middle class, and government workers. Since 65 per cent of the delegates to the Congress were themselves unemployed, part of that great army of jobless now approaching a million in Canada (and about forty million world-wide), it seemed quite appropriate for the Congress to single out as a central task of the revolutionary trade union movement the organization of the everyday struggles of the unemployed.

In addition to that central task, Litterick presented a dizzying array of projects to be taken up by the Workers' Unity League: building its own unions, rooting itself in the factories and mine pits, winning over members of other unions through creating 'opposition groups,' warning against the class collaboration tactics and 'left manoeuvres' of the reformist leaders (as in the railway industry), helping to organize united front strikes against wage cuts, demanding government relief for those on short time or temporarily out of work, opposing Bennett's 'forced labour camps' where single unemployed worked for $5.00 to $7.50 per month, demanding non-contributory unemployment insurance for workers on long-term unemployment, and fighting against imperialist war and defending the Soviet Union, the heartland of socialist construction. There were so many urgent, 'main tasks' to be pursued. The main point, according to the final resolution of the Congress, was for the WUL to develop 'the independent leadership of the working class,' bypassing the established but inert trade unions. If properly understood and applied, this was thought of as a non-sectarian approach to the class struggle that grew out of the Strassburg Resolution's insistence on 'elected committees of action and elected strike committees' including everyone involved as the means to develop the 'fighting strength and initiative of the workers.'[5]

Litterick was mildly positive about the progress made by the Workers' Unity League in spite of many shortcomings. He commented that the league in 1930 was but a propaganda sect, but now it had passed into the stage of 'fighting for the independent leadership of the working class.' He claimed that out of eighty-eight strikes that took place in Canada in the previous year (according to government statistics), thirty-six were conducted by the WUL and 'most of these were won.'[6] He placed the membership of the WUL at between 14,000 and 15,000, composed of the three large affiliated unions – lumber, miners, and garment workers – as well as a number of smaller unions such as food workers, domestic

servants, marine, metal, and furniture workers, fishermen, and groups
and leagues such as in the railway, pulp and paper, and building trades,
and the Women's Labour League.[7] The credential committee's report
indicated a certain broadening out in terms of 'national composition':
Anglo-Saxons 29, Jewish 29, Finns 26, Ukrainian 8, French Canadian 5,
others 43. Eighty per cent of the participants were male, 20 per cent
female.

With almost fifty delegates making speeches in the plenary sessions
as well as those taking part in the various commissions established for
the lumber industry, railways, building trades, needle trades, youth, and
women, the delegates were constantly busy. But everyone came to attention in the middle of Saturday morning when something extraordinary
happened. The session chair, Jack Stevenson, a building trades worker
from North Burnaby, BC, suddenly introduced 'J. Burns, national committee member' to make a 'main contribution.'

Who was this Burns? No one had ever heard of such a person and delegates wondered as a young man in his twenties with blue eyes and a full
head of light brown hair took the podium. As soon as 'Burns' began to
speak, however, many delegates recognized the voice: 'Burns' was Stewart Smith in a wig.

As acting general secretary of the quasi-illegal Communist Party, Smith
had kept himself from the public eye, hoping to avoid the fate of his
colleagues presently sitting in jail. In spite of his assumption that his
whereabouts escaped police surveillance, the RCMP noticed that he travelled about 'in disguise,' and while they were sure that he worked as
an organizer undercover on 'orders from the heads of the Communist
Party in Moscow,' they did nothing to stop him.[8] Smith appeared now, at
the national congress of the Workers' Unity League, with the honorific
title of 'national committee member,' as the Canadian communist considered most likely capable of making a theoretically sophisticated and
authoritative analysis of the tasks at hand.

If the delegates expected to hear some 'fire and brimstone,' attacks
on 'social fascists' or 'renegades,' they would be disappointed. Smith
delivered what was for him a subdued address, more like the censorious
professor that Salsberg had once complained of than a revolutionary
agitator. His topic was building 'the united front – some errors and shortcomings,' the twin dangers of 'right opportunism' and 'left sectarianism.'

Fully a third of the speech, at least as it was published,[9] dwelt on errors
made during the Crowsnest Pass miners' strike, a strike led by Harvey
Murphy and still in progress. The educational purpose of Smith's heavy

emphasis on the 'left sectarianism' and failure to develop 'a real united front' in this negative example may have had the subsidiary aim of reining in a growing admiration for the as yet insufficiently unrepentant Murphy.

A crass example of 'right opportunism,' in Smith's exposition, was how a revolt of garment workers in Montreal against wage cuts, in which Joshua Gershman had a leading hand, played out. In a joint struggle led by communists and social democrats, many workers abandoned the corrupt American union run by Sydney Hillman from New York City, but then they joined a new Canadian union affiliated to the social democratic All-Canadian Congress of Labour. A 'revolt against class collaboration,' Smith exclaimed, had been diverted back 'into channels of class collaboration,' a move that some local communists justified as 'a necessary step in the direction of affiliation to the WUL.' To Smith the left wing 'was strangled' by this theory. If not resisted it would mean the 'liquidation of the Needle Trades Workers' Industrial Union' and, without 'a fighting program,' the workers would be no further ahead. A well-understood, well-executed united front policy entailed both unity and struggle – an idea that was not always easy to grasp and was harder still to perform.

The most astonishing part of Smith's address concerned the struggles of the unemployed and the recognition that he accorded the efforts of the reformists in this connection. He reiterated a self-criticism of the Workers' Unity League presented in George Winslade's report, which was that by trying to build an organization of the unemployed, the National Unemployed Workers' Association, with membership cards and a constitution, the WUL was following a narrow, sectarian path. But then he went further to suggest that the reformists were actually doing a better job with the unemployed than the Workers' Unity League. 'Today there are hundreds of independent neighbourhood unemployed organizations,' he said, 'almost every large city has one or more ... *most of them under reformist ideology and leadership* [emphasis added] some of whom are putting up militant struggles over the heads of their leaders.' A proper approach to unemployed work, according to Smith, would 'draw these organizations into struggles on the basis of the united front' with democratically elected neighbourhood councils and relief committees. In other words, the purpose of the united front was not a sectarian one, not to bring the unemployed into the WUL via the NUWA, but rather '*to develop the independent leadership of the workers.*' As indicated above, this phrase became a much cited, and possibly not entirely understood, concept of the Congress. Through leading the unemployed into militant struggles for their needs, the WUL would thoroughly expose the expected 'treachery of the reformist leaders, the shams and hypocrisy of bourgeois democracy and government.' This was the way that the WUL organizations and adherents should understand and apply the united front to the struggles of the unemployed. This was the way that, indirectly, the WUL would grow in prestige and in numbers. This was the way for the WUL to shed its inceptive sectarian skin.

Although Smith did not refer to the founding of the Co-operative Commonwealth Federation, the delegates were aware of the surge in popularity of Canadian social democracy in 1932, a surge that had grown in response to the increasingly militant, anti-capitalist rhetoric of several of its main leaders. Smith fretted about the 'reformists strengthening their position' and the 'rapid growth' in social democratic ideology, a concern echoed by a Canadian in the Anglo-American Secretariat, in Moscow, who wrote that 'the social-fascists [have] practically taken over our entire set of demands.'[10]

It is not difficult to imagine why the communists were nervous about the new-found confidence of their rivals. The eight policies adopted by the founding convention of the CCF in Calgary on 1 August 1932 embraced some important tenets of socialism:

(1) the establishment of a planned system of social economy for the production, distribution and exchange of all goods and services; (2) socialization of the banking, credit and financial system of the country together with the social ownership, development, operation and control of utilities and natural resources; (3) security of tenure for the worker and the farmer in his home; (4) retention and extension of all existing social legislation and facilities, with adequate provision for insurance against crop failure, illness, accident, old age and unemployment; (5) equal economic and social opportunity without regard to sex, nationality or religion; (6) encouragement of all co-operative enterprises aiming at the achievement of the Co-operative Commonwealth Federation; (7) socialization of health services; (8) acceptance by the Federal Government of responsibility for the unemployed through the supplying of suitable work or adequate maintenance.

Leading members of the CCF hailed the new party as the alternative to revolution, the 'surest way of preventing the encroaching cataclysm' foretold by the communists.[11]

The communists, of course, did not believe the social democrats were sincere in their support for socialism; they thought the CCF would abandon their platform in due time. All the same, many left-thinking workers were heartened by the support for socialist ideology that the CCF platform showed, and this may help to explain the measure of restraint in the language used by the Canadian communists in the summer of 1932 in defining the differences between reformist socialism and their own concept of Marxist 'class struggle' revolution.

When Litterick summed up the general discussion of the congress he picked up on the recurrent, underlying question that Smith had tried to bring to the centre of attention: how to struggle against reformists and at the same time try to build a united front with them? How to have unity as well as struggle? Litterick thought not enough had been said on exposing the policies of the 'fakirs' that 'betray the workers to the bosses' and disarm the workers for the struggle. At the same time, he said, 'we cannot do it by shouting and calling them names,' after having perhaps inadvertently just called them one, but by 'pointing out all the small things ... explaining, by giving examples ... by bringing forward our policy.' It was an appeal for reasonableness. The main resolution adopted by the WUL Congress called for persuasion and a 'comradely approach' to workers of 'all political convictions and all organisations' as the means of working for a united front.[12] Given the continued use of the sectarian term 'social fascist' to describe social democratic reformists by the Red International in Europe,[13] it is remarkable, in retrospect, that there was virtually no such exaggerated rhetoric in the resolutions and published documents of the First National Congress of the Workers' Unity League.[14] This absence goes some distance to undermine claims about Canadian communists' automatic 'subservience to Moscow' so often aired in criminal trials and by representatives of the capitalist class.

Something not so well documented is a significant change that occurred in the relationship of the Workers' Unity League and the Red International during this period. The congress of the WUL, in adopting the report of its program committee, actually reiterated the existing relationship, namely that the WUL was the Canadian section and placed itself 'under the leadership of the Red International of Labour Unions.'[15] But later, in December, Joshua Gershman, one of the WUL authorities on the Red International, made reference in an article in the *Worker* suggesting that at its congress the WUL had, in fact, adopted a 'broader International policy ... by establishing *fraternal relationship* with the Red International of Labour Unions' (emphasis added). Henceforth, according to the amended constitution, the WUL would not be 'entering into any organic relations or connections' with the Red International.[16] Was this a casual announcement of divorce? What had happened in the intervening four months to cause a separation that Tom Ewen had once vowed would never be allowed?[17]

What seems obvious is that the communists were thinking about the probability of further attacks on their legality and on the Workers' Unity League, and the possible use which the government might make of the claim that the league and its organizers were not only subservient to a foreign power but also advocates of force and violence in making social change.[18] This concern took on added urgency when, after the trial and conviction of the eight top communist leaders in Ontario on such charges, the attorney general of that province, William H. Price, began contacting the attorneys general of the other provinces in an effort to encourage them to follow Ontario's example. To support his campaign he had his office prepare a pamphlet called *Agents of Revolution: A History of the Workers' Unity League, Setting Forth Its Origin and Aims*, alleging that 'the whole organization was a mere subordinate branch' of the illegal Communist Party of Canada and citing captured letters and telegrams between the WUL in Toronto and the RILU to illustrate the case.[19] Price's offensive spelled trouble and led the league's organizers to think of ways to blunt his attacks. This eventually resulted in a redrafting of their constitution and stripping it of such phrases as 'the final overthrow of capitalism' and the establishment of 'a Revolutionary Workers' Government,' which had such an ominous ring in the ears of jurors when read out in a court of law.

Already by 1932 there were hesitant but unmistakable signs that, under the insistent prodding of the capitalist class, governments were further stiffening their attitudes toward the militant workers' organization. This was true in Manitoba and particularly so in British Columbia.

The lumber operators in British Columbia, described by one of their own number as 'tough, selfish, and ruthless employers,'[20] were especially active not only in slashing their costs at the expense of their employees but also in urging the provincial government to repress any countermeasures by the workers. The operators had grown anxious in the spring as they watched Arthur 'Slim' Evans, newly appointed district organizer of the Workers' Unity League, and Arne Johnson, secretary of the league's Lumber Workers' Industrial Union, mobilizing organizers to distribute tens of thousands of leaflets calling workers to oppose the 30 per cent wage cuts instituted by firms such as Timberland Mills in New Westminster. The operators realized that the unions' ranks were swelling and, dissatisfied by lack of punitive action by the provincial attorney general, they had sent one of their number, J.G. Robson, president of Timberland, to Ottawa to seek the intervention of the ideologically congenial General MacBrien, commissioner of the RCMP. MacBrien assured his visitor that 'if the Attorney-General of B.C. would declare the Communist Party an illegal organization and request our assistance, this Force would clean up 61 Cordova Street in 24 hours.'[21] The address given was the British Columbia headquarters of the Workers' Unity League and several of its affiliated unions. This was the message the lumber operators wanted to hear. MacBrien ordered that the relevant RCMP files needed to make such a prosecution under Section 98 of the Criminal Code be sent to the BC attorney general.

Nothing much happened until the union led most of the 140 workers at Timberland Mills out on strike in September 1932. According to a report of RCMP superintendent S.T. Wood, of the strikers involved '90 [were] Japanese, 20 Hindu and the remainder Whites,' and following an established pattern the Workers' Unity League had sent a truckload or two of unemployed workers from Vancouver to bolster the picket line on the first few mornings in order to discourage the company from trying to bring in scabs. Mill owner Robson was furious as he watched while several provincial police stood on the other side of the street and a picket line peacefully circled his plant with placards demanding a 10 per cent wage raise.

The attorney general was understandably cautious about 'cleaning out 61 Cordova Street West,' since the best legal advice he could obtain told him there was no evidence in MacBrien's files that would ensure a successful prosecution under Section 98 of the Criminal Code. There was nothing in the reports of the police undercover operatives or in the materials seized in police raids on Cordova Street that expressed the purpose of bringing about governmental, industrial, or economic change in Canada 'by use of Force, Violence or Physical injury to person or property'; there had to be evidence bringing the accused within these words before a conviction 'could stand the test of the Courts.'[22] The provincial government's solicitor, W.H. Bullock-Webster, proposed an alternative, which was to have the chief constable of Vancouver, the superintendent of the RCMP at Vancouver, and the commissioner of British Columbia police, acting together, confront the landlord of the premises and tell him verbally that an unlawful association was using his building and unless he terminated their tenancy 'as soon as possible' action would be taken against him under Section 98 of the Criminal Code. This empty threat could be repeated just as often as new premises were occupied.

'I admit,' said Bullock-Webster, 'that this procedure would be bluff, but I think it can be so strongly presented that the effect would be satisfactory.' This method of denying people with 'undesirable thoughts' a place to propagate them became standard procedure in British Columbia and before long the WUL and its unions found themselves scrambling to find new headquarters.

Meanwhile delegations of angry mill owners and the executive of the BC Lumber and Shingle Manufacturers' association repeatedly interviewed the provincial premier and the attorney general, demanding that the province make a definite request to the RCMP for help in a strike situation which, they said, was threatening to engulf the province's largest industry. This plea was successful and in short order a large force, including thirty-five Mounties as well as provincial and local police, was on the scene at Timberland, smashing the picket line with clubs and whips and defeating the strike. Such a large and co-ordinated attack by local and national forces had not been seen before by the labour movement in British Columbia and it was an ominous sign to the Workers' Unity League.

Another straw in the wind indicating tougher times ahead for the Workers' Unity League was the arrest of Arthur Evans, its organizer in BC, his trial and conviction under Section 98 of the Criminal Code, and especially the way this was accomplished in the midst of a formidable coal miners' strike in Princeton, British Columbia.

Evans had been returning from the national congress of the WUL in Montreal and, at the invitation of a coal miners' committee, stopped over in Princeton to help the miners find a way to challenge the wage-cutting, speed-up campaign of the bosses and to correct the dismal safety record of mines that, in the busy season, employed up to 600 men. The miners, many of them Yugoslavs, were nervously eager to hear from him. At first, fearing retaliation and deportation, they met after dark, 300 of them, in a vacant lot. 'It had got so dark,' Evans wrote afterwards, 'that no one was recognizable, so with nothing but a flash light to read the notes with I started.' Since it was a well-grassed lot and he wanted to talk 'for at least an hour and a half,' he suggested that they should all sit down and 'therefore not tire themselves too much.' After outlining the policies of the Workers' Unity League and explaining its unique strike tactics in which 'the miners themselves must actively participate in order to make it a success,' Evans left for Vancouver, promising to come back when the weather turned cold and the mines would have many orders to fill.[23]

When Evans returned in mid-November, hundreds of workers, the employed as well as the unemployed, jammed into meetings night after night at the Scandinavian Hall, the Orange Hall, the Princess Theatre, and other places to hear him speak. He advertised various topics, including 'Fifteen Years of Building Socialism in the U.S.S.R.,' to remind the townspeople that there was a working alternative to capitalism. Evans established committees to refine the demands of the miners, to prepare demonstrations by the unemployed for better relief from the local government, and to create women's and youth auxiliaries. Even a wedding dance at the Independent Order of Oddfellows' hall turned into a mobilization at which Evans spoke and sang 'The Internationale,' reportedly to great effect.

'Evans is gaining a large following of miners and unemployed,' wrote Sergeant G.J. Duncan, in charge of Boundary District for the Provincial Police, adding that 'while a good deal of the substance of his speeches is of an inflammatory nature,' it would not be an easy matter to convict Evans under the Criminal Code. Duncan's superior agreed and wrote to the RCMP for help, saying, 'This man seems to be establishing himself as quite a danger, and if there is any way of removing him it would help considerably.'[24]

In preparation for the expected strike, Attorney General R.N. Pooley ordered thirty members of the Provincial Police to Princeton and the Mounties sent a force of ten; supporters of the mine owners formed a Citizens' League to combat 'industrial hooliganism' and to protect 'British democracy'; a hastily created branch of the Ku Klux Klan burned crosses on the mountain and pasted notes on the doors of union leaders, saying, 'Take Note. The Fiery Cross Has Spoken. Agitators Take Warning and Move On or Suffer the Consequences.' In this case no one was arrested for intimidation. The police imported into the area, wrote the *Unemployed Worker*, 'brutally clubbed the workers, entering their homes and intimidating them.'[25] When the strike began, on 1 December, the police at first tried escorting scabs into the mines, but when that proved futile against the shouting and booing of hundreds of men, women, and children on the picket lines, they attacked the picketers with clubs and whips as they had done at Timberland. The workers had established their capacity to stand up to the boss class, but a number were arrested, including Evans, who was whisked away to Penticton on 7 December, charged under Section 98 of the Criminal Code, and taken to Oakalla Jail near Vancouver, far from the scene of the strike, to be held without bail for six weeks. In preparation for the trial the commissioner of the British Columbia Police, J.H. McMullin, took the view that this case 'might have quite a bearing' on the activity of organizers of demonstrations in the coming winter, and in seeking the support of the RCMP said he was 'anxious that no stone is left unturned to bring it to a successful conclusion.'[26] The crown prosecutor, the same Bulloch-Webster, scoured the materials of the First National Congress of the WUL, taken from Evans's suitcase, hoping to make a case that would establish the WUL as an illegal organization under the control of Moscow, but could find nothing and eventually had to settle for getting Evans sentenced to eighteen months with hard labour for seditious utterances. Tom Bradley, who had been so successful during the Fraser Mills strike, came up immediately from Vancouver to replace the imprisoned Evans, and within a few days the union was able to win its demands at the largest mine. This was cause of great satisfaction to the workers: a 10 per cent raise in wages, the company recognized the Pit Committee, the Pit Committee asked the mine inspector to stop haulage during the changing of shifts as a safety measure, all strikers were to be re-employed without discrimination during the term of the agreement, and there would be no production of coal on Sundays.[27]

The victory was welcomed by the miners and established a solid base for the Mine Workers' Union in Princeton. But for the Workers' Unity League the increasing intensity of attacks by the state in 1932 and the probability of more costly challenges in the courts caused its leaders to amend the legal form, though not the ideological ties, of the organization's association with the Red International of Trade Unions. This change, they calculated, would remove a trump card in the prosecution's attack, and the amendment appeared as one of several carefully considered alterations to the constitution that the league formally adopted the following year at its second national congress.[28] Whether the constitutional change actually helped buffer the league and its unions against attacks through the Criminal Code is unknown, but it is certain, as later events proved, that their champion organizer, Arthur 'Slim' Evans, emerged from jail at the end of 1934 a folk hero and more effective than ever.

9

Women of the Workers' Unity League: Taking Their Place Side by Side as Activists in the Labour Market

The women workers have no interests apart from those of the working class generally. There is no room for 'feminism' in our movement.

– Leslie Morris, editor of the *Worker*, 28 February 1931

Communism will raise women for the first time in human history to full equality with men, and do away with the capitalist enslavement of women.

– *Worker*, 22 July 1933

It is true that, primarily in the CPC, some activists personally challenged the inequalities of traditional marriage and family life, but these experiments represented a courageous minority rather than the prevailing majority.

– Joan Sangster, historian[1]

With the deepening of the crisis of capitalism in the 1930s, the lives of working-class women became all the more difficult. Women were already paid lower wages than men, and were often employed in mechanized industries where they faced the constant threat of speed-ups. As well, they frequently had to work a double day, balancing their paid work with their unpaid work of raising a family and managing a household. During the 1930s, things got worse. On the situation of employed women in the 1930s, the report of the first Workers' Unity League National Congress stated: 'The average earnings of women workers have decreased from $12 per week in 1926 to $9 per week in 1930; at the same time the hours of labour have increased from 48 per week to 52 hours per week.'[2]

On top of this, employed women, especially those who were married, faced a general social attitude that saw women as stealing work away from men. Full-time housewives endured hardship as well. The wife of a working-class man often saw her family's income reduced as her husband's wages were cut, and many families endured long strike struggles as a result; if husbands became unemployed the families could face a life of relief handouts, eviction, and hunger.

During this time working-class women struggled to improve the conditions of their existence. Many stood up and fought for a better life for themselves and for their families, challenging popular stereotypes of frivolous girls and obedient housewives. And some stood up to the capitalist system itself by participating in activities led by the Workers' Unity League.

One of the means through which the Workers' Unity League could potentially reach out to working women was an existing organization known as the Women's Labour Leagues. At first, however, the WUL had difficulty making the connection.

The Women's Labour Leagues had started in Winnipeg around the time of the General Strike in 1919, like many other labour organizations. The cross-class alliances that had developed around the suffrage struggles dissolved when suffrage for a majority of women was won in the years between 1916 and 1925.[3] For class-conscious working-class women the large, established organizations like the YWCA, women's auxiliaries in the churches, the Women's Christian Temperance Union, the Imperial Order Daughters of the Empire, the Navy Leagues, and the National Council of Women had little direct appeal. The Communist Party recognized that such organizations were 'directed toward the alleviation of human suffering,'[4] but it believed that working-class women needed an organization with a focus on trade unionism for women, equal pay for equal work, and the enforcement and expansion of minimum wage laws, if they were to find freedom from oppression.[5] With the CP's help, by 1924 there were eleven branches of the Women's Labour Leagues across the country.[6] That year the scattered groups held a convention in London, Ontario, out of which was formed the Federation of Women's Labour Leagues, a national body that would lead the organization for the next five years. The federation, under the guidance of Communist Party organizer Florence Custance, continued to grow, and, in 1926, the first edition of the *Woman Worker* appeared, with Custance as the editor. By 1929 there were around sixty affiliates, including some groups of maids organized in the Domestic Workers' Union. The relationship of the Women's Labour Leagues to the Communist Party is slightly opaque, but it seems clear that the party considered them to be the expression of the activities of its women's department, a department that consisted mainly, if not entirely, of Custance. At the same time it also seems clear that, in 1929, the Federation of Women's Labour Leagues considered itself a non-sectarian, non-party movement, and was working actively with leftist non-communist groups and individuals.[7] These contradictions would play out in 1929, a year of great change for the Women's Labour Leagues.

In 1929 a letter from the women's secretariat of the Third International arrived in Toronto harshly criticizing the Communist Party for its lack of leadership and supervision of the women's department.[8] The letter was discussed during the party's sixth national convention in June of that year, and members of the executive committee were highly critical of themselves for allowing 'the gravest of errors to be committed by the director of this department without any attempts at correction.'[9] With regard to the director of the women's department, Custance, the convention concluded:

> The orientation of the Director of the Women's Dept. has not been based on winning the masses of working women for the revolutionary movement, it has been rather an orientation of conniving stratas of the petit bourgeoisie. The approach has been mainly to housewives while little has been done towards reaching the masses of organized and unorganized factory women, and we have looked upon the Women's Labour Leagues as practically our sole basis for this work. The propaganda put forth has been petit-bourgeois, pacifist in character, impermissible in the Communist party.[10]

The essential issue, divorced from the somewhat dramatic style of the party literature, was that Custance had been guiding the women's department and the Women's Labour Leagues in a path too conciliatory to other women's organizations, giving air to reformist arguments, rather than condemning them while promoting the view that true emancipation for both sexes could only come with the end of capitalism. Custance had gone too far astray and the 1929 convention resolved, in a sectarian fashion, that 'the former friendly attitude towards these [reformist] organizations (inviting speakers to address the WLL meetings, etc.) must be condemned.' As for the *Woman Worker*, the 'impermissible social democratic ideology' that had permeated the policy of the magazine was seen as the main evidence of the unacceptable direction of the women's department.[11] It was resolved that the paper be reworked to ensure that all of the articles reflected the militant stance of the class struggle. As if these strong criticisms of 'Ma Custance' weren't enough to shake up the women party members and the Women's Labour Leagues membership, in mid-July of 1929 Florence Custance died, leaving the women's department, the Federation of Women's Labour Leagues, and the *Woman Worker* without a leader, and leaving Custance without a chance to respond to her critics.

Within six months, a new executive of the Federation of the Women's Labour Leagues was hastily formed, based on an emergency convention held in Toronto by just two local branches of the league, one English-speaking and the other Yiddish-speaking. At this gathering Alice Buck took over as interim leader.

The decision to hold an emergency convention in Toronto and to elect Buck was significant for at least two reasons. Firstly, in 1929, of the sixty local groups affiliated to the Federation of Women's Labour Leagues, only four were English-speaking (Toronto, Calgary, Vancouver, and Regina), and two Yiddish (Toronto and Montreal), and the rest, representing 98 per cent of individual membership, were Finnish and mainly centred in Sudbury and other parts of Northern Ontario.[12] Holding a rump convention was a violation of democratic practice and it rankled in members' minds. Secondly, the choice of Alice Buck, wife of Tim Buck, as the new leader of the federation was a clear statement that the Women's Labour Leagues would move in line with the new leadership of the Communist Party at a time, in 1929, when the internal politics of the party were in transition, with prominent party members, especially among the Finns in Sudbury, in revolt against the central party leadership in Toronto.[13] Bitter words and some muddled thinking coloured the process by which the Women's Labour Leagues became part of the Workers' Unity League.

Nevertheless, more locals of the Women's Labour Leagues began responding to the appeals of Rebecca (Becky) Buhay, who emerged as the leading communist woman organizer of this period.

Educated in the British school system before emigrating to Canada in 1913, Buhay retained her British accent and had the didactic manner of a proverbial high school Latin teacher – there was so much to do, so much to learn, so little time. Always searching and self-critical, from her posts as head of the women's departments of both the Communist Party and, for a short while, the Workers' Unity League, she berated her comrades on the central committee, saying the 'party as a whole has never placed women's work in its correct perspective.'[14] She sent letters to local organizers and communist fractions in the Women's Labour Leagues and Workers' Unity League typically giving instructions for half a dozen urgent campaigns all at once, with the word 'must' appearing in every other sentence. These communications would be followed up by complaining letters asking why she wasn't getting any reports of work accomplished from her harried or baffled correspondents. By her unflagging dedication, her courage in the face of danger, and her influence upon other women, Buhay undoubtedly qualifies as a pioneer socialist feminist in Canada. The sleuths of the government's secret service, who compiled a large dossier on her activities, discerned her as a person of 'refined manner ... good habits ... well-liked by most of the extreme element,' with 'good knowledge of Marxian socialism, first class speaker and good agitator ... particularly noted for her open air speeches.'[15]

As a result of Buhay's efforts, in the winter of 1931 units of the Women's Labour Leagues began to affiliate to the Workers' Unity League with groups in Sylvan Lake, Canmore, and Blairmore, Alberta, leading the way under the leadership of local organizer Mary North. Meadow Portage, Manitoba, followed their lead and joined by early February. Affiliation of the large Finnish contingent in Northern Ontario was more difficult to achieve. The Sudbury party organizer, A. Newman, articulated the concerns of the local women in a letter sent to the party office in Toronto. Newman claimed that the women in Sudbury 'seemed to be against such an affiliation.' He himself did not see any point in affiliating to the Workers' Unity League at that time, especially since the Women's Labour Leagues were made up of mostly housewives and the unity league was meant to be a centre for trade union activity.[16] More promisingly, Aino Lahti, active in the Kirkland Lake area, wrote to Toronto near the end of January to ask for more information so that she could be better able to appeal to the local women to join, especially since 'many branches are not aware of what the Workers' Unity League stands for.'[17] On 24 March, likely as a response to Newman's earlier letter, Buhay sent a letter to the Sudbury area convention, explaining why, in her view, even Women's Labour Leagues composed largely of housewives ought to affiliate:

> The WLL, while consisting in the main of housewives, can play an important role in the economic struggles of the workers. As housewives they feel the full effect of the crisis through wage cuts, unemployment, and increased cost of living, and through their organization they can materially assist in building up an effective resistance against the capitalist offensive if, instead of being isolated as in the past, they link themselves up with the general stream of the revolutionary movement.[18]

But, two days later, Tim Buck received another letter from Newman protesting the abrupt and high-handed manner in which the affiliation of the Women's Labour Leagues to the Workers' Unity League had been carried out. Buck admitted that mistakes had been made and said that they would be corrected. But he noted that as far as he knew from his conversations with Ewen, head of the Workers' Unity League, and Buhay, Sudbury was the only place to have offered any protest, and, in fact, Ewen had already received many requests for membership cards.[19] Based on the record of correspondence, apart from a letter from Bessie Schacter in Montreal, this appears to be true.[20] Indeed, a letter from Catherine Lesire, a communist organizer in Vancouver, far from questioning why the Women's Labour League should want to affiliate with the Workers' Unity League, implied the opposite: she expressed frustration that the Women's Labour Leagues in her area had become full of 'white pink and very little red,' and thus not appealing to the class-conscious working-class woman.[21]

In any event, by mid-April, Lyyli Toivonen, secretary of the Sudbury district Women's Labour League, had ordered one hundred membership cards from the Workers' Unity League, and, by the end of May, most Women's Labour Leagues in the Timmins, Sudbury, and Kirkland Lake areas had affiliated. As well, the national leadership in Toronto prepared a draft new constitution for the Women's Labour Leagues, and, possibly as a way of mending relations with the Finns, mailed it to Sudbury for revision and approval before sending it out nationally. By mid-June, Toivonen in Sudbury reported that the draft was being circulated and was being well received and 'generally approved of.'[22] The transition of the Women's Labour Leagues to the Workers' Unity League was certainly rough and too hurried, and the communist leaders involved were forced to recognize their faults.[23] But the party and its champion, Becky Buhay, were highly reluctant to lose the opportunity to lead an already established and generally progressive group of women into battle against capitalist exploitation.[24]

In the end, joining the Workers' Unity League gave the Women's Labour Leagues a new unifying focus: to strive for the improvement of the living and working conditions of working-class women through vigorous support of various economic and social issues and the drive for industrial trade unionism. And the process, in fact, helped to clarify and strengthen the views of the Communist Party and Workers' Unity League on the important place women could have in the class struggle. Though the major gains of women in the Canadian workforce were made during the Second World War, the events of the Great Depression, the period during which the Women's Labour Leagues and women's auxiliaries were affiliated with the Workers' Unity League, occupy an enormous place in the working-class culture of Canada. This period was also key as workers developed the organizing skills, the language of demands, and the political solidarity that led to the subsequent gains. The hundreds of strike struggles, long lines for relief provisions, home foreclosures, massive protests and marches for civil rights, and campaigns for unemployment insurance all defined that era and influenced the state of the nation for decades afterwards. And it becomes evident that women, as active participants and as significant leaders in the campaigns of the Workers' Unity League, played a prominent role in this process.[25]

At the beginning, in 1930, the main focus of activity for the Women's Labour Leagues was a campaign organized by Buhay to send a delegation of working women to the Soviet Union to learn about the new social and economic system being constructed there. The motivations underlying this campaign were to inspire people with the possibility of having an alternative to the capitalist system and to defend the world's socialist heartland by helping the Soviet Union break out from international isolation. At that time, as frequent articles in the daily press and an outpouring of books attest, the desire for news about the Soviet Union, both for and against, spread far beyond the confines of existing political parties. It was a fiercely contested topic but one in which left-wingers could receive an increasingly sympathetic hearing as the capitalist world spiralled downward in the Depression. As a result, concerted efforts to send in nominations and to raise funds for delegations to the Soviet Union became a constant feature in the life of the Women's Labour Leagues and of all related organizations during these years. Despite the subsequent revelations about some of the actual problems in the USSR and the related torrents of criticism, it is important to realize how powerful the vision of socialist life in the USSR was for working people elsewhere in the 1930s.

The six members of the Women's Labour Leagues who departed for Soviet Russia in August 1930 included two trade union activists: Bessie Schacter from Montreal, and Pearl Wedro from Winnipeg. The delegation also included Elsa Tynjala, a Finnish domestic worker from the Timmins area; Annie Whitfield, a Women's Labour League activist from Glace Bay in Cape Breton; Annie Zen, a Ukrainian Labour Farmer Temple Association member from Alberta, and Buhay.[26] During and after the trip, the members of the delegation wrote essays for the *Worker* based on their experiences, covering topics such as the role of youth, women in mining, support for mothers, women's emancipation, and health care in the Soviet Union.[27] These articles portrayed a positive view of the lives of workers, including women workers, though at least one member of the Canadian delegation, Annie Whitfield, privately expressed dismay at some conditions, particularly the long lines for food and supplies.[28] Publicly though, she wrote in the *Worker* that 'we were greatly impressed by the great change that the revolution has brought to women … Woman in the Soviet Union is equal socially and economically to man. She receives the same pay for the same kind of work. Motherhood is protected and the best possible is done for children.'[29]

Upon their return to Canada the participants spoke publicly about what they had seen in the Soviet Union, and even though organizers expressed some disappointment about the extent of their tours, these women undoubtedly talked to thousands of attentive Canadians, from Cape Breton to Vancouver.[30] As well, and perhaps this was the main practical objective of the trip, the women's delegation helped to inspire the founding of the Friends of the Soviet Union, a non-party organization dedicated to spreading information about 'the truth of what is going on in the Soviet Union, and to popularize her achievements in the building of Socialism.'[31] For this purpose the Vancouver Women's Labour Leaguers brought together around twenty participants from a range of organizations, including the American Federation of Labour, the All-Canadian Congress of Labour, and other union groups.[32] Within a few months there were several regional groupings of Friends of the Soviet Union and an established national organization.

There is no doubt the numerous reports of the successes of Soviet women in overcoming stereotypes and isolation in the home to become full members in society inspired many women in Canada. Apart from the many articles in the *Toronto Star* and in the *Worker* about the achievements of women in the Soviet Union (with such titles as 'Where Women Are Free,' 'Help the Working Women of the Soviet Union Build a New World of Social Economic and Sex Equality,' 'Conditions of Maternity Are Best in Entire World'),[33] other sources such as the *Canadian Unionist*, organ of the social democratic All-Canadian Congress of Labour, had reports in a similar vein. Even the arch-conservative Toronto *Mail and Empire* ran an article in 1931 extolling the great gains of women in the Soviet Union.[34] With accounts such as these confirming what their delegates had seen with their own eyes, progressive women in Canada had no reason to doubt that women in the USSR were making great advances. More importantly, the images these accounts provided of life for women in the USSR gave substance to their own ideas of what they wanted to see happen in Canada.

Historian Karen Petrone, reviewing the hard-lived experiences of women in the USSR during the 1920s and 1930s, concludes in a similar positive vein that one must argue for a nuanced reading of the Soviet gender system under Stalin's leadership. 'The enormous burdens that the system placed on women (and men) are undeniable,' she notes, 'yet this system also produced dynamic public, social, and professional identities for women that many actively embraced.'[35] The policy of the Soviet state, as economist Sarah Ashwin reminds us, was never directed at the liberation of women from men; rather it was aimed at breaking the subordination of women to the patriarchal family in order to free both sexes to serve the collective cause.[36] The beliefs of the most prominent members of the Women's Labour Leagues relating to ending women's subordination were along the same lines.[37]

The greatest public debate relating to women in Canada at this time was about whether or not married women should be allowed to work for pay.[38] In 1929, at the start of the Great Depression, there were about 130,000 unemployed workers in Canada, but by 1933 this figure had risen to well over 800,000.[39] For working-class people the situation was becoming increasingly desperate, as they struggled to feed themselves, and stay warm. As unemployment increased, the general attitude in society towards women, especially married women in the workforce, deteriorated. Even some members of liberal middle-class women's organizations such as the Councils of Women of Canada and the Business and Professional Women's Clubs were against the employment of married women, supporting the idea that women in the workplace were taking jobs away from unemployed men.[40] The Liberal premier of Ontario, Mitchell Hepburn, said, in 1936, 'We take the position, as have all previous governments, that if a woman marries, her husband should keep her.'[41] And to back up this statement, Hepburn fired six women public servants who had been hiding their marital status. He was not alone in his opinion. Three years earlier, the former mayor of Montreal, Mederic Martin, had written the following in *Chatelaine*:

> Wouldn't national life be happier, saner, safer if a great many of these [unemployed] men could be given work now being done by women, even if it meant that these women would have to sacrifice their financial independence? Go home to be supported by father, husband, or brother as they were in the old pre-feministic days?[42]

Clearly the Depression, with its mass unemployment, had provided fertile ground for a regression in society's acceptance of women, especially married women, being in the workplace or even being the principal breadwinner. Considerable sections of popular opinion had returned to the view that a woman's place was in the home, and that women ought to be obedient to men, who should be the major breadwinners. Officials from various bodies encouraged this Victorian, middle-class ideal of women, including the mayor of Winnipeg, who commended unemployed women who 'suffer in silence, not demanding this that and the other thing' and said that 'this is what makes our womanhood what it is.'[43] As historian Margaret Hobbs says, women could either take the role of 'dutiful daughter' or 'martyr mother.'[44]

But the reality of the employment situation for women was far more complex than the popular debate reflected. The main motivation for employers to hire women during the 1930s was that they were a source of cheap labour, generally being paid 50 per cent less than men doing the same work.[45] There was often, thus, a motivation for owners to lay off men, only to rehire women at a lower rate, which happened especially in the textile industry and the needle trades. By the mid-1930s there were minimum-wage laws for women, but it was widely known that these laws were not always followed; the British Columbia Department of Labour reported that, in 1932, a third of women were receiving below the minimum wage.[46] In this context, what was the attitude of the Workers' Unity League to the struggle of unemployed women and for pay equity? What role did women themselves play in the campaigns?

In 1931, near the beginning of the struggles to organize the unemployed, the *Worker* editorialized:

> In Canada, the only agitation around this matter [of Unemployment Insurance for women], apart from a few isolated instances where local Unemployed Councils take it up, is the brazen hard-bitten bourgeois demand that married women shall withdraw into that place in which God and bourgeois morality see fit to shove them – the home – and it is illustrative of the need for explanation by the Communists and left-wingers that many workers fall for this dusty Victorian prejudice.[47]

Perhaps a practical place to gain a true understanding of 'the place of women' in the lexicon of the Workers' Unity League and its activists is in the campaign they waged in the Depression to achieve a national system of non-contributory unemployment insurance – a campaign which began in 1931 with the formation of the National Unemployed Workers' Association. What, if anything, did this organization say or do about women's rights during this militant struggle in which they mobilized thousands of their members and supporters, both men and women? While Leslie Morris, editor of the *Worker*, once wrote, 'There is no room for "feminism" in our movement,' detailed records show that the Workers' Unity League and its supporters exhibited strong elements of the commitment to women's all-round liberation that the next wave of the feminist movement after the Second World War would demand.[48]

Rebecca Buhay, in her role as head of the women's department of the Communist Party, sent a memo in February 1931 to all district executive committees and district women's departments saying: 'We must combat the ideology that married women are responsible for much of the unemployment by taking the place of men workers and must fight against any attempts forbidding married women the right to work. We must also combine with our slogans on unemployment, the slogan of Equal Pay for Equal Work for all women workers and equality in relief measures.'[49] The communist activists, both men and women, seem to have taken this message to heart, at least in principle, given that, from the earliest days of the non-contributory unemployment insurance campaign of the Workers' Unity League and the National Unemployed Workers' Association, they explicitly decried discrimination on the basis of sex or marital status. Even the earliest drafts of the Workers' Unity League's 'Non-Contributory Unemployment Insurance Bill' endorsed insurance for both 'single unemployed girls' and unemployed married women.[50] Later drafts of their proposed unemployment insurance legislation would continue to strengthen this commitment. Many women at the grassroots level, likely as a result of this inclusive stance, were attracted to the work of the unemployed organizations. Indeed, many women played a significant role in both the leadership and the on-the-ground work of the unemployment campaigns of the Workers' Unity League. Given that the WUL was the main leader in organizing unemployed workers, this meant that women played a major role in unemployed organizing in the 1930s.

There was, for example, Lillian Wilkinson, in North York, Ontario.

In August 1932 when the Dominion government hosted the Imperial Economic Conference in Ottawa to strengthen trade relations with other countries of the British Empire, the Workers' Unity League, affronted by this international assemblage of millionaire capitalists, took the opportunity to organize a rival, working-class event, called the 'Workers' Economic Conference' (see chapter 7). Delegates arrived from all over the country to discuss the problems facing the working class, including unemployment. Through its agitation the conference managed to get Prime Minister Bennett to meet with a delegation.

Wilkinson, representing unemployed women, was included in the group chosen to interview the prime minister. During the audience with him, she proceeded to speak up in no uncertain terms, banging her fist on his desk while declaring: 'We women of Canada are not going to let our children starve for you or any government in Canada.' And when Bennett called her 'bitter,' Wilkinson retorted, 'If we are bitter, it is you who have made us bitter. We women can't go on bringing kids into the world just for them to starve.'[51] Bennett attempted to console her, and promised personal attention to her situation. Wilkinson was arrested by the police later that day during a demonstration. She remained active over the following years, and, in 1935, the National Committee of Unemployed Councils chose a new national executive in which two women were elected to high positions: Wilkinson as president and Mrs Elmore Philpott from the East York CCF club as the national financial secretary.[52]

And then there was Flora Hutton, member of the Capitol Hill (Burnaby) Women's Labour League and a representative of the Unemployed Girls' Club in Vancouver.

A year after the Workers' Economic Conference, a large national congress of unemployed workers took place in Ottawa.[53] Hutton was chosen by the conference to be on the committee sent to see the prime minister. The millionaire Bennett, having made arrangements to be away from Ottawa during the congress, sent his representative Sir George Perley, the deputy prime minister, to meet with the unemployed delegates. When Hutton's turn came to address Perley, she declared that unemployed girls of Vancouver 'have starved while the Prime Minister has been away living in luxury.' Referring to a speech made by Bennett, she demanded to know whether Bennett thought 'law, order, and good government means girls walking the streets, selling their bodies for a meal.'[54] Immediately following the unemployed workers' congress, the Workers' Unity League held its second national congress. Hutton attended this as well, and was elected as a member of the national executive board of the league, along with four other women: Becky Buhay, Julia Carr, Ann Walters, and Bertha Dolgoy.[55] When Hutton arrived back in Vancouver she received a hero's welcome, with 300 workers gathered on the platform to meet her as she stepped off the train at 9 a.m. Hutton, normally a humble, quiet woman, and tired from her trip, was ushered off to speak at a meeting at the Majestic Hall, where she delivered a short

into unions, and for improving working conditions for women workers in factories, including demanding sanitary conditions in the shops, no night work, time off for nursing mothers, and fighting against speed-up as a detriment to the health of working women. Banners at Women's Day marches included slogans such as: 'For a 7 hour Day and 5 day Week!' and 'Fight against Hunger, Imperialist War and Exploitation!'[74]

Buhay had hoped that the 1931 International Women's Day campaign would mark a turning point in organizing work among women, and in spite of the mistakes, there were indeed some positive results to report on, with about 15,000 people attending 8 March events across the country.[75] The largest gatherings took place in Vancouver, where an afternoon rally at the Cambie Street grounds drew a crowd of 2,000 to listen to speeches by, among others, Jean Stevenson of the Capitol Hill branch of the Women's Labour League. Later that same day, in the Royal Theatre, Annie Zen, also of the working women's USSR delegation, spoke to a large crowd about the conditions of women in the Soviet Union, where 8 March had received official recognition as 'a day of rebellion of working women against kitchen slavery.'[76] In addition to the prominent women speakers, members of the Women's Labour Leagues and others circulated through the crowds distributing nearly 25,000 leaflets and collecting hundreds of signatures for the Non-Contributory Unemployment Insurance petition. These activities left the women involved feeling an overall sense of success and optimism, which is evident in Buhay's report when she wrote:

> The good efforts of the campaign are that it has strengthened many of our Women's Departments, and made our women comrades gain confidence in their ability ... The objective conditions of our work among women was never better than it is today.[77]

In the following years, after the Communist Party was banned and had gone underground, the celebrations of International Women's Day were somewhat muted and reduced in size. Nonetheless, throughout these years the militant tradition of 8 March was kept alive in Canada by progressive-minded people.

Another preoccupation of the Workers' Unity League was to encourage the formation of women's trade union auxiliaries, especially for its affiliates in the lumber and coal mining settlements. In the course of bitterly fought strikes in these industries in Bienfait/Estevan, Saskatchewan, in New Westminster, BC, in Northern Ontario, on Vancouver Island, and in Flin Flon, Manitoba – which are the subject of close scrutiny in other chapters of this book – the role of the women and their auxiliaries was of central importance to the struggle.

Replacing striking workers with strike-breakers was a common tactic used by owners to try to defeat strikes. In many instances, wives of strikers would join the picket lines in order to bolster numbers and keep scabs out. In at least a few cases, working-class women associated with women's auxiliaries organized by the Workers' Unity League took the defence of the picket line further, physically confronting workers attempting to steal their men's jobs. The value of the strike for the political and social awakening of women in the community, such as the miners' wives interviewed by Meg Luxton for her book *More Than a Labour of Love*, is tangible. 'Before the strike I stayed home with my family,' said one woman participant to Luxton. 'I didn't know many people and I wasn't interested in the union. But during the strike I got to know a lot of other women and afterwards I felt more part of the town.'[78] The daughter of another woman picketer recalled to Luxton how her mother used to say that, before the strike, 'my father never paid her much heed. He always told her not to bother with "men's work." But after he saw her on the picket line yelling at the police, he used to always ask her opinion. And he used to say "My wife is smart and tough."'[79]

While women's auxiliaries were not a new idea, the Workers' Unity League conceived of them not just as adjuncts of the unions but as having a wide range of work, and not only at the time of strikes. If properly understood, they would be organizations in their own right 'as a force of inestimable value to the community' and for the women themselves. In a wide-ranging memorandum on women's work, in 1936, a communist organizer, probably Alice Cooke, who succeeded Buhay as head of the Communist Party's National Women's Department, summed up the case for building such organizations: a women's auxiliary functioned, she wrote, as an educational and social centre, as a medium of bringing men and women closer to trade unionism, and as an instrument to campaign for good housing for the workers and for educational and health facilities for the children. These auxiliaries could also 'be a factor in the campaign for the union label' and agitation for union-made products. In strike situations, women's auxiliaries had proved to be 'of decisive importance in preserving the morale of the workers'; women had participated in picketing, taken charge of canvassing for food and distributing it to the strikers, and in the organization of meetings and socials to popularize the demands of the strikers.[80]

Table 9.2 Women's Labour Leagues: Reported membership in November 1935

Place	Members	Secretary
Toronto	40	V. Rock
Montreal	40	Mrs Kangas
Vancouver	500	Mrs Wilson
Regina	20	Mrs Pakkela
Sointula, B.C.	50	T. Puhtala
Yorkton	22	Tynni Neimi
Meadow Portage	15	Mrs Duncanson
Saskatoon	23	
Sudbury	300	Mrs Erickson
Timmins	285	Mrs Suksi
Port Arthur	113	
Total	1,408	

Sources: 'Membership in Workers' Unity League Unions – Women's Labour Leagues,' 7 November 1935, LAC, CI Fonds 495, list 72, file 200, reel 2, K-270. The Vancouver figure includes twenty-three local units in British Columbia. The above list remains incomplete as it omits Alberta and such places as Kitchener, London, Gogama, Sault Ste Marie, Windsor, and Kirkland Lake in Ontario that had active units within the previous year and a half. See 'WUL Union Directory,' 7 August 1934, LAC, CSIS Records, RG146, access request 92-A-00088, 'WUL – Canada,' Interim Box 1; 'London Women Win Back Relief Cuts,' *Worker*, 27 April 1935; 'Unity Pays in Gogama,' *Unity*, January–February 1936.

The activities of women's auxiliaries, guided by the fighting spirit of activists in the Women's Labour Leagues, helped to combat the image of housewives as docile, submissive, and apolitical; and, just as important, they contributed to improving the material and spiritual well-being of the women involved.

Women members of the Workers' Unity League worked to support the unionization of women workers in canneries, textile and garment factories, and restaurants and domestic service, and helped to create women's auxiliaries in the Mine Workers' Union of Canada, the Lumber Workers' Industrial Union, and the Fishermen and Longshoremen's unions. They also built the membership of the Women's Labour Leagues. In 1929 there were at most sixty Women's Labour Leagues, mostly Finnish and mostly in Northern Ontario, with a total membership of around 1,000.[81] By the end of 1935, as the figures in table 9.2 show, there were local branches scattered across Southern Ontario, the prairies, and British Columbia, with a total membership of around 1,500. Since this listing omits many local leagues that were active within the previous year and a half, it seems certain that, at the very least, the Women's Labour Leagues did not shrink during the Workers' Unity League period. If anything, they grew and diversified, especially in British Columbia.

As for the women's auxiliaries, even though many hundreds of women took an active part in their husbands' strike struggles, in 1936 Alice Cooke reported that 'we cannot claim that there are functioning women's auxiliaries throughout the country.'[82] At the same time, though, the women's auxiliaries of Workers' Unity League–affiliated unions that did exist offered invaluable experience to the same women who subsequently built auxiliaries in the 1940s and 1950s.[83]

At its final convention at the end of 1935, the Workers' Unity League, once again under the active leadership of Tom Ewen, decided to encourage its members to join with the AFL and other existing union centrals to build a 'united front against war and fascism.'[84] This decision led, by mid-1936, to the disbandment of the Workers' Unity League (see chapter 15). Although there were attempts to keep the Women's Labour Leagues going in some places, they largely died out with the Workers' Unity League. Historian Betty Griffin interviewed former Women's Labour League activist Edna Sheard, who recalled the attempts to save the organization in British Columbia: 'We fought terribly to keep the Women's Labour League, we fought awfully hard to keep the League going. But decided that it should die a natural death. Then the House-wives' League came in, but I don't know if they were ever as strong as the WLL.'[85] In hindsight, the content of Annie Stewart's address to the tenth BC convention of the Women's Labour Leagues, in December 1935 (which claimed thirty-six delegates and nine 'fraternal delegates' who 'represented 10,802 persons'), has the ring of a eulogy about it. Stewart spoke of how the WLL branches 'helped to gain a $5 maternity grant from the government; how we helped to get relief for the camp boys; how we helped to form the Women's Auxiliaries of the unions, and the work we did to form the Domestic Servants' Union.'[86] The 1936 Communist Party document on women's work contained not a single mention of the Women's Labour Leagues,[87] and the report Alice Cooke delivered a year later at the Communist Party's eighth convention also had no reference to them.[88] The Women's Labour Leagues had already vanished into history.

Nipigon River Power Plant
Harold A. Pearl, artist, in R.S. Rivers et al., *The Canadian Story* (Toronto: Ryerson Press, 1939).

Nickel Smelter, Copper Cliff, Ontario
Harold A. Pearl, artist, in R.S. Rivers et al., *The Canadian Story* (Toronto: Ryerson Press, 1939).

Logging in British Columbia
Harold A. Pearl, artist, in R.S. Rivers et al., *The Canadian Story* (Toronto: Ryerson Press, 1939).

Fishing Fleet at Prince Rupert, BC

Harold A. Pearl, artist, in R.S. Rivers et al., *The Canadian Story* (Toronto: Ryerson Press, 1939).

AMONG THE MANY KNIGHTED CAPITALISTS AT THE FOREFRONT OF CANADA'S INDUSTRIAL REVOLUTION

Sir Edward Beatty
For 25 years from 1918 to 1943 Beatty was president of the Canadian Pacific Railway, Canada's largest and most powerful corporation.
Ville de Montréal, gestion de documents et archives, Canadian Historical Portraits, P0119.

Sir Herbert Holt
President, Royal Bank of Canada. Holt was also a director of the CPR, Dominion Textiles, Montreal Light, Heat and Power, and a host of other corporations. In the 1930s he was said to be Canada's richest person. Wikipedia.org.

FOREIGN INVESTORS MULTIPLIED

Alfred Mond/Lord Melchett
A British tycoon with nickel, chemical, and other investments in Canada.
Wikipedia.org.

Cornelius Vanderbilt Whitney
American investor born to wealth, major owner of the Hudson Bay Mining and Smelting Co., at Flin Flon, Manitoba.
Artist sketch.

Richard B. Bennett
Prime minister of Canada from 1930 to 1935, Bennett was a prominent lawyer,
businessman, and member of parliament from Calgary.
City of Toronto Archives/William James Collection, f1244-8130.

Solving the Bosses' Unemployment Problem
A sketch from a branch of the Progressive Arts Club depicting the terror of a
charge by mounted police into a demonstration of unemployed workers.
The Worker, 7 February 1931.

The Worker, 28 March 1931.

Bosses' Reply to Demand For Bread

(February 25th Demonstration in Toronto)

Unemployed Demonstration in Toronto
Mounted police wade into a crowd demonstrating for unemployment relief, a
common sight across Canada in the spring of 1931 when over 150,000 people
took part in such gatherings.
The Worker, 7 March 1931.

10 C 2170   No 7407

"Workers Unity League of Canada"

Workers' Demand for
Non-Contributory State Unemployment Insurance

The undersigned workers from the shops, mills, mines and factories, members of Trade Unions, Language cultural organizations, Women's Labor Leagues and other working-class organizations demand the immediate enactment of legislation for a Bill providing STATE UNEMPLOYMENT INSURANCE for all Unemployed Workers resident in Canada, irrespective of age, sex, race or color. This Bill must be applicable to ALL UNEMPLOYED workers, and to Workers only partially employed, through inability to find Work, or because of sickness, accident, old age or other disability.

Pending the enactment of such legislation, we also demand that the Federal Government of Canada assume the responsibility of the Municipal Administrations, and grant immediate relief in the form of sufficient food, clothing, shelter and other necessaries of life to all Unemployed workers and their dependents, without discrimination or favor.

WE DEMAND:

1. NON-CONTRIBUTORY STATE UNEMPLOYMENT INSURANCE.
2. THE 7-HOUR DAY—5-DAY WEEK IN ALL INDUSTRIES.
3. A GUARANTEED WORKING WEEK AND A MINIMUM WAGE OF $25.00.

NAME	ADDRESS	CITY	INDUSTRY
T. Anderson	7 ave. 316.	Calgary	Labourer
John Koren	316-7 ave Ea.	Calgary	Fr. Laborer
Austin Kcha	316-7 ave. Ea.	Calgary	Laborer

The Unemployment Insurance Petition

Workers' Unity League supporters across Canada gathered almost 100,000 signatures to this petition which was presented to Prime Minister R.B. Bennett in Ottawa on 15 April 1931.

OA, RG4, MS367, reel 7, 10-C-2170.

Winnipeg, 15 April 1931
The line-up of policemen confronting 15,000 workers demonstrating in
support of the Workers' Unity League delegation to Ottawa presenting the
unemployment insurance petition to Prime Minister Bennett.
The Worker, 25 April 1931.

Starvation Bennett
In denying the unemployment insurance petition the
prime minister said, 'We will not put a premium on idleness.'
Text from the *Montreal Gazette*, 17 April 1931. Cartoon in *The Worker*, 19 November 1932.

Annie Buller
Needle trades organizer and member of the National Executive Board of the Workers' Unity League.
Jim Buller Collection.

Annie Buller addressing a public meeting in Bienfait, Saskatchewan, during the coal miners' strike of 1931
Seated on the platform is Dan Moar, president of Local 27 of the miners' union. This photo, taken by RCMP detective Walter Mortimer, was later produced in the court in Estevan as evidence supporting the charge that Buller urged the miners to riot.
SAB R-A3258-4.

"WORKERS OF THE WORLD UNITE"

FIGHT FOR:—
Non-Contributory State Unemployment Insurance.
The 7-Hour Day, 5-Day Week.
A Guaranteed Working Week and a Minimum Wage of $25.00.
Immediate Cash Relief; Food, Clothing and Shelter for All Unemployed Workers and Their Dependants.

All the Forces and the whole energy of the Red International of Labor Unions must at the present time be concentrated on the following two points:—
(a) The Organization of Mass Economic Struggles, and
(b) The Strengthening of the Revolutionary Trade Union Movement.

—Thesis. V Congress, R.I.L.U.

WORKERS' UNITY

Vol. 1, No. 2   Official Bi-Monthly Organ — "WORKERS' UNITY LEAGUE OF CANADA" — Canadian Section, R.I.L.U.   Price 5c   August

Organize Against Deportatio

Martin Day
An outstanding leader of the Bienfait miners; deported to Britain
with his family by the federal government following the 1931 strike.
Stephen Endicott Collection.

Lest We Forget!
Avrom cartoon in *The Worker*, 29 September 1934.

Headstone of the grave of the three miners shot and killed in Estevan, Sask., by
the RCMP during the Bienfait miners' strike of 1931.
SAB R-A6697-1.

Hans Sula
Secretary of the National
Committee of Unemployed
Councils.
The Worker, 26 August 1933.

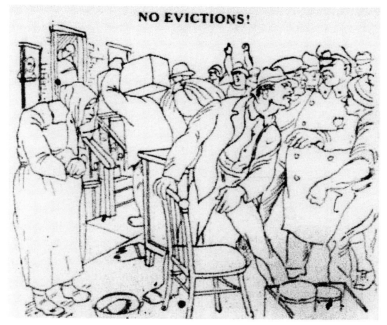

Unemployed Councils Resisting an Eviction.
The Worker, 7 January 1933.

THE PRINCIPAL NATIONAL LEADERS OF THE
WORKERS' UNITY LEAGUE OF CANADA

J.B. McLachlan. President.
Jim Buller Collection.

Tom Ewen. General Secretary.
Jim Buller Collection.

Sam Scarlett. Vice-president.
OA, F1412, Gershman Collection, no.
220, I0031429 (detail).

Nick Thatchuk. Vice-president.
The Worker, 22 July 1933.

THE PRINCIPAL NATIONAL LEADERS OF THE
WORKERS' UNITY LEAGUE OF CANADA

Charles Sims. Executive Board
Secretary, 1933–5.
OA, F1412, Gershman Collection, no.
220, I0031429 (detail).

Julia Carr (*pseud:* Julia Collins).
National Secretary-Treasurer.
Nancy Carr Collection.

Joshua Gershman.
Executive Board Member.
OA, F1412, Gershman Collection, no. 251.

James Litterick. National Secretary
1931–2.
University of Toronto Fisher Rare Book
Library, R.S. Kenny Collection, F5604
(detail).

LEADERS IN THE RED INTERNATIONAL

Otto Kuusinen (left) and **Dimitri Manuilsky** were two of the main leaders of the
Third International from 1930 to 1935.
The Worker, 23 April 1935.

MARX
and the
TRADE
UNIONS

A. Lozovsky

Alexander Lozovsky. Lozovsky was general secretary of the Red International
of Labour Unions from 1921 to 1937. His book, *Marx and the Trade Unions*, was
published in English by International Publishers (New York, 1933).
Artist's sketch from *Workers' Unity*, 15 July 1931.

CANADIAN REFERENTS

Stewart Smith

Norman Freed

Principal Canadian referents at the RILU were Stewart Smith, alumnus of the International Lenin School, from 1930 to 1931, and Norman Freed, garment worker, from 1932 to 1935.

Image of Stewart Smith from *The Worker*, 29 May 1935.
Image of Freed from OA, F1405, Sylvia Schwartz Collection.

Pearl Wedro
Organizer of needle trades workers in Winnipeg and spokesperson for the Canadian delegation at the Fifth RILU Congress in Moscow in 1930.
OA, F1405, Sylvia Schwartz Collection.

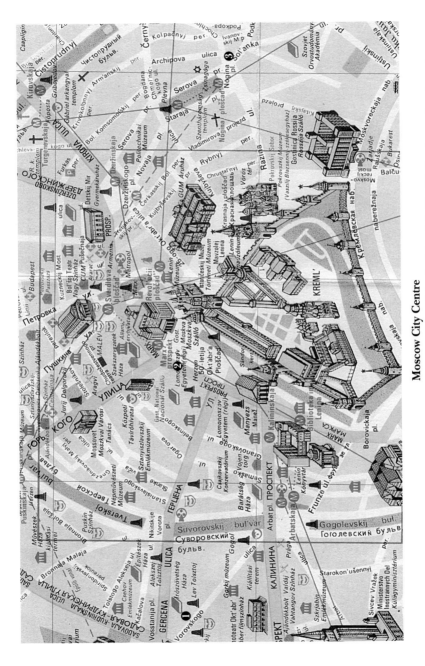

Moscow City Centre

Showing the Kremlin and the locations of (1) the International Lenin School (left); (2) Comintern headquarters (centre); and (3) Red International of Labour Unions (right).

Kartografiai Vallalat, Budapest, 1976.

10
Hard Rock Miners:
Anyox – Noranda – Flin Flon

If the conduct of the provincial police and Dominion Government cruiser during the strike at Anyox was British justice, then I am a Red. I felt ashamed of our Attorney-General ...

– H.F. Kergin, Liberal MLA for Atlin, BC,
quoted in the *Victoria Times*, 30 March 1933

The property is well guarded, being fenced in ... there are two men employed as agents underground and care is being taken in the hiring of new men. There are two machine guns available on the property in case of serious trouble. There are three watchmen on the property at night. They do not anticipate any strike.

– RCMP report on McIntyre Mine, Schumacher, Ontario,
employing 1,150 men, 25 June 1934[1]

In the proud history of mining industry of Canada probably no individual development has reached such substantial proportions in so brief a period of time as that of Noranda Mines Limited – the outstanding producer in the Province of Quebec.

– *Canadian Annual Review 1933*, 727

The miners' union is going like wildfire here in Timmins and Rouyn.

– Report of District 4, Communist Party, 21 April 1934[2]

It was with a slight sense of nervous anticipation that 'J.T.' (Tom) leaned on the rail of the SS *Catala* of the Union Steamships Line while the boat churned its way up the narrow passage of Observatory Inlet. As end-of-January snow squalls blew off the mountains of the Alaska panhandle, he squinted into the chill wind, looking for the appearance of lights, and tried not to get into conversation with other passengers. Finally the ship reached her last port of call, which was ninety miles northeast of Prince Rupert, the nearest habitation of any size. This was Anyox, a company town. He had heard that nobody got off the ship unless they were expected, since a company policeman met every arrival at the wharf and anyone seeking employment without prearrangement or coming for some other unauthorized reason was not allowed to land. J.T. had reason to be nervous. He had no letter from the approved Vancouver employment agency of Leighton Thomas on Burrard Street and he certainly was not expected. He had made his own arrangements. But still, he could not help but wonder, would his 'arrangements' materialize? Was the plan he had in mind feasible? Was change a real possibility?[3]

According to its records, the Granby Consolidated Mining, Smelting and Power Company owned an array of companies producing copper, iron, gold and silver, coal, and electric power in British Columbia. It had been incorporated in 1901 by a group of American capitalists based in Boston and New York City, and, armed with a British Columbia charter, they bought up existing mining claims that white men had staked in the territory of the Nisga'a people in the Nass River district of northern British Columbia.[4] In the years 1911–14 the Granby Company constructed a vast mining and smelting complex at Anyox to exploit the copper, gold, and silver deposits. Aided by the demands of the First World War, it soon had a profitable industry in operation. While devastating the environment – trees blighted by the sulphur fumes and the water poisoned by the cyanide wastes dumped into the creek – Granby continued to prosper through the 1920s until the depression struck in 1930 and prices for metal, especially copper, temporarily collapsed. Even then, in 1931 the company reported $15 million in assets and paid up to a $7 dividend per share.[5] In 1932, the mill at Anyox still produced 38 million pounds of copper, 260,000 ounces of silver, and 4,000 ounces of gold. With an annual payroll of $1,500,000 and yearly purchases of supplies, machinery, explosives, coal, transportation services, etc., worth about $2,500,000, this 'immense industrial activity,' according to the Vancouver Board of Trade, had far-reaching influence on 'the business and domestic life of the entire Province.'[6] As company towns went, it was a decided success. By 1933 Anyox had approximately 2,500 residents.

Actually Anyox was two communities, as Peter Loudon explained in his richly detailed account of ten childhood years spent growing up there:

The plant workers, office workers and people involved with the business section lived and worked in the waterfront area while the mine people lived almost two miles away at the head of the valley. They had their own bunk houses and mess house as well as a number of private homes. They had movies there and the United Church minister ... would go up there ... to conduct Sunday School. I know because he would often take me with him ... These trips were about all I knew of the mine and it was more than most kids at Anyox experienced. We knew the mine kids because we all attended the same school halfway between the beach and the mine, but as far as we were concerned, the action was at the beach.

The residents of the 'beach,' although distinct from the miners, were not themselves of one kind, being divided along ethnic and income lines. There were separate quarters for the Chinese workers who maintained the bunkhouses and mess houses and served as domestic help for the upper crust. Two huge three-storey frame and concrete bunkhouses on the flats by Hidden Creek housed 300 production workers employed in the smelter, the blacksmith shop, machine and boiler shops, the foundry, sawmill, carpentry and shoemaker's shops, and the klim plant and coke furnace; a bridge over the creek led through a no-man's-land of large oil storage tanks and the foundry to the hill section of town in the centre of the valley. Here there were cabins and two-storey residences for the minor functionaries, shop-keepers, and administrative employees, two 'harbour-fronting apartments' for the senior white-collar families and four or five 'large and stylish homes on the highest ground' where, according to Loudon, the bosses lived. Mingled among the town houses were the Anglican, Catholic, and United churches, and between them and the harbour were the bank, the government agent's office, the police station, the pool hall, the movie house, the community hall, the Pioneer Hotel and Café, and an eighteen-bed hospital.[7]

Although Anyox had no road or rail connections to the outside world, it had two miles of roads, mostly made of two-inch planks 'laid crosswise to the traffic,' and seven miles of railway tracks and an aerial cable to connect the mines to the smelter and harbour where the docks, equipped with an overhead travelling crane and derricks, could accommodate several deep sea freighters or coastal passenger ships at the same time. Adjoining the wharf were the general store, the butcher shop, the liquor store, the freight shed, a lime storage shed, 'the floats where everyone kept a boat,' and the morgue. To complete the picture, just outside the town line, beyond the slag heap, a Chinese merchant, Lu Lun, known locally as 'Frank the Chinaman,' ran a store to supply the Chinese workers with the food and spices they enjoyed as well as various items of clothing and haberdasheries for the general community; there was a bootlegger named Leo, and a collection of half a dozen cabins, known as 'disorderly premises,' that constituted the red light district. A few years earlier, before a fire burned it to the ground, there had also been a small dance hall and cabaret.[8]

Many of the town residents, including Loudon's family, considered themselves to be well off. Looking back, Loudon felt that 'there could have been few better places for a boy to spend those years where love and comfort and security are so necessary to his development.' 'Our company town,' Loudon wrote, 'offered benefits which were usually attributed to a socialist state.'[9] There was no unemployment. When a worker arrived he came with a job and accommodation for himself and his family. An employee had access to the company store, pool room, café, library, theatre, gym, and dance hall operated by the company-sponsored 'Community League,' to which one could pay dues by payroll deduction. There was an excellent school with good teachers. The hospital was 'adequate,' according to Loudon, and doctors made house calls under a medical and surgical insurance plan through payroll deduction of $1 per month for single people, $2 for families; hospital stay, drugs, and x-rays were extra.

To enhance their monopoly of power and fend off any challengers, the company managers encouraged certain kinds of social organizations among the residents. Apart from the Community League with its many activities, the most important of these was the Anyox Branch of the Canadian Legion, which was run by the postmaster. Anyox had sent 400 men to fight for 'King and Empire' during the First World War; all but 30 came back, although many were wounded. Given light duty jobs, the legionnaires constituted a loyal core of company supporters, vigilant to detect any who were thought to be otherwise. Then there were the Elks, Oddfellows, Scouts, and other 'youth guidance' and service organizations as well as the three church congregations which could work to provide social cohesion. If, in spite of all these supports, trouble came, the company had every reason to expect that the member of the BC legislative assembly for the area, H.F. Kergin, a member of the Liberal Party first elected in 1920, would stand them in good stead. They had, therefore, a formidable blockade against any hostile social forces of the outside world. But trouble came nevertheless.

From its inception a prime objective of the Workers' Unity League had been to spread union organization to the hard rock metal mines. These centres in Trail and Anyox, BC, Sudbury, Ontario, Noranda, Quebec, Flin Flon, Manitoba, and elsewhere produced the nickel, copper, lead, zinc, gold, silver, and their by-products that lay at the base of industrializing economies, and they had mushroomed across the country in Canada's Second Industrial Revolution. Although these industries provided jobs for 20,000 or more people,[10] the quarries, mines, and mills were usually located in remote places where companies, often American-owned and under an umbrella of some form of 'welfare capitalism,' could exercise arbitrary control over the lives of their workers. Moreover, the metals they produced fed the armaments factories of many powers in a time of foreign wars and interventions. The mines were also dangerous workplaces with many fatal accidents.[11] For these reasons the Workers' Unity League felt it a special challenge to help the workers defend their living standards, their health and safety, and by waging class struggle weaken what the league considered to be a particularly virulent form of boss rule.

In the spring of 1932 their chance came at Anyox. With the price of copper falling on the New York market, the Granby Company decided to cut the workers' wages. They made three cuts totalling $1.50 per day over the course of several months so that the lowest-paid miners found themselves earning $2.10 per eight-hour shift instead of $3.60. With Granby doing nothing to reduce its charges for lodging and food, at $1.10 per day, the miners, working twenty to twenty-two shifts per month but having to pay their upkeep thirty or thirty-one days, ended each eight-hour day of 'loading sixteen tons' with a miserable 50 cents in their pockets instead of $2.00. There were other grievances as well: 'lousy bunks, dirty blankets and no pillows,' very poor board, and discrimination and favouritism in job assignments without regard to seniority.[12]

The Workers' Unity League had to devise a plan to overcome, in its own words, 'one of the most hostile and labour-hating companies in Canada,' a company that from its inception had had the support of the federal and provincial police to keep out people the police alleged to be 'crooks and agitators.'[13]

The league's strategy was to go to the 'language mass organizations' in Vancouver, many of whom had halls in the vicinity of its headquarters at 61 Cordova Street West: the Ukrainian Labour Temple on Pender Street, the Yugoslav hall on Keefer, the Swedish hall on East Hastings, the Finn hall on Clinton Street, and the Chinese Workers' Protective Association on Main Street, to mention some of the most prominent. In early 1932 a

WUL organizer smuggled himself into Anyox with a list of contacts from these organizations and before leaving a few weeks later he had dented the company's blockade by secretly organizing three groups in the mines and smelter — forty workers altogether. Then began ten months of 'difficult and skilful work' by the mine and mill employees until they decided the time was ripe 'to come up for air.' Organizing secretly in teams of five where everyone knew each other personally, dubbed 'the Anyox system,' by now they had 325 members, all without the boss finding out, and they requested the Workers' Unity League to send in another organizer.[14]

Of the 'mass language organizations' in Vancouver, one with special importance in the Anyox operation was the Chinese Workers' Protective Association. Unlike the Chinese Free Masons nearby on Pender Street with their links to the merchant class and to the old warlords in China, this organization was composed of railway builders and retired workers from the lumber and mining camps of British Columbia; its members were apt to be heartened by news from China of the victories of Mao Zedong's peasant armies. Their main preoccupation was to look after sick and elderly workers who had no family to help them, but the organization also took part in Vancouver May Day rallies and other activities of the labour movement. Its leaders were retired camp cooks Luo Toy and Wang Fook, and as they told me when I came to know the group there in the 1940s, they were well aware of the campaigns of the Workers' Unity League and had been willing to help when possible.

After the SS *Catala* pulled into the Anyox dock early that evening in the last days of January 1933 and began unloading visitors and cargo onto the wharf from its starboard side, Lu Lun, as was his custom, pulled his launch up to a hatch on the other side of the ship to take on his supplies and a few cartons for Leo the bootlegger. By prearrangement with the Chinese Workers' Protective Association, J.T. was there too and he dropped down into the launch. Much relieved, J.T. Bradley, one of the WUL's most daring young organizers and fresh from the successful Princeton coal miners' strike, thus evaded Granby's blockade to find lodging in one of the 'disorderly premises.' From here he hoped to launch the strike of 600 mine and smelter workers.[15]

After a few days of intensive organization following Bradley's arrival, the union miners decided to come out in the open and to call a public meeting in the Community Hall for Sunday, 29 January. The company got the surprise of their lives. Superintendent W.R. Lindsay hurried over and tried to take charge of the overflow meeting. When unsuccessful he called in the company's policeman to clear the hall, saying that it was company property. The miners refused to budge, shouting out, 'What do we pay our 50 cents a month for? Is it for candy?' By now the union had grown to 450 members and instead of leaving the hall they demanded that Lindsay and the constable depart, which they did as the workers shouted, clapped, and jeered. In the business meeting which followed, lasting from 9:15 p.m. to 2:15 a.m., the workers proceeded to discuss the demands which the union would place before the company. The general thrust indicated a feeling and experience far removed from the concerns of the company-sponsored 'Community League,' and, apart from wages, rents, and cost of board, included hiring procedures, seniority in lay-offs, no discrimination, recognition of a Grievance Committee, bunkhouse and mess hall conditions – the 'right to eat where we choose.'[16] The chairman introduced Bradley, who said he represented the Mine Workers' Union of Canada, which was affiliated to the Workers' Unity League and the Red International of Labour Unions; it was no longer a time for camouflage. He told of other strike struggles, outlined in detail the strategy of the Workers' Unity League for a situation such as was present at Anyox, stressing the importance of full, democratic participation, and offered, if chosen, to be part of a delegation to meet the boss the next day.[17]

The elected committee of three placed the union's minimum demands before management at 8 o'clock the next morning: a 50 cents per day increase in wages and a 20 per cent reduction in board and in bunkhouse and home rents. The demands were refused. The management told the *Alice Arm Herald* that it was impossible to meet the union requests because of the low price of copper.[18] Another meeting, open to all workers, was called later that day and it decided that if the company did not comply with the demands by the last day of January a strike would take effect Wednesday, 1 February at 8 a.m. It was critical to act quickly before the state could send in its troopers. This meeting elected a strike committee of twenty-one members representing the different work groups and the committee established sub-groups to take responsibility for relief, picketing, and publicity.[19] A womens' auxiliary of fourteen was also established. All this was in accordance with the Workers' Unity League strike strategy. Next day, 1 February, the strike began at the mine, to be joined by the workers at the beach two days later.[20]

Peter Loudon, a schoolboy at the time, remembered the drama of the moment: 'We were all milling about in the schoolyard waiting the bell which would line us up to march into classes,' he wrote. 'Suddenly all fooling around stopped and there was a strange silence. All the kids were looking up the plank road to the mine ... the road was filled with men, hundreds of men. They were wearing their hard hats and walking purposefully in a tight body. They weren't talking but you could hear their feet pounding the boards. You could smell their determination as they headed past us toward the beach. None of us had seen anything like it. It was so ominous that some of the kids verged on tears, scared without knowing why. At that moment everything changed for us in Anyox.'[21]

The union held several meetings in the week after the strike began and it was reported that some of the beach workers, most of whom had families in town, were willing to go back to their jobs. The miners, however, 'most of whom were single, were adamant. They felt that if the wages couldn't be improved the plant might as well be closed.' They took up their picket signs.[22]

By 2 February, the day after the strike started, the union claimed to have 600 members. But by now there were also twenty-seven provincial police in town, and more arriving by ship and plane. In face of this development the miners decided to make a show of solidarity and several hundred men marched down the plank road again, 'seven or eight abreast,' planning to parade in front of the company offices at the beach. Half a dozen police officers met them on a bridge at Kelly's Cut, where Hidden Creek pierced a deep gully, and ordered them to halt. According to some officers' testimony at a subsequent trial, 'the marchers refused to halt and stated they were going through to the beach.' The police drew their revolvers and fired into the air. This infuriated the men and they rushed forward. After a scrimmage in which one worker lost an eye and the officers had their weapons thrown into the creek, the police gave way to the miners, permitting them to march, and preceded the men in their walk to the beach. 'A good many people in Anyox,' according to Loudon, said that 'the police should have done that in the first place.'[23]

More police arrived, some aboard the former HMCS *Malaspina*, a naval ship that had been converted into a fisheries patrol vessel.[24] Over 100 uniformed officers, according to H.F. Kergin, some of them hastily recruited from the ranks of the unemployed, were on site in an 'unnecessary show of force.' The police mounted machine guns in front of the bunkhouses, carried rifles and clubs. The company once again refused to negotiate, and, in a move calculated to frighten the miners, on 6 February the general manager posted notices saying the mine would be closed permanently. At the same time the police arrested five of the strikers – Kenneth Montgomery, Matt Jurgevich, Giovanna Sanvido, Angus McIver, and Joseph Sarich – charging them with unlawful assembly and rioting, and shipped them out to Prince Rupert aboard the *Malaspina*. Many others, under the orders of the Dominion government, were arrested as well for possible deportation. When, on the same day, the company sent back a large order of foodstuffs placed by the Women's Auxiliary in Prince Rupert, the hungry miners had little choice but to accede to the company's demand that they vacate the property. Many Anyox people observed how the police officers 'herded the unwanted young men along the docks,' wrote Loudon, 'made them open their suitcases and parcels and searched their possessions with the toes of the high leather boots,' and they 'could well believe this was a private army of the company.' Such incidents, he concluded, 'probably did more to create political dissidents, agitators and outright Communists than all the writings of Karl Marx, so far as Anyox was concerned.'[25]

The strike, however, was not over and continued to reverberate, from picket lines on the docks at Prince Rupert and Vancouver, around the court house, in the relief offices, and at the BC legislature, until the union called it off three months later after the company had made some concessions.

Meanwhile governments at all levels moved into high gear in support of the Granby Company.

In Vancouver, Deputy Police Chief Murdock and twenty-five policemen walked into the Workers' Unity League centre at 61 Cordova Street W. with a search warrant and proceeded to turn everything upside down. They helped themselves to leaflets and pamphlets, arresting William Kendrick, organizer of the Workers' International Relief, and taking him to the Immigration Office, where he was threatened with deportation. Brigadier James Sutherland Brown, army commander for the Pacific Coast and in charge of federal relief camp efforts there, told Attorney General R.H. Pooley that relief payments for men who went on strike should be stopped, especially 'for foreigners.' And sixty-five of the foreign-born workers who had been evicted and kidnapped without charge from Anyox by the police were haled before the immigration inspector in Prince Rupert, on instructions from the minister in Ottawa, and given their choice of returning to work at Anyox as strike-breakers or of being deported. Many were put on the train for the deportation sheds at Halifax, there to join the 7,131 people who were shipped out of the country by the government in the fiscal year 1932–3.[26]

By now the Workers' Unity League was well accustomed to such intimidation tactics and refused to panic. Instead it set out to aid the strikers with 'the full power of the working class,' as an editorial in the

Unemployed Worker described it: appeals for strike relief funds, demonstrations in the cities, pickets at the docks in Vancouver, delegations to the government, resolutions to workers' organizations across the country for endorsement, protests against the terror tactics, and legal defence for those arrested.[27] The campaign found support in some apparently unexpected places. A former mines inspector, T.J. Shenton, agreed to speak to a mass meeting in Prince Rupert about the reckless behaviour of Granby in 'its greed for profits.' The mine at Anyox, he said, 'is absolutely honeycombed, the company ... having failed to leave sufficient columns to support the enormous weight of rock.' The mine was 'a regular death trap'; any day 'the whole mountain may collapse, and miners will not have a ghost of a chance.'[28]

The miners' union appointed a delegation to interview the provincial government and to lobby members of the legislature in Victoria. This delegation included strike leaders Joseph Sarich (out on bail) and Russell Barr as well as Harvey Murphy, national mines director of the Workers' Unity League. The men demanded a full independent investigation into the working and safety conditions in the Anyox mines and an end to deportation proceedings against sixty-five strikers. As already mentioned, they found strong support for their case in H.F. Kergin, MLA for Atlin since 1920, who poured scorn on the attorney general's justifications for sending armed police into Anyox and defended the strikers in a stirring speech to the legislature.

The BC legislature did not have a Hansard in those days and relied on newspaper reporters to record the debates. The *Victoria Times* gave Kergin a big spread. The man who went to work in this desolate smelter town, he had said, found that a foreign company controlled everything. It was 'his employer, his landlord and his merchant.' The workers had taken three pay cuts in the previous year without any corresponding cuts for rent and board charged by the company. They had a real grievance and declared a strike, but within twenty-four hours were confronted by heavily armed provincial police arriving from Vancouver. He described how police with rifles had gone into the men's rooms without a search warrant and opened their baggage. They had arrested men suspected of being in a scuffle and 'sent them to Prince Rupert on a cruiser. They did not try them in Anyox.' What followed 'he likened to the times of Evangeline': the representatives of 'this foreign company, who are not citizens of Canada,' he said, began to expel scores of men from the town, while the police, although not putting a hand on them, lent their moral support. Men were held in custody on boats for forty-eight hours by foreigners and sent out to sea at night, and efforts were made to land them at Alice Arm, where they had no friends. 'I call that kidnapping,' said Kergin. 'If they call that British justice, then I am a Red,' he added. He pleaded for an independent investigation into conditions at the mine and to see that board and rental charges were fair and 'that a living wage was paid.'[29] That speech was probably Bert Kergin's finest hour, for which the Liberal Party denied him its nomination at the next general election, and he went down to defeat as an independent.[30]

The police arrested Bradley, placed him on the *Malaspina* bound for Prince Rupert, and charged him with 'unlawful assembly,' but the case did not proceed for lack of evidence. Such was the force of public senti-ment in Prince Rupert that the government, relying on the evidence of police officers, was unable to send any of the strikers to jail, including the five indicted for 'unlawful assembly' and 'rioting.' In a trial before the Supreme Court of British Columbia, where defence counsel Gor-don Grant, hired by the Canadian Labour Defense League, persuasively argued that the five men had not been arrested for participating in a riot but for having been leaders in the strike, a jury acquitted them all.[31]

In spite of the staunch three-month fight put up by the Mine Workers' Union of Canada and its allies, the Granby Company, supported by the Bennett and Tolmie governments, had gradually recruited 300 strike-breakers, and by April the smelter was operating three days a week. The union claimed that of the 700 workers who struck on 1 February, less than 20 had returned. But in a public statement calling off the strike it admitted that it had made mistakes by underestimating the terror and by the lack of preparation for the mass eviction that took place. The strike had taken place under 'tremendous difficulties.' It had occurred in a war industry and the strikers had faced the 'full fury of the capitalist class,' with airplanes, machine guns, rifles, a war vessel, and large police forces being brought in to crush the strike. In spite of the 'utmost terror,' the campaign against the strikers in all the capitalist newspapers, the threatened mass deportations, and the cutting off of relief from work-ers who refused to scab, the ranks of the strikers had remained solid and the recruiting of scabs was slow. The company had been forced to reduce the price of board and rent, the filthy and insanitary bunkhouses were cleaned up, and fresh blankets and pillows were now furnished. The company was anxious to obtain experienced miners and the union believed it would have to win them from among those who had refused to scab. According to the union, the miners were calling off the strike 'in order that the strike may not end in debacle,' and 'the militant miners' could return to Anyox and reorganize their ranks so that the mistakes made on this occasion could be avoided in the future and the Granby Company would be compelled to recognize the power of the organized workers. 'Anyox,' the union predicted, 'will fight again.'[32] And it did, but not on the edge of the Alaska panhandle.[33]

The other hard rock mine and smelter operations that the Workers' Unity League had set its mind on organizing included the Consolidated Mining and Smelting Company at Trail, BC, owned by the Canadian Pacific Railway (with $50 million in assets in 1933), the much larger International Nickel Company operations at Sudbury, Ontario ($196 million assets), the Hudson's Bay Mining and Smelting Company at Flin Flon, Manitoba ($33 million assets), and the Noranda Mining Company in northeastern Quebec near Rouyn ($29 million assets). The first two proved to be virtually impenetrable for union organizers in the 1930s.

At the CPR operations in Trail, BC, the management had foreseen the attempt to contact its employees and had taken strong defensive measures early on, offering various forms of 'welfare capitalism' as at Anyox. These included low-interest building loans to encourage employees to own their own homes, building sites made available to employees for summer camps at a nearby lake, private health insurance and pensions, free apprentice training, profit sharing, and bonus pay. All this was overseen by Workmen's Co-operative Committees elected through secret ballot every year by over 5,000 fellow workers and with a representative from every department in the plants. The company boasted that there had been 'no serious labour troubles or strikes of any kind' for twenty years.[34] The trouble with all this, according to Al King, an early campaigner for the Mine, Mill and Smelter Workers' Union, was that the general manager, Selwyn Blaylock, was himself the chairman of the workmen's committees, ensuring the 'cozy fellowship' of a company union where grievances, complaints about favouritism, and other discriminations were easily swept aside. In at least one case when workers' representatives went to Blaylock with complaints against a foreman, he fired the whole crew on the spot and kept the foreman. It wasn't until after almost ten years of underground organizing and the changed conditions of the Second World War that Local 480 of the Mine-Mill Union won a certification vote in Trail. After that vote Harvey Murphy, district organizer, arrived from Vancouver in 1944 to negotiate and sign the first collective agreement forcing Blaylock and the Consolidated Mining and Smelting Company to recognize a real union.[35]

The International Nickel Company of Canada, known as 'Inco' for

short, was a large and powerful organization. After it acquired the Sudbury assets of Alfred Mond Nickel Company in 1929, it controlled 90
per cent of the world's production of nickel, a vital component in the
modern armaments industry. Its shareholders and board of directors,
dominated by American financiers, included a few wealthy Canadian
families – the Richardsons of Winnipeg, the Bicknells, Cockshutts, and
McLaughlins of Ontario – but such international luminaries as the lawyer John Foster Dulles of New York City and the Rt. Hon. Lord Melchett
(Mond) of Great Britain directed affairs. The company's world-wide
operations, employing more than 8,000 people in 1933, were concentrated in Ontario with mines and mills on a huge acreage in the Sudbury
district and at a refinery in Port Colborne.[36]

More so than many other companies, Inco had a reputation for ruling with an iron hand and continuous 'slave driving' of its miners. 'Only
those workers of exceptional physical strength,' wrote the *Worker*, 'could
stand the grind for any length of time.'[37]

Although the company had never missed a dividend payment since its
inception in 1894, its fortunes took a nosedive when world markets for
nickel and copper collapsed in the early 1930s. But in the spring of 1933
the industry began to experience a 'boom,' with production and profits quickly returning to historic levels. This was after Hitler had seized
power in Germany and the I.G. Farben Industrie placed an exceptionally
large order in Sudbury for 1,200,000 pounds of nickel matte – enough
raw material to make 160,000,000 lbs. of nickel alloy suitable for an ambitious rearmament program. Other, even larger, exports of the metal
routed through Holland found their way to Germany.

In the light of this information, the Workers' Unity League circulated agitational material about 'German fascists need[ing] nickel for
bullets!' and warning that 'the nickel ... now being feverishly mined in
Sudbury and exported across the ocean may in a few months or a year
shatter the bodies of Canadian workers again conscripted into uniforms
to wage a new war for markets, profits and colonies.' It urged the miners to organize solidly to improve their conditions and 'at the same time
prepare the means to strike a body blow to the profit-hunting inciters of
a new world slaughter,' whether it be the Germans or 'other imperialist
governments.'[38]

Inco did not take kindly to such views and it went to extraordinary
lengths to screen out or get rid of employees who might hold pro-union
sentiments. For this purpose it hired the U.S.-based Pinkerton's detective agency. This agency, operating through an organization in Toronto

called 'The Auxiliary Co., of Canada Limited,' offered services that ranged from supplying goons and thugs to disrupt workers' meetings, to hiring on 'auxiliaries' as decoys in the mines to inform on their fellow workers, to more subtle means of intimidation. The Sudbury Mine and Smelter Workers' Union famously captured the instructions of one of the Auxiliary Company's spies who posed as a door-to-door salesman peddling stain remover to gain information on family sympathies. The agency gave its spy examples of the kind of reports he should turn in:

> James Novack, 36 Cedar St., employed at Frood Mine. Wife says that husband belongs to Party, but is afraid to attend meetings or picnics. Donates money occasionally. Subscribes to Clarion.
>
> John Zielenski, 467 – 18th St. Employed as carpenter in smelter. Wife says he has a good job and gets good treatment. Lives in Company house and thinks rent is reasonable. Hates reds and says they do nothing but cause trouble.[39]

Given these realities, the Workers' Unity League was forced to proceed cautiously. A functioning miners' union in the Sudbury area with cards, a constitution, and dues stamps claimed to have 300 members by the end of 1930, but most of these were only on paper with few actually paying dues.[40] After the experience of the Anyox miners, the union resolved to employ all the lessons learned there 'to successfully pit our organizational efforts against the intimidation, discrimination and stool pigeon system of Inco.' The organizational structure of necessity would have to be of 'illegal form' until the union was 'strong enough to prevent any man from being fired for being a union man.' The illegal form would take as its basis small groups 'with only those of the same language and well known to each other in the same group.' No miner would be known as a union man outside of his own group. Each group would have an elected leader and the leaders of the groups in one enterprise would meet together regularly to make general decisions. The efforts of all union members would be directed to securing new members and setting up new groups, agitating on the issues in the enterprise, writing for publications (local and general) popularizing the union. The union would utilize 'all possible methods' to win concessions from the company and popularize the union on the job, carrying persistent agitation on the large issues such as speed-up, the bonus system, and payment for walking time from the mine entrance to the work areas. Foremost in all this was the task of developing mine and smelter newspapers. In addition, unemployed miners would be organized to carry out 'the more open work involved in spreading union literature,' and in 'developing contacts in their homes.'[41]

To spur enthusiasm for building the metal miners' union, the Workers' Unity League council for the area decided to endorse a proposal to have a three-month 'social competition' among the Sudbury, Timmins, Kirkland Lake, and Rouyn locals where the one getting the most adherents would elect a rank and file member to go to Moscow for 1 May to be financed by all four districts.[42]

But with Inco steadily increasing its pressure on union activists, the bulk of the miners had a dispiriting impression of the unconquerable strength of the company. Only about a third of the union membership paid their dues. They did so, according to Sam Carr, visiting Sudbury on a national organizing tour, as their revolutionary tribute to unionism rather than as an expression of a belief that a union would help them to fight Inco – 'they pay their cents,' he wrote to Ewen, 'as a religious jew drops his pennies into the Palestine fund box.'[43] As the company hoped and expected, there was little chance of the union becoming effective as long as it was forced to remain a small sect functioning illegally, not known to the workers as an organization actually fighting for their daily needs.

The Workers' Unity League was more successful at the two remaining hard rock mines in that its union was able to build up its strength as at Anyox until it could force the companies to consider its proposals and then to back up its demands by strike action that involved a majority or substantial part of the workforce.

It was in the spring of 1934 when the WUL organizer for the northern district reported that the miners' union was 'going like wildfire' in Timmins and Kirkland Lake, Ontario, and especially in nearby Rouyn, Quebec. After a three-month organizing drive, the union membership in the district had reached 900, of which the Noranda mine near Rouyn, employing about 1,300 miners and smeltermen, had over 500, 30 of whom joined or were already members of the Communist Party.[44] This place, described in 1930 as no more than 'a little frontier town, huddled around a copper mine, without paved streets or sidewalks ... the forest ... still nearby,'[45] was the jewel of the mining industry, praised in financial circles for being 'the outstanding producer,' the 'most rapid development in production and dividend payments among Canadian mining developments.' In the three-year period ending 1932 it paid an astonishing $8 million dividends on $11 million worth of shares.[46]

According to the local union's research, most people working in the mine were from Anglo-Saxon families and were native-born Canadians, followed by Yugoslavs, Ukrainians, French Canadians, and finally Finns. The foreign-born workers from Eastern Europe, who usually did the 'bone and muscle' jobs, made up about 30 per cent of the workforce in the mines of the district,[47] and it was among these men that the union had its first contacts. As at Anyox and Inco, to minimize the effect of company spies, the union organized the men into small groups, men who felt more secure all speaking the same language. At the end of May 1934 it had fifty such groups, including about thirty Anglo-Saxon and French-Canadian groups, and was beginning to contemplate the possibility of going to the employer with a list of grievances and demands to be backed up by strike action if necessary.[48]

It was just at this moment that the company began to discriminate against union activists. The first to be fired for being 'an agitator and trouble maker' was the president of the local union, an Anglo-Saxon. The workers wanted the union to take some action, but it was not ready yet. Soon another four were discharged for the same reason. After that the work of building the union slowed down and came to a standstill. 'The members want some action,' wrote the WUL organizer, 'and if we don't have it soon, we will not be able to hold what we have now.' A major difficulty, however, was that the union organizers had reason to suspect that the local president was actually a company agent. After being discharged he began working full time for the union at $30 per week but did not show much interest in the work of the organization. He threatened his comrades that if he didn't get his $30 per week he would go back to the company, tell them everything, and ask to be rehired.[49]

Although the district WUL organizer was now unsure whether or not a strike sentiment actually existed at Noranda, the union decided, after small group consultations, to proceed with open meetings of the miners to discuss the issues and to prepare for strike action. The miners adopted a list of demands relating to conditions at the workplace, hours and rates of pay, the right to organize into a union of the miners' own choice, and recognition of mine and smelter committees, and chose a delegation to present them to the general manager of the mine, H.L Roscoe.

What happened next has been well described by historian Evelyn Dumas in *The Bitter Thirties in Quebec*.[50] The manager rejected the demands, saying he would never deal with any union and especially one that was no more than 'a bunch of communists'; he pleaded that he could not afford any wage increase as he had to split profits among 1,800 shareholders, and he dared workers to 'go ahead and strike.'

Next morning there were a thousand miners and sympathizers including wives and children on the picket line. But by noon the company had a hundred 'special constables' sworn in by the municipal authorities, and together with the regular police, and supported by officers of the RCMP, they accompanied mine foremen who went about in trucks to collect strike-breakers and convey them through the picket line, visiting the homes of the foreign-born and threatening that if they didn't go to work they could face deportation.

The strike committee carried on bravely for a week, issuing a daily strike bulletin, holding open air meetings every afternoon by the lake-side, running a soup kitchen for strikers and their families, trying to bolster morale. But on the seventh day of the strike a fight broke out on the picket line. By then 150 armed police had arrived in town and they were waiting for just such an occasion. They swooped onto the scene, laying charges against strikers for rioting, intimidation, vagrancy, illegal distribution of leaflets, etc., railroading sixty-six of the most active members off to jail – without bail – some of them to be condemned to St Vincent de Paul penitentiary for two years.

'The strike has been smashed,' conceded Nick Thatchuk, district organizer of the Workers' Unity League, 'and the profit-greedy bosses are gleeful.' But heavy arrests and 'brutal police terror,' he said, had not been able to cow the Rouyn-Noranda workers in the past and neither would they this time. As he described the justice of the workers' cause for the *Worker*, and analysed how the strike was smashed, he predicted that the bosses would not exult for long, as the workers would consolidate their ranks and 'prepare determinedly for the next time.'[51]

Simultaneous with the Noranda strike was the hard rock miners' struggle at Flin Flon, Manitoba. This clash was larger in scale and longer in duration than the one at Noranda. Here, the heavy state intervention on behalf of the mine owners took on a no less military and even more political colouring, resulting once again in defeat for the miners and smelter workers. But the month-long confrontation became one of those legends that captured the imagination of workers in Manitoba and across the country for a generation.

The multi-millionaire Cornelius Vanderbilt Whitney, of Wall Street fame, and his family had the controlling interest in the Hudson's Bay Mining and Smelting Company, which was incorporated as recently as 1927. The Whitney interests held almost 6,000 acres of land straddling the Saskatchewan-Manitoba boundary eighty-five miles north of The Pas, Manitoba, at Flin Flon Lake. As an inducement to invest there, the government in Ottawa excused the company from paying royalties on the natural resources of Canada's north country for twenty years. By that time the patch of muskeg and rock in Manitoba had become the third-largest city in the province.[52]

The top managers of the Hudson's Bay Mining and Smelting Company were all Americans (R.H. Channing, Jr, president; R.E. Phelan, superintendent and chief engineer; and W.A. 'Baldy' Green, general manager), and they were adamant in not tolerating a union that might challenge their absolute control of the workplace. This was made clear early on, when a group of union carpenters presented Green with a petition signed by all sixty carpenters on the job requesting the removal of a certain capricious foreman who bullied the workers mercilessly. Once again, as at Trail, British Columbia, the managers did not hesitate a moment, firing the whole crew on the spot and retaining the foreman.[53]

A number of accounts of the Flin Flon strike have been written, of which the most natural and balanced presentation is the small book by James D. Mochoruk, *Mining's Early Years: An Historic Look at Flin Flon's Mining Pioneers*, published around 1984.[54] Fifty years after the strike, Mochoruk, a graduate history student, interviewed a cross-section of thirty-four Flin Flon residents about their recollections of those times on behalf of the Provincial Archives of Manitoba and the Manitoba Labour Education Centre.[55] Two of those interviewed were organizers for the Workers' Unity League: Mitch Sago, and Bill Ross, who was arrested in Flin Flon and sentenced to hard labour for his part in supporting the miners' union.

From these oral interviews and corroborated by other primary sources, we learn that the miners' union, using 'the Anyox method' of organizing, signed up a majority of the 1,300 miners and smeltermen into the union by June 1934. The union then held an election for a strike committee, which drew up a list of demands encompassing such basic trade union goals as better pay, the eight-hour day, seniority rights, the right to have all job-related accidents investigated by the union, and union recognition.[56] The company rejected the workers' overture, announcing, instead, that the plant could be closed for ten years rather than have anything to do with 'a handful of communist agitators.' From then on the strike committee, organizing from the community hall, mounted strong picket lines which closed down the mining operations, while the foreign-owned company orchestrated a Red-bogeyman campaign about 'outside agitators.' The company appealed to the provincial government to uphold 'law and order,' and it was behind the formation of an organization that called itself the 'Anti-Communist League of Flin Flon.' The irony of an anti-communist league campaigning in support of a U.S. company around the slogan 'Put Canada First' did not pass unnoticed at the strikers' rallies.

It happened that the Manitoba provincial government, headed by Premier John Bracken, who was also the sitting member of the legislature for the district, was unhappy about recent communist successes in local elections: communists elected included reeves, councillors, school trustees, and even an alderman in Winnipeg. Bracken and his government were only too willing to respond to the company's propaganda about the supposed threat posed by the Reds. The government added its own dire warnings of chaos and increased the number of police on the site. After an altercation in front of the community hall, where pro-company forces were organizing a back-to-work vote, the government ordered the police into action. Scores of strikers and their leaders were arrested and put into a makeshift jail. Bracken personally ordered 'back to work' posters to be printed and tacked up throughout the town. On 9 July, the whistle blew at the plant, and, under the watchful eye of steel-helmeted, rifle-bearing RCMP officers and the premier, several hundred men returned to work.[57] The strike was effectively over. The miners, here as elsewhere, had to accept the fact that they still had a long road to travel before they would be able to force the capitalist corporations and their supporting politicians onto the defensive. At the same time, the bold strike strategy of the Workers' Unity League provided invaluable experience in ways to participate in the class struggles that lay ahead.

Almost sixty years after the Flin Flon strike, in 1993, I located someone who had joined the Workers' Unity League in the course of that struggle. This was Oscar Dexter Brooks. When we met he had just written a book, *Legs: An Authentic Story of Life on the Road*, which described his youthful experiences as a hobo, farm labourer, horse handler, carnival barker, and mechanic, but which stopped just short of his arrival in Flin Flon.[58] Our conversation,[59] which took place thirty-five years after Brooks had given up his labour connections to sell real estate, provides a window not only into the awakening mind of a young worker who rose to become a leader of the strike, but also into the way in which Lozovsky's strike strategy actually operated on a major battleground.

Brooks, aged twenty-nine, was working part-time as a garage mechanic in Saskatoon in the summer of 1933, but climbed aboard a freight train for the north country when he heard a rumour about hirings in Flin Flon.

'It took about two months to get a job,' Brooks recalled. While he was waiting he cut wood, did odd jobs, and built a little log cabin along with another chap who was also on the skids. He recalled liking the atmosphere in the town; he could get everything he wanted. 'The mine, mill, smelter and power house were fully operating, [so there was] lots of activity,' he said. 'There were three hotels with beer parlours and several whore houses that also engaged in bootlegging.'

Eventually Brooks got a job labouring on a bull gang and later as a millwright's helper in the smelter. 'I was versatile,' said Brooks. 'I could adapt.' At the time of the strike he was driving a locomotive with two flat cars, getting sand for the smelter.

In response to my question about how he found out about the union, and his attitude to it, he replied:

'At the time I knew someone was organizing the men. I wanted to get in. But they figured that since I worked hard and diligently at any job I was given – that I was competitive; had the attitude of wanting to be the best on any job – that I might not look favourably on collective action. They were afraid to invite me in.'

The night before the strike the organizers called a mass meeting. Brooks heard about it and discovered that the men were electing representatives or shop stewards for the different departments of the mine, the mill, and the smelter to be on the strike committee. He spoke up even though he wasn't in the union. 'Son of a gun,' he said, 'if they didn't turn around and elect me to the strike committee.'

He talked of the Communist Party and its role in the strike:

'I knew there was someone planning operations,' Brooks said. Then, one day, organizers Mabel Marlowe and Bill Ross took him aside and talked to him for an hour about this 'organization,' including its aims and structure. 'They didn't mention its name until the very end, and then they asked me if I'd like to join. I was happy to,' Brooks said. 'I could remember the Winnipeg General Strike, and for a while I had carried a Wobbly [IWW] card. I had a labour background so it was natural that I would be attracted to the party.' Brooks was active in the party for the next twenty years. 'The party,' he said, 'gave me a great intellectual stimulus.'

Marlowe was with the Canadian Labour Defense League and Ross was doing relief work among the unemployed. Others in the communist group whom Brooks recalled included Alex Stewart, who had been in

the Independent Labour Party and was chairman of the strike committee; Earl Sedberg, a good speaker who did much of the early organizing
of the union in Flin Flon; Jim Coleman, secretary of the Workers' Unity
League, and Peter Barclay, both of whom were deported after the strike;
and Mitch Sago, who was also doing relief work. Brooks also recalled
'Whispering' Smith, a huge fellow with a booming voice who had a background in the ILP.

These were the people who built the union. They would begin with a
few contacts, perhaps people who belonged to other friendly organizations, such as the Ukrainian Labour Farmer Temple Association, finding
out about their leanings through those channels. Then, at somebody's
house, with four or five invited people present, they would explain the
drive by the Mine Workers' Union of Canada to set up a local. Brooks
recalled a Métis fellow who always had a bundle of copies of the *Worker*,
which he distributed from his one-room home. 'He wasn't in the party,'
said Brooks, 'but he promoted the paper, and he would tell the union of
likely prospects.' That was how Sedberg and the others worked to build
the union: 'in little groups so that any company spy would not be able to
give in the names of very many workers.'

The strike itself, as recounted by Brooks, showed the determination
and resourcefulness of the strikers, and the flimsy grounds for the subsequent arrest of their leaders.

'We did a very conscientious job of organizing the strike,' Brooks said.
'We allowed the pump men into the mines to keep them from flooding;
allowed a shift to go in to clean out the settling tank in the smelter, and
for the smelter to cool down properly.' The organizers also closed down
the three beer parlours and the bootlegging operations. 'We threatened
that they would get no business afterwards if they didn't close,' Brooks
recalled.

From the start the strikers wanted to use the Community Recreation
Hall as a headquarters. It was large building in which badminton and
other sports activities took place, as well as dances. Plus, importantly, it
had a good kitchen and, said Brooks, 'would be the place for us to organize food relief.' Since the workers had contributed by payroll deduction
to the building of the hall, they felt a sense of ownership. But the people
in charge of the hall were all company officials, and they barred the
strikers.

Before Brooks and Alex Stewart went to meet the officials about this,
Brooks read the by-laws carefully and knew that if he posted a list with
enough names, a new election for community hall officers would have to

be held within seven days. The president of the community hall was also head of the Zinc Plant, and Brooks gave him a hard time.

'I don't have to take this from you, Brooks!' he objected. 'I'm in charge here.'

'If you won't allow us the use of the facility which we have paid for,' Brooks responded, 'then we will challenge you. I'll have your job as president.' Brooks read him the by-laws on the spot and, seven days later, he was president. 'They never got us out of the community hall,' said Brooks, 'at least not until they had brought about 100 Mounties to town, and by then I was in jail.'

The strikers held a meeting every day in the hall. 'We wanted to negotiate with the company but they ignored the union,' said Brooks. Then, one day, a dentist came into the office when four or five of the strikers were there, including Brooks. The dentist made a pitch to set up a meeting with Channing, company president, and ended by asking: 'What am I going to tell Mr Channing?' 'We didn't trust him,' said Brooks. 'I said, "Go fuck yourself."' Challenged by Stewart as well, the dentist left.

After a week the police started arresting everybody who spoke at the daily meetings, charging them with anything they could think of, including intimidation, making threats, 'bringing false news,' and unlawful assembly. The strike committee kept urging Brooks to speak at the meetings, 'but,' he said, 'I was afraid of making an asshole of myself.' Finally he decided that he'd have to speak, since all the other speakers (Bill Ross, Mabel Marlowe, Jim Coleman, and Pete Barclay) had been arrested and the company was organizing a back-to-work vote. He worked on a speech all night, memorizing it. The next day he stood up and started out: 'Fellow strikers, comrades and friends ...' – then he forgot everything. In desperation he switched into the kind of free-wheeling talk he was used to at carnivals. 'I spoke for twenty minutes from my gut and created quite an uproar,' said Brooks. After that he spoke for three evenings in a row, until he, too, was arrested.

The authorities decided to go ahead with a back-to-work vote at the town hall. By now there were quite a few Mounties present and they created a wedge between the picketers to open up the way for the strike-breakers. But the union had some tough people, including Sig Sundquist, who was a wrestler, and a couple of boxers, and they surged in behind. Several strikers got arrested. 'Not too many got in to vote,' said Brooks, 'so it was not a valid result.' But the company claimed otherwise.

The assay office for testing ore samples became the temporary jail, with about forty prisoners, including Brooks. Bail bond hearings took place in the schoolhouse, where brave people came and put up their houses for surety. The Canadian Labour Defense League brought a lawyer up from Winnipeg to help in the defence. When Brooks's turn came the judge said, 'This man is a rabble rouser; he has the ability of a Hitler. I've watched him in action. He'll have to stay in jail until the strike is over.' Brooks was charged with thirteen offences. All were dropped except one: he received a year's suspended sentence for being part of an unlawful assembly according to Section 98 of the Criminal Code. Stewart won his case in a rather humorous fashion, getting his look-alike brother Jock to come to the courthouse dressed in his clothes and putting him on the stand. Said Brooks: 'He convinced the judge that it was Jock, not himself, who the police witness had identified.'

Still, as already indicated, the strike was broken. Bolstered by the anticommunist hysteria orchestrated by Premier Bracken and his attorney general, W.J. Major, and supported by the presence of the Royal Canadian Mounted Police, the company breached the picket line, jailed the union's leaders, and smashed the strike after thirty days. The company made a few concessions – restoring half of the 18 per cent wage cut; reducing light charges; and introducing a twice-a-month pay cycle – enough to allow Mabel Marlowe and Bill Ross to observe that the 'struggle had not been entirely fruitless.'[60] Nevertheless, the Hudson's Bay Mining and Smelting Company restored its dominance, instituting an elected 'Workmen's Welfare Board,' much as the other hard rock mining companies had done, in an ultimately futile effort to stem the growing discontent of an awakened workforce.

11
1933: Gaining Momentum

En dépit de ces difficultés, la L.U.O. constitue ... pour notre periode le fer de lance du movement ouvrier canadien.

— Béatrice Richard, '*Péril Rouge*' (1993)[1]

Those who go to radical organizations to get accomplished what well-established labour unions have failed to do are flying in the teeth of providence.

— Attorney General W.H. Price, 6 October 1933,
after ordering the armed militia into Stratford, Ontario[2]

Agitation is not a crime, or it used not to be. The very structure of British liberties which we all talk so loudly about but so often forget to defend is founded on the deeds of agitators.

— *Ottawa Evening Citizen*, 10 July 1933

When the Workers' Unity League met in its second national congress, in September 1933, it could record some enviable gains since its first congress a year earlier. In spite of government repression, especially in Ontario, 170 delegates gathered in Toronto, and according to their new national secretary, Charles Sims, the league could claim to have about 30,000 adherents – double that of a year earlier. This membership figure may well have been an exaggeration.[3] Nevertheless, new unions were being organized, especially in Ontario;[4] many strikes had been fought against wage and relief payment cuts, blacklisting, and violation of agreements, and in support of wage increases, shorter working days, and other union conditions; out of 250 strikes of employed and unemployed workers in the year since the first congress in August 1932, the league, according to Sims, had led 190, of which 155 were won or partially successful.[5] The Department of Labour in Ottawa kept track of all these occurrences and in 1933, confirming the gist of Sims's claims, it produced an elaborate chart on the spreading influence of supporters of the Third International in Canada.[6] (See appendix 2.)

Of course the achievements were insufficient and Sims warned against overestimating the successes gained under the banner of the WUL. Our work, and our successes, said Sims, 'are simply drops in the bucket – the bottom of the bucket is hardly wet.' In a country with a workforce of 2.5 million, only about 27,000 workers, he stated, were engaged in the successful strikes of the employed workers and only about 75,000 unemployed workers had taken part in the relief strikes.[7] It was a sobering thought.

Nevertheless, the past year, Sims claimed, had been 'exceptionally favourable for the development of militant industrial unionism and for the building up of a powerful movement of the workers around the issues that arise from mass unemployment.' The workers of Canada, he said, were 'in a ferment of indignation and resentment against the inhuman attacks showered upon them by the employers and the government authorities.' As Premier Bennett continued to accord first priority to paying bondholders in New York City, London, and Toronto, a million poverty-stricken and often hungry unemployed workers had their endurance tested to the breaking point with relief cuts, forced labour schemes, evictions and foreclosures, and shootings. 'Pent-up bitterness,' Sims asserted, 'is boiling over.'[8] This view was substantiated in a general way by the deputy minister of labour of Ontario, who stated in his annual report of October 1933 that 'the change in attitude on the part of industrial workers' in the province, the increase in 'strikes and protests' by both the unemployed and those 'whose wages and salaries have been reduced to the point where a decent standard of living cannot be maintained,' had been the most significant development of the year.[9]

The new leader of the Workers' Unity League, already proving himself to be an effective speaker, was a self-educated man, energetic, and although young, was fast developing as an organizer, according to his closest colleagues. Originally a coal miner from Newcastle, England, Sims had emigrated to Canada in the 1920s to work in the Alberta mines. From there the Communist Party recruited him as a student to the International Lenin School and for a time he was a roommate of Stewart Smith. 'Charlie enjoyed talking,' Smith recalled. 'Once when I was sleeping in the same bed I woke up two hours later and Sims was still talking.'[10] Unfortunately, surviving records of the second WUL congress are scarce, making it impossible to know the exact effect of Sims's speech there, but from contemporary articles in the *Worker* an impression of the work of the congress emerges.

J.B. McLachlan was re-elected president even though he was unable, or perhaps did not wish, to nudge the radical Nova Scotia miners and their newly formed Red union, the Amalgamated Miners of Nova Scotia, now 7,000-strong, to join the league. McLachlan was flanked by vice-presidents: Nick Thatchuk from northern Ontario, Joseph Forkin from Manitoba, George Drayton from British Columbia, Sam Scarlett, the famed IWW orator, from Saskatchewan, and the resurgent Albertan, John Stokaluk. Less than a year after the Crowsnest Pass strike, Stokaluk had regained favour and had replaced the jailed and quietly smouldering Harvey Murphy as the league's lead person among the coal miners.[11]

The co-reports to the congress were given by a new set of activists: Anne Walters reported on the results of the textile campaign, Kalle Salo on work among lumber workers, Hans Sula on the trade unions and unemployment, Meyer Klig on the needle trades, G. Wright on the pulp and paper industry, George Marceau on work among French-Canadian workers, Joseph Forkin on the work done among railway workers, and John Stokaluk on the miners.[12]

A comparison of the resolutions and programs adopted in 1932 and in 1933 reveals both continuities and change. There was the same emphasis on a militant, united-front struggle to beat back the economic attacks of the employers and the governments on the living standards of the working class – both employed and unemployed. There was self-criticism about failures to penetrate the basic, unorganized factories and mines of Canada, and about the lack of vigorous rank and file movements in the railway and other mainstream trade unions. As well, weak efforts to organize women and youth were mentioned. The congress continued its demands for a system of social and unemployment insurance financed by government and employers; for the right of labour to organize, to strike, and to picket; for equal rights for all foreign-born workers; for the release of all working-class political prisoners; for democracy and rank and file control in all trade unions; for the resumption of normal trade relations with the Soviet Union and against all imperialist war preparation.[13]

But this time there was a change in tone which was both more confident and more guarded; plans were more precise, less wordy. The league was learning how to concentrate its forces and finances in decisive places more efficiently so as to win some victories.

A revised constitution adopted by the congress had some noteworthy features designed to please the rank and file, to strengthen democracy within the union, and to improve relations with other sectors of the labour movement: officers' salaries in affiliated unions were not to exceed the average wage in the industry, and the principle of 'democratic central-ism' was spelled out as (1) democratic elections and right of recall of all executive organs, (2) inner-union democracy based upon maximum ini-tiative and activity of the entire membership, and (3) an authoritative executive board to lead the work in the union. As well, pejorative sectar-ian references to work in 'reformist, craft, patriotic or Catholic unions' were replaced by references simply to 'work in non-affiliated unions.'

Two other constitutional changes reflected deep concerns of the lead-ership about increasing attacks on the league by the Canadian state and its court system and threats to outlaw the organization on the supposed grounds of seditious conspiracy to overthrow the government under the direction of a foreign power.

When Norman Freed went to Moscow in the summer of 1932 he initi-ated discussions in the Anglo-American Secretariat of the Third Inter-national on steps that could be taken to blunt the attacks of the owning class and help communists to operate more effectively in the conditions of illegality or semi-illegality that had been imposed on them by the Canadian state. There is a large file on this subject in the archives of the Red International containing reports and theses, but unfortunately minutes of the discussions are not included.[14] The conclusions of these talks, however, may be inferred from at least two changes in the constitu-tion of the WUL.

The change of greatest immediate import was the section redefining and relaxing the league's relationship with the Red International, which has been referred to in chapter 8. Informed by careful discussion in the Anglo-American Secretariat and to make it more difficult for the enemy to threaten the organization's legal existence, the Congress adopted two paragraphs that clearly defined the league's position as being in control of its own foreign relations on the basis of fraternal co-operation, mutual benefit, and subservience to none. No doubt written with an ear to how the words would sound if read out in a capitalist courtroom, they did not reveal the underlying hierarchy of influence at the Third International and gave away little of importance in the actual practice of international solidarity, at least as it affected Canada:

FRATERNAL RELATIONS: The Workers' Unity League of Canada shall

maintain the closest fraternal relationships with all other Trade Union
Organizations pursuing the same or similar objects that the WUL stands
for, and will, without entering into any organic connections with them,
strive to maintain the closest relationship with, and to cooperate with such
organizations. This will be carried on, according to the decisions of the
National Executive Board, by maintaining and developing correspondence
with such organizations, an exchange of fraternal delegates where this is
deemed advisable and by mutually cooperating in the various National and
International campaigns that may render such mutual fraternal cooperation advisable and necessary in the interests of the Workers' Unity League
and its affiliated organizations and any other trade union organizations that
the National Executive Board consider should be approached with offers
for, or requests for fraternal aid or mutual cooperation from time to time
as occasion may arise.

The Workers' Unity League of Canada shall strive to strengthen and
improve its existing fraternal relationships with the Red International of
Labour Unions, the Minority Movement of Great Britain and the Trade
Union Unity League of the U.S.A. (without entering into any organic
relations or connections with any of these organizations) and will seek to
achieve fraternal cooperation with these organizations in the various trade
union campaigns in the course of the struggles.

The second change was to tone down the revolutionary rhetoric: the
WUL stripped its constitution of virtually all references to long-term
aims and objectives about overthrowing capitalism; the word 'revolutionary' appeared but once in the amended document. There is a deep irony
here, given the almost simultaneous publication by Canadian social
democracy of high-sounding rhetoric in the 'Regina Manifesto' promising that no CCF government would rest content until it had 'eradicated
capitalism' and eliminated the 'exploitation of one class by another.'[15]
Once again, as in 1932, the Congress discussed the proper relation of
class struggle communists to gradualist social democrats. For the communists, what took any sting out of the CCF's threat to capitalism was
that it promised peace, and said it did 'not believe in change by violence'
and would pursue its ends 'solely by constitutional methods.'[16] In other
words, it would never break the law. Earlier in the year, Stewart Smith,
acting head of the Communist Party, had written, in line with statements
of the Third International, that in spite of left-sounding phrases by CCF
leaders, 'only over the dead body of SOCIAL REFORMISM, could the
workers' cause be victorious.'[17] But communists in Europe had begun to

have second thoughts about their bad relations with social democracy after Hitler won a national election and came to power legally late in January 1933.

When the Nazi leader started, 'according to the law,' to decimate the Jews and his socialist and communist enemies on the left (and proceeded to withdraw Germany from the League of Nations), the sparring working-class parties in Germany belatedly began thinking seriously about organizing a united front of resistance. This sentiment was endorsed by the Third International in March 1933 after an overture from the Second International (in Amsterdam),[18] and it called upon communists everywhere to forge a united front against fascism. In the common struggle it urged its members to 'refrain ... from making attacks on social democratic organizations.' This attitude opened the door to the 'united front from above' as well as 'from below.' In this way, in 1933, there began a gradual, historic shift in the Canadian Communist Party's view of how the transition to socialism could occur in a liberal democracy like Canada, away from the insurrectionary model of the Russian revolution in favour of 'the mobilization of the democratic struggle and choice – election and the development of the peoples' front' as the means to achieving the strategic aim of working-class state power. The Communist Party began a process leading to advocacy of 'a peaceful transition to socialism within the framework of the historically-evolved Canadian parliamentary institutions.'[19]

In line with the new situation and the changing attitude of some of the leading members of the Third International (but not including Lozovsky as yet),[20] Canadian communists started telling themselves that they had to 'sit at the same table with reformist leaders' and not stick 'to the old methods' of exposing them through 'name-calling' and other forms of sectarianism.[21] In this connection the national executive board of the Workers' Unity League addressed an open letter to the leaders of Canada's largest trade union centres, in April 1933, inviting them to join in organizing a national united front conference to deal with the acute problems thrown onto workers as a result of the Depression, by the rise of fascism and by the 'growing danger of new imperialist wars.'[22]

Not unexpectedly, since the league's letter included a clumsy and stinging sentence assigning major responsibility for 'the present serious situation of the working class' to the 'class collaboration' policies of the Trades and Labour Congress (AFL) and the All-Canadian Congress of Labour, the leaders of the TLC and ACCL rejected the overtures of the Workers' Unity League. With disdain. W.T. Burford, secretary-treasurer of the ACCL, wrote that his organization was not convinced that 'a convention such as you contemplate is necessary or desirable.' And when Hans Sula, organizer of the WUL's unemployed work, approached J.S. Woodsworth, MP, the leader of the CCF huffily replied that 'we prefer to work along our own lines.' Woodsworth did not believe that unemployment insurance measures could be secured by means of resolutions or deputations, 'but rather by sending men to parliament,' who as their numbers increased would be able 'more and more effectively to demand rather than to beg.'[23] The delegates to the WUL congress were predictably infuriated by such responses but resolved, nevertheless, to persevere by sending representatives to the annual gatherings of the reformist labour movement to press their united front proposals. They also resolved to continue marching on the streets with their banners.[24]

Working-class activity in the previous year made its mark on the second national congress, leading Sims to predict that 'we stand on the threshold of great historic struggles.' This was especially true for the '*central task*,' which was to take the lead in organizing a nation-wide movement to force the government to accede to working-class demands on unemployment, and for the '*major task*,' requiring 'every ounce of energy,' which was to organize unions in some of the 'decisive industries of Canadian capitalism' – steel and automobile, metal mining, pulp and paper, and textiles, where so far the WUL had got 'a mere toehold.'[25]

The momentum felt by the league derived in the first place from the increasing effectiveness of the unemployed movement.[26] In mid-January 1933, with an almost unimaginable 30 per cent of the Canadian workforce unemployed, Hans Sula, secretary of the National Committee of Unemployed Councils, led yet another unemployed delegation to call upon Premier Bennett in Ottawa. This meeting followed hard on the heels of the December 'Alberta Hunger-March,' a massive demonstration of 12,000 unemployed workers and indebted farmers in the home base of the prime minister, an event that has been described as 'the biggest single manifestation of class conflict in Alberta during the entire decade of the 1930s.'[27] Bennett, whose RCMP had helped the Edmonton police to forcibly disperse the march with horse and club – for lacking a parade permit – was not pleased to receive the deputation and he rejected all their demands. There would be no full and free unemployment insurance, relief expenditures would have to be reduced, more investigators would be hired to catch cheaters, and Bennett promised sterner measures to keep the unemployed quiet. Sula promised to come back with a national hunger march when parliament was sitting, and they both kept their promises.[28]

In the spring of 1933 Bennett announced a 50 per cent cut in the federal government's relief appropriations to the provinces (and municipalities) with the claim that warmer summer weather reduced the needs of the destitute. As well, his government took over the relief camps in British Columbia, Manitoba, Ontario, and Quebec and placed them under the Department of National Defence, where the single unemployed worked for 20 cents a day. These actions unleashed a wave of relief struggles.[29] There were about twenty hard-fought strikes in towns and municipalities that involved married men. These ranged across the country from such places as Halifax and Reserve Mines in Nova Scotia; Oshawa, Hamilton, Lakeview, St Catharines, Sudbury, Kirkland Lake, Parry Sound, and Windsor in Ontario; Winnipeg and Brandon in Manitoba; Saskatoon; Calgary and Drumheller in Alberta; and several places in British Columbia, according to the leader of the Workers' Unity League. There were an equal number in what became known as the 'slave camps' of the single unemployed. 'We can expect more and bigger struggles,' wrote Sims in the *Worker*'s new section on theory, 'and we must organize for them better, have the employed workers support them, and utilize this growing wave of discontent to force the government to grant full and free unemployment insurance.'[30] That was the central task of the revolutionary trade union centre.

In his wide-ranging article Sims devoted himself to the lessons of the relief strikes, seeking to make clear what was meant by *revolutionary* in the work of the league. He said it was to become involved with all the available progressive social forces in society, and without being dictatorial, to unite them and mobilize them to participate in activities of great importance to their daily well-being and to their future. In contrast to a non-revolutionary or reformist way of settling things comfortably by talks within accustomed channels, conciliations, and arbitrations conducted in suitably 'neutral' surroundings, the Workers' Unity League wished to encourage the hungry to make a noise in the streets and marketplaces, to trouble the dreams of their exploiters, to invade the council chambers with their urgent demands, and to defend their right of free speech and assembly on all occasions including defiance of the forces of 'law and order' if and when necessary. Sometimes the league found approval in unexpected places: 'Agitation is not a crime, or it used not to be,' editorialized the *Ottawa Evening Citizen*, adding that 'the very structure of British liberties which we all talk so loudly about but so often forget to defend is founded on the deeds of agitators.'[31]

Of all the relief struggles in 1933 perhaps the most successful was the six-week strike against the relief cuts in Calgary during April and May;

this also happened to be the home town and political base of the prime minister. Sims analysed the success of the strike in considerable detail as a model for others to follow.

According to city officials, Calgary, a city of 80,000, had 10,727 people on relief in the spring of 1933 and relief costs there had risen from $53,000 in 1929 to $334,000 in 1932. To keep such an immense body of people from starvation, city hall was both raising taxes, to the outrage of the home owners, and harassing the jobless citizens, cutting them off relief for infractions of petty rules and generally making their lives even more miserable. The unemployed received 30 cents a day for food ($10 a month) and for this meagre sum they were expected to put in forty hours' manual labour each month at special, often meaningless, work projects created by city officials.[32] Even this standard of relief was cut by 20 per cent on the first of April.

That was the background to the formation of large organizations of unemployed ex-servicemen, and of married and single unemployed men and women in different parts of the city. Until Bennett announced his relief cuts, a dozen or more of these organizations were led by workers with reformist ideas, pledged to a policy of 'passive disobedience,' and therefore were often spurned by the communists as hopeless. 'Some of our comrades had to be expelled from our revolutionary organizations,' wrote Sims, 'because they refused to carry out united front work, because they refused to work within the Married Men's Unemployed Association.' Gradually the Calgary leadership of the Workers' Unity League worked out plans that became the policies and tactics of the strike. It was a genuine united front, according to Sims, not one where the communists entered 'as dictators with a ready-made, typed-out program,' which demanded that the others conform 'lock, stock and barrel' with the league's ideas of tactics and slogans, but as part of a movement. It was hard work, he said, mistakes were made,'but great steps ahead were taken.'[33]

The various organizations agreed to form a Central Council of Unemployed to direct the strike; large open-air meetings took place at which WUL leaders Harvey Murphy and Pat Lenihan, an immigrant worker from Ireland, were among the featured speakers; disciplined street parades – four marchers abreast in the style of coal miners and thousands strong – put great pressure upon the city and the Brownlee provincial government to restore the unemployment relief rates. Of over 3,000 unemployed supposed to be at work on relief projects, less than 200 showed up; at one site more than a thousand strikers swept aside

Table 11.1 Schedule of relief in Calgary, 1 July 1933

Family	Amount per week for food	Amount per month for rent, light, and gas
Man and wife	$4.50	$16.00
Man and wife and 1 child	$6.00	$17.35
Man and wife and 2 children	$6.90	$19.95
Man and wife and 3 children	$7.65	$22.10
—	—	—
Man and wife and 9 children	$9.90	$28.60
Married men, in return for their relief, work for the city at the rate of 50 cents/hour.		

Source: Worker, 1 July 1933, LAC, Department of Labour, RG27, v. 358, T-2969. See also James Struthers, No Fault of Their Own, appendix 4, for relief rates in selected Canadian cities by 1936.

50 policemen and shut down a relief job where 70 strike-breakers were at work; arrests and trials followed. The strikers brought the schoolchildren into action and got church congregations to bring pressure on the authorities, they invaded the big restaurants and department stores at the busy hours on 'shopping tours.' The City Council settled the strike (and eventually persuaded the attorney general to have a stay of proceedings against the strike leaders) when it became clear that the employed workers were stirring for action, 'when whisperings about a general strike grew louder and louder.' 'The Calgary relief strike showed how to win,' said Sims. Calgary had maintained its standards of relief – the highest in Canada (see table 11.1).[34]

The high point of the unemployed movement in 1933 was the National Congress on Unemployment that took place in Ottawa after Labour Day when Parliament was in session. There 321 delegates claiming to represent over 300,000 workers in more than 200 organizations met to share their experiences under a large banner that read 'Unite against Hunger.' After hearing of conditions of undernourishment and near-starvation, as well as examples of militant actions in getting better relief, preventing evictions, and conducting relief strikes, they adopted a 'Charter for the Right to Live' and a program of action to win the charter. This charter[35] embodied the fundamental demands of the unemployed movement for the rest of the hungry thirties and is reproduced in appendix 3. The congress also chose a delegation of fifteen, headed by Alderman Reginald Morris of East Windsor, to present its demands to the government of Canada. After some difficulty in arranging for the meeting, the delegation was received in the prime minister's office by the Honourable Sir

George Perley, acting prime minister in Bennett's absence, as well as six other cabinet members – the ministers of justice, national defence, national revenue, fisheries, the attorney general, the solicitor general, and the postmaster general – all in the presence of reporters from the *Toronto Star,* the Canadian Press, the *Ottawa Journal,* and the *Worker.* It was a curiously impressive collection; either the cabinet members, apparently, wished to have a good look at their quarry or perhaps there was not much else to do on a day when their boss was away. Noticeable by his absence in this parade of ministers was the Honourable W.A. Gordon, minister of labour and immigration (and deportations), who by the ancient rite of banishment held a dire threat over many Workers' Unity League members. In any event, after hearing Alderman Morris and several others, including a passionate speech by Flora Hutton of Burnaby, British Columbia, Perley replied in a surprisingly subdued and conciliatory manner, saying he would discuss what they had said with the prime minister upon his return but adding, 'I should like to say this, that in my judgment, much that you ask is entirely impractical'; he declined to specify any examples.[36] The delegation returned to their congress suitably indignant, and determined to work even harder.

After the Workers' Unity League's second congress, in the autumn of 1933, there took place several 'great historical struggles' of the kind that Sims had predicted. These were in Stratford and Hespeler, Ontario, and in the lumber camps of northern Ontario and Quebec. In all of them the 'red bogey,' the 'péril rouge,' was the main ammunition and battle-cry of a worried capitalist class. But there were variations as well.

The most famous battles, invoking military aid to civil power, were the strikes of 650 furniture workers and 100 chicken-pluckers in Stratford, Ontario. The furniture workers, engaged in making radio cabinets for such giant corporations as Rogers-Majestic and the Philco Radio Company, had seen their wages fall below subsistence level (some getting only 10 cents an hour or $5 a week, the majority making $10 or $11 at a time when the federal government said an average-size family required $16 per week to survive),[37] and took heart from news of a successful strike by a newly formed furniture workers' union in Toronto. This was the Chesterfield and Furniture Workers' Industrial Union of the Workers' Unity League, led by Fred Collins and Isadore Minster, which had won 20 to 40 per cent wage increases for 275 Toronto workers, a forty-four-hour week with overtime pay after forty-eight hours, recognition of the union and its shop committees, and hiring through the union. It was a stunning advance.[38]

When the Workers' Unity League's organizers came to Stratford to extend the union drive, they received an attentive hearing which led to the rapid formation of a local union. Collins, thirty-five, had some unusual credentials.[39] He was a Scottish Presbyterian, married, and a war veteran who had served twelve years in the Imperial Army, followed by three years in the Glasgow police force, two years with the Niagara Falls city police, and then work as a part-time Toronto street car conductor until getting fired in the spring of 1933 for some newly acquired radical sympathies. Although a recent recruit to the movement, Collins, with his upright military bearing, Scottish accent, ruddy complexion, and booming yet friendly voice and manner, could command attention in a community settled by Anglo-Celts such as Stratford, and he already knew how to hold an audience. Considered a rabble-rouser by some, he would be remembered by furniture workers as a 'great fighter.'[40]

Collins spoke to increasingly large audiences of workers, telling them how the Toronto furniture workers won their strike and urging the Stratford workers to follow their example. He warned that the employers would use every possible means to combat a union, including the claim that it was a communist organization, controlled by Moscow. Within three weeks the *Beacon-Herald* reported that 90 per cent of the workers in six of the seven local furniture factories had joined the union, elected local officers and shop committees, formed a central council and publicity, relief, picket, and other committees, and decided upon five demands to put before the employers. The struggle was shaping up in the now classic mode of Lozovsky's 'Strassburg Resolution.' The demands were similar to the conditions recently accepted by the employers in Toronto: recognition of the union and its shop committees; a 30 per cent wage increase (45 cents an hour for unskilled workers, 50 cents for semi-skilled, and 65 cents for skilled workers), a forty-four-hour work week with time and a half for overtime and holidays, equal distribution of work among departments, and no discrimination against any employee for union organizing.[41] According to Nancy Stunden, who has made a detailed and fair-minded study of the strike in her MA thesis, in the final union meeting before confronting the employers the workers gave Collins a 'rousing reception':

He discussed the Unity League's strike record and the necessity of organizing all the furniture workers in Canada. Referring to the possibility of a local strike, Collins urged the workers to be as vigilant on the picket lines as they had been during the war. 'A strike is a war,' he said. 'In war, what do you do with a man who shirks? A spy gets the same dose. A man who doesn't recognize a strike is a traitor to himself and his class – a man who scabs is a spy. There are only two sides to every question ... Either a man is with the strikers or with the employers. Anyone who tries to be a connecting link is going to be a sick man ... The front line of trenches will be your picket line. A strong front line is essential. The war is a just war and right one – fought for the benefit and safe-guarding of your homes. You are the troops.'[42]

When the employers failed to respond to the union demands, the strike of 650 workers began on Wednesday morning, 14 September.[43] From then on events moved rapidly with the mayor seeking to bring the parties together face to face as the union demanded. The employers were adamant that they would not recognize the union or negotiate with its officers. Collins replied that union organizers would only be advisory members of any negotiating committee and that any agreement would have to be ratified by members of the union. Later Collins agreed to stay off the negotiating committee, whereupon the employers met with their shop committees on Monday, 18 September. While this was happening the central strike committee organized a parade of 1,000 workers headed by a recently organized fourteen-piece band. 'From factory to factory they paraded,' wrote the *Worker*, 'being greeted with cheers from the workers' homes.' Prominent among the many slogans was one carried by the women and girls: 'We demand the minimum wage for girls.'[44] Hundreds of unionized workers at the large Stratford railway shops of the Canadian National Railways, who had received two pay cuts in the previous sixteen months, showed their support for the strikers.

That same day one of the companies hired strike-breakers and at midnight they started to remove partly finished radio cabinets for shipment to other factories; a crowd of 300 strikers arrived, the first clash with strike-breakers erupted, and the shipment was stopped. The *Beacon-Herald* demanded to know why no arrests were made and the local police chief was suspected of being too friendly with Collins and the striking workers. To complicate matters the militant chicken-pluckers at the Swift Canadian plant, who were demanding to be paid 3 cents instead of 2 cents per chicken, began a strike the next day that would raise tempers on the picket lines.

When the negotiations between the furniture manufacturers and their respective shop committees broke down, the central strike committee made a surprising concession, offering an 'open shop' (the employer free to hire anyone he liked) in return for 'recognition of the union as a bona-fide union with shop committees,' no discrimination against those presently out on strike, and on that basis negotiation about wages and conditions. After conferring with the mayor and other government officials, the manufacturers agreed to accept the union's proposals. They met the central strike committee that evening and arranged to confer with the respective shop committees. Still later at a mass meeting that evening, Thursday, 21 September, the strikers greeted the central committee's report of the negotiations with 'deafening applause,' according to the *Beacon-Herald*. The newspaper was optimistic on the prospect of the strike being settled soon.[45]

The next morning, Friday, 22 September, the union led a parade of 2,000 people, including delegations from the railroad workers' unions and the unemployed association, through the city for a rally at Lakeside Park. At that time the total population of Stratford was little more than 17,000. With Collins acting as chair, rousing speeches were made, pledges of financial support given, and warnings issued to guard against 'sly tricks and dirty dealings of the bosses.'[46]

That afternoon the shop committees reported the offers of the companies to the workers. For some reason the details did not become public knowledge, but according to Stunden they appeared to include a wage increase of only 10 per cent, a fifty-hour week, and a clause whereby companies could specify certain workers 'disabled' or 'less than normal capacity' and pay them less than the standard rate. At a mass meeting that evening Collins and Isadore Minster, a more experienced organizer who had recently come to Stratford to assist Collins, spoke of the employers' proposals in scathing terms, arguing that the large Stratford manufacturers could afford wage raises equal to those conceded by the small Toronto companies. The employees rejected the offers of the manufacturers, whereupon the companies broke off all negotiations with the union, blaming the Unity League organizers for being more interested in promoting class conflict than in improving the situation of the furniture workers.

Over the weekend of 23–4 September the situation took an ominous turn as the furniture manufacturers and Swift requested more police protection for strike-breakers. The Stratford police commission, consisting of the county judge, the mayor, and the police magistrate, attempted to do this by swearing in special constables, but Stratford being 'a great labour town,' they were unable to recruit any.[47] Whereupon the mayor called another meeting of the police commission for Monday morning, 25 September. This meeting was attended by top company officials and by Joseph Sedgewick, a solicitor in the attorney general's department in Toronto. It was a busy day. Although Sedgewick had barely arrived on the scene, he lost no time in requesting twenty-six additional provincial police from Toronto, and later the same day the local police commission, undoubtedly on Sedgewick's urging, made a formal request to the attorney general appealing for military forces.[48] Lieutenant-Colonel William H. Price, attorney general, was not reluctant to respond. Sedgewick, thirty-five, who two years earlier was prosecutor in the trial of the eight communist party leaders, increasingly assumed command. The Workers' Unity League organizers sensed that the 'forces of capitalism' were gathering and warned the workers that an attack was imminent.

As it happened, the most serious trouble of the two strikes broke out Monday afternoon, not at the furniture factories but at Swift, where there was as yet no union organized but where the workers had acted spontaneously. Since there were 14,000 chickens in the plant that had to be fed, the strikers agreed to have four of their number remain on the job. But when these workers took time out to join the parade, the meat-packing company seized the moment to bring in a carload of strike-breakers from Toronto. The strikers tried to remove the scabs. By 9:30 that evening the chief of police estimated 1,000 people were milling about the plant, eggs and rocks were thrown, the power lines cut, a few windows smashed. With the appearance of Sedgewick's police reinforcements the crowd dispersed. In spite of the violent behaviour and the presence of a large police force, no arrests were made at that time. Nevertheless, thirty-six hours later the army arrived – two companies of the Royal Canadian Regiment consisting of 129 soldiers, four tanks, two machine gun platoons with eight guns each and other equipment – and proceeded to billet itself ostentatiously in the centre-town armouries behind hastily erected barbed wire entanglements. The commanding officer, Lieutenant-Colonel R.J.S. Langford, met with Sedgewick, who told him the situation was quiet.[49] The townspeople, who according to the police commission were 'largely favorable to the strikers,' quickly understood that the presence of the army was not to quell a 'riot' or 'disturbance of the peace' that might be 'beyond the powers of the civil authorities to suppress, or to prevent, or to deal with,' as set forth in the Militia Act, but to take sides in a labour dispute.

The people of Stratford expressed their shock at the deployment of the army, and the union was incensed. That evening a protest rally at Lakeside Park, variously estimated to have attracted between 3,000 and 8,000 people, heard angry speeches by the leaders of the Chesterfield and Furniture Workers' Industrial Union, and a wide variety of other people expressed their opposition and dismay. A resolution supported by a thunderous roar from the crowd denounced 'the action of importing troops for the purpose of the attempted intimidation of the striking workers, whose only desire and aim is for the immediate improvement of their conditions,' and demanded 'immediate and unconditional withdrawal.' The *Beacon-Herald* joined in condemning the government for its 'rank stupidity,' and predicted that 'no self-respecting man is going to carry on negotiations while such a condition exists.'[50]

When the furniture factories opened their doors the next morning not a single worker went in.

The striking workers continued their parades and rallies in the following days, singing songs deriding the mayor and the police commission and Attorney General Price, whom they saw as responsible for calling in the army; their placards carried slogans such as 'the soldiers don't go hungry, why should we?', 'machine guns bring death, higher wages, life,' and 'we fight against starvation and slave labour.'

When the security provided by the presence of soldiers and police failed to undermine the union and bring the workers back, Sedgewick orchestrated a second strategy: a 'Red scare.' After having initially agreed to negotiate with the Chesterfield and Furniture Workers' Industrial Union,[51] the furniture manufacturers suddenly announced that they could no longer meet with the union because it was a communist organization. In a lengthy joint statement framed in consultation with the agent of the attorney general, they said that the industrial union was affiliated to the Workers' Unity League, which 'is the Canadian branch of the Red International of Labour Unions with headquarters in Moscow. It is a revolutionary organization which rejects and ridicules the principle of conciliation or collaboration adopted by established trade unions ... it advocates and promotes class war ... declaring that the interests of the so-called capitalists and workers are diametrically opposed.'[52]

Collins and Minster responded not by denying these statements or that there were communists in the league but by arguing that the league was an economic and not a political organization, that it fought for workers' rights and accepted all wage workers regardless of race, creed, colour, sex, age, craft, or political affiliation as members; it was controlled by its members, who had the responsibility to ratify or reject all contract proposals by a democratic, majority vote. And, since the Second National Congress of the Workers' Unity League, they could truthfully say that it was not affiliated to the Red International. Collins managed to persuade

Charles Dingman, the editor of the *Beacon-Herald*, to publish the newly amended constitution of the Workers' Unity League in its entirety to prove his point. The 'Red bogey,' they said, was a 'red-herring to distract from the real issues.'[53]

The argument went on through the month of October. During that time the employers sent private letters to all their employees emphasizing the threat of communism. The leaders of the established trade union centres, Tom Moore and A.R. Mosher, also issued statements calculated to undermine the Unity League, warning that its 'sole purpose' was 'to stir up strife and foster the aims and objects of the Communist Party.'[54] In spite of these attacks on the union, the companies were unable to persuade the workers to return to work. But with the heavy police protection and the threat of intervention by the army, they proceeded to weaken the effectiveness of the strike by emptying the factories of the inventory of radio cabinets.

On its side, the union spread its organization to other towns in Ontario, such as Hanover, Preston, Neustadt, and Hespeler;[55] it organized meetings across other areas of the province to publicize the issues and to raise funds to support the strikers. It won many new friends and large amounts of relief, including municipally approved tag days, but still it was not enough to sustain 700 strikers and their families indefinitely. Having to supply $1,000 of food and fuel every week, the funds raised by the union were on the verge of depletion. In mid-October the Shop Committee at one of the furniture plants signed an agreement with the employer and the workers there returned to their jobs against the advice of Collins and Minster. After that the government appointed a 'special investigator' to undermine the union leaders and to persuade the rest of the workers to give up. Gradually the resolve of the workers weakened and they returned to work on 3 November with an agreement that did not recognize the Chesterfield and Furniture Workers' Industrial Union. Nevertheless, the union could claim a partial victory in that contracts, signed by union shop committees, contained provision for a wage increase (12 ½ per cent), a shorter work week (forty-four hours), all strikers to retain their jobs, and the right of workers to form a union of their own choice. The workers at the Swift Canadian Company, now organized into the Food Workers' Industrial Union, returned to work on the same day with a 10 per cent raise.[56]

Nancy Stunden concludes her study by observing that while the Stratford strikers achieved some substantial improvements in their working conditions, they did not win their strikes in 1933. Nevertheless, they demonstrated their determination and ability to stand up to their employers, which, she says, 'is probably the most critical step in working class development.' As in Blairmore, Alberta, a year earlier, their moment of triumph came when one of the local strike leaders led a slate of labour candidates to victory over the Property Owners' Association in 'the most hotly-contested municipal election ever witnessed in the city.'[57]

And members of the middle class, too, had some kind of awakening. One Sunday, after the strikes, a Canadian missionary on furlough from China passed through Stratford to preach at the central United Church. In the middle of his sermon when he came to describing the sweatshops in Shanghai 'from which foreign investors have reaped the benefit because of the lack of "vexatious factory laws"' and the presence of child labour, causing 'a certain amount of dumping on the market here with the effect on unemployment,' an old gentleman in the congregation called out, 'Gude for you, laddie! Tell 'em the truth!'[58]

Hard on the heels of the Stratford strikes came the strike and lockout of 700 workers at the Dominion Woollen and Worsted Mill in Hespeler, population 2,900. When a request for help came to the Workers' Unity League, Anne Walters, organizer for the fledgling Textile Workers' Industrial Union of Canada, hurried over from Toronto. Dominion Woollen and Worsted was one of those textile giants that the league aspired to organize. It was the dominant manufacturer of woollen yarn and cloth in Canada, a conglomorate with over $5 million in assets which controlled a fistful of other companies such as Canadian Woollens Ltd., Otonabee Mills, Milton Spinners Ltd., Orillia Worsted Company, and R. Forbes Company, Ltd, all located in small towns scattered across Ontario, making it difficult to mount a co-ordinated union organizing drive. Protected by Prime Minister Bennett's 33 per cent tariff wall in 1933, these companies were a formidable force.[59]

The turbulent thirty-day strike saw the participation of many of the Unity League's most experienced organizers – Fred Collins, who by now had the status of a folk hero in southwestern Ontario, James Houston, who was to spend sixty days in jail for his efforts, J.B. Salsberg of the Workers' Unity League's Toronto Council, and Joshua Gershman of its National Board. These organizers helped the elected strike committee and its chairperson, Albert Proud, make their case, first to the management and, when it rejected the union's demands, to a large meeting in the town theatre and along the mass picket lines that were formed. It was a familiar story: workers faced with speed-up, new looms being added, workers doing more for the same and sometimes less pay; the minimum wage law flouted – some girls earning as little as 10 cents an hour; older workers laid off and replaced by apprentices; unbearable sanitary conditions in the factory; straw bosses lording it over the workers like despots. Twice the company attempted to reopen the plant and twice it failed. The police complained that they were unable to make arrests because hundreds of women workers were on the picket line.

But after some initial victories in stopping strike-breakers from crossing the picket line, the union was unable to counteract the determined pressure of the state in its support of the textile firm. 'Our business,' said Attorney General Price, 'is to see that people wanting to work shall not be molested.'[60] Local and provincial police combined forces to intimidate the strikers and to urge a return to work, a task in which they were assisted by the rectors of the Catholic and Anglican churches, a retired school principal, the mayor, and a retired organizer of the Trades and Labour Congress. After a violent free-for-all on the picket line in the third week of the strike, the police went to the union's headquarters with a blanket warrant to arrest the entire strike leadership and take them off to jail in Kitchener without allowing bail; for good measure they arranged to have the strikers evicted from their headquarters.

The odds against the union, including the burden of strike relief, were too great, and after a month a newly elected strike committee ended the conflict, saying that an 'organized retreat is forced upon us through conditions that we cannot remedy at this moment.'[61] The company had made concessions on working and sanitary conditions but on the larger questions of wages and union recognition it had refused to budge. It was a disappointing result for the Unity League but at least it had increased the size of its toe-hold in the textile industry.

The other big struggle of this time took place in the bush camps supplying pulpwood to the pulp and paper industry in Ontario and Quebec. The industry, still the largest manufacturing sector in Canada, had 7,000 bushworkers in 241 camps strung across northern Ontario in 1933 and a similar concentration in neighbouring Quebec.[62] Starting in June of that year, at Onion Lake, not far from where union organizers Rosval and Voutilainen had been murdered four years earlier, and lasting until June 1935 at Nipigon, there took place in the boreal forests of the Canadian Shield a dozen or more co-ordinated strikes whose size and intensity have seldom been matched in the country's history.[63] In all cases, win, lose, or draw, a major catalyst was the Unity League and its affiliate, the Lumber Workers' Industrial Union of Canada, whose ultimate aim was to achieve an industry-wide collective agreement covering all the employers. If a strike became necessary under this strategy, the picket line would stretch for a thousand miles from Fort Frances near the Manitoba border to the Saguenay district of Quebec. It was an ambitious plan that took another decade and wartime conditions to achieve but this was the beginning.

The time was ripe for action because of a promising upturn in the economy in the second half of 1933 that brought improved pulp and paper exports. The logging camps 'have sprung into activity overnight,' noted the *Ottawa Evening Citizen*, as seventy pulp mills across the country sought to replenish their exhausted woodpiles.[64] Bushworkers, eager to fill the jobs, lined up at the employment agencies, but many soon found the wages and conditions being offered by the operators not to their liking. Some companies had forms similar to 'yellow dog contracts' whereby each individual had to sign agreeing to forfeit wages owing if he failed to stay the whole season (i.e. if he found a better job elsewhere, or went on strike); operators charged for mail delivery, for coal oil and blankets; bunkhouse and sanitary conditions often fell below standards required by provincial laws; there were exorbitant prices in camp commissaries and for transportation to the camps; the daily charges for board were too high and monthly wages too low. After deductions it was not uncommon for lumberjacks to end up with net pay of 5 to 10 cents an hour for their exhausting labour.[65]

The pulpwood cutters' campaign followed the now familiar pattern of the Workers' Unity League's *revolutionary strike strategy*, although now, for tactical reasons in the face of court trials, the league moderated its rhetoric: an editorial in the *Worker* called it simply 'the New Unionism.' The content of this particular brand of 'new unionism,' however, remained the same.[66] It was defined as militant struggle, rejection of arbitration and conciliation, the widest democracy among the strikers, the strictest discipline in face of the enemy, mass pickets and mass action, the building of a united front of the rank and file of all working-class organizations, of employed and unemployed.[67] It entailed gathering workers' opinions at camp meetings; holding united front wage scale conferences, the conclusions of which were to be sent to the companies and by wide publicity in various languages to the workforce; after a suitable interval – in this case two to three months – further united front conferences to vote on specific demands and on a strike mandate (face-to-face meetings with employers, if possible, with a short strike deadline); election of strike committees as well as publicity, picket, relief, social, and other committees to involve large numbers of workers in active strike work; the creation of solid picket lines to deter strike-breakers; and work to support those arrested by the police and to frustrate the tricks of the employers who seeded disruptive agents into the union.[68]

The heart of the campaign took place in simultaneous strikes in November and December 1933 against the operations of Great Lakes Paper in the Thunder Bay district, Spruce Falls Pulp and Paper in Kapuskasing, Abitibi Pulp and Paper in the Cochrane area, and the Canadian International Paper Company in the Temiscaming region of Quebec. Most of these companies had gone into receivership as a result of over-investment in the booming 1920s and now the great trust companies of Toronto, Montreal, and New York represented and jealously guarded the interests of their shareholders and bondholders.

The united front wage scale conferences, which included elements of the Industrial Workers of the World (IWW), who still had a consider-able presence among the bushworkers,[69] took place in Port Arthur and in Cochrane where delegates agreed on sets of demands to be placed before the operators; speeches at Port Arthur were translated into Eng-lish, Finnish, Ukrainian, and Yugoslav. The demands, as recorded at Cochrane, included $3.50 for a double cord of unpeeled eight-foot logs (up from $2.50 or $2.75), board at 75 cents per day (down from $1); for those on monthly salaries (teamsters, loaders, road gangs, cooks, etc.) a minimum of $35 and board, twenty-six work days each month, and a working day of not more than nine hours including travel time; the right for the workers to hold meetings in the camps, to elect camp commit-tees, and to join and organize a union without interference on the part of the companies or the police.[70]

The union achieved a quick breakthrough at Kapuskasing, where the Kimberly Clark Company of New York, owner of Spruce Falls Power and Paper, which supplied newsprint to the *New York Times* and the *Wash-ington Post*, had 950 men out in bush camps along the Smokey River. Half of them were French Canadians who had never had much previous experience of union organization. When the company's rejection of the union's demands became known and a strike vote was taken, the strike machinery, under the direction of Jack Gillbanks, the English-speaking secretary from the national office of the Lumber Workers' Industrial Union, William Lehtinen, a Finn, as well as Nick Thatchuk, district sec-retary of the Unity League, went into high gear. Hundreds of workers poured out from the camps, and under the watchful eye of a detach-ment of provincial police, an RCMP constable, and an intelligence agent of the Canadian Army's General Staff, established pickets at every road, railroad, and entry point.

Within a few days the army man had gained a strong impression that everyone realized the men's wage demands were justified and he reported by telephone to the General Staff that the company was preparing to meet them, while refusing 'to recognize alleged red element.'[71]

The Kapuskasing strike lasted but a week. With support coming from the townspeople and neighbouring settlers and from the co-operative store in Timmins, the union could announce that it had two months' supply of food to sustain the strike. When eighty additional men came down from camp after a few days and a truck with a ton and a half of beef drove past the City Hall, the mayor, who was also the general manager of the Spruce Falls Company, decided, according to Gillbanks, that 'it would be better to grant more of the demands or ... soon be forced to close the paper mill.' The end of the strike came unexpectedly when the company accepted all the workers' demands. This was a remarkable victory for the strike tactics of the Workers' Unity League – winning wage increases from 20 to 50 per cent – and it was like a beacon to workers across the district and into Quebec. 'The majority of the workers,' wrote one organizer, 'did not mind to be called "reds." Especially among the French Canadians is this noticeable,' he added. 'They seem to be more militant and active than any other nationality in the lumber camps or among the settlers.'[72] For the first time in the North country, according to Gillbanks, a large company had been forced by mass pressure to sign a wage agreement with a strike committee of lumberjacks, and they could 'well be proud to possess such a document.' The union claimed to have recruited 400 new members in the district during these eventful days and another 2,000, mostly French Canadians, by the end of the year.[73]

Things did not go so smoothly for the union in other places, especially in the Thunder Bay district, where 1,500 men were on strike, even though the lumberjacks there also had a large measure of public opinion on their side. 'The people of Canada will not tolerate a starvation standard for the workmen in any industry,' thundered the *Winnipeg Tribune* in an editorial titled 'Trouble in the Woods.'[74] Faced with public support for the workers, the smaller timber operators and the Chamber of Commerce in Port Arthur favoured reaching an early agreement along the lines of the Kapuskasing settlement. But that was decidedly not the view of the National Trust Company, which held a receivership over the Great Lakes Mill and was a large shareholder in the biggest source of pulpwood in the region, the Pigeon River Timber Company.

From his office in Toronto, J.M. Macdonnell, general manager of the National Trust Company, defended the trust's position, saying the Pigeon River Company was fair, conditions there were good, and he was unwilling to be a party to negotiations with the United Front Strike Committee. Macdonnell believed that many workers were satisfied with their lot and were anxious to go back to work 'if they [could] be protected against interference.' 'You should also know,' he wired the Port Arthur Chamber of Commerce, 'that under our contract with Pigeon timber company any increase in labor charges whether from increase in pay or decrease in charges for board and lodging must be borne solely by us.' But for 'these disastrous labor troubles,' Macdonnell said, 'general improvement in conditions would have given newsprint industry a chance to pull itself out of the mire.'[75]

The National Trust thought that it could find a means to break the union and was determined to try. Its first weapon was a company union, the anti-communist Canadian Bush Workers' Union, headed by a Port Arthur alderman. This organization's manifesto declared that 'we decline to belong ... to any ... camouflaged political despotism,' and 'we prefer to do business the Canadian way – by collective bargaining assuming responsibility for our agreements, and fighting politically as we individually please.' Like Macdonnell, it claimed that there was very little dissatisfaction among the workmen of the district, 'except as they are inspired, or through fear and threat, are led by these agitators.' It affiliated with the All-Canadian Congress of Labour and joined in the recruitment of strike-breakers.[76]

More decisive for the National Trust strategy was the political power of the Ontario provincial government. A close association between government and the industry had a long and intricate history, as discovered by Professor H.V. Nelles of York University when he wrote his landmark work on the politics of development in Ontario. Men like Edward Wellington Backus from Minneapolis, described by admirers as 'an empire builder,' 'a modern Napolean of finance, diplomacy and astuteness,' who had established the Great Lakes Mill at Thunder Bay, 'knew exactly what they wanted,' wrote Nelles, 'how to get it, and were accustomed to getting their own way.' Under pressure from industrial promoters, 'government became an extension of management, bending and twisting its regulations to suit private interests.' And further, 'industrialists used the government ... to provide key services at public expense, promote and

protect vested interests, and confer the status of law upon private decisions.' In an analysis that bore striking similarities to that of the Unity
League, Nelles concluded that paternal government departments and
political friendships 'permitted businessmen to use the state to stabilize,
extend and legitimize their economic power.'[77]

It was not out of character, therefore, that Macdonnell would lean on
the provincial government for support, demanding police and armed
militia to keep the roads open for strike-breakers, and in response that
Attorney General Price, while ignoring the requests for the army in the
wake of the Stratford experience, would send a large contingent of provincial police. Considerable tumult resulted from this action, as scores
of strikers were arrested for 'unlawful assembly,' 'intimidation,' 'begging
without a permit' (as they tried to raise strike funds); forty-seven were
given jail sentences and a dozen or more held for deportation to Finland
and Poland.[78] An eyewitness participant recalled the time:

> It was a dirty strike, with RCMP, Ontario Provincial Police and Lakehead
> local police forces involved. The RCMP used horses a lot.
>
> One morning, when strikebreakers tried to take out horses from a stable
> belonging to a Port Arthur timber contractor, known as Pigeon-River-John-
> son of the Pigeon River Timber Company, a vicious anti-union operator, the
> RCMP tried to disperse well over 1,000 pickets by running their horses over
> them. But they got showered with stones by angry pickets until they fell out
> of their saddles and were forced to beat a retreat.
>
> However, the next morning about 4 a.m., after boozing all night, several
> hundred of the local constabulary surprised hundreds of workers, sleeping
> in two halls adjacent to the previous day's skirmish, by driving the workers
> out of the halls and into the streets in 25 degree below zero temperature
> (about –31 degrees Centigrade) attacking them with their billies as they
> fled out into the icy streets. Many workers suffered from frightful beatings
> and some became invalids for years; one Norwegian worker died a few years
> after as a result of this merciless brutality.[79]

Police action was not enough to break the strike; but Macdonnell and
his co-directors had other demands to put upon the state. If the government could not end the strike by force, then certainly it would have
to protect the investors by other means. While another director of the
National Trust, R.H. Major, assured a public hearing in Port Arthur that
the company was 'entirely impartial' in the dispute and that it was 'actu-
ated wholly and solely from sound business principles,'[80] in private it was

another matter. Soon enough, after some hard bargaining, the government announced a special subsidy. The cabinet approved a 28 per cent reduction of stumpage fees on spruce pulpwood – from $1.40 a cord to $1 – for the current year.[81] With the investors' interest secured, a strike settlement followed immediately.

Macdonnell and the National Trust had failed to break the union, and hundreds of lumberjacks jammed into the Finnish Hall in Port Arthur to celebrate their victory. They had won the 'Kapuskasing settlement' with some modifications and they relished a banner headline on the front page of the Port Arthur press: 'DISTRICT BUSHWORKERS WIN IN WAGE DISPUTE.' But even if National Trust had lost the war in the bush for the moment, it had kept its grip on the powers of the state and that same evening all timber operators in the district were guests of the National Trust Company at a dinner in the Prince Arthur Hotel; after all, they had something to celebrate as well, having secured their pocketbooks at the public's expense.[82] This was the kind of bailout the capitalists most appreciated.

The extension of the pulp cutters' strike into Quebec proceeded with the same hue and cry about the 'Red peril' that permeated government, business, and media in Ontario. The reality, however, as demonstrated by scholar Béatrice Richard, was that in all likelihood few communists were on the scene. Utilizing the report of a commission of inquiry appointed afterwards by the Quebec government, Richard has made a detailed, objective analysis of the strike and its participants. The impetus for the strike came from French-Canadian lumberjacks who had worked in Ontario and who were well aware of the gains made by the strike movement there. This was especially true of men working in the camps of Raoul Turpin, men known as 'voyageurs,' mobile workers often without a fixed address who had no other sources of income (such as from farming) and thus were highly motivated to enter the struggle for a living wage. While working in Ontario, the 'Turpin men' had become acquainted with, and in many cases had joined, the Lumber Workers' Industrial Union. That was how the union came to Quebec.

The Workers' Unity League sent three young people over from the Timmins district to help the executive of the new local union. These were Harry Racketti, twenty-four, a Finn born in the United States, Jerry Donahue, from Kirkland Lake, and Jeanne Corbin, twenty-five, from Timmins. They all played active roles in helping the strike committee and all went to jail for their efforts. The part taken by the bilingual Corbin, whose health was fragile, was especially noteworthy. She had been a schoolteacher in Alberta, then worked as editor of the Communist Party's paper, *L'ouvrier canadien*, in Montreal, and now was organizer for the Canadian Labour Defense League in Timmins and a member of the Workers' Unity League's district executive. Politically developed and a 'passionate and convincing speaker,' according to Richard's research, 'she enjoyed great popularity among the workers.'[83] The police wanted to charge her with sedition.

When the strike by 800 of the 2,000 lumberjacks supplying pulpwood to the Canadian International Paper Company began on 26 November 1933, 'the news,' according to Richard, 'spread like a powder wick enveloping the political scene of the province.'[84] The provincial Liberal government of Premier Louis A. Taschereau moved swiftly to have police disperse the picket lines, using tear gas, clubs, arrests, and in one case the Riot Act to justify its actions. Mass trials took place. Thirteen of the leaders were sentenced to from four months to a year and another sixty-four workers given six months' suspended sentence. In spite of the repression, the strike lasted almost three weeks, long enough for a disturbed public opinion to force the government to establish a commission of inquiry into conditions in the forest industry. Some changes were made in the laws. Nevertheless the strike was lost. The company was able to keep the workers at $26 per month, plus board, as well as lower piece rate prices, and the union was severely damaged.

It was a harsh experience, to be repeated when the largely immigrant workforce in the Noranda mines attempted to establish a miners' union in the same area six months later. The Workers' Unity League, however, tried to see a positive side to this and other experiences in Quebec as it congratulated French-Canadian fellow workers on their magnificent work during the loggers' strikes, showing that the workers of Quebec were 'uniting, organizing and struggling as never before': the knell was being sounded, Charles Sims predicted, 'to the age-old boast and slander of the Canadian employing class "that Quebec offers docile and cheap labor."'[85]

12

Sweatshops and Militancy in the Needle Trades

We cannot, in frankness, refrain from stating that the labour and wage conditions in this branch of Canada's industrial activity are such as to merit the most emphatic condemnation ... the worker in the clothing industry can expect neither comfort nor security; in many cases, he can, indeed, expect only hopeless poverty.

– Report of the Royal Commission on Price Spreads, 1934[1]

The Industrial Union of Needle Trades Workers led by the Communist Party of Canada, was the first union to succeed in organizing large numbers of women workers in the dress trade; ... [its] shop-focused structure ... which allowed rank and file control over shop issues, was more accessible to women than that of any other union.

– Mercedes Steedman, historian[2]

Although the Communist-led Industrial Union of Needle Trades Workers made some notable gains for certain groups of workers, the main impact ... was to undermine the workers' struggles for better conditions by pitting worker against worker and union against union.

– Ruth A. Frager, historian[3]

Canadian politics experienced an unusual turn of events in 1934. No sooner had the New Year dawned than one of the senior cabinet ministers parted company with the prime minister over how to cope with the lingering economic depression. This was the Honourable Henry Herbert Stevens of British Columbia, minister of trade and commerce and a sometime Methodist preacher. Stevens demanded that the government intervene to set things right and save a capitalist system that had gone badly off the rails. He created such a storm that Prime Minister Bennett was forced to appoint him head of a parliamentary Select Committee on Price Spreads and Mass Buying to investigate business abuses. The hearings of the Select Committee soon created more outcries, obliging Bennett to raise its status to that of a royal commission, again with Stevens in charge.[4]

Taking his inspiration from the example of President Roosevelt's New Deal program, Stevens sought to stir up public opinion through a series of speeches in which he stated, among other things, that Canadian laws had 'holes big enough for millionaires to crawl through and company laws that permitted the fleecing of the public, on the one hand, and sweatshops on the other.' While not sparing the 'pulp and paper barons,' the meat packers and tobacco monopolists and other leaders in industry and finance for their 'disregard for ethics,' he was particularly aggressive in denouncing the large department stores (such as Eaton's and Simpson's) with their practice of 'mass buying' and 'predatory price cutting' which pushed down the wages of employees in the manufacturing sector 'to a starvation point.'[5] Witnesses from the garment industry, boot and shoe manufacturing, furniture factories, meat packing industry, tobacco, baking, and canning industries, chain stores, textile industries, and others, who spoke about low wages, terrible working conditions, long hours of work, and high profits, supplied ample corroboration for Stevens's charges. In the words of his final report, wages in the needle trades were 'exceedingly low,' hours of employment 'oppressively long,' and violations of the laws about employment conditions 'frequent and continuous.'[6]

In the wake of public indignation stirred up by the Stevens inquiry and a growing strike wave by aggravated workers, provincial governments began passing laws to establish 'hours of work' and 'fair wage' codes for the conduct of business. British Columbia formed a Board of Industrial Relations and passed a Special Powers Act, allowing a panicky government to do whatever it wished without first passing any bill in the Legislature; supporters of the Workers' Unity League called this legislation the 'Slave and Pauperization Act.'[7] Alberta set up a board with the right to issue orders fixing minimum wages and conditions in all industries, and overriding existing collective agreements in the coal industry. The Arcand Bill in Quebec gave the crafty provincial cabinet the power to make an agreement arrived at by any one group of employees (no matter how small in number) with any one employer binding upon everyone else in the trade. From the workers' point of view, this was an alarming development. Already an order of this kind in the shoe industry existed; it made no mention of hours of work, established a wage scale ranging from 12 ½ cents an hour to 40 cents, and further stated that for those on piece-work, it was only necessary for 80 per cent of the workers to reach the average hourly rate stipulated. Ontario, too, announced plans to introduce codes fixing wages and hours. In all cases the governments had no intention of enforcing the regulations; that would be left to joint bodies of employers and 'responsible' or 'sensible' unions. Involving unions in this way, and giving them increased status, was an attempt to 'keep our streets clear of strikers,' according to Ontario's deputy minister of labour. It was, as another commentator has written, a method to 'take the wind from the sails of the troublesome communist-led Workers' Unity League' with its class-struggle unionism, by favouring 'tame' unions.[8]

Alarmed by these developments, considering them a form of incipient fascism, the league decided to participate in the Stevens inquiry with a brief of its own. Theirs was a hard-hitting, militantly left statement that called into question the sincerity of the inquiry and took the opportunity to criticize the social reformists who supported it. The differences between Stevens and Prime Minister Bennett, it said, while significant, were 'not differences in principle.' The league suggested that the inquiry was basically a cover-up by the government to gull the working class into thinking it was doing something about sweatshop conditions even while it was hounding, terrorizing, deporting, and shooting workers who were trying to change things for the better, at a moment when there were 200 workers in jail for combating sweatshops. The federal government itself, the statement continued, set the standard for sweatshop conditions by paying only 20 cents a day for work by 40,000 people on roads and airports. Apart from that, it was the biggest corporations and monopoly trusts in the textile, railroad, steel, auto, pulp and paper milling, and match industries that were the most guilty of paying little and pushing hardest, and they were not even on the agenda of the inquiry. The basic remedies against sweatshops, according to the Workers' Unity League, were readily at hand: federal enactment of a seven-hour day, five-day work week and a minimum wage law of $12.50 per week for the young, unskilled male and female workers, and the election of Action Committees against Sweatshop Conditions in every city and town; there was no need for codes 'to bind and hog-tie' workers in the manner of Hitler and Mussolini.[9] If there were to be codes for industry, they should be generated with the participation of labour; the Workers' Unity League and its affiliates would propose drafts of the content for such codes.[10] The league continued to advocate that workers could only defeat sweatshop conditions 'through shop committees, through powerful unions, by means of a class struggle policy ... and [being] prepared to strike to enforce their demands.'[11]

When vice-president Sam Scarlett and national secretary Charles Sims of the Workers' Unity League sought, in March 1934, to present their brief, Stevens curtly refused, saying it was irrelevant to the work of his committee.

The Industrial Union of Needle Trades Workers had taken shape in Canada in 1928. It was founded on the initiative of communist-minded workers and their allies in three local unions – cloakmakers in Montreal, dressmakers in Toronto, and capmakers in Winnipeg. Their decision to try to form an *industrial* union in the garment industry paralleled a similar move in the United States and was in keeping with urgings from Alexander Lozovsky at the Red International. Until then, the workers involved, predominantly Jewish immigrants from Eastern Europe, had been members of one of the four large American international garment workers' unions – the Amalgamated Clothing Workers (male clothing), the International Ladies' Garment Workers' Union, the International Fur Workers' Union, and the United Cloth Hat, Cap and Millinery Workers' International Union. But after years of factional struggles in these organizations, the communists, in many cases, found themselves without influence through exclusion or blacklisting by the anti-communists who controlled the upper echelons. In the journal of the New York Historical Society, Stanley Nadel describes how in the 1920s, the International Ladies' Garment Workers' Union 'came within a hair's breadth' of becoming the first major communist-led labour union in North America. Only an exhausting struggle which the author describes as a civil war of 'Reds versus Pinks,' which cost the union half of its membership and left it deeply in debt, 'turned back the Communist advance.' Since history is written by the victors, Nadel observed, it is essentially their version that appears every time a new book refers to those events, a version that falls short of explaining the bitter feelings of the losers and their subsequent determination to build anew outside the established unions. Nadel writes:

Perhaps most striking in these events was the readiness of the Socialist leaders of the ILGWU to 'sort of stay away from the demands of democratic

rules.' They barred left wing [i.e. communist] candidates from elections
and from office, then they suspended them from membership in the union.
When the left wingers were elected in sufficient numbers to control local
executive boards, the administration suspended local self-government. In
the final battle of 1927, the Socialists allied themselves with employers, the
police, and even with gangsters to restore their control over the union. In
the end, they were even prepared to destroy the ILGWU in order to 'save'
it.[12]

The struggles of the 1920s, which also played out in Toronto and
Montreal, help to explain the move of the communists to establish a
Canadian union in the needle trades and are part of the background
for understanding the suspicion, rancour, and high level of vituperation
that characterized strained relations between themselves and the social
democrats in the needle trades unions for decades to come.[13]

In Canada, a brief alliance of the communist-led Industrial Union of
Needle Trades Workers with the social democratic All-Canadian Congress of Labour occurred in 1928–9 but was soon dissolved. By 1931, at
the time of its second national convention, the IUNTW affirmed, instead,
its affiliation with the newly formed Workers' Unity League. Although by
this time the industrial union had already established twelve local unions
in Montreal, Toronto, and Winnipeg for mens' cloakmakers, fur workers, capmakers, glove and raincoat makers, and custom tailors (ironically still along traditional *craft* lines), it was the dressmakers' locals in
Montreal, Local 4, and Toronto, Local 2, that became the focus of its
attention and offered the greatest opportunities for its chosen mandate
to organize the unorganized.[14]

Led by Annie Buller, the IUNTW launched its first organizing campaign among dressmakers in downtown Toronto, where there were
about 3,000 workers in the trade. The rival International Ladies' Garment Workers' Union soon became aware of Buller's activities and under
the leadership of Bernard Shane, sent up from New York, began organizing the same field in what became an acrimonious conflict in 1931. The
two types of unionism competed for support among the dressmakers:
shop-floor, class-struggle unionism advocated by the industrial union,
in contrast to a unionism that 'no longer saw manufacturers and workers as adversaries but as partners working together,' as promoted by the
ILGWU.[15]

Buller and her team of organizers campaigned around a program of
higher wages, shorter hours, and better working conditions, and elected

shop committees to handle grievances and to enforce collective agreements with the companies. After many months of patient work, they succeeded in signing up a number of workers, mainly young women, in each of 100 out of 150 of the smaller dress manufacturers' shops in Toronto. The union expected, or at least hoped, that when it called for a general strike, this nucleus would succeed in bringing out the dressmakers *en masse*. But they were in for a rude awakening, since only about 300 workers responded to the strike call, and the walkout had to be called off after six days.[16] Given the deplorable conditions exposed by the Stevens inquiry, what happened?

There was, of course, a campaign of intimidation by the employers, supported by municipal officials, and arrests by the police which damaged morale. There was also sabotage by the rival international union. Bernard Shane was reported in the Toronto *Globe* as going around to the shops influenced by the industrial union, cautioning the workers that there was a *proper* way to handle disputes with the employer. The *Worker*, in response, assailed Shane and the International Ladies' Garment Workers' Union as a scab-herding, company union.[17]

And there were other opinions on reasons for the failure. 'We certainly had plenty of preparations for the Toronto strike,' said Tom Ewen, general secretary of the Workers' Unity League, 'but nobody knew anything about it. It was too secret.' In his view, the union leaders were so apprehensive of any counter-move the international union might make that 'they kept all preparations to themselves'; there was little publicity, even among the needle trades workers themselves, 'so we had no chance of carrying through a really successful strike.' He scolded the strike leaders for talking about a little strike of about 300 as if it were a few thousand.[18]

Perhaps the most important reason for failure was the fact, expressed by Buller, that the strategy of building shop-floor committees in the union was far from general. 'We talked about turning our faces to the factory,' she said, 'but we did not colonize our comrades'; the union had only been put on a shop-delegate system a few months earlier, and 'while the re-organization injected new life into our work,' Buller said, 'it is difficult to catch up on lost time.'[19]

The next month, Shane and his international union, which had also signed up about 300 members, launched their own dressmakers' strike in Toronto and, to the surprise of many, 1,800 workers from seventy shops heeded the call. By prearrangement, a few of the shops quickly made agreements with the international union, but the strike dragged on for several months and it, too, according to historians Frager and McLeod, was a failure.[20] As Mercedes Steedman comments, 'collective agreements collapsed before the ink was even dry.'[21] After this, the international union lost interest in the dressmakers. The industrial union, however, licked its wounds, and soldiered on in the class war along Toronto's Spadina Avenue. After a while its perseverance led to some victories for the dressmakers, especially in a general strike in 1934.

Before the dressmakers' strike of 1934, and leading to its effectiveness, there was a rise in the prestige of the industrial union through a series of small strikes and shop floor stoppages in the various crafts – cloakmakers, furriers, capmakers, dressmakers, and others – in Winnipeg and Montreal as well as Toronto. Joshua (Joe) Gershman, general organizer of the union, claimed that since its second national convention in 1931, the union had led about 200 shop strikes in which over 4,000 workers were involved. This activity led to a thousand new members for the industrial union. The results of such struggles in the needle trades industry were encouraging and, according to Workers' Unity League leader Charles Sims, had 'lessons for all workers in Canada.'[22]

Gershman, general organizer for the garment workers, explained how the union worked, emphasizing that it concentrated its efforts on the lowest paid, who were mainly women. It was through the medium of the shop committee, he said, that 'we reached out to the women [and] gave them the initiative in forming the union.' Once everyone in the shop had signed up, a shop committee elected 'shop chairladies and grievances were reported to her,' he said, 'then she reported it to the union [and] if it was necessary we called a shop meeting to see what to do.'[23] The executive of the union was composed of representatives from the shops. In this way, the union won the loyalty and active participation of large numbers of the lowest-paid workers in the sweatshops the better to defend the collective agreement, while keeping a day-to-day watch on the activities of the boss. This was the class struggle up close and a signal success for the industrial union, 'the first union,' says historian Mercedes Steedman, 'to succeed in organizing large numbers of women workers in the dress trade.'[24]

Great drum rolls of publicity heralded the looming Toronto dressmakers' general strike on Spadina Avenue in January 1934 when the Toronto Council of the Workers' Unity League staked its reputation on the outcome. The strike against the 'low wages and rotten conditions' of the sweatshops, the league declared, would be 'the greatest single strike' in the district and it would pave the way for thousands of unorganized workers. In a flurry of activity the league mobilized all its members in the city to assist the garment workers in organizing a strike kitchen and various other action committees.

The league was not disappointed. At ten a.m. on the appointed day, over 1,500 workers in seventy dressmaking shops poured out onto the streets to gather at the nearby Standard Theatre for the first general strike meeting. Showing 'a fine spirit of enthusiasm and confidence,' according to the *Worker*, the men and women – cutters, pressers, machine operators, and finishers – reaffirmed the central strike demands, discussed plans, and then marched through the fashion district. Sixty per cent of the strikers were women, most of whom held the more unskilled jobs as sewing machine operators.

The strike continued to gain in momentum, leading to a decisive and stunning result within six days. The dress manufacturers conceded virtually all the demands.

The collective agreement, joyously celebrated by union members, provided wage increases of from 10 to 40 per cent. Other significant points summarized by the *Labour Gazette* included stipulations that only members of the industrial union could be employed. No work was to be done for individual firms against which the union was conducting a strike. Work was to be for eight hours per day, four on Saturday, with a forty-four-hour week. No overtime would be permitted if other help could be obtained from the union and if there was room and extra machinery for such extra help. No one would work on legal holidays or on 1 May. Minimum wages were established for workers paid by the week (mostly skilled male labour): $12.50 for finishers and drapers, and up to $30 for fully qualified cutters; 20 to 27.5 cents per garment. Piece rates (mostly unskilled, female labour) were to be settled between employer and shop committee; in case of disagreement, a union representative was to be called in; no additional apprentices were to be employed until all unemployed union members had been absorbed; no work would be contracted out; no employer, foreman, or designer was to work as a cutter, operator, presser, or finisher except under specified conditions; no employee would be discharged without sufficient cause, and without the consent of the union; a shop committee was to be chosen at a meeting of the employees, and any disputes which could not be settled between the manufacturer and the shop chairman were to be referred to the union representative for settlement.[25] The list of gains for the workers went on and on.

One is left to wonder what the difference was between the success of this general strike and the failure of the one three years earlier. In part, it was the result of a modest up-swing in the economy in 1934. But this alone would not have led to a larger share for the workers or an increase in their control of conditions in the workplace. The decisive factor was the success of the union in spreading the shop floor delegate system through the industry in the years since the first failed strike.

The shop-delegate system had been particularly important for drawing in women, who were the largest part of the workforce. As union delegates right on the shop floor, they had learned to battle face to face with the boss over setting piece rates in the ever-changing fashions of the dress trade. This process, which often led to temporary work stoppages if the boss tried to fire the spokesperson, had produced such spirited fighters as Pearl Wedro, Bessie Kramer, Sadie Hoffman, and other mainly Jewish communist women, who emerged as strong, highly capable, and assertive union leaders.[26]

In Montreal, by contrast, it was not as easy to win victories. The number of wage earners in the garment industry here had mushroomed in the 1930s – many of whom were working in 'runaway shops,' trying to escape from the more militant labour market in Toronto. By the early 1930s, Montreal had the largest aggregation of dressmakers in the country – over 10,000.

In her book *The Bitter Thirties in Quebec*, Evelyn Dumas provides detailed information about the Montreal dress trade, its workers, and their union organizations. She points out that although the garment industry was one of the main sources of employment in Montreal during the years of economic crisis, the industry was far from being solidly established. 'On the flanks of a few "big" companies,' she wrote, 'tens and hundreds of little ones swarmed, often set up by ex-workers who first hired brothers, sisters and cousins, resisting for better or worse and more often for worse the shrinking of the market due to the depression and to the seasonal fluctuations of the industry. Bankruptcies abounded and few enterprises survived ten years.'[27]

This chaotic market did not make it easy to find stable recruits for an industrial union. The workforce was mainly French-Canadian women, and men and women of Jewish origin, with other ethnic groups having little representation. Since most of the French Canadians were from conservative Catholic families, and the existing membership of the Industrial Union of Needle Trades Workers consisted mainly of socialist-minded Jewish immigrants from Eastern Europe, there would have to be much patient work to bridge the language barriers, to overcome ethnic biases, and to mute differing ideological preferences, if the union were to be built. It was a daunting task, especially as the union had a serious lack of French-speaking organizers. The rival International Ladies' Garment Workers' Union had little taste for the job, considering the Montreal dress trade as 'practically an unorganizable field.'[28]

A difficult situation was made worse by the role of the Catholic priests, not to mention the anti-communist Tashereau provincial government. In a much-cited incident, Gershman illustrated the malign influence of the *curé* on union activists. 'The very same women who were militants in the shop,' he said, 'were, at home, under the influence of the Church and the priest. In one shop strike, where we won an increase for the finishers, drapers and operators, we got a raise of $2.50 a week. Then on Monday, the women came back to the office to tell us they were going to give the money back to the manufacturers because the priest had told them at Sunday mass that the money was sinful money. This is the kind of thing we had to fight against.'[29]

When Gershman, a young man of twenty-six, arrived in Montreal in 1929 to organize the industrial union, he went to the Communist Party headquarters where he found unemployed people 'sleeping all over the place.' 'From them,' he said, 'we set up the union ... We would form shop committees from the sections of the shop. If only operators and pressers were interested then we used to meet. From them we would hope to organize the whole shop.' After some experimentation with these small dressmakers' groups, especially among the skilled cutters on whom every shop depended, the union changed its tactics and formed a Montreal Dress Cutters' Union as an independent organization with Frank Breslow, a cutter and a member of the Workers' Unity League, as general manager. After months of fruitless talks with the manufacturers, this union called a general strike of 500 cutters in the summer of 1933. The union demanded a forty-four-hour week, a minimum wage scale with time and a half for overtime, union recognition, and an unemployment insurance fund equal to 2 per cent of the payroll. Heated exchanges took place in the Montreal Jewish press between the union and the manufacturers, but with the entire dress trade paralysed, the strike was over in two weeks. The cutters gained all their demands except the unemployment fund, and their success gave a strong impetus to the unionization campaign among the rest of the workers.

On 21 August 1934, in an auditorium on Ontario Street West, a crowd of working men and women in the dressmaking trades, led by the Industrial Union of Needle Trades Workers, voted to begin a general strike. The workers called for wage increases, especially for the lowest paid; a minimum of $12.50 a week for finishers and $30 for cutters; a forty-four-hour week; the abolition of penalty clauses and the recognition of their union. The next day 3,500 workers, mainly women, were out on the sidewalks and about ninety shops along St Catherine, Bleury, and Peel streets were shut down. Never had so many women demonstrated in Montreal. The police guarding the doors of the establishments looked on with sympathy, according to Evelyn Dumas, 'regarding the unexpected picketers as pretty girls.' The police were also sympathetic because members of their own families were among the strikers, and they were aware how hard it was to live on the low wages of the Depression years.

It wasn't long, however, before men armed with 'bludgeons, lead pipes and rubber hoses filled with sand' attacked the picket lines. The Montreal *Herald* stated that these were American goons who had invaded Montreal to break the strike. Government officials spoke of riots and sent in provincial police on horseback, leading to the arrest of twenty-three picketers, including eleven women. The union replied to the gangster attacks and the arrests by a mass meeting of 4,000 people in the local arena and by organizing larger picket lines. 'It was a most wonderful spectacle to see a picket demonstration over a half a mile long,' wrote the *Worker*'s correspondent, 'blocking all the streets and thousands on the street showing their sympathy.' The 'militancy of the French-Canadian working class,' the *Worker* predicted, 'is established for all time.'[30] This opinion may have been too optimistic, but as sociologist Tom Langford has written, a major strike is undoubtedly a momentous occasion in workers' lives, 'involving emotion-laden moments of intergroup conflict and ingroup solidarity, which are not commonplace in working-class life,' and which led some workers to report that their whole world view had been changed as a result of strike participation.[31]

A see-saw battle raged as the strike progressed. A gang of hoodlums armed with sticks and blackjacks invaded union headquarters and ransacked the place looking for Gershman, Leo Robin, and the other leaders. The strikers drove the invaders back into the street. 'Clubs and fists flew until police squads arrived to break up the crowd.' The *Ottawa Citizen* called it a third day of riots in the Montreal dress trade strike.[32]

That same day the strikers received an unexpected boost when the government's Minimum Wage Commission issued a statement revising upward the rates of women working in the garment industry, and reducing the work week from fifty-five to forty-eight hours. In making his announcement, Gustave Francq, president of the commission, scolded the employers:

'It is a disgrace,' he said. 'I have brought almost every one of you, one by one, before the courts of justice to make you pay the minimum wage. I have hauled more firms into court from the dress-making sector than from any other sector. I do not know of another industry which allows such flagrant violations of the law.'[33]

But the newly formed union was no match for the combined power of the government, the Church, and the manufacturers, and after two weeks, amid conflicting reports and rumours, the strike gradually lost its effectiveness. Quebec's labour minister, C.J. Arcand, further weakened the strike by proposing third-party arbitration, an offer that the bosses accepted immediately but which they knew the union would reject. The union said that twenty-five out of ninety companies had already concluded agreements directly with the union and that it favoured continued face-to-face negotiations with the employer. The question of arbitration pushed by Arcand, according to the union, was only another attempt on the part of the provincial authorities to break the powerful mass strike of the dress workers and leave them to the mercy of a so-called impartial committee whose judgment 'in all cases favours the bosses.' The arbitration in the case of the railwaymen, the Vancouver dockers, and the Montreal cutters, the union said, 'proves our thesis.'[34]

The employers' association countered by saying that no agreements had been reached with the union, and besides, since the union was communist-dominated, no talks would ever occur. To frighten the workers with permanent loss of jobs, employers were quoted in the press as saying they were planning to move their shops out of the city into the suburbs for a more peaceful future.

In the midst of these debates, the impending trials of those arrested, and rumours that the majority of the ninety establishments affected were voluntarily giving a wage increase of about 20 per cent, many strikers began drifting back to work.[35] Claiming that the strike was broken, Bernard Shane of the rival International Ladies' Garment Workers' Union saw his opportunity and started to recruit the more conservative of the skilled workers into his union; he told his leader in New York City that 1,500 Jewish workers in Montreal had been completely excluded from the dress trade and the chances were 'that they shall never be able to come back since the employers blame them for all their troubles.'[36]

A month after the strike began, on 21 September, the dressmakers' strike committee conceded defeat. It issued a lengthy, carefully worded statement, undoubtedly crafted by Gershman, which, while recognizing the defeat of the strike, proposed to consolidate the union by advising its members to return to work. The statement sought to reassure the workers about the value of the recent struggle: after four weeks the strike was over but 'not without some gains and valuable experiences.' Approximately 2,700 workers were back in their jobs; in cases where manufacturers set up blacklists and would not reinstate workers, the strike would continue; in twenty-five shops union agreements contained increased wages, a forty-four-hour week, and union recognition; although the workers had returned without a union agreement to many of the other shops, the manufacturers had felt compelled to grant them higher wages and shorter hours; the strike had taken 'the lid off the horrible conditions' that existed in the trade – wages as low as $5 and $6 per week, mother and daughter punching one time card – a scheme by the bosses to avoid paying wages in accordance with the Women's Minimum Wage Law. The French-Canadian workers had smashed 'the old boast of Canadian capitalism that Quebec labour is docile, cheap and against militant trade unionism.' This militancy had prompted the biggest capitalists and the government to unite their power against the dressmakers, hoping to 'teach all Quebec labor a bitter lesson.'[37]

When the smoke of battle cleared, the union members could say to each other that they had won a moral victory plus, in some cases, raises of 20 per cent. These were tenuous gains but not without significance. And even though the industrial union never recovered from its defeat in Montreal, the five years of IUNTW efforts there made the job easier for later efforts to build a union. Under the industrial union, said organizer Leah Roback in a 1972 interview, 'the workers had developed a militancy that they didn't know existed. For the first time there was this militancy of the French girls.'[38]

The other important centre of activity for the garment industry and for the Workers' Unity League's industrial union was in Winnipeg – the storied prairie city with a high concentration of socialist-minded workers and supporters of the Communist Party who were, as already described, capable of creating considerable turbulence in the labour market.

The main work of the garment shops in Winnipeg was to produce work clothes and uniforms, and these trades, along with others in the clothing industry, had suffered grievously from 1930 to 1935 when wages were cut to about 50 per cent of their pre-1929 levels.[39] Slowly at first but with increasing frequency by 1933, and in the face of heavy repression from the government, the industrial union of the Workers' Unity League led groups of workers who still had jobs to rebel against their fate. In addition to the uncounted random work stoppages and mini-strikes, the Department of Labour recorded seventeen strikes that 'rocked the needle trades'[40] in Winnipeg between 1930 and 1935, most of them mobilized and led by WUL organizers Louis Vassil, Bertha Dolgoy, Isadore Minster, and Meyer Klig.[41]

These organizers started the industrial union's drive in Winnipeg at the plant of the Jacob and Crowley Manufacturing Company. This firm was the largest and wealthiest in the industry, with up to 200 workers, and as the company launched another round of wage cuts, it counted on the support of the anti-communist mayor, Ralph Webb, and the threat of firings to frustrate any attempt by the union to make headway into its imposing premises on Portage Avenue. Its calculations were not mistaken.

When about a hundred workers in the cloak-making shop voted by secret ballot to declare a strike in February 1931, and a picket line supported by members of the Unemployed Association reached 300, police reinforcements arrived to clear the way for 'non-sympathetic' workers to enter the plant. In what the press described as a 'near riot,' the police chased the strikers down lanes and adjacent streets, wielding their batons and arresting several of the leaders for 'disorderly conduct.' When another eighty workers in the fur and dress shops of Jacob and Crowley joined the strike, and other garment workers began talking about a general sympathy strike, Mayor Webb went on the radio to blame a few 'Toronto communists' for the trouble, and the City Council, prompted by an Independent Labour Party alderman, put forward a committee to arbitrate the dispute. Newspapers ran blaring headlines predicting that the strike would be over in forty-eight hours. Gershman, who was in Winnipeg to help the local union, replied that the Shop Delegate Council would sit in at any conference the City Council organized, but insisted that 'the decisive vote on the terms of settlement rests in the hands of the strikers.'[42]

Because of the clamour that arose, Gershman and the district executive of the Workers' Unity League, led by Joseph Forkin, took the occasion to circulate a 'statement of enlightenment' elaborating their negative view of arbitration as a method to solve a dispute between capital and labour. Since the interests of the workers were diametrically opposed to the interests of the bosses, they argued, there could be no 'impartial arbitration' standing above the interests of both parties. That was an illusion. The capitalist class wanted more work to be done per worker per hour, higher profits, and lower wages to pay; the workers wanted less exploita-

tion, better working conditions, higher wages, and, eventually, the abolition of capitalism. The boss class, they said, uses arbitration to beat off
the attack of the workers, to kill their spirit by prolonged talk, to mislead
the workers, to give the press a chance to spread propaganda against the
workers' supposed 'unjust' demands, and eventually, by weakening the
ranks, to give less than the workers would have gained by direct negotiations with the boss. That was why the union leaders opposed proposals
for arbitration and urged the workers to stand firm.

As for Mayor Webb, Gershman and the league were defiant. Webb had
announced to the wide world that the communists were to blame for
the dispute in the Jacob-Crowley shop, and not the wage cut. 'Well,' said
Gershman, 'some people would like to blame the communists for the
earthquake in New Zealand, but this does not stop the earthquake, and
the fulminations of Mayor Webb and the vicious police terror cannot
stop the working class.'[43]

This was the kind of rhetoric that the radical workers of Winnipeg
enjoyed immensely. But in spite of strenuous efforts, which included
financial support from local AFL unions to the tune of $1,400, the com-
pany, with the intervention of the mayor, the city council, and the police,
was able to stare down the union. After three weeks the strike had to be
called off.

In point of fact the balance of forces had been extremely unfavour-
able to the union. Although a majority of the workers had voted to go on
strike, when the strike was called the industrial union actually had only
a handful of members in the employ of the company, and it had fewer
than forty members in the whole city. Jacob and Crowley was free to continue on in its role as 'the champion in wage-cutting.'[44]

Two years later, however, starting in March 1933, matters turned
around briefly for the Workers' Unity League. Joseph Forkin, Winnipeg district secretary, was able to report to the third national convention of the organization that the league in Winnipeg had grown from
a mere 120 members to 1,431 members in the first six months of the
year, including a needle trades section that had increased in membership from 40 to 500.

This impressive increase was due in part to the successful efforts of
the leaders of friendly organizations, such as the Ukrainian Labour
Farmer Temple Association, in convincing their members to be more
active in the affairs of the trade union movement. These organizations
established 'industrial committees' to canvass their members, to identify
their occupations, and to make wider contacts in the industry. 'You can

imagine the vast amount of information that would come into the Workers' Unity League office,' said Forkin, 'when every member of the mass organization is on the job to find out about wage cuts and what is going on in the different industries.'[45]

The rapid rise in the strength of the needle trades union was also due to a change in tactics, and to concentration on some of the smaller shops with thirty or fewer workers where victories could be won. The organizing campaigns were prepared more carefully. 'We adopted every means in order to win demands without a strike,' Forkin explained, 'and only when we were convinced and when the workers were convinced that there was absolutely no other way out of it did we take strike action.' But whenever the workers went to place their demands before the boss, they had already elected a strike committee as backup. Forkin also spoke about women workers. 'It does not need to be a separate task any more,' he stated, 'they are organizing just as the men are and are even better fighters on the picket line.'[46]

Following Forkin's lead, in the summer and autumn of 1933, organizers Louis Vassil and Bertha Dolgoy successfully led half a dozen strikes in the Winnipeg needle trades. These victories, including substantial wage increases, abolition of the contracting out system, a check against speed-up measures, recognition of the union or of shop committees, and reinstatement of workers fired for union activity,[47] thoroughly alarmed the boss class. Especially important was the success of the league in turning the unemployed from a potential pool of scab labour for employers into a reliable ally of striking workers. In the case of thirty workers on strike at the Hertig Company in August 1933, 1,000 garment workers and unemployed sympathizers showed up one day to march on the picket line.

In the trials that resulted from the arrest of several people during that strike (on the charge of 'unlawful assembly' or the 'watching and besetting' clause in Section 501 of the Criminal Code, which virtually forbade picketing), county court judge H.W. Whitla took a narrow view of the right to picket, and found the defendants guilty, sentencing them accordingly.[48] Under this legalistic regime, a later attempt by the industrial union to organize a general strike of Winnipeg garment workers in 1934 ended in failure.

To catch the spirit of the times, however, it is worth remembering that Judge Whitla's intervention in the contests between capital and labour contrasted sharply with that of another county court judge just a year earlier. After hearing the case of six striking workers arrested and charged with 'unlawful assembly, riot and aggravated assault' in a box factory strike at that time, Judge Lewis St George Stubbs, in a lengthy statement arguing that there was something 'very radically wrong' with the training of the police force, acquitted the accused and, in doing so, said that the trouble on this occasion was caused by the 'arbitrary, officious and provocative conduct' of the police. In turn, the audacious judge was both removed from his judgeship the following year for alleged 'judicial misbehaviour' and then elected to the provincial legislature from Winnipeg, winning his seat on the second try with an unprecedented popular vote.[49] Also at this time, Joseph Forkin joined fellow communist Alderman Jacob Penner in gaining electoral support in Winnipeg, becoming Alderman Forkin, a post he held with only one short interruption until his death twenty-eight years later in 1962.

Attempts of historians to assess the campaigns of the needle trades workers under the leadership of the Workers' Unity League reveal mixed feelings. James Mochoruk and Donna Webber credit the industrial union's 'willingness to organize women and propel them to positions of authority' as being responsible for bringing this union 'to the forefront of every struggle in the needle trades between 1931 and 1935.' But in the final analysis, they say, the union let the workers down with 'a sad record of defeats and disappointments,' and 'for all of its activity,' the industrial union 'could claim very few victories of any lasting value.' James H. Gray, reporter for the *Winnipeg Free Press*, was categoric: 'The Communists had failed.' Historian Ruth Frager is more nuanced. In her judgment, 'the Communist-led Industrial Union of Needle Trades Workers made some notable gains for certain groups of workers.' But she places a heavy burden of guilt on the union. 'The main impact,' she writes, 'was to undermine the workers' struggles for better conditions by pitting worker against worker and union against union.' Mercedes Steedman, although cautious, shows more empathy for the efforts of the industrial union, noting that with its 'shop-focused structure,' it allowed more democratic, rank and file control over shop issues, and 'was more accessible to women than … any other union.'[50]

Of most interest, perhaps, is the reflection of Joshua Gershman, national executive board member of the Workers' Unity League and general organizer of the militant union. Fifty years later, when interviewed by Irving Abella, he said that the experience of attempting to organize a radical trade union centre 'outside the orbit' of the established trade union movement had been 'a mistake.' But he qualified this opinion by adding: 'it's a very ticklish kind of question' because of the WUL's undoubted contributions to the labour movement. He said the WUL had some 'terrific achievements,' helping to organize close to 50,000 workers, and leading the majority of these workers in important strikes that not only sharpened the class struggle but also won better conditions for the workers in these industries. He also believed that the experience gained in organizing on an industrial rather than on a craft basis was of 'tremendous value' in helping to found the Congress of Industrial Organizations in the later 1930s. The CIO, it will be remembered, was another trade union centre 'outside the orbit' of the established labour movement. Many of the best CIO organizers came out of the Workers' Unity League. They were not chair fillers, they built unions – mine, mill and smelter workers, the United Electrical Radio and Machine workers, the Canadian Seaman's Union, fur and leather workers, food and tobacco workers, the woodworkers' union, the fishermen and cannery workers, the longshore and warehousemen's union, and yes, automobile and steel workers too. These were huge achievements of the veterans of the league. For Gershman, it could be said, the experiment of the Workers' Unity League and its affiliated unions was 'a mistake' not because it was a failure, 'outside the orbit,' but because it was too short-lived.[51]

To sum up: the activities of the Workers' Unity League in the garment industry put some serious dents into the sweatshop system here and there and from time to time. The league charted a new direction, especially for women workers. Thousands of women, including many in French Canada, experienced the emotions of solidarity on an embattled picket line in the struggle for a living wage. The communists themselves gained valuable experience in refining their approach to working with others, in gaining election to public office without abandoning Lozovsky's revolutionary unionism, and in employing humour and irony to stand firm against the 'Red scare' tactics of the bosses.

But in the words of the Stevens Commission with which this discussion began, wages in the needle trades generally continued to be 'exceedingly low,' hours of work 'oppressively long,' and violations of the laws on employment conditions 'frequent and continuous,' and they remained so until the demands and opportunities of a wartime economy five years later gave workers some powerful new leverage.

13

Woodsmen of the West

... when I read these apparently dreadful tales of the men's leaders ... my mind jumps back and I see Mr Mackin and Mr Humbird, gross and over-bearing, bullying and conceited, and I wonder to myself in whose hands I would sooner be – the workmen's leaders or the employers' leaders! ... there's got to be some pretty tough stuff going around in order to influence [the employers] and increase the remuneration of the workers.

– Montague Meyer (London) to H.R. MacMillan, 9 July 1935[1]

In the early years of the depression, when other unionists were on the defensive, only the communists were willing to organize and manage a union drive in coastal logging camps ... In the 1934 strike the communists earned the respect of coastal loggers.[2]

– Gordon Hak, historian, July 1989

In the midst of the Great Depression the pace of the natural resource industries of British Columbia unexpectedly picked up in 1933, especially in the lumber business. Production did not return to the level of the peak year of 1929 but it made a 'notable recovery,' according to the *Canadian Lumberman*. In spite of the usual talk about the virtues of private enterprise, this recovery was made possible by the help of the federal and provincial governments through tariff preferences, subsidized shipping services, and financial assistance.[3] As orders from Britain and other countries multiplied under the Empire preference agreements (which offset the stiff Smoot-Hawley tariff that the Americans had erected in 1930 to protect their flagging industry), lumber exports increased

100 per cent over the previous year. Shipping circles reported that 1933 'was the busiest year in a decade,' and employment in the coastal logging camps of British Columbia rose that year from 2,350 to 4,625 men.[4]

This welcome trend, however, did not translate into better wages and living standards for most of those who worked in the forests and sawmills. The employers, determined to put off any sharing of the new-found prosperity, introduced a 14 per cent wage cut in the first part of 1933, which followed a 13 per cent cut the previous year.[5] Sensing a favourable opportunity to challenge the lumber operators, Workers' Unity League organizers were more determined than ever to mobilize a struggle in the woods.

The loggers of British Columbia had some history of successfully confronting the lumber operators, especially after the First World War, and the memory of those days lingered on. A veteran organizer of the Workers' Unity League who lived through that period recalled the situation prior to the organization of a union in 1919:

> The life of the logger ... was worse than chattel slavery. From dark to dark, 10, 12, 14 hours of slavish, backbreaking, soul-destroying labor; the vilest of food, discarded remnants of the slaughterhouses and the canneries; overloaded bunkhouses with vermin-infested, muzzle-loading, double-deck bunks, three decks in some cases, and for which the logger had to pack his own blankets; no sanitary conditions or wash-houses; swindled and robbed by employment sharks, grafting foremen and the steamboat companies. Such was the lot of the timber-beasts in B.C.'s banner industry![6]

In 1919, at a time of general labour unrest, the lumber workers organized the Lumber Workers' Industrial Union and, within a year, had about 15,000 members. Through a series of strikes the union managed to improve the quality of life for the woodsmen. Among other improvements they won higher wages and an eight-hour day; compelled the companies to clean up the bunkhouses and provide showers and drying houses for wet clothes; and obliged the government to enforce existing sanitary regulations. The union affiliated itself with the Red International of Labour Unions in Moscow. But, after six years, the union fell apart, victim of aggressive employer tactics and the RCMP (who created a blacklist by seeding informers into the workforce to identify the most active union men), and of internal dissension between the anarchist-syndicalists of the IWW and the communists.[7] The employers, described by their own kind with such adjectives as 'selfish and ruthless,' 'gross ... overbearing, bullying and conceited,' soon returned unimpeded to their old ways of managing the industry.[8]

By 1931, as a result of company intimidation and some faulty strike tactics, the Lumber Workers' Industrial Union was at an all-time low, with only thirty-one members in the entire timber-cutting industry of British Columbia. But, by this time, the union, with headquarters in Ontario, was already affiliated to the Workers' Unity League, and its handful of British Columbia activists were well acquainted with the revolutionary strike strategy of Alexander Lozovsky and the Red International, the famous 'Strassburg Resolution.' They understood the need for carefully planned strike action to supplement or replace fly-by-night work stoppages over particular irritations and grievances, stoppages that often took the form of discontented workers dropping their tools and taking off to find a new boss without effecting any dent in the arbitrary power of the employer. Instead of fighting 'one camp at a time,' the WUL organizers determined to build a movement.

Their strategy called for identifying a point of concentration and, for this, the union men chose the largest, most modernized company on the coast: Bloedel, Stewart and Welch. Bloedel's, as it was known for short, owned the licences for vast tracts of the best timber on Vancouver Island, employed over a thousand woodsmen in its camps, and had as its head Sydney Garfield Smith, one of the more ruthless and intimidating managers in the business. According to Arne Johnson, member of the WUL district council and secretary of the industrial union, the American-owned Bloedel's was 'the most hated outfit on the coast';[9] it set the standard for the subsistence wages paid in the industry. The Workers' Unity League calculated that if the workers could successfully confront Bloedel's, a strike would rapidly spread to the other camps and logging companies, possibly taking a giant step towards the aim of 'a unionized lumber industry' in coastal British Columbia. It was a work for dreamers, and a great case study of how the WUL operated.

In July 1933 the lumber workers' union on Vancouver Island began sending two organizers on weekly visits into Bloedel's camps, especially Camp 3 and Camp 4, located four miles apart about sixteen miles outside of Campbell River, the nearest settlement. This started a process that would lead to an epic strike struggle six months later, in 1934, involving over 2,500 loggers in eighteen camps and lasting three months. While the Lumber Workers' Industrial Union fell short of its objectives, this struggle became a central reference point in the loggers' history, and in the course of militancy in the British Columbia labour movement. Why is this the case? How did it happen?

The chief organizer of the Lumber Workers' Industrial Union on Vancouver Island in the early 1930s was Ted Gunerud, a blond Scandinavian logger, tall and wiry. Writer Myrtle Bergren, whom I met in the winter of 1949 during a stay at Cowichan Lake, later described this impressive man in her 1979 book, *Tough Timber*:

> ... he was the agitator supreme. His expression was one of truth, simple, unaccepting ...
>
> Outside some logging camp in a clearing he would stand, where only the trees and the ragged loggers could hear, away from the management's ears, he would speak, his hands speaking too, his eyes meeting theirs.
>
> 'Loggers are second class citizens. You are a skidroad bum! You don't get enough pay to live like humans, they treat us like animals ... We don't have any choice, boys, we have to organize!'
>
> He was a logger himself. And every man experienced the shock of recognition and his blood quickened and his heart beat faster and something happened to him inside.[10]

Union organizers often went through untold hardships to reach the lumber camps, travelling muddy roads for twenty or thirty miles over a day and a night; sometimes taking untrodden paths at night through snow-covered bush to avoid detection; occasionally threatened by the police and by the employers' men. In the case of the Bloedel camps in 1933, it was different. At least, at first. For a time the company hired policemen to trail the organizers, but soon organizers were free to go into the camps at will. The union was aware that Smith, the general manager, had hired secret service agents to work among the men as loggers and let him know about the union's plans. From his office in the Standard Bank Building, high over Vancouver's Hastings Street on Victory Square, Smith watched and waited, as if he had a trap to spring.[11]

At the end of six months the union organizers were selling about a hundred copies of the *Worker* on each visit to the camps and had gained fifty members for the LWIU (three of whom joined the Communist Party). The new union members, however, did not get together, as the company constantly watched the men. Thus, although the organizers believed that the militancy of the men was great, they feared that, in the heat of a strike, they might be 'very weak.'[12]

The union placed its hopes on educational activity and a wage scale conference in Vancouver during the Christmas season; this was a time when practically every logger came to the city. Although plans to hold a short school, or at least a few lectures for union members, failed to materialize (on the theory that 'the logger comes to town to get boozed up and it is impossible to get them together to meet'), about forty loggers, most of them from Bloedel's, attended a lively wage scale conference which took place at 52 ½ Cordova Street East, near Main, an area commonly known as 'skidroad.' This meeting heard many complaints from the loggers about working and living conditions in the camps: about the speed-up, the disregard of health and safety regulations and the perils of working in the woods,[13] prices at company stores, blacklists, and other concerns. A short program of demands was adopted for possible strike action, including a 15 per cent wage increase, a minimum wage of 40 cents an hour ($3.20 for an eight-hour day), no Sunday work, reasonable prices for commissary supplies, and recognition of camp committees.[14]

In early January 1934, John Thomas Bradley, twenty-eight, by now a seasoned Workers' Unity League organizer from the campaigns at Fraser Mills, Anyox, and Princeton,[15] BC, joined the veteran Ted Gunerud in making his way to Campbell River. There the two men found leaflets about the wage scale issue already posted in Camps 3 and 4 of Bloedel's, and the men 'loudly ... discussing the contents of the leaflet.' They were talking strike, having discovered that the company had stolen 2,000 feet of their log scale (measurement of timber) within a day or two.[16] In mid-January, Bradley and Gunerud called a conference for both camps. Although self-appointed, the forty men who attended represented every line of work. They joined the union, formed camp committees, and decided to collect the entire crew's signatures on a petition to present to the company with a program of demands similar to that adopted at the wage scale conference in Vancouver. They set a tentative deadline of 5 February, which was a day after the next pay day.[17]

Smith, well informed of these developments and not inclined to acquiesce, exerted his influence in every possible direction to thwart the efforts of the union. Large employers in the British Columbia Loggers' Association, of which Smith was a director, were unanimous in believing that the best policy was not to change existing wage schedules and to 'await developments.'[18] Smith was also head of the organization's most important committees: 'Price, Production, and Curtailment,' 'Timber Royalties,' and 'Labour.' To help him on labour policies, the association operated a hiring office on Burrard Street called the 'Loggers' Agency,' where one William Black supplied labour to the association's camps, maintained a blacklist of potential pro-union troublemakers, and had an easy and close relationship with the British Columbia Provincial Police. 'It would be a good idea,' he told a detective, 'if a number of officers in logger's clothes could proceed to the camps, in order that evidence could be obtained against the ringleaders for intimidation.'[19] He could find them a suitable position.

Smith began his counter-attack carefully, spreading a rumour that the company would be offering a 10 per cent wage increase on 1 February. Then, immediately after the workers' conference in his camps, Smith had two of the active men fired and 'shipped out of the camp so skilfully that the rest of the men found out only after they left.' Allowing a few days for that blow to sink in, Smith then abruptly laid off forty fallers on 26 January, all of them active union members. At the same time he ordered replacements from Black's agency. That was 'the spark that blew the whole thing up,' said Bradley, and, by the next morning, 300 men were out on strike.

According to Bradley's graphic account, still kept in the archives of the Red International in Moscow, Bradley and Gunerud waited in the woods after dark that night, where they were joined by activists from Camp 3, who told them about the firings.[20] The organizers split up, with Gunerud going to Camp 4 and Bradley going to Camp 3, with the understanding that they would call meetings in both camps, take a strike vote, and elect strike committees.

At Camp 4, ninety-four men voted for an immediate strike, with twenty-five against, and a few spoiled ballots. At Camp 3 the activists decided not to take a vote, since the loggers were broke, the weather was uncertain, and they feared they would lose. Bradley talked to them for nearly two hours, but couldn't convince them. Not accepting defeat, he and two other activists brought Camp 4's committee to Camp 3 and, by 11:30 p.m., they had gone through every bunkhouse, waking up the men. A meeting was called to order in the dining room, which was filled to capacity. There was little hesitation. The committeemen from Camp 4 asked whether the Camp 3 men 'were going to back them up or scab on them.' A secret vote produced ninety-seven votes in favour of a strike, twenty-two against, and four spoiled ballots. The meeting also decided that all the fallers who had been laid off should remain in the camp, and that the whole crew would walk down in the morning to meet the men from Camp 4. From there, they would go, together, to the Beach Camp and present their demands to management. Gunerud drove his old truck to Campbell River to telephone the news to union headquarters in Vancouver.

In the morning 'everything went smoothly,' wrote Bradley. 'And let me tell you, 'it was a great procession. It is quite a walk from Camp 3, and it seemed that the more we walked (the snow is quite deep in these parts of the woods) the higher the spirit.'[21]

They met the men from Camp 4 and a strike committee was elected: twenty-five from each camp. Then they walked to the Beach Camp, where the workers there joined them as well. The steam plant was shut down, and, at the meeting called, the men approved several demands additional to those already on the petition: no discrimination, abolition of the blacklist system, and the immediate reinstatement of all those who had been laid off.

In his letter, Bradley described how the committee of 50 crowded into the company's office. The high-earning men, backed up by another 250 men outside, presented their demands to a nervous Mr Daly, superintendent. Daly, who had good reason to be nervous, asked the men to return to their camps, saying he would be back in the afternoon to give them a reply.

Outside the office door another meeting took place and the workers adopted several decisions crucial to the cohesion of their strike: no one was to speak on their own with management; the camp committees were to be in charge of negotiations; the strike committee, representing both camps, had to receive the approval of all the men at a joint meeting before making a settlement with management; no man was to accept his paycheque; and no one was to leave the camp without the permission of the strike committee.

The meeting invited Bradley and Gunerud to sit on the strike committee and, since this was pay day for the coal miners of Cumberland, it was decided that a delegation of four would go there to collect money for strike relief. In a quixotic mood, the loggers also agreed that the company should be asked to transport the strike committees from camp to camp in the speeder, 'as it is quite a walk.' (A speeder was typically a hand-operated jitney that ran along railway tracks.)

The exact form of the management's rejection of the workers' petition is not recorded, but, according to a favourite anecdote among the loggers, one of the company officials met the waiting committee and said:

'This company is not going [to] accede to any demands of you fellows. This company is paying a fair wage scale, and losing money and we can't afford to pay any more.' He lifted his head and spoke clearly: 'If you fellows think you are going to get anything out of *this*' – stretching out his hand arrogantly at the mass assembly – 'you are crazy! You will never work in the B.C.

woods again!' With these words he tore the paper into pieces and threw it at their feet.[22]

Even if these were not the exact words, the message was clear.

In the late afternoon Bradley and other members of the strike committee went to Campbell River to draft a strike-support call to the loggers of British Columbia, and to make dues-collection lists. When Gunerud returned from Cumberland that evening, they would head up to the camps with the company's reply and meet the strike committees. The momentum was strong; there was little time to lose before extra police forces arrived to bolster the company. This was tough yet democratic revolutionary strike strategy, well understood and executed with vigour.

Likely exhausted from a lack of sleep the night before, Bradley, nevertheless, found energy to compose a lengthy report to the Workers' Unity League in Vancouver. 'We must analyse the first few hours of the strike activities,' he tapped out on his typewriter, 'and the perspectives.'

> 'It is clear,' he said, 'that we have undisputed leadership in the situation and that the workers are looking towards us and will gladly follow us. The spirit is good. The decisive step was made and the boys are determined to go thru with it. The slogan advanced is "We are out to win."'[23]

The strike could be won, he said, on two conditions: (1) as long as it spread out to other camps, particularly the association's camps, and; (2) as long as the strikers received sufficient relief.

The two organizers believed it crucial to keep the strikers on site at Campbell River for picket duty at the point of production, and, for this, they needed food and accommodations in a hurry. 'We are in a hell of a fix,' wrote Bradley in his report to the WUL in Vancouver, worried that tents wouldn't arrive on time for the men, and that the workers would be run out of the camps the next day. 'What we will do with the men if they are chased out tomorrow, I don't know,' he wrote. 'The worst thing is that two boats are leaving tomorrow for Vancouver. If we have no place where to house the [men] they may take a notion to beat it to Vancouver.' Bradley knew a hard struggle was ahead of the strikers and urged supporters in Vancouver to respond quickly, saying: 'We cannot afford to lose this strike. The possibilities are here. The slogan of the strikers "We are out to win" must become a reality.'

As for spreading the strike, Bradley urged his comrades in Vancouver to send 'a flock of organizers' to get into the camps, call meetings, and take strike votes. 'It is really too bad,' he wrote, 'that we are not prepared in the camps, but that is the situation and we therefore have to rely upon quick bold action, advancing the strike slogan to the very forefront.'[24]

The Workers' Unity League in Vancouver immediately began mobilizing support for the strike, asking such experienced and class-conscious woodsmen as Hjalmar Bergren, Ernie Dalskog, Andy Hogarth, Eric Graf, Mark Mackinnon, and others to go to Campbell River to work with the central strike committee. At the same time, the WUL established a sub-strike committee in Vancouver under the guidance of Arne Johnson, the industrial union's BC secretary. Within twenty-four hours the Lumber Workers' Industrial Union sponsored a public meeting in the Vancouver Orange Hall, where Jack Brown and Glen Lamont, two of its best-known speakers, appealed to the capacity crowd for volunteers to mount picket lines on the Vancouver waterfront to prevent strike-breakers being shipped to the area. They also called for people to support the efforts of the Workers' International Relief to raise funds, and to collect food, tents, blankets, and other supplies. And, they appealed for the loan of a truck to pick up vegetables, meat, eggs, and fruit from farmers in the Fraser Valley. Brown announced that the union's intention was to establish a field kitchen outside the limits of the Bloedel Camp to feed the men on the picket line. The first shipment, he said, would be leaving in the morning on the *Z Brothers*, a fifty-ton seiner leased for the duration of the strike from sympathetic fishermen. Sitting in the audience, undercover RCMP officer Leland Graham estimated the attendance at around 700 and noted that the meeting closed with the singing of the 'Red Flag.' His superior informed General MacBrien, the RCMP commissioner in Ottawa, that preparations for the strike appeared 'to be more complete than on any former occasions.'[25]

Within two weeks several other large association camps near Bloedel's joined the strike, and, by the end of February, the strikers' ranks had swelled to 1,500. By the end of March another 1,000 men had joined the strike and twice that many had joined the union, signing membership cards.[26]

From the union's point of view there were two outstanding features of the struggle. The first was the high level of participation by the men in the daily strike activity. In addition to the picket camp at Campbell River, they established another further down the east coast of Vancouver Island, at Bowser, and a third on the west coast at Port Alberni, places where hundreds of strikers could live while picketing the camps in the forest clearings. The picket camps, home to the central strike committee, were a 'deadly weapon' against the employers' attempts to bring in strike-breakers.[27] Anticipating an attempt by the government to close down the camps on the grounds of health hazards, the men dug latrines, made root cellars for their vegetables, and maintained a standard of cleanliness that impressed the inspectors as a model for the logging companies. The strikers agreed there would be no drinking of alcoholic beverages for the duration of the strike.

In Vancouver, the sub-strike committee published a daily one-page strike bulletin – a source of information, mobilization, and counter-attack to the employers' propaganda. It generated wide public interest in the struggle, reaching a hand-distributed circulation of 4,000 at the height of the strike. Arne Johnson, the editor, kept in touch with the central strike committee by receiving a daily telephone call from Campbell River. From this source it is possible to sense the pulse of the strike and also to keep track of the scene in Vancouver, which included daily meetings of the strike committee and of picket captains, regular strikers' meetings on Monday, Wednesday, and Friday at the Eagles Hall, meetings of the strikers according to local (Bloedel's every Tuesday, Elk River Timber on Saturday, Lambs Camp on Thursday, and so forth), announcements of dances and concerts at the Majestic Hall, Orange Hall, or the Ukrainian Labour Temple, and notices of radio broadcasts by strikers on Station CKKO or CJOR, sponsored by the Rainier Hotel, Ye Old Empire Fish and Chips, and the Grand Union Public Market. An unlikely notice for a Lumber Workers' Dance at the Orange Hall promised the winning ticket-holder in a draw a free trip to Moscow for May Day celebrations. The mobilization of the strikers' forces was quite overwhelming.

The other outstanding feature of the struggle was the high level of public support. For example, a mass meeting of 1,500 people was sponsored by the *Commonwealth*, the official organ of the Co-operative Commonwealth Federation. The editor, William A. Pritchard, who was also the social democratic reeve of Burnaby, called upon all CCF clubs to support the strike and decried the policies of forest licence holders, saying: 'Nowhere on this globe has there been such rapine and slaughter of the natural resources of a country as is recorded in the history of the lumber industry on this Pacific Coast of Canada.'[28] In spite of protests by the employers, the mayor of Vancouver authorized two tag days on the streets of the city, which allowed the union to emerge debt-free at the conclusion of the struggle. Over the course of three months, the Workers' International Relief raised $28,000 as well as several hundred tons of foodstuffs from Fraser Valley farms; organizers found that Japanese and Chinese farmers were especially generous, as were members of the Finnish halls that dotted the area. Loggers at several camps that were still working voted to donate a day's pay to the cause, which added hundreds of dollars to the strike relief funds. Merchants in the vicinity of the strike-bound operations were often sympathetic to the loggers: the *Vancouver Sun*'s roving reporter Bob Bouchette cited, as an example, Stanley J. Issacs, proprietor of the Willows Hotel in Campbell River, who supplied the strikers with lumber for their picket camp, and 'yesterday he sent out 35 pies baked by Mrs Issacs.' Bouchette found the strike being conducted peaceably everywhere and wrote that the operators who raised the 'red bogey' did so in an effort to deceive the public as to where the responsibility for the strike lay.[29]

In a similar vein, the representative of the federal Department of Labour in Vancouver wrote to his superiors that he believed 'most emphatically' that the lumber operators were alone to blame for the strike 'for not voluntarily granting a goodly share of the increased revenues to the men rather than forcing them to strike for it.' He expressed a degree of admiration for the men, saying: 'One has to take his hat off to these guys in their *modus-operandi* as they stick together like glue and never quit.' The 'one big fly in the ointment,' according to this official, was the fact that the strike was being engineered and conducted by communists and aliens (immigrants) instead of 'those of the English-speaking race.'[30]

Supporters of Smith and the Loggers' Association tried unsuccessfully to divide the workers by organizing a 'Maple Leaf Club,' open only to those of Canadian-born, Anglo-Celtic extraction. These efforts were exposed and roundly condemned by the Lumber Workers' Industrial Union as an attempt to break the strike by pitting Canadian-born workers against foreign-born workers, and against the strike leadership. 'Bloedel worked us and robbed us and killed many regardless of nationality,' speakers told a packed meeting held, perhaps ironically, in the hall of the Orange Order on Hastings Street. 'We worked together, came out on strike together, now let us all stick together, and rebuff any attempt to recruit strikebreakers.' That they urged the case with strong effect was shown by an audience that rose to its feet yet again to sing the 'Red Flag,'[31] the unofficial anthem of the British labour movement.

Three weeks into the strike, with 1,500 men holding the picket lines and more threatening to join them, representatives of the federal and provincial departments of labour, led by Adam Bell, British Columbia's deputy minister of labour and chair of the Board of Industrial Relations, met with the Loggers' Association to work out a negotiating position. The association readily agreed with Bell's suggestion of $2.45 as a minimum wage, which was well below the strikers' demand of $3.20 for an eight-hour day.[32] Bell proceeded to Campbell River but he got nowhere with the central strike committee. The strikers would settle for nothing less than $3.20 and the right to have camp committees.

The next attempt at negotiations occurred in the second week of March, with the mayor of Vancouver joining Bell in bringing six members of the Loggers' Association to the table. The central strike committee adopted a draft agreement outlining the powers of a camp committee and selected a negotiating team of twenty-five loggers plus the executive of the Lumber Workers' Industrial Union. When Bell saw the list he insisted that the union's executive members be taken off the committee. To show their sincerity about negotiating the strikers agreed, while pointing out that they were all union members themselves and insisting, once again, on the right to have a union of their own choosing.[33] While this was going on Smith rented a room in the Hotel Vancouver, where representatives of the six struck companies met with a number of working loggers. Smith had a scheme. The operators should accede to the demand for camp committees, but also support the creation of a rival union. Then they should give recognition to *its* camp committees, and shut out the industrial union and the Workers' Unity League. This scheme was agreed to by the employers, and a new union, the Coastal Loggers' Union, came to life, at least on paper.[34]

The next day, 8 March, at the courthouse in Vancouver, the Honourable George Pearson, BC minister of labour, who had come over from Victoria to take charge of the negotiations, triumphantly announced to the strikers' negotiating committee that the operators had agreed to the demand for camp committees. Pearson said they had also promised no discrimination against any of the 1,500 strikers. He had a signed agreement to that effect in his pocket. The only thing remaining, Pearson said, was the wage scale. The operators had persuaded him that they could go no further than the government's proposal for a $2.45 minimum wage. Pearson asked if the men would accept it.

Not about to be stampeded, Tom Kelso, chairman of the central strike committee, questioned the sincerity of the operators. He pointed out that only yesterday they had held a meeting in Room 155 at the Hotel Vancouver with certain loggers and planned to form their own union and camp committees to undermine the industrial union.

Pearson, a little rattled, replied that he was not informed on this point, but gave his personal assurance (which turned out to be worthless) that if the operators failed to stand by their agreement, 'the government would force them to do so.' He quickly returned to the wage scale. Would the men accept it? The answer of the strikers' negotiating team was a unanimous 'No,' but they promised to submit the proposal to a secret vote of all the men.

As the meeting ended Pearson is reported to have said: 'You with your union have a power; you have also a strong public support; but we have a greater power and we will use it to its fullest extent, including that of the press.' It was a bare-knuckle threat validating the observation of historian Stephen Gray that 'the provincial state ... at least insofar as forestry policy was concerned, had become ... by the mid-1920s, a mere instrument of the lumbermen.' One of the operators moved adjournment of the negotiations for four days.[35]

The union quickly moved again into high gear. There was no time to lose. It issued a leaflet titled 'We Will Win!,' hailing the right to have camp committees as a victory for the central strike committee, and urging that now was the time for loggers in all camps to elect their committees.[36] In addition, the union announced meetings in Campbell River, Port Alberni, Horne Lake, and Vancouver for the strikers to vote on the government's wage proposal.

In Vancouver the meeting took place in the Royal Theatre, with Tom Kelso, chairman of the central strike committee, presiding. Three members of the negotiating committee reported on the negotiations and their speeches were translated into Finnish, Swedish, Ukrainian, and Yugoslavian. Jack Stevenson, veteran Workers' Unity League trade unionist of North Burnaby, gave a persuasive summing up just before the vote. 'If the bosses hold out against the wage scale demanded by the loggers, more camps,' he predicted, 'will join the ranks of the strikers. We are well on the way to victory!' The result of the secret ballot, from all locations, reflected a decisive rejection of the government's proposal: 789 voted 'No'; 49 voted 'Yes.'[37]

Adam Bell confessed to a federal government counterpart that he didn't know how things would turn out, as 'the Red organizers' had 'got control of the situation';[38] ominously the provincial government introduced a Special Powers Act in the legislature which, if passed, would give it wide powers to act in emergencies.

The operators, headed by Smith, were actually relieved at the result of the vote because, as the representative of the department of labour observed, their Coastal Loggers' Union had 'died ... almost before it was born.' Smith wrote to Pearson, saying that, in view of the workers' rejection of the proposed wage scale, the major logging companies had decided to withdraw 'in their entirety' the acceptances and agreements they had signed. They would keep operations closed down until conditions were ripe to resume.[39]

As predicted by the Workers' Unity League, 1,000 workers from eight more camps came out on strike in the last three weeks of March, bringing the total number of strikers to 2,500. This put enormous pressure on the government and, by the end of the month, it had raised its offer: it now proposed to pass a law making $2.75 the minimum daily wage in the logging industry. The strikers still would not budge. A week later, Bell was forced to announce a minimum daily wage of $3.20 for those engaged in logging operations. This was a stunning political victory for the strikers.

But the government's announcement did not actually match the union's demand for a minimum of $3.20 for *all* those working in the woods, including kitchen helpers, bedmakers, and others in the lowest categories, including the few women who worked in the woods. One of the association operators, Henry Mackin of Fraser Mills and Comox Logging, had insisted on a wage differential between white and 'oriental' (Asian) workers. The central strike committee drafted a firm but conciliatory letter to Pearson saying that they believed that the $3.20 minimum could apply to the whole lumbering industry and that they were ready to resume negotiations with the employers on that basis; such negotiations to include 'an agreement on camp committees, and no discrimination against any worker who took part in the strike.' A mass meeting of strikers in Vancouver's Royal Theatre endorsed the strike committee's letter.[40]

Smith and the Loggers' Association had already received advance notice from the government containing the terms of its new offer to settle the strike. In its telegram to Smith, the government said it was proposing a minimum wage of $3.20 for an eight-hour day for males working in the logging operations; $2.80 for sawmill workers (except for 25 per cent of the workforce [Asians] who would work at a rate 'not below' $2.00 per day), and cookhouse occupations would receive a minimum of $2.75 per day.[41] But Smith was in no mood to restart talks with the union workers. Instead, believing the government's announcement would cause confusion and uncertainty within the ranks of the union, he thought the time was ripe for a new effort to resume operations. Avoiding the union stronghold at Campbell River, he began his strike-breaking effort at Great Central Lake in the more isolated Clayoquot Land Division near Port Alberni.

In a secret exchange of messages, Labour Minister Pearson supported Smith in his strike-breaking activities, urging him to open his camps 'in the public interest.' In view of the serious unemployment situation, he said, 'speedy resumption' would go far 'to offset the unmistakable public demand for further Government action if the strike is unduly prolonged.' Smith replied two days later, on 12 April, saying: 'We were successful in running the picket lines and conveying 15 men with their baggage through to Great Central last evening, and yesterday afternoon we sent in four other men by aeroplane, and are shipping out 12 more men this afternoon by the same method.' He said he would be opening other camps by the same methods 'in the very near future.'[42]

The hard-set alliance between the government and the BC Loggers' Association would thwart the drive to unionize the logging industry of British Columbia at this stage. But, in the final two weeks of the strike, there took place a dramatic series of moves and counter-moves between the antagonists that, through wide media coverage, captured the attention of the general public and fired the imagination of the working class. The union sent sixty-eight men overland from the Port Alberni picket camp to Smith's Great Central Lake operation and, at their approach, the strike-breaking crew fled into the woods. In looking through the bunkhouses, the union men claimed to have found various clubs and pieces of iron pipe. Smith had already made arrangements with the attorney general's department to confront the union with a detachment of the provincial police. As planned, the police arrived and proceeded to drive the pickets out of the camp.[43]

On 20 April, in response, several hundred strikers and their families set out on a forty-mile march across Vancouver Island, from Parksville to Port Alberni on the way to the Great Central Lake camp, with the announced aim of clearing out the strike-breakers, now grown to seventy in number, who were being protected by forty provincial police.[44]

Gunerud, the union's district organizer, made a speech to encourage the marchers before they entered Port Alberni. He said the loggers would not be the cause of violence; if given a chance to talk to the strike-breakers, they would take them out of there peacefully. But the police, he said, 'are not going to stop us from tying up that camp. That's what we came here for and that's what we're out to do!'

As the loggers marched resolutely into Port Alberni, where Smith, guarded by four policemen, stood watching, they sang 'Hold the Fort,' the song of the British transport workers, set to the music of an old hymn:

We meet today in freedom's cause
And raise our voices high;
We'll join our hands in union strong
To battle or to die.
   Chorus: Hold the fort, for we are coming,
     Union men be strong;
     Side by side we battle onward,
     Victory will come.
Look, my comrades, see the union,
Banners waving high;
Reinforcements now appearing
Victory is nigh.

See our numbers still increasing,
Hear the bugles blow;
By our union we shall triumph
Over every foe.[45]

In spite of the workers' militancy, however, it soon became apparent that they couldn't get past Smith and the police, who had blocked the road to Great Central Lake.

Two days later, undaunted and with wide media coverage, 250 strikers set out on foot from Port Alberni on the first lap of an eight-mile journey to Great Central Lake through the dense bush and mountainous terrain, carrying blankets, utensils, and a supply of food. It was a stupendous effort to keep the strike intact and it became the excited topic of conversation in the places where workers gathered around the province.

After the marchers emerged from the bush at 11:00 a.m. on 24 April at the Great Central Lake camp, a delegation requested management to immediately fire the strike-breakers. This was refused, but the delegation was given permission to speak to the strike-breakers briefly at lunch time. After the talk, four of the strike-breakers changed sides to join the ranks of the picketers. Following this, picketers moved up to the perimeter, which was being guarded by the police, whose weaponry included a machine gun. It was then that Sergeant Russell, of the Nanaimo detachment of the British Columbia provincial police, stepped forward to remind the pickets that the police were there to see that the camp stayed open, saying: 'Whatever you start, the police will finish.'[46] This was the line in the sand. The Liberal government in Victoria was, apparently, prepared to have Canadian workers shot in order to protect the interests

of a foreign investor. However, men able to climb to the top of 150-foot
fir trees, fully equipped, weren't easily intimidated – or provoked. So far
there had been no violence during the strike.

The next day, 28 April, the union executive and the central strike committee announced, in a public statement, that the strike committee had
decided to withdraw the pickets to Alberni, reasoning that 'to attempt to
drive the scabs out of the camp would mean blood-shed,' especially as
'many of the scabs' were 'bulls camouflaged as loggers.' In addition, the
fire season, which began on 1 May, would give the provincial police an
excuse to drive out the pickets.[47] The march to Great Central Lake was
over, but such was its impact that, even six decades later, when the story
of British Columbia woodworkers and their successful struggles to build
an industrial union was written, the images of that trek and of the strike
of 1934 were proudly displayed on the cover of a handsome volume of
union history.[48]

Although the trek was over, the strike continued, and in an even more
heated atmosphere. The worried BC Loggers' Association began spending thousands of dollars to place large advertisements in the daily newspapers attacking the union. And a special committee of the Vancouver
Board of Trade met to hear Bloedel's representative say that the central
strike committee was so strong that it was preventing willing loggers from
returning to work. The issue for Bloedel and the Loggers' Association,
he said, was not wages or conditions but the demand for the recognition
of camp committees, which he interpreted as 'the attempt by the strikers
to secure control of the camps.' What the strikers wanted was not 'camp
committees' but 'camp soviets,' according to the Bloedel representative,
and the Loggers' Association declared that 'no logging business could
operate successfully under agitator control.' Camp committees, it was
said, would be under the control of the Lumber Workers' Industrial
Union, which was affiliated to the Red International of Labour Unions
through the Workers' Unity League, an organization whose constitution
committed it to 'the final overthrow of capitalism.' The Board of Trade
sent a deputation to scold the mayor of Vancouver for allowing the members of such an organization a tag day on the streets of the city.[49]

The central strike committee issued a spirited reply, defining camp
committees as 'about 12 men out of 100 in a logging camp, democratically elected from all the workers in the camp regardless of union or
non-union men, and irrespective of their political or religious belief, to
represent all departments and occupations in order to bring before the
management any grievance that may arise, and to be responsible for the

welfare of the men on the job.' Indeed, the committee declared, it was the job of the camp foreman, 'hired for that purpose,' to run the camps, not the workers. The strike committee pointed out that the principle of camp committees had already been accepted by the major operators in a signed agreement that had been guaranteed by the government. But, they had gone back on their word. This, it said, was the only obstacle to a settlement of the strike.[50]

In the midst of this controversy and to emphasize their point, 400 strikers marched to the office of Smith, leader of 'these bombastic timber Mussolinis,' and a delegation pressed their case for camp committees. Smith reiterated his stand, telling the men that he would never recognize camp committees.[51]

The strike had been a long and trying time, especially for those strikers who had no previous experience with such a class confrontation. With the resumption of work in those camps that had signed agreements with camp committees and with others trickling back to work, as well as the government's wage law coming into effect at the end of April, the central strike committee and the union's executive decided it was time to end the strike, and to do so in a credible manner. As the *Strike Bulletin* put it: 'We realized that an organised return to work would be preferable to hanging on while camps filled up with scabs leaving a large number of Union members outside holding the bag.'[52] At a meeting in the Royal Theatre in Vancouver on 6 May, the leaders put forward two proposals: hold out for a signed agreement for all the demands, and, in doing so, 'see the gradual disintegration of the organisation which had been built ... during the strike period'; or return to work on the basis of the government's Minimum Wage Law and the Bell scale for higher ratings, and set up the camp committees on the job to fight discrimination where it occurred. The vote was two to one for a return to work.[53]

To some observers, while the strike made some 'minor gains' for the loggers, it was 'a complete defeat' for the industrial union, since camp committees were 'effectively disposed of' and the blacklist system was still in effect.[54] Even the editor of the union's paper, the *B.C. Lumber Worker*, thought it was 'a toss up' after the strike as to whether 'our strengths outweigh our weaknesses.' The employers' determined efforts to block the union made the union's consolidation in the camps 'next to impossible' except in two districts: the Queen Charlotte Islands and Lake Cowichan, where camp committees persisted. These two camps became the 'backbone of unionism in the industry,' keeping it from extinction until the next surge of organizing a few years later.[55]

The Lumber Workers' Industrial Union recognized that the failures and shortcomings of the strike were many; no major struggle is without them. But the union was prepared to learn from its mistakes. The major ones identified were the failure to involve the sawmill workers from the start, thus allowing the employers to keep on filling their foreign orders with logs already in the water, and later to keep the mills operating with logs imported from the United States; the lack of a strike relief fund prior to the commencement of the strike; and how some of the picketing lacked 'the militant and swift action necessary to defeat scab herding,' especially in the Vancouver area. As well, although many strikers were married, few attempts had been made to engage the women in the strike, through women's auxiliaries. A lack of educational activity, with speakers and classes, was felt to be another serious weakness.

Nevertheless, the three-month strike had been historic, proving 'the loggers could and would stick together in a common fight' for better living and working conditions. Not only the loggers but the sawmill workers as well had benefited economically from the strike; a minimum wage for both the camps and the mills had been established, and the entire working-class movement in British Columbia had been lifted up.[56] The strike, which helped unions like the International Woodworkers of America to establish themselves on the BC coast in the next decade, developed a large group of capable, trusted leaders, many of them communists. Although the Communist Party cautioned the organizers not to be 'giddy with success,' their accomplishment in mobilizing the woodsmen of the West in 1934 was undoubtedly one of the outstanding achievements of the Workers' Unity League.[57]

14

Fishers in the Salish Sea*

The commercial fisheries of British Columbia ... present the picture of a highly competitive, speculative industry in which labour unrest and conflict are endemic.

– Stuart Jamieson and Percy Gladstone (February 1950)[1]

The New England Fish Co. at Butedale, B.C. paid 22½¢ each for sockeye, 4¢ per pound for dog-salmon, 3¢ for humpback; after deductions for nets, gas, oil and a $70 licence fee there was nothing left to reward the fishermen for their work. After slaving two months they arrived in Vancouver $25 in the hole to the company. Being out of town they will be classed as transients and refused relief by the City.

– *Unemployed Worker* 3.48 (12 September 1931) (abridged)

Much has been said about the complexities of the fishing industry in British Columbia. This vital primary economy, stretching along 750 miles of coastline and farther into 13,000 miles of waterways around coastal islands and inlets, was fractured in many ways.

The fish of commercial interest that swam these waters, for example, appeared in multiple species requiring a study of their separate and particular habits, calling for different angles of approach, and special gear for their capture.

---

* The waters off the south coast of British Columbia were officially named the Salish Sea by both First Nations and the B.C. Provincial Government on 15 July 2010. The new name which refers to the language of the First Nations groups who traversed the area for thousands of years is used to refer to the whole area including the Straits of Georgia, Juan de Fuca Strait and Puget Sound. (*CBC News*, 15 July 2010)

By way of illustration, the salmon, the most valuable part of the catch and involving the largest number of fishermen and shore workers, sorted themselves into such stocks as sockeye, chinook or spring, coho, chum or 'dog' salmon, pink or humpbacks, steelheads, blueback (young coho), and several sub-groups, each having its own locations and runs at certain times and fetching its own price on the market depending upon the geographic district and the way it was caught.

The fishing fleet consisted of three kinds of vessels: numerous small boats with a crew of two – one to row and tend the sail, the other to control the gill-nets; trollers that dragged weighted lines with baited hooks and lures; and larger seine boats with a crew of half a dozen or more employing large drag nets and heavy equipment. Since fish stocks were subject to depletion, each boat required a government licence regulating its allowable catch and its fishing ground for conservation purposes. The workforce of small, independent proprietors competing with each other, and wage labourers employed directly by the processing companies, was further divided by wide differences in language and in ethnic and racial origin – Native Indian, Japanese, and white (mainly Finns, Yugoslavs, Norwegians, Swedes, Italians, Greeks, and a minority of Anglo-Canadians)[2] – a fact that would be manipulated by the fish companies for their own advantage and could lead to misunderstandings and sometimes to fierce racial conflicts. In the decades before the Great Depression there were more than forty strikes, some of them involving as many as 8,000 fishermen.[3] During that period there were also many fishermen's associations, craft unions, and co-operatives jostling for advantage and working at cross-purposes as they attempted to represent the thousands who plied the coastal waters in search of a livelihood or worked on shore in the widely scattered canneries, salteries, and frozen fish plants. And at all times, as scholars of the subject have pointed out, the industry, dependent as it was on export markets, was 'extremely vulnerable to economic crises and unstable in output and price.'[4]

When the Workers' Unity League emerged onto this scene in 1930 it had few contacts and little apparent influence among the primary and secondary workers in the British Columbia fishing industry. It may seem all the more surprising, therefore, that by the middle of the next decade, in the 1940s, the organizers who emerged from the experience of the Workers' Unity League succeeded in establishing a substantial industrial union encompassing 8,000 members that was able to bargain with the processing companies across all jurisdictions on an industry-wide basis. This was the United Fishermen and Allied Workers' Union, which became a powerful force in the British Columbia labour movement under the leadership of, among others, George Millar and Homer Stevens, the latter a man of mixed Native Indian and Yugoslav background and a communist, who was active as a teenage fisherman at the time of the Workers' Unity League.[5]

Agitation and conflict between fishermen and the fish-processing companies reached new and unprecedented proportions during the depression years of the 1930s. This unrest occurred in part from changes in technology – the introduction of gas and diesel engines – that revolutionized the way fishermen could operate and vastly increased their productivity. These changes also increased the fishermen's costs at a time when canneries sought to cut the prices paid for raw fish in the face of shrinking export markets. Many fishermen went heavily into debt. In addition, taking advantage of improved transportation and refrigeration facilities, the fish packers soon consolidated their operations along the coast, reducing the number of their canneries from seventy-six to forty-four (down to eight by 1960)[6] and forcing the fishermen into a market controlled by fewer and fewer large monopolies.

An *ad hoc* strike[7] affecting about 300 men at Barkley Sound, on the west coast of Vancouver Island, in the autumn of 1931 showed the need for better organization. The men were fishing chum salmon for salteries with contracts in Japan. The price offered per fish, which sometimes had reached 40 cents in the past, was only 5 cents – a hopeless level. The previous year, when the price was 6 cents, 'most of the men,' according to the local member of parliament, 'finished the season in debt after working for nothing.'[8] But on a promise from the government to relax the conservation rules by allowing the big seine boats to fish in the Alberni Canal and to operate five instead of four days a week, the strike was broken after ten days.

Following this experience the Workers' Unity League saw an opportunity to mobilize the former members of the Vancouver local of the BC Fishermen's Protective Association who had already been dropped by their parent body for their 'embarrassing' militancy.[9] In early 1932 sixty fishermen gathered at the Finnish Hall in Vancouver and voted to form 'one union for all fishermen.' They acted quickly, electing a district committee of seven to draft a constitution and to draw up a schedule of prices for the next season.[10] Unlike the BC Fishermen's Protective Association and other dominant unions affiliated to the Trades and Labour Congress, who spent much of their energy trying to persuade the government to limit or eliminate Canadian fishermen of Japanese origin from the waters of British Columbia, this union set up shop on an entirely different footing. In the words of one historian, the creation of the Fishermen's Industrial Union of the Workers' Unity League 'marked the beginning of a new era' in the history of fishermen's unions in British Columbia.[11]

According to its constitution, the purpose of the FIU was to organize all workers in the industry whether at sea or on shore, regardless of race, gender, and particular occupation, into a single industrial union. No other union had claimed such a broad constituency. Its founding document dedicated the union to actively engage in the struggle for the immediate needs of the workers – a living wage – as well as 'social insurance, adequate old age pensions, compensation for disability, sickness, maternity and so forth, and to give every assistance to the organizing of unemployed workers in the fight for adequate relief measures and for non-contributory state unemployment insurance.' In common with all unions organized and chartered by the Workers' Unity League at that time, its constitution subscribed to 'the strategy and tactics of revolutionary class struggle ... repudiating arbitration and class collaboration in all price, wage and working disputes, relying entirely upon the militant activity of the organized fishermen and workers employed in the industry, and the mass support of the revolutionary working class as the final arbitrator between Capital and Labour.'[12]

Although their guidelines were clearly spelled out, the Fishermens' Industrial Union and its successor, the Fishermen and Cannery Workers' Industrial Union, were less sure-footed in their actual operations. According to a knowledgeable insider, they were 'constantly in the stage of organizing.' The unions had a hard core of support from convinced socialists among the Finns and Yugoslavs 'with a smattering of British and Scandinavians,' and included the Japanese Workers' Protective Association, the Chinese Workers' Protective Association, and the Indians of North Vancouver, but the bulk of their members were recruited during 'specific disputes which generated "flash militancy"'; the membership was never secure from season to season.[13]

A 'specific dispute' in 1932, led jointly by the BC Fishermen's Protective Association, the United Fishermen of BC (a newly formed body said to be organized 'by anti-communist elements among the fishermen'),[14] and organizers of the Fishermen's Industrial Union based in the radical Finnish community of Sointula, saw 3,200 gill-netters out on strike in northern BC along the Skeena and Nass Rivers and in the central coastal area at Rivers and Smith Inlets. In these struggles, which lasted up to

Table 14.1 Agreed schedule for salmon prices in British Columbia by fishing method, 1933

Gill-net (Fraser River exempted)	Purse seine	Trolling
Sockeye 45¢	Sockeye	Red Salmon (dressed) 10¢/lb
Red Spring (round weight) 7¢/lb	North of Queen	White Spring (dressed) 5¢/lb
White Spring (round weight) 1¢/lb	Charlotte Islands 45¢	Coho (dressed) 6¢/lb
Coho 25¢	West Coast and	Blueback (dressed) 7¢/lb
Steelhead 25¢	Johnson Straights 50¢	Dog Salmon (Nipkish) 25¢
Humpback 5¢	Humpback	
Chum 5¢	North of Queen	
Jack Spring 10¢	Charlotte Islands 4¢	
	West Coast and	
	Johnson Straights 5¢	
	Summer Chum 8¢	
	White Spring 1¢/lb	
	Red Spring 5¢/lb	
	Coho 5¢/lb	
	Dog Salmon	
	Nanaimo (fall) 15¢	
	Deep Water Bay 20¢	

thirty days in some cases, the Native Indian, Japanese, and white fishermen mainly supported each other in preventing price cuts. But fishermen blamed the BCFPA for the modest achievement.

Later in the year, after various propaganda meetings in which speakers decried the worsening conditions in the fishing industry and the efforts of the bosses to deprive the fishermen of 'the fruits of their toil,' the Fishermen's Industrial Union organized a Fishermen's Convention on 'a United Front basis' to set price demands for the next season. Through intense, detailed discussions over a number of days, the delegates (including representation from the Native Brotherhood of BC and from the Amalgamated Association of Fishermen [Japanese]) set out an agreed schedule to be negotiated with the fish companies (see table 14.1).[15]

By 1933 the Fishermen's Industrial Union began emerging as the leading fishermen's organization in British Columbia.[16] Veteran fisherman and organizer Elgin Neish toured through Ladner, Sointula, Sunbury, Port Alberni, Bella-Bella, and Prince Rupert trying to establish local executive committees.[17] The union soon had functioning locals in Prince Rupert, Sointula, and Port Alberni as well as in Vancouver. The organization felt strong enough to bring out 250 trollers on the west coast of Vancouver Island in solidarity with a strike of American fishermen from

Oregon and Washington;[18] it also began to pay attention to the wages and working conditions of cannery workers.

A majority of cannery employees were Native Indian and Chinese workers. 'The big boys sure have control of the Indians,' wrote a union delegate, in describing the conditions of work and rates of pay especially for women. With the assistance of local chiefs who received $2 per man and $1 per woman hired for the season, the cannery owners expected the women to work from ten to twenty hours a day in unsanitary conditions and required them to fill 4,500 cases of fish to make $6; on Sundays they had to cut cord wood for a song, or 'get out.'[19]

The male Chinese cannery workers were no better off. Since white company managers had difficulty with the Chinese language, they dealt through a Chinese contractor; once signed up, the workers were compelled under police guard to proceed to the cannery. Under the terms of a document resembling a yellow dog contract, the company could threaten legal action. Since the wages of the Chinese workers were paid by the contractor at the end of the season, there was no room to back out. Terms of one contract that fell into the hands of a union organizer included agreement to an eleven-hour day at 15 cents an hour; 20 cents for overtime; piece work for cleaning nets and loading ships but not for unloading coal or emptying tin cans. A worker could leave the employ of the cannery only in case of sickness, and was required to pay his own way home.[20]

The case of the Japanese women workers in the canneries was little different. But in 1933, a small but capable Japanese group in the Communist Party in British Columbia discussed the matter and resolved to assist the Workers' Unity League in contacting and organizing the Japanese women employed in the Great Northern, London, and New England canneries.[21]

Appropriately, at its next convention in December 1933, when Frank Kiviharju was elected full-time national secretary, the Fishermen's Industrial Union changed its name to the Fishermen's and Cannery Workers' Industrial Union. The union purchased a boat for organizing purposes and began a publication called the *Voice of the Fishermen and Cannery Workers*. Claiming 1,700 members, the newly named organization announced that it was taking up the battle of fishermen and cannery workers 'irrespective of race, creed or color,' pointing out that its ranks included many Japanese, Chinese, white, and Indian cannery workers. Its platform, to be negotiated with the fish companies, was detailed and emphatic. 'Wages of women workers,' it said, 'shall be increased in the same proportion as other workers' wages with a guaranteed monthly minimum of between $52.20 and $72.80. Twenty-eight days or 208 hours shall be considered one month. Working time to be from 8:00 a.m. to 5:00 p.m. and anything over this to be paid at time and a half; rubber boots, aprons, gloves, oil skins, knives etc., shall be furnished by the company without any charge to the workers; wood shall be supplied direct to the camp, also coal, electric light, fish salt, kitchen supplies; a cook shall be supplied for every 20 workers; a $12 food allowance shall be furnished by the company for all cannery workers.'[22]

A first test of strength came in the summer of 1934 at the St Mungo Cannery, operated by the Nelson Brothers in Sunbury on the delta of the Fraser River. By now prices on the fish market had picked up, but women were averaging only 10 to 15 cents per hour – about half the union demand. After some preliminary organizing, nine women, claiming to represent eighty women workers, presented a petition for better rates to the management and were immediately fired by the foreman. The ensuing sequence of events closely followed the militant strike strategy that served the organizers of the Workers' Unity League so well: a mass meeting of all the cannery workers, a set of demands adopted, a strike vote, necessary committees elected, plans for twenty-four-hour picket duty established, a relief committee to begin collecting food and finances from local farmers and workers. The Bayview Hall was rented by the strike committee to quarter the pickets, Japanese and Chinese organizers worked to bring out their constituents in support of the white women, and all fishermen on the Fraser River were notified of the imminent strike for the purpose of gaining their support.

By day three, after the firings, the strike committee was ready to meet the operators over wage rates and a demand for the immediate reinstatement of the nine workers. As expected, the company refused all demands. The strike machinery went into effect with mass picketing, police arrived to escort a minority of workers into the cannery, and the fishermen stopped selling their catch to Nelson Brothers. After three days of strike the operator felt compelled to meet the workers' negotiating committee. When the committee arrived it found Nelson in the company of the local police chief, the reeve, and a councillor of Delta, an 'evident display of municipal authority' to assist the company in achieving a favourable settlement. But the strike committee held its ground, saying that the final decision would be up to a vote of all the workers in the plant. The *Voice of the Fishermen and Cannery Workers* (and the Department of Labour) reported a settlement favourable to the workers including a minimum wage of 25 cents an hour and the reinstatement of the nine discharged workers. The paper also noted that at the close of the workers' meeting a cannery committee 'was elected to consolidate the gains and to attend to the grievances that may come up in the future.'[23] This strike, although small in scale, was another successful example of the revolutionary strike strategy promoted by the Workers' Unity League.

The following year, in 1935, amid some intense inter-union rivalries, there were a number of fishermen's strikes. The most significant one for the Workers' Unity League was that of 750 trollers for the blueback salmon in the Strait of Georgia, since it won the first signed agreement of recognition between the industrial union and a fish company, the Deep Bay Packing Company. The settlement brought a 20 per cent raise for those fishing salmon in the area of Bute Inlet and substantial benefits to the company's cannery workers.[24] But BC Packers Ltd., and the other large operators who were organized together in the powerful Canned Salmon Section of the Canadian Manufacturers' Association, owned virtually all the boats, the gear, the housing in the fishing camps, and the supplies of food, and they continued to remain virtually unscathed by the scattered efforts at unionization.

In recognition of the need for greater unity, and in light of broader unity discussions taking place within the Workers' Unity League in 1935 (see chapter 15), the fourth annual convention of the Fishermen's and Cannery Workers' Industrial Union, in December 1935, decided to disaffiliate from the Workers' Unity League in favour of creating an all-inclusive BC Federation of Fishermen and Cannery Workers that would apply for affiliation to the Trades and Labour Council of Canada.

Earlier the Workers' Unity League had helped create a Fishermen's Joint Committee. This committee, representing five of the twelve major organizations of fishermen in British Columbia – the Fishermen's and Cannery Workers' Industrial Union, the BC Fishermen's Protective Association, the Native (Indian) Brotherhood of British Columbia, the United Fishermen's Federal Union, and the Amalgamated Association of Fishermen (Japanese) – regrouped to launch a major campaign to challenge the Canned Salmon Group of the Canadian Manufacturing Association in the 1936 fishing season.[25] By an overwhelming secret vote, the joint committee succeeded in bringing out 2,500 white, Native Indian, and Japanese fishermen from the seining, gill-net, and trolling fleets in the central coastal area with demands for a living wage – a 50 cent sockeye – but difficulties in communications and some defections strengthened the hand of the packers. When the provincial government and the provincial police came to the aid of the companies, amid cries that the strikers were bringing about 'the ruination of the fishing industry,' the three-week strike was broken. In spite of the strike in the central coastal area, the companies managed to land the largest catch of salmon on record to that date – 92,210 tons.[26] As a result of these events, the vision of the Workers' Unity League for an industrial union covering the entire fishing industry lay in tatters for the moment, and the league itself was no more. But the organizers the league had trained continued to hold the dream of an industry-wide, all-encompassing union, including men as well as women, workers of all ethnic groups, a dream that would be fulfilled within their lifetimes.[27]

15

Not Hot Cakes or Foremen:
On to Ottawa!

If a surplus labouring population is a necessary product of accumulation or of the development of wealth on a capitalist basis, this surplus population becomes, conversely, the lever of capitalistic accumulation, nay, a condition of existence of the capitalist mode of production. It forms a disposable industrial reserve army, that belongs to capital quite as absolutely as if the latter had bred it at its own cost ... it creates ... a mass of human material always ready for exploitation.

– Karl Marx, *Capital*, v. 1, ch. 25

When this Government commenced to send the single men and transients to the work camps from the large centres such as Vancouver ... it was found that a great majority of these men were temporarily physically unfit owing to the fact that they had been undernourished and had been living on the verge of starvation for some considerable time.

– N.A. McKenzie, Ministry of Public Works, Victoria, BC, November 1931[1]

It is the hopelessness of life these people are kicking about, not the camp conditions.

– Arthur Evans, to Regina Riot Inquiry Commission[2]

Evans always insisted that you've got to do something new, you can't go on marching and singing and begging with tin cans. You've got to do something new, surprising, something with daring if you're going to attract people's support. I've always admired his ability to do this ...

– Steve Brodie, a leader of Division 3 in the relief camp workers' general strike, 1935[3]

Early attempts by the Workers' Unity League to take up the cause of Canada's unemployed have already been alluded to, beginning with the formation of a National Unemployed Workers' Association in 1930 and the staging of demonstrations across the country in response to a call from the Red International for an international day of protest to demand 'work or maintenance' for the unemployed.

There followed a national petition proposing that the federal government enact a bill for non-contributory unemployment insurance for all unemployed workers to be paid for by a levy on military appropriations and a steep tax on all incomes above $5,000; the Workers' Unity League took a petition to that effect, bearing almost 100,000 signatures, to the prime minister in 1931. There were many other public activities organized in the name of the National Unemployed Workers' Association: rallies of a size rarely seen in Canada bringing attention to the needs of 470,000 unemployed workers – 18.6 per cent of the labour force according to the Census of 1931;[4] local actions to stop bailiff sales of household furniture and to prevent the eviction of jobless families who could not pay their rent or farm families who fell behind on their mortgages; deputations to municipal relief offices; numerous demonstrations by mobile squads offering solidarity and support to the picket lines of workers protesting wage cuts, speed-ups, and arbitrary actions in their workplaces. These activities led a commissioner of the federal government to warn her superiors that 100,000 unemployed transients in Western Canada were beginning to form a movement that was 'organizing itself, comparing treatment in different centres, demanding conferences with public bodies, putting forward demands for service and standards and generally becoming a menace to law, order, property and security.'[5]

In British Columbia the National Unemployed Workers' Association, guided by Arthur Evans, district organizer of the Workers' Unity League,[6] was especially active. It had individual membership cards with a constitution and a dues-paying structure. Nowhere was the spirit of this organization more evident than in the lively eight-page mimeographed weekly, the *Unemployed Worker*, published by the BC section. The threepenny paper, appealing especially to the young, restless, half-starved, homeless migrant workers, had a large 'hammer and sickle' emblazoned on its masthead.[7] It ran political cartoons, short articles, letters to the editor reporting on bad conditions in the relief camps (called 'prison' or 'concentration' camps), criticizing the inaction or misdirection of governments in face of the desperate needs of the population, exposing the actions of police in clubbing demonstrators on the picket lines, and

protesting the imprisonment or deportations of workers' leaders; articles pointing to the contrast between successes of socialism in the Soviet
Union and the economic mess in capitalist countries; notices about
forthcoming social events, concerts, meetings, hunger marches, and
May Day rallies; celebrations of a more partisan political character such
as the 'Great October Revolution in Russia,' or the 'Lenin, Liebnecht,
Luxemburg Memorial Meeting' organized by the Communist Party.
What is more, the circulation of the *Unemployed Worker* steadily increased
until it was over the 3,000 mark and the unemployed association grew
until it had branches in more than twenty locations in British Columbia.[8]
Although it was most successful in BC, the association also took root
in many other centres across the country. According to participant and
Communist Party member Ron Liversedge, the young people involved
thought of themselves as part of 'the family,' whose 'organization and
fine discipline, whose refusal to accept intimidation, and whose unceas-
ing fight against oppression throughout the whole of the thirties' helped
to make life a little more bearable.[9]

Imagine then the acute disbelief of the Workers' Unity League and
leading Canadian communists when a letter arrived from Moscow, in
April 1931, suggesting that building the National Unemployed Workers' Association had been a mistake, one of a series of 'leftist quirks'
by the Workers' Unity League. The letter proposed that the unemployment organization should immediately be disaffiliated from the Workers' Unity League and not be subordinate to it in order 'to embrace
the widest possible masses of unemployed.' The letter was from Stewart
Smith, the ranking Canadian communist who was then working in the
Anglo-American Secretariat of the Red International in Moscow. Smith
indicated he was helping to draft an official letter to this effect.[10]

Tom Ewen, Sam Carr, Tim Buck, and the other leading communists
in Canada were incensed. What was the organizational or political principle, they wanted to know, that made 'affiliation of the revolutionary
unions to the WUL imperative, but of the *organized* unemployed workers
inadvisable [emphasis added]'? They were of the opinion that the situation in Canada and the needs of the unemployed were such that 'the
bogey of communism' was 'not a great detriment' to the development
of the movement, and they argued that a thousand unemployed workers
organized as an integral part of the revolutionary movement (i.e. the
Workers' Unity League) was better than two thousand organized in a
movement which was 'independent' and provided 'a stamping ground
for every faker and social fascist in the country.'[11]

The argument went on for eighteen months. Smith and the Anglo-American Secretariat of the Red International contended that the National Unemployed Workers' Association and its paper failed to respect the united front approach and that tens of thousands of unemployed workers would not join the movement because they looked upon the unemployed association as 'an adjunct of the Communist Party,' and because its agitation was '*mainly* the same as the agitation of the party.' The NUWA should be disbanded, they thought, or merged into a loosely knit system of block committees and united front neighbourhood unemployed councils in which the Workers' Unity League's leading role (and its concern to combat the increasingly vocal leaders of 'parliamentary' social democracy) would be 'ensured thru the most energetic organizational and political activity' of its members.[12]

The Canadian side accepted the notion of loosely organized united front neighbourhood councils in towns and cities and popularized it,[13] but continued to insist on the important role of the National Unemployed Workers' Association, especially for penetrating the relief camps being organized by the provincial and federal governments. These camps, mainly for single men, were places where thousands of unemployed were 'to be herded like cattle into camps under semi-military prison discipline' and at 'slave wages,' through which the trans-Canada highway and other projects were to be constructed. This situation, they argued, demanded 'immediate attention' and the sending of 'definite numbers of unemployed comrades' to seek employment and to work from within these camps.[14] This was the kind of work that the National Unemployed Workers' Association had shown it could accomplish.

The local organizers in British Columbia were particularly adamant. The NUWA was so well known, they said, and had such a place in the conscience of the masses, that it could not be 'liquidated' or 'merged in the wider movement' as proposed; thousands had already enrolled in the NUWA – residential workers in rural and city areas as well as transient workers – and thousands more would be enrolled. 'United Front Action on a wide scale,' they insisted, had been secured in Vancouver and in the 'prison camps' in the remote areas, which were organizing rapidly. The NUWA was widely respected and 'the masses would resist it being obscured': 'The workers,' they declared, 'want an organization, a card and a constitution.'[15]

Eventually Smith and the Anglo-American Secretariat of the Red International appeared to get their way. This was after the Communist Party was outlawed and its leadership jailed in 1932. At that time Smith returned to

Canada from Moscow to lead the illegal party and, as previously related, he turned up in disguise at the national congress of the Workers' Unity League in August that year. Under his guidance the congress adopted an uncompromising resolution deciding, in effect, that there would be no more NUWA. The resolution stated: 'The WUL has no separate program for the unemployed, and does not organize any separate or special organizations of unemployed as a substitute for the united front unemployed organizations. The WUL or affiliated organizations do not build their "own" unemployed movement.'[16] Shortly after this, the *Unemployed Worker* became the organ of the Vancouver Unemployed Councils; it moved from 61 Cordova Street West to a more respectable address on south Granville Street, and the 'hammer and sickle' disappeared from its masthead in favour of the slogan 'The Organization of Class Solidarity.'

But this was not the end of the story. Within a few weeks, by some undocumented process, the Workers' Unity League established two new organizations in Vancouver, the Single Unemployed Protective Association and the British Columbia Relief Camp Workers' Union, into which the National Unemployed Workers' Association members could simply transfer their memberships and which allowed them to carry on as usual. This was the dialectical fox trot in the dance hall of international solidarity. The seal on the charter given by the Workers' Unity League of Canada to the BC Relief Camp Workers' Union bore the date 'November 1932,' confirming the sequence of events. The BC Relief Camp Workers' Union began to publish its own mimeographed eight-page three-penny weekly, the *Relief Camp Worker*, from an address back on Cordova Street with the slogans 'Maintain Our Right to Organize,' and 'Organize into a Fighting Union with the WUL.'[17] The constitution of the RCWU described the organization succinctly, using terms similar to all affiliates of the Workers' Unity League:

> To organize all relief camp workers into the Union. To promote and lead the struggles of the relief camp workers for higher living standards. To rely upon the principles of Trade Unionism and the democratic decisions of the membership to forward our policy of struggle and if need be, to use the form of strike if so decided. To actively support all measures that will give the right of franchise to all camp workers. To give assistance to all workers in their struggle for Non-Contributory Unemployment Insurance, adequate old age pensions, compensation for disability, sickness, etc. In the spirit of the Trade Union movement to resist all efforts to enforce our participation in Imperialist War.[18]

The formation of the Relief Camp Workers' Union happened to coincide with a new and bold development in the federal government's relief program. Suggested to the prime minister by the chief of staff of the Canadian army, General Andrew McNaughton, the plan involved army-run labour camps where, in return for food, clothing, shelter, medical care, and 20 cents a day, single, physically fit jobless men would work at assigned tasks. Often the clothing supplied was surplus military issue, some of it dating from the First World War; some of the shelter was initially canvas tents and even much later 'shack tents' – wood-frame walls with canvas roofs. Although not strictly run according to military discipline, the Department of Defence camps emerged as places to impose a work ethic, with an overarching political objective of taking the men out of the cities to remove the active elements on which the 'Red' agitators could play. Without such camps, the military leadership believed it would only be a matter of time until the government would have to resort to arms to restore and maintain order. By the summer of 1933 scores of Department of Defence relief camps and a few 'camps of discipline' had popped up across Canada like mushrooms after rain, especially in British Columbia.[19] In this way the stage was set for a gathering storm.

After two years of trial and error, the BC Relief Camp Workers' Union, buttressed by a constantly widening circle of public support, was able to launch a two-month general strike followed by an 'On-to-Ottawa Trek,' have a confrontation with Prime Minister Bennett, and endure a police riot in Regina, all of which seized the imagination of the entire country and helped to rout the discredited Conservative Party in the general election in the autumn of 1935. Six decades later the Saskatchewan Federation of Labour would hail these events as 'pivotal ... in Canadian history; events that led to social reform and a stronger Canada'; the Historic Sites and Monuments Board raised a plaque in Regina's Scarth Street Mall recognizing the trek as 'a defining moment of the Great Depression.' For the leader of the Workers' Unity League the historic confrontation between Arthur Evans and his On-to-Ottawa delegation with the Tory prime minister marked the 'nodal point' of Bennett's well-deserved and 'rapid down-hill slide into political oblivion.'[20]

A number of original and scholarly accounts have appeared, including Ronald Liversedge's *Recollections of the On to Ottawa Trek* (1973), edited by Victor Hoar (Howard), Ben Swankey and Jean Evans Sheils's *'Work and Wages!'* (1977), Lorne Brown's *When Freedom Was Lost* (1987), Bill Waiser's *All Hell Can't Stop Us* (2003), and more recently Jim Warren and Kathleen Carlisle's *On the Side of the People* (2006), which document and analyse the efforts of the Relief Camp Workers' Union. They show, in general, that the union owed its historic success to having a clear political program that attracted public support, to the conscious discipline and loyalty it instilled in its young members, to the inspiring qualities of its leading figures, and, of course, to the considerable political failures and moral blindness of its adversaries in the face of the great tragedy of a private enterprise economy – by 1933 the unemployment level in Canada was unprecedented, encompassing close to 30 per cent of the workforce; 1,500,000 people were subsisting on meagre and intermittent social support.

There were other, specific reasons for the rapid growth of the Relief Camp Workers' Union. One of the most obvious was that a private in the Canadian Army received $1.10 per day while a civilian in the Department of National Defence relief camps received only 20 cents for eight hours' labour, a contrast that could not fail to stir indignation among the camp inmates. This made them eager to support the union and its demand for work at trade union rates of pay, perhaps giving them the possibility of saving some money for a better future. Then there was the often mindless and seemingly punitive nature of the work they were assigned. As Matt Shaw, a young inmate in DND Camp No. 333 at Beaver Ranch, BC, and future leader of the union, explained: 'seems the boys at this camp were picking out a pass through the mountains with much the same tools the Egyptians used five thousand years ago. Yes, the bosses had the lads tackling the bare rock with picks and sledges. They'd been at it three years and had only got 300 yards. Practically no blasting whatever was done – you just slugged away like the old Georgia chain gang.'[21] Apart from usual grievances about the quality of food, poor washing facilities, and bunkhouses, there was the matter of the isolated situation of the camps, far from centres of normal social life, and the deliberate policy of the Department of Defence to have no government-sponsored recreational or education programs; one department official boasted in an internal memo that 'not one cent of public money has been spent ... on reading material and recreational equipment.'[22] It was little wonder the men referred to these places as slave camps. 'If a lad had a word with the slave-driving straw boss,' according to Shaw, 'or was caught organizing, down the road he was sent.'[23] Shaw's real family name was Surdia; he opted for the alias to avoid the blacklist maintained by the camp officials.

Ron Liversedge, another camp inmate who was also a leader of the union and editor of the *Relief Camp Worker*, had another insight on camp life. Although the Department of National Defence had rules prohibiting organization of any kind, he said, it was as if the regulations did not exist, 'so complete and final was the disregard for them by the men of the RCWU.' Each camp where Liversedge worked was a local of the union, with elected chairman, secretary, and grievance committee, and held weekly meetings conducted by 'Robert's Rules of Order.' The foremen would not recognize the committee and would call in police to arrest the ringleaders. There would be much 'strife and hardship.' But when one executive was expelled another would be elected: 'the union was always there, and always had to be reckoned with.'[24]

In Vancouver the union had a headquarters on Cordova Street with Ernest Cumber taking care of business. It was a bustling place. Liversedge describes the scene, explaining how 'the family' took shape:

There was never a lack of activity, and the men at 52½ Cordova were rapidly becoming the shock troops of the unemployed movement as a whole: handing out leaflets on the streets, advertising meetings or demonstrations, selling the ... mimeographed newspaper, and the periodicals of the Friends of the Soviet Union, which at the time were in great demand.

Two or three nights a week, open forums would be held at the hall, with speakers from the Communist Party, CCF, Friends of the Soviet Union, and later from the League against War and Fascism. These meetings were always crowded affairs with all available space occupied. The unemployed were avid questioners, the question periods being always lively.

The young men wanted to know why there were no jobs, why they had to leave home so that the still younger ones could have a crust more, what caused the depression, and hundreds of other questions.

The unemployed learned the answers quickly. They learned that the worker never is paid enough to buy back the goods he produces, so that a point is reached when goods start piling up, and workers start getting laid off, which means less and less money to buy goods with less and less goods produced, more layoffs, until chaos is reached. Then it is called a 'crisis of overproduction,' and economic depression.

There was also plenty of literature in the hall, working class papers, trade union papers and Marxist pamphlets, and these were not neglected. The young men were class conscious and rapidly becoming politically conscious. They were not ready to lay [sic] down and die because the boss had no jobs for them. They seemed to realize right away that they would have to fight the bosses and their executive committees, the parliaments, if they wanted to maintain decency and human dignity. The challenge was calmly accepted.

There was no defeatism, and in the darkest periods of the depression these men refused to be intimidated.

The family was emerging, the family of over one thousand members who formed the hard core, around which the B.C. Relief Camp Workers was to be built, the On to Ottawa trek was to be organized ... [25]

The aim of the Relief Camp Workers' Union was to plan a general strike in the camps and bring the workers down to Vancouver to negotiate new terms with the authorities. After two years of organizing, such a strike took place, in December 1934, in which more than a thousand men came to Vancouver; but after three weeks the strike was defeated by government manoeuvres, and by hunger, which drove the men back to the hinterlands. Police and government officials congratulated themselves on what they thought would be the collapse of the union. But they were mistaken. The men treated the defeat as a learning experience and determined to try again.

It was at this moment, after eighteen months inside, that Arthur Herbert 'Slim' Evans (forty-four) walked out the door of Okalla Prison Farm to resume his post as district organizer of the Workers' Unity League in British Columbia. Since what followed is so closely bound up with this man, a reminder of his background and outlook is pertinent.

Originally from Toronto, where he was born of Anglo-Celtic parents, Evans travelled west in search of work as a qualified carpenter at the age of twenty-one and landed in Winnipeg in 1911. From here he moved to the United States for five years. There he became acquainted with the militant, anarchist, and socialist-orientated syndicalism of the Industrial Workers of the World. The moral force and errant outlook of the IWW stayed with him the rest of his life, even after he accepted the discipline of becoming a communist. The first three sentences of the IWW constitution summed up Evans's world view: 'the working class and the employing class have nothing in common. There can be no peace so long as hunger and want are found among millions of working people, and the few who make up the employing class, have all the good things of life. Between these two classes a struggle must go on until the workers of the world organize as a class, take possession of the earth and the machinery of production, and abolish the wage system.'

On returning to Canada he worked at the mines in Alberta and British Columbia, becoming an organizer for the One Big Union. Following this he took part in campaigns attempting to turn the United Mine Workers of America into a militant miners' union. During the course of one strike, instead of sending the miners' dues money as 'per capita' to an unresponsive international union headquarters in Indianapolis, he used union funds to feed starving strikers and their families. For this he was arrested, charged with fraudulent conversion of funds. His enemies called it theft; the court sentenced him to three years at Prince Albert Penitentiary in 1924. He was released on probation the next year. With his wife and daughter, Evans moved to Vancouver for a fresh start. Here he joined the Communist Party of Canada in 1926, while finding work as a union carpenter; recognizing his leadership qualities, the carpenters' union soon elected him as a delegate to the Vancouver Trades and Labour Council.

Because of his experience as a labour organizer, his quick mind, and his gifts as a public speaker, the newly formed Workers' Unity League appointed him BC organizer of the National Unemployed Workers' Association. In this capacity, according to a Vancouver daily paper, he organized a hunger march along Hastings Street, in February 1932, that culminated in an immense meeting of 30,000 people at the Cambie Street grounds. This was at a time when the total population of Vancouver was only 245,000. The civic authorities and the police commission took alarm and denied further demonstrations without a permit. In response Evans helped to organize and became secretary of a municipal Free Speech Committee. If denied permits this committee resolved to 'call demonstrations in all congested areas in the downtown district' until the right to free speech and assembly was re-established. This was a tactic Evans had learned from the Wobblies during his stay in the United States ten years earlier and one that he would soon apply to promoting the demands of unemployed youth in British Columbia.[26] Evans was a man of restless energy, always on the move.

The first challenge in the spring of 1935 was to help regain the initiative for the unemployed in their struggle with the federal government and its Department of National Defence. With the blessing of Bob Kerr, provincial secretary, and other members of the Workers' Unity League executive in British Columbia, Evans set about the task with his accustomed vigour. The result was breath-taking and sometimes alarming to the other members of the executive.

On Evans's advice, and to start the ball rolling, the Relief Camp Workers' Union called a general conference in Kamloops, for 9–11 March 1935. This gathering attracted about sixty-five delegates from the DND camps, who came from places such as Salmon Arm, Revelstoke, Nelson, Princeton, and Hope. With Ernest Cumber as secretary and rotating chairpersons, the delegates made reports of conditions in the camps and drew up demands for presentation to the government. The central demand was for a program of work with wages at trade union rates, as well as a minimum wage, on the basis of a six-hour day, five-day week. Other points included demands for coverage by the Workmen's Compensation Act in case of injury, abolition of military control and the system of blacklists, recognition of democratically elected camp committees, the right to vote in elections, implementation of a system of non-contributory unemployment insurance, and repeal of anti-working-class legislation such as vagrancy laws, Section 98 of the Criminal Code, and the deportation clauses of the Immigration Act. These seven items, later reduced to six, became the bargaining points throughout the strike up to and including the meeting with the prime minister that summer. The conference decided upon a walk-out from the camps to Vancouver, 'where greater pressure could be brought upon the authorities,' and set the date of 4 April. Ever determined to practise rank-and-file democracy, the union made this action subject to ratification by the camp workers when the delegates returned to report on the Kamloops conference. The *Relief Camp Worker* of 19 March reported that Evans had tendered greetings from the Workers' Unity League and 'pledged support of that organization and its various affiliates.' He had expressed the hope that the experiences of previous strikes would 'stand us in good stead in the coming struggle,' and stressed 'the necessity of extended preparations so as to eliminate confusions.' One delegate, an 'old-timer,' reminded delegates not to forget Lozovsky's advice on how to conduct strike struggles.

As organizers fanned out to the camps, Evans was confident the walk-out would be ratified, and in the three-week interval between the Kamloops conference and 4 April he and the leadership of the RCWU busied themselves in making preparations for 'organized militant struggle' in Vancouver.

When the day arrived and the strikers began assembling in the city, a welcoming committee assigned them to one of four divisions with about 400 men in each. A division's membership clustered around men from the most active areas – Revelstoke and Princeton – the already blacklisted men living in Vancouver, and then the others. Each division had a chairman, a secretary, and a captain or marshal to look after discipline and to lead the division out onto the streets; the divisions were subdivided into groups of twelve with an elected leader; each member received a personal identification card with his number, group, and division. Evans made it clear that if anyone misbehaved or engaged in theft or hooliganism he faced expulsion and his card would be lifted. These tightly knit small groups where everyone knew each other and could offer mutual support were a key to maintaining high morale. And they were a way to minimize the danger of infiltration by secret police agents or provocateurs who might seek by word or deed to tarnish the reputation of the strikers. Each division had a headquarters in the downtown core – the Ukrainian Labour Temple on East Pender Street, the Orange Hall on Hastings, and vacant warehouses on Cordova Street – where they were billeted. Every division elected a finance committee that gave out meal tickets and bed locations at daily noon-hour meetings. The divisions also chose various committees for publicity, for collecting and dispersing food donations, a card committee, a bumming committee, which collected funds from the citizens, and a movie ticket committee. All these committees gave reports at the daily division meetings. This was the bedrock of the strike. The all-important publicity committee, headed by Matt Shaw, also had an invitations subcommittee. The job of this committee was to coach and then assign speakers to visit trade unions, schools, churches, and community organizations to explain the background and purposes of the strike and to seek support.

To complete the democratic structure of the organization the divisions elected a strike committee of about eighty people – fifteen from each division plus the executive of the RCWU and Evans. This was the steering committee of the strike where major decisions were made and where the divisions could report on their problems or raise questions. The strike committee had rotating chairmen, a signal of its collective leadership.

At the very top of the structure was the strategy committee, which made the day-to-day, even hour-to-hour, policy decisions. Its membership varied but generally included Evans, Cumber, the heads of the divisions such as James 'Red' Walsh, Robert 'Doc' Savage, Mike McCauley, Peter Nielson, and Steve Brodie; Matt Shaw; and John Cosgrove, the head marshall, George Black, and Stewart O'Neill, the latter three all war veterans and members of the Workers' Ex-Servicemen's League.

Parallel to but outside the strikers' organization there grew up another structure, the Action Committee. This committee represented community support for the strikers. It was the united front element that was so important for mobilizing public sympathy and financial aid. The action committee grouped together forty-two members representing varied labour, ethnic, religious, education, political, and other community groups in Vancouver, as well as a mothers' group. The phenomenon of a Mothers' Committee, which existed in both Vancouver and Regina, was especially important in the support of relief camp strikers and the trekkers both individually and as a group; the mothers would take the striking camp inmates home for meals, often treating them as sons.[27] Also significant was the participation of the CCF movement, which was a rising force and had recently elected some members to the British Columbia provincial legislature. While the members of the CCF generally supported the strikers in a wholehearted way, their leaders, with some exceptions, were ambivalent because they wished to avoid identification with the militant mass actions set in motion by Evans and the other communist organizers. As a result, according to participant and historian Ben Swankey, the CCF both 'aligned themselves with public sentiment on the relief camps' and joined in 'the anti-Communist tirade' coming from 'the establishment of the day.' This contradictory policy fostered tensions in the action committee, leading the unemployed and their leaders to both condemn and welcome the stands taken by the leading social democrats.[28]

After the relief camp workers assembled in Vancouver and their strike organizations had been established, the Relief Camp Workers' Union called a conference of delegates and community organizations at the Lumber Workers' Hall on Hastings Street to decide on how to proceed. This was on 7 April. Joe Kelly, the one-armed district organizer of the union, explained the background of the strike and that its aim was to gain public support to open negotiations with the federal authorities on the seven demands drawn up at the Kamloops conference. Since the strikers had no funds of their own, he pointed out, they also had to bring their situation to the attention of the municipal and provincial governments as well as to the citizenry in short order to gain immediate financial and food support.

With Kelly's words in mind, the action committee decided to send a delegation to Victoria to interview the premier. This deputation found the provincial government sympathetic but unwilling to offer any help, claiming that unemployment relief was the responsibility of the federal government. The next day the strikers organized a parade through the downtown area of Vancouver to protest the provincial government's 'buck-passing.' After it reached the Cambie Street Grounds, a delegation of fifty was chosen to call on the mayor. The strikers sought permission for a tag day. No permit was granted but there was a tacit understanding. The tag day, on the following Saturday, was a great success, netting $5,000, a strong reflection of the attitude of the citizens. It was a great beginning, but with 1,500 hungry men to feed the funds would not last more than a few days.

Evans then appeared before a commission hastily arranged by the federal government to inquire into conditions in the Department of Defence Camps. The commission was headed by Justice W.A. MacDonald, the same judge who had sentenced Evans to a year in Okalla prison for organizing the coal miners. When Evans raised the seven demands of the strikers, MacDonald ruled Evans out of order. His demands, the justice said, were outside the terms of reference of his commission. It was concerned only with conditions in the camps, the quality of food, the cleanliness of the bunkhouses, and the nature of the foreman. Evans protested. The complaints of the strikers, he said, 'were not just against foremen and hot cakes.' These were minor matters. 'It is the hopelessness of life that these camp strikers are kicking about,' Evans insisted, 'not the camp conditions. They want to live like human beings with decent wages and these minor grievances would be eliminated if these demands were granted.'[29]

The strikers continued with their parades, demonstrations, and mass meetings, issuing daily strike bulletins, and speaking over the radio. The snake parades often included chants of 'We Want Work and Wages' or 'When Do We Eat?' – common slogans of the relief camp strikers. The young militants were determined to keep the public informed of developments, pressing their demand for negotiations to begin, making appeals for relief, all the while impressing everyone by their discipline and orderly behaviour. When spirits flagged or the momentum dissipated Evans would try to give a new lead. Steve Brodie, a division leader, remembered Evans saying, 'You can't go on marching and singing and begging with tin cans. You've got to do something new, surprising, something with daring if you're going to attract people's support.'[30] As a result of Evans's ideas there were several moments of high drama in the two-month struggle.

In one case the strikers, led by Division 3, known to the unemployed workers as 'the shock troops' because of its higher percentage of experienced union men who were familiar with police-initiated violence, marched through the streets and into the large department stores, snaking in and out of the displays, taking care not to damage anything. By the time they got to the giant Hudson's Bay Store on Granville Street this was too much for the authorities and the police intervened, creating mayhem and considerable damage. The strikers held their ranks and marched out of the store down to Victory Square, which was close by the city hall then on Hastings Street. A huge crowd gathered to hear speeches and

to cheer the election of a delegation to interview the mayor. The delegation was promptly arrested for vagrancy, after which the mayor stepped
into the scene. He appeared to be reading the Riot Act, although no
one could hear what he was actually saying. Refusing to be provoked
or intimidated, the strikers lined up in fours and marched out of the
square to their divisional headquarters singing their trademark hymn,
'Hold the Fort For We Are Coming.' To the chagrin of the authorities,
the arrested 'vagrants' all had permanent Vancouver addresses. That
night the police raided the offices of the Relief Camp Workers' Union,
confiscating their banners, posters, and papers, and, for good measure,
they waded into a crowd of protesters in the street, injuring a number of
strikers and citizens.

As a result of these events the action committee remobilized itself, calling upon the trade union movement to come out in a one-hour general
sympathy strike. In response to the call for solidarity with the strikers, the
Vancouver longshoremen voted to contribute 1 per cent of a month's
pay to the camp men; a mothers' committee organized a tag day in
which women only collected the money; the *Relief Camp Worker* reported
that the May Day parade from Cambie Street Grounds to Stanley Park
that year attracted 35,000 people.

Three weeks later when funds were once again exhausted and still no
progress made in negotiations on the strikers' demands, one division,
under Evans's direction, stormed into the city museum on the top floor
of the central library at the corner of Main and Hastings Streets and held
it for an afternoon. Thousands of citizens gathered on the street below
and cheered as baskets of food were hauled up by a rope dangling from a
window; all the while the other three divisions paraded in fours through
other areas of the downtown district. In the course of these actions Evans
negotiated enough money from the city to give the 1,500 men two meals
a day for several days.

But by the end of May the strikers had come to an impasse. They had
not succeeded in forcing the government in Ottawa to negotiate their
demands and they had failed to persuade the provincial or municipal
governments to finance a delegation to meet the prime minister; they
could not rely endlessly on the generosity of the people of Vancouver to
sustain their cause; their numbers were beginning to dwindle. The strike
would have to be brought to an end, in orderly fashion if possible.

It was just at this moment that somebody, no one can quite remember
who, put forward a motion at an overflow meeting in the Avenue Theatre on 30 May saying that since the federal government 'won't come to

us, I say let us go to them,' and he moved that 'we go to Ottawa, to discuss work and wages with the federal cabinet.' There was reportedly a sudden silence, broken after a long pause by Evans, who, on an impulse, seconded the motion.[31] With his endorsement the motion caught fire. The idea of an On-to-Ottawa trek seized the imagination of the strikers and rapidly took shape. Two thousand men, with more gathered along the way, according to the plan, would travel across half a continent to parade on Parliament Hill demanding an audience with the prime minister to negotiate the six demands.

The suggestion of a trek to Ottawa was a move that allowed the British Columbia provincial and Vancouver municipal governments to heave a sigh of relief. They were only too willing to facilitate the departure of the camp men from their jurisdictions.

The sudden turn of events caught the Communist Party by surprise. At the time the national leaders of the party were gathering in Toronto for one of their periodic central committee meetings and when they received the news of the proposed trek by wire they wondered if the idea was another risky and perhaps irresponsible notion of Evans. They worried that the authorities might shunt the trekkers' train onto a siding in some remote place, surround it with military forces, and disperse the strikers in humiliating and possibly brutal fashion.[32] Their first response, therefore, was a note of warning that the trek could 'easily result in the liquidation of the strike,' since it was only when concentrated in large numbers in the main centres that it had its leverage. The party urged consideration from all points of view before deciding on the proposed plan.

But within three days, as the strikers boarded the freights to leave Vancouver with the full support of the BC District Bureau of the Communist Party, the national party leaders in Toronto reconsidered their position and publicly urged their members and friends all across Canada to give fullest support to the youthful trekkers on their historic mission to Ottawa. 'We vacillated,' said Ewen, but 'got over the knotty spot because we were confronted again with facts.'[33]

Evans's senior colleagues in British Columbia, while supporting the trek, insisted that Evans not leave the province and that he return to Vancouver after waving the trekkers off to Alberta at Golden. A police report suggests that they were worried Evans would not be allowed back into the province.[34] Some veterans of the trek have suggested that the impending dockers' strike was the reason for Evans being recalled to the coast.[35] Possibly it was concern about Evans's unpredictable tendencies causing trouble for the trek at some point. The BC secretary of the Workers' Unity League, Bob Kerr, hinted at this when he recalled that Evans had 'too much energy sometimes' and gave an example: on one occasion when it was proposed to take a large contingent of unemployed across the Strait of Georgia to Victoria to lobby the provincial government, Evans allegedly suggested hijacking a Canadian Pacific ship. Evans, according to Kerr, proposed 'to take it away from the dock and then we would have all the supplies and everything.' 'We would discuss [his] ideas in the executive,' said Kerr, 'and it often became my job to argue one way or the other ... If you didn't go along with his ideas, well, he didn't like it.' Kerr, though, recognized that Evans was 'the driving force' of the trek to Ottawa. It would have 'fizzled out,' he said, 'if it hadn't been for the energy of Art.'[36]

Evans left the trek at Golden, high in the Rocky Mountains, as his colleagues demanded, and returned to the coast, but not before arranging a rousing reception, a public meeting, and a parade along the banks of the Kicking Horse River. He was able to join in a satisfying meal for the 1,400 men prepared by the people of Golden, and to witness the choice of army veteran George Black as his successor to lead the trek.

There is no record of the discussion when Evans got back to Vancouver, but he was able to reassure his comrades. After two days they provided him with money for a ticket and he was back on board an eastbound train, aiming to catch up to the trek again in Medicine Hat, Alberta. Steve Brodie, a leader of Division 3, described his dramatic arrival:

> Out of the dark shadows at the entrance of the park came a man. Somebody looked up and said, 'Well, here's Arthur.' He was absolutely bone-weary, almost staggering from tiredness and weakness ... he looked like a living skeleton. He had pulled on a pair of overalls over his suit. His face was black with soot and his eyes were red with cinders and from tiredness ... 'Steve,' he said, 'for god's sake, give me a cup of that coffee, please.'

As the trek's all-night security detail sat around a blazing fire, Evans recounted the story of his trip. Brodie recalled his account: sure that the police would be watching him and ready to foil his plans, Evans had had a friend drive him to a small station outside Vancouver where he boarded the train. Presently he saw two men who looked suspiciously like policemen come into his coach and he sensed that he would be arrested on some pretext long before reaching Medicine Hat. At the next stop he casually walked into the station restaurant and bought a sandwich and a cup of coffee, aware that he was being watched from the train window. Then he went out through a side door, took off uptown, ran ahead of the train, got into the local 'jungle' area where freight and passenger trains were normally boarded by the rod-riders, and jumped on the tender of his own train. As far as the policemen who had been sent to watch him were concerned, he had disappeared from that train. At any rate his manoeuvre was successful. He rode the tender all the rest of the way, which would be a matter of over 700 miles. It was 2:00 in the morning when that train arrived in Medicine Hat where he appeared in front of his comrades.[37]

As Evans's dramatic story circulated, most trekkers eagerly believed it, a few thought him paranoid about the presence of policemen, but there is little doubt that it added to an already romantic image of a hero in the minds of the young people. In short order the BC district organizer of the Workers' Unity League found himself once more chosen to be the principal leader of the trek.

Some observers were inclined to mock the trek, calling it 'a comic opera revolution,' or a 'revolution on wheels,' the 'Rollicking Regiments of Reliefers.'[38] But Prime Minister Bennett took it seriously and decided to terminate it in Regina before it could link up with similar hunger marches being organized in Ontario, Quebec, and the Maritimes. Bennett's decision led to the final drama of the trek.

The prime minister was busy in his office in the winter of 1935, having been converted to the need for parliament's intervention to save the economy. In a radio address to the nation on 2 January, Bennett had said that the Great Depression, with its untold sufferings for the people, had proved that free enterprise capitalism was no longer workable and it had to be reformed. 'In my mind,' he told a startled nation, 'reform means Government intervention. It means Government control and regulation. It means the end of *laissez-faire*.' 'I nail the flag of progress to the masthead,' he proclaimed with dramatic flourish, 'I summon the power of the State to its support.' Among the items he introduced to parliament in rapid succession were measures to establish a Bank of Canada as the central regulator of the nation's finances, a national broadcasting system, a national airline, the Wheat Board, a broadened Natural Products Marketing Act, the Dominion Housing Act, and others.

For the workers Bennett offered an unemployment insurance bill but with a catch: they would have to pay for it. As a biographer of Bennett noticed, the draft bill 'was intended to enforce working-class savings, not redistribute income on a large scale'; it 'did nothing for those already unemployed' and it excluded seasonal workers.[39] There was no emergency plan for work with liveable wages.

Bennett's announcements were a case of too little and too late to influence the minds of the relief camp workers and their supporters across the country. They would march on. By mid-June Bennett, with the co-operation of the railway companies, had assembled eighty-five railway policemen and approximately 300 of the RCMP in Regina to forcibly remove the strikers from eastbound trains on the pretext of preventing further illegal trespassing on railway property.

As the primary leader of the trek and as a tactician who had taken courses at Communist Party schools, Evans certainly had no intention of heading his unemployed army into a violent confrontation with the armed forces of the state. He knew the trek might have to retreat and that the worst thing would be to drag it out to the point of complete exhaustion and disorganization of the trekkers. If he wished, he could find comfort in the words of Lozovsky, who in addressing the Red International had said, 'We must not think that every struggle is a final and decisive battle, they are only skirmishes ... defeat is not a disgrace.' But Evans's personality was such that as long as there existed a glimmer of possibility he would strive and not yield in his determination to have the trek reach its objectives. He would do all he could to keep up morale and gather public support in a united effort.

After catching up to the trek, Evans left Moose Jaw to travel eastwards to Regina on 13 June in advance of the trekkers. There he found a broadly representative Citizens' Emergency Committee, already aware of the federal government's intentions, preparing a warm welcome. He also met the provincial premier, James Gardiner, who was angry at Bennett's arrogant disregard of Saskatchewan's jurisdiction in deciding unilaterally to terminate the trek in that province and who offered shelter for the trekkers in the city's exhibition grounds stadium and two meals per day for several days. With this information Evans returned to Moose Jaw to prepare the strike committee and the trekkers for what lay ahead, and to urge even greater discipline in the ranks and the avoidance of any provocative actions. Discipline during the trek was to a large extent the responsibility of Elof Kellnor, a big, normally mild-mannered Scandinavian immigrant who talked the young men into behaving well and thereby impressing the public, whom they had to count on for support.[40]

The trek proceeded according to plan. After a grand reception in Regina – a rally of 6,000 addressed by the national secretary of the CCF, the head of the Regina Ministerial Association, a priest representing the

Catholic Church, the president of the Regina Trades and Labour Council, the provincial leader of the Communist Party, and Evans, plus a tag day netting $1,500 and many donations in kind, and the support shown by the provincial premier – Prime Minister Bennett was forced to temporize. He sent two cabinet ministers to meet the strikers in the capital of Saskatchewan. The ministers were not prepared to negotiate on the six demands. They declared they had no such mandate. But they said that the federal government was ready to finance a small delegation to Ottawa and would supply relief to the trekkers for the duration of the delegation's absence from Regina.

When the strike committee discussed the federal government's proposal, Evans was opposed. He thought it was a ruse to get the leaders separated from the trekkers, a plan to hold a kangeroo court in Ottawa and then to throw the leadership in jail.

But the strike committee felt it could not refuse. A stormy meeting of all the strikers overruled Evans and accepted the proposal.[41] Following this a delegation of eight, headed by Evans, left Regina to meet the prime minister in the nation's capital. They were joined on the train in North Bay, Ontario, by Tom Ewen, national secretary of the Workers' Unity League, and his secretary, Lil Greene, who came to offer support for a difficult assignment.

The meeting with the prime minister was a tense and turbulent affair. On one side of the room sat Bennett with eleven of his ministers – twelve disciples of 'capitalism on the rocks' one might say – and the official debates recorder of parliament; on the other sat Evans, an unemployed carpenter, with seven of the strike leaders and Lil Greene – a setting of strangely mixed biblical flavour. For all the disparities in social status, education level, and size of pocketbooks, the two sides were remarkably well matched: Bennett, the multi-millionaire, blusterer, and master of shrewd argument, pitted against Evans, bearer of scars from many class battles, a convinced socialist and a man of inexhaustible energy.

One of Bennett's strategies was to undermine the credibility of the unemployed movement and its leader in every way possible. This was apparent in the course of the hour-long interview and in his speech to the House of Commons afterwards. By asking each of the unemployed men to state his place of residence and birth, he hoped to undermine their legitimacy as real Canadians, a move that fell flat, since, although seven were foreigners by birth, all but one had been born in the United Kingdom or in a British colony and the family of their leader had lived in Canada for 112 years. The prime minister wanted the unemployed, many of whom he felt were innocent and badly deceived young people, to know that their leader was a criminal and a thief and that the Workers' Unity League was a conspiracy trying to overthrow 'law and order.' In violation of the law, he said, the trekkers had trespassed on railway property, endangering human life. The Workers' Unity League wanted recognition of camp committees, but these, Bennett claimed, were really Soviet committees, a form of government that Canada would not tolerate. These people had come to Ottawa asking for 'work and wages,' but he doubted if they had 'much anxiety to get to work.' That is the one thing you do not want, he said. 'What you want is this adventure in the hope that the organization which you are promoting in Canada may be able to over-awe government and break down the forces that represent law and order.'

Bennett's other strategy was an attempt to defend his efforts at coping with the crisis of unemployment. It was a world-wide crisis, he liked to emphasize, and Canada was doing as well as or better than the other industrialized countries. As for the relief camps, there was no compulsion or military discipline about them, he insisted. They had not been established to provide regular work with wages but only as temporary emergency places to provide food, clothing, shelter, and a little gratuity for otherwise homeless and hungry single young people. Discontent with this arrangement was the fault of 'agitators representing Communism.' Bennett wanted to know if the trekkers thought they were playing the part of good citizens in a country with the difficulties Canada faced in view of the government's vigorous efforts to restore normal conditions. What could be the purpose of a march on Ottawa?

When the prime minister invited the spokesman of the delegation to speak, Evans stood up. He said that he had a copy of the six points with respect to the relief camps which he would like to provide to the prime minister and that he would give an oral summary of the reasons for drawing up such a list. These camps, he said, represented a 'hopeless outlook' for the men: no opportunity for them to marry, have a home or normal life. Not in three years had some of them been inside the four walls of a home, and at the present time 'they are forced to work eight hours per day for twenty cents per day.' That was why the main demand was for 'work and wages' with a minimum wage and at trade union rates of pay for skilled workers. This would allow men hope for a better future. He gave a brief history of the Relief Camp Workers' Union and its unsuccessful attempts to change the situation and explained how from that experience there had arisen the other demands, namely, coverage by the

Workmen's Compensation Act in case of injury, abolition of military control and the system of blacklists, recognition of democratically elected camp committees, the right to vote in elections, and the implementation of a system of non-contributory unemployment insurance. He described the various attempts of the Relief Camp Workers' Union and the strike committee to open negotiations on the six points and to gain relief but said that their efforts had become a political football between the various levels of government. And now in leading a disciplined trek to Ottawa they wished to bring legitimate grievances to 'the proper quarters' and to take them up 'in a proper manner.' Except for a few argumentative interjections, the prime minister listened quietly until Evans concluded his twenty-minute introduction.

After Bennett made his equal-time rebuttal, the interview became something of a free-for-all scrum. The volatile exchanges between the prime minister and a group of working men reflected the temper of the two sides:

STEWART 'PADDY' O'NEILL (36, division leader): You have accused us of all kinds of things – wanting to set up Soviet committees.

BENNETT: Nobody has told you the facts and I am trying –

O'NEILL: I have ridden in box cars in France, too, and in cattle cars. You call us foreigners.

JOHN COSGROVE (35, trek marshal): I take exception to any personal attack on this delegation and will not –

BENNETT: Sit down, Mr Cosgrove.

COSGROVE: I will not.

BENNETT: Then you will be removed.

EVANS: Then the entire delegation will be removed.

BENNETT: Sit down Mr Cosgrove.

COSGROVE: I will when I have said this. I fought in the war as a boy fifteen years old. I have the interests of this country as much at heart as you have.

BENNETT: That is good enough.

Evans tried to keep the discussion focused on the main demand of the trekkers, that the government should institute a program of work and wages, and this led to an outburst that electrified the country:

BENNETT: We have made it perfectly clear so far as we are concerned that these camps were not established for that purpose.

EVANS: That is passing the buck. We want work and wages.

BENNETT: Just a moment –

EVANS: You referred to us not wanting work. Give any of us work and see whether we will work. This is an insidious attempt to propagandize the press on your part, and anybody who professes to be Premier and uses such despicable tactics is not fit to be Premier of a Hottentot village [a colloquial name for the Khoikhoi people living in the southwest corner of Africa].

BENNETT: I come from Alberta. I remember when you embezzled the funds of your union and were sent to penitentiary.

EVANS: You are a liar. I was arrested for fraudulently converting these funds to feed the starving, instead of sending them to the agents at Indianapolis, and I again say you are a liar if you say I embezzled, and I will have the pleasure of telling the workers throughout Canada I was forced to tell the premier of Canada he was a liar. Don't think you can pull off anything like that. You are not intimidating me a damned bit.

BENNETT: I know your record in the penitentiary at New Westminster, your record in the penitentiary elsewhere.

EVANS: I was never in penitentiary at New Westminster. You do not know what you are talking about.

BENNETT: Where was it?

EVANS: I know your –

BENNETT: You are at present on ticket of leave?

EVANS: I am.

BENNETT: It has lapsed now?

EVANS: There are a lot of things you don't know.

BENNETT: You are here deluding a number of young men.

EVANS: I have stated I used the funds for hungry people instead of sending them to Indianapolis to a bunch of pot-bellied business agents. For you to bring this question up shows the absolute groundlessness of your position. You have raised the question that we did not start this for work and wages. We want work and wages.

BENNETT: I was referring to the second time you were sent to penitentiary.

EVANS: Where was the second time and where was the ticket of leave? I was never sent a second time to penitentiary.

BENNETT: Jail.

EVANS: Under Section 98 for leading miners in a strike.

After a few more minutes of the scrum Evans sought to return the discussion to the purpose of the interview.

EVANS: I propose we do not interject any more. We have heard enough of these idle statements from our Prime Minister so we will take the rest of what he has to say and go out and back to the workers and the citizens of Canada

BENNETT: That is your privilege so long as you keep within the law, and the minute you step beyond it, Mr Evans, you will land where you once were ...

Bennett then went through the six demands, categorically rejecting them one by one, concluding with his warnings of suppression and prison:

BENNETT: That is all that can be said. I want to warn you once more, if you persist in violating the laws of Canada [by riding the rails] you must accept full responsibility for your conduct.

EVANS: And you also.

BENNETT: I am prepared for that.

EVANS: So are we.

BENNETT: And I suggest to those who have misled and are continuing to mislead their fellow-citizens that they have a great responsibility, for the government of this country proposes to govern, which means that the laws of Canada will be enforced so long as there is government ... Good day, gentlemen.

Not to be so easily dismissed, the spirited leader of the unemployed had the last word.

EVANS: In conclusion, you brought the question up that we should seriously consider our responsibility. We realize the responsibility we are confronted with. We are confronted to-day with a greater responsibility than when we first came here in view of the statement of the Prime Minister that the government will not deal with the questions raised here. In place of that they attempt to raise the red bogey ... Our responsibility is we must take this back to the workers and see that the hunger programme of Bennett is stopped.

BENNETT: I have nothing more to say. Good morning gentlemen. We have been glad to listen to you.[42]

The next day Evans and the leaders of hunger marches from Ontario and Quebec spoke to an overflow meeting at the Rialto Theatre in Ottawa, telling the dramatic stories of their interviews with the prime minister, and announcing their intentions to continue organizing pressure on the government of Canada to meet the demands of the legions of unemployed. The western delegates then departed for Regina, mak-

ing brief stopovers in Sudbury, Port Arthur, and Winnipeg before receiving a tumultuous welcome in the capital of Saskatchewan on 26 June at
a mass meeting with about 7,000 people attending.

But the euphoria was short-lived. The federal government had cut off
relief payments and 2,000 men had to be fed. More than that, Bennett
had turned Regina into something of an armed encampment: in addition to sending about 800 railway, federal, and other police to enforce an
order-in-council (which turned out to be fictitious) preventing the strikers from leaving Regina by train, truck, or on foot, and threatening anyone who offered food, transportation, or other assistance to the strikers
with arrest, the government had proposed the building of a high-security
holding camp near the town of Lumsden in the Qu'Appelle Valley north
of Regina for securing control of the trekkers.[43] The government showed
that it had extensive plans to terminate the trek by force.

In order to avert a bloodbath, Evans and the trekkers offered a compromise. They would agree to end the strike, provided the government
conveyed them back to Vancouver as a group under their own leadership and from there to the relief camps from which they originally came.
They also asked for reassurance that there would be no arrests. On the
morning of Dominion Day, 1 July, Evans and the division leaders negotiated with the RCMP assistant commissioner, S.T. Wood, as well as with a
member of the federal government and the premier of Saskatchewan,
but without result. Wood insisted the men must go to the government's
barbed-wire concentration camp near Lumsden, eighteen miles north of
Regina, to be decommissioned, or else face the consequences.

In the evening of that day the Strike Strategy Committee scheduled
a meeting in Regina's Market Square to report on the state of negotiations for the retreat from Regina. The rally, attended by about 300 strikers (the rest were at a baseball game in the Exhibition Grounds) and
about 1,500 citizens, had barely got underway at 8:00 p.m. when it was
subjected to a co-ordinated surprise attack by city police and the RCMP,
led by the latter. Plain-clothes detectives immediately and easily arrested
Evans and the other leaders on the platform, but the uniformed and hel-
meted police, some of them on horseback, charged through the square
swinging their batons. The people were driven into the side streets but
then anger erupted. Trekkers and citizens barricaded themselves with
overturned cars and pelted the police with anything lying at hand while
the police fired their revolvers and spread tear gas. Store front windows
were smashed. The battle in the streets raged for several hours as the day-
light faded. By next morning when the smoke had cleared scores of local

citizens and trekkers and a number of policemen had been wounded, one plain-clothes police detective, Charles Millar, killed, and 120 citizens and trekkers arrested. One trekker, Nick Schaack, also died after the riot of head wounds and being kept in police custody for many hours rather than getting medical attention as his cell-mates requested and then demanded. There was almost no looting after hundreds of store windows were broken.

Armed police surrounded the exhibition stadium where the trekkers were billeted and a barbed-wire stockade encircled its perimeter. The trekkers within were denied food and water. News of the police riot flashed across the country with the prime minister claiming his government had saved the country from an 'uprising,' a 'revolutionary effort on the part of a group of men to usurp authority and destroy government.'[44]

The Saskatchewan premier, anxious to have the trekkers removed from his jurisdiction and still furious with Bennett for usurping control of police functions in his province, came to the support of the trekkers by negotiating an agreement for their retreat from Regina, the same one that Evans, now arrested again under section 98 of the Criminal Code, had initiated. As a result of these negotiations the Saskatchewan provincial government issued meal tickets and chartered two special trains at its own expense to take the trekkers back to British Columbia. The court trials and the hearings of a commission of inquiry dragged on for months, but eventually many of the charges, including those against Evans, were dropped 'for lack of evidence' and because of widespread public protests. Nine men, however, were sentenced to jail on charges of rioting or assault, while the RCMP escaped without a note of censure.

The judges who conducted the trials and the inquiry into the Regina riot exonerated the Bennett government. They defended the police in their assault on Market Square on 1 July, saying that the government was justified in stopping the trek in Regina because it had been controlled by 'vicious characters,' led by 'scoundrels,' and threatened the nation with the spectre of communism.[45] These judgments, aimed at tarnishing the image of the trek and its organizers, the Relief Camp Workers' Union and the Workers' Unity League, had the effect of demonizing the communists in some sectors of public opinion.[46]

But other sections of the public held a contrary opinion. The labour movement and some of its historians offered a more positive verdict: the real spectre facing Canada had not been communism but mass unemployment and the loss of civil liberties. After the passage of fifty years the activists who built the Relief Camp Workers' Union and who led the trek presented quite a different impression to the mind of historian Lorne Brown in his well-researched book *When Freedom Was Lost.* The 'scoundrels,' who had 'withstood some of the most severe state repression ever seen in Canada during peacetime,' Brown wrote, were for the most part 'dedicated, self-educated working people … courageous and skillful in day-to-day struggle and no issue or grievance was too big or too small to demand their attention. They could operate effectively on a political stage as small as the smallest relief camp or as large as all of Canada. Their political judgement was usually sound and those who worked with them seldom questioned their devotion to the cause. They were not limited by the narrow confines of Parliamentary politics … They did not allow the powers that be to define what was legitimate and illegitimate in either political ideas or tactics and strategy. These activists earned the trust and respect and often the devotion … of countless thousands of the Canadian people.'[47]

On the sixtieth anniversary of the On-to-Ottawa Trek and Regina Riot in 1995, the Saskatchewan Federation of Labour declared these events to be pivotal moments in Canadian history, events that led to social reform – unemployment insurance, social welfare, medicare, union rights – and a stronger Canada.

The trekkers had arrived in Regina 'riding the rods' and breathing coal smoke. In leaving, after grievous tribulations, they marched to the Regina train station, heads held high and in accustomed formation, singing their hymn, 'Hold the Fort For We Are Coming.' They had not reached their goal but they had not been beaten either. And as a bonus they rode home on cushions paid for by the Saskatchewan government.

The On-to-Ottawa Trek had been stopped short all right, but in its duration the Relief Camp Workers' Union and its many friends had conveyed a potent message of hope to the people of Canada. And by returning to the coast with their organization intact, they offered a sound rebuke to an increasingly unpopular prime minister and his trigger-happy advisors.

The upshot of the struggle was a better result than many in the leadership of the Workers' Unity League could have expected: militarized relief camps as a means of dealing with mass unemployment and Section 98 of the criminal code as an instrument of state repression both became important issues in the next general election. Four months after Bennett's violent suppression of the On-to-Ottawa Trek, he led the Conservative Party to its worst general election result since Confederation, a clear warning to future governments to heed the demands of 'the reserve army of labour.' And at the local level, as in the case of struggles led by unions of the Workers' Unity League in Blairmore, Alberta, in 1932, and in Stratford, Ontario, in 1933, the workers and their allies in Regina exercised their democratic rights in an act of poetic justice to elect a pro-labour majority to City Council in the autumn of 1935, including T.G. McManus, leader of the local Communist Party. When McManus was subsequently unseated by the business crowd for owing the city of Regina money – relief debt – he was replaced as councillor in a by-election won by the Rev. Sam East, the United Church minister who had had the temerity to champion the cause of the strikers.

The On-to-Ottawa Trek and the events surrounding it were an encouraging foretaste of the popular front that the Workers' Unity League was hoping to accomplish and to which it devoted its efforts leading up to the third and final convention of the organization in November 1935.

16

Changing Times:
The Final Convention of the
Workers' Unity League

The relative strength of the revolutionary unions compared with the reformist unions is extremely favourable ... The strength and prestige of the revolutionary unions, won in the course of strike struggles, are excellent means for the fight for unity and against the trade union bureaucracy.

– Letter of the Red International of Labour Unions to
Canadian Communist Party, April 1935[1]

It is paramount in any country when the militant movement of the working classes had to analyse their position and having done so it is sometimes advisable to retreat. We have reached this position now in Canada ... A year ago we were on the offensive everywhere, but the situation has changed to such an extent that the ruling classes in Canada are now on the offensive and attacking us from every angle from Vancouver to the Atlantic Coast.

– Report of Vancouver delegate after attending
CPC Central Committee meeting, 4 July 1935[2]

For all the romantic appeal of their campaigns ... in the majority of cases [the Workers' Unity League] failed, leaving a heritage of violence, martyrdom, and misery.

– Desmond Morton, historian[3]

When the delegates assembled in Toronto for the third and, as it turned out, the final convention of the Workers' Unity League, in November 1935, the organization was completing its sixth year of existence. Much had changed since the previous convention two years earlier and there were many things to consider.

As they greeted each other in the brightly decorated Pythian Castle Hall on College Street, most delegates believed they could be justly proud of the league's achievements, and they looked ahead with confidence; yet in their minds they also carried the knowledge of failures, and future uncertainties.

Many of the familiar figures were there: J.B. McLachlan from Nova Scotia in the chair, and calling the meeting to order; Tom Ewen delivering the main report; T.C. Sims, acting national secretary while Ewen had been in the penitentiary; Sam Scarlett, Fred Collins, and J.B. Salsberg, the gifted Southern Ontario organizers; Joe Gershman, Pearl Wedro, and Max Dolgoy from the needle trades; Nick Thatchuk and Carl Palmgren from the North; Harvey Murphy and John Stokaluk, old rivals from the Alberta coal fields; Ted Gunerud, woodsman from British Columbia; Annie Buller; Julia Carr, national secretary-treasurer, and Jeanne Corbin, leading the contingent of women activists; altogether 146 delegates, including a score of fraternal guests.

From all outward appearances it was a normal convention with plenary sessions and small group meetings to consider resolutions and to recommend courses of action, a special issue of *Unity* with a reassuring message from President McLachlan, and display advertisements with warm greetings from affiliated unions and fraternal organizations across the country; a gala dance at the Pythian Hall; a group photograph of the delegates.

In his opening report, Ewen laid out for the convention an indictment of the prevailing economic system. It was a system that favoured the Big Interests, he said, while wreaking havoc on workers, farmers, women, youth, and urban middle-class people. Supported by official government statistics, Ewen pointed out that national income was rising again, profits in many firms were up, and the rich were prospering while workers were 'having their noses ground harder than ever against the millstone of poverty, low wages, speed-up, unsafe working conditions and malnutrition.' Very few earned $25 a week, the amount the Department of Labour calculated an average family needed to maintain itself in food, rent, clothes, and sundries. As a result of 'the maddening speed-up systems' and violations of the safety laws of the land, approximately 100 workers were killed every month in Canadian industry. Thousands of willing workers remained unemployed while hundreds of factories stood idle. When unemployed workers asked the government to open up the closed factories or provide adequate relief and genuine unemployment insurance – 'What do we hear?' Ewen asked rhetorically. 'We hear the well-fed politicians and manufacturers and stock exchange sharks and reactionary newspaper editors howling about agitators from Moscow … about the need for more jails, more R.C.M.P.s and more deportations. That's what we hear.'[4] This was the now familiar background upon which the delegates framed the justice of their cause, and formulated their ideas, their resolutions, and their plans of action.

By the time the gathering concluded three days later, at midnight, with the singing of 'Hold the Fort' (a departure for delegates accustomed to raising their fists and singing the more revolutionary 'Internationale' or 'The Red Flag' on such occasions), a reporter from the Associated Labour Press described the convention as 'the most successful in the history of Canada's fighting trade union organisation.'[5]

Apart from electing a dominion council of fifty members and a national executive board of fifteen members headed by McLachlan and Ewen to lead the organization for another year,[6] the delegates had debated and adopted a host of decisions and resolutions. These ranged from a constitutional amendment to raise the per capita initiation fee to one dollar and per capita dues from one cent to two cents per month, to advocating a huge building program of slum clearance and construction of working-class homes, at trade union rates, and not to include military construction, such as armouries and barracks. They called upon all unions to aid the strike of the British Columbia longshoremen, supported the house workers' union (domestic workers) in their struggle for decent pay, and called upon the Ontario Department of Labour to enforce the minimum wage in this field. They advocated the six-hour day and the five-day week as a step toward full employment, and demanded increased compensation for injured workers, and the setting up of an appeal board (on which there would be worker representation) to which injured workers could appeal when they felt themselves treated unjustly by the provincial compensation boards. They also advocated a complete boycott of all goods from Nazi Germany and pledged every aid and support to such a boycott. All this and much more.[7] By all appearances, the WUL was prepared to soldier on. But this was actually 'Plan B.'

There was one policy resolution of such prime import that this convention would later be judged as one of 'the most important meetings in the history of the Canadian left,'[8] and this was 'Plan A.' The resolution in question centred on the issue of trade union unity.

Introduced on behalf of the national executive board by J.B. Salsberg, it proposed 'One Union – One Industry,' and instructed the newly elected dominion council of the Workers' Unity League to seek the assistance and co-operation of its erstwhile adversaries, the Trades and Labour Congress, the affiliates of the American Federation of Labour, the All-Canadian Congress of Labour, and the Catholic and independent unions, to achieve this end. On the basis of conditions prevailing in each industry, the convention proposed that to help maintain and improve the living standards of Canadian workers, to defend against a rising tide of reaction and company unionism, and to keep Canada at peace, the Workers' Unity League should encourage its affiliated unions to join hands with other related or parallel unions 'in the speediest fashion.' 'We are prepared to agree that W.U.L. unions shall merge with other unions,' said Ewen, 'even if this means that W.U.L. unions would sever their affiliation with us and affiliate to the A.F.L.' The only conditions were that such a move served the interests of the working people over the interests of the employing class and that democracy – the will of the majority – prevailed in the trade unions.[9] Although this was not said, it was implied that the WUL was prepared to go as far as ending its separate existence as a trade union centre under these conditions and to lead its 35,000 members, including 6,000 or 7,000 communists, back into the AFL and the Trades and Labour Congress of Canada.

On the face of it, this was an astonishing turnabout. Was it an admission that the decision to build the Workers' Unity League as a revolutionary trade union centre six years earlier had been a terrible mistake? That the league's efforts had been a dismal failure, as former leaders, now followers of Trotsky, and some future historians, maintained? Was it a case, as some suggested, of policy suddenly being turned around 'on instructions from Moscow'?[10] Or are there other explanations, other ways to consider this historic change of tactics?

To gain perspective on these questions, it is helpful to turn back a year to 1934 to consider how the Workers' Unity League viewed several important developments on the international stage, certain stirrings in the United States, and new challenges in Canada.

Originally, the Workers' Unity League's third convention had been scheduled to take place in the first week of September, 1934. It had been announced in the spring during the euphoria of the largest and most successful strike wave in fifteen years, much of it led by the league.[11] With this background, the affiliated unions had drafted their resolutions and elected their delegates to the convention, when, with barely three weeks' warning, it was abruptly postponed for six months. And then it was postponed again.

Something had gone amiss, but what? The official reason – that affiliated unions had requested delay so that they could prepare for their own meetings[12] – was little more than an attempt at saving face. More to the point, perhaps, was a notice sent out from the national office earlier in the summer, which spoke of a 'critical financial situation'; the centre requested unions to send in their per capita dues without delay, otherwise it would be 'virtually impossible' to send out the preparatory materials for the convention.[13] But the Workers' Unity League was accustomed to operating on a shoe-string budget and had seldom allowed financial shortages to stand in the way of important projects.

There was something more fundamental involved here, some uncertainty or conflict of opinion triggering an uncharacteristic hesitation and last-minute decision to postpone the annual convention.

From the vast outpouring of documents preserved in the recently opened archives of the Third International, what surfaces more clearly than ever is an emerging difference of opinion among leading communists, between a 'sectarian left' and a 'non-sectarian left,' not only in Canada but around the world, on how effective working-class politics and trade union organization should proceed within what was perceived to be an increasingly dangerous and harsh political environment, both internationally and in Canada. It was a time of considerable confusion and debate about the next step.

There was no doubt that the international situation had changed radically since the Workers' Unity League's previous convention in 1933. Hitler's coming to power that year and the rise of fascism on a world scale, including in Italy and Japan, signalled this change. The once formidable trade unions in those countries, both the social democratic and the communist, had been crushed, and no one knew where the spread of fascist ideas and organization would stop. Hitler had smashed all the political parties but his own; in his anti-Semitic frenzy, he had driven the Jews out of public life and had taken Germany out of the League of Nations to begin a rearmament program that would soon propel the German army over the borders of many countries. Japan had already invaded China and, from its puppet state in Manchuria, had its guns pointed at the Soviet Union. These developments made some kind of reorientation unavoidable, and the Third International and the Red International of Labour Unions began reconsidering their strained relations with the world-wide liberal reformist and social democratic movements with a view better to resist the advance of fascism and the growing threat of war.

This reconsideration and subsequent transition from the strident 'class against class' analysis of the 'third period' to a 'fourth period' took place gradually over the early months of 1933 and on into the summer of 1935. In the third period, communists had targeted social democrats in particular as the chief social prop of the bourgeoisie and the *main enemy* of revolutionary advance. In the fourth period they decided to *embrace* social democrats as a vital part of a progressive alliance to enhance working-class unity as part of an anti-fascist Popular Front. Through most of this time, supporters of both the 'old' and 'new' analyses of the role of social democracy and the possibilities for unity jostled for support.

This was the case even at the highest level. On one side were important leaders of the executive committee of the Third International, including Bela Kun (Hungary), Wang Ming (China), and Alexander Lozovsky, who clung to warnings about the reformists and continued to call them 'social fascists' as late as the autumn of 1934. On the other side were Georgi Dimitrov, the Bulgarian communist leader widely known for successfully defending himself against the charge of setting fire to the Reichstag building in 1933, and his supporters (who eventually included both Manuilsky and Kuusinen). Dimitrov argued, with increasing success, for an end to narrow sectarian quarrels in view of the alarming growth of the Nazi Party in Germany and signs of fascism in many countries. He favoured building a broadly based 'united front against fascism.'

E.H. Carr, the former member of the British Foreign Office and eminent historian of the Third International, pointed to 'an anomalous situation in which officials of the Comintern spoke with different voices, and directives issued to communist parties were conflicting and indecisive.' In his view, it was the pressure of external events rather than 'pressure from ... Moscow' which drove the Third International 'along the path of a united, and later the popular, front.'[14]

In Canada the same arguments were put forward. Stewart Smith, the leader of the Communist Party, was on the sectarian path, while on the other track was Leslie Morris, editor of the *Worker*, and his friends, who were finding their way to advocate a non-sectarian popular-front perspective. Somewhere in between, but more with Morris, were Charles Sims, and, after his release from prison in the autumn of 1934, Tom Ewen, the two men chiefly responsible for piloting the course of the Workers' Unity League.

The presence of leading communists in the workings of the league was so important – the major influence – that some understanding of their policy debates and their thinking will help clarify the dilemmas facing the trade union centre, which caused its leadership to postpone its annual convention for fifteen months before launching out on a new path.

For those who wish to trace the course of the struggle between the 'sectarian left' and the 'non-sectarian left' in the communist movement in Canada, a good place to start is the recently discovered controversy that occurred over an editorial appearing in the *Worker* in the spring of 1934.[15] According to Norman Freed, the Canadian representative to the Anglo-American Secretariat of the Third International, the editorial implied that the social democratic Co-operative Commonwealth Federation was a working-class party and that splitting the CCF was synonymous with splitting the working class.

After this editorial reached Freed, he wrote an excited letter to Smith, complaining about it, reiterating the dangers of 'social fascism,' and recalling the recently expressed resolve of the Canadian party to 'hinder the growth of the influence of the CCF and to commence to smash some of its already won positions.' Freed suggested that the party issue a self-critical statement retracting the editorial.[16] Smith ignored the suggestion but stepped up promotional activities for his new book, *Socialism and the CCF*, in which he tried to persuade Canadians that 'a fundamental community of ideas' existed 'between the fascism of Hitler and the social-fascism of the CCF' then led by the Reverend J.S. Woodsworth.[17]

In the summer of 1934, Smith organized a secret national convention of the still small and illegal but growing Communist Party of Canada to rally members to his viewpoint. (The convention was so covert that the RCMP, in spite of all its sleuths, did not find out about it until its resolutions were published in the *Worker* several weeks later.)

The convention's Manifesto, which in a general way followed the earlier resolutions of the executive committee of the Third International, reflected the position of Smith:

> ... capitalism was bringing to the labouring people of Canada the catastrophe of poverty, fascism and a new war; while poverty stalked the land over a million unemployed stood idle outside of closed factories; under schemes of 'labour codes' the capitalist governments were putting controls on the market place that would ostensibly curb sweatshop conditions but which would tend to reduce wages to a minimum level and take away the right of workers to protest by strike action; in this semi-fascist strategy the capitalist class was aided by the class-collaboration attitudes of the leaders of reformist unions and the social-democratic Co-operative Commonwealth Federation (CCF); these leaders, stigmatized as agents of the capitalists, and sometimes as 'social fascists' – socialist in words, fascist in deeds – stood in the way of a united working-class struggle. Only the Communist Party

had led the fight of workers and farmers 'against the hunger offensive of capitalism' and 'the only way out of the crisis of capitalism' was to abolish it by the 'establishment of Socialism through the power of a revolutionary workers' and farmers' government, a Soviet government.

There were many other ringing phrases, composed in Smith's characteristic style, which, in the words of T.C. Sims, firmly anchored the party's political program with the 'ball and chain of sectarianism.'[18]

The party's economic program, as proposed by Smith, was modest by comparison and actually reduced the centrality of independent Red trade unions. The need for modesty was dictated by forthright recognition of the fact that the recent strike wave led by the Workers' Unity League had touched only 'the fringe of the organized workers of Canada.' In addition, of the quarter of a million unionized men and women, only 26,000 were in unions affiliated to the WUL. Furthermore, the successful strikes led by the Workers' Unity League had mainly been in plants owned by small manufacturers; the league had been largely unsuccessful in penetrating the large corporation-controlled plants such as in the auto industry, where the greatest numbers of factory workers found employment, and which were 'the strongholds of Canadian capitalism.' As in the mining and lumbering fields, these workers, in Smith's words, were up against the 'big corporations, the big bourgeoisie, the banks and through them the government, which now had an intimate interest in bringing the full weight of terroristic pressure to bear on the workers to crush them into submission.' This was seen in the Anyox, Noranda, and Flin Flon metal mines, the Crowsnest Pass and Stellarton coal mines, the British Columbia loggers' strike and those of the pulpwood cutters of Ontario and Quebec, where, at various times, military forces, aeroplanes, machine guns, gas bombs, concentrations of heavily armed police, and mass arrests with imprisonment and deportation were used as a means of cowing the workers.

All these matters suggested a serious problem with strike strategy and tactics, according to Smith, and, in particular, past mistakes in 'organizing the united front as a weapon in the hands of the workers to win strikes.' In this respect, Smith now doubted the advisability of continuing to build small Red trade unions by breaking off pieces of reformist unions. That approach, he said, was 'merely bluffing the workers,' did not lead to developing a wide opposition movement, and promoted 'the conception among the workers that the Communists are union wreckers.' Such tactics led 'not to the growth of the revolutionary trade-union

movement, but to [its] further isolation and strengthening of the position of the reformists.' Instead, in urgent tones, he called upon communists to enter the reformist unions and to attack the 'social fascists' on
all fronts because the greatest challenge to mobilizing the workers for a
united struggle was the influence of the social-fascists and 'insufficient
exposure' of their manoeuvres.[19]

Smith's views would not find much favour with Sims and the other
leaders of the Workers' Unity League who were still dedicated to building
up the revolutionary, class-struggle unions.[20] Still, they were put before
the Anglo-American Secretariat of the Third International by Freed,
and three weeks later, in Toronto, on 29 August 1934, they became the
essence of the resolution of the 6th Session of the Central Committee of
the Communist Party on work in the reformist unions.[21]

In the other camp, as already mentioned, the most prominent member of the 'non-sectarian left' in the Communist Party was Leslie Morris,
age thirty, editor of the *Worker*, the main labour newspaper in the country at the time and the unofficial voice of the Communist Party.

The rift between those who wanted to work with the social democrats
and those who didn't was unmistakable, even though no open break
occurred. Scarcely a month after the seventh CPC convention, which
declared itself 'a completely united party,' Smith called together the full
meeting of the Central Committee of the Communist Party, the 6th Session, at which Morris was forced to read out a lengthy self-criticism about
his 'failure to bring questions to the PB [political bureau] for frank discussion' and his inability to get along with Smith ever since their days
at the International Lenin School, with promises to do better in the
future.[22]

Humiliated, no doubt, but still sure of his ground, Morris continued
as editor of the paper and worked on other important political assign-
ments, especially the task of helping to build a broad united front against
war and fascism. In that job he was having considerable success. Together
with A.A. McLeod, he associated closely with such personalities as Rev.
Salem Bland, Rabbi Maurice Esiendrath of the Holy Blossom Temple in
Toronto, Elizabeth Morton, Dr Rose Henderson, and others whose political views spanned the spectrum from liberal to left, and who included
the valued participation of some prominent members of the CCF in
Ontario. A large and broadly representative Canadian Congress against
War and Fascism held in Toronto early in October, at which Morris presented the communist point of view, was a major accomplishment. Morris himself reported on the gathering in the *Worker*, emphasizing that

working-class unity for an urgent cause had received a great impetus and that revolutionary workers could not but see in the program adopted at the congress 'a step towards unity in action between the Communist Party and the C.C.F.' He continued his political momentum as principal speaker at a rally of 1,800 people in Massey Hall, the beloved concert venue and meeting place on Shuter Street in downtown Toronto. In a secret report to the government, the RCMP estimated that the communists had cause to be well satisfied with the result of the congress and that indeed it was 'one of the outstanding achievements in the history of the Communist Party in Canada.'[23]

Not to be outdone, Smith appeared three weeks later before an overflow meeting of 3,500 at the same venerable building to celebrate the seventeenth anniversary of the Russian Revolution. It was an incredible, pulsating scene in the heart of the city. According to a police report, on a platform decorated with giant sketches of Karl Marx, Joseph Stalin, V.I. Lenin, and Tim Buck, which had been created by local artists and members of the Progressive Arts Club, Smith waited five minutes before the cheering, foot-stamping crowd, singing 'The Internationale,' made it possible for him to be heard. He then explained how the Communist Party would remedy the economic system of Canada.[24] The Massey Hall rallies reflected a passionate concern of many Canadians about the threat of war and fascism and suggested a growing impatience for an alternative to capitalism.

By October, an important shift had taken place in the leadership of the Third International, and the forces led by Dimitrov had won the upper hand. The political commission of the Third International, now headed by Dimitrov, sent a letter to the Communist Party of Canada raising a question which, it said, was 'of central importance.' The commission suggested that there was much sincerity in the leftward thinking of many in the reformist, social democratic movements, and that it was futile to repeat constantly the term 'social fascist,' which helped convince no one in the reformist organizations. 'Repeated use' of the term 'social fascist' was incorrect and, in proposing joint action, the communist side should be willing to put forward fewer demands and thus not place obstacles in the way of approaching reformist-thinking workers. In short, the CCF was no longer the main enemy. The letter concluded by requesting that the communists consider how the problem of trade union unity on the basis of the class struggle could best be raised in Canada.[25]

One can imagine Smith's dismay when he read this letter, representing, as it did, a repudiation of his way of thinking. Without doubt it helped pull the rug out from under his dominant position in the Canadian party. Morris, who had long resented Smith's 'gratuitous insults, uttered in the name of bolshevism,' and who compared Smith's creation of 'illusory theories' to 'a conjurer spiriting white rabbits out of empty top-hats,'[26] was soon on his way across the Atlantic Ocean, together with his wife, Sonia, to replace Freed as the Canadian representative at the Third International in Moscow. At the same time, Charles Sims set out on an organizing tour of Western Canada to bolster flagging spirits among some members of the Workers' Unity League.

Another noteworthy event in the autumn of 1934 was the release of Tom Ewen from Ontario's Kingston Penitentiary, three years after the date of his arrest, and his return to the post of general secretary of the Workers' Unity League. He was quick to appreciate the growth and achievements of the league during his long absence and to orient himself to the changing scene. Aligning himself with the 'non-sectarian left,' Ewen joined McLachlan, on behalf of the national executive board of the WUL, in issuing a public appeal proposing the amalgamation of all existing trade unions into one all-inclusive labour union federation on a broad program of resistance against 'the new attacks of capital,' a 'crusade for 100 per cent unionism' across the country, based on 'full trade-union democracy.'[27]

From his prestigious position in the Anglo-American Secretariat of the Third International and in close contact with the new leadership there, Morris promoted the non-sectarian left position, going beyond the appeal of Ewen and McLachlan, and proposing an altered set of tactics and way of thinking about workers' 'reformist unions' that were far removed from those of Smith.

After conversations with Lozovsky and others, Morris drafted a letter suggesting that the scope of the appeal of Ewen and McLachlan be extended by adopting the bold general slogan '*One Union in Each Industry.*' On the basis of '*class struggle policies and full trade union democracy,*' the two conditions set out in the Workers' Unity League appeal, this, he explained, would be achieved by examining the situation industry by industry and 'determining how best to proceed.' Revolutionary workers in reformist unions should not conceive of themselves as narrow oppositionists, he said. Rather, they should become 'exemplary trade unionists, taking a leading part in the daily life of the unions, fighting to build the unions, winning positions in the unions because of their devoted work, and in this manner becoming in fact the leaders of the trade unions.' All 'sectarian tendencies' that 'regarded the reformist-led workers as scabs,' or that conceived of trade union unity as being possible only within the WUL unions, 'must be combated.' The tone of the press with regard to the reformist union officials should be 'carefully determined in order to convince and not antagonize the members of the reformist unions,' he wrote. If, despite the best efforts, company unions were formed, the militants should not under any circumstances allow themselves to be isolated from them by a boycott policy, but should join them for the purpose of winning workers to a policy of class struggle and into 'genuine trade union organizations.'

Backing up these ideas, the leadership of the Red International of Labour Unions expressed the opinion that the strength and prestige of the revolutionary unions as compared with the 'reformist unions ... [was] extremely favourable for a broad fight for trade-union unity.'[28]

Smith had raised the question about whether the Red trade unions of the Workers' Unity League should continue at all. Pressure in Canada in support of the idea of disbanding came from the United States and the experience of the Trade Union Unity League, the counterpart of the Workers' Unity League. Following President Roosevelt's proclamation of the National Industrial Recovery Act, in June 1933, which gave labour some rights 'to organize and bargain collectively free from interference, restraint or coercion by employers,' and some signs of economic recovery, over one million American workers had taken part in strike activities – mainly coal miners and garment and textile workers, and there was a general strike of the San Francisco longshoremen and waterfront workers. These militant strikes, in which left-wingers took active and sometimes leading parts, and which often reflected the principles, strategy, and tactics that had been so vigorously propagated by Lozovsky and the Red unions, led to spectacular gains in union membership, especially in the United Mine Workers of America under John L. Lewis, in the Amalgamated Clothing Workers under Sydney Hillman, and in the International Ladies' Garment Workers' Union led by David Dubinsky. The 'biggest mass movement of the workers in American history,' according to William Z. Foster, leader of the Trade Union Unity League, 'began to get under way,' and, by the end of 1933, the TUUL was releasing its 'parallel' unions to fold into the newly activated unions of the American Federation of Labour. Within a year, the American Red unions had been effectively disbanded with the approval of the Third International.

In Toronto the leaders of the Workers' Unity League had studied these developments carefully, but, since there was no similar upsurge of militancy within the Canadian mainstream unions, they concluded there was no reason to copy the actions of the Trade Union Unity League. Nevertheless, since American trends often flowed into Canada at a later date, the events south of the border added a note of uncertainty when making convention plans for the longer-range future of the Workers' Unity League.[29]

In spite of uncertainties, as delegates to the WUL's third convention listened to regional reports and surveyed the organization's development since the previous national gathering, there was an understandable sense of achievement. The members of the league had developed a substantial and militant union movement in harsh circumstances.

They had attained this goal by insisting on keeping their distance and independence from the employers' ways of thinking; by constantly attempting, through a policy of 'a united front from below,' to strengthen their contact with social forces beyond their own ranks; and by seeking to promote rank and file trade union democracy.

From the miners of Anyox, Flin Flon, and Noranda and on the Workers' Council of Blairmore, to pulp cutters in the boreal forests of Northern Ontario and Quebec and the loggers of Vancouver Island, and in the largest cities of the country, the league had trained scores of organizers to challenge non-union conditions, to create new industrial unions in often perilous circumstances, and to assist workers in building hope for an alternative way of life in the face of the unprecedented violence of a floundering economic system.

The league's organizers – whether they came out of the Women's Labour League in North Burnaby, BC, or from Calgary, or from Crowland, Ontario – had shown great courage in taking up the cause of workers struggling to keep their families alive while on relief.

On the picket lines in Saint Boniface, Manitoba, or during the historic On-to-Ottawa Trek, the Workers' Unity League had helped transform unemployed young people from a passive industrial reserve army of capitalism to an active and conscious reserve army for labour.

At prolonged confrontations with powerful companies in Fraser Mills, BC, in Stratford, Ontario, or in Montreal, the league had learned lessons in strike strategy, and within it, the principles of trade union democracy in which broadly elected strike committees took charge of the battle.

Among the garment workers of Toronto, the militant workers had taken positive steps for women's rights by promoting 'shop-floor unionism,' which sought to place bargaining power directly in the hands of the workers, who were predominantly female.

Defying the possibility of arrest and deportation, league members had organized May Day rallies in towns and cities across the country and had circulated petitions to win political influence for the rights of labour; and all the while they argued about, and spread the news of, the advantages of an alternative to capitalism as seen first-hand in the experience of building socialism in the Soviet Union. Throughout the years, the league had given meaning to the term 'revolutionary unionism,' and in spite of Red scares and the threat of jail sentences, many members were willing to campaign for international workers' solidarity through association with the Red International of Labour Unions. All these were considered to be the underlying, long-term achievements of the Workers' Unity League.

But, for the convention delegates, there were the negative experiences to consider as well. By the summer of 1934, the spurt of growth for the Workers' Unity League was over. The league's efforts were meeting greater resistance, and it was losing a higher number of strikes than usual. It was these circumstances, as much as anything else, which led it to search for a new footing.

In seeking to analyse their reversal of fortune, WUL leaders at first had singled out three major factors: poor strike preparations, insufficient participation by workers during the struggles, and the organized opposition forces which included 'the bosses, the banks, the governments and their police forces, the press and the mis-leaders of labor.'[30] After a pause to analyse the WUL's own failings, and to take into account the changing tactics of owners in promoting company unions and industry 'codes of conduct,' as well as to assess the increased use of force by governments (there had been 2,700 workers arrested in strike struggles in Canada since the beginning of 1933)[31] and the victimization of its members, the league decided, nevertheless, to carry on as before, only with renewed energy and greater concentration. This strategy proved to be of short duration. Although a campaign to double the Ontario membership in six weeks was announced in a flurry of press publicity in October, and twenty-four organizers were dispatched to recruit members in auto, steel, textile, chemical, and other unorganized basic industries,[32] by the end of 1934 little was actually accomplished. A slightly demoralized league leadership was forced to recognize that it did not have the financial resources or the personnel to do a job that 'is 100 times as hard as to what we have done until now.'[33] To accomplish such a task, the Workers' Unity League would have to discover some way to find common cause with the rest of the labour movement.

It was shortly after this that Tom Ewen joined J.B. McLachlan in issuing an appeal on behalf of the national executive board of the Workers' Unity League, proposing a federation of all existing labour unions, united around a broad program of resistance to the attacks of capital, and aiming to achieve 100 per cent unionism across the country.[34] At this point the executive board still hoped to maintain the league as a separate revolutionary trade union centre. But, as related earlier, the appeal evolved into a proposal presented to the final convention for 'one union – one industry' and, to further the cause of labour unity, the willingness of the WUL to have its unions give up their separate identity under certain conditions and merge with unions affiliated with the American Federation of Labor.

In retrospect, the decision of the Workers' Unity League to merge its unions with the AFL unions at this moment in history was a tactical error, since a new, dramatic, more progressive development was in the offing. A powerful group of eight dissident AFL unions led by John L. Lewis, the fiery, anti-communist president of the United Mine Workers of America, had signalled its intention to challenge the AFL and, perhaps, to start a new labour centre much as the Workers' Unity League had done five years earlier.[35] And for the same basic reason. Lewis and his colleagues declared that their Committee for Industrial Organizations would be dedicated to 'the organization of the unorganized workers in the mass production and other industries on an industrial basis.' As it turned out, within two years, many of the former WUL unions found themselves moving away from the AFL once again, this time to the newly constituted Congress of Industrial Organizations, and they became an important part of the most successful unionization drive in North American history. It was the beginning of a new era in the mass production industries of the Second Industrial Revolution.

But at the time of the WUL's third national convention, the dissident American unions who had recently formed the Committee for Industrial Organizations were still part of the AFL, and their ferment, no doubt, served as an encouragement to many in the WUL for proceeding with their plan to merge with AFL unions. Some members, though, had doubts, fearing 'that something they have may be lost.'[36]

Among the doubters was none other than J.B. McLachlan, newly re-elected president of the Workers' Unity League. McLachlan had supported the unity movement because he believed it would strengthen labour's position. But he also believed that, while the miners of Nova Scotia were for one union, they were not ready to unite with the United Mine Workers of the AFL. Lewis's dictatorial behaviour, treacherous betrayals, and anti-communism during the Nova Scotia miners' strikes in 1923–5 remained firmly etched in McLachlan's mind and he was certain that there could be no unity or popular front acceptable to the coal miners until the UMWA changed its leadership. He was also alarmed by certain leaders of the Workers' Unity League urging what amounted to 'unity at any cost.' That, he feared, would lead to the sacrifice of the important principles of rank and file democracy and local autonomy – essential elements in any worthwhile united front. As the drive for unity picked up speed in the spring of 1936, these worries led him to withdraw from the leadership of the league, resign from the Communist Party, and retire to his farm in Cape Breton, where he died the following year. As the large portrait of McLachlan on the cover of the special convention edition of *Unity* had shown, this staunch revolutionary fighter symbolized the Workers' Unity League, and his departure was sorely felt.[37]

Other league leaders, such as coal miner Charles Sims, shared the dislike of Lewis and his followers. Lewis, Sims said, had carried out 'the rottenest policies of class collaboration, wage reductions, expulsion of militants like J.B. McLachlan,' and suspensions and expulsions of whole districts. 'No man can deny this,' Sims exclaimed, 'and no miner can forget this either.'[38] But, while the UMWA was less than a model union, Sims joined Ewen in arguing that Lewis had changed his tune in favour of progressive trade union policies. Although the change had been forced upon him by rank and file militancy, he was, nevertheless, becoming a towering figure in the North American labour movement, leading militant struggles and now prepared to work with communists in an all-out drive to unionize the mass-production industries. In other words, he should be supported. Sims and Ewen persuaded the WUL delegates to adopt the far-reaching unity proposals that Salsberg had introduced to the convention. As a gesture in preparation for such a transition, even the terms of address among communists changed to correspond with Canadian trade-union custom: 'Comrade' became 'Brother' or 'Sister.' Previous habits of branding an opponent as 'a labour fakir' were rejected as a 'terrible mistake.'[39] 'It goes without saying,' Ewen promised, that the broad questions of policy would be laid before 'the entire membership of the WUL unions' and 'before the workers in general' for their discussion, amendment, and approval.[40]

There was no single pattern for achieving 'one union in each industry.' Ewen urged the league organizers to 'utilize their horse-sense on the basis of the concrete condition' when applying for charters with the relevant AFL unions.[41]

As negotiations proceeded, a series of letters from its national unions began arriving at the league's office proposing disaffiliation in order to apply formally for charters with the AFL. There were letters from most of the large WUL–affiliated unions, including the Industrial Union of Needle Trades Workers, the Mine Workers' Union of Canada, the Lumber Workers' Industrial Union, the Fishermen and Cannery Workers' Industrial Union, and the Furniture Workers' Industrial Union. There were others from the smaller and local organizations, too.[42] McLachlan called it a 'sad march to the right.'[43] Negotiations to merge with AFL unions were intense, requiring compromises, and organizers who had given their heart and soul to building the Workers' Unity League felt 'it was like losing a dream.'[44] But, as a next step, it appears the agreements, in most cases, were not as harmful to the league's core principles as McLachlan had feared.

Perhaps the most difficult time was in the garment industry. Organizer J.B. Salsberg reported to the national executive board of the Workers' Unity League that 'the sharpness of differences' among the leadership of their Industrial Union of Needle Trades Workers was 'greater than among any other section' of the league. The problem was that the relevant AFL unions wanted to admit the membership of the industrial union only on an individual basis – so that they could weed out certain members. In Winnipeg this demand was successfully resisted and the units entered the international unions without such conditions, sometimes as entire units, and without having to pay initiation fees. The dressmakers of Montreal, however, still suffering from the defeat of the 1934 general strike, were not as fortunate and had to apply to join the International Ladies' Garment Workers' Union (AFL) as individuals. Many were blacklisted and had to find other work. In Toronto, the full-time organizers of the IUNTW, Myer Klig and Joshua Gershman, were put out of office, but in spite of this, according to Salsberg, the dressmakers were entering the international union 'as a solid body,' determined 'to carry forward their militant traditions and policies.'[45]

The leaders of the Lumber Workers' Industrial Union hesitated, too, about applying to join the AFL, fearing that 'something is going to be taken away.' But, on Ewen's urging them to use their 'horse-sense,' and without waiting for an ideal blueprint, the union negotiated a merger with the United Brotherhood of Carpenters and Joiners (AFL-TLC) through its Lumber and Sawmill division. They joined as a block with full rights and no initiation fee. The American sister organization did likewise.

The newcomers, however, were not given a vote in convention, and felt treated as second-class members. The Canadians used their 'horse-sense' in different ways in response. The Ontario district of Lumber and Saw, led by former Workers' Unity League organizers Carl Palmgren and Bruce Magnuson, decided to stick it out in the AFL union and, under this arrangement, the lumber workers still made considerable progress.[46] But the West Coast district (which included American local unions) held a referendum vote of its members on whether to withdraw from the carpenters' union and join the newly forming Congress of Industrial Organizations. The result was 76 per cent in favour of leaving the carpenters.

The conservative and vehemently anti-communist leaders of the carpenters' union, with the help of the lumber companies and local governments, refused to accept this result, and running battles took place, sometimes turning violent. But the West Coast lumber workers were aided by the labour provisions of Roosevelt's National Recovery Act, which stipulated that workers had 'the right to organize and bargain collectively free from interference, restraint or coercion by employers,' and no employee, as a condition of employment, could be required to join a company union or prevented from joining a labour organization of his own choice.[47] The loggers and sawmill workers won the battle the following year, forming the Federation of Woodworkers, and, in 1937, they voted to affiliate with the CIO. With Harold Pritchett, former WUL organizer, elected as first international president, the International Woodworkers of America (IWA) soon gained 100,000 members, and the dream of the Workers' Unity League of 'one union in wood' was on the horizon in this district.[48]

As already mentioned, the road to unity among the coal miners also faced many obstacles. Quite a few members of the Mine Workers' Union of Canada in Western Canada, as well as the radical miners in Nova Scotia, had doubts about merging with the United Mine Workers of America while it was still led by John L. Lewis. Earlier attempts to achieve unity, in 1935, had not been at all reassuring when the incumbent leaders of the UMWA in Alberta (Lewis supporters) warned about 'the intruders in our ... ranks.'[49]

To gain acceptance of the decisions of the WUL convention, Tom Ewen embarked on a four-month tour of Western Canada, spending a month in the coal-mining districts. After visiting the mining camps, Ewen made his pitch for unity at a convention held under the auspices of the Calgary Trades and Labour Council. According to his memoirs, there was some hard bargaining, as the international union had wanted to admit the Mine Workers' Union of Canada members piecemeal (so that individuals, as in the case of the garment workers, could be screened out by the leaders). But Ewen successfully argued that the return should be on the basis of a local union with its elected officers intact and without paying new initiation fees. This proposal was put to a referendum vote of the MWUC miners on 30 June 1936. Over 80 per cent of those who voted – 2,257 out of a total membership of 2,800 in thirteen locals – confirmed the return of the unionized coal miners to a single organization in Alberta and British Columbia.[50] In Nova Scotia the unity process took another two years, and occurred only after the UMWA had left the AFL to lead the way in establishing the Congress of Industrial Organizations.[51]

By the time Ewen returned from his 15,000-mile tour of Western Canada, most of the unions affiliated to the Workers' Unity League had completed merger arrangements with their American Federation of Labour counterparts. As a result, when Ewen stood before the national executive board in June 1936, it was to make his final report, summing up the experience of the league and making a last appeal to its members.

The origin and life of the league, he said, was 'an epic in the great chain of trade unionism in Canada that shattered the dogmas of class-collaboration, and servile surrender to bourgeois cupidity.' This epic, he continued, had 'written a glorious page into the records of Labour's struggles,' and it was a page for which 'no single member of the WUL, man or woman, need ever apologize.' The strike weapon, he said, had been characterized by some as 'an obsolete weapon,' as a 'weapon of the jungle,' as a 'destructive force,' but the 'deadly alliance' of hunger, fascism, and war that stalked 'throughout the entire capitalist world,' and that menaced the 'life, liberty and well-being of every Canadian worker,' he said, would not permit 'the conception of a trade union organization as a quiet sheep-fold.' He appealed to the 35,000 members now within the AFL to carry with them the traditions that made the Workers' Unity League 'a mighty factor in recharting the course of trade unionism in Canada' and called upon them to be 'constructive builders, consistent fighters and courageous critics,' so that the AFL in Canada could become a 'centre of economic struggle serving the interests of all toilers.'[52]

His parting words ranged over a wide spectrum of ideas and activities central to the experience of the league. He recalled the indignities that had been heaped upon the organization and its members: the raids on its offices and wanton destruction of its property at the hands of capitalist governments; its organizers and members imprisoned, clubbed, shot down, persecuted, and beaten by the police, victims of vicious espionage and terror. Still, he pointed out, the statement of a trial judge in Saskatchewan, in 1931, declaring the WUL an illegal organization, had only temporarily hindered its prestige and growth. Through the energy and resourcefulness of the men and women leading the organization in all parts of the country, it had become 'a living body' that carried trade unionism into new fields and broke through 'outworn theories that had served to hamstring' trade union organization. That same energy and resourcefulness would now enter the AFL to enrich and help transform it into a living centre of struggle for the betterment of its members and the working class as a whole. Ewen declared that the closing of the Workers' Unity League marked the beginning of a new era and predicted that the satisfaction of those who had 'misinterpreted the passing of the WUL' would be short-lived.

The minutes of the national executive board record that Sister Annie Buller raised the question of giving up the national office and renting a post-office box. This suggestion was duly moved by Brother Salsberg and seconded by Brother Collins to take effect the end of April 1936.[53] With that, the legendary Workers' Unity League became a part of history.

Charter of WUL, Issued to The British Columbia Relief Camp Workers Union in 1932

SAB, Transcript of Preliminary Hearing of *Rex vs Bell … Evans et al*, Regina, July 1935, 747–9, exhibit P22.

Blairmore, Alberta, in 1932

This townsite, with Crowsnest Mountain in the background (right), was the centre of a bitter, seven-month coal miners' strike led by the Workers' Unity League that swept through the Crowsnest Pass in 1932. Miners were resisting conditions of extreme privation and demanded the right to belong to a union of their own choice.

Glenbow Archives, NC-54-4298.

Crowsnest Pass Miners' Strike Committee, 1932
John Stokaluk, organizer of the Mine Workers' Union of Canada,
is third from the left with hand on his knee.
Glenbow Archives, NC-54-4339.

Workers' International Relief

Unloading supplies from L. Pozzi's truck for the Crowsnest Pass strikers,
Blairmore, Alberta, 16 April 1932.

Glenbow Archives, NC-54-4340.

Blairmore, Alberta, 1 May 1932 May Day Demonstration
Harvey Murphy, WUL organizer, leads the parade along with a piper.
Greenhill Hotel is in the centre background.
Glenbow Archives, NC-54-4389.

Sweet Revenge: Blairmore Town Administration, 1934

Although the 1932 strike was defeated, afterwards the miners made a clean sweep of the municipal election and appointed the WUL organizer, Murphy, as town solicitor. Above is the official photograph of the new administration. Included in the photograph, front row left to right, are Harvey Murphy; Joe Aschcaher; Angelo Pagnucco; William Knight, mayor; Joe Krkosky Sr; Jack Packer; and Evan Morgan.

Glenbow Archives, NC-54-1970.

UNITY OF ALL MINERS   ONE UNION OF MINERS IN CANADA

The Western Miner

Organ of the Miners Section of the Workers Unity League of Canada

Vol. I. No. I.   Lethbridge, Alberta, Thursday, February 20th, 1930.   Price 5 Cents

Organ of the Miners Section of the Workers' Unity League

Harvey Murphy was the editor of this newspaper.

OA newspaper collection.

Anyox, BC, 1932: Forbidden Territory
Owned by Granby Consolidated Mining, Smelting and Power Co., this isolated, closely guarded company town near the Alaska panhandle had many facilities to serve 2,500 residents: Elks Hall in the centre; three-storey building to the right housed a movie theatre and the pool hall; the cemetery with its white crosses was on the old road leading up to the mine.
BC Archives, D-01311.

Anyox Harbour
Union organizers had to smuggle themselves in and work
secretly to avoid arrest.
BC Archives, A-00462.

Women's Labour League

The Capitol Hill branch was one of the most active in the league. Front (l): Mrs Peden, Mrs Campbell, Jean Stevenson, Mrs Hepburn. Back: unknown, Olena Nelson, Catherine Marsh, Mrs Kerr, Florence Strachan, Mrs Chappel, Mrs Brigden, Mrs Hector, Flora Hutton, Elizabeth Wilson.

Margaret Boyd (Nelson) Collection.

Flora Hutton (left), national executive board member, Workers' Unity League, and **Elizabeth Wilson**, secretary, Provincial Workers' Council, in 1933.

Margaret Boyd (Nelson) Collection (detail).

Bertha Dolgoy
Organizer of garmet workers in
Winnipeg, on a visit to the Soviet
Union in 1932.
Reva and Len Dolgoy Collection.

Becky Buhay
Leader of the WLL delegation to
visit the Soviet Union in 1930.
OA, F1405, Annie Buller Collection.

Women's Labour League Delegation to the Soviet Union in 1930
Left to right: Elsa Tynjala, Mrs Zen, B. Colle (sitting), Anne Whitfield,
Becky Buhay, and Bessie Shecter.
The Worker, 8 August 1931.

Soviet Poster on International Women's Day, 1932
'8 March. Day of rebellion of working women against kitchen slavery.
Say NO to the oppression and Babbitry of household work.'
Wikipedia: 8-Marta.

'The issue is socialism versus capitalism.'
Editorial cartoon, *Unemployed Worker* 4.4 (7 November 1931).
LAC, Department of Labour Collection, RG27, v. 349.

Fred Collins
WUL organizer in Stratford strike
of 1933.
LAC, RG146, v. 1058, RCMP Collection.

J.B. Salsberg
Southern Ontario organizer of the
Workers' Unity League.
OA, F1412, Gershman Collection, no.
220 (detail).

Price's Providence after Ordering the Army to Stratford
'Those who go to radical organizations to get accomplished what
well-established trade unions have failed to do are flying in the teeth of
providence.' From report of speech by Attorney General Price.
The Worker, 14 October 1933.

Jeanne Corbin
Militant French-speaking organizer
of the Workers' Unity League, Corbin
helped in the pulp cutters' and miners'
strikes in Northwest Quebec in 1933–4,
and was arrested and sentenced to
three months in jail for 'incitement to
unlawful assembly.'
OA F1405, MSR 6671, Annie Buller
Collection.

The Worker, 16 December 1933.

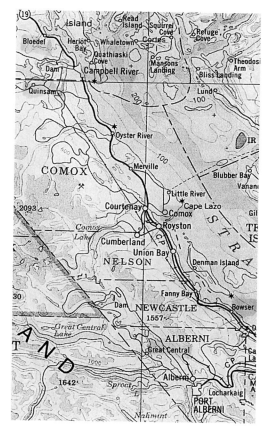

Vancouver Island Loggers' Strike

Sites of the great loggers' strike in 1943 ranging from Port Alberni/Great Central Lake north 60 miles along Route 19 from Bowser to Campbell River and Bloedel. BC Department of Energy, Mines and Resources, NM-9/10 (1949).

Centre for Socialist Education, Vancouver.

Strikers' Picket Camp at Campbell River, July 1934
IWA Local 1-80, Duncan, BC/Kaatza Station Museum and Archive.

Striking BC Loggers on the March
Their aim is to close down operations staffed with Bloedel's strike-breakers at
Great Central Lake, Alberni District, BC
IWA Local 1-80, Duncan, BC/Kaatza Station Museum and Archive.

Demand Withdrawal of Charges Against Flin Flon Arrested!

THE TRUE FACTS ABOUT THE FLIN FLON STRIKE

By MABEL MARLOWE & BILL ROSS

| Mabel Marlowe | Bill Ross | Oscar Brooks | Jim Coleman |

For a month the rain fell in Flin Flon, a slow, cold, miserable drizzle that pierced the bones of the men and women who stoutly stood by their posts on the picket line. Here and there along the three mile picket-line little tin and wood structures had been built, a crude

grip of the company demagogy and their threats the miners were finally forced to return to work under the same conditions, with only promises of future improvements.

The fifteen arrested workers are not criminals. They are the finest of their class who to the best of their

**Workers' Unity League Organizers Arrested during the Flin Flon Strike
in July 1934.**

Canadian Labour Defense League, Bill Ross Collection.

Department of National Defence Camp No. 333 at Beaver Ranch, BC
'The bosses had the lads tackling the bare rock with picks and sledges. They'd
been at it three years and had only got 300 yards. Practically no blasting whatso-
ever was done – you just slugged away like the old Georgia chain gang.'
Drawing by anonymous, text by Matt Shaw, in *The Worker*, 20 July 1935.

Matt Shaw. Chairman of the
Trekkers Publicity Committee.
The Worker, 13 July 1935.

Relief Camp Strikers Ottawa Bound
Matt Shaw drawing, CI Fonds 495, list 98, file 182A, *Relief Camp Worker* 3.15, 8 June 1935.

Arthur H. Evans. BC organizer of
the WUL and leader of the On-to-
Ottawa Trek of 1935.

Swankey and Sheils, *Work and Wages.*

Hungry 30s Red Riders Hop Trains
City of Toronto Archives/William James Collection, f1244-2181.

On-to-Ottawa Hunger Marchers from Eastern Canada, 1935

City of Toronto Archives/William James Collection, f1244-1684.

'Fall In!'

In an effort to quell discontented youth, the prime minister assigned the
department of National Defence, headed by General MacNaughton, to operate
Relief Camps for the Single Unemployed.

Avrom cartoon in *The Worker*, 31 August 1935.

Forward March!

Avrom cartoon in *The Worker*, 27 June 1935.

Delegates to Third National Convention, Workers' Unity League of Canada, Toronto, 9–11 November 1935 (partial view)
Among those attending are (1) Joshua Gershman, (2) Meyer Klig, (3) J.B. Salsberg, (4) Sam Scarlett, (5) J.B. McLachlan,
(6) Fred Collins, (7) Tom Ewen, (8) Patrick Lenihan, (9) Bill Ross, (10) Sam Lepedes, (11) Annie Buller,
(12) Marion Noodelman (Magnuson), (13) Lily Steinman (Greene), (14) Jeanne Corbin, (15) Max Dolgoy,
(16) Ted Gunarud, (17) Izzie Minster.

Photo: OA F1412, Gershman Collection I0031429.

Afterword

The circumstances and political culture have changed ... what remains constant is that progressive social change will by necessity have to be preceded by agitation, organization, and militant struggle.

– Lorne Brown, *When Freedom Was Lost* (1987), 15

The Workers' Unity League originated in 1930 during a period of retreat in the labour movement in Canada. Its closure six years later coincided with the start of vibrant growth for industrial unionism. The league's existence, its stimulation of worker class consciousness and militancy in Canada, acted as a bridge between those times of retreat and advance. It made important contributions to workers' rights and was, indeed, with its 35,000 members, a Canadian success story. But because of its openly declared revolutionary aspirations and its international connections, the league has sometimes been misrepresented, and its achievements questioned. This study suggests that the Workers' Unity League's experience merits another look.

At the birth of the Workers' Unity League, the activists forming its core considered themselves no more than a small 'propagandist sect ... weakly connected with the workers in heavy industry.'[1] With such a self-image, they hardly expected to see themselves leading the overthrow of the capitalist system in an imminent revolutionary crisis, as argued by some historians in order to explain the league's militant tactics.[2] Although the Third International and the Red International of Labour Unions spoke of 'revolutionary surges' in different parts of the world, Canada was not mentioned as one of those places, and the immediate tasks of affiliated trade unionists here were on a lesser scale: to champion the economic demands of workers for better wages and conditions of work; to organize the unorganized into industrial unions; to lead the unemployed in gaining adequate relief and government unemployment insurance; to oppose discrimination on the grounds of race, gender, or immigrant origin; to defend the right to organize, strike, and picket, and to free speech and assembly; and to oppose war preparations – and to do so in a way that raised the political and class consciousness of working people about their lives and the world they lived in. In performing these 'lesser tasks,' the Workers' Unity League still considered itself to be a 'revolutionary trade union centre' – a 'revolutionary industrial union movement' dedicated to the overthrow of the capitalist system – and it defined itself in that manner.[3] In view of its more mundane activities, could the league truthfully be viewed as *an agent of revolutionary transformation?*

When the Workers' Unity League arrived on the scene, its ideas and methods of operation alarmed the corporate owners and displeased the government.[4] It had large ideas. It was definitely trying to shift the boundaries between management rights and workers' rights, between property rights and people's needs. One way or another, all strike struggles are about the right to control the terms and conditions of labour, but these matters can be negotiated in different ways. Management called for a 'co-operative' and 'responsible' attitude on the part of its employees, preferring that there be no union of any kind, but, if necessary, they would recognize one whose leaders were, by tacit understanding, safely under their control or influence. Governments and the more conservative unions tended to resort to conciliation and mediation boards where both sides stated their case and a third party made non-binding, unenforceable recommendations. Militant or radical unions, like those affiliated with the WUL, preferred direct negotiations with the bosses supported by social pressure, and the election of shop or pit committees to enforce the results of agreements. In taking this stance, the WUL went some distance in defining itself as a revolutionary trade union centre.

Many WUL organizers went to jail or were deported on the grounds that they advocated or threatened 'force and violence' to overthrow the existing social and political order. In reality, while the league was prepared to engage in civil disobedience, to ignore questionable injunctions about picketing, or otherwise to break the law when necessary to make their strikes effective, it was not planning armed insurrection. Not even on such occasions as when 15,000 unemployed workers and their supporters paraded through Vancouver's Victory Square behind a red flag in the spring of 1932. Or when the league's organizers led thousands of hunger marchers to assemble, in defiance of government orders, on the steps of a provincial legislature with more red flags, to hear their leaders demand state-sponsored unemployment insurance, and meal and bed tickets for the out-of-town marchers.[5] Such demonstrations, and there were hundreds of them all across the country in those years, were in the nature of desperate and daring people exercising their constitutional right to petition and to gain relief from His Majesty the King and his constituted authorities. The league never argued (though some members may have imagined and at some point Stewart Smith apparently believed) that it was heading for armed insurrection and barricades on the streets.

Still, for propaganda purposes – and to set the stage for jail sentences and deportations – the government of Canada never tired of charging the Workers' Unity League, and especially the communists, with advocating 'force and violence,' even though it knew perfectly well, through its own security forces, that the supposed agents of violent revolution were not training members to confront the armed forces of the state, nor were clandestine shipments of arms appearing off the coast of Nova Scotia to make possible any such aims.[6] The league had no arms, and, in that sense, it was non-revolutionary. In a liberal democracy all power did not come from the barrel of a gun (as was common in most parts of the world); some of it came from the tradition of parliamentary struggle. This was the point that Friedrich Engels made in his preface to the first English translation of *Capital* as well as in his introduction to Marx's *The Class Struggles in France 1848–1850*, and it would have saved members of the Third International in Western democracies considerable grief if the 'general staff' of that organization had made the same distinction instead of universalizing Lenin's teaching that 'only the forcible overthrow of the bourgeoisie' could lead to the submission of the exploiters to the will of the majority.[7]

In addition to its strong strike strategy, the league had two other characteristics that might suggest it was of a revolutionary nature, allowing it to claim that honour or suffer such rebuke. The first was that it tried to raise political issues in the context of economic struggles. Whereas more conservative unions prided themselves on, and were praised by the capitalist owners for, keeping to bread and butter issues and accepted methods, WUL organizers tried by various means – such as parades, public meetings, petitions, mass picketing – to involve the wider community, including other unions, farmers' organizations, the unemployed, home-

makers, schoolchildren, and professional people. They did this both for
strike support and to increase political and social consciousness. This
concept of union activity became widely practised in Canada after the
Second World War and is now known as 'social unionism' rather than
'revolutionary unionism.' A fruit of the pressure created, in no small
measure, by 'social unionism' was a body of law passed in support of the
right to collective bargaining and the substantial Canadian social safety
net put into legislation by various political parties between 1941 (unemployment insurance) and the 1960s (medicare).

The second additional revolutionary characteristic of the WUL was
that it proposed not only reform but more far-reaching transformation
of existing society. As we have seen in chapters 2 and 4, it was in this
sense that the WUL offered the results of the Russian Revolution as an
alternative to capitalism: as a form of commonwealth without landlords,
capitalists, and millionaires that it believed worked well and operated to
the benefit of the working class. Such a view of the socialist experiment
has been challenged with the passage of time. But, as this account has
shown, the dream has not been vanquished – except, perhaps, in the
minds of those who accept the travesties of easy caricatures in preference
to the kind of scientific research conducted by historians like Stephen
Kotkin in his book *Magnetic Mountain: Stalinism as a Civilization.*

Whether these three areas of revolutionary practice qualify the league
to be considered a 'revolutionary trade union centre' is up to the reader
to decide.

Another area of controversy concerns the nature of the connection
of the Workers' Unity League to the Red International of Trade Unions.
The complexities of this topic (which have been explored in the early
chapters of this book) continue to occupy the attention of historians.

Some scholars hold that while the communists made a contribution
to 'building a better world,' a policy of following the 'twists and turns'
of the Third International was their central weakness and limited their
effectiveness.[8] These scholars concentrate on the idea that the relationship was that of master and servant, of 'subservience to Moscow.' That is
what the Canadian government, through its undercover agent Sergeant
John Leopold (alias Jack Esselwein), tried to prove in the 1931 trials of
the communist leaders. But as the Cold War recedes in time, this line of
inquiry begins to exhaust itself. Perhaps it will be replaced, as historian
Kevin Morgan has suggested, by a plurality of perspectives 'from which
alone one can make sense of so volatile and contradictory a phenomenon' as the world of the Third International.[9]

The point of view advanced from the research upon which this book is based is that in the six years of the Workers' Unity League's association with the Red International of Labour Unions and the Third International, the relationship was collegial in nature, mutually supporting, and of great political and psychological value, especially to the league's leading members and organizers. Uncertainties about what attitude to take at the commencement of the Second World War, and knowledge about the scale of repression practised by the Soviet government, emerged later as major troubling questions. But in the 1930s, the opportunities for study abroad and the alliance of like-minded trade unionists gave rise to feelings of attachment and power which, in moments of doubt or distress, could offer considerable reassurance. The sense of solidarity with a rising socialist society which promised a different, better, fairer way of living for ordinary people helps to explain the extraordinary confidence with which a sizeable group of Canadian working-class men and women met and challenged their social superiors, whether on the platform, as elected members of city councils, in the hallways of parliament, around a bargaining table, on the picket line – or in court.

It was this confidence and energy that so infuriated Prime Minister Bennett and his friends and led them to apply Section 98 of the Criminal Code against the Communist Party in 1931. Hurriedly passed by Parliament at the time of the Winnipeg General Strike in 1919 but not used until 1931, Section 98, as previously noted, was aptly described by McGill University law professor F.R. Scott as a part of the Criminal Code which, 'for permanent restriction of rights of association, freedom of discussion, printing and distribution of literature, and for severity of punishment, is unequalled in the history of Canada and probably of any British country for centuries past.'[10] The leaders of the liberal-democratic state that was Canada were neither liberal nor democratic when they felt that the interests of their class were significantly challenged by the left in 1919 and again in the 1930s.

Inevitably, the international affiliation of the WUL gave the employers an excuse to cry about 'patriotism' and 'undesirable foreigners' in the multi-ethnic workforce, and those charges often raised tensions to dangerous levels, leading to such spectacles as the hooded Ku Klux Klan (of U.S. inspiration, really white men in business suits) marching through Canadian cities, and their fiery crosses burning on the mountainsides. From its early experiences in this regard, the league dropped its formal affiliation with the Red International of Labour Unions at its second national convention. This happened without any great fanfare and a fra-

ternal relationship was put in its place. It was not necessary, the Workers' Unity League's leaders considered, to swing at every ball. While the
change did not reduce the Red-baiting to any extent, the majority of
league members felt more comfortable; it was an easier relationship to
defend and it still allowed the important practical, emotional, and moral
aspects of international connections to find expression in the activities
of the league and its affiliated unions. At the same time, the Workers'
Unity League's insistence on the value of international solidarity among
working people and on the right to choose freely the channels of opti-
mal mutual benefit were important legacies.

A major fault of the Communist Party during this period was its sectarian attitude to social democracy, deeming it, in line with the lead given
by the Third International, the main social support of the capitalist class,
and calling its leaders 'social fascists.' In their trade union work, however, and in the conventions of the Workers' Unity League, it was to
their credit that the Canadian communists mainly avoided the sectarian
excess of such name-calling.

The essence of revolutionary, class-struggle trade unionism, as conceived by the Workers' Unity League, meant a commitment to practise
democracy in union affairs. This was not only the crucial way to advance
workers' political understanding; it was also the league's answer to those
who talked of 'communist conspiracies' (businesses, churches, the state,
and anti-communist trade-union leaders).

Democratic involvement, which the WUL espoused so strongly, was
especially important when a union faced the task of organizing successful strike action. In an industrial union action, as in the cases of the
Fraser Mills strike (1931), the Stratford (1933) and the Vancouver Island
Loggers' (1934) strikes, and the many battles of the unemployed, the
WUL trained its organizers to insist that it was the right of all workers in a
factory, mill, or camp, irrespective of race, sex, nationality, colour, creed,
or union membership, to take part in the decision – by secret ballot if
possible – to start a strike or to terminate one. This was not an easy step
for eager, young organizers such as Harvey Murphy, especially when they
were faced with the underhanded tricks of intransigent corporations as
in the Crowsnest Pass strike (1932). Still, the WUL insisted on it. It was
a commitment learned from studying well-thumbed copies of the Strassburg Resolution of the Red International on the strategy and tactics of
strikes, and, in terms of the continuing struggles even today, this determination to practise democracy in the heat of battle represents the most
significant and enduring contribution of the Workers' Unity League to

the Canadian labour movement. This conclusion, demonstrated time after time, may come as a surprise to readers who, in the past, have been led to believe that anything related to communists was a negation of democracy.

Finally, underlying the experience of 'Red trade unionism' is the perennial question: when, if ever, is it in the wider class interest of workers to split away from a long-established labour movement to form a splinter group? The norm in trade union thinking and instinct has always been to unite, to achieve maximum strength through greater unity. But was it sometimes justified to divide first around some principle, the better to make future gains?

From the narrative of the Workers' Unity League presented and analysed in this book, the answer to this question must surely be 'rarely, but sometimes and in certain circumstances, yes.' This had been the answer of the Industrial Workers of the World and the One Big Union early in the twentieth century when they led inspiring challenges to the 'robber barons' of capitalism and to the passivity and 'business unionism' of the established leaders of the American Federation of Labour.

In the late 1920s and early 1930s, the question had posed itself again when the 'second industrial revolution' took shape and the subsequent hardships of widespread unemployment during the Great Depression created new challenges for the working class. The established labour leaders in the craft unions failed to develop a strategy to unionize the great mass-producing industries that employed tens of thousands of new industrial workers. They also declined to consider the problems of unemployed labourers as part of their mandate. These were the large issues of the day demanding leadership.

Reluctantly at first, but with increasing vigour and success, the communists took up the challenge to build a new union central that would do what was necessary – even while affirming that their aim was unity. They had not always won the day by any means, but they led the way. Earlier splinter groups had sometimes tried to carry on beyond their time of power and usefulness to become jaded sects. It was to the credit of the Workers' Unity League that it escaped such a fate and freed its members to rejoin the mainstream of an awakening North American labour movement. There, enriched by their experiences in the Red unions, they were able to play a vital role in their new home.

Appendices

APPENDIX I

Draft Constitution

WORKERS' UNITY LEAGUE OF CANADA[1]

Name. – This organization shall be the Workers' Unity League of Canada; the Canadian Section of the Red International of Labour Unions.
Purpose. – To organize the Canadian workers into powerful revolutionary Industrial Unions created on the axis of the widest rank and file control; to fight for the defense and improvement of the conditions of the working class, mobilizing and organizing the Canadian workers for the final overthrow of capitalism and for the establishment of a Revolutionary Workers Government. Towards this end, the Workers' Unity League of Canada lays down the following organizational structure:

It shall be the task of the WUL to initiate aggressive campaigns of organization in every field of industry, where no organization obtains. The organization of the unorganized must be the main and central task of the Workers' Unity League of Canada.

In all campaigns unemployed workers must be organized and their activities linked with the general activities of the revolutionary working class struggle. The unemployed workers must become an integral part of the revolutionary working class movement.

The Workers' Unity League of Canada shall organize left wing oppositional groups in the reformist unions; these oppositional groups must be regarded as the nuclei of industrial unions within the frame work of the craft and patriotic unions, and every effort shall be made to win the membership of the reformist unions for the revolutionary industrial unions.

The accompanying draft constitution will govern until the first national convention, when an elected committee on law and constitu-

---

1 The text reproduced here, which first appeared in the *Worker*, 28 June 1930, is from Department of Labour, *Labour Organizations in Canada for 1930* (Ottawa: King's Printer), 162–3. Discussion of its draft constitution at the first national convention, in 1932, was inconclusive and the WUL adopted no report on the matter. The second national convention, in 1933, eliminated the part on '*Purpose*' entirely and it formally amended the organization's relation to the Red International of Labour Unions from being 'a section' to having a 'fraternal relationship.' See discussion in chapter 8 of this book. The amended 'Constitution of the Workers' Unity League' (1933) is in Tom McEwen, *The Forge Glows Red* (Toronto: Progress Books, 1974), 247–56.

tion will present amendments acceptable to the convention of the WUL of Canada.

The Workers' Unity League of Canada is the Canadian section of the Red International of Labour Unions, pledged to a program and policy of revolutionary struggle for the complete overthrow of capitalism and its institutions of exploitation, and the setting up of the State power of the workers and poor farmers through a workers' and farmers' government.

CONSTITUTION WORKERS' UNITY LEAGUE OF CANADA

The Workers' Unity League of Canada shall consist of:–

(a) Affiliated revolutionary unions, now independent of the reformist centres (AF of L and ACC of L).

(b) New industrial unions organized by the WUL of C.

(c) Industrial leagues of the WUL of C. These shall be the basis for organization where no industrial union exists.

(d) Local industrial leagues of the WUL of C., in isolated areas.

(e) General leagues of the WUL of C. consisting of workers from various industries where special conditions render their organization by industry difficult.

(f) Shop councils, committees of action, and other oppositional forms, organized within the reformist unions (AF of L., national and Catholic unions) to propagate industrial unionism and put forward a policy of militant struggle against the policies and tactics of the reformist trade union bureaucracy.

(g) Women's labour leagues and women's trade union auxiliaries.

(h) Local delegate councils.

(i) Unemployed councils from every centre linked up through a national movement.

(j) Wherever necessary, the WUL shall create special youth forms of organizations, such as youth sections, in the new industrial unions, economic youth associations, and youth sections in the old unions. Youth committees on a national, district and local scale shall be created, elected by national, district and local conferences of youth.

Revenue. – The revenue of the WUL of C. shall be derived from a per-capita tax as follows:–

(a) Affiliated national unions, 5 cents per member per month.

(b) Local unions directly chartered by the WUL of C. shall pay dues not less than 50 cents per month per member. Of this amount, 20 cents shall be paid per month to the WUL of C. These unions shall also pay an initiation fee of 50 cents per member, except where conditions warrant a lower rate.

(c) Industrial and local leagues of the WUL of C. shall pay 40 cents per month per member, and initiation of 50 cents.

(d) General leagues of the WUL of C. shall pay dues at the rate of 40 cents per month per member, as well as an initiation fee of 50 cents per member. The general leagues shall remit 25 cents per month per member to the WUL of C.

(e) Women's labour leagues and women's trade union auxiliaries shall pay a per capita of 5 cents per month per member.

(f) Shop councils, committees of action, and opposition groups, in the reformist unions, shall pay the WUL of C. 5 cents per member, as well as maintain the dues in the union they hold membership in.

(g) Fifty per cent of all initiation fees shall be forwarded to the WUL of C.

(h) The per capita fees of all affiliated unions, leagues and opposition groups, shall be paid to the Executive Secretary of the WUL of C. not less than every 3 months.

(i) Individual membership in the WUL of C. shall be 50 cents per month and 50 cents initiation fee; full amount to be remitted to the national executive secretary of the WUL of C. Upon the securing of 15 members in a given industry the rates defined in clause 'c' shall become applicable.

Representation.– At annual or special convention of the Workers' Unity League of Canada representation shall be as follows:–

(a) Affiliated national unions: one delegate for every 500 or fraction thereof.

(b) Affiliated local unions: one delegate for every local unit, except in cases where membership exceeds 400.

(c) Industrial local and general leagues: one delegate for each group.

(d) Women's labour leagues and women's trade union auxiliaries: one delegate for each unit.

(e) Shop councils and opposition groups, committees of action: one delegate for each unit.

(f) Youth sections, economic youth associations, national, district and local youth committees: one delegate for each group.

All delegates to the National Convention must be members in good standing in their respective unions, leagues or groups. Two local unions, leagues or opposition groups may be represented by one delegate, if such is desired.

National Executive. – The national executive of the Workers' Unity

League of Canada shall be elected at the national convention and shall consist of one member from each basic industry represented from among the delegates present, officers of the WUL to be elected by the national executive.

Duties of the National Executive. – The decisions of the national executive on all matters pertaining to the organization shall be binding between conventions, and shall be determined upon the express desires of the rank and file. No officer or member of the national executive can usurp the decision of any affiliated section, when that decision embodies a line of strike action or revolutionary struggle in conformity with the general line of the WUL of C.

All paid functionaries of the WUL of C. shall not be paid in excess of $5 a day, and expenses not to exceed $3 a day, plus transportation.

The books and accounts of the national executive shall be open to inspection by any member of the executive and shall be audited by a chartered accountant, not less than once a year.

Wherever possible members of the N.E.C. shall be appointed organizers for the industry they represent and shall be available also for organizational work in other industries, whenever necessity arises.

This draft constitution will govern until the first national convention, when an elected committee on law and constitution will present amendments acceptable to the convention of the WUL of C.

The Secretary of the League is Tom Ewen, Room 58, 70 Lombard St., Toronto, Ont.

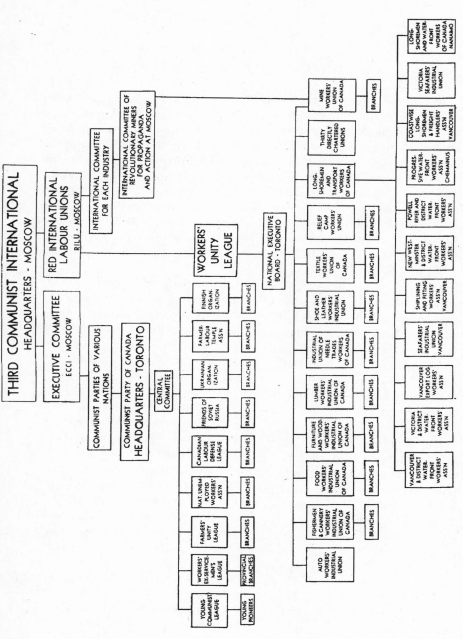

THIRD COMMUNIST INTERNATIONAL
HEADQUARTERS - MOSCOW

RED INTERNATIONAL LABOUR UNIONS
RILU - MOSCOW

EXECUTIVE COMMITTEE
ECCI - MOSCOW

INTERNATIONAL COMMITTEE FOR EACH INDUSTRY

INTERNATIONAL COMMITTEE OF REVOLUTIONARY MINERS FOR PROPAGANDA AND ACTION AT MOSCOW

COMMUNIST PARTIES OF VARIOUS NATIONS

COMMUNIST PARTY OF CANADA
HEADQUARTERS - TORONTO

WORKERS' UNITY LEAGUE

CENTRAL COMMITTEE

NATIONAL EXECUTIVE BOARD - TORONTO

YOUNG COMMUNIST LEAGUE

WORKERS' EX-SERVICE-MEN'S LEAGUE

FARMERS' UNITY LEAGUE

NAT. UNEMPLOYED WORKERS' ASS'N

CANADIAN LABOUR DEFENSE LEAGUE

FRIENDS OF SOVIET RUSSIA

UKRAINIAN ORGANIZATION

FARMER-LABOUR TEMPLE ASS'N

FINNISH ORGANIZATION

YOUNG PIONEERS

PROVINCIAL BRANCHES

BRANCHES

BRANCHES

BRANCHES

BRANCHES

BRANCHES

AUTO WORKERS' INDUSTRIAL UNION

FISHERMEN & CANNERY WORKERS' INDUSTRIAL UNION OF CANADA

FOOD WORKERS' INDUSTRIAL UNION OF CANADA

FURNITURE AND WOOD WORKERS' INDUSTRIAL UNION OF CANADA

LUMBER WORKERS' INDUSTRIAL UNION OF CANADA

INDUSTRIAL UNION OF NEEDLE TRADES WORKERS OF CANADA

SHOE AND LEATHER WORKERS' INDUSTRIAL UNION

TEXTILE WORKERS' UNION OF CANADA

RELIEF CAMP WORKERS' UNION

LONG-SHOREMEN AND TRANSPORT WORKERS OF CANADA

THIRTY DIRECTLY CHARTERED UNIONS

MINE WORKERS' UNION OF CANADA

BRANCHES

BRANCHES

BRANCHES

BRANCHES

BRANCHES

BRANCHES

BRANCHES

BRANCHES

VANCOUVER & DISTRICT WATER-FRONT WORKERS' ASS'N

VICTORIA & DISTRICT WATER-FRONT WORKERS' ASS'N

VANCOUVER EXPORT LOG WORKERS' ASS'N

SEAFARERS' INDUSTRIAL UNION VANCOUVER

SHIPLINING AND FITTING WORKERS' VANCOUVER

NEW WESTMINSTER & DISTRICT WATER-FRONT WORKERS' ASS'N

POWELL RIVER AND DISTRICT WATER-FRONT WORKERS' ASS'N

PROGRESSIVE WATER-FRONT WORKERS' ASS'N CHEMAINUS

COASTWISE LONG-SHOREMEN & FREIGHT HANDLERS' ASS'N VANCOUVER

VICTORIA SEAFARERS' INDUSTRIAL UNION

LONG-SHOREMEN AND WATER-FRONT WORKERS OF CANADA NANAIMO

APPENDIX II The Federal Department of Labour Diagram of the Workers' Unity League, c. 1933. (LAC, RG27, v. 835, file 1-28-1, pt. 1)

APPENDIX III

CHARTER FOR THE RIGHT TO LIVE

The National Congress on Unemployment regards it as its task to lay down a programme upon which the whole Canadian working class can unite in struggle against the present conditions of the unemployed workers, which directly and inevitably bears upon the conditions of the employed workers. The National Congress proceeds from the fundamental position that the capitalist class and its governments, who own and control all the means of production, are responsible for the full and adequate maintenance of every man, woman and child of the working class, who are without means of life as a result of the capitalist crisis. The Congress puts forward these demands as the *Charter of Our Right to Live*:

1. The immediate enactment by the Federal and Provincial governments of the Workers' Unemployment and Social Insurance Bill providing benefits to all workers who are unemployed or who are unable to work because of sickness, disability or old age, at the expense of the government and the capitalist class.

2. Pending this enactment, cash relief for all unemployed workers and their dependants (including part-time workers) of not less than $10 per week for a family of two, $2 for each dependant and $6 for all single unattached persons over 16 years of age. This scale must be raised to conform to every rise in prices. Widows and widowers with dependants to receive equal rates of relief as married persons with same number of dependants.

3. Immediate provision for the winter needs in clothing, etc., of all unemployed at the rate of $50 for a family of two and $10 additional for each dependant and $25 for all single unattached persons over 16.

4. Trade union rates of wages and conditions on all so-called 'relief' work. Abolition of all forced labour and task work. The Workmen's Compensation to be applied to all relief work. The Compensation Board to be composed of workers, elected by the workers. Unrestricted right to organize, strike and picket.

5. The immediate launching of a national billion-dollar building programme by the Federal government for the constructing

of workers' homes, hospitals, children's recreation centres and irrigation in drought-stricken areas. All labour to be employed at trade union rates and conditions.

6. **P**rohibition of all evictions, seizures, foreclosures or forced sales of homes or furnishings of unemployed or part-time workers and farmers for non-payment of rent, interest, principal, taxes or other debts.

7. **F**ree medical and health service and free light, gas, water and transportation services (to school relief work etc.) for all unemployed and their dependants.

8. **S**ix-hour day and five-day week for all employed workers without reduction in their weekly wages.

9. **A**bolition of all child labour under 16 years of age. The Federal and Provincial governments to establish free schools for vocational training or any other education the young workers or students may choose and provide necessary maintenance for these students.

10. **I**ncreased Department of Soldiers Civil Re-Establishment relief for all veterans, veterans' wives and dependants up to the age of 21 and the abolition of the unfair clauses in the Pensions Act dealing with War Widows.

11. **R**epeal of Section 98 of the Criminal Code and freedom of organization and assembly for all workers with free use of public parks, buildings and other public places for meetings and activities of all workers and their organizations. Abolition of all deportations of British or other foreign-born workers.

12. **I**mmediate repeal of the embargo against Canadian-Soviet trade and immediate restoration of normal trade relations with the Soviet Union.

SOURCE: LAC, Bennett Papers, M-1326, #402393; *Worker*, 9 September 1933, reporting on the National Congress on Unemployment held in Ottawa, September 1933.

Notes

Preface

1 Karl Marx and Friedrich Engels, *The Communist Manifesto* (New York: International Publishers, 1948), 9.

2 *Workers' Unity League: Policy, Tactics, Structure, Demands* (Toronto: WUL National Office, pamphlet, 50 pages, n.d. circa 1932), 46, UBC Special Collections, SPAM 12030.

3 Commissioner A.B. Perry, Royal North West Mounted Police, circulars 807, 807a, 807b, 6 January 1919, 5 February 1920, Library and Archives Canada (LAC), Records of the Canadian Security Intelligence Service (CSIS), RG146, access request 1925-9-91024, 'Historical Paper on Security Services Involvement in Labour,' 43pp. Gregory S. Kealey has written extensively on the RCMP's intelligence section, and especially relevant for the present discussion is his Introduction to the *RCMP Security Bulletins: The Depression Years, Part I, 1933–1934* (St John's: Canadian Committee on Labour History, 1993), 8–18. The CBC program 'The Fifth Estate' aired a program on 15 October 2010 called 'Enemies of the State,' showing that detailed secret plans of the RCMP to harass and round up thousands of Canadians on political grounds in the 1950s lasted until the mid-1980s.

4 Marx and Engels, *The Communist Manifesto*, 13.

5 See for example Irving Abella, *The Canadian Labour Movement 1902–1960* (Ottawa: Canadian Historical Association, Booklet 28, 1975), 16–17, and Bryan Palmer, *Working-Class Experience: The Rise and Reconstitution of Canadian Labour, 1800–1980* (Toronto: Butterworth and Co., 1983), 212–13, 217. Palmer is one of the more prolific writers on the working-class experience in Canada, and commands respect for his contributions to the subject. He has not published extensively on the Workers' Unity League but in his writ-

ings he has pointed to the efforts of the communists in that regard, saying 'a great deal of historic importance must be attached to their activities in the 1930s.' He is disappointed, however, believing that the communists substituted 'ritual exhortations of revolution' for their 'larger responsibility' to provide political leadership to the left. Up to this point Palmer joins those who think that from beginning to end the WUL was characterized by 'sectarian and irrational adventurism,' the product of 'subservience' and 'slavish adherence' to the Comintern.

6 John Manley, 'Red or Yellow? Canadian Communists and the "Long" Third Period, 1927–1936,' in Matthew Worley, ed., *In Search of Revolution* (London: I.B. Tauris, 2004), 238–9. Manley, whose unpublished doctoral thesis, 'Communism and the Canadian Working Class during the Great Depression: The Workers' Unity League, 1930–1936,' was written at Dalhousie University, Halifax, in 1984, has since published a series of articles on the same subject. Most of these are in *Labour/Le Travail* from 1986 to 2005. In 1994 Manley made a presentation at the annual meetings of the Canadian Historical Association held in Calgary. His paper, titled 'Canadian Communists, Revolutionary Unionism, and the "Third Period": The Workers' Unity League, 1929–1935,' summarizes his thesis. His conclusion is that 'massive achievements' cannot be claimed for the WUL, but 'what it did achieve cannot be casually dismissed.' He argues that while the WUL was 'an unusually – but not uniquely – militant brand of labour unionism,' whose 'tactics were designed for victory not heroic defeat,' it was never a revolutionary union movement. *Journal of the Canadian Historical Association* 5 (1994), 190.

7 Norman Penner finds that the WUL went 'beyond the confines of ordinary trade-union activism' but he found no reason to put it in a 'revolutionary frame of reference.' *The Canadian Left: A Critical Analysis* (Scarborough: Prentice-Hall, 1977), 137.

8 Raphael Samuel, ed., *People's History and Socialist Theory* (London: Routledge and Kegan Paul, 1981), xviii.

9 For the first ten years of my project CSIS declined to produce its index of available files so that a search for documents was like poking around in a haystack. This led to much frustration for me and for the staff at Library and Archives Canada. Even after a lucky strike on the name of a file, CSIS could take months, perhaps a year or more, to produce the photocopied and censored document. It was time-consuming work. Antonio Lechasseur, an access officer at LAC, advised me that if nothing showed up for a long time I could make an identical request directly to CSIS. I did this (and perhaps others did too), and that led Canada's spy agency to establish a reading room in its own headquarters. This way, perhaps, it could keep 'freedom

of information' under closer surveillance. I went there by appointment
in September 1992 and was ushered into a spacious office that had been
stripped down to a large desk and two chairs. Presently an older man in a
conservative business suit wheeled in a stack of photocopied and censored
documents. This was Erwin Pethick, who said he was 'an access officer.' He
sat down in the other chair and read a newspaper for several days while I
read through the files on some of Canada's most famous revolutionaries
– Malcolm Bruce, Bill Bennett, Arthur 'Slim' Evans, Sam Scarlett, Annie
Buller, Jeanne Corbin, Joseph Forkin, Matthew Popovich – and chose the
pages for which I wished copies. Occasionally Pethick was spelled off by Norman Sirois, a younger man dressed in the kind of leather jacket bikers wear,
who introduced himself as 'the supervisor of access officers.' Sirois had an
informal, easy manner and we had some conversation. He told me that I was
about the only one who came in to read and select from the documents; the
others ordered and paid for the whole bundle. 'Perhaps,' he said, 'they have
a bigger budget than you.'

Unless CSIS was thinking of going into the film business, another experience I had in trying to obtain access to declassified documents suggests the
existence of an ongoing struggle over policy about releasing historical documents at the higher levels of the organization. Copies of the Weekly Summary of reports on 'Revolutionary Organizations and Agitators in Canada'
that the RCMP prepared for the prime minister's office during the Depression years had come to me as a result of a Freedom of Information Request
and I was reviewing them in the section of the reading room at Library and
Archives Canada which stayed open late for the convenience of researchers.
There were three or four other researchers there as well, when suddenly
the door burst open and in came some men dressed as workers carrying a
tall extension ladder, cameras, and lighting equipment. They said they had
come to check the lighting system in the reading room. To the astonishment of everyone, they proceeded to focus their cameras and lighting on
me from every angle, including close-ups of the sixty-year-old material I was
reading. After ten minutes of this performance they packed up their equipment and left without a further word. The irony is that CSIS had already
cleared the Weekly Summaries and (unknown to me) the censored version
of these documents would soon be published in book form by the Canadian
Committee on Labour History of the History Department of Memorial
University in St John's, Newfoundland. When I made inquiries of the person
in charge of the reading room at Library and Archives Canada about any
'lighting problems,' he was mystified, saying the intrusion had been 'a most
unexpected and unusual happening.'

1. Workers in Canada's Second Industrial Revolution

1 John Herd Thompson and Allen Seager, *Canada 1922–1939: Decades of Discord* (Toronto: McClelland and Stewart, 1985), 78; *The Canadian Annual Review of Public Affairs 1932*, 489–90, 503–4; John A. Guthrie, *The Newsprint Paper Industry: An Economic Analysis* (Cambridge: Harvard University Press, 1941), 57–75; H.H. Stevens, *The Stevens Pamphlet* (Toronto: West Toronto Printing House, 1934), LAC, CPC Papers, MG28 IV4, v. 61, file 25; Tim Buck, 'Report on the Canadian Party Situation,' 23 January 1930, 1, LAC, CI Fonds 495, list 98, file 101, reel 11, K-279.

2 www.museumnorth.org/iroquois_falls/mill (2005).

3 *Worker*, 20 December 1930. LAC, Department of Labour, RG27, v. 346, file 86, reel T-2757.

4 Satu Repo, 'Rosvall and Voutilainen: Two Union Men Who Never Died,' *Labour/Le Travailleur* 8/9 (Autumn/Spring 1981–2), 79–102; Taimi Davis, '70 Years Ago: Murder in the Woods,' *People's Voice* (Vancouver, December 1999); 'Viljo Rosvall and John Voutilainen,' *Lumber Worker* 1 (3 December 1932), Ontario Archives (OA), RG27, v. 344, file 98, reel T-2755.

5 K. Finn, 'On the Situation in Canada,' *Viesti*, New York, May 1932. LAC, CI Fonds 495, list 98, file 142, reel 16, K-284.

6 Thompson and Seager, *Canada 1922–1939*, 81, 139.

7 'The Campaign to Organize the Automobile Industry in Canada (Preliminary Report),' 16 October 1928, encl. in Tim Buck, trade union department, Communist Party of Canada to A. Lozovsky, executive secretary, Profintern, Moscow, 24 October 1928, LAC, CI Fonds 534, list 7, file 334, reel 45, K-313; Thompson and Seager, *Canada 1922–1939*, 85–8.

8 Phillip Bonosky, *Brother Bill McKie: Building the Union at Ford* (New York: International Publishers, 1953), 9; Harvey Murphy to Local Unions of Automobile Workers in Canada, 16 October 1928, LAC, CI Fonds 534, list 7, file 334, reel 45, K-313.

9 *Report of the Royal Commission on the Textile Industry* (Ottawa: King's Printer, 1938) 176, 143.

10 *Who's Who in Canada 1934–35* (Toronto: International Press, 1935), 393, 1307, 336; Watt Hugh McCollum, *Who Owns Canada?* (Regina: Saskatchewan CCF Research Bureau, 1935), 39–40; 'Women Workers in Canadian Industry,' n.d. circa 1931, National Women's Department, CPC, LAC, CI Fonds 495, list 98, file 126, reel 14, K-282.

11 J.B. McLachlan at a district miners' convention, Sydney, NS, 15–16 March 1930, LAC, CPC Papers, MG28 IV4, v. 52, file 52, 'Minutes,' p. 6.

12 Quoted by Angus MacInnis, *Debates: House of Commons* (Ottawa: King's Printer), 1946 vol. 5, 5611.

13 'Women Workers in Canadian Industry.'

14 J.C. McRuer, 'Brief to the Royal Commission on the Textile Industry,' Ottawa, 2 February 1937, p. 426. Copy in the University of Toronto Law Library.

15 Craig Heron, ed., *The Workers' Revolt in Canada 1917–1925* (Toronto: University of Toronto Press, 1998), 4; Gregory S. Kealey, '1919: The Canadian Labour Revolt,' *Labour/Le Travail* 13 (Spring 1984), 11–44.

16 *Canadian Unionist* 2.6 (December 1928), 104. Until 1935 the ACCL journal gave mainly favourable coverage of developments in the Soviet Union, i.e. 'What Is Happening in Russia?' 4.9 (February 1931); 'A Great Achievement,' 6.8 (January 1933); 'The March of Labour,' 7.6 (November 1933).

17 Department of Labour of Canada, *Twentieth Annual Report on Labour Organization in Canada (1930)* (Ottawa: King's Printer, 1931), 72.

18 Tim Buck, 'National Trade Union Centre Established in Canada,' 29 April 1927, LAC, CI Fonds 534, list 7, file 333, reel 45, K-313.

19 'Where We Stand,' editorial in *Canadian Unionist* 1.9 (February 1928); 'The "Honourable" Gid,' ibid. 1.12 (May 1928).

20 Colin McKay, 'The Conceits of the Communists,' *Canadian Unionist* 4.3 (August 1930); Raymond Postgate, 'The Revulsion against the Communists,' ibid. 1.9 (February 1928); ibid. 3.6 (November 1929), 59.

21 Tim Buck, 'Report on Trade Union Activity in Canada,' October 1927, LAC, CI Fonds 534, list 7, file 333, reel 45, K-313.

22 *Western Miner* 1.8 (27 June 1930). The vote against Wheatley was almost two to one.

23 Communist Party of Canada, *Canada's Party of Socialism: History of the Communist Party of Canada 1921–1976* (Toronto: Progress Books, 1982), 33.

24 Tim Buck, industrial director of the Communist Party, wrote in 1928 that the centre of the left wing in the labour movement had been reduced to 'no more than the trade union department of the party.' Buck to Guy, Organization Department, Profintern (Moscow), 2 August 1928, LAC, CI Fonds 534, list 7, file 334, reel 45, K-313.

25 Formed in Moscow in 1919 under Lenin's leadership in opposition to the second, or social democratic international, located in Amsterdam. See Kevin McDermott and Jeremy Agnew, *The Comintern: A History of International Communism from Lenin to Stalin* (London: Macmillan, 1996), introduction and chapter 1.

2. The Red International

1 *Agents of Revolution: A History of the Workers' Unity League, Setting Forth Its Origin and Aims* (Toronto: Attorney General's Office, n.d. circa 1934), 6. See

R.B. Bennett Papers, LAC, reel 1324, frames 388406–14; *Winnipeg Free Press* (morning edition), 19 February 1934, 3, 'To Inform Workers in Ontario of Unity League.'

2 E.H. Carr, *The Twilight of Comintern, 1930–1935* (London: Macmillan, 1982), 6. For an opposite view of the Comintern as a monolithic structure under the tight control of Stalin and his close associates see Franz Borkenau, *World Communism: A History of the Communist International* (Ann Arbor: University of Michigan Press, 1938/62)) and F.L. Firsov, 'What the Comintern's Archives Will Reveal,' *World Marxist Review* no. 1 (1989), 52–7.

3 See *Why Every Worker Should Join the Communist Party* (Toronto: Canadian Workers' Pamphlet Series No. 3) June 1930, 7–9. LAC, CPC Papers, MG28 IV4, v. 60, file 37.

4 Cable of greetings to the Communist International from the Central Committee of the Communist Party of Canada, meeting in plenary session in Toronto, in February 1931. Ontario Archives, MS367, RG4, reel 5, 8-C-0447.

5 'Theses on fundamental tasks of the Second Congress of the Communist International' (1920), in V.I. Lenin, *Collected Works*, 4th English ed. (Moscow: Progress Publishers, 1965), v. 31, 185.

6 See, for example, *Payroll* (Winnipeg) 1.2 (April 1922); Citizens' League of British Columbia, 'Communism in British Columbia,' pamphlet, n.d., c. 1935, BC Provincial Archives, Premier's Office, GR1222, box 7; *Agents of Revolution: A History of the Workers' Unity League, Setting Forth Its Origin and Aims* (Toronto: Attorney General of Ontario, n.d. circa 1934), LAC, R.B. Bennett Papers, reel M-1314.

7 In the post-Soviet era the name of Vorovsky Street was changed to Povarskaya Street, but number 25a still houses the Gorky Institute of World Literature, which succeeded the International Lenin School as the tenant of this handsome structure.

8 Interview with Stewart Smith in Fergus, Ontario, 24 September 1992.

9 See for example John Hladun's article in *Maclean's* in 1947, 'They Taught Me Treason: The First-Hand Story of a Canadian Farm Boy Trained by Moscow as a Storm Trooper of a World-Revolution.' Hladun, a farmer's son and coal miner from Alberta, was a student briefly at the ILS in 1930. Years later, during the Cold War against Communism, Hladun emerged briefly on the national stage in Canada when the sensational article purportedly relating his experiences in Moscow appeared in *Maclean's*. This happened to coincide with Communist Party leader Tim Buck's annual public lecture at the University of Toronto sponsored by the student communist club. The amphitheatre in the McLennan Physics Building was packed for the event, of which I was the unsuspecting chairperson. After Buck's talk there

was a question period during which someone asked him to comment on the *Maclean's* article. No sooner had Buck begun to reply than a man in the audience stood up and shouted: 'You can stop right there, Tim! I am John Hladun!' There ensued pandemonium as the cameras of the *Toronto Evening Telegram* flashed and chants of 'We want Hladun! We want Hladun!' filled the hall. Having no other reasonable option, I invited Hladun to the stage and told him he could have five minutes. But after he had uttered two or three semi-articulate sentences in broken English it became clear that the famous Cold War editor of *Maclean's*, Blair Fraser, had had someone else write the polished article. Amidst a growing chorus of guffaws and catcalls from the students, I invited a deflated Hladun to take his seat, for which he was visibly grateful, and the meeting continued.

10 Joseph Freeman, *An American Testament: A Narrative of Rebels and Romantics* (London: Victor Gollancz, 1938), 521.

11 Smith's contact with Joseph Stalin, who, according to historian E.H. Carr, rarely visited the CI headquarters by the late 1920s (see Carr, *The Twilight of Comintern, 1930–1935*, 5), was limited to one or two brief encounters. Smith, interview (1992).

12 Freeman, *An American Testament*, 520.

13 Smith, interview (1992).

14 Among many examples, see Sam Carr (Moscow) to Tim Buck, 11 April 1929, LAC, CPC Papers, MG28 IV4, v. 8, p. 6.

15 Smith, interview (1992).

16 Smith acted as underground general secretary of the Communist Party while Tim Buck was in Kingston Penitentiary from 1932 to 1934; later while working as Toronto CP organizer he was elected to the Toronto City Council as alderman for ward 5 in 1937 and then to the Board of Control with over 40,000 votes during the Second World War. LAC, CSIS Records, RG146, v. 849, box 96 (access request 96-A-00149).

17 Leslie Morris (Dagestan Soviet Socialist Republic) to Stewart Smith (Toronto), 25 May 1929, LAC, CI Fonds 495, list 98, file 97, reel 11, K-279. Morris became national leader (general secretary) of the Communist Party after Tim Buck retired in 1961.

18 E.H. Carr, *A History of Soviet Russia: Foundations of a Planned Economy, 1926–29*, v. 3, part 2 (London: Macmillan, 1976), 318–21.

19 Harvey Klehr, John Earl Haynes, and Kyrill M. Anderson, *The Soviet World of American Communism* (New Haven: Yale University Press, 1998), 132.

20 Smith, interview (1992).

21 C. Starnes to O.D. Skelton, under-secretary of state for external affairs, 27 August 1930, LAC, R.B. Bennett Papers, reel M-989.

22 According to a sceptical report from U.S. Brigadier General Armstrong
to Canada's Department of National Defence of July 1932, there was 'no
concrete evidence of money coming from Moscow to the United States at
the present time.' Enclosed in H.H. Matthews, Department of National
Defence, Ottawa, to Lt.-Colonel T.S. Belcher, deputy commissioner, RCMP,
Ottawa, 9 August 1932, LAC, CSIS Records, RG146, v. 3305/2.

23 Smith, interview (1992).

24 Carr, *A History of Soviet Russia*, v. 3, part 1, 214.

25 J.R. Knight's report to the OBU, 13 January 1922, LAC, CI Fonds 534, list 7,
file 329, reel 44, K-312.

26 A. Lozovsky, *Marx and the Trade Unions* (New York: International Publishers,
1942), 8. See also his pamphlet *The Workers' Economic Struggles and the Fight
for Workers' Rule: Some Challenging International Lessons* (Montreal: Contemporary Publishers, n.d. circa 1932) in the Bill Bennett Memorial Library,
University of British Columbia, Special Collections, SPAM 122523. After the
RILU faded away in 1937, Lozovsky became a deputy foreign minister of
the Soviet Union, and chief co-ordinator of various Anti-Fascist Committees
during the Second World War. Then following the founding of the state of
Israel in 1948, the Soviet Jewish Anti-Fascist Committee members, including Lozovsky, were charged on various counts, tried in secret, and executed
in 1952. For this tragic story see Joshua Rubenstein, *Stalin's Secret Pogrom:
The Postwar Inquisition of the Jewish Anti-Fascist Committee* (New Haven: Yale
University Press, 2001).

27 A. Losovsky (*sic*), *The Workers' Economic Struggles and the Fight for Workers' Rule*,
20– 1. This was Lozovsky's speech to the Twelfth Plenum of the Executive
Committee of the Communist International, August 1932.

28 Lozovsky, *Marx and the Trade Unions*, 12.

29 Carr, *A History of Soviet Russia*, v. 3, part 1, 168. Chapter 69 of this book,
'Profintern and the Trade Unions,' is a well-informed account of the development of Lozovsky's program and its opponents during this period.

30 Fraser Ottanelli, *The Communist Party of the United States: From the Depression
to World War II* (New Brunswick, NJ: Rutgers University Press, 1991), 21;
William Z. Foster, *From Bryan to Stalin* (New York: International Publishers,
1937), 213–15.

31 Carr, *A History of Soviet Russia*, v. 3, part 2, 599.

32 Foster, *History of the Communist Party of the United States* (New York: Inter-
national Publishers, 1952), 257–9 and Foster, *From Bryan to Stalin*, 216ff;
Ottanelli, *The Communist Party of the United States*, 21; 'TUUL Formed in
Cleveland,' *Worker* (Toronto), 21 September 1929.

33 Foster, general secretary of the TUUL, records that twenty-three workers

were murdered by police, company gunmen, and vigilante thugs in the many struggles led by the TUUL over the next three years. Hundreds more were slugged and jailed. TUUL headquarters were raided repeatedly and effective organizers deported. *History of the Communist Party of the United States*, 285.

34 See LAC, CI Fonds 534, list 7, file 334, reel 44, K-312, for documents relating to forming Red unions among auto workers, needle trades workers, and miners, in 1928.

35 Secretary, Red International of Trade Unions (Moscow) to Dear Comrades (Toronto), 15 February 1929, LAC, CI Fonds 495, list 98, file 80, reel 9, K-277. See also Tim Buck (Toronto) to A. Lozovsky, 23 February 1929, enclosing 'Trade Union Thesis of the Communist Party of Canada,' which contained many similar suggestions. LAC, CI Fonds 534, list 7, file 335, reel 45, K-313. The amended 'Trade Union Thesis,' n.d. (May 1929), is in CI Fonds 495, list 98, file 77, reel 9, K-277.

36 'Closed Letter from the Political Secretariat of the ECCI to the Central Committee of the Communist Party of Canada,' 8 April 1929, LAC, CPC Papers, MG28 IV4, v. 11, file 26.

37 'Report of the Sixth National Convention of the Communist Party of Canada,' 31 May to 7 June 1929, LAC, CPC Papers, MG28 IV4, v. 11, file 26, 16.

38 'Minutes of Central Executive Meeting, Communist Party of Canada,' 12 July 1929, 20–1, LAC, CI Fonds 495, list 98, file 77, reel 9, K-277.

39 The number of workers involved in strikes in Canada in 1929 – 12,946 – was the lowest figure for any year since the First World War. Ontario Archives, RG7, 12-O-263, 'Strikes and Lockouts'; see also Douglas Cruikshank and Gregory S. Kealey, 'Strikes in Canada, 1891–1950,' *Labour/Le Travail* 20 (Fall 1987), 85–145, who put the figure at 13,120. However, this figure did not necessarily reflect a contented workforce since the prosperity of the Second Industrial Revolution was spread unevenly and a complacent trade union movement was making little effort to contact two-thirds of the industrial workforce which remained unorganized. Many of these wage-earners worked in sweated industries, faced wage cuts, short shifts, lay-offs, and other adverse situations.

40 Leslie Morris, 'A Critical Review of the Party,' 20 May 1930, LAC, CI Fonds 495, list 98, file 97, reel 11, K-279.

41 See Carr, *A History of Soviet Russia*, v. 2 and 3, part 2, note C 'Social-Fascism' for an explanation of the evolution of the phrase, which 'both in its origins and consequences ... remained predominantly a German concept' (643). Stewart Smith, who had been greatly influenced by his German roommate

at the International Lenin School, tried to make it a Canadian concept in a book published under the alias G. Pierce called *Socialism and the C.C.F.* (Montreal, 1934), 142–3, and it gained some currency during the period of his leadership 1932–4. In his autobiography, *Comrades and Komsomolkas: My Years in the Communist Party of Canada* (Toronto: Lugus, 1993), Smith attempts to present himself as a consistent opponent of ultra-leftism within the Communist Party; when I asked him, in 1992, about his 1934 book he waved it off as a mistake, a temporary aberration.

42 The most comprehensive description of its work ever published by the WUL, a pamphlet titled *Workers' Unity League: Policy, Tactics, Structure, Demands* (1932), does not employ the term 'social fascists' when referring to social democracy and neither do the reports to their three national conventions in 1932, 1933, and 1935; this suggests that in the past historians have exaggerated the prevalence of this abusive term in the actual workings of the league in Canada.

43 Maurice Spector, 'Report on the Political and Economic Situation in Canada and the Tasks of the Communist Party,' proceedings of the 5th National Convention, CPC, June 1927, LAC, CPC Papers, MG28 IV4, v. 11, file 23.

44 Cited in David Reynolds, 'Rethinking Anglo-American Relations,' *International Affairs* 65.1 (Winter 1988–9), 91–2; see also 'The War Danger,' editorial, *Canadian Unionist* 2.7 (January 1929).

45 Jack MacDonald, 'The Sixth Convention of the Communist Party and the War Danger,' *Canadian Labour Monthly* 2.14 (August 1929), 15, LAC, CI Fonds 495, list 98, file 85, reel 10, K-278.

46 *Toronto Star*, 27 December 1928, LAC, CSIS Records, RG146, v. 849, box 96, access request 96-A-02149, part 1.

47 Leslie Morris, 'Canada and the Anglo-American Conflict,' *Canadian Labour Monthly* 2.14 (August 1929), 45. For similar statistics see *The Canadian Annual Review of Public Affairs, 1930–1931*, 565. See also Tim Buck's spirited refutation of Leslie Morris's claims in 'Statement on Political Perspectives in Canada, 31 January 1930,' 9–14, LAC, CI Fonds 495, list 98, file 101, reel 13, K-279.

48 Political Secretariat, ECCI, 'Closed Letter to the Central Committee of the Communist Party of Canada,' paragraph 11, 8 April 1929, LAC, CPC Papers, MG28 IV4, v. 11, file 26. This letter was drafted and discussed over a period of six weeks by Sam Carr and the members of the Anglo-American Group of the A-A Secretariat. See Jack Davis/Sam Carr (Moscow) in letter to Toronto of which the salutation and date are torn off. Ibid., v. 8, file 6.

49 As head of the Comintern, Bukharin had defined and defended the new, leftist, 'third period' policy at the 6th CI Congress in the summer of 1928, but for an account of his growing tension with Stalin over the rate of

industrialization and rural collectivization in the Soviet Union's First Five
Year Plan, and his withdrawal or removal from the Russian delegation to the
Comintern in the autumn of 1928, see Carr, *A History of Soviet Russia*, v. 2,
75–82 and v. 3, part 1, 221–36.

50 Smith, interview (1992).

51 Carr, private conversation with the author.

52 The most important and valuable documents for following the bitter 'status
of Canada' controversy are: in the Communist Party Papers, LAC, MG28
IV4, v. 11, files 25, 26, 28, 29, 30, 31, 32, and 33; in the Comintern archives,
LAC, CI Fonds 495, list 98, file 97, reel 11, K-279, including personal letters
of Tim Buck (Moscow) to Stewart Smith (Toronto) of January and February
1930, letter of Canadian students at the International Lenin School to the
CEC of the CPC 29 January 1930; file 94, letter from Political Secretariat of
ECCI to the Central Committee, CPC, n.d. (28 February 1930); file 101 with
two lengthy documents composed in Moscow by Tim Buck when he was
trying to get a hearing with the CI, 'Report on the Canadian Party Situation,
23 Jan 1930,' 7–9, and 'Statement on Political Perspectives, 31 Jan 1930';
'Resolutions of Enlarged Plenum of Communist Party of Canada,' February
1931, LAC, CPC Papers, MG28 IV4, v. 11, file 35, 21.

53 According to Lozovsky, the countries where the RILU concentrated its spe-
cial attention were Germany, Japan, France, China, Poland, Czechoslovakia,
Great Britain, the United States, India, and Spain. Lozovsky, *The Workers'
Economic Struggles and the Fight for Workers' Rule*, 24.

54 [Stewart Smith] (Moscow), 'Report on the Situation of the Work of the
Communist Party of Canada during the Year of July 1929 to July 1930,' n.a.,
18 August 1930, LAC, CI Fonds 495, list 98, file 101, reel 11, K-279.

55 K.E. Heikkinen (ECCI), 'On the Organizational Questions of Canada,' 15
March 1931, LAC, CI Fonds 495, list 98, file 122, reel 14, K-282. Heikkinen
was a Finn from the United States CP, working in the secretariat of the
Comintern.

56 John Williamson, 'Material on Situation in Canada,' 5 March 1929, 6, CI
Fonds 495, list 98, file 86, reel 10, K-298; 'Letter from the Organization
Department of the ECCI to the Canadian Party Convention,' 31 May 1929,
4, 12, LAC, CPC Papers, MG28 IV4, v.11, file 26.

57 See John Kolasky, *The Shattered Illusion: The History of Ukrainian Pro-Communist Organizations in Canada* (Toronto: PMA Books, 1979), 244.

58 The 'Report of the Communist Work among Finnish Workers,' 25 May 1929,
states that of about 50,000 Finns in Canada, at last count in 1927, there were
2,640 in the Communist Party via membership in the Finnish Organization
of Canada. Another report notes that many of these were only nominal mem-

bers of the party, 'fictitious members,' who in reality joined the FOC for sport and social purposes, CI Fonds 495, list 98, file 77, reel 9, K-277, 3; 'Letter from the Organization Department of the ECCI to the Canadian Party Convention,' LAC, CPC Papers, MG28 IV4, v. 11, file 26, 4; 'Canada – Revolutionary Press,' LAC, CI Fonds 495, list 98, file 120, reel 13, K-281.

59 Sam Carr, 'Draft Resolution on Work in Language Mass Organizations,' minutes of Political Bureau, 22 January 1931, LAC, CI Fonds 495, list 98, file 117, reel 13, K-281.

60 John Boychuck, quoted in 'Report of District 3 Convention of the Communist Party,' taking place in the Finnish Hall on Broadview Avenue, 9–13 March 1929, LAC, CI Fonds 495, list 98, file 81, reel 10, K-278.

61 Ahlqvist, Wirta, et al. Executive Committee, Finnish Organization of Canada to Executive Committee Communist International, 29 December 1929, LAC, CI Fonds 495, list 98, file 82, reel 10, K-278.

62 The Smith-FOC conflict may be followed in LAC, CI Fonds 495, list 98, files 81, 82, and 84, reel 10, K-278.

63 Smith (Moscow) to Buck (Toronto), 14 August 1930, LAC, CI Fonds 495, list 98, file 97, reel 11, K-279.

64 Buck (Moscow) to Secretariat, Communist Party of Canada, 13 January 1930, LAC, CI Fonds 495, list 98, file 97, reel 11, K-279.

65 Buck (Moscow) to Smith (Toronto), 31 January 1930, LAC, CI Fonds 495, list 98, file 97, reel 11, K-279.

66 'Trade Unionism Marches On,' editorial, *Canadian Congress Journal* 8.9 (September 1929), 32.

67 Report of the Executive to the Third Convention of the ACCL, 4 November 1929, *Canadian Unionist* 3.7 (December 1929).

68 Political Secretariat of Executive Committee Communist International (ECCI) to Central Committee, Communist Party of Canada, 3 October 1929, LAC, CPC Papers, MG28 IV4, v. 11, file 33, 3.

69 Acting general secretary of the RILU to Central Committee, Communist Party of Canada, 19 October 1929. LAC, CI Fonds 495, list 98, file 111, reel 12, K-280 and draft of same letter, dated 26 September 1929, by the Anglo-American Section of the RILU, LAC, CI Fonds 495, list 98, file 88, reel 10, K-278. For the significance of 'the Strassburg Resolution,' see chapter 4, note 13.

70 'Minutes of Political Committee,' Communist Party of Canada, 16 December 1929, LAC, CI Fonds 495, list 98, file 98, reel 11, K-279.

3. Getting Started

1 Quoted by Tom McEwen in *The Forge Glows Red* (Toronto: Progress Books, 1974), frontispiece.

2 Ewen to C. Bradley (Calgary), 12 June 1931, OA, RG4, MS367, reel 2, 3-A-2210.

3 Thomas A. Ewen, 'Personal History File,' 1 April 1931, CSIS Records, LAC, RG146, file 175/P2459, public access box 17. The report also notes that Ewen had a 'complete set of false teeth,' his own having been smashed out by Toronto policemen.

4 McEwen, *The Forge Glows Red*, 7–8.

5 See Ruth Wright Millar, *Saskatchewan Heroes and Rogues* (Regina: Coteau Books, 2004), 88, which suggests that Taylor's death was from tuberculosis and possibly from despair.

6 McEwen, *The Forge Glows Red*, 78–82.

7 Ibid., 11, 27, 34, 39, chapters 4 to 9. In the late 1930s Ewen changed his surname to that of his mother, Agnes McEwen.

8 Acting general secretary, RILU, to Central Committee, CPC, 19 October 1929, LAC, CI Fonds 495, list 98, file 111, reel 12, K-280; minutes, Political Committee, CPC, 16 December 1929, ibid., file 98, reel 11, K-279; minutes, National Trade Union Department, CPC, 25 December 1929, OA, RG4, reel 7, 10-C-1813–14.

9 OA, RG4, reel 3, 4-A-2491. There was a curious slip in the masthead: instead of 'Provisional National Executive,' it read 'Provincial National Executive.'

10 'Draft Constitution,' *Worker*, 28 June 1930. Also available in the *Western Miner*, 18 September 1930; 'Twentieth Annual Report on Labour Organization in Canada' (Ottawa: King's Printer, 1931), 162–3; LAC, R.B. Bennett Papers, reel M-989, #94441; the draft was on the agenda of the Polcom of the CPC on 26 May 1930, 'Minutes,' LAC, CI Fonds 495, list 98, file 98, reel 11, K-279.

11 In translations of the *Manifesto*, this phrase is often translated as 'Working-men of All Countries, Unite!'

12 McEwen, *The Forge Glows Red*, 137. The minutes and full report of this conference, 'Workers' Unity League, Southern Ontario Conference, May 24th and 25th, 1930' (25 pages) are available in the RCMP files, LAC, CSIS Records, RG146, access request 92-A-0086, file 175/6811.

13 Ewen to J. Barker (Sudbury), 24 December 1930, OA, RG4, reel 1, 1-A-0439.

14 Ewen to Lil Greene (Toronto) 8 June 1955, UBC Special Collections, Lil Greene Papers, box 1.

15 See 'Souvenir Program of the First National Convention of the Industrial Union of Needle Trades Workers of Canada,' 7, LAC, CI Fonds 495, list 98, file 88, reel 10, K-278.

16 Stenogram of the Sixth Convention of the CPC, 31 May–7 June 1929, LAC, CPC Papers, MG28 IV4, v. 11, file 26, 79.

17 J.B. Salsberg (1903–98) came to Canada from Poland with his parents at

age eleven, settling in Toronto. At first he studied to be a rabbi, but at age sixteen decided to join a secular Zionist workers' group while working as a hatter in the garment industry. His participation in the labour movement led him to join the Communist Party of Canada in 1926, where he became a leading member and organizer for the Workers' Unity League. A colourful speaker and charismatic personality, Salsberg was elected to Toronto City Council in 1938 and then in 1943 to the Ontario Provincial Parliament, where he represented the Labour Progressive (Communist) Party and the people living around Spadina Avenue in the heart of Toronto until he was defeated in 1955. After Nikita Khrushchev's speech, in 1956, denouncing Stalin and revealing the decimation of the Soviet Jewish Anti-Fascist Committee, Salsberg left the Communist Party and the United Jewish People's Order, to become active in the Canadian Jewish Congress. Salsberg's papers are located at Queen's University, Kingston, Ontario.

18 'Trade Union Report,' Industrial Department, CPC, 30 June 1930, p. 14, LAC, CPC Papers, MG28 IV4, v. 51, file 21.

19 M. Klig, national secretary, IUNTW, to A. Lozovsky, secretary, RILU (Moscow), 30 December 1930, LAC, CI Fonds 495, list 98, file 335, reel 45, K-313.

20 See Catherine McLeod, 'Women in Production: The Toronto Dressmakers' Strike of 1931,' in Janice Acton, ed., *Women at Work, Ontario 1850–1930* (Toronto: Canadian Women's Educational Press, 1974), 309–30.

21 See Mercedes Steedman, 'The Promise: Communist Organizing in the Needle Trades, the Dressmakers' Campaign 1928–1937,' *Labour/Le Travail* no. 34 (Autumn 1994), 40–1.

22 J. Gershman (Montreal) to Ewen, 26 November 1930; Ewen to Gershman, 28 November 1930, OA, RG4, reel 1, 1-A-0282; 0284–5.

23 Ewen, report on the Eighth Convention of the Lumber and Agricultural Workers' Industrial Union (LAWIU), Port Arthur, May 1931, LAC, CI Fonds, 495, list 98, file 129, reel 14, K-282; George Drayton (Vancouver) to Ewen, 30 June 1930, LAC, CPC Papers, MG28 IV4, file 52–74.

24 From an appeal by Ewen to working-class organizations to support the Shabaqua strike of the Lumber Workers' Industrial Union (LWIU), 15 November 1929, LAC, CI Fonds 495, list 98, file 80, reel 9, K-277.

25 Bruce Magnuson, *The Untold Story of Ontario's Bushworkers: A Political Memoir* (Toronto: Progress Books, 1990), preface.

26 Minutes, Seventh Annual Convention of the Lumber Workers' Industrial Union of Canada, held in Port Arthur at 316 Bay St, 7–9 April 1930, 2, LAC, CPC Papers, MG28 IV4, v. 51, file 65. This proposal came from the executive of the International Land and Forest Workers' Union affiliated to the Red International of Labour Unions.

27 See Ian Radforth, *Bushworkers and Bosses: Logging in Northern Ontario, 1900–1980* (Toronto: University of Toronto Press, 1987), 125; Minutes, 7th Annual Convention of LWIU, 7–9 April 1930, 7, LAC, CPC Papers, MG28 IV4, v. 51, file 65; Newman (Sudbury) to Buck, 1 April 1931, OA, RG4, reel 2, 2-A-1480–1; Buck to Newman, 10 April 1931, ibid.; Industrial Department, CPC to A. Hautimaki (Port Arthur), 2 November 1929, ibid., reel 1, 1-A-0126.

28 David Frank, *J.B. McLachlan: A Biography* (Toronto: James Lorimer, 1999), 300–15.

29 Minutes of the District Convention, convened by Sub-District No. 1, District 26, UMWA, 15–16 March 1930, 12, LAC, CPC Papers, MG28 IV4, v. 52, file 52.

30 Ewen to Jim Barker (Glace Bay), 13 June 1930, OA, RG4, reel 1, 1-A-0234–6; Ewen, Reply to Discussion, CPC Plenum, 7 February 1931, OA, RG4, reel 5, 8-C-0485–6.

31 Ewen to Barker, 13 June 1930, OA, RG4, reel 1, 1-A-0236.

32 See Wheatley's article, 'Mining Conditions in Alberta,' *Canadian Unionist* 3.9 (February 1930).

33 McEwen, *The Forge Glows Red*, 141.

34 Murphy was active in forming the Automobile Workers' Industrial Union in Windsor in 1928, the steel railcar riveters' seven-week strike in Hamilton, and the bushworkers' strike in the Port Arthur area in 1929.

35 Allen Seager, 'Memorial to a Departed Friend of the Working Man,' *Bulletin of the Committee on Canadian Labour History* 4 (Autumn 1977), 9–14. Seager's fulsome tribute, though brief, is the best available account of Murphy's life.

36 Murphy to Stewart Smith (Toronto), 28 January 1930, OA, RG4, reel 1, 1-A-0549; 'Trade Union Report,' Industrial Department, Communist Party of Canada, 1 June 1930, LAC, CPC Papers, MG28 IV4, v. 8, file 7, 8–10.

37 Jack [Sam Carr] (Moscow) to Buck, 27 May 1930, LAC, CPC Papers, MG28 IV4, v. 8, file 7; Buck to J. Davis [Sam Carr] (Moscow) 3 August 1930, ibid. Arthur Horner (Moscow) to Buck/Ewen, 11 May 1930, appendix to Hon. W.H. Price, attorney general for Ontario, *Agents of Revolution* (Toronto, n.d. circa 1933 or early 1934). 'Program and Policy of W.U.L. in Canadian Mining Industry,' 12 May 1931, OA, RG4, reel 7, 10-C-2126. The Profintern was having similar arguments with Palmiro Togliatti of the Italian and H. Brandler of the German CPs; see Aldo Agosti, 'The Italian Communist Party and the Third Period,' in Matthew Worley, ed., *In Search of Revolution: International Communist Parties in the Third Period* (London: I.B. Tauris, 2004), 95 and A. Lozovsky, 'Report to the 5th Congress of the RILU,' *International Press Correspondence* 10. 42 (11 September 1930), 896.

38 Ewen to Arthur Horner (Anglo-American Secretariat, Profintern), 15 June 1930, OA, RG4, reel 3, 4-A-2724–7.

39 The debate over mining policy may be followed through the voluminous stack of letters, telegrams, and position papers on the subject from 1929 to 1934 located in the Ontario Archives Record Group 4, and Library and Archives Canada, MG28, IV.4, CPC Papers, as well as the Comintern Fonds, MG 10 K3, Fonds 495, list 98, file 80, reels 9 and 12, and file 111. They begin with the instructions to Murphy on going to Alberta in 'The Tasks of the Party in the Mining Districts of Alberta and Nova Scotia,' n.d., n.a., probably written by Ewen circa December 1929, LAC, CI Fonds 495, list 72, file 80, reel 9, continue with the contrary proposals from the Anglo-American Section, RILU, 'To the TUEL of Canada,' n.d., circa December 1929 in ibid., file 111, reel 12, and end with a national conference report by Harvey Murphy, 'Montreal Conference of Miners and Smelter Men Plans to Organize and Unite All Canadian Mine Workers,' *Worker*, 21 July 1934. A clear and succinct example of this kind of discourse occurs over tactics in the unemployed movement in 'Pol. Bureau minutes,' 21 July 1931, 7, LAC, CI Fonds 495, list 98, file 117, reel 13, K-281. For a somewhat frivolous example of the subservient/obedience argument in CI relations see John McIlroy and Alan Campbell, '"Nina Ponomareva's Hats": The New Revisionism, the Communist International, and the Communist Party of Great Britain, 1920–1930,' *Labour/Le Travail* 49 (Spring 2002), 147–88. Other historians who argue in this vein include Theodore Draper, Irving Howe, Harvey Klehr, and John Earl Haynes.

40 There were 1,600 miners on the Alberta side of the pass. Christen Junget (Lethbridge, commanding Southern Alberta District, RCMP) to the commissioner (Ottawa), 30 January 1932 (Secret), LAC, CSIS Records, RG146, v. 3616 [box 81, access request 96-A-00189, pt. 6].

41 *Western Miner*, 20 February 1930, quoted in Allen Seager, 'A History of the Mine Workers' Union of Canada 1925–1936' (MA thesis, Department of History, McGill University, March 1977), 89.

42 Murphy (Edmonton) to Stewart Smith, 28 January 1930, OA, RG4, reel 1, 1-A-0550.

43 Murphy to Ewen, 15 February 1930, Murphy to Smith, n.d. circa 20 March 1930, OA, RG4, reel 1, 1-A-0558, 1-A-0821. 'Nationalize the Coal-Mines,' by Frank Wheatley, vice-president, All-Canadian Congress of Labour, *Canadian Unionist* 1.1 (June 1927); 'Russia Sells Her Coal,' ibid., 3.12 (May 1930).

44 Murphy (Drumheller) to Ewen, 15 February 1930, OA, RG4, reel 1, 1-A-0558; Murphy (Edmonton) to Stewart Smith (Toronto), n.d. circa 20 March 1930, ibid., 1-A-0821.

45 Ewen to Murphy, 19 February 1930, OA, RG4, reel 1, 1-A-0560.

46 Daneliuk (Drumheller) to Central Executive Committee, CPC, 2 February 1930. This letter included complaints that the district organizer was 'idling around,' spoiling the workers' movement by his gambling at slot machines and 'losing hard earned money of the workers.' OA, RG4, reel 1, 1-A-0746. Later the author apologized for spreading unfounded gossip.

47 Murphy (Edmonton) to Stokaluk (Coleman), 6 March 1930, OA, RG4, reel 1, 1-A-0752.

48 Murphy to Ewen, 18 March 1930, OA, RG4, reel 1, 1-A-0771.

49 Secretariat, CPC (Toronto) to Murphy (Calgary), 12 March 1930, OA, RG4, reel 1, 1-A-0560.

50 'Statement of the Communist Party of Canada on the expulsion of J. Stokoluke [sic],' Western Miner, 4 April 1930; 'Minutes of PolCom Meeting,' 4 April 1930, LAC, CI Fonds 495, list 98, file 98, reel 11, K-279.

51 The Stokaluk case may be followed in the Comintern archives, CI Fonds 495, list 98, file 108, reel 12, K-280. See also CPC PolCom Minutes of 22 May, 19 June, 22 July 1930, and the Worker, 5 September 1931.

52 Murphy (Calgary) to Ewen, 24 April 1930, OA, RG4, reel 1, 1-A-0798; Murphy (Calgary) to Buck, 15 September 1930, LAC, CPC Papers, MG28 IV4, v. 51, file 73.

53 Western Miner, 27 June 1930.

54 The registered membership of the Mercoal local at the Fifth Annual Convention of the MWUC in September 1930 was sixty (out of a workforce that ranged between eighty and a hundred, depending on the season). OA, RG4, reel 7, 10-C-2081.

55 The Mercoal strike may be followed in the records of the Department of Labour, LAC, RG27, v. 345, no. 44, T-2757.

56 'Peace and Order Restored at Mercoal,' Edmonton Journal, 1 August 1930.

57 Edmonton Bulletin, 25 September 1930.

58 LAC, RG27, v. 345, no. 44, reel T-2757, 'Jailings Fail to Dampen Mercoal Strikers Spirit,' Worker, 4 October 1930.

59 Worker, 11 October 1930.

60 'Russia Sells Her Coal,' Canadian Unionist 3.12 (March 1930); 'United Effrontery,' ibid. 6. 12 (May 1933). The Edmonton Journal gave credit to the leaders of the MWUC for restraining the miners: 'believing as they did that a great injustice was being done them, the least hint of rough tactics by the leaders would have resulted in a wholesale cleanup of the camp long before the police arrived.' 1 August 1930.

61 'Workers' Unity League Monthly Letter, June 1931,' OA, RG4, reel 7, 10-C-1781.

62 M. Gilmore to Ewen, 3 February 1931, OA, RG4, reel 2, 3-A-2020.

63 Malcolm Bruce (Vancouver) to Ewen, 16 May 1930. OA, RG4, reel 1, 1-A-0809; 29 April 1931, reel 2, 3-A-2144.

64 Murphy (Calgary) to Ewen, 24 April 1930, OA, RG4, reel 1, 1-A-0798.

65 Murphy (Coleman) to Ewen, 22 May 1930, OA, RG4, reel 1, 1-A-0610. See also Murphy (Drumheller) to Buck, 4 September 1930, LAC, CPC Papers, MG28 IV4, v. 51, file 73.

4. Going to 'Mecca'

1 A.A. Santalov and Louis Segal, eds., *Soviet Union Year-Book 1930* (London: Allen and Unwin, 1930), 188–213; Stephen Kotkin, *Magnetic Mountain: Stalinism as a Civilization* (Berkeley: University of California Press, 1995), 43 ff.

2 See Paul Hollander, *Political Pilgrims: Travels of Western Intellectuals to the Soviet Union, China, and Cuba 1928–1978* (New York: Harper Colophon Books, 1981/3); David Caute, *The Fellow Travelers* (London, 1973).

3 For reports of the subsidiary conferences see Beckie Buhay, 'World's Working Women Plan Big Struggles,' and T. Ewen, 'The Ninth International Miners' Conference,' *Worker*, 11 October 1930, and Miners' International Committee, 'Build a Coast-to-Coast Militant Miners Union!' *Worker*, 8 November 1930.

4 *International Press Correspondence/World News and Views* 10.42 (11 September 1930), 900.

5 Sectarianism is understood here as putting the interests of a small group, a sect, ahead of the general interests of a class, in this case the working class; sectarian behaviour leads to isolation from the mainstream of social and political action, to a lack of solidarity across ideological lines.

6 E.H. Carr, *The Twilight of Comintern, 1930–1935* (London: Macmillan, 1982), 5; Matthew Worley, ed., *In Search of Revolution: International Communist Parties in the Third Period* (London: I.B. Tauris, 2004), 10.

7 A. Lozovsky, 'Report to the 5th Congress of the R.I.L.U,' *International Press Correspondence* 10.41 (4 September 1930), 867–71.

8 Ibid. 10.42 (11 September 1930), 894.

9 Ibid. Political issues included such matters as the right to organize unions and to strike, freedom of speech and assembly, the demand for workmen's compensation, unemployment insurance, etc.

10 Ibid., 895.

11 Ibid. 10.41 (4 September 1930), 872; 10.42 (11 September 1930), 895, 892.

12 Ibid. 10.43 (18 September 1930), 919.

13 Ibid. 10.42 (11 September 1930), 89443; (18 September 1930), 919; *Workers' Unity* no. 2 (August 1931), 5. See also *Problems of Strike Strategy: Decisions of the International Conference on Strike Strategy Held in Strassburg, Germany, January, 1929* (New York: Workers' Library Publishers, n.d. circa 1930), foreword by A. Lozovsky, preface to American edition by Bill Dunne, 49 pages, and Jane Degras, *The Communist International*, v. 3 (London: F. Cass, 1971), 64. The official language of the Comintern was German, hence the use of the German spelling for Strasbourg.

14 See Carr, *The Twilight of Comintern*, 21–2.

15 *International Press Correspondence* 10.42 (11 September 1930), 895.

16 Ibid. 10.41 (4 September 1930), 874, 870; 10.35 (31 July 1930), 676.

17 Carr, *The Twilight of Comintern*, 433ff.

18 Ibid., 85.

19 Smith to Buck, 13 October 1930, LAC, CPC Papers, MG28 IV4, v. 8, file 7.

20 'Draft Resolution of the Anglo-American Section of the Profintern on the Situation and Tasks of the Workers' Unity League of Canada,' 28 November 1930, LAC, CI Fonds, reel 12, file 111. A copy of this document and a shorter, simplified version, 'Profintern Resolution on the Canadian Situation and the Tasks of Workers' Unity League of Canada,' n.d., is in OA, RG4, reel 7, 10-C-1850–6, 10-C-1909–16.

21 Carr (Moscow) to Buck, 10 September 1930, LAC, MG28 IV4, v. 8, file 7. By February 1931, according to Tim Buck, all members of the CPC Central Committee had copies of Kuusinen's speech, OA, RG4, reel 5, 8-C-0457.

22 Smith (Moscow) to Buck, 8, 27 September, 18 October 1930, 11 January 1931, LAC, MG28 IV4, v. 8, file 7.

23 Ewen, 'Reply to Discussion,' CPC Plenum, 7 February 1931, OA, RG4, reel 5, 8-C-0501–2. The 'Condensed Report of the Canadian Delegation to the Fifth Congress of the RILU' appeared in the *Worker*, 29 November 1930.

24 For a classic example see Joseph Freeman, *An American Testament: A Narrative of Rebels and Romantics* (London: Victor Gollancz, 1938), 327–32.

25 Sidney and Beatrice Webb, *Soviet Communism: A New Civilisation?* (London: Longmans, Green and Co., 1935/6), v. 2, 1, 103. See also the *Worker*, 12 November 1932, 5, for the Webbs' report on returning from their first visit to the Soviet Union.

26 David Lewis and F.R. Scott, *Make This Your Canada: A Review of C.C.F. History and Policy* (Toronto: Central Canada Publishing Co., 1943), 24–5, 31, 84; E.H. Carr, *The Soviet Impact on the Western World* (London: Macmillan, 1946), vii.

27 Kotkin, *Magnetic Mountain*, 355, 358, 364.

5. 1931: Trial by Fire

1 Ewen to Victor Friedman (Winnipeg), 17 December 1930, OA, RG4, reel 1, 1-A-525.
2 Ewen to Alf Hautimaki (Port Arthur, secretary, Lumber Workers' Union), 3 December 1930, OA, RG4, reel 1, 1-A-0469.
3 Ewen to J. Barker (Sudbury), 24 December 1930, OA, RG4, reel 1, 1-A-0439.
4 4 Workers' Unity League, Bulletin No. 1, 9 December 1930, OA, RG4, reel 1, 1-A-0526.
5 Ewen to J. Barker (Sudbury), 25 November 1930, OA, RG4, reel 1, 1-A-0426.
6 Workers' Unity League of Canada, 'Monthly Letter June 1931,' OA, RG4, reel 7, 10-C-1783; 'Minutes of Southern Ontario Conference of WUL,' 24 May 1930, LAC, CPC Papers, MG28 IV4, v. 52, file 75.
7 Ewen (WUL) to industrial organizers of CP and YCL (Winnipeg), 12 December 1930, OA, RG4, reel 1, 1-A-0527–9.
8 'Build the Workers' Unity League,' *Worker*, 28 February 1931.
9 Ewen to V. Friedman (Winnipeg), 17 December 1930, OA, RG4, reel 1, 1-A-525; 'Police Protected Thugs Slugging Strike Pickets,' *Worker*, 20 December 1930.
10 G. Drayton (Vancouver) to Ewen, 27 March 1931, OA, RG4, reel 3, 4-A-2374; ibid., 4-A-2472, reel 2, 3-A-1809, 3-A-1741–3, 3-A-1786–8.
11 Ewen to G. Drayton, 18 April 1931, OA, RG4, reel 3, 4-A-23 87–8.
12 Ewen to A. Meronyk (Cranbrook, BC), 27 June 1931, OA, RG4, reel 3, 4-A-2472; Ewen to J.M. Baker (Burnaby, BC), 22 June 1931, OA, RG4, reel 3, 4-A-2455; Ewen, 'Reply to Discussion' at CPC Plenum, February 1931 (Toronto), OA, RG4, reel 5, 8-C-0505.
13 Ewen to Steve Forkin (Saskatoon), 2 April 1931, OA, RG4, reel 2, 3-A-1809; Judy Fudge and Eric Tucker, *Labour before the Law: The Regulation of Workers' Collective Action in Canada, 1900–1948* (Toronto: University of Toronto Press, 2001/4), 154, 164, 190.
14 Ewen to Ben Winter (Winnipeg), 17 March 1931, OA, RG4, reel 2, 3-A-1752.
15 Ibid., 30 March 1931, 3-A-1789.
16 Ibid., 17 March 1931, 3-A-1752.
17 Ibid., 7 May 1931, 3-A-1847.
18 See CPC Organization Department document, 'Face to the Shops,' 21 April 1931, which includes a detailed 14-page mimeographed pamphlet on the subject of 'The Work of Factory Nuclei' issued by the Comintern and mainly sharing recent experience in Germany, OA, RG4, reel 38, 29-L-0636.
19 Ewen to Ben Winter (Winnipeg), OA, RG4, reel 2, 3-A-1790.
20 Ewen to Jack Clarke (Saskatoon), 7 January 1931, OA, RG4, reel 1, 1-A-0531;

RCMP, 'Personal History File 175/P2459,' 1 April 1931, LAC, CSIS Records, RG146, public access box 17; 'Workers Savagely Beaten by Toronto Police Thugs, Tom Ewen Arrested at Election Meeting and Almost Killed by Murderous Assault at Station,' *Worker*, 3 January 1931.

21 See Workers' International Relief (Toronto), letter to the Convention of the Lumber Workers' Industrial Union, 30 April 1931, in LAC, CSIS Records, RG146, v. 2 of 'open records available for research,' access request 1025-9-9019.

22 *Manitoba Free Press*, 15 September 1931.

23 The Dominion Wheel and Foundry strike may be followed in the *Labour Gazette*, October 1931, 1068ff; the Department of Labour's strike file, LAC, RG27, v. 348, no. 71, T-2759; the *Worker*, 19, 26 September 1931, 16 December 1934; and the *Manitoba Free Press*, 14, 15, and 19 September 1931. John Manley, who recounts this strike in his PhD thesis, 'Communism and the Canadian Working Class during the Great Depression: The Workers' Unity League 1930–1936' (Dalhousie University, 1984), 178–81, suggests that the strikers had to use tactics forbidden by the WUL ('conciliation'), and be bold enough 'to manipulate official guidelines' in order to win; given the high level of 'struggle' in the strike, this is a narrow reading of 'revolutionary strike strategy' as advocated by the Strassburg Resolution, a strategy that never ruled out negotiation or seeking third-party help in collective bargaining.

24 A. Rosenberg (Montreal) to Tim Buck, 7 March 1931; Buck to Rosenberg, 10 March 1931, OA, RG4, reel 1, 2-A-0899–0902, 2-A-0903–4.

25 Ewen to A. Rosenberg, 19 March 1931, Ewen to Jeanne Harvey [Corbin], 20 March 1931, OA, RG4, reel 1, 2-A-0908, 2-A-0912.

26 Fred Rose, 'Report of Cowansville Strike', n.d., OA, RG4, reel 1, 2-A-0922–6. Part of this report is printed in Irving Abella and David Millar, eds., *The Canadian Worker in the 20th Century* (Toronto: Oxford University Press, 1978), 260–4.

27 'Textiles: Statement of the National Fraction of the WUL on the Cowansville (P.Q.) Strike Based on the Report of Comrade F. Rose.' 1 April 1931, OA, RG4, reel 7, 10-C-2057–8. Historian Andrée Lévesque discusses the dilemmas of Rose in face of Ewen's intransigence and concludes that the Cowansville strike illustrates the difficulty, if not the futility, of applying an international doctrine such as communism in a local setting that is far away from the centres of decision. See 'Le Québec et le monde communiste: Cowansville 1931,' *Revue d'histoire de l'Amerique française* 34.2 (September 1980), 171–82.

28 These records include two thousand pages of a Royal Commission investigation, six hundred pages of secret police records, transcripts of the trials of

those arrested, especially the self-defence of Annie Buller, records of the
Communist Party in Library and Archives Canada, local newspaper accounts
and oral interviews with participants stored at the Saskatchewan Archives
Board. See Stephen L. Endicott, *Bienfait: The Saskatchewan Miners' Struggle of
'31* (Toronto: University of Toronto Press, 2002). This discussion, all direct
quotations, and other sources on the Bienfait strike are found in the book
and in Stephen Endicott, 'Bienfait: Origins and Legacy of the Coal Miners'
Strike of 1931,' *Prairie Forum* 31.2 (Fall 2006), 217–32.

29 Endicott, *Bienfait*, 137–8.

30 Garnet Dishaw, 'Trade Union Heroes,' *Our Times*, December 2002, 42–3;
according to a UMWA 'Memorandum re Formation of the Mine Workers
Union of Canada' n.d. circa 1932, 7–8, located in RCMP files, the history
of MWUC efforts was 'one of failure, disruption and dissension in the coal
mining fields of the West,' and 'of treachery' against the workers in the
Estevan coal field in 1931, LAC, CSIS Records, RG146, access request 92-A-
00056 [original file 175/6261] part 1, International Union of Mine Mills
and Smelter Workers' Union of Canada, Correspondence 1926–36, vol. 1.

31 See *Workers' Unity League: – Policy – Tactics – Structure – Demands* (Toronto,
circa June 1932), 31–5 for a contemporary Canadian exposition of the
meaning of the 'united front from below.'

32 Smith's autobiography is *All My Life* (Toronto: Progress Books, 1949). For
examples of workers' self-defence see pamphlets *Workers' Self-Defence in the
Courts* and *The Frame-up of Allan Campbell* (Toronto: National Executive Committee, CLDL, n.d.). See also J. Petryshyn, 'Class Conflict and Civil Liberties: The Origins and Activities of the Canadian Labour Defense League,
1923–1940,' *Labour/Le Travailleur* 10 (Autumn 1982), 39–63.

33 See Endicott, *Bienfait*, 111–13.

34 Al Parkin, 'Labor and Timber: A Brief History of Trade Unionism in British
Columbia's Lumber Industry,' chapter 11, in *The B.C. Lumber Worker*, 10
February 1947.

35 Jeanne Meyers, 'Class and Community in the Fraser Mills Strike, 1931,' in
Rennie Warburton and David Coburn, eds., *Workers, Capital, and the State in
British Columbia* (Vancouver: University of British Columbia Press, 1988),
chapter 8, 141–60.

36 Ibid., 145.

37 'Fraser Mills Strike Committee Log Book,' entry for Sunday 4 October,
UBC Special Collections, Harold Pritchett–IWA Papers, box 10, files 11, 12;
George Drayton, 'Some Lessons in Strike Strategy from the Coast,' *Worker*, 3
October 1931.

38 Meyers, 'Class and Community in the Fraser Mills Strike, 1931,' 146–8. By

1931 the average wage (median) was $615.00, compared to $959.37 in 1930 and $1,085.00 in 1929.

39 Ibid., 151.

40 'Lumberworkers: What Is This Union?', leaflet issued by the Lumber and Agricultural Workers' Industrial Union of Canada, BC District, in UBC Special Collections, Pritchett–IWA Papers, box 10, files 11, 12.

41 J.H. McMullin (commissioner, BC Police) to Premier S.F. Tolmie (Victoria), 5 October 1931, UBC Special Collections, Tolmie Papers, box 9, file 41.

42 On one occasion a group of Japanese farm workers donated 15 tons of vegetables; Fraser Mills Strike Committee Log Book, Sunday, 11 October.

43 Meyers, 'Class and Community in the Fraser Mills Strike, 1931,' 151; F.E. Harrison to H.H. Ward (deputy minister of labour, Ottawa), 7 October 1931, LAC, Department of Labour, RG27, v. 348, file 72 (Strikes and Lockouts).

44 Strike Committee Log Book, entry of Tuesday, 17 November. In a secret poll 466 mill workers voted, 406 yes, 55 no, and 5 spoiled ballots.

45 *Worker*, 21 November 1931.

46 *Canada Year Book 1934–1935*, 836; James Struthers, *No Fault of Their Own: Unemployment and the Canadian Welfare State 1914–1941* (Toronto: University of Toronto Press, 1983), 55.

47 *Canadian Annual Review of Public Affairs* (Toronto, 1932), 399, 652.

48 Quoted in John Herd Thompson and Allen Seager, *Canada 1922–1939: Decades of Discord* (Toronto: McClelland and Stewart, 1985), 213.

49 Struthers, *No Fault of Their Own*, 3–5, 48.

50 Ibid., 10. See H.M. Cassidy, 'Unemployment Insurance for Canada' (1931), in the papers of the prime minister, for a detailed academic discussion on how an unemployment insurance system could work in Canada, LAC, R.B. Bennett Papers, reel M-1460, 502239ff.

51 R.H. Pooley to R. Stewart (Victoria, BC) 11 April 1931, OA, RG4, reel 3, 4-A-2469.

52 Struthers, *No Fault of Their Own*, 9.

53 N.A. McKenzie, chairman of the Committee of the Executive Council on Unemployment Relief, Ministry of Public Works, Victoria, BC, to Senator G.D. Robertson, minister of labour, Ottawa, 24 November 1931, LAC, RG27, v. 2041, BC file X1-8.

54 Struthers, *No Fault of Their Own*, 46, 54, 52.

55 Claiming that the Russians had an unfair trade advantage by using 'forced labour' and state-monopoly trading organizations, Bennett rejected an offer of the Soviet Union's trade agent in Canada, Lt.-Col. Herbert J. Mackie, former Conservative MP for North Renfrew, (ret), to swap $10 million

worth of Canadian agricultural machinery for one-third anthracite coal and two-thirds payments in gold, a favourable proposition for Canada. Instead, backed by the intervention of Sir Herbert Holt, president of the Royal Bank of Canada, and others, Bennett placed an embargo on imports from the USSR in February 1931, *Canadian Annual Review 1930–1931*, 518; 'Bear and Beaver,' *Canadian Unionist* 4.10 (March 1931).

56 'Draft Constitution of the Workers' Unity League,' OA, RG4, reel 7, 10-C-1804; 'W.U.L. Calls upon Provinces to Rally Unemployed for a National Association,' *Worker*, 31 May 1930; Minutes of the Executive Committee, Workers' Unity League, 21 June 1930, OA, RG4, reel 7, 10-C-1815; 'Minutes of Workers' Unity League Conference of Southern Ontario,' 24 May 1930, LAC, CPC Papers, MG28 IV4, v. 52, file 75.

57 Ewen to J. Millar (Montreal), 20 December 1930, OA, RG4, reel 1, 1-A-0246; Leslie Morris, 'The Unemployment Crisis and Our Party,' *Worker*, 19 April 1930.

58 Plans for this campaign were formulated by Ewen and discussed in the Political Bureau of the Communist Party of Canada on 10 January 1931. See 'Minutes of Political Bureau CPC,' LAC, CI Fonds 495, list 98, file 117, reel 13, K-281.

59 Buck to Smith (Moscow), 15 January 1931, CPC Papers, LAC, MG28 IV4, v. 8, file 7; 'Summary Report on International Day against Unemployment in Canada, (February 25th),' n.a. [Sam Carr, Central Organization Department, CPC], OA, RG4, reel 6, 9-C-0805.

60 'The Next Step – A Trade Union Press,' WUL Bulletin, n.d., LAC, CI Fonds 495, list 98, file 129, reel 14, K-282. The first issue of the paper appeared 15 July 1931.

61 Cohen Papers, LAC, MG30A94, v. 1, file 5.

62 'Ewen's Reply to Discussion,' CPC Plenum, 7 February 1931. In contrast to the police, Ewen believed the militia 'could be appealed to' and worked with through contacts to support the workers' cause, OA, RG4, reel 5, 8-C-0497, 8-C-0498. 'Resolutions of Enlarged Plenum of Communist Party of Canada,' February 1931, pamphlet, 30 pages, LAC, CPC Papers, MG28 IV4, v. 11, file 35.

63 The leaders of these unemployed delegations were Thomas A. Ewen (1931), James Litterick (1932), Hans Sula and Alderman Reginald Morris (1933), Sula and Alderman Thomas Raycroft (1934), Workers' Congress on Unemployment and Social Insurance, Ottawa (17 February 1935), Arthur Evans (July 1935).

64 T.A. Ewen to Prime Minister R.B. Bennett, 15 April 1931, LAC, Bennett Papers, reel M-1459, 501983–5. The WUL petition proposed a minimum weekly wage of $25, equal to the average of a skilled worker in 1931. Later,

more realistically, this demand was changed to that of an unskilled worker, $14 weekly for a family of two plus $2.50 for each dependent; not less than $8.00 weekly for single unemployed above the age of sixteen. See 1931 Petition in Bennett Papers, reel M-1459, 501937; M.C. Urquhart, ed., *Historical Statistics of Canada* (Toronto: Macmillan, 1965), 96; WUL 'Educational Leaflet No. 2, Unemployment Insurance,' n.d. circa February 1935, UBC Special Collections, Pritchett–IWA Papers, box 11, files 25, 27. See also table 5.1.

Table 5.1 Canadian male average annual earnings, weeks employed, and weekly salary by occupation groups, 1931

	Labourers			Clerical		
	Non-primary	Semi-skilled	Skilled	Commercial and financial	Professional	Managerial
Average annual earnings (dollars)	480.00	791.00	1,042.00	1,192.00	1,924.00	2,468.00
Average weeks employed	32.5	38.5	40.1	47.2	48.7	50.1
Average weekly earnings (dollars)	14.74	20.52	25.96	25.21	39.48	40.22

Source: Census of Canada, 1931, adapted from M.C. Urquhart, ed., Historical Statistics of Canada (Toronto: Macmillan, 1965), 96.

65 'Personal History File: Thomas A. Ewen,' 1 April 1931, LAC, CSIS Records, RG146, public access box 17, file 175/P2459, also LAC, Bennett Papers, reel M-989, 94306–7. The RCMP supplied the prime minister with lists and descriptions of thousands of Canadian communists – their addresses, activities, places of employment, immigration and citizenship status, and criminal records, if any. There were 760 names from Winnipeg alone, LAC, Bennett Papers, file C-650/1932, reel M-988, 92975–93008.

66 Workers' Unity League, 'Bulletin #9,' 28 April 1931, OA, RG4, reel 7, 10-C-1763–8, also in LAC, CI Fonds 495, list 98, file 129, reel 14, K-282; A.E. Smith, *All My Life* (Toronto: Progress Books, 1949), 119–20; Montreal *Gazette*, 17 April 1931.

67 Lorne Brown, 'Unemployed Struggles in Saskatchewan and Canada, 1930–1935,' *Prairie Forum* 31.2 (Fall 2006), 201–2; Workers' Unity League, 'Bulletin #9,' OA, RG4, reel 7, 10-C-1763, 'Addendum to Report of February 25, 1931,' ibid., reel 6, 9-C-0788; 'Workers Pour into Streets April 15,' *Worker*, 18, 25 April 1931.

68 Kassian (Vegreville, Alberta) telegram to the *Worker*, 26 February 1931, OA, RG4, reel 2, 3-A-2043–4.

69 A. Newman to 'Dear Boys!' (Toronto), 1 March 1931, OA, RG4, reel 2, 2-A-1444–50.

70 Mayor David Croll (Windsor), to Hon. R.B. Bennett, 15 April 1931; Charles F. Roland, managing secretary, the Employers' Association of Manitoba, to Hon. Hugh Guthrie, minister of justice (Ottawa), 14 April 1931, LAC, Bennett Papers, reel M-1459, 501989, reel M-989, 94524–5.

71 Brown, 'Unemployed Struggles in Saskatchewan and Canada, 1930–1935,' 203.

72 Lita-Rose Betcherman, *The Little Band: The Clashes between the Communists and the Canadian Establishment 1928–1932* (Ottawa: Deneau, 1982), 167.

73 A.E. Smith (Canadian Labour Defense League) to International Labour Defense (New York City), 4 July 1931, OA RG4, reel 3, 4-A-2871; Fudge and Tucker, *Labour before the Law*, 156–7; Stewart Smith to Anglo-American Secretariat of the Comintern, 27 January 1932, LAC, CI Fonds 495, list 98, file 140, reel 16, K-284.

74 Quoted by Betcherman, *The Little Band*, 171.

75 Prime Minister R.B. Bennett, 29 July 1931, Hansard, 4278.

76 W.H. Price, 'Communism in Canada,' introduction to 'The King vs. Buck and Others: The Judgement of the Court of Appeal of Ontario concerning the Communist Party in Canada' (Toronto: Attorney General for Ontario, n.d. [1932]), 2, in LAC, CSIS Records, RG146, v. 907 [box 64, 96-A-0911, pt. 3].

77 F.R. Scott, 'The Trial of the Toronto Communists,' *Queen's Quarterly* 39 (August 1932), 512–13. See also Betcherman, *The Little Band*, 183–286; Fudge and Tucker, *Labour before the Law*, 157; Tim Buck, *Yours in the Struggle* (Toronto: NC Press, 1977), 168–89.

78 Thompson and Seager, *Canada 1922–1939*, 227.

79 For this case see Oscar Ryan, *Deported!* (Toronto: Canadian Labour Defense League, 1932), pamphlet; Barbara Roberts, 'Shovelling Out the "Mutinous": Political Deportation from Canada before 1936,' *Labour/LeTravail* 18 (Fall 1986), 77–110; A.L. Jolliffe, commissioner of immigration and colonization, 'Memorandum: Deportation of Members of the Communist Party,' 1 December 1931, LAC, CSIS Records, RG146, box 60, file/access request 96-A-00110, pt. 1.

80 Scott, 'The Trial of the Toronto Communists,' 527.

81 Betcherman, *The Little Band*, 206; Harvey Murphy, 'Judge Ousley's Outlawing of W.U.L. and Mine Union,' *Worker*, 12 December 1931; 'Protest against Judge Ousley's Illegal Statement!' *Canadian Miner*, 12 December 1931; 'Legal Opinion Denies Judge Ousley's Ruling,' *Worker*, 9 January 1932.

6. Red Blairmore

1 Glenbow Archives, West Canadian Collieries (WCC) Papers, file 102, cor-

respondence 1925–35, G.A. Vissac on 'General Situation in the Country,' 12 January 1932.

2 Glenbow Archives, WCC Papers, file 102, February 1934.

3 Quoted by C.F. Steele, 'That Town of Blairmore,' *Toronto Star Weekly*, 18 May 1935.

4 Quotation is from page 23 of an unidentified, undated transcript of an interview with Harvey Murphy loaned to me by his son, Rae Murphy, January 1993. Murphy's detractors liked to portray him more as a 'belligerent, often inebriated, rabble-rouser,' wrapped up in 'authoritarian arrogance,' Peter McInnis, 'Big Lives,' *Labour/LeTravail* 45 (Spring 2000), 276; Mercedes Steedman, Peter Suschnigg, and Dieter K. Buse, eds., *Hard Lessons: The Mine Mill Union in the Canadian Labour Movement* (Toronto: Dundurn Press, 1995), 45.

5 R.G. Dun, *The Mercantile Agency Reference Book, 1929* (Toronto: Hunter Rose, 1929); Norman Knowles, '"A Manly, Commonsense Religion": Revivalism and the 1909 Kootenay Campaign in the Crowsnest Pass,' in Wayne Norton and Tom Langford, eds., *A World Apart: The Crowsnest Communities of Alberta and British Columbia* (Kamloops: Plateau Press, 2002), 3–4.

6 Glenbow Archives, WCC Papers, file 102, correspondence 1925–35, G.A Vissac, on 'General Situation in the Country,' 31 July 1930.

7 Ibid., 22 May 1930, 12 January 1932.

8 Ibid., 31 July 1930.

9 Ibid., 12 January 1932.

10 Dominion Bureau of Statistics, *Coal Statistics for Canada, 1931–1933*, tables 26, 29; *Coal Statistics, 1935*, graph, 'Canadian Coal Moved under Assisted Rates 1928–1935'; Glenbow Archives, WCC Papers, file 102, 31 July 1930.

11 Glenbow Archives, WCC Papers, file 102, Vissac letters of 25 June 1930, and to minister of mines, W.A. Gordon, February 1934; file 101, 11 January 1932.

12 Ibid., file 102, 12 January 1932.

13 Ibid., file 101, 10 March 1932.

14 M.C. Urquhart, ed., *Historical Statistics of Canada* (Toronto: Macmillan, 1965), Series D232–237, 96.

15 *Canadian Miner*, 31 December 1931; Dominion Bureau of Statistics, *Coal Statistics* for 1930 and 1931, table 124. Glenbow Archives, WCC Papers, file 102, 'Labour Situation,' 12 January 1932.

16 *Report of the Department of Labour for the Fiscal Year Ending March 31, 1931* (Ottawa: King's Printer, 1932), 190, gives the MWUC's membership as 4,380; also see *Labour Organizations in Canada, 1931*, 175.

17 *Western Miner*, 8 September 1930, 4; *Constitution, the Mine Workers' Union of Canada*, as amended September 1931, art. 15, see LAC, CI Fonds, 495, list

98, file 129, reel 14, K-282; Ewen to Malcolm Bruce, 12 May 1931, OA, RG4, reel 2, 3-A-2155.

18 Ibid.; *Constitution, the Mine Workers' Union of Canada*, art. 32, 34.

19 Ibid., art. 28.

20 'Officers Report to Seventh Annual Convention of the Mine Workers' Union of Canada,' 12 September 1932, 3, LAC, CI Fonds 495, list 98, file 145, reel 17, K-285. Mine operators also opposed the 'equal division of work' as it afforded the unions an opportunity, in their view, to intrude into the managers' right to manage. See Glenbow Archives, WCC Papers, file 101, 'Labour Situation,' 27 February 1932.

21 Ibid.; *Constitution, the Mine Workers' Union of Canada*, art. 24. For discussion on the 'equal division of work' and 'stagger system,' see CPC Plenum, February 1931, OA, RG4, CPC Records, reel 5, 8-C-0294–5, 8-C-0298–0300; Malcolm Bruce (Calgary) to Ewen, 2 May 31, OA, RG4, reel 2, 3-A-2139–42, Ewen to Bruce (Calgary), 12 May 1931, 3-A-2154; LAC, CI Fonds 495, list 98, file 117, reel 13, K-281, 'Pol-Bureau Minutes,' 8–9 May 1931; Winters (Winnipeg) to Ewen, 3 June 1931, OA, RG4, reel 2, 3-A-1887–91, Ewen to Winters, 3-A-1892–3.

22 *Canadian Miner*, 12 October 1931; Ewen, draft of WUL letter to MWUC Convention, CPC 'Pol-Bureau minutes,' 24 August 1931, LAC, CI Fonds 495, list 98, file 117, reel 13, K-281.

23 See the *Canadian Miner*, 30 January 1932 and subsequent six issues to 21 April 1932.

24 Ibid., 12 March 1932; Glenbow Archives, WCC Papers, file 101, 'Labour Situation,' 25 February 1932.

25 Glenbow Archives, WCC Papers, file 101, 'Labour Situation,' 27 February 1932; E. Humphrys, general fuel agent, CPR, to J.R. Smith, West Canadian Collieries, Blairmore; ibid., file 101, 4 March, 22 March 1932; LAC, RG 27, Department of Labour, v. 350, file 22, Strike T-2761, 'Memo,' n.d. [26 February 1932].

26 LAC, CI Fonds 495, list 98, file 145, reel 17, K-285, has a document without title, or author, or date but received at the Anglo-American Secretariat of the Comintern on 26 June 1932 giving a cool analysis of the Crowsnest Pass strike and clearly the product of a leading person or committee in 'the centre' in Toronto. After the Communist Party was officially declared illegal in Ontario, following the conviction of the eight leaders, the communist organizations there were more careful about giving names or other identities to their communications.

27 'Some Lessons of the Crows Nest Pass Strike,' *Canadian Miner*, 21 April 1932.

28 'What We Are Striking For,' leaflet issued by the Strike Committee, Crow's Nest Pass, 18 April 1932, in Glenbow Archives, WCC Papers, file 101.

29 Rolf Knight, 'Harvey Murphy – An Unfinished Biography,' 33, manuscript in UBC Special Collections, Rolf Knight Papers.

30 *Canadian Miner*, 21 April 1932; Knight, 'Harvey Murphy – An Unfinished Biography'; for a later report see the *Worker*, 7 May 1932

31 LAC, CSIS Records, RG146, v. 1191, file 175/p2972, Const. E.B. Davis (Coalhurst detachment), 18 May 1932.

32 LAC, R.B. Bennett Papers, reel M-989, nos. 94840–1, 94846–51.

33 Glenbow Archives, WCC Papers, file 101, 'Citizens League Hears Stirring Pleas, Blairmore,' 15 June 1932.

34 LAC, Bennett Papers, reel M-989, no. 94539 ff., J.R. Smith, business superintendent, West Canadian Collieries, Blairmore, to Prime Minister R.B. Bennett, 24 June 1932, Bennett's reply 28 June 1932, and several other exchanges of correspondence in the file.

35 One occasion many years later, when Murphy and I were among the May Day speakers at Lumberman's Arch in Vancouver's Stanley Park, he gave me some advice on how to make an effective speech. Nervous before a crowd of 5,000 and newly graduated from the department of history at the University of Toronto where I had learned that an effective speech included a beginning, a middle, and an end, I held a small note in my hand to help keep track. When the rally was over Murphy put his arm around my shoulder. 'That was a good speech, son,' he said, 'but next time throw away that bit of paper; with that in your hand workers will never believe that you are convinced of what you are saying.' It was good advice, I thought, provided you didn't need structure, and had the personality to put it over.

36 UBC Special Collections, VF #298.

37 The main RCMP file of correspondence on the day-to-day happenings and police analysis of the Crowsnest Pass strike, file no. 175/7177, has apparently been destroyed. According to Doug Luchak, a retired Canadian Security Intelligence Service [RCMP] officer attached temporarily to the National Archives of Canada in the 1990s, this destruction took place during a 'general housekeeping' in 1963–4. Luchak told me that only a few files of strikes and radical demonstrations in the 1930s were retained. They are generally called 'Historically Valuable' (HV) files, such as the invaluable one on the Bienfait/Estevan miners' strike in 1931, LAC, CSIS Records, RG146, v. 817, file HV7, parts 1 to 6. On the other hand, many of the 'personal history files' on communist and other radical leaders are still retained and may be accessed twenty years after the person is deceased. Murphy's file is no. 175/p2972 in v. 1191 of RG146.

38 LAC, CSIS Records, RG146, v. 1191, file 175/p2972, 'Report,' 4 April 1932; *Edmonton Journal*, 24 March 1932 for reference to 'uniformed thugs'; CSIS

Reading Room, Personal History file 175/p962, Malcolm Bruce, 12 October 1934 for reference to Halsbury.

39 LAC, CSIS Records, RG146, v. 1191, file 175/p2972, 25 January, 3 April 1932.

40 Ibid., 22 February, 6, 18 May 1932.

41 Ibid., 6, 18, 22 May, 3 April 1932.

42 Murphy's words quoted here are a composite from the reports of Constable F.B. Bailey (2 May 1932) and Sergeant J.T. Jones (3 May 1932) in LAC, CSIS Records, RG146, v. 1191, file 175/p2972.

43 Ibid., 8, 10 May 1932.

44 Ibid., 3 February, 25 July 1932, 22 April 1930, 25 January 1932, 27 February 1933.

45 *Worker*, 7 May 1932.

46 Glenbow Archives, WCC Papers, file 101, 'Labour Situation,' 17 May 1932; LAC, CSIS Records, RG146, v. 1191, file 175/p2972, 4 May 1932.

47 Glenbow Archives, WCC Papers, file 101, 'Labour Situation,' 17 May, 15 July 1932.

48 Murphy, 'Some Lessons of the Crows Nest Pass Strike,' letter to the editor, 13 April, printed in the *Canadian Miner*, 21 April 1932.

49 *Lethbridge Herald*, 14 April 1932, 'Coleman Radicals Win Mine Vote.'

50 *Edmonton Journal*, 16 May 1932; *Worker*, 21 May 1932.

51 *Lethbridge Herald*, 21 May 1932; *Vancouver Province, Edmonton Bulletin*, 18 May 1932. Vissac, commenting on the events at Coleman, wrote: 'Coleman has returned to work by surprise thanks to a group of enterprising British, who had the courage to create an active opposition; a new union was created and by artificial methods had succeeded by surprise in taking control.' Glenbow Archives, WCC Papers, file 101, 'Labour Situation,' 1 June 1932.

52 Allan Seager, 'The Pass Strike of 1932,' *Alberta History* 25.1 (Winter 1977), 6.

53 Glenbow Archives, WCC Papers, file 101, 'Labour Situation,' 24 June, n.d. July.

54 *Worker*, 11 June 1932.

55 Glenbow Archives, WCC Papers, file 101, G.A. Vissac, general manager, WCC, to Hon. J.E. Brownlee, premier of Alberta, 12 July 1932; Brownlee to Vissac, 15 July 1932. When the strike committee met Vissac in June to seek a settlement, he had offered to reduce his blacklist to fifty men, but the strikers rejected this as a concession, ibid., 'Labour Situation,' 24 June 1932.

56 *Lethbridge Herald*, 18 July 1932.

57 LAC, RG27, v. 350, no. 22, T-2761, 'Agreement,' 5 September 1932; Calgary *Albertan*, 22 August 1932; *Worker*, 10 September 1932; Glenbow Archives, WCC Papers, file 101, G.A. Vissac to Honourable J.E. Brownlee, 19 August 1932.

58 J. Krkosky, Jr, 'Diehard Coal Barons More Human Than UFA,' *Worker*, 5 November 1932.

59 'Pass Workers Hold Meeting; File Demands,' *Lethbridge Herald*, 4 October 1932; article by J. Krkosky Jr, secretary of the Blairmore local, MWUC, *Worker*, 5 November 1932.

60 Glenbow Archives, WCC Archives, file 101, 'Labour Situation,' 25 August 1932.

61 Ibid.

62 LAC, CSIS Records, RG146, v. 1191, file 175/p2972 (personal history file on Murphy), 'Report on Preliminary Hearing,' Blairmore, 27 May 1932, submitted by Sergt. J.T. Jones, copy forwarded to the commissioner.

63 See Stephen Endicott, *Bienfait: The Saskatchewan Miners' Struggle of '31* (Toronto: University of Toronto Press, 2002), 119–20.

64 The documents where this debate may be followed include a mildly worded two-page analysis with no title or author that was received at the Anglo-American Secretariat of the CI on 26 June (LAC, CI Fonds 495, list 98, file 145, reel 17, K-285), a didactic five-page letter of the Political Bureau (undoubtedly by Smith) to the Alberta district of the party dated 26 August 1932 (LAC, CI Fonds 495, list 98, file 140, reel 16, K-284), and an uncomfortable, self-critical article, 'The Party's Policy in the Mining Industry and Our Mistakes and Tasks in the Alberta Coalfields' (undoubtedly by Murphy), in *Communist Review* no 4 (July–August 1934) in LAC, CPC Papers, MG28 IV4, v. 78, file 11. Working under conditions of illegality, identities are omitted in many documents but can be recognized by other references and in some cases by the style of writing and argument, especially in the case of Smith.

65 CPC Political Bureau to the Alberta district of the party dated 26 August 1932, LAC, CI Fonds 495, list 98, file 140, reel 16, K-284.

66 A memorandum written from the point of view of the United Mine Workers of America in 1932 states that as a result of 'the many childish efforts' of the Mine Workers' Union of Canada, 'working conditions have been lost and a state of chaos prevails.' The history of their 'treachery' was said to be 'one of failure, disruption and dissension,' LAC, CSIS Records, RG146, access request 92-A-00056, part 1, file 175/6261, International Union of Mine, Mill and Smelter Workers – Canada, Correspondence to 7 - 12 - 36, 'Memorandum. Re formation of the Mine Workers Union of Canada,' n.a., n.d., 7.

67 LAC, CI Fonds 495, list 98, file 145, reel 17, K-285, 'Report of the Seventh Annual Convention of the Mine Workers' Union of Canada Held in the Oddfellows Hall, Calgary, September 12th to 16th, 1932,' 10.

68 Ibid., 'Officers' Report,' 1.

69 Allen Seager, 'A History of the Mine Workers' Union of Canada 1925–1936' (MA thesis, Department of History, McGill University, 1978), 168.
70 Glenbow Archives, WCC Papers, file 101, 'Situation Ouvrière,' 30 May 1934, 13 February 1933; 'Agreement,' 2 April 1934.
71 Ibid., le président to Vissac, 13 June 1932, 29 August 1933.
72 'Blairmore – A Union Camp,' by J.W. (probably John Weir), *Worker*, 3 June 1933; Seager, 'A History of the Mine Workers' Union of Canada 1925–1936,' 166–8.
73 LAC, CSIS Records, RG146, v. 3616, RCMP file 175/6805 (Communist Party, Blairmore), box 81, access request 96-A-00189, pt. 5, 24 March 1935.
74 C.F. Steele, 'That Town of Blairmore,' *Toronto Star Weekly*, 18 May 1935.
75 See David Frank, 'Company Town/Labour Town: Local Government in the Cape Breton Coal Towns, 1917–1926,' in D. Bercuson, ed., *Canadian Labour History* (Toronto: Copp-Clark Pitman, 1987), 138–55, for other experiences of coal miner town councils in Canada.

7. August 1932: Confronting the Prime Minister

1 *Canadian Annual Review of Public Affairs 1932* (Toronto), 320–1.
2 Ibid., 322.
3 Ian Drummond, 'Empire Trade and Russian Trade: Economic Diplomacy in the Nineteen-Thirties,' *Canadian Journal of Economics* 5 (February 1972), 36, 39, 41. See also Sir Curtis Keeble, *Britain, the Soviet Union and Russia* (London: Macmillan, 2000), 114–19 for discussion of Anglo-Soviet relations in 1932–3.
4 'Britain Drafting Restrictions on Soviet Trade – Point Insisted on by Premier in Discussions,' *Evening Citizen* (Ottawa), 3 August 1932.
5 *Canadian Annual Review of Public Affairs 1932*, 324.
6 'Against Terror and Persecution!' National Executive Committee, CLDL, n.d. circa June 1932, University of Toronto Fisher Rare Book Library, Robert S. Kenny Collection, box 39, file 18; 'Class Terror in Canada, 1932' (CLDL), LAC, CSIS Records, RG146, v. 826, HV35; *Worker*, 18 June 1932; 'Report, Ukrainian Fraction Bureau of CPC,' 27 June 32, 5, LAC, CI Fonds 495, list 98, file 142, reel 16, K-284; 'CLDL Press Release,' *Worker*, 2 January 1932; S. Smith (Toronto) to Dear Friends [Anglo-American Secretariat, CI], 27 January 1932, LAC, CI Fonds 495, list 98, file 140, reel 16, K-284.
7 *Manitoba Free Press*, 14 May 1932.
8 K. Finn, 'On the Situation in Canada,' May 1932, LAC, CI Fonds 495, list 98, file 142, reel 16, K-284.
9 'Report on Canadian Question,' 2 July 1932, LAC, CI Fonds 495, list 72, file

176, reel 1, K-269; 'Meeting on Canada,' Anglo-American Secretariat, 23 July 1932, LAC, CI Fonds 495, list 72, file 190, reel 2, K-270.

10 LAC, CI Fonds 495, list 98, file 140, reel 16, K-284, 'Dear Friends' [S. Smith (Toronto) to Anglo-American Secretariat of the CI], 27 January 1932, 11.

11 LAC, CI Fonds 495, list 98, file 138, reel 16, K-284 contains such papers as 'The W.U.L. of Canada' and 'Strikes in Canada – 1931–1932,' both by C. Watt; 'Work amongst Women,' by [Ann] Walters; 'The Economic Situation in Agriculture and the Condition of the Poor Farmers in Canada,' by 'Carnegie.' File 136, reel 15, K-283 has a series of substantial papers on the problems and tactics of working in conditions of illegality.

12 LAC, CI Fonds 495, list 98, file 135, reel 15, K-283, 'Norman' to CP Canada, Secretariat, 31 July 1932.

13 'The First W.U.L. Congress and Its Tasks in Canada,' *International Press Correspondence* 12.32 (21 July 1932), 670–2. This article, attributed to 'J. Gray (Toronto),' was based on periodic reports from Stewart Smith, acting general secretary of the CPC, to the CI Anglo-American Secretariat, i.e. 27 January, 22 February, and 26 June 1932 in LAC, CI Fonds 495, list 98, file 140, reel 16, K-284.

14 This committee was formed after a delegation from a Hunger March and National Unemployed Conference in Ottawa, attended by 220 participants and reportedly backed by 'an enormous crowd of more than 10,000 Ottawa workers,' interviewed Prime Minister Bennett in the Railway Committee Room of the House of Commons on 3 March 1932. James Litterick, national secretary of the Workers' Unity League, presented the demands to Bennett. 'Hunger March Delegation in Ottawa,' *Worker*, 12 March 1932, and 'National Unemployment Day Set for March 3rd,' *Worker*, 16 January 1932.

15 'Workers' Economic Conference August 1st,' LAC, CSIS Records, RG146, v. 826, HV31, v. 2; *Workers' Unity* no. 10 (June 1932); G. Winslade, 'W.E.C. Initiates Fighting Campaign,' *Workers' Unity* no. 12 (August–September 1932); 'History of the Conference,' 'Workers Must Take Up and Answer the Arrogant Reply of Bennett,' 'Jim McLachlan Beards Bennett the Millionaire,' 'The Representation at the Conference,' which claims 214,000 are represented, *Ottawa Journal*, 2 August 1932, *Toronto Star* and *Mail and Empire*, 3 August 1932, *Worker*, 6 August 1932; 'WEC Closes, but Real Work Begins,' 'Make This Program of Action Be Your Guide in Struggle!,' *Worker*, 13 August 1932.

16 LAC, CI Fonds 495, list 98, file 145, reel 17, K-285, 'Resolution on Future Tasks Unemployed Councils,' n.d., received in Moscow 15 November 1932, 'Manifesto: Toilers of Canada! Workers and Small Farmers!', n.d.

17 *Worker*, 28 May, 18 June, 25 June, and 9 July 1932; *Workers' Unity* no. 10 (June 1932), 4.

18 *Evening Citizen* (Ottawa), 27 July 1932.

19 LAC, CSIS Records, RG146, v. 826, HV31, v.1, encl. in Supt. J.W. Spalding to the commissioner, 16 July 1932.

20 LAC, CSIS Records, RG146, v. 826, HV31, v. 1, A.H. Cadieux (CPR) to Brig. Gen. E. de B. Panet, 8 July 1932, G.L. Jennings, director, criminal investigation, to G.A. Shea (CNR), 11 July 1932 (personal and secret). *Toronto Star*, 25 July 1932.

21 LAC, CSIS Records, RG146, v. 826, HV31, v. 1, 'Memorandum,' 11 July 1932.

22 *Unemployed Worker* 4.38 (9 July 1932), LAC, RG27, v. 358A, reel T-2969.

23 *Evening Telegram* (Toronto), 23 July 1932, said 'noticeable is the immediate increase in the number of women traveling in company of men for Ottawa on freight trains.'

24 *Toronto Star*, 26 July 1932.

25 Sergt. E.W. Greenley (Regina) to assistant commissioner, RCMP (Ottawa), LAC, CSIS Records, RG146, v. 826, HV31, v.2, 27 July 1932.

26 *Evening Telegram* (Toronto), 23 July 1932.

27 The hall of the Ukrainian Labour Farmer Temple Association on Arlington Avenue, located between one and two miles southwest of Parliament Hill.

28 J.W. Phillips (RCMP superintendent, Ottawa) to the commissioner, 26, 23 July 1932, LAC, CSIS Records, RG146, v. 826, HV31, v. 2.

29 'Communist Demonstration in Ottawa Well in Hand,' *Mail and Empire* editorial, 1 August 1932.

30 *Evening Citizen* (Ottawa), 25 July 1932.

31 *Ottawa Journal*, 2 August 1932.

32 *Toronto Star*, 3 August 1932.

33 *Mail and Empire*, 31 July 1932.

34 'Report' of undercover agent, enclosed in T. Dann, superintendent 'C' Division (Montreal), to the commissioner, 2 August 1932, LAC, CSIS Records, RG146, v. 826, HV31, v. 3.

35 *Worker*, 6 August 1932.

36 Ibid.

37 *Toronto Star*, 3 August 1932.

38 The dialogue of the interview with Bennett is reconstructed from the reports of the *Toronto Star, Ottawa Journal, Evening Citizen* (Ottawa), *Mail and Empire*, and *Worker*, of 2, 3, and 6 August, 1932.

39 Through his intelligence service, Bennett probably already knew that on the request of the fledgling Indian Communist Party and the invitation of the Third International in 1931, the Canadian party had sent one of its best

organizers, William (Ol' Bill) Bennett, of Vancouver, on a two-year assignment to Bombay to help with Marxist training and union organization.
See Tom McEwen, *He Wrote for Us* (Vancouver: Tribune Publishing, 1951),
77–81.

40 *Mail and Empire,* 3 August 1932.

41 Ian Drummond says that Bennett may have thought 'dumping' was a real
problem, but if so he and his advisors had got their information crucially
wrong: 'In fact, the Soviet Government did not fix prices: Soviet timber sold
in Britain under a "fall and rise clause," by which, if market prices differed
from contract prices, the USSR would receive the former instead of the latter.' 'Empire Trade and Russian Trade,' 38.

42 David Frank, *J.B. McLachlan: A Biography* (Toronto: James Lorimer, 1999),
462.

43 LAC, CSIS Records, RG146, v. 826, HV31, v. 2.

44 'Arrest North York Woman with 12 Others,' *Toronto Star,* 3 August 1932.

45 *Toronto Star,* 3 August 1932.

46 *Workers' Unity* 2.12 (August–September 1932), 7.

8. The First Congress of the Workers' Unity League 1932

1 A. Lozovsky, *Marx and the Trade Unions* (New York: International Publishers,
1933/42), 41–2, 101.

2 'Report of Credential Committee, W.U.L. Congress,' Montreal, 5–7 August
1932, LAC, CI Fonds 495, list 98, file 144, reel 17, K-285.

3 For some reason the constitution committee did not make a published
report at the Congress, and yet, according to Joshua Gershman, it made a
significant proposal that the Workers' Unity League change its relationship
to the Red International. Instead of being an affiliate, henceforth, 'without
entering into any organic relations or connections' with the international,
it would engage in 'fraternal co-operation.' J. Gershman, 'Workers' Unity
League to Hold Important Session,' *Worker,* 31 December 1932; 'Constitution of the Workers' Unity League' as amended at the Second National
Congress in September 1933, Tom McEwen, *The Forge Glows Red* (Toronto:
Progress Books, 1974), 247ff; LAC, CSIS Records, RG146, interim box 193,
access request 92-A-00088, 'WUL – Canada.'

4 'Report of First National Congress Workers' Unity League of Canada,' 5–7
August 1932, Montreal (48 pages), file copy, Anglo-American Secretariat,
LAC, CI Fonds 495, list 98, file 144, reel 17, K-285; Irving Abella, 'Portrait
of a Jewish Professional Revolutionary: The Recollections of Joshua Gershman,' *Labour/LeTravail* 2 (1977), 202.

5 'Resolution Adopted at WUL Congress,' 6, 'Report of First National Congress, Workers' Unity League of Canada,' 5–7 August 1932, Montreal, LAC, CI Fonds 495, list 98, file 144, mfm reel 17, K-285.

6 'Report of First National Congress Workers' Unity League of Canada,' 5–7 August 1932, Montreal (48 pages), file copy, Anglo-American Secretariat, LAC, CI Fonds 495, list 98, file 144, reel 17, K-285, 'Litterick Report,' 2. Litterick's statement is vague probably because, as Douglas Cruikshank and Gregory S. Kealey demonstrate in their article 'Strikes in Canada, 1891–1950: Methods and Sources,' *Labour/Le Travail* 20 (Fall 1987), 123–45, there are many difficulties and ambiguities in any attempt to establish accurate strike statistics in Canada. According to the 'Dominion of Canada, Report of the Department of Labour,' 31 March 1933, there were 116 strikes in Canada in 1932, the largest number since 1921.

7 A memorandum of 1932 in the archives of the Anglo-American Secretariat (Moscow) entitled 'Organizational Notes on Workers' Unity League' places the membership total at 10,234 plus 1,000 in the Women's Labour League. This document does not mention the unemployed workers organized by the WUL, which Litterick may have included in his total. LAC, CI Fonds 495, list 98, file 145, reel 17, K-285.

8 Stewart Smith, *Comrades and Komsomolkas: My Years in the Communist Party of Canada* (Toronto: Lugus, 1993) 145; RCMP, 'Weekly Report on Revolutionary Organizations and Agitators in Canada, Summary No. 679' (secret), 3 November 1933, LAC MG30 E-163 v. 12, file 124 (Norman Robertson Papers); LAC, CSIS Reports, RG146, v. 849, pt. 1. Most of the RCMP 'Weekly Reports on Revolutionary Organizations' for the years 1931–3 were destroyed before the series was sent to the National Archives in 1964.

9 J. Burns [pseud. for S. Smith], 'The United Front – Some Errors and Shortcomings,' *Workers' Unity* 2.12 (August–September 1932).

10 Smith to Anglo-American Secretariat (Moscow), 27 January, 26 June 1932, LAC, CI Fonds 495, list 98, file 140, reel 16, K-284; 'Additional Material on Work among Unemployed in Canada,' 17 July 1932, ibid., file 138.

11 *The Canadian Annual Review of Public Affairs 1933* (Toronto: Canadian Review Company), 36–7.

12 James Litterick, 'Concluding Remarks'; 'Resolution Adopted at the First Congress of the Workers' Unity League,' 7, LAC, CI Fonds 495, list 98, file 144, reel 17, K-285, 'Report of First National Congress,' 5–7 August 1932.

13 See 'The First W.U.L. Congress and Its Tasks in Canada,' *International Press Correspondence* 12.82 (21 July 1932), 670–2, which was slightly amended as 'R.I.L.U. Greets 1st National Congress of the Workers' Unity League,' *Workers' Unity* 2.12 (August–September 1932), 20–4.

14 There is an exception where the term 'social fascist leadership' appears once on page 2 of the 'Lumber Workers' Program,' which was a report from the sub-committee on the lumber industry, 'Report of First National Congress Workers' Unity League of Canada,' 5–7 August 1932, Montreal (48 pages), file copy, Anglo-American Secretariat, LAC, CI Fonds 495, list 98, file 144, reel 17, K-285.

15 *Workers' Unity League: Policy, Tactics, Structure, Demands* (Toronto, n.d., circa June 1932), 43, 42, UBC Special Collections, William Bennett Papers, SPAM 12030; 'Report of First National Congress WUL of Canada,' 3, LAC, CI Fonds 495, list 98, file 144, reel 17, K-285.

16 J. Gershman, 'Workers' Unity League to Hold Important Session,' *Worker*, 31 December 1932. 'Constitution of the Workers' Unity League of Canada' as amended on 3 January 1933, LAC, CI Fonds 495, list 98, file 153, reel 18, K-286.

17 In his statement ('Workers' Unity League to Hold Important Session'), Gershman backdated the decision to no longer be a section of the RILU to the WUL Congress, but that claim is contradicted by the recommendations of the Program Committee which were approved by the Congress. The minutes of the Congress note that the report of the Constitution Committee was 'adopted as amended,' but no detail is provided. See chapter 11, note 14 for further explanation.

18 See reports of police undercover agents in the Lumber Workers' Industrial Union (LWIU), British Columbia, in LAC, CSIS Records, RG146, v. 2 of 'open records available for research,' access<?> request 1025-9-9019, S.T. Wood (RCMP superintendent, British Columbia) to the commissioner (Ottawa), 27 January 1933, paragraph 5, and 'Lumber Workers' Industrial Union, Report II,' 3 December 1932.

19 See LAC, R.B. Bennett Papers, reel M-1314, #388406. This pamphlet is undated but was being widely distributed by early 1934. See 'Price Holds Threat over WUL Leaders,' and Charles Sims, 'WUL Leader Replies to the Attack of the Ontario Attorney-General, W.H. Price,' both in *Worker*, 27 February 1934.

20 H.R. MacMillan to Montague Meyer, 28 July 1935, UBC Special Collections, MacMillan-Bloedel Papers, box 411, file 25.

21 LWIU, British Columbia, 1929–37, LAC, CSIS Records, RG146, v. 2 of 'open records available for research,' access request<?> 1025-9-9019, S.T. Wood, commanding 'E' division, to the commissioner, Ottawa, 23 September 1932. Information for the Timberland incident is mainly taken from this police file.

22 LAC, CSIS Records, RG146, LWIU file access request 1025-9-9019, W.H. Bullock-Webster, barrister, solicitor, and notary (Victoria), to the commissioner, British Columbia Police, 27 September 1932.

23 Arthur H. Evans (Vancouver) to National Office, WUL, 25 September 1932, LAC, CI Fonds 495, list 98, file 145, reel 17, K-285.

24 LAC, CSIS Records, RG146, personal history file 175/P1072 [Arthur H. Evans], Sergt. G.J. Duncan, Boundary District, to J. MacDonald, officer commanding 'B' Division, BC Police, Nelson, BC, 23 November 1932; J.H. McMullin, commissioner, BC Police, to S.T. Wood, officer commanding 'E' Division, RCMP, Vancouver, 24 November 1932. See also the *Princeton Star*, during this period and April–May 1933.

25 LAC, RG27, v. 353, no. 170, T-2764, F.E. Harrison, western representative, Department of Labour, to H.H. Ward, deputy minister of labour (Ottawa), 3 December 1932; Ben Swankey and Jean Evans Sheils, *Work and Wages! Semi-Documentary Account of the Life and Times of Arthur H. (Slim) Evans* (Vancouver: Trade Union Research Bureau, 1977), 42; *Unemployed Worker* (Vancouver), 10 December 1932 (see LAC, RG27, v. 353, no. 170).

26 J.H. McMullin to Major S.T. Wood, commanding 'E' Division, RCMP, Vancouver, re: 'Strike at Princeton' (Secret), 9 December 1932, in Arthur H. Evans, personal history file no. 175/p1072, read at CSIS headquarters, Ottawa, May 1992.

27 'Agreement between the Princeton Local of the Mine Workers Union of Canada and the Tulameen Coal Mines Ltd., of Princeton, British Columbia for a period of one year terminating on the 1st day of December 1933,' LAC, RG27, v. 353, no. 170, T-2764. The union was unable to prevail over the other coal operators in Princeton at this time.

28 An amended WUL Constitution was adopted on 3 January 1933 at a meeting of the National Executive Board, and then again after further amendments at the Second National Congress of the WUL held in Toronto on 9 to 12 September 1933, LAC, CI Fonds 495, list 98, file 153, reel 18, K-286.

9. Women of the Workers' Unity League

1 Joan Sangster, *Dreams of Equality* (Toronto: McClelland and Stewart, 1989), 235.

2 'Report of WUL First National Congress,' 5–7 August 1932, LAC, CI Fonds 495, list 98, file 144, reel 17, K-285.

3 Though women in Quebec gained the right to vote in federal elections in 1918, they had to wait until 1940 to gain the vote provincially. First Nations people did not gain the federal franchise until 1960. For full details on the history of the vote franchise see *A History of the Vote in Canada* (Ottawa: Minister of Public Works and Government Services Canada, for the Chief Electoral Officer of Canada, 1997).

4 'Memorandum on Women's Work' (1936), LAC, CI Fonds 495, list 98, file 183A, reel 22, K-290.

5 Alma Norman, 'Getting It Together, Part II: Working Women and the Women's Labour Leagues,' *Upstream* 2.4 (May 1978).

6 'Thesis on Work amongst Women,' CPC, Central Executive Committee, 27 May 1929, 7, LAC, CI Fonds 495, list 98, file 77, reel 9, K-277.

7 Ibid.

8 The letter is the topic of a resolution at the sixth CPC convention (cited below) and is referred to in the 'Closed Letter to the Central Committee of the Communist Party of Canada,' which was reprinted in the convention materials, LAC, CPC Papers, MG28 IV4, v. 11, file 26, p. 19.

9 'Resolution of the Sixth National Convention of the CPC on the Letter from the Women's Secretariat of the CI on Women's Work, CPC Convention, 1929,' 68, University of Toronto Fisher Rare Book Library, Kenny Collection, MS179, box 2, folder 2.

10 Ibid.

11 Ibid. See also 'Thesis on Work amongst Women,' where Custance describes the vision of the paper: 'the magazine must be changed from an entirely organizational paper into a popular paper for working women generally.'

12 'Minutes of Political Committee,' 24 November 1929, LAC, CI Fonds 495, list 98, file 75, reel 9, K-277.

13 See chapter 2. Also Varpu Lindstrom-Best, *Defiant Sisters: A Social History of Finnish Immigrant Women in Canada* (Toronto: Multicultural History Society of Ontario, 1988), chapter 7, 'Women in Socialist Organizations,' 138–62, for the points of view of Finnish women's leaders on the WLL.

14 'Resolution on Women's Work,' CPC, Central Committee Plenum, February 1931, LAC, CI Fonds 495, list 98, file 126, reel 14.

15 'Personal History File re: Rebecca Buhay,' 175P/1254, n.d., LAC, CSIS Records, RG146, v. 10, file access request 92-A-00012, pt. 2 (declassified November 1992).

16 A. Newman (Sudbury) to 'Dear Boys' (Toronto), 3 January 1931, OA, RG4, reel 2, 2-A-1444–50.

17 Aino Lahti (Kirkland Lake) to Becky Buhay, 20 January 1931, OA, RG4, reel 2, 2-A-1316.

18 Women's Department, WUL, to Sudbury Convention of the Women's Labour Leagues, 24 March 1931, OA, RG4, reel 2, 2-A-1466.

19 Tim Buck to Newman (Sudbury), 28 March 1931, OA, RG4, reel 2, 2-A-1475.

20 National Women's Department to Bessie Schacter, 21 April 1931, OA, RG4, reel 2, 2-A-0969.

21 Catherine Lesire (Vancouver) to J. Collins, 21 May 1931, OA, RG4, reel 3, 4-A-2446.

22 Lyyli Toivonen (Sudbury) to J. Collins, 15 June 1931, OA, RG4, reel 2, 2-A-1509.

23 See Buck to Newman (Sudbury), 28 March 1931, OA, RG4, reel 2, 2-A-1475; Buhay to Lahti, 29 January 1931, ibid., 2-A-1315; Ewen to Sula (Calgary), 15 June 1931, ibid., 2-A-2215–18.

24 See Ewen to Sula (Calgary), 15 June 1931, ibid. In this letter is talk and strategy related to the leadership by the WUL of the Women's Labour Leagues in Alberta. Ewen is pleased that 'we have got this National Federation [of Women's Labour Leagues] broken up and won many of those sections of the WLL into the WUL, where under our direction they can take a more aggressive part in the general class struggle than a mere gossip circle.' This shows that even in June 1931 the WUL still did not have the leadership of all the Women's Labour Leagues.

25 For another interpretation of the reorganization of the Women's Labour Leagues see Sangster, *Dreams of Equality*, 63–4. Sangster sees the period of WUL leadership as leaving the leagues in a 'no-win dilemma,' since the 'Comintern-inspired critique of the WLLs denigrated their reformist auxiliary work, but the CPC offered few workable directions for change and gave little time to the upkeep of the WLLs.'

26 For details of what the women did in the Soviet Union see this book, chapter 4.

27 Elsa Tynjala, 'The Working Class Youth in Canada and the Youth in the Soviet Union,' *Worker*, 28 February 1931; Annie Whitfield, 'Canadian and Soviet Union Compared,' *Worker*, 14 March 1931; Elsa Tynjala, 'Women in the Mining District of Donbas,' *Worker*, 8 August 1931; Bessie Schachter, 'Revolution Frees Mohomeden Women,' *Worker*, 8 August 1931; Annie Zen, 'Where Women Are Free,' *Worker*, 8 August 1931.

28 See Sangster, *Dreams of Equality*, 69–71, for her views on the 1930 women's delegation, including the selection process and the Whitfield problem. Sangster, broadly speaking, presents the whole project as unsuccessful, and cites an internal CP document saying that the party 'had failed to make any concrete organizational gains from the project.' See also this book, chapter 4, 'Going to Mecca,' 63.

29 'Nova Scotia Miner's Wife Nails "Forced Labor" Lie,' *Worker*, 22 November 1930. This seems to contradict to some extent Ruth Frager, who comes out against feminist gains in the Soviet Union in *Sweatshop Strife: Class, Ethnicity, and Gender in the Jewish Labour Movement of Toronto 1900–1939* (Toronto: University of Toronto Press, 1992), 176–8. Frager says that when she interviewed

the women who had been on the delegation, forty years later, 'none of them stressed the idea that women were achieving equality in the Soviet Union in the interwar period.'

30 See Pearl Wedro to Becky Buhay, 6 January 1931, OA, RG4, reel 2, 3-A-1683, in which Wedro writes about having spoken to 2,300 people at three separate events; also, 'Women's Day Celebrated by Workers of Vancouver,' *Worker*, 14 March 1931, and 'Pol Bureau Minutes,' 17 April 1931, LAC, CI Fonds 495, list 98, file 117, reel 13, K-281, which show that Annie Zen talked to a few thousand people around International Women's Day, 1931.

31 Agenda of 'First Canadian Conference of Friendship with the Union of Socialist Soviet Republics,' 1935, LAC, CI Fonds 495, list 98, file 183, reel 22, K-290.

32 'Friends of the Soviet Union Launched in Vancouver,' *Worker*, 28 February 1931.

33 See note 35; 'Where Women Are Free,' *Worker*, 8 August 1931; 'Help the Working Women of the Soviet Union Build a New World of Social Economic and Sex Equality,' *Worker*, 8 August 1931; 'Conditions of Maternity Are Best in Entire World,' *Worker*, 15 September 1934.

34 See Colin McKay, 'What's Happening in Russia?' *Canadian Unionist* 4.99 (February 1931); editorial, 'A Great Achievement,' ibid. 6.8 (January 1933); 'Moscow Celebrates Women's Liberation,' *Mail and Empire*, 10 March 1931.

35 Anna Krylova, 'Stalinist Identity from the Viewpoint of Gender: Rearing a Generation of Professionally Violent Women-Fighters in 1930s Stalinist Russia,' *Gender and History* 16.3 (November 2004), 628. The footnote following this quote in Krylova's article discusses the 'scholarly tendency to "dismiss" a particular aspect of gender politics in the Soviet Union – the 1930s wife-activists' movement – as neo-conservative.' See also Karen Petrone, 'Soviet Women's Voices in the Stalin Era,' *Journal of Women's History* 16.2 (Summer 2004), 207.

36 Sarah Ashwin, Introduction to *Gender, State, and Society in Soviet and Post-Soviet Russia* (London: Routledge, 2000).

37 See Meg Luxton, 'Feminism as a Class Act: Working-Class Feminism and the Women's Movement in Canada,' *Labour/LeTravail* 48 (Fall 2001), for a clear explanation of place of socialist feminism in the women's movement deriving mainly from the experiences of the 1960s and later.

38 See editorial, 'Should Married Women Work?' *Canadian Unionist* 4.8 (January 1931).

39 M.C. Urquhart, *Historical Statistics of Canada* (Toronto: Macmillan, 1965), 61, column C54.

40 See Margaret Hobbs, 'Gendering Work and Welfare: Women's Relationship

to Wage-Work and Social Policy during the Great Depression,' PhD thesis, OISE, 1995, 96 ff; Ruth Roach Pierson, 'Gender and the Unemployment Debates in Canada 1934–1940,' *Labour/Le Travail* no. 25 (Spring 1990), 82.

41 'Six Provincial Jobs Are Given to Single Girls,' clipping from *Toronto Star*, 4 July 1936, in OA, RG3, Prime Minister's Office, Hepburn Papers, appendix N, box 367, file: dismissals, etc; original citation in Hobbs, 'Rethinking Antifeminism in the 1930s: Gender Crisis or Workplace Justice? A Response to Alice Kessler-Harris,' *Gender and History* 5.1 (Spring 1993), 4–15

42 'Go Home Young Women,' *Chatelaine*, September 1933, 10, as quoted in Victoria Strong-Boag, *The New Day Recalled: Lives of Women and Girls in English Canada 1919–1939* (Toronto: Copp Clark Pitman, 1998).

43 'For a Women's Section in NUWA,' *Workers' Unity*, 30 October 1931, 5 (available from Ontario Archives, Department of Labour, Ontario, mfm N-100); the editors of the paper respond, saying, 'Alas for the working class womanhood of Winnipeg if that were true – what a spineless, crawling, despicable, miserable species they would be.'

44 Hobbs, 'Gendering Work and Welfare,' abstract, i.

45 Anne Walters, 'Work amongst Women,' 15 July 1932, LAC, CI Fonds 495, list 98, file 138, reel 16, K-284.

46 Betty Griffin and Susan Lockhart, *Their Own History: Women's Contribution to the Labour Movement of British Columbia* (Vancouver: UFAWU/CAW Seniors Club, 2002), 69.

47 'About Jobless Women,' *Worker*, 17 October 1931.

48 Leslie Morris, 'International Women's Day,' *Worker*, 28 February 1931. The interpretation taken here is that Morris was referring to the prevalent middle-class Victorian view of what it meant to be womanly, namely that married women should not be looking for paid employment, that their proper place was in the kitchen. Later feminist historians, however, have seized upon Morris's statement as evidence of a lack of concern within the program of the Communist Party and its supporters for the rights of women, for their liberation from oppression, and for equality with men in all aspects of life. There have been many academic essays written on this topic.

49 'International Day of Struggle against Unemployment,' 4 February 1931, LAC, CI Fonds 495 list 98 file 126, reel 14.

50 This contradicts Hobbs, who in 'Gendering Work and Welfare,' 107, asserts that 'Ultimately, Communists were arguing not for married women's right to work but for their right not to work, a right they assumed would follow once a socialist economic system paid men a proper family wage.' For the earliest draft of the UI Bill, see 'Polcom Minutes,' 30 January 1931, LAC, CI Fonds 495, list 98, file 117, reel 13, K-281. The draft bill says, 'State

unemployment insurance for all unemployed workers resident in Canada, irrespective of age, sex, race, or color.' And, 'Section 3 – Workers Eligible for Unemployment Insurance – All unemployed married or single workers irrespective of sex or national extraction shall receive social insurance immediately.' ' Unemployed women workers, for four weeks previous and after child-birth shall receive full social insurance prescribed by the act.' 'All young workers irrespective of sex.'

51 'Woman Defies Premier,' *Worker*, 6 August 1932.

52 'NUC Elects New National Committee,' *Worker*, 23 February 1935.

53 For more on the National Congress of Unemployed Workers, see this book, chapter 7.

54 'Jobless Delegation Takes Up Challenge of Bennett's Millionaire Cabinet,' *Worker*, 16 September 1933.

55 'Tom Ewen Elected National Secretary at Congress of Workers' Unity League,' *Worker*, 16 September 1933.

56 'Flora Hutton Welcome,' *Unemployed Worker* 5.48 (20 September 1933), from Department of Labour, LAC, RG27, v. 352, no. 125, T-2765.

57 'Flora Hutton Told the Truth!' ibid.

58 'Memorandum on Women's Work,' 1936, 5, LAC, CI Fonds 495, list 98, file 183A, reel 22, K-290.

59 'What Mrs Wilkinson Meant,' *Worker*, 6 August 1932.

60 'Working Women Force City Council to Provide Relief,' *Worker*, 6 February 1932.

61 'London Women Win Back Relief Cuts,' *Worker*, 27 April 1935.

62 'May Vote to Cease Relief Strike Today,' *Toronto Star*, Friday, 10 May 1935, reported a 10 per cent increase offered by Premier Hepburn; see also Carmela Patrias, 'Relief Strike: Immigrant Workers and the Great Depression in Crowland, Ontario, 1930–1935,' in Franca Iacovetta, ed., *A Nation of Immigrants: Women, Workers, and Communities in Canadian History, 1840s–1960s* (Toronto: University of Toronto Press, 1998).

63 See 'Unity Pays in Gogama,' *Unity* (January–Febuary 1936), LAC, CPC Papers, MG28 IV4, v. 78, file 51.

64 'Militancy of Unemployed Forces Immediate Relief,' *Worker*, 31 December 1932.

65 'Burnaby in the Vanguard for Amnesty and Relief,' *Unemployed Worker*, 24 December 1932, from Department of Labour, LAC, RG27, v. 353, no. 197, T-2764.

66 Gregory S. Kealey and Reg Whitaker, eds., *RCMP Security Bulletins: The Depression Years, Part I, 1933–1934* (St John's: Canadian Committee on Labour History, 1993–5), no. 737, 20 December 1934.

67 Kealey and Whitaker, eds., *RCMP Security Bulletins: The Depression Years, Part II, 1935*, no. 756, 22 May 1935.

68 Ibid.

69 Temma Kaplan, 'On the Socialist Origins of International Women's Day,' *Feminist Studies* 11.1 (Spring 1985).

70 Ibid. It may seem strange that the February revolution began on International Women's Day, 8 March, but this oddity is due to the difference between the Western calendar and the Gregorian calendar in use in Russia at the time, which in 1917 would have placed 8 March as 3 February.

71 'ZU,' International Women's Secretariat to Women's Department of CPC, 25 January 1931, LAC, CI Fonds 495, list 98, file 116, reel 13, K-281; for an example of the complaint see 'International Women's Day in Border Cities,' *Worker*, 22 March 1930.

72 National Women's Department, CPC, 'to all party fractions in the Women's Labour Leagues,' 16 February 1931, LAC, CI Fonds 495, list 98, file 126, reel 14, K-282.

73 'Minutes of Pol Buro, 3 Feb. 1931,' 'Resolution on Women's Work,' 9, LAC, CI Fonds 495, list 98, file 117, reel 13, K-281; A. Newman (Sudbury) to Tim Buck, 26 March 1931, OA, RG4, reel 2, 2-A-1472–3; Buck to Newman, 28 March 1931, ibid., 2-A-1475–6.

74 List drawn from documents in LAC, CI Fonds 495, list 98, files 126 and 127, reel 14, K-282: National Women's Department to All District Committees, 14 February 1931; National Women's Department to All Party Fractions in the Women's Labour Leagues, 16 February 1931; promotional poster 'Working Women of Montreal,' 8 March 1931.

75 'Minutes of Pol Bureau, 17 April 1931,' reports 14,315 people and twenty-six locations, with some places not reported yet, LAC, CI Fonds 495, list 98, file 117, reel 13, K-281. 'Report on International Women's Day March 8 1931,' n.d., claims thirty-eight meetings in about thirty locations with 15,000–16,000 people, LAC, CI Fonds 495, list 98, file 126, reel 14, K-282.

76 'Women's Day Celebrated by Workers of Vancouver,' *Worker*, 14 March 1931; for the text of the 1932 Soviet poster dedicated to 8 March, see Wikimedia Commons, 8 marta.jpg.

77 'Minutes of Pol Bureau 17 April 1931,' LAC, CI Fonds 495, list 98, file 117, reel 13, K-281.

78 Meg Luxton, *More Than a Labour of Love: Three Generations of Women's Work in the Home* (Toronto: Women's Press, 1980), 218.

79 Ibid.

80 'Memorandum on Women's Work,' 1936, LAC, CI Fonds 495, list 98, file 183A, reel 22, K-290.

81 'Resolution on Trade Union Work amongst Working Class Women,' from 'Report of the First National Congress of the Workers' Unity League,' 5–7 August 1932, LAC, CI Fonds 495, list 98, file 144, reel 17, K-285.
82 'Memorandum on Women's Work,' 1936, LAC, CI Fonds 495, list 98, file 183A, reel 22, K-290.
83 Dorothy Sue Cobble, *The Other Women's Movement: Workplace Justice and Social Rights in Modern America* (Princeton: Princeton University Press, 2004), 23.
84 See this book, chapter 15.
85 Griffin and Lockhart, *Their Own History*, 61.
86 'B.C. Women in Convention,' *UNITY*, January–February 1936.
87 'Memorandum on Women's Work,' 1936, LAC, CI Fonds 495, list 98, file 183A, reel 22, K-290.
88 'Work amongst Women,' from '8th National Convention CPC,' 8–12 October 1937, University of Toronto Fisher Rare Book Library, Kenny Collection, MS0179, box 2, folder 6. This report talks of fighting price rises, anti-fascism, building women's auxiliaries, and recruiting women to the CPC.

10. Hard Rock Miners: Anyox – Noranda – Flin Flon

1 RCMP, Timmins, Ontario Detachment, 'Report on Communist Activities,' LAC, CSIS Records, RG146, v. 32361, pt. 1/1, 25 June 1934.
2 District 4, CP, report of 21 April 1934, LAC, CI Fonds 495, list 98, file 163, reel 19, K-287.
3 Pete Loudon, *The Town That Got Lost* (Sidney, BC: Gray's Publishing, 1973), 90; 'Death Stalks at Anyox,' *Unemployed Worker*, 15 March 1933.
4 *Canadian Mines Handbook 1934* (Toronto), 67–8; (*1935*), 103. The company was reincorporated by a special act of the BC Legislature in 1931, with an authorized capital stock of 500,000 shares par $100.
5 *Canadian Mines Handbook, 1934*, 67, and *1935*, 103.
6 W.E. Payne, secretary, Vancouver Board of Trade, to Hon. T.D. Pattullo, premier, 18 March 1935, BC Archives, GR1222, Premier's Office, box 11/5.
7 Loudon, *The Town That Got Lost*, 53–5.
8 Ibid., 56–9.
9 Ibid., 100.
10 M.C. Urquhart, ed., *Historical Statistics of Canada* (Toronto: Macmillan, 1965), table on 'The Labour Force,' 65, shows 60,000 in 'mining, quarrying and oil wells' in 1931, of which about 26,400 were employed in coal mining. See also table 36, 'Employment and Earnings in the Coal Mines of Canada 1927–1931,' *Coal Statistics for Canada, 1931* (Ottawa, 1932), 30.
11 The Bonanza and Hidden Creek mines at Anyox between them reported

fatal accidents every year, sometimes as many as three of them. See the annual *Report of the Minister of Mines* for British Columbia (Victoria: King's Printer).

12 *Unemployed Worker*, 22 February 1932; 'Letter from Anyox Miner,' ibid., 8 February 1933, LAC, RG27, v. 354, no. 5, reel T-2764; 'A Strike of Outstanding Importance,' *Worker*, 18 February 1933; H.F. Kergin, MLA for Alice Arm, *Victoria Times*, 30 March 1933, *Prince Albert Herald*, 31 March 1933.

13 *Worker*, 18 February 1933; LAC, CSIS Records, RG146, v. 1916, H.M. Hewson, 'E' Division, to the commissioner, 30 October 1919, with enclosures.

14 'A Strike of Outstanding Importance,' *Worker*, 18 February 1933.

15 The account given in this paragraph is suggestive and circumstantial.

16 'Letter from Anyox Miner,' *Unemployed Worker*, 8 February 1933; *Worker*, 18 February 1933.

17 *Alice Arm Herald* as cited by Loudon, *The Town That Got Lost*, 88; *Worker*, 18 February 1933; *Unemployed Worker*, 8, 15 February 1933, LAC, RG27, v. 354, no. 5, reel T-2764.

18 The correspondence of the Granby Company relating to the Anyox operation does not appear to have been deposited in a public archive and therefore it is not an easy matter to assess the company's real financial situation. According figures sent to the *Canadian Mines Handbook* (Toronto) for 1934 and 1935 (pages 67–8 and 103), the company declared accounting losses 'after depreciation and depletion' in 1930, 1931, 1932, and 1933. On the other hand, with 450,000 shares issued, it apparently paid dividends in the first three of these 'deficit' years. The reported dividend was as much as $7 per share in 1931 and fell to 12 ½ cents per share on 1 February 1932. In another context the Honourable Justice M.A. Macdonald, in reporting for the Coal and Petroleum Products Commission of British Columbia in 1937, comments on the practice of some BC mining companies of hiding their profits by employing questionable accounting conventions, 'Synopsis of the Main Features,' *Report of the Commissioner, Coal and Petroleum Products Commission (British Columbia)*, v. 2 (Victoria: King's Printer, 1937), xv.

19 Loudon, *The Town That Got Lost*, 89; *Worker*, 18 February 1933.

20 Loudon, *The Town That Got Lost*, 89.

21 Ibid., 87–8.

22 Ibid., 89, 90.

23 *Worker*, 18 February 1933; M. Solski and J. Smaller, *Mine Mill* (Ottawa: Steel Rail, 1985), 52; Loudon, *The Town That Got Lost*, 90.

24 LAC, Bennett Papers, reel M-989, telegram from R.H. Pooley (BC attorney general) to Prime Minister R.B. Bennett, 4 February 1933, requesting urgent dispatch of the *Malaspina* to Anyox since 'condition is critical.'

According to archivists Paul Marsden and Brien Brothman, references to the *Malaspina*'s role at Anyox are sparse in official government documents, but 'there are numerous allusions ... in several newspaper accounts to a "gunboat", "warship" and "armed naval vessel" being sent to "terrorize" or "intimidate" the workers. It is not clear, however, whether any vessel despatched to Anyox was already armed, or whether the provincial police armed the vessel by mounting machine guns once it had arrived at the scene – or whether both are true.' Brothman (Government Archives Division, LAC) to Stephen Endicott, 28 April 1993; Marsden (Government Archives Division, LAC) with enclosures, to Endicott, 18 March 1993.

25 Loudon, *The Town That Got Lost*, 95–6.

26 Kerry Badgley, archivist, Government Archives and Records Disposition Division, National Archives of Canada, to Stephen Endicott, 15 September 1998, gives the figure in an e-mail on the subject of 'Deportations in the 1930s,' *Unemployed Worker*, 1 March 1933; Sutherland Brown (Department of National Defence) to R.H. Pooley (BC attorney general), LAC, RG27, v. 2045, 3 February 1933 and H. Hereford, Dominion commissioner of unemployment relief, to W.A. Carrothers, acting chairman, Special Relief Commission, Vancouver, 8 March 1933, LAC, RG27, v. 2045, file Y2-1, section #1; *Unemployed Worker*, 29 March 1933; *Worker*, 22 April 1933; Hansard, 4 April 1935, where Hon. W.A. Gordon, minister of labour and immigration, stated, 'At that time, I took steps to remove from Canada and to return to their native country a number of agitators who fomented that strike.'

27 *Unemployed Worker* 5.18 (15 February 1933).

28 *Worker*, 11 March 1933. Earlier, as a inspector for the Northern Inspection District, Shenton had felt able to write favourable reports on Granby's safety measures. See, for example, *British Columbia, Report of the Minister of Mines, 1931* (Victoria: King's Printer, 1932), A 197–8.

29 *Victoria Times*, 30 March 1933. See also the *Daily Colonist* (Victoria) and the *Province* (Vancouver), 30 March 1933, and *Alice Arm Herald*, 8 April 1933.

30 T.J. Shenton, the retired mines inspector, ran for the CCF, receiving 308 votes while Kergin got 267; by this split the winning official Liberal candidate, a mill superintendent, got elected with 419 ballots. See www.elections.bc.ca for results of the eighteenth BC General Election, 2 November 1933. See also the *Alice Arm Herald*, 4 November 1933, for detailed poll returns.

31 *Prince Rupert News*, 10 May 1933, LAC, RG27, v. 354, no. 5, reel T-2764.

32 *Worker*, 6 May 1933.

33 A year later, in 1934, the company had about 450 men working, but of them 'no more than 25 of the original miners' were employed; the rest were let go after the company had broken in 'new and green men.' 'Report on

Anyox,' in letter from District #9 (British Columbia) to 'Dear Friends,' LAC, CI Fonds 495, list 98, file 163, reel 19, K-287. In 1935 the Granby Company, not finding enough new ore bodies, decided to abandon Anyox. Consolidated Mining and Smelting Company of Trail, BC, dismantled the operation for its parts and salvage. *Vancouver Province*, 29 October 1935. Seven years later the ghost town burned to the ground, ibid., 7 July 1942. The miners, meanwhile, went on learning to organize hard rock mines in Manitoba, Ontario, and Quebec, employing 'the Anyox system.'

34 'The Consolidated Mining and Smelting Company of Canada Limited,' Supplement, *The Canadian Annual Review 1935 and 1936*, S48–S50.

35 Al King, *Red Bait! Struggles of a Mine Mill Local* (Vancouver: Kingbird Publishing, 1998), 27–9, 49.

36 *Canadian Mines Handbook* (Toronto, 1935), 121–2; Jamie Swift and the Development Education Centre, *The Big Nickel: Inco at Home and Abroad* (Kitchener: Between the Lines, 1977), 13–31.

37 'Nickel Prosperity,' *Worker*, 11 November 1933.

38 'Nickel for War,' *Worker*, 9 December 1933, and 'Nickel Prosperity,' ibid., 11 November 1933.

39 Fred Rose, *Spying on Labor* (Toronto: New Era Publishers, 1939), 14; see also Swift and the Development Education Centre, *The Big Nickel*, 36.

40 Ewen to Jim Barker (Sudbury), 24 December 1930, OA, RG4, reel 1, 1-A-0439–40; 'Organization Campaign in Metal Mining Industry,' 23 September 1930, OA, RG4, reel 7, 10-C-1775.

41 'Sudbury District Conference on Nickel Industry – Pre-conference Discussion Material,' report of District 5, 21 November 1933, LAC, CI Fonds 495, list 98, file 152, reel 18, K-286.

42 'Notes from Captains' Meeting, 3 Dec 1933,' District 5, LAC, CI Fonds 485, list 98, file 152, reel 18, K-286.

43 Carr (Sudbury) to T.E. Ewen, 17 June 1931, LAC, CI Fonds 495, list 98, file 127, reel 14, K-282.

44 Report from District #4, 21 April 1934, LAC, CI Fonds 495, list 98, file 163, reel 19, K-287; Dear Friends, 28 May 1934, LAC, CI Fonds 495, list 98, file 162, reel 19, K-287.

45 Evelyn Dumas, *The Bitter Thirties in Quebec* (Montreal: Black Rose, 1975), 28.

46 'Noranda: One of Canada's Greatest Mines,' *Canadian Annual Review 1932*, 727; *Canadian Mines Handbook 1935* (Toronto), 180.

47 Timmins Detachment, RCMP, 'Report re: Communist Activities Northern Ontario,' 25 June 1934, LAC, CSIS Records, RG146, v. 3261, pt. 1/1.

48 'The Causes of the Noranda Defeat,' *Communist Review* (mimeo) no. 4 (July–August 1934), 26, LAC, CPC Papers, MG28 IV4, v. 78, file 11;

Dear Friends, 28 May 1934, LAC, CI Fonds 495, list 98, file 162, reel 19, K-287.
49 Dear Friends, 28 May 1934, LAC, CI Fonds 495, list 98, file 162, reel 19, K-287.
50 Dumas, *The Bitter Thirties in Quebec*, 28–42.
51 *Worker*, 7 July 1934.
52 *The Financial Post Survey of Mines 1929*, 78–9; *Canadian Mines Handbook 1935*, 117–19; J.S. Woodsworth, speaking in the House of Commons throne debate 31 January 1928, as cited in *Canadian Unionist* 1.9 (February 1928).
53 James D. Mochoruk, *Mining's Early Years: An Historic Look at Flin Flon's Mining Pioneers* (Manitoba Labour Education Centre, n.d. circa 1984), 11.
54 Other accounts include Robert S. Robson, 'Strike in the Single Enterprise Community: Flin Flon, Manitoba – 1934,' *Labour/Le Travail* 12 (Fall 1983), 63–86, and Valerie Hedman, ed., *Flin Flon* (Altona: Flin Flon Historical Society, 1974), 121ff.
55 Flin Flon Oral History Project (1984), Provincial Archives of Manitoba, Moving Images and Sound Division.
56 Mochoruk, *Mining's Early Years*, 19.
57 Ibid., 20.
58 Oscar D. Brooks, *Legs: An Authentic Story of Life on the Road* (Toronto: Key Porter Books, 1991).
59 Interview with Oscar D. Brooks in Toronto, 28 January 1993, by Stephen Endicott. Mr Brooks reviewed the transcript of his interview and approved of it without amendment.
60 Mabel Marlowe and Bill Ross, 'Demand Withdrawal of Charges against Flin Flon Arrested!' August 1934, leaflet given to author by Bill Ross, 14 October 1995.

11. 1933: Gaining Momentum

1 Translation: 'In spite of these difficulties the WUL ... was the spearhead of the Canadian workers' movement for our period,' Béatrice Richard, '*Péril Rouge' au Témiscamingue: la grève des bûcherons de Rouyn-Noranda 1933–1934* (Montreal: Collection RICHTQ Études et Documents, 1993), 45. This book is a seminal study of the political economy of the forest industry in Quebec, rich in analysis, centring on a two-week strike against a pulp and paper conglomerate, and was sponsored by the departments of history at the University of Montreal and the University of Quebec at Montreal.
2 *Worker*, 7 October 1933.
3 'Statement of the Second National Congress of the Workers' Unity League,

. 1933,' LAC, RG27, v. 835, file 1-28-1, pt. 1, Department of Labour, 2. For a similar figure see the Anglo-American Secretariat's estimate in table 11.2.

Table 11.2. Workers' Unity League Membership, circa December 1933 (as estimated by the Anglo-American Secretariat, RILU)

Logging and sawmill	10,000	Building trades	1,500
Pulp and paper	100	Rubber	200
Metal mining	400	Boot, shoe, leather	1,000
Coal mining	2,200	Textiles	800
Fisheries & canning	1,000	Cleaners & dyers	200
Railroads	300	Furniture & upholstery	3,000
Automobiles	300	Relief camps	5,000
Garments (women)	3,000	Other trades	800
Food workers	1,000		
		Total	30,800

Source: LAC, CI Fonds 495, list 98, file 153, reel 18, K-286 with this note: 'This information was gathered from government reports, newspapers, and personal information, will therefore have to be considered as approximate figures.'

But lesser estimates of WUL membership, at around 14,000, were suggested by Julia Collins [Julia Carr], national organizational secretary, who was possibly relating membership to actual dues payments to the national office, and at 21,253 by the deputy minister of labour. See 'There Are Valuable Experiences,' *Worker*, 26 August 1933, and *Canadian Annual Review 1934*, 529. See LAC, RG27, vols. 354–8, 358A, reels T-2764–T-2969 for the government's list of strikes in the calender year 1933, totalling 243. WUL unions allowed their unemployed members to continue in good standing without keeping their dues payments up on the understanding that they took part in the unemployed movement; this policy made it difficult for the league (and for historians) to know precisely how many members it had at any given time. The most complete listing of the affiliates of the WUL when it was at its peak, as given by its national secretary, appears in *Labour Organizations in Canada, 1934* (Ottawa: Department of Labour), 138–42.

4 Fred Collins, 'Toronto District Will Bring New Experience,' on organizing the chesterfield and furniture workers, boot and shoe workers, leather industry, cleaning and dyeing trades, and opposition shop groups in the railway industry, *Worker*, 26 August 1933.

5 'Some Lessons from the 2nd National Congress of the Workers' Unity League,' *Worker*, 23 September 1933.

6 LAC, RG 27, v. 835, file 1-28-1, pt. 1 (in photo folder).

7 'For Unity and Action,' *Worker*, 12 August 1933; 'Some Lessons from the 2nd National Congress of the Workers' Unity League,' *Worker*, 23 September 1933. Although the calender year 1933 saw the largest number of strikes since

1925, involving the most workers (26,558), the 'per cent of estimated working time lost' for the whole workforce was only .07, according to M.C. Urquhart, ed., *Historical Statistics of Canada* (Toronto: Macmillan, 1965), 107.

8 'Some Lessons from the 2nd National Congress of the Workers' Unity League,' *Worker*, 23 September 1933; 'No Money for Jobless Says Bennett but Millions for Coupon Clippers,' *Worker*, 4 February 1933. See also Anglo-American Secretariat, 'Unemployed and Unemployed Struggles in Canada,' 1933, an analysis based on articles appearing in the *Worker* and other sources, LAC, CI Fonds 495, list 98, file 153, reel 18, K-286.

9 Quoted by Nancy Stunden, 'The Stratford Strikes of 1933' (MA thesis, Carleton University, 1975), vii.

10 Interview with Stewart Smith at Fergus, Ont., 24 September 1992, by S. Endicott. Smith claimed Sims as a supporter of his. Later, in the 1940s, when Smith became a member of the Toronto Board of Control, the city's Ward 5 elected Sims to city council as its alderman; see also Tim Buck letter, July 1929, OA, RG4, reel 5, 8-C-0259.

11 'Statement of the Second National Congress of the Workers' Unity League, 1933,' LAC, Department of Labour, RG27, v. 835, file 1-28-1, pt. 1, 3. 'Calgary Relief Strike Leaders Are Sent to Prison by C.C.F. Govt.,' *Worker*, 8 July 1933.

12 'The Agenda for 2nd National Congress of the Workers' Unity League,' *Worker*, 19 August 1933.

13 'Second Congress of WUL Plans Action to Win Great Struggles,' *Worker*, 23 September 1933.

14 Morgan [Norman Freed], 'Methods of Illegal Work in the Communist Party of Canada,' (Strictly Confidential), 8 August 1932, and sundry other reports. LAC, CI Fonds 495, list 98, file 136, reel 15, K-283. The dates of the documents in file 136 run from 16 July to 2 September 1932, thus overlapping the 1st Congress of the WUL, which helps to explain why that Congress did not adopt or report on an amended constitution. When J. Gershman, a National Executive Board member, returned from a visit to Moscow in the autumn of 1932, he brought the results of the discussion on file 136 in time for an enlarged national executive board meeting. This gathering proceeded to adopt an amended draft constitution in early January 1933. In a little deception, probably to avoid talk of 'talking orders from Moscow,' Gershman, interviewed by the *Worker* on 31 December 1932, spoke as if the amended constitution had already been adopted at the 1st Congress (in August). In September the following year (1933), the 2nd Congress of the WUL adopted the amended constitution in finalized form. See chapter 8, notes 16 and 17.

15 David Lewis and F.R. Scott, *Make This* Your *Canada: A Review of C.C.F. History and Policy* (Toronto: Central Canada Publishing Co., 1943), 199–207, appendix A, 'Regina Manifesto adopted at First National Convention Held at Regina, Sask. July, 1933,' LAC, CPC Papers, MG28 IV4, v. 78, file 44, *Saskatchewan C.C.F. Research Bureau* 1.2 (August 1933).

16 Ibid., 199.

17 G. Pierce (pseud. for S. Smith), 'Canada and the End of Capitalist Stabilization,' *Worker*, 28 January 1933.

18 E.H. Carr, *The Twilight of Comintern, 1930–1935* (London: Macmillan, 1982), 109.

19 Leslie Morris lectures on 'Strategy and Tactics,' National Training School of the Labour Progressive Party, at Sudbury, Ontario, 2, 3 August 1949 (unpublished notes in possession of the author). See also Morris, 'Canada's Road to Socialism,' *National Affairs Monthly* 9.3 (1952), 24ff, and *The Road to Socialism in Canada: The Program of the Communist Party of Canada* (Toronto: Progress Books, 1960), 22.

20 Carr, *The Twilight of Comintern, 1930–1935*, chapter 7, 'Divided Counsels,' 123ff.

21 Communist Party of Canada, 'Information Material,' District 3 (Toronto), 20 June 1933, LAC, CI Fonds 495, list 98, file 152, reel 18, K-286; 'Letter from "Dick" (Moscow),' 7 May 1933, saying to 'stop shouting against the social-fascist leaders,' ibid., file 147; CI Political Commission letter to CP of Canada, 17 October 1934, ibid., file 156.

22 22 'Manifesto of the Executive Committee of the Comintern,' 5 March 1933, *Worker*, 1 April 1933, also in Jane Degras, *The Communist International*, v. 3 (London: Oxford University Press, 1965), 252–4; LAC, CSIS Records, RG146, CSIS file on WUL-Canada, access request 92-A-00088, pt. 1, access box 193 'WUL to Fellow Workers and Brothers, 28 April 1933'; 'Workers Unity League Calls United Front,' *Worker*, 6 May 1933; 'Action against Fascism,' *Worker*, 8 July 1933; '25,000 Workers in Mighty Mass Meeting Unite against Fascism, Hunger and War,' *Worker*, 15 July 1933; 'Capitalist World Thrown into Turmoil As Germany Withdraws from the League of Nations,' *Worker*, 21 October 1933.

23 'Woodsworth and Mosher Oppose National Congress on Unemployment,' *Worker*, 22 July 1933.

24 'Statement of the Second National Congress of the Workers' Unity League, 1933,' LAC, Department of Labour, RG27, v. 835, file 1-28-1, pt. 1, 5.

25 'Some Lessons from the 2nd National Congress of the Workers' Unity League,' *Worker*, 23 September 1933.

26 See National Committee of Unemployed Councils, *Building a Mass Unemployed Movement* (Toronto, April 1933), 32 pages, for a discussion of the

transition from an individual membership organization of the unemployed, such as the National Unemployed Workers' Association, to loosely structured urban block committees and neighbourhood councils as the most effective way to build a mass movement, LAC, CPC Papers, MG28 IV4, v. 61, file 10. See also 'Unemployed and Unemployed Struggles in Canada,' n.d., circa July 1933, 22 pages, for an authoritative analysis including a clear exposition of the united front unemployment movement from the point of view of the Workers' Unity League, likely prepared by a researcher at the Anglo-American Secretariat of the Red International of Trade Unions, LAC, CI Fonds 495, list 98, file 153, reel 18, K-286.

27　Gilbert Levine, ed., *Patrick Lenihan: From Irish Rebel to Founder of Canadian Public Sector Unionism* (St John's: Canadian Committee on Labour History, 1998), 64–5. See also *The Alberta Hunger-March and the Trial of the Victims of Brownlee's Police Terror* (Toronto: Canadian Labour Defense League, n.d., c. January 1933), 39 pages, LAC, CPC Papers, MG28 IV4, v. 61, file 7.

28　'Give Bennett a Fitting Reply!' *Worker*, 28 January 1933. Bennett's chief concern was to preserve the country's credit 'at whatever sacrifice,' by keeping up enormous interest payments to the bondholders. *Canadian Annual Review, 1933*, 28–9; James Struthers, *No Fault of Their Own: Unemployment and the Canadian Welfare State 1914–1941* (Toronto: University of Toronto Press, 1983), 67; 'No Money for Jobless Says Bennett but Millions for Coupon Clippers,' *Worker*, 4 February 1933.

29　'A Few Lessons to Be Drawn from the Relief Strikes,' *Worker*, 1 July 1933; Struthers, *No Fault of Their Own*, 103, 99–100.

30　'A Few Lessons to Be Drawn from the Relief Strikes,' *Worker*, 1 July 1933.

31　*Evening Citizen* (Ottawa), 10 July 1933.

32　Larry Hannant, 'The Calgary Working Class and the Social Credit Movement in Alberta, 1932–1935,' *Labour/Le Travail* 16 (Fall 1985), 101–2.

33　'A Few Lessons to Be Drawn from the Relief Strikes,' *Worker*, 1 July 1933.

34　This account of the Calgary relief strike is taken from LAC, RG27, v. 359, T-2969, no. 11 (newspaper clippings); C. Sims, 'A Few Lessons to Be Drawn from the Relief Strikes,' *Worker*, 1 July 1933; Levine, ed., *Patrick Lenihan*, 65–74.

35　See copy in LAC, R.B. Bennett Papers, reel M-1326, #402393.

36　Andrew D. Maclean, 'Memorandum,' 7 September 1933, LAC, Bennett Papers, reel M-1326; *Worker*, 9, 16 September 1933.

37　Stunden, 'The Stratford Strikes of 1933,' 7–9.

38　LAC, RG27, v. 355, no. 78, T-2766; 'How the Toronto Furniture Workers Organized and Won,' *Worker*, 2 September 1933.

39　LAC, CSIS Records, RG146, v. 1058, access request 1025-9-92014, Frederick A. Collins 'Personal History File,' RCMP file p175/4462.

40 Joy Parr, *The Gender of Breadwinners* (Toronto: University of Toronto Press, 1990), 215.

41 Stunden, 'The Stratford Strikes of 1933,' 23; 'Workers' Union Sends Demands to Companies,' *Beacon-Herald*, 13 September 1933 (2nd edition).

42 Stunden, 'The Stratford Strikes of 1933,' 16–17, quoting the *Beacon-Herald*, 12 September 1933; see also James Leach, 'The Workers' Unity League and the Stratford Furniture Workers: The Anatomy of a Strike,' *Ontario History* 60.2 (1968), 41.

43 The following brief summary of the strike relies mainly on Stunden's account in 'The Stratford Strikes of 1933,' chapters 2 and 3.

44 'Tremendous Militancy and Great Enthusiasm in Stratford Strike,' *Worker*, 23 September 1933.

45 'Prospects of Ending Strike Are Better,' *Beacon-Herald*, 22 September 1933.

46 'Nearly 2,000 Took Part in Large, but Orderly Demonstration To-day,' *Beacon-Herald*, 22 September 1933 (2nd edition).

47 C.A. Pearson, Office of the Minister of Justice, to Miss A.E. Millar, secretary to the prime minister, 14 November 1933, LAC, Bennett Papers, reel M-1090, 267621–2.

48 Stunden, 'The Stratford Strikes of 1933,' 61, citing an implication by the mayor of Stratford. The documents of the Office of the Attorney General pertaining to the Stratford strikes appear to have been destroyed before the archives were transferred to the Ontario Archives. See explanations on Ontario Archives website with respect to record group RG4-2, 'Office of the Attorney-General correspondence and subject files.' A few documents, such as Attorney General W.H. Price's letter to the secretary of state, Ottawa, of 7 October 1933, in RG13, v. 389, file 1313, Ministry of Justice, accounting for his request for army intervention, survive in Library and Archives Canada; several points in this 'explanation' are misleading. There are a few relevant documents in the Department of National Defence: see Desmond Morton, 'Aid to the Civil Power: The Stratford Strike of 1933,' in Irving Abella, ed., *On Strike* (Toronto: Oxford University Press, 1975), 79–91.

49 Stunden, 'The Stratford Strikes of 1933,' 50, quoting Langford to Defensor, Department of National Defence, 27 September 1933, Canadian Forces Historical Section, file 161.009 D 56.

50 *Beacon-Herald*, 28 September 1933.

51 See W.M. Dickson (private secretary) to Rt. Hon. R.B. Bennett, prime minister, 22 September 1933, enclosing a report on the strike negotiations in which it is said that the manufacturers will recognize the union, LAC, Bennett Papers, reel M-1090, 267577–80.

52 Stunden, 'The Stratford Strikes of 1933,' 56–7, quoting 'Employers With-

draw Recognition,' *Beacon-Herald*, 29 September 1933, and 'Stratford Employers Heave "Red" Charge against Strike Leaders,' Toronto *Globe*, 30 September 1933.

53 Stunden, 'The Stratford Strikes of 1933,' 72–3; a copy of the WUL constitution may be found in LAC, CPC Papers, MG28 IV4, v. 52, file 78 and as an appendix in Tom McEwen, *The Forge Glows Red* (Toronto: Progress Books, 1974). Later in an arcane theoretical commentary entitled 'The Economic Struggles and Our Work, Weaknesses and Main Problems and Tasks,' Stewart Smith, acting leader of the Communist Party of Canada, accused the organizers of backing away from the 'Red scare' and for flatly denying that they were communists. *Communist Review*, March 1934, LAC, CPC Papers, MG28 IV4, v. 78, file 10.

54 Stunden, 'The Stratford Strikes of 1933,', 57–60; 'Unity League Denounced by Labor Leader,' *Beacon-Herald*, 2 October 1933.

55 See Parr, *The Gender of Breadwinners*, 214–18; LAC, RG 27, v. 357, file 96.

56 *Labour Gazette*, October 1933, 986; November 1933, 1075, 1076, 1124; Charles Sims, 'The Stratford Victory,' *Worker*, 25 November 1933. A copy of the 1933 agreement between Kroehler Co. and its employees is in LAC, CPC Papers, MG28 IV4, v. 51, file 27.

57 Stunden, 'The Stratford Strikes of 1933,' 105; 'Kerr Elected Mayor with 291 Majority; Six Labour Candidates on New Council,' *Beacon-Herald*, 5 December 1933.

58 Mary Austin Endicott (Toronto) to her family, 22 January 1934, LAC, Endicott Papers, MG30 C130, v. 49, file 1054.

59 Watt Hugh McCollum, *Who Owns Canada?* (Regina: Saskatchewan CCF Research Bureau, 1935), 40.

60 'Hespeler Rioters Batter Policemen,' *Mail and Empire* (Toronto), 21 December 1933. The events of the strike may be followed through the newspaper collection in the Department of Labour file on 'Strikes and Lockouts,' LAC, RG24, v. 358, #151, reel T-2968.

61 'Strike Called Off in Hespeler,' *Worker*, 6 January 1934.

62 *The Canadian Annual Review of Public Affairs, 1933*, 170

63 This struggle has been studied in detail by Ian Radforth, *Bushworkers and Bosses: Logging in Northern Ontario, 1900–1980* (Toronto: University of Toronto Press, 1987), 124–33, and by Richard, *'Péril Rouge' au Témiscamingue*. See also Radforth's 'Finnish Radicalism and Labour Activism in the Northern Ontario Woods,' in Franca Iacovetta, ed., *A Nation of Immigrants* (Toronto: University of Toronto Press, 1998), 293–316.

64 'Logging Camps Look for Good Season's Work,' *Ottawa Evening Citizen*, 30 November 1933; *Canadian Annual Review, 1934*, 434.

65 'Signed Statements of Bushmen Received,' *Fort William Times-Journal*, 11
December 1933. For average weekly earnings for semi-skilled workers in
Canada, according to the census of 1931, see chapter 5, note 64. In the
labour movement a 'yellow dog contract' is a paper that an anti-union
employer asks workers, particularly new hires, to sign stating their intention not to sign an application for membership card in a union. These
documents, now illegal in most societies, often went on to provide for the
employees to forfeit their jobs if they did sign a union card.

66 For a discussion of 'new unionism' as a term to describe the type of *concili-
atory* unionism embraced by AFL unions during this period see Mercedes
Steedman, 'The Promise: Communist Organizing in the Needle Trades, the
Dressmakers' Campaign, 1928–1937,' *Labour/Le Travail* 34 (Fall 1994), 45ff.

67 *Worker*, editorial, 18 November 1933.

68 In 'Report of District #4 (Timmins),' 26 March 1934, a communist organizer describes the challenges of coping with spies, stools, betrayers, and just
plain adventurers during the lumber workers' strike, LAC, CI Fonds 495, list
98, file 163, reel 19, K-287.

69 See J. Peter Campbell, 'The Cult of Spontaneity: Finnish-Canadian Bushworkers and the Industrial Workers of the World in Northern Ontario,
1919–1934,' *Labour/Le Travail* 41 (Spring 1998), 117–46. See 'Summary
of Proceedings and Decisions' of the Enlarged National Executive Board
meeting of the Workers' Unity League on 11 December 1934 for criticism
of the LWIU's sectarian approach to the IWW in strikes of that year as a bad
example of united front work and poor strike preparation, p. 17, LAC, CSIS
Records, RG146, 'Workers' Unity League – Toronto, Ontario, 1930–1936,'
file 175/6811, access request 92-A-00086.

70 'Thunder Bay Pulpwood Cutters' Conference,' *Worker*, 3 September, 1933;
'Loggers Union Holds Conference up North,' *Worker*, 21 October 1933;
J. Gillbanks, 'Lumberjacks Victorious in Kapuskasing Strike,' *Worker*, 18
November 1933.

71 'Memorandum,' by (undecipherable), Lt-Colonel, G.S., (Ottawa), 6 November 1933, LAC, RG27, v. 356, file 154.

72 'Report from District #4' (Timmins, Ontario), 31 January 1934, LAC, CI
Fonds 495, list 98, file 163, reel 19, K-287.

73 J. Gillbanks, 'Lumberjacks Victorious in Kapuskasing Strike,' *Worker*, 18
November 1933. See also *Porcupine Advance* (Timmins), 16 November 1933,
in LAC, RG27, v. 356, file 154. Report of District #4 (Timmins, Ontario), 31
January 1934, LAC, CI Fonds 495, list 98, file 163, reel 19, K-287.

74 *Winnipeg Tribune*, 15 December 1933. See also 'No Wonder They Revolt,'
editorial of 23 November 1933.

75 J.M. Macdonnell, telegram to C.W. Cox, president of Port Arthur Chamber of Commerce, and vice-president of the Lakehead Timber Association, printed in the *Fort William Times-Journal,* 7 December 1933.

76 *Fort William Times-Journal,* 7 December 1933; Radforth, *Bushworkers and Bosses,* 130.

77 *Fort Frances Times* and *Rainy Lake Herald,* 15 April 1913 and Fort Frances Museum site on the internet, 7 November 2007; H.V. Nelles, *The Politics of Development: Forests, Mines and Hydro-Electric Power in Ontario 1849–1941* (Toronto: Macmillan, 1974), 394, 398, ix, 428.

78 Department of Labour, LAC, RG27, v. 357, file 127, T-2967.

79 Bruce Magnuson, *The Untold Story of Ontario's Bushworkers: A Political Memoir* (Toronto: Progress Books, 1990), 9.

80 'Signed Statements of Bushmen Received,' *Fort William Times-Journal,* 11 December 1933.

81 'Timber Strikes at Port Arthur, Cochrane Over,' *Winnipeg Tribune,* 14 December 1933.

82 *Port Arthur News-Chronicle,* 14 December 1933.

83 Richard, *'Péril Rouge' au Témiscamingue* 147; See also Andrée Lévesque, *Red Travellers: Jeanne Corbin and Her Comrades,* trans. Yvonne M. Klein (Montreal and Kingston: McGill-Queen's University Press, 2006), 95–108.

84 Richard, *'Péril Rouge'au Témiscamingue,* résumé.

85 T.C. Sims, 'Strike Strategy and Tactics' (1934), 2–4, LAC, CPC Papers, MG28 IV4, v. 61, file 28.

12. Sweatshops and Militancy in the Needle Trades

1 *Report of the Royal Commission on Price Spreads* (Ottawa: King's Printer, 1937), 111.

2 Mercedes Steedman, 'The Promise: Communist Organizing in the Needle Trades, the Dressmakers' Campaign, 1928–1937,' *Labour/Le Travail* 34 (Fall 1994), 37.

3 Ruth A. Frager, *Sweatshop Strife: Class, Ethnicity, and Gender in the Jewish Labour Movement of Toronto 1900–1939* (Toronto: University of Toronto Press, 1992), 215.

4 *Canadian Annual Review of Public Affairs 1934* (Toronto: Canadian Review Company), 38–43.

5 H.H. Stevens, text of speech to the Conservative Study Group in Ottawa, 27 July 1934, printed as 'Stevens Booklet' (Toronto: New Commonwealth, 1934), LAC, CPC Papers, MG28 IV4, v. 61, file 25; Richard Wilbur, *H.H. Stevens 1878–1973* (Toronto: University of Toronto Press, 1977), 157, 118;

Larry A. Glassford, *Reaction and Reform: The Politics of the Conservative Party under R.B. Bennett 1927–1938* (Toronto: University of Toronto Press, 1992), 148.

6 *Report of the Royal Commission on Price Spreads,* 110–11.

7 *Resolution of the 2nd District Convention – April 1934 (District 9),* LAC, CI Fonds 495, list 98, file 163, reel 19, K-287.

8 J.F. Marsh, 8 May 1935, OA, Labour, RG7 115-O-19; Marcus Klee, 'Fighting the Sweatshop in Depression Ontario: Capital, Labour and the Industrial Standards Act,' *Labour/Le Travail* 45 (Spring 2000), 23, 24.

9 T.C. Sims, *Sweated Labor: A Piercing Analysis of the Purposes and Aims of the Stevens Inquiry* (Toronto: Workers' Unity League, 1934), pamphlet, 15 pages, LAC, MG28 IV4, v. 61, file 30; 'Statement,' 15 March 1934, LAC, CI Fonds 495, list 98, file 153, reel 18, K-286; 'Sims Shows WUL Only Force Fighting against New Chains,' *Worker,* 10 October 1934.

10 See the *Worker,* 15 August, 29 September, 6 October 1934 for codes being drafted by WUL unions for the mining, lumber, auto, and (13 October 1934) needle trades – J. Gershman, 'Industrial Union Makes Bid for United Action: Text of Letter Sent to AF of L Unions in Needle Trades Calling for Conference on Code for Industry.'

11 *Worker,* editorial, 29 September 1934.

12 Stanley Nadel, 'Reds versus Pinks: A Civil War in the International Ladies' Garment Workers' Union,' *New York History,* January 1985, 71.

13 In *Sweatshop Strife,* Ruth Frager places the burden of guilt for losses caused by the inter-union conflict in Canada most heavily upon the shoulders of the communists. See augury to this chapter, footnote 3.

14 *Convention Souvenir: First National Convention of the Industrial Union of Needle Trades Workers,* Montreal, 10–12 May 1929, LAC, CI Fonds 495, list 98, file 88, reel 10, K-278.

15 Steedman, 'The Promise,' 45–7. Steedman has an enlightening discussion of the changing nature of the dress trade, the effect of the Depression on that trade including the 'steep decline in wages,' and how these factors influenced the development of different forms of unionism (40–5).

16 LAC, RG27, Department of Labour, v. 346, file 3, T-2758.

17 Catherine McLeod, 'Women in Production: The Toronto Dressmakers' Strike of 1931,' in Janice Acton, ed., *Women at Work: Ontario 1850–1930* (Toronto: Canadian Women's Educational Press, 1974), 323; *Worker,* 24 January 1931.

18 OA, RG4, reel 5, 8-C-0493, Communist Party of Canada Records, 'Ewen's Reply to Discussion,' February 1931.

19 *Worker,* 7 February 1931.

20 Frager, *Sweatshop Strife*, 196; McLeod, 'Women in Production,' 314; LAC, RG27, Department of Labour, v. 347, file 14, T-2758.

21 Steedman, 'The Promise,' 51.

22 'Some Important Lessons of the Needle Trades Strikes,' *Worker*, 2 September 1933; 'Needle Trades Union in Discussion of Its Work,' *Worker*, 7 July 1934.

23 Steedman, interview with Joshua Gershman in 1986, 'The Promise,' 55, 64.

24 Steedman, 'The Promise,' 37.

25 *Labour Gazette*, February 1934, 107–9, 193; LAC, RG27, v. 359, file 9; *Mail and Empire*, 22 January 1934.

26 Frager, *Sweatshop Strife*, 154–67.

27 Evelyn Dumas, *The Bitter Thirties in Quebec* (Montreal: Black Rose, 1975) 44–5.

28 Steedman, 'The Promise,' 63, citing ILGWU *Report and Proceedings of the 21st Convention*, 1932.

29 Ibid., 64 (interview with Gershman, 1986); Dumas, *The Bitter Thirties in Quebec*, 46; Irving Abella, 'Portrait of a Jewish Professional Revolutionary: The Recollections of Joshua Gershman,' *Labour/Le Travail* 2 (1977), 200.

30 *Worker*, 5 September 1934.

31 Tom Langford, 'Strikes and Class Consciousness,' *Labour/Le Travail* 33 (Spring 1994), 110.

32 *Ottawa Citizen*, 30 August 1934.

33 Dumas, *The Bitter Thirties in Quebec*, 51; *Ottawa Citizen*, 30 August 1934.

34 'Declaration by the Montreal Dressmakers' Strike Committee,' 21 September, published in the *Worker*, 29 September 1934.

35 E. McG. Quirk, [labour] departmental representative (Montreal), to C.W. Bolton, chief, Statistical Branch (Ottawa), 17 October 1934, LAC, RG27, v. 364, no. 197B.

36 Shane to David Dubinsky, 17 and 5 September 1934, as quoted in Steedman, 'The Promise,' 66–7.

37 'Montreal Dressmakers Call ...' *Worker*, 29 September 1934.

38 Steedman, interview with Leah Roback, 'The Promise,' 67.

39 Steedman, 'The Promise,' 40.

40 James Mochoruk and Donna Webber, 'Women in the Winnipeg Garment Trade, 1929–1945,' in Mary Kinnear, ed., *First Days, Fighting Days: Women in Manitoba History* (Regina: Canadian Plains Research Centre, 1987), 135.

41 LAC, RG27, vols. 344–71, T-2756–T-2981.

42 *Star-Phoenix* (Saskatoon), 5 February 1931; *Tribune* (Winnipeg), 16, 26 February 1931; *Worker*, 21 February 1931.

43 *Worker*, 4 April 1931.

44 'Report on the Strike at the Jacob & Crowley Manufacturing Co., in Winnipeg,' in Gershman to the National Fraction of the Workers' Unity League, n.d. OA, RG4, reel 2, 3-A-1778–81.
45 Joe Forkin, 'Reasons for the Successful Work of the Workers' Unity League in Winnipeg,' *Worker*, 23 September 1933.
46 Ibid.
47 LAC, RG27, Department of Labour Records, v. 354, 355, 356, 357, nos. 38, 71, 79, 100, 134, 157, T-2765–T-2966, T-2967–T-2968.
48 LAC, RG27, Department of Labour Records, v. 355, no. 71, T-2766.
49 *Winnipeg Free Press*, 27 October 1932; LAC, RG27, Department of Labour Records, v. 351, no. 77, T-2762; Roy St G. Stubbs, *Prairie Portraits* (Toronto: McClelland and Stewart, 1954).
50 Mochoruk and Webber, 'Women in the Winnipeg Garment Trade, 1929–1945,' 139–40, 145–6; James H. Gray, *The Winter Years: The Depression on the Prairies* (Toronto: Macmillan, 1966), 137; Frager, *Sweatshop Strife*, 215; Steedman, 'The Promise,' 37.
51 Abella, 'Portrait of a Jewish Professional Revolutionary,' 203.

13. Woodsmen of the West

1 UBC Special Collections, MacMillan Bloedel Papers, box 411, file 24.
2 G. Hak, 'Red Wages,' *Pacific Northwest Quarterly* 80 (July 1989), 90.
3 *Canadian Lumberman*, Toronto, 15 February 1934, in UBC Special Collections, Pritchett–IWA Papers, box 1, file 1, 'Research Material on B.C. Lumber Situation,' n.d. The BC government paid half the salary for a full-time industry lobbyist in England, UBC Special Collections, Tolmie Papers, box 9, file 41, 'Memorandum re: Lumber,' 3 January 1933.
4 *Canadian Annual Review 1934*, 433; 'The "Industry" through the Crisis,' *B.C. Lumber Worker*, 1 September 1934; *Canadian Lumberman*, 1 February 1934, Pritchett–IWA Papers, box 1, file 1; Hak, 'Red Wages.'
5 *Canadian Annual Review 1933*, 452.
6 William Bennett, *Builders of British Columbia* (Vancouver: Broadway Press, 1937), 92.
7 Ibid., 93–5.
8 H.R. MacMillan to Montague Meyer (London), 28 July 1935, UBC Special Collections, MacMillan Bloedel Papers, box 411, file 25; Montague Meyer to H.R. MacMillan, 9 July 1935, ibid., file 24.
9 Andrew Neufeld and Andrew Parnaby, *The IWA in Canada: The Life and Times of an Industrial Union* (Vancouver: New Star Books, 2000), 44.
10 Myrtle Bergren, *Tough Timber: The Loggers of British Columbia* (Vancouver:

Elgin Publications, 1979), 32. For some reason Bergren used a pseudonym, 'Pete Hanson,' for Gunerud in her book.

11 *Communist Review* no. 4 (July–August 1934), LAC, CPC Papers, MG28 IV4, v. 78, file 11, 37; LAC, CI Fonds 495, list 98, file 163, reel 19, K-287, District #9 letter, 'Dear Friends,' 26 January 1934.

12 District #9 letter, 'Dear Friends,' 26 January 1934.

13 Of 18,200 reported accidents in British Columbia in 1933, 36 per cent or 6,552 were in the lumbering industry and included many of the 97 fatalities of that year. *Daily Province*, (Vancouver), 28 February 1934.

14 Bergren, *Tough Timber*, 34; District # 9 letter, 'Dear Friends,' 26 January 1934; Thomsen and Clark Timber Co. to F.E. Harrison, Department of Labour, 28 February 1934, LAC, RG27, v. 359, file 23.

15 The work of this talented organizer does not appear in any of the historical accounts of these great struggles by either the left or the right, for reasons that have become partially clear. At the start of the anti-communist Cold War following the Second World War, Bradley switched sides and joined the social democrats in their successful effort to drive the communists out of the leadership of the lumber workers' union; he quickly became organizer and first vice-president of the BC district of the union. Then three years later the table officers of that organization unceremoniously 'discontinued' him and he disappeared from public view. Letter of J. Stewart Alsbury, president, BC District Council #1, IWA to T.J. Bradley, 4 April 1951, UBC Special Collections, IWA Western Canadian Regional Council No. 1, reel 14, file 1951, 'Tom Bradley, first vice-president.'

16 In a letter to the *News Herald*, 30 January 1934, Arne Johnson, secretary, Sub-Strike Committee in Vancouver, cited an even larger figure, claiming that the scale (measurement of timber) stolen was 20,000 feet.

17 District #9 letter, 'Dear Friends,' 26 January 1934.

18 UBC, Special Collections, Council of Forest Industries of British Columbia Records, Minutes of Board of Directors, BC Loggers' Association, 23 January 1934. Another active member of the Loggers' Association at this time was M.A. Grainger, an Englishman, owner of Alberni Pacific Logging Co., and author of a celebrated novel set in Canada, *Woodsmen of the West* (1908).

19 UBC, Special Collections, S.F. Tolmie Papers, box 6, file 20, Correspondence of the Attorney General's Department, 4 March 1934.

20 'Organizer's Report, Campbell River, B.C.,' 27 January 1934, LAC, CI Fonds 495, list 98, file 163, reel 19, K-287.

21 District #9 letter, 'Dear Friends,' 26 January 1934.

22 Bergren, *Tough Timber*, 35.

23 'Organizer's Report, Campbell River, B.C.,' 27 January 1934.

24 Ibid.

25 LAC, CSIS Records, RG146, access request 1025-9-9019, RCMP HQ File 175/7035, Lumber Workers' Industrial Union 1928–37 (on open shelves), 29 January 1934.

26 A. Johnson, list of companies involved in the strike, 30 April 1934, part of Thornley letter/memo received in the Department of Labour, Ottawa, 7 May 1934, LAC, RG27, v. 359, no. 23; the union claimed an increase of 3,000 members by the end of the strike, 'Statement of LWIU on Loggers Strike,' *B.C. Lumber Worker* 4.8 (26 May 1934), UBC Special Collections, Pritchett–IWA Papers.

27 *Communist Review* no. 4 (July–August 1934), LAC, CPC Papers, MG28 IV4, v. 78, file 11, 39.

28 *Vancouver Sun*, 27 February 1934. Pritchard tried, unsuccessfully, to exclude any known Reds from speaking at the meeting, LAC, CI Fonds, file 163, letter of District #9, 19 February 1934.

29 Ibid.

30 Hugh Thornley to C.W. Bolton, 2, 31 March 1934, Thornley to F.E. Harrison, 5 March 1934, LAC, RG27, v. 359, no. 23.

31 Leaflet, 'Break the Organised Disrupters!,' UBC Special Collections, Pritchett–IWA Papers, box 1, file 3, n.d.; LAC, CSIS Records, RG146, access request 1025-9-9019 'Lumber Workers' Industrial Union, Vancouver, B.C.' (on open shelves), 7 February 1934.

32 F.E. Harrison to W.M. Dickson, deputy minister of labour (Ottawa), 19 February 1934, LAC, RG27, v. 359, no. 23.

33 *Unemployed Worker*, 7 March 1934, LAC, RG27, v. 359, no. 23.

34 *Worker* (Toronto), 17 March 1934; *Vancouver Sun*, 8 March 1934.

35 *Strike Bulletin* no. 33, Monday, 12 March 1934, LAC, RG27, v. 359, no. 23; Stephen Gray, 'Forest Policy and Administration in British Columbia, 1912–1928' (MA thesis, Department of History, Simon Fraser University, 1982), 7.

36 UBC, Special Collections, Pritchett–IWA Papers, leaflet 'We Will Win!' and a draft agreement on camp committees, 'Record of Agreement re Discrimination and Blacklist,' box 1, file 3; A. Johnson, signatories to 'Agreement Accepting the Principle of Camp Committees,' 30 April 1934, part of Thornley letter/memo received in the Department of Labour, Ottawa, 7 May 1934, LAC, RG27, v. 359, no. 23.

37 *Strike Bulletin* no. 33, 13 March 1934, LAC, RG27, v. 359, no. 23.

38 Bell to F.E. Harrison, 19 March 1934, LAC, RG27, v. 359, no. 23.

39 Smith to Pearson, 15 March 1934, UBC, Special Collections, Bloedel, Stewart, and Welch Papers, correspondence, box 26, file 2.

40 'Sawmill Workers!' leaflet, UBC, Special Collections, Pritchett–IWA Papers, box 1-3, n.d.; *News Herald* (Vancouver), 9 April 1934.

41 Adam Bell to S. Smith, telegram, 7 April 1934, UBC, Special Collections, Bloedel, Stewart, and Welch Papers, correspondence, box 26, file 2.

42 Hon. George S. Pearson to S.G. Smith, telegram, 10 April 1934; Smith to Pearson, 12 April 1934, UBC, Special Collections, Bloedel, Stewart, and Welch Papers, correspondence, box 26, file 2.

43 *Strike Bulletin* no. 60, 13 April 1934, LAC, RG27, v. 359, no. 23; Smith to Pearson, 12 April 1934, UBC, Special Collections, Bloedel, Stewart, and Welch Papers, correspondence, box 26, file 2; Bergren, *Tough Timber*, 48.

44 The account of the encounter at Great Central Lake which follows is taken from the *Vancouver Province*, 24 April 1934; *Strike Bulletin* no. 70, 25 April 1934, and no. 72, 27 April 1934, LAC, RG27, v. 359, no. 23; *Strike Bulletin* no. 73, 28 April 1934, LAC, CSIS Records, RG146, access request 1025-9-9019, 162; *Worker*, 5, 12 May 1934.

45 For the music see *The People's Song Book* (New York: Boni and Gaer, 1948), 67.

46 *Strike Bulletin* no. 72, 27 April 1934.

47 *Strike Bulletin* no. 73, 28 April 1934, LAC, CSIS Records, RG146, access request 1025-9-9019, 162; *Worker*, 12 May 1934.

48 Neufeld and Parnaby, *The IWA in Canada*.

49 *Vancouver Sun*, *Vancouver Province*, 27 April, *News-Herald*, 28 April 1934; Vancouver City Archive, Vancouver Board of Trade additional manuscript 300, Special Committee Minutes, v. 148, 26 April 1934; *Strike Bulletin* no. 73. For the 'camp soviets' remark see Bouchette, '2 Sides of Loggers' Strike,' *Vancouver Sun*, 1 March 1934.

50 *Vancouver Sun*, 26 April 1934; *Strike Bulletin* no. 73.

51 *Strike Bulletin* no. 73; *Worker*, 28 April 1934.

52 *Strike Bulletin* no. 80, 8 May 1934.

53 *Strike Bulletin* no. 79, 7 May 1934.

54 Ronald Shaw, 'Organized Labour and the Co-operative Commonwealth Federation in British Columbia 1932–1937' (1973), 32, UBC Special Collections; see also John Manley, 'Communism and the Canadian Working Class during the Great Depression: The Workers' Unity League 1930–1936' (PhD thesis, Dalhousie University, Halifax, 1983), 308.

55 *Worker*, 30 October 1934.

56 'Statement of L.W.I.U. on Loggers' Strike,' *B.C. Lumber Worker* 4.8 and 9 (26 May, 5 June 1934), UBC Special Collections, Pritchett–IWA Papers.

57 'The Lessons from the Loggers' Strike in British Columbia,' *Communist Review* no. 4 (July–August 1934), 38, 51. For favourable verdicts on the strike

by labour historians see Hak, 'Red Wages,' 90, and Clay Perry, cited in Neufeld and Parnaby, *The IWA in Canada*, 45.

14. Fishers in the Salish Sea

1 Stuart Jamieson and Percy Gladstone, 'Unionism in the Fishing Industry of
British Columbia' (part 1), *Canadian Journal of Economics and Political Science*
16.1 (February 1950), 5.
2 Ibid., 7.
3 Percy Gladstone and Stuart Jamieson, 'Unionism in the Fishing Industry of
British Columbia' (part 2), *Canadian Journal of Economics and Political Science* 16.2 (May 1950), 146–52; for graphic descriptions of the fishermen's
strikes of 1900 and 1901 see BC Workers' Unity League organizer William
Bennett's *Builders of British Columbia* (Vancouver: Broadway Press, 1937),
53–9.
4 Jamieson and Gladstone, 'Unionism in the Fishing Industry of British
Columbia' (part 1), 4; Percy Gladstone, 'Industrial Disputes in the Commercial Fisheries of British Columbia' (MA thesis, University of British Columbia, 1959), 125ff.
5 See Homer Stevens and Rolf Knight, *Homer Stevens: A Life in Fishing*
(Madeira Park, BC: Harbour Publishing, 1992); 'Homer Stevens 1923–2002:
Union Hero Fought for Fishermen,' obituary, *Globe and Mail*, 14 November
2002.
6 Stuart Jamieson, 'Native Indians and the Trade Union Movement in British
Columbia,' *Human Organization* 20.4 (Winter 1961), 222.
7 Nominally, according to Percy Gladstone, the strike was led by the BC
Fishermen's Protective Association ('Industrial Disputes in the Commercial
Fisheries of British Columbia'); A.W. Neill, MP for the area, commented
that the fishermen 'had no Union and no organisation, only a committee
elected for the occasion,' A.W. Neill (House of Commons) to W. McGirr,
Nanaimo, 16 October 1931, in LAC, RG27, v. 349, no. 76.
8 Ibid.
9 George North and Harold Griffin, *A Ripple, a Wave: The Story of Union
Organization in the B.C. Fishing Industry* (Vancouver: Fisherman Publishing
Society, 1974), 9.
10 'Fishermen Organize in Workers' Unity League,' *Unemployed Worker* 4.9 (20
February 1932).
11 John Peter Frecker, 'Militant and Radical Unionism in the British Columbia
Fishing Industry' (MA thesis, University of British Columbia, 1973), 96.
12 'Constitution and By-laws of the Fishermen's Industrial Union,' as cited

by Gladstone, 'Industrial Disputes in the Commercial Fisheries of British Columbia,' 172–3.

13 John Peter Frecker, interview with Harold Griffin, 6 December 1971, 'Militant and Radical Unionism in the British Columbia Fishing Industry,' 104; Gladstone, 'Industrial Disputes in the Commercial Fisheries of British Columbia,' 174.

14 Jamieson and Gladstone 'Unionism in the Fishing Industry of British Columbia' (part 1), 163.

15 Table adapted from 'Fishermen,' in the *Unemployed Worker* 5.13 (14 January 1933); 5.17 (15 February 1933), LAC, RG27, v. 353, no. 196.

16 Jamieson and Gladstone, 'Unionism in the Fishing Industry of British Columbia' (part 1), 163.

17 LAC, CI Fonds 495, list 98, file 151, reel 17, K-285, 'Tasks of District 9,' 22 February 1933.

18 LAC, RG27, v. 355, no. 44, June–July 1933.

19 *Worker*, 6 May 1933.

20 *Worker*, 23 December 1933; 15 September 1934.

21 Ted Morino, 'The Movement among Japanese in Canada,' 7 October 1933, 4, LAC, CI Fonds 495, list 98, file 151, reel 17, K-285; 'Report of District 9,' to Central Executive Committee, n.d. (c. Spring 1932), 1; see also research paper, 'Oriental Labor in Canada' (1934), LAC, CI Fonds 495, list 98, file 164, reel 20, K-288 for further background.

22 *Worker*, 26 May 1934.

23 *Voice of the Fishermen and Cannery Workers*, 16 August 1934, LAC, RG27, v. 364, no. 192.

24 'Agreement entered into by the Deep Bay Packing Co., Limited and the Fishermen & Cannery Workers' Industrial Union of Canada, acting for the fishermen at Bute Inlet as adopted by the majority meeting of the fishermen at Bute Inlet, B.C. this 11th day of September, 1935,' LAC, RG27, v. 371, no. 149; 'Department of Labour. Re-reported strike of Blueback Trollers at Heriot Bay, Deep Bay, Lasqueti Island, Pender Harbour, Egmont, Quathiaska Cove, etc., commenced May 16th 1935,' LAC, RG27, v. 368, no. 70.

25 George Miller, president, FCWIU, 'Fishermen on Road to Unity,' *Unity* 6.14 (January–February 1936).

26 'Fishermen's 1936 Strike,' by the Executive Committee, FCWIU, October 1936 (mimeo pamphlet, 23 pages, with introduction by Tom Ewen), UBC Special Collections, Tom McEwen Papers, box 2/3; D.J. Noakes, R.J. Beamish, and R. Gregory, 'British Columbia's Commercial Salmon Industry,' Department of Fisheries and Oceans, Sciences Branch, Pacific Region, Nanaimo, BC (doc. 642, NPAFC, September 2002), 3

27 UBC Special Collections, United Fisherman and Allied Workers' Union Records, 'Our History: How the Union Began.'

15. Not Hot Cakes or Foremen: On to Ottawa!

1 N.A. McKenzie, chairman of the Committee of the Executive Council on Unemployment Relief, Ministry of Public Works, Victoria, BC, to Senator G.D. Robertson, minister of labour, Ottawa, 24 November 1931.
2 Quoted in R. Liversedge, *Recollections of the On to Ottawa Trek* (1973), 125.
3 Testimony to the Regina Riot Inquiry Commission, cited in Ben Swankey and Jean Evans Sheils, *'Work and Wages!': Semi-Documentary Account of the Life and Times of Arthur H. (Slim) Evans* (Vancouver: Trade Union Research Bureau, 1977), 98.
4 James Struthers, *No Fault of Their Own: Unemployment and the Canadian Welfare State 1914–1941* (Toronto: University of Toronto Press, 1983), 61–2.
5 Charlotte Whitton, 'Report *re* Unemployment and Relief in Western Canada' (1932), quoted in ibid., 79.
6 Swankey and Sheils, *'Work and Wages!'* 35
7 At first the paper was published by the 'Workers' Unity League of Canada, Vancouver, B.C,' but later, in December 1931 when there was a possibility the WUL would be declared illegal, the publisher changed to 'Organ of the Vancouver Central Council, National Unemployed Workers' Association,' surprisingly with a more militant format. A year later, in 1932, reflecting further political changes, it became 'Organ of the Vancouver Unemployed Councils, 61 Cordova Street, W., Vancouver, B.C,' minus the 'hammer and sickle.' Copies of the publication can be found in LAC, RG27, Department of Labour, v. 349–54, 358A, reels T-2760–5, T-2969.
8 'Unemployed Work in District #9,' p. 3, April 1932, LAC, CI Fonds 495, list 98, file 141, reel 16, K-284.
9 Liversedge, *Recollections of the On-to-Ottawa Trek,* 15.
10 Smith to Buck, 9 April 1930 [actually 1931], OA, RG4, reel 3, 4-A-2721; also CPC Political Bureau Minutes, 8–9 May 1931, 4, LAC, CI Fonds 495, list 98, file 117. For the RILU letter of 28 May 1931 to the Workers' Unity League, see LAC, CI Fonds 495, list 98, file 117, reel 13, K-281, minutes of CPC Political Bureau meeting of 21 July 1931.
11 Buck to Smith and to Anglo-American Secretariats of the CI and the RILU, 11 May 1931, LAC, CI Fonds 495, list 98, file 121, reel 13, K-281.
12 Smith to Buck, 17 June 1931, LAC, CPC Papers, MG28 IV4, v. 8, file 7; RILU letter to WUL, 28 May 1931, see LAC, CI Fonds 495, list 98, file 117, reel 13, K-281, minutes of CPC Political Bureau meeting of 21 July 1931.

13 See, for example, 'What Is a Neighbourhood Council?' *Unemployed Worker* 4.30 (14 May 1932); Liversedge, *Recollections of the On to Ottawa Trek*, 31–2.

14 LAC, CI Fonds 495, list 98, file 122, reel 14, K-282, CPC, 'Weekly Organization Letter #25,' 15 September 1931; CPC, Political Bureau, 'Three Month Plan of Work,' 15 September 1931; ibid., file 129, National Executive, WUL, 'Re-organisation Programme of N.U.W.A.,' 16 September 1931.

15 LAC, CI Fonds 495, list 98, file 129, reel 14, K-282, 'Unemployment Work in District #9,' April 1932, 3. See also comprehensive reports prepared for the Anglo-American Secretariat by Canadian students at the International Lenin School, such as by 'C. Copeland,' 'Unemployment and the Unemployed Struggles in Canada 1931–1932,' 5 July 1932, and 'Additional Material on Work among Unemployed in Canada,' (Confidential), 17 July 1932, noted as read by members of the CI Political Secretariat, ibid., file 138.

16 'Resolution and Directives on the Role of the WUL Unions and Opposition Groups in the Movement of the Unemployed,' *Workers' Unity* 2.12 (August–September 1932), 6.

17 LAC, MG30A94, J.L. Cohen Papers, v. 5, file 1, transcript of Preliminary Hearing of *Rex vs Bell … Evans et al,* Regina, July 1935, pp. 747–9, exhibit P.22; LAC, CI Fonds 495, list 98, file 182A, reel 22, K-290.

18 From the files of the Vancouver City Police Department and the Regina Riot Inquiry Commission as cited by Liversedge, *Recollections of the On to Ottawa Trek,* 325, and Victor Howard, *We Were the Salt of the Earth!* (Regina: Canadian Plains Research Center, 1985), 14–15; another more militant version of the RCWU constitution, as amended in August 1934, speaks of supporting trade unionism 'in the final overthrow of capitalism and the establishment of a workers' government.' See Swankey and Sheils, *'Work and Wages!'* 80.

19 Lorne Brown, *When Freedom Was Lost: The Unemployed, the Agitator and the State* (Montreal: Black Rose Books, 1987), 47–56.

20 Saskatchewan Federation of Labour, *The 60th Anniversary of the On-to-Ottawa Trek* (pamphlet, 1995), 13; Tom McEwen, *The Forge Glows Red* (Toronto: Progress Books, 1974), 165. The Regina Riot began in Market Square and moved west into the downtown, with severe fighting taking place at Scarth and 11th and 12th avenues. The actual site of the beginning of the riot is now underneath the new Regina police headquarters and parking lot. On advice from the labour movement, the Historic Sites and Monuments Board placed a plaque in the Scarth Street Mall immediately south of the intersection of Scarth Street and 11th Avenue (Garnet Dishaw, letter to author, 21 March 2010).

21 Pat Forkin, 'Meet Matt Shaw!' *Worker*, 20 July 1935.

22 Quoted in Struthers, *No Fault of Their Own*, 100.

23 Forkin, 'Meet Matt Shaw!'

24 Liversedge, *Recollections of the On to Ottawa Trek*, 39.

25 Ibid., 18–19.

26 For a fuller account of Evans see Swankey and Sheils, *'Work and Wages!'* 6–37.

27 Evans, testimony to the Regina Riot Inquiry Commission (1935) as cited in ibid., 86–7. See also interviews with surviving strikers by Victor Howard in the 1960s in *We Were the Salt of the Earth!* 34–8.

28 Swankey and Sheils, *'Work and Wages!'* 93.

29 *B.C. Workers' News*, 18 April 1935; Conference with Mayor McGeer, 25 April, cited in Swankey and Sheils, *'Work and Wages!'* 89, 93; see also interview with Prime Minister Bennett, 22 June 1935, in Liversedge, *Recollections of the On to Ottawa Trek*, 201.

30 Quoted in Swankey and Sheils, *'Work and Wages!'* 98.

31 Liversedge, *Recollections of the On to Ottawa Trek*, 84.

32 Bob Kerr, BC secretary of the WUL, quoted in Swankey and Sheils, *'Work and Wages!'* 289; Tim Buck speaking at Montreal election rally, in Gregory S. Kealey and Reg Whitaker, eds., *RCMP Security Bulletins: The Depression Years, Part II, 1935* (St John's: Canadian Committee on Labour History, 1995), 375.

33 *Worker*, 1, 4, 6, 8 June 1935; Central Committee, CPC to all district secretaries ('Dear Friends'), 6 June 1935, LAC, CI Fonds 495, list 98, file 179.

34 RCMP 'E' Division, Criminal Investigation Bureau (Secret), 5 June 1935, 'Arthur H. Evans – Communist,' personal history file 175/p1072, Freedom of Information Act request, read at CSIS headquarters, Ottawa, in May 1992.

35 Garnet Dishaw, letter to the author, 21 March 2010.

36 Quoted in Swankey and Sheils, *'Work and Wages!'* 289.

37 Steve Brodie in ibid., 113

38 RCMP 'E' Division, 13 June 1935; *Worker*, 1 October 1935, quoting Humphrey Mitchell speaking at the Trades and Labour Congress in Halifax.

39 Larry A. Glassford, *Reaction and Reform: The Politics of the Conservative Party under R.B. Bennett 1927–1938* (Toronto: University of Toronto Press, 1992), 160.

40 Dishaw letter, 21 March 2010.

41 Swankey and Sheils, *'Work and Wages!'* 137–8.

42 H. Oliver, official debates reporter, 'Report of Interview between Delegation of Strikers and Dominion Government, June 22nd 1935,' cited in Liversedge, *Recollections of the On to Ottawa Trek*, 194–216.

43 Dishaw letter, 21 March 2010.

44 Prime Minister R.B. Bennett, in the House of Commons, 2 July 1935, cited in Swankey and Sheils, *'Work and Wages!'* 197.

45 Bill Waiser, *All Hell Can't Stop Us: The On-to-Ottawa Trek and Regina Riot* (Calgary: Fifth House, 2003), 258, 264.

46 In *All Hell Can't Stop Us*, Waiser, projecting an aura of even-handedness, perhaps, balances his sympathy for the strikers against a denigration or misrepresentation of the activity and policies of the communists in the struggles of the single unemployed. 'For [Tim] Buck,' he writes, 'the trek never happened' (273). See also 36, 40, 58, 62, 112, and 167.

47 Brown, *When Freedom Was Lost*, 204–5.

16. Changing Times: The Final Convention of the Workers' Unity League

1 Bureau Fraction of RILU, 'Letter to Canadian CP on Trade Union Work,' 28 April 1935, LAC, CI Fonds 495, list 98, file 182, reel 22, K-290.

2 Sir Edward Beatty, chairman and president, Canadian Pacific Railway (Montreal), to Prime Minister R.B. Bennett (personal), 28 July 1935, enclosing a report 'Re: Party Policy, 4 July 1935' consisting of 'a fairly authentic – indeed almost verbatim – transcription of a speech' made by a leading British Columbia communist who had attended a recent CPC Central Committee meeting in Toronto, LAC, Bennett Papers, reel M-1090, 267493–5.

3 Desmond Morton with Terry Copp, *Working People: An Illustrated History of the Canadian Labour Movement* (Toronto: Deneau, 1984), 144.

4 Thomas Ewen, *Unity Is the Workers' Lifeline*, report to the Third Dominion Convention of the WUL, 9 November 1935, 7, LAC, CPC Papers, MG28 IV4, v. 61, file 42.

5 *Worker*, 14 November 1935.

6 The National Executive Board consisted of J.B. McLachlan, president, Thomas E. Ewen, national secretary, Thomas C. Sims, executive board secretary, Julia Collins [Carr], national secretary-treasurer, and George Drayton, British Columbia, Sam Scarlett, Ontario, Joshua Gershman, Quebec, Myer Klig, Toronto, John Stokaluk, Alberta, Nicholas Thatchuk, Northern Ontario, Martin J. Forkin, Winnipeg, Edward Sarman, (?), Annie S. Buller, Toronto, Frederick Collins, Southern Ontario, and Jacob Penner, Winnipeg. See letterhead, 14 June 1935, in LAC, CI Fonds 495, list 98, file 182, reel 22, K-290.

7 *Worker*, 12, 14, 19, November 1935.

8 See David Frank, *J.B. McLachlan: A Biography* (Toronto: James Lorimer, 1999), 500.

9 Ewen, *Unity Is the Workers' Lifeline*, 19, 17.

10 Irving Abella, *Nationalism, Communism and Canadian Labour* (Toronto: University of Toronto Press, 1973), 3–4.

11 Douglas Cruikshank and Gregory S. Kealey, 'Strikes in Canada, 1891–1950,' *Labour/LeTravail* 20 (Fall 1987), 101, 114–16; citing various sources, John Manley estimates that the WUL led over 50 per cent of the strikes during the upsurge of 1933–4, embracing half of all strikers, occupying 71 per cent of striker days, and in the process winning improvements in wages and/or conditions in almost 75 per cent of all strikes, 'Canadian Communists, Revolutionary Unionism, and the "Third Period": The Workers' Unity League, 1929–1935,' *Journal of the Canadian Historical Association* no. 5 (1994), 179.

12 *Worker*, 8 August 1934.

13 'WUL Bulletin #50,' 19 July 1934, LAC, CI Fonds 495, list 98, file 165, reel 20, K-288.

14 E.H. Carr, *The Twilight of Comintern, 1930–1935* (London: Macmillan, 1976), 124–8.

15 *Worker*, 3 March 1934.

16 Freed (Moscow) to Smith, 7 April 1934, LAC, CI Fonds 495, list 98, file 162, reel 19, K-287.

17 G. Pierce (pseudonym), *Socialism and the CCF* (Toronto: Contemporary Publishing Association, 1934), 160.

18 'Manifesto of the Seventh Convention of the Communist Party of Canada, July 23–28, 1934,' *Worker*, 29 August 1934; Gregory S. Kealey and Reg Whitaker, eds., *RCMP Security Bulletins: The Depression Years, Part I, 1933–1934* (St John's: Canadian Committee on Labour History, 1993–5), 247–51; T.C. Sims, representative of the Trade Union Commission, 'Trade Union Unity and Our Party,' in *Toward a Canadian People's Front* (November 1935), 119, University of Toronto Fisher Rare Book Library, Kenny Collection.

19 'Strike Struggles in Canada and the Work of the Communist Party,' 8 August 1934. There are two drafts of this 22-page document. The first one, dated 15 May 1934, mentions 'social fascism' only in passing, and is generally positive about the strike wave, about the growth of the revolutionary unions of the WUL and their influence among workers in the reformist-led unions. The second draft, three months later on 8 August, is attributed to 'Barnes.' By its content, and the style, authority, and sophistication of this author, it can almost certainly be assumed that 'Barnes' was a pseudonym for Smith, LAC, CI Fonds 495, list 98, file 158, reel 19, K-287.

20 See T.C. Sims, 'Strike Strategy and Tactics,' from his report on the National Executive Board of the Workers' Unity League, 4, 5 September 1934, LAC, CPC Papers, MG28 IV4, v. 61, file 28.

21 'Directives on Work in the Reformist Unions,' adopted at the 6th Central Committee sessions in August 1934, LAC, CI Fonds 495, list 98, file 160, reel 19, K-287.

22 'Minutes – 6th Central Committee Session,' 28/9 August 1934, LAC, CI Fonds 495, list 98, file 160, reel 19, K-287.

23 Leslie Morris, 'What Faces Us Now in the Struggle to Defeat War and Rising Fascism,' *Worker*, 17 October 1934; Kealey and Whitaker, *RCMP Security Bulletins: The Depression Years, Part I, 1933–1934*, 332, 366.

24 Insp. A.E. Reames, 'O' Division, to the commissioner, Ottawa, 9 November 1934, LAC, CSIS Records, RG146, v. 849. Access request 96-A-00149, access box 96 pt. 2: Stewart Smith.

25 Political Commission (ECCI) to CP Canada, 17 October 1934 (Confidential), LAC, CI Fonds 495, list 98, file 156.

26 Morris, in Toronto, to Johnny [Weir], in Moscow, 22 April 1931, LAC, CI Fonds 495, list 98, file 103, reel 11, K-279.

27 'An Open Letter and Appeal,' 28 February 1935, LAC, CI Fonds 495, list 98, file 182, reel 22, K-290.

28 Bureau Fraction of RILU, 'Letter to Canadian CP on Trade Union Work,' 28 April 1935, LAC, CI Fonds 495, list 98, file 182, reel 22, K-290; for an earlier draft of this document dated 31 March 1935, see ibid., file 169, reel 20, K-288 and letter of L. Morris, no. 5 to Dear Friends (Toronto), 28 March 1935, ibid., reel 21, K-289; see also 'Red International Urges World Trade Union Unity,' *Worker*, 26 March 1935.

29 For developments in the USA see H.U. Faulkner, *American Political and Social History* (New York: F.S. Crofts and Co., 1947), 697ff; Fraser Ottanelli, *The Communist Party of the United States: From the Depression to World War II* (New Brunswick, NJ: Rutgers University Press, 1991), 44 ff; William Z. Foster, *History of the Communist Party of the United States* (New York: International Publishers, 1952), 297–307.

30 J.B. Salsberg, 'W.U.L. Organizer Explains the Loss of Certain Strikes at Present Time,' *Worker*, 13 October 1934. See also T.C. Sims, *Strike Strategy and Tactics*, report to WUL, Toronto, 4–5 September 1934, LAC, CPC Papers, MG28 IV4, v. 61, file 28.

31 Ibid., 21. See also Canadian Labour Defense League, 'Class Terror in Canada, 1934,' LAC, CI Fonds 495, list 98, file 183, reel 22, K-290.

32 'Klig Announces Campaign,' *Worker*, 13 October 1934; 'A Summary of Proceedings and Decisions,' Enlarged National Executive Board, WUL, Toronto, 11 December 1934, LAC, CSIS Records, RG146, access request 92-A-00086 (file 175/6811).

33 Meyer Klig, acting national secretary, WUL, ibid., 2, 'The Unionization Campaign and the Struggle for the United Front.' See also 'Material for Canadian Report on Trade Union Work,' 7 February 1935, LAC, CI Fonds 495, list 98, file 171, 4, reel 20, K-288.

34 'An Open Letter and Appeal,' 28 February 1935, LAC, CI Fonds 495, list 98, file 182, reel 22, K-290.

35 'Executive of A.F.L. Acts against Twelve Unions,' *Labour Gazette* (Ottawa) (August 1936), 680.

36 Ewen (fraction secretary), *Toward a Canadian People's Front: Reports and Speeches at the 9th Plenum of the Central Committee, CPC, November 1935*, 125, LAC, CPC Papers, MG28 IV4, v. 11, file 39; also University of Toronto Fisher Rare Book Library, Kenny Collection, CAN 0373.

37 For the circumstances surrounding McLachlan's withdrawal from the Workers' Unity League, see David Frank and John Manley, 'The Sad March to the Right: J.B. McLachlan's Resignation from the Communist Party of Canada, 1936,' *Labour/LeTravail* 30 (Fall 1992), 115–34.

38 *Unity* (January–February 1936).

39 Ewen, 'Unity is the Workers' Lifeline,' 30.

40 Ibid., 19. In his memoirs, Ewen states that 'in all W.U.L. unions the decision to return to the AFL-TLC unions was carried out by a referendum vote of the membership.' McEwen, *The Forge Glows Red* (Toronto: Progress Books, 1974), 149.

41 'The W.U.L. Fights for Unity,' *Toward a Canadian People's Front*, 125.

42 Minutes of the Executive Board, Workers' Unity League, 7 December 1935, 4, 22 January and 4 April 1936, UBC Special Collections, Angus MacInnis Papers, box 35.

43 McLachlan to Tim Buck, 13 June 1936, cited in Frank and Manley, 'The Sad March to the Right,' 134.

44 Interview with Joshua Gershman in 1986 in Mercedes Steedman, 'The Promise: Communist Organizing in the Needle Trades, the Dressmakers' Campaign 1928–1937,' *Labour/Le Travail* no. 34 (Autumn 1994), 69

45 I. Minster, 'We Fight for Unity of Winnipeg Labor,' *Unity* (January–February 1936), 18; Steedman, 'The Promise,' 68; 'Minutes of Executive Board Meeting, [W.U.L.], 73 Adelaide St W., Toronto,' 4 April 1936, rm. 207, 73 Adelaide St W., Toronto, UBC Special Collections, Angus MacInnis Papers, box 35, 2–3.

46 *Toward a Canadian People's Front*, 124–5; Bruce Magnuson, *The Untold Story of Ontario's Bushworkers: A Political Memoir* (Toronto: Progress Books, 1990), 22; Ian Radforth, *Bushworkers and Bosses: Logging in Northern Ontario 1900–1980* (Toronto: University of Toronto Press, 1987), 134–58.

47 Faulkner, *American Political and Social History*, 701.

48 See Andrew Neufeld and Andrew Parnaby, *The IWA in Canada: The Life and Times of an Industrial Union* (Vancouver: IWA Canada/New Star Books, 2000), 50ff; Magnuson, *The Untold Story of Ontario's Bushworkers*, 48.

49 See Robert Livett and A.J. Morrison, 'Officers' Report to the 20th Consecutive Constitutional Convention, District 18, United Mine Workers of America, Calgary, Alberta,' 9 January 1935, 5, in·LAC, RG27, v. 117, file 600-02-130.

50 McEwen, *The Forge Glows Red*, 149–50; Allen Seager, 'A History of the Mine Workers' Union of Canada 1925–1936,' appendix E, table 7, 'The "Unity" Referendum, June 30, 1936' (MA thesis, McGill University, 1977/8).

51 Ibid., 229.

52 Ewen, 'Final Statement of W.U.L. Executive Board to Those Trade Unionists Who Constituted Its Membership, and Who Have Now Merged within the Unions of the A.F. of L,' Toronto, 18 June 1936, LAC, CPC Papers, MG28 IV4, v. 52, file 79.

53 Minutes, 4 April 1936, rm. 207, 73 Adelaide St. W., Toronto, UBC Special Collections, Angus MacInnis Papers, box 35.

Afterword

1 Draft Statement of the Political Bureau, CPC, *Worker*, 3 January 1931.

2 Norman Penner, *Canadian Communism* (Toronto: Methuen, 1988), 106, 141.

3 *Workers' Unity League: Policy, Tactics, Structure, Demands* (Toronto: WUL National Office, n.d., circa spring 1932), 48-page pamphlet, 21, UBC Special Collections, SPAM 12030; *Constitution of the Workers' Unity League* (as amended in September 1933), Tom McEwen, *The Forge Glows Red* (Toronto: Progress Books, 1974), appendix II, 255.

4 This section of the text, slightly modified, was first inserted in *Bienfait: The Saskatchewan Miners' Struggle of '31* (Toronto: University of Toronto Press, 2002), 128–30.

5 *Unemployed Worker* 4.20 (27 February 1932), LAC, Department of Labour, RG27, v. 358A, mfm T-2969.

6 Corlandt Starnes, commissioner, RCMP, to W.S. Edwards, deputy minister of justice, re 'Alleged Smuggling of Arms by Communists,' 8 November 1930, LAC, RG13, Department of Justice, v. 346, file1750. Starnes dismissed the rumours of arms smuggling, commenting that 'these people have no organization in the Maritime Provinces capable of carrying through any such operations.'

7 In passing, it is of interest to note that the difference between the approach of Engels and Lenin was acknowledged by Ontario's attorney general, W.H. Price, in 1932, even as he advocated the use of Section 98 of the Criminal Code to put communists in jail because, he claimed, they 'rely on force.' See W.H. Price, 'The Possibility of Peaceful Economic and Political Develop-

ment with a Consideration, in that Regard, of Section 98 of the Criminal Code,' 9 September 1933, 7, in OA RG4, box 4, file 27; Frederick Engels, 'Editor's Preface to the First English Translation' of Karl Marx, *Capital*, 1886 (Chicago: Charles H. Kerr and Co., 1906), 32. The communists, in defence, said that was not their position, but they did not cite Engels's views to bolster their defence, nor did they break ranks to stand up in court and say that Lenin's model did not necessarily apply to a parliamentary democracy like Canada.

Years later, in the early 1950s, after wide consultations, including with the senior members of the Communist Party of the Soviet Union, all the communist parties in the English-speaking liberal democracies revised their programs to say explicitly that they thought a peaceful, parliamentary transition from capitalism to socialism was possible. Yet even then many communists continued to have credible doubts about such possibilities because the liberal democracies, if they felt able, showed themselves quite prepared to abandon their principles and either forcibly or covertly overthrow the results of democratic elections in numerous countries rather than accept an elected leftist or socialist government coming to power. A short list of such expected 'pro-slavery rebellions,' as Marx put it, would include the overthrow of democratic election results by the United States and its allies in Guatemala (Arbenz's government, 1954), British Guiana (Jagan, 1961), Chile (Allende, 1973), and Haiti (Aristide, 1991, 2004). U.S. involvement in the overthrow of Prime Minister Jagan is revealed in the *New York Times* obituary of his widow on 1 April 2009 in these terms: 'According to long-classified documents, President John F. Kennedy ordered the Central Intelligence Agency in 1961 to destabilize the Jagan government. The CIA covertly financed a campaign of labour unrest, false information and sabotage that led to race riots and, eventually, the ascension of Forbes Burnham, a London-educated lawyer and a leader of the People's Progressive Party, who had become a rival of the Jagans.'

8 Errol Black and Jim Silver, *Building a Better World: An Introduction to Trade Unionism in Canada*, 2nd ed. (Halifax: Fernwood Publishing, 2008), 144.

9 Kevin Morgan 'The Trouble with Revisionism: Or Communist History with the History Left In,' *Labour/Le Travail* 63 (Spring 2009), 152, 155.

10 F.R. Scott, 'The Trial of the Toronto Communists,' *Queen's Quarterly* 39 (August 1932), 512–13.

Bibliography

The sources listed below are those items which proved most helpful in yielding the information and insights that went into producing this book.

Primary Sources

Archival Collections

British Columbia Archives, Victoria
   Attorney General's Department GR429, box 21
   Premier's Office – GR1222, boxes 7, 11, 12

Glenbow Archives, Calgary
   Gushel Family Fonds
   Western Canadian Collieries Ltd., Fonds

Library and Archives Canada, Ottawa (LAC)
   Canadian Security Intelligence Service (formerly RCMP) Records, RG146
   Communist International Fonds, MG10 K3
   Communist Party of Canada, MG28 IV4
   Department of Immigration, RG76
   Department of Justice, RG13
   Department of Labour, 'Strikes & Lockouts,' RG27
   Personal Papers: R.B. Bennett MG26K; J.L. Cohen MG30A94

Ontario Archives, Toronto (OA)
   Communist Party of Canada Collection, RG4, Appendix 3, MS367
   Department of Labour, RG7
   Multicultural History Society of Ontario Fonds

Provincial Archives of Manitoba, Winnipeg
  Flin Flon Oral History Project (1984)

Saskatchewan Archives Board, Regina
  Department of Labour: Estevan strike file 1931
  Oral History Collection, Nos. R-319, R-326-27, R-1020-21, R-1964, R-1966
  Records of the Royal Commission on the Estevan-Bienfait Mining Dispute,
    1931
  Regina Riot Inquiry Commission, proceedings and *Report* (1935)
  Rex vs. Anne Buller, transcripts of preliminary hearing (1931), trial (1932),
    and appeal (1933)

University of British Columbia, Special Collections, Vancouver
  Willilam Bennett Papers
  Bloedel, Stewart and Welch Collection
  Council of Forest Industries of British Columbia Records
  Arthur H. Evans Papers
  Lil Greene Papers
  Angus MacInnis Papers
  MacMillan Bloedel Papers
  Tom McEwen Papers
  Harold Pritchett/IWA District Council No. 1 Papers
  IWA Western Canadian Regional Council Records
  Rolf Knight Papers
  S.F. Tolmie Papers
  United Fishermen and Allied Workers Union Records, 1934 ff.

University of Toronto Fisher Rare Book Library
  Robert S. Kenny Collection

Vancouver City Archives
  Board of Trade Records

Government Documents

British Columbia. *Report of the Commissioner, Coal and Petroleum Products Commis-*
  sion, v. 2 (1937)
Canada. Department of Labour. *Labour Gazette*
Canada. Department of Labour. *Labour Organizations in Canada*
Canada. Department of Labour. *Annual Report*

Canada. Dominion Bureau of Statistics. Canada Year Book
Canada. Dominion Bureau of Statistics. *Coal Statistics for Canada*
Canada. *Report of the Royal Commission on Price Spreads* (1937)
Canada. *Report of the Royal Commission on the Textile Industry* (1938)

Newspapers and Periodicals

Alice Arm Herald
The B.C. Lumber Worker
The Canadian Annual Review of Public Affairs
The Canadian Labour Monthly

The Canadian Unionist
Communist Review
International Press Correspondence/World News and Views
The Unemployed Worker
The Western Miner/The Canadian Miner
The Worker
Workers' Unity

Pamphlets

The Alberta Hunger-March and the Trial of the Victims of Brownlee's Police Terror.
   Toronto: Canadian Labour Defense League, n.d. circa January 1933
Lozovsky, A. *The Workers' Economic Struggles and the Fight for Workers' Rule: Some*
   Challenging International Lessons. Montreal: Contemporary Publishers, n.d.
   circa 1932
Price, W.H. *Agents of Revolution: A History of the Workers' Unity League, Setting Forth*
   Its Origin and Aims. Toronto: Attorney-General's Office, n.d. circa 1934
Problems of Strike Strategy: Decisions of the International Conference on Strike Strategy
   Held in Strassburg, Germany, January 1929. Foreword by A. Lozovsky. New York:
   Workers' Library Publishers, n.d. circa 1930
The Regina Manifesto. Regina: Co-operative Commonwealth Federation, 1933
Ryan, Oscar. *Deported!* Toronto: Canadian Labour Defense League, 1932, 12
   pages
The Stevens Pamphlet: Why? Toronto: West Toronto Printing House, 1934
Workers' Self-Defense in the Courts. Toronto: Canadian Labour Defense League,
   n.d. circa 1933
Workers' Unity League: Policy, Tactics, Structure, Demands. Toronto: WUL National
   Office, n.d. circa 1932, 50 pages

Secondary Sources

Books

Abella, Irving. *The Canadian Labour Movement 1902–1960.* Ottawa: Canadian Historical Association, Booklet 28, 1975.

– *Nationalism, Communism and Canadian Labour.* Toronto: University of Toronto Press, 1973.

Abella, Irving, and David Millar, eds. *The Canadian Worker in the 20th Century.* Oxford: Oxford University Press, 1978.

Acton, Janice, ed. *Women at Work, Ontario 1850–1930.* Toronto: Canadian Women's Educational Press, 1974.

Bennett, William. *Builders of British Columbia.* Vancouver: Broadway Press, 1937.

Bercuson, David. *Fools and Wise Men: The Rise and Fall of the One Big Union.* Toronto: McGraw-Hill Ryerson, 1978.

Bergren, Myrtle. *Tough Timber: The Loggers of British Columbia.* Vancouver: Elgin Publications, 1979.

Betcherman, Lita-Rose. *The Little Band: The Clashes between the Communists and the Canadian Establishment 1928–1932.* Ottawa: Deneau, 1982.

Black, Errol, and Jim Silver. *Building a Better World. An Introduction to Trade Unionism in Canada.* 2nd ed. Halifax: Fernwood Publishing, 2008.

Bonosky, Phillip. *Brother Bill McKie: Building the Union at Ford.* New York: International Publishers, 1953.

Borkenau, Franz. *World Communism: A History of the Communist International.* Ann Arbor: University of Michigan Press, 1938/62.

Brown, Lorne. *An Unauthorized History of the RCMP.* Toronto, James, Lewis and Samuel, 1973.

– *When Freedom Was Lost: The Unemployed, the Agitator and the State.* Montreal: Black Rose Books, 1987 .

Buck, Tim. *Thirty Years: 1922–1952.* Toronto: Progress Books, 1952.

Canadian Mines Handbook. Toronto: Northern Miner Press, 1934.

Caragata, Warren. *Alberta Labour: A Heritage Untold.* Toronto: Lorimer, 1979.

Carr, E.H. *The Twilight of Comintern, 1930–1935.* London: Macmillan, 1982.

– *A History of Soviet Russia: Foundations of a Planned Economy, 1926–29,* vols. 2 and 3, parts 1 and 2. London: Macmillan, 1976.

– *The Soviet Impact on the Western World.* London: Macmillan, 1946.

Communist Party of Canada. *Canada's Party of Socialism: History of the Communist Party of Canada 1921–1976.* Toronto: Progress Books, 1982.

– *The Road to Socialism in Canada: The Program of the Communist Party of Canada.* Toronto: Progress Books, 1960.

Creighton, Donald. *Canada's First Century 1867–1967*. Toronto: Macmillan, 1970.

Degras, Jane. *The Communist International*. Vol. 3. London: Oxford University Press, 1965.

Dumas, Evelyn. *The Bitter Thirties in Quebec*. Montreal: Black Rose, 1975.

Endicott, Stephen. Bienfait: *The Saskatchewan Miners' Struggle of '51*. Toronto: University of Toronto Press, 2002.

Foster, William Z. *From Bryan to Stalin*. New York: International Publishers, 1937

– *History of the Communist Party of the United States*. New York: International Publishers, 1952.

– *Outline Political History of the Americas*. New York: International Publishers, 1951.

Frager, Ruth. *Sweatshop Strife: Class, Ethnicity, and Gender in the Jewish Labour Movement of Toronto 1900–1939*. Toronto: University of Toronto Press, 1992.

Frager, Ruth, and Carmela Patrias. *Discounted Labour: Women Workers in Canada, 1870–1939*. Toronto: University of Toronto Press, 2005.

Frank, David. *J.B. McLachlan: A Biography*. Toronto: James Lorimer, 1999.

Freeman, Joseph. *An American Testament: A Narrative of Rebels and Romantics*. London: Victor Gollancz, 1938.

Friesen, J., and H.K. Ralston. *Historical Essays on British Columbia*. Toronto: McClelland and Stewart, 1976.

Fudge, Judy, and Eric Tucker. *Labour before the Law: The Regulation of Workers' Collective Action in Canada, 1900–1948*. Toronto: University of Toronto Press, 2001/2004.

Glassford, Larry A. *Reaction and Reform: The Politics of the Conservative Party under R.B. Bennett 1927–1938*. Toronto: University of Toronto Press, 1992.

Griffin, Betty, and Susan Lockhart. *Their Own History: Women's Contribution to the Labour Movement of British Columbia*. Vancouver: United Fishermen and Allied Workers Union/Canadian Autoworkers Union Seniors Club, 2002.

Hedman, Valerie, ed. *Flin Flon*. Altona: Flin Flon Historical Society, 1974.

Heron, Craig. *The Canadian Labour Movement: A Short History*. Toronto: James Lorimer and Co., 1996.

Heron, Craig, ed. *The Workers' Revolt in Canada 1917–1925*. Toronto: University of Toronto Press, 1998.

Hobsbawm, E.J. *Revolutionaries: Contemporary Essays*. London: Weidenfeld and Nicholson, 1973.

Hollander, Paul. *Political Pilgrims: Travels of Western Intellectuals to the Soviet Union, China, and Cuba 1928–1978*. New York: Harper Colophon Books, 1981/83.

Howard, Victor. '*We Were the Salt of the Earth!*' Regina: Canadian Plains Research Centre, 1985.

Jamieson, Stuart. *Industrial Relations in Canada.* 2nd ed. Toronto: Macmillan, 1973.

Kealey, Gregory S., and Reg Whitaker. *RCMP Security Bulletins: The Depression Years.* Parts I and II. St John's: Canadian Committee on Labour History, 1993–5.

Kinnear, Mary, ed. *First Days, Fighting Days: Women in Manitoba History.* Regina: Canadian Plains Research Centre, 1987.

Klehr, Harvey, John Earl Haynes, and Kyrill M. Anderson. *The Soviet World of American Communism.* New Haven: Yale University Press, 1998.

Kolasky, John. *The Shattered Illusion: The History of Ukrainian Pro-Communist Organizations in Canada.* Toronto: PMA Books, 1979.

Kotkin, Stephen. *Magnetic Mountain: Stalinism as a Civilization.* Berkeley: University of California Press, 1995.

Kuusinen, Aino. *The Rings of Destiny.* New York: William Morrow, 1974.

Lenin, V.I. *Collected Works.* Vol. 31. 4th English ed. Moscow: Progress Publishers, 1965.

– *Women and Society.* New York: International Publishers, 1938.

Lévesque, Andrée. *Red Travellers: Jeanne Corbin and Her Comrades.* Trans. Yvonne M. Klein. Montreal and Kingston: McGill-Queen's University Press, 2006.

Levine, Gilbert, ed. *Patrick Lenihan: From Irish Rebel to Founder of Canadian Public Sector Unionism.* St John's: Canadian Committee on Labour History, 1998.

Lewis, David, and F.R. Scott. *Make This Your Canada: A Review of C.C.F. History and Policy.* Toronto: Central Canada Publishing Co., 1943.

Lindstrom-Best, Varpu. *Defiant Sisters: A Social History of Finnish Immigrant Women in Canada.* Toronto: Multicultural History Society of Ontario, 1988.

Liversedge, Ron. *Recollections of the On to Ottawa Trek.* Toronto: McClelland and Stewart, 1973.

Livesay, Dorothy. *Right Hand, Left Hand: A True Life of the Thirties.* Erin: Press Porcepic, 1977.

Loudon, Pete. *The Town That Got Lost.* Sydney, BC: Gray's Publishing, 1973.

Lozovsky, A. *Marx and the Trade Unions.* New York: International Publishers, 1933/42.

Luxton, Meg. *More Than a Labour of Love: Three Generations of Women's Work in the Home.* Toronto: Women's Press, 1980.

Magnuson, Bruce. *The Untold Story of Ontario's Bushworkers: A Political Memoir.* Toronto: Progress Books, 1990.

Marx, Karl. *Capital.* 1886. Chicago: Charles H. Kerr and Co., 1906.

Marx, Karl, and Friedrich Engels. *The Communist Manifesto.* New York: International Publishers, 1948.

McCollum, Watt Hugh. *Who Owns Canada?* Regina: Saskatchewan CCF Research Bureau, 1935.

McDermott, Kevin, and Jeremy Agnew. *The Comintern: A History of International Communism from Lenin to Stalin.* London: Macmillan, 1996.

McEwen, Tom. *The Forge Glows Red.* Toronto: Progress Books, 1974.

McKay, Ian. *Rebels, Reds, Radicals: Rethinking Canada's Left History.* Toronto: Between the Lines, 2005.

McKay, Ian, ed. *Working-Class Culture.* St John's: Canadian Committee on Labour History, 1996.

Mochoruk, James D. *Mining's Early Years: An Historic Look at Flin Flon's Mining Pioneers.* Winnipeg: Manitoba Labour Education Centre, n.d., circa 1984.

Morton, Desmond, with Terry Copp. *Working People: An Illustrated History of the Canadian Labour Movement.* 1st ed. Toronto: Deneau, 1984.

Nelles, H.V. *The Politics of Development: Forests, Mines and Hydro-Electric Power in Ontario 1849–1941.* Toronto: Macmillan, 1974.

Neufeld, Andrew, and Andrew Parnaby. *The IWA in Canada: The Life and Times of an Industrial Union.* Vancouver: IWA Canada/New Star, 2000.

North, George, and Harold Griffin. *A Ripple, A Wave: The Story of Union Organization in the B.C. Fishing Industry.* Vancouver: Fisherman Publishing Society, 1974.

Ottanelli, Fraser. *The Communist Party of the United States: From the Depression to World War II.* New Brunswick, NJ: Rutgers University Press, 1991.

Palmer, Bryan. *Working-Class Experience: The Rise and Reconstitution of Canadian Labour, 1800–1980.* Toronto: Butterworth and Co., 1983.

Patrias, Carmela. *Relief Strike: Immigrant Workers and the Great Depression in Crowland, Ontario.* Toronto: New Hogtown Press, 1990.

Penner, Norman. *Canadian Communism.* Toronto: Methuen, 1988.

– *The Canadian Left: A Critical Analysis.* Scarborough: Prentice-Hall, 1977.

Phillips, Paul. *No Power Greater: A Century of Labour in British Columbia.* Vancouver: BC Federation of Labour/Boag Foundation, 1967.

Pierce, G. *See under* Smith, Stewart.

Radforth, Ian. *Bushworkers and Bosses: Logging in Northern Ontario, 1900–1980.* Toronto: University of Toronto Press, 1987.

Rees, Time, and Andrew Thorpe, eds. *International Communism and the CI 1919–1943.* Manchester: Manchester University Press, 1998.

Richard, Béatrice. *'Péril Rouge' au Témiscamingue: la grève des bûcherons de Rouyn-Noranda 1933–1934.* Montreal: Collection RICHTQ Études et Documents, 1993.

Rodney, William. *Soldiers of the International: A History of the Communist Party of Canada 1919–1929.* Toronto: University of Toronto Press, 1968.

Rose, Fred. *Spying on Labour.* Toronto: New Era Publishers, 1939.

Ryan, Toby. *Stage Left: Canadian Theatre in the Thirties.* Toronto: CTR Publications, 1981.

Samuel, Raphael, ed. *People's History and Socialist Theory*. London: Routledge and Kegan Paul, 1981.

Sangster, Joan. *Dreams of Equality*. Toronto: McClelland and Stewart, 1989.

Santalov, A.A., and Louis Segal, eds. *Soviet Union Year-Book 1930*. London: Allen and Unwin, 1930.

Smith, A.E. *All My Life*. Toronto: Progress Books, 1949.

Smith, Doug. *Joe Zuken: Citizen and Socialist*. Toronto: James Lorimer, 1990.

Smith, Stewart. *Comrades and Komsomolkas: My Years in the Communist Party of Canada*. Toronto: Lugus, 1993.

– pseud. G. Pierce. *Socialism and the C.C.F.* Montreal, 1934.

Sonier-Newman, Lynne. *Policing a Pioneer Province: The BC Provincial Police 1858–1950*. Vancouver: Harbour Publishing, 1991.

Stafford, Ellen. *Always and After: A Memoir*. Toronto: Viking, 1999.

Struthers, James. *No Fault of Their Own: Unemployment and the Canadian Welfare State 1914–1941*. Toronto: University of Toronto Press, 1983.

Swankey, Ben, and Jean Evans Sheils. *'Work and Wages!': Semi-Documentary Account of the Life and Times of Arthur H. (Slim) Evans*. Vancouver: Trade Union Research Bureau, 1977.

Swift, Jamie, and the Development Education Centre. *The Big Nickel: Inco at Home and Abroad*. Kitchener: Between the Lines, 1977.

Thompson, John Herd, with Allen Seager. *Canada 1922–1939: Decades of Discord*. Toronto: McClelland and Stewart, 1985.

Urquhart, M.C., ed. *Historical Statistics of Canada*. Toronto: Macmillan, 1965.

Waiser, Bill. *All Hell Can't Stop Us: The On-to-Ottawa Trek and Regina Riot*. Calgary: Fifth House, 2003.

Warburton, Rennie, and David Coburn, eds. *Workers, Capital, and the State in British Columbia*. Vancouver: University of British Columbia Press, 1988.

Warren, Jim, and Kathleen Carlisle. *On the Side of the People*. Regina: Coteau Books, 2006.

Warwaruk, Larry. *Red Finns on the Coteau*. Saskatoon: Core Communications, 1984.

Webb, Sidney and Beatrice. *Soviet Communism: A New Civilization?* London: Longmans, Green and Co., 1935/1936.

Worley, Matthew, ed. *In Search of Revolution: International Communist Parties in the Third Period*. London: I.B. Tauris, 2004.

Who's Who in Canada 1934–35. Toronto: International Press, 1935.

Articles

Abella, Irving. 'Portrait of a Jewish Professional Revolutionary: The Recollections of Joshua Gershman.' *Labour/Le Travail* 2 (1977), 185–213.

Brown, Lorne. 'Unemployed Struggles in Saskatchewan and Canada, 1930–1935.' *Prairie Forum* 31.2 (Fall 2006), 193–216.

Cruikshank, Douglas, and Gregory S. Kealey. 'Strikes in Canada, 1891–1950: Methods and Sources.' *Labour/Le Travail* 20 (Fall 1987), 123–45.

Drummond, Ian. 'Empire Trade and Russian Trade: Economic Diplomacy in the Nineteen-Thirties.' *Canadian Journal of Economics* 5 (February 1972), 35–47.

Firsov, F.L. 'What the Comintern's Archives Will Reveal.' *World Marxist Review* no. 1 (1989), 52–7.

Gladstone, Percy, and Stuart Jamieson. 'Unionism in the Fishing Industry of British Columbia.' Part 2. *Canadian Journal of Economics and Political Science* 16.2 (May 1950), 146–71.

Hak, G. 'Red Wages.' *Pacific Northwest Quarterly* 80 (July 1989), 82–90.

Hannant, Larry. 'The Calgary Working Class and the Social Credit Movement in Alberta, 1932–1935.' *Labour/Le Travail* 16 (Fall 1985), 97–116.

Henson, Tom. 'Ku Klux Klan in Western Canada.' *Alberta History* 25.4 (Autumn 1977), 1–2.

Heron, Craig. 'Towards Synthesis in Canadian Working-Class History.' *Left History* 1.1 (Spring 1993).

Hladun, John. 'They Taught Me Treason: The First-Hand Story of a Canadian Farm Boy Trained by Moscow as a Storm Trooper of a World-Revolution.' *Maclean's*, 15 October 1947.

Hobbs, Margaret. 'Rethinking Antifeminism in the 1930s: Gender Crisis or Workplace Justice: A Response to Alice Kessler-Harris.' *Gender and History* 5.1 (Spring 1993), 4–15.

Jamieson, Stuart. 'Native Indians and the Trade Union Movement in British Columbia.' *Human Organization* 20.4 (Winter 1961), 219–25.

Jamieson, Stuart, and Percy Gladstone. 'Unionism in the Fishing Industry of British Columbia.' Part 1. *Canadian Journal of Economics and Political Science* 16.1 (February 1950), 1–11.

Kealey, Gregory S. '1919: The Canadian Labour Revolt.' *Labour/Le Travail* 13 (Spring 1984), 11–44.

Klee, Marcus. 'Fighting the Sweatshop in Depression Ontario: Capital, Labour and the Industrial Standards Act.' *Labour/Le Travail* 45 (Spring 2000), 13–51.

Langford, Tom. 'Strikes and Class Consciousness.' *Labour/Le Travail* 34 (Spring 1994), 107–37.

Lévesque, Andrée. 'Le Québec et le monde communiste: Cowansville 1931.' *Revue d'Histoire de l'Amerique Française* 34.2 (September 1980), 171–80.

Levine, Gilbert. 'Patrick Lenihan and the Alberta Miners.' *Labour/Le Travail* 16 (Fall 1985), 167–78.

Luxton, Meg. 'Feminism as a Class Act: Working-Class Feminism and the
   Women's Movement in Canada.' *Labour/Le Travail* 48 (Fall 2001), 63–88.
Manley, John. 'Canadian Communists, Revolutionary Unionism, and the "Third
   Period": The Workers' Unity League, 1929–1935.' *Journal of the Canadian
   Historical Association* 5 (1994), 167–94.
– 'Red or Yellow? Canadian Communists and the "Long" Third Period, 1927–
   1936.' In Matthew Worley, ed., *In Search of Revolution*. London: I.B. Tauris,
   2004, 220–46.
McIlroy, John, and Alan Campbell. '"Nina Ponomareva's Hats": The New Revi-
   sionism, the Communist International and the Communist Party of Great
   Britain 1920–1930.' *Labour/Le Travail* 49 (Spring 2002), 147–87.
Morgan, Kevin. 'The Trouble with Revisionism: or Communist History with the
   History Left In.' *Labour/Le Travail* 63 (Spring 2009), 131–55.
Morris, Leslie. 'Canada's Road to Socialism.' *National Affairs Monthly* 9.3 (1952),
   24–38.
Norman, Alma. 'Getting It Together, Part II: Working Women and the Women's
   Labour Leagues.' *Upstream* 2.4 (May 1978).
Patrias, Carmela. 'Relief Strike: Immigrant Workers and the Great Depres-
   sion in Crowland, Ontario, 1930–1935,' in Franca Iacovetta, ed., *A Nation of
   Immigrants: Women, Workers, and Communities in Canadian History, 1840s–1960s*.
   Toronto: University of Toronto Press, 1998.
Petrone, Karen. 'Soviet Women's Voices in the Stalin Era.' *Journal of Women's
   History* 16.2 (Summer 2004), 000–000.
Pierson, Ruth Roach. 'Gender and the Unemployment Debates in Canada
   1934–1940.' *Labour/Le Travail* 25 (Spring 1990), 77–103.
Price, Col. William H. 'Political Changes by Force and Violence: An Address
   Given before the Liberal-Conservative Summer School at Newmarket,
   September 1933.' 16-page reprint from *Canadian Problems As Seen by Twenty
   Outstanding Men of Canada*. Toronto: Oxford University Press, 1933.
Repo, Satu. 'Rosvall and Voutilainen: Two Union Men Who Never Died.'
   Labour/Le Travailleur 8/9 (Autumn/Spring 1981–2), 79–102.
Roberts, Barbara. 'Shovelling Out the Mutinous: Political Deportation from
   Canada before 1936.' *Labour/Le Travail* 18 (Fall 1986), 77–110.
Robson, Robert S. 'Strike in the Single Enterprise Community: Flin Flon, Mani-
   toba – 1934.' *Labour/Le Travail* 12 (Fall 1983), 63–86.
Scott, F.R. 'The Trial of the Toronto Communists.' *Queen's Quarterly* 39 (August
   1932).
Seager, Allen. 'Memorial to a Departed Friend of the Working Man.' *Bulletin of
   the Committee on Canadian Labour History* 4 (Autumn 1977), 9–14.
– 'The Pass Strike of 1932.' *Alberta History* 25.1 (Winter 1977), 1–11.

Steedman, Mercedes. 'The Promise: Communist Organizing in the Needle
   Trades, the Dressmakers' Campaign 1928–1937.' *Labour/Le Travail* no. 34
   (Autumn 1994), 37–73.

Unpublished Material

Endicott, Stephen. Interview with Oscar D. Brooks. Toronto, 28 January 1993.
– Interview with Stewart Smith. Fergus, Ontario, 24 September 1992.
– 'Theory and History.' Lecture notes at the National Training School, Labour
   Progressive Party, Sudbury, June–August 1949.
Frecker, John Peter. 'Militant and Radical Unionism in the British Columbia
   Fishing Industry.' MA thesis, University of British Columbia, 1973.
Hobbs, Margaret. 'Gendering Work and Welfare: Women's Relationship to
   Wage-Work and Social Policy During the Great Depression.' PhD thesis,
   OISE, 1995.
Manley, John, 'Communism and the Canadian Working Class during the Great
   Depression: The Workers' Unity League 1930–1936.' PhD thesis, Dalhousie
   University, 1984.
Radforth, Ian. 'The Workers' Unity League in Ontario.' MA thesis, York Univer-
   sity, 1979.
Rankin, Phillip. 'The Workers' Unity League: An Historical Paper.' BA paper
   for Prof. Martin Robin, Simon Fraser University, 1973.
Seager, Allen. 'A History of the Mine Workers' Union of Canada 1925–1936.'
   MA thesis, Department of History, McGill University, 1977/1978.
Stunden, Nancy. 'The Stratford Strikes of 1933.' MA thesis, Carleton University,
   1975.
Toews, Anne Frances. 'For Liberty, Bread, and Love: Annie Buller, Beckie
   Buhay, and the Forging of Communist Militant Femininity in Canada
   1918–1939.' MA thesis, Simon Fraser University, 2009.

Note on Absences

The Department of Labour in Ottawa recorded 1,500 strikes of employed and
unemployed workers in the years 1930–6, many of them inspired or led by the
Workers' Unity League. In addition, the league organized countless meetings,
issued scores of manifestos, and conducted hundreds of demonstrations. To
encompass such a vast canvas this book would have had to be something in the
nature of an encyclopaedia – a concept that was never contemplated. Inevitably
the selection process eliminated or underrepresented items that easily merited
more attention but whose absence, in the opinion of the author, does not flaw

a comprehensive understanding of the outlook and practice of the league. But in fairness to the reader, to the participants themselves, and for the historical record, some of the more important of these absences, beginning from the West Coast and moving eastward to Maritime Canada, are noted as follows.

British Columbia

The Longshore Strike of 1935. This major struggle was not led by the WUL, but many of the league's members shared close links with the longshoremen's union through concurrent memberships in the Communist Party, and they participated in that conflict. The longshore insurgency of 1935 is recorded in Andrew Parnaby's *Citizen Docker: Making a New Deal on the Vancouver Waterfront 1919–1939* (Toronto: University of Toronto Press, 2008).

Coal miners' strikes on Vancouver Island and at Corbin, BC in 1934–5. For these memorable strikes, led by the Mine Workers' Union of Canada, see Allen Seager's accounting in 'A History of the Mine Workers' Union of Canada 1925–1936' (MA thesis, McGill University 1977), 187–213, and Sean Griffin, ed., *Fighting Heritage: Highlights of the 1930s Struggle for Jobs and Militant Unionism in British Columbia* (Vancouver: Tribune Publishing Co., 1985), 75–84.

Prairie Provinces

The Farmers' Unity League, the sister organization of the Workers' Unity League, had its headquarters in Saskatoon. For a wide-ranging discussion of the FUL see David Monod, 'The Agrarian Struggle: Rural Communism in Alberta and Saskatchewan 1926–1935,' *Social History* 18.35 (May 1985), 99–118.

Sugar Beet Workers in Alberta. For this dramatic episode see John Thompson and Allen Seager, 'Workers, Growers and Monopolists: the "Labour Problem" in the Alberta Beet Sugar Industry during the 1930s,' *Labour/Le Travailleur* 3 (1978), 153–74.

Ontario and Quebec

Auto Workers Industrial Union. See John Manley, 'Communists and Auto Workers: The Struggle for Industrial Unionism in the Canadian Automobile Industry, 1925–36,' *Labour/Le Travail* 17 (Spring 1986), 105–33. While the WUL was unable to make a breakthrough in this important industry, the strikes it organized, Manley writes, 'gave workers the experience of struggle that fostered class consciousness, undeniably awakening the passive majority to the possibility of challenging industrial subordination.' He believes that the communists laid most of the foundations for the growth of the United Automobile Workers union in Canada.

Steel Workers Organizing Committee. See Craig Heron, *Working in Steel: The Early Years in Canada 1883–1935* (Toronto: McClelland and Stewart, 1988).

Food Workers' Industrial Union of Canada
Shoe and Leather Workers' Industrial Union of Canada
Building Trades Workers' Industrial Union, Toronto
Cleaners, Dyers and Laundry Workers' Industrial Union, Toronto
Domestic Servants' Union, Toronto
General Workers' Union, Toronto
Journeymen Barbers and Hairdressers' Union, Toronto
Rubber Workers' Industrial Union, Toronto
Steel and Metal Workers' Industrial Union, Toronto
Textile Workers' Union, Toronto

Maritimes

Coal miners in Nova Scotia did not affiliate with the WUL. See Michael Earle, 'The Coalminers and Their "Red" Union: The Amalgamated Mine Workers of Nova Scotia, 1932–1936,' *Labour/Le Travail* 22 (Fall 1988), 99–132, and David Frank, *J.B. McLachlan: A Biography* (Toronto: James Lorimer, 1999).

Index

Abitibi Power and Paper Co.: at Iroquois Falls, 4–5, 220; pulp cutters' strike at, 5, 30

All-Canadian Congress of Labour (ACCL), 8, 9–10, 24, 37, 42, 149, 205–6, 308; attitude to USSR, 164, 343n16; doubts about strike weapon, 10, 30–1

American Federation of Labour, 9, 23, 24, 50, 164, 205, 240, 319, 394n66; business unionism, 327; complacency of, 8, 76; financial connections of, 20; Lozovsky on, 22; mergers with, 176, 303, 311, 314–18; opposition groups in, 36, 69

anarchists, 63, 93, 145. *See also* Industrial Workers of the World

Anglo-American Secretariat, 30, 40, 130, 150, 354n38; and status of Canada, 26; on mining policy, 369n64; estimate on size of WUL, 388; 'social fascism' arguments, 306–10; structure of, 17–18; on working underground, 203, 366n26; work among the unemployed, 274–6, 390n26, 405n15. *See also* Third International

Anyox, BC, 3, 178–80; the 'Anyox system,' 182

– and Granby Consolidated Mining and Smelting and Power Company, 178; miners' strike at, 183–7; Chinese workers in, 179–80, 181–2; WUL strike strategy, 183

Bell, Adam (deputy labour minister, BC), 254; negotiations to end loggers' strike, 255, 256, 257

Bennett, R.B. (prime minister): Alberta coal subsidy, 103–4; Alberta hunger march, 206, 371n19; and Crowsnest Pass strike, 111; the Eight imprisoned, 99; embargo of Soviet Union, 9, 128–9, 131, 141, 361n55, 373n41; on limits to freedom, 67; and On-to-Ottawa Trek, 134, 136, 289, 290–5, 298; H.H. Stevens inquiry, 227–8; Section 98 of the Criminal Code, 325; and war in Asia, 141; meets workers' delegations, 138–41, 168, 206; and Workers' Economic Conference, 132–2, 134, 137

– and unemployment crisis, 89–91,